The New Testament

OF THE JERUSALEM BIBLE

READER'S EDITION

WITH ABRIDGED INTRODUCTIONS AND NOTES

•

General Editor

ALEXANDER JONES, L.S.S., S.T.L., I.C.B.

IMAGE BOOKS

A Division of Doubleday & Company, Inc.
Garden City, New York

Image Books edition 1969
by special arrangement with Doubleday & Company, Inc.

Image Books edition published February 1969

The abridged introductions and notes of this Bible
are based on those which appear in *La Bible de
Jérusalem* (one volume edition) published by Les
Editions du Cerf, Paris. The English text of this Bible,
though translated from the ancient texts, owes a
large debt to the work of the many scholars who col-
laborated to produce *La Bible de Jérusalem*, a debt
which the publishers of this English Bible gratefully
acknowledge.

ISBN: 0-385-06569-8
Library of Congress Catalog Card Number 69-11018
© 1966 and 1967 by Darton, Longman &
Todd, Ltd. and Doubleday & Company, Inc.

". . . a lasting monument to the industry and sound judgment of a group of scholars who have been in the vanguard of Biblical research . . . . the reader has direct access to a richness of Biblical scholarship that is without parallel in any other single volume."

James B. Pritchard, Professor of Religious Thought,
University of Pennsylvania

". . . . the definitive edition of Scriptures for the English-speaking world."

Most Rev. Fulton J. Sheen, Bishop of Rochester

"The Reformation was in part a rebellion against policies that kept the Bible out of the language and the reach of the laity; the *Jerusalem Bible*, on the other hand, is a masterful example of scriptural translation in lay language linked to skillful attempts to place it in the hands of millions . . ."

Martin E. Marty in Chicago Sun-Times

"This scholarly work is of high quality, and the quantity of information placed at the disposal of student and scholar alike is quite remarkable." *The London Times*

EDITOR'S FOREWORD

When the Jerusalem Bible was first published in English in 1966, the Foreword to the complete Standard edition announced its objects: to serve two pressing needs facing the Church, the need to keep abreast of the times and the need to deepen theological thought. This double program was carried out by translating the ancient texts into the language we use today, and by providing notes to the texts which were neither sectarian nor superficial. In that Foreword also, the dependence of the translators on the original pioneer work of the School of Biblical Studies in Jerusalem was acknowledged, and the English version was offered as an entirely faithful rendering of the original texts which, in doubtful points, preserved the text established and (for the most part) the interpretation adopted by the School in the light of the most recent researches in the fields of history, archaeology and literary criticism. With the text, the Standard edition presented the full explanatory notes that would enable any student to confirm for himself the interpretations that were adopted, to appreciate the theological implications drawn from them, and to understand the complex relations between different parts of the Bible.

However the Bible is not only for students undergoing a formal course of study, and there has been an immediate demand for an edition of the Jerusalem Bible which would bring the modern clarity of the text before the ordinary reader, and open to him the results of modern researches without either justifying them at length in literary and historical notes or linking them with doctrinal studies. For this reason, the present edition has been prepared. The full Introductions of the Standard edition are here greatly abridged, to serve simply as brief explanations of the character of each book or group of books, their dates and their authorship; and the full Notes of the Standard edition have been greatly reduced in number and length, to restrict them to the minimum which are necessary for understanding the primary, literal meaning of the text; to explain terms, places, people and customs; to specify dates, and to identify the sources of quotations. In short, the brief Introductions and Notes are here only to help the ordinary reader to understand what he is reading and do not assume in him any wide literary, historical or theological knowledge or interests.

ALEXANDER JONES

Christ's College, Liverpool

TYPOGRAPHICAL NOTE

Chapter numbers

The beginning of a chapter is usually marked by a large bold
numeral. A smaller bold numeral is used when a chapter begins inside a paragraph.

Verse numbers

The beginning of each verse is indicated in the line by a dot •
preceding the first word, except when a verse starts at the
beginning of a line or begins a chapter. Where two verses
begin in the same line, the verse numbers in the margin are
placed one slightly above and the other slightly below the line.
In a few places, the text adopted by the Editors differs from
the Vulgate, A.V., and other previous versions by omitting
a verse which those versions include. The verse numbering of
the previous versions has nevertheless been retained for ease
of reference; certain verse numbers are therefore omitted from
their sequence in the margin, or appear in parentheses.

Italics in the text

Italic type is used in the text to distinguish words which are
quotations from or close allusions to another book of the
Bible. The origins of such quotations or allusions are given
as references in the footnotes (except in cases in which the
source is obvious to any Bible-reader), and are not necessarily
repeated when the same passage is quoted more than once in
a single book.

Punctuation of biblical references

Chapter and verse are separated by a colon, e.g. Ex 20:17.
In a succession of references, items are separated by a
semicolon, e.g. Ex 20:17; Lv 9:15. The same practice is
followed in a succession of references to different chapters of
one book, e.g. Ex 20:17; 21:3 or Ex 15;17;20.

CONTENTS

LIST OF ABBREVIATIONS

The books of the Bible in biblical order

Genesis	Gn	Obadiah	Ob
Exodus	Ex	Jonah	Jon
Leviticus	Lv	Micah	Mi
Numbers	Nb	Nahum	Na
Deuteronomy	Dt	Habakkuk	Hab
Joshua	Jos	Zephaniah	Zp
Judges	Jg	Haggai	Hg
Ruth	Rt	Zechariah	Zc
1 Samuel	1 S	Malachi	Ml
2 Samuel	2 S		
1 Kings	1 K	Matthew	Mt
2 Kings	2 K	Mark	Mk
1 Chronicles	1 Ch	Luke	Lk
2 Chronicles	2 Ch	John	Jn
Ezra	Ezr	Acts	Ac
Nehemiah	Ne	Romans	Rm
Tobit	Tb	1 Corinthians	1 Co
Judith	Jdt	2 Corinthians	2 Co
Esther	Est	Galatians	Ga
1 Maccabees	1 M	Ephesians	Ep
2 Maccabees	2 M	Philippians	Ph
Job	Jb	Colossians	Col
Psalms	Ps	1 Thessalonians	1 Th
Proverbs	Pr	2 Thessalonians	2 Th
Ecclesiastes	Qo	1 Timothy	1 Tm
Song of Songs	Sg	2 Timothy	2 Tm
Wisdom	Ws	Titus	Tt
Ecclesiasticus	Si	Philemon	Phm
Isaiah	Is	Hebrews	Heb
Jeremiah	Jr	James	Jm
Lamentations	Lm	1 Peter	1 P
Baruch	Ba	2 Peter	2 P
Ezekiel	Ezk	1 John	1 Jn
Daniel	Dn	2 John	2 Jn
Hosea	Ho	3 John	3 Jn
Joel	Jl	Jude	Jude
Amos	Am	Revelation	Rv

The books of the Bible in alphabetical order
of abbreviations

Ac	Acts	Lk	Luke
Am	Amos	Lm	Lamentations
Ba	Baruch	Lv	Leviticus
1 Ch	1 Chronicles	1 M	1 Maccabees
2 Ch	2 Chronicles	2 M	2 Maccabees
1 Co	1 Corinthians	Mi	Micah
2 Co	2 Corinthians	Mk	Mark
Col	Colossians	Ml	Malachi
Dn	Daniel	Mt	Matthew
Dt	Deuteronomy	Na	Nahum
Ep	Ephesians	Nb	Numbers
Est	Esther	Ne	Nehemiah
Ex	Exodus	Ob	Obadiah
Ezk	Ezekiel	1 P	1 Peter
Ezr	Ezra	2 P	2 Peter
Ga	Galatians	Ph	Philippians
Gn	Genesis	Phm	Philemon
Hab	Habakkuk	Pr	Proverbs
Heb	Hebrews	Ps	Psalms
Hg	Haggai	Qo	Ecclesiastes
Ho	Hosea	Rm	Romans
Is	Isaiah	Rt	Ruth
Jb	Job	Rv	Revelation
Jdt	Judith	1 S	1 Samuel
Jg	Judges	2 S	2 Samuel
Jl	Joel	Sg	Song of Songs
Jm	James	Si	Ecclesiasticus
Jn	John	Tb	Tobit
1 Jn	1 John	1 Th	1 Thessalonians
2 Jn	2 John	2 Th	2 Thessalonians
3 Jn	3 John	1 Tm	1 Timothy
Jon	Jonah	2 Tm	2 Timothy
Jos	Joshua	Tt	Titus
Jr	Jeremiah	Ws	Wisdom
Jude	Jude	Zc	Zechariah
1 K	1 Kings	Zp	Zephaniah
2 K	2 Kings		

INTRODUCTION TO
The Synoptic Gospels

The first three gospels are called synoptic ("with the same eye") because their narratives are all built on the same events in the life of Jesus and indeed many passages from all three of them can be placed side by side as evident parallels. From the earliest times, Matthew, Mark and Luke respectively have been named as the writers of them.

According to a tradition dating from the second century, St. Matthew was the first to write a gospel and he wrote "in the Hebrew tongue." Our Greek "Gospel according to St. Matthew" is not identified with this early Aramaic book, which is lost, though there are times when it appears to represent a more primitive text than Mark.

Some parts of the gospel story assumed a fixed and stereotyped pattern in the oral tradition founded on the preaching of the apostles; the similarity of the Passion in all four gospels suggests a common oral tradition very firmly fixed. But the relationships between the three synoptic gospels are too close and too complex to be explained by a common oral tradition underlying all of them. It is clear that Luke depends on Mark, and although it was held for a long time that Mark depends on Matthew, a number of indications now suggest the reverse. Luke and Matthew also have a number of non-Marcan passages common to both, and these probably have a common source or sources; in addition, each of these gospels includes episodes and sayings not found in the other.

Mark, said to have been Peter's interpreter, is mentioned in St. Paul's letters as one of his companions, and described in Acts as a disciple from Jerusalem. Luke is also mentioned in St. Paul's letters and when writing Acts incorporated parts of a first-person travel diary. Mark's gospel can be dated before A.D. 70, perhaps about 64. Our Greek Matthew and Luke are later and probably date from 70-80.

The arrangement and presentation of the historical facts in the synoptic gospels are dictated by the purposes of a written gospel: to convert, to edify, to infuse faith, to enlighten it and defend it against its opponents.

Mark

The shortest of the gospels, it is not concerned with elaborating Christ's teaching and it records few of his sayings; the real point of its message is *the manifestation of the crucified Messiah*. While on the one hand Jesus is seen by the writer as the Son of God, acknowledged by the Father and vindicating his power and his mission by miracles, on the other hand he chooses to appear to the world under the mysterious title "Son of Man," and the gospel puts great emphasis on his apparent frustration and rejection by the people. The "messianic secret" is a basic idea of Mark's gospel.

Matthew

This gospel is divided into five books, each consisting of a discourse introduced by painstakingly selected narrative matter which follows the same broad outline as in Mark. These are preceded by the story of the Infancy and followed by that of the Passion. The fact that this gospel reports Christ's teaching much more fully than Mark and stresses especially the theme of the "kingdom of heaven" makes it *a dramatic account in seven acts of the coming of the kingdom*. Matthew, writing for Jewish Christians, makes a special point of demonstrating, by the use of Old Testament quotations, that *the scriptures are fulfilled* in the person and work of Jesus.

Luke

The plan of this gospel follows Mark's outline as a rule, but the narrative is controlled and edited to bring in much teaching, including the longer parables, and to omit episodes that would not interest Luke's non-Jewish readers. The originality of Luke is in *his religious mentality*: he is the faithful recorder of Christ's loving kindness, he emphasizes the necessity for prayer and he is the only one of the synoptic authors to give the Holy Spirit the prominence which we find in Paul and in Acts.

Greek style

Mark's Greek is rough, strongly Aramaic and often faulty, but it is fresh and frank. Matthew's Greek is also rather Aramaic but smoother and more correct than Mark's, though less picturesque. Luke's style is variable: excellent when he is writing independently but at other times incorporating the peculiarities of his sources; as in Acts he suits the style to the subject and occasionally he goes out of his way to give a good imitation of Septuagint Greek.

THE GOSPEL ACCORDING TO
Saint Matthew

I. THE BIRTH AND INFANCY OF JESUS

The ancestry of Jesus

1 A genealogy of Jesus Christ, son of David, son of Abraham:[a]

2 Abraham was the father of Isaac,
Isaac the father of Jacob,
Jacob the father of Judah and his brothers,

3 Judah was the father of Perez and Zerah, Tamar being their mother,
Perez was the father of Hezron,
Hezron the father of Ram,

4 Ram was the father of Amminadab,
Amminadab the father of Nahshon,
Nahshon the father of Salmon,

5 Salmon was the father of Boaz, Rahab being his mother,
Boaz was the father of Obed, Ruth being his mother,
Obed was the father of Jesse;

6 and Jesse was the father of King David.

David was the father of Solomon, whose mother had been Uriah's wife,

7 Solomon was the father of Rehoboam,
Rehoboam the father of Abijah,
Abijah the father of Asa,

8 Asa was the father of Jehoshaphat,
Jehoshaphat the father of Joram,
Joram the father of Azariah,

9 Azariah was the father of Jotham,
Jotham the father of Ahaz,
Ahaz the father of Hezekiah,

10 Hezekiah was the father of Manasseh,
Manasseh the father of Amon,

1 a. Showing the descent of Joseph, legally the father of Jesus, from Abraham and David, to whom the messianic promises were made.

Amon the father of Josiah;

11 and Josiah was the father of Jechoniah and his brothers.
Then the deportation to Babylon took place.

12 After the deportation to Babylon:
Jechoniah was the father of Shealtiel,
Shealtiel the father of Zerubbabel,

13 Zerubbabel was the father of Abiud,
Abiud the father of Eliakim,
Eliakim the father of Azor,

14 Azor was the father of Zadok,
Zadok the father of Achim,
Achim the father of Eliud,

15 Eliud was the father of Eleazar,
Eleazar the father of Matthan,
Matthan the father of Jacob;

16 and Jacob was the father of Joseph the husband of
Mary;
of her was born Jesus who is called Christ.

17 The sum of generations is therefore: fourteen from
Abraham to David; fourteen from David to the Babylonian deportation; and fourteen from the Babylonian deportation to Christ.

The virginal conception of Christ

18 This is how Jesus Christ came to be born. His mother
Mary was betrothed to Joseph;[b] but before they came to
live together she was found to be with child through the
19 Holy Spirit. ·Her husband Joseph, being a man of honor
and wanting to spare her publicity, decided to divorce her
20 informally. ·He had made up his mind to do this when
the angel of the Lord appeared to him in a dream and
said, "Joseph son of David, do not be afraid to take Mary
home as your wife, because she has conceived what is in
21 her by the Holy Spirit. ·She will give birth to a son and
you must name him Jesus, because he is the one who is
22 to save[c] his people from their sins." ·Now all this took
place to fulfill the words spoken by the Lord through the
prophet:

23 *The virgin will conceive and give birth to a son
and they will call him Immanuel,[d]*

24 a name which means "God-is-with-us." ·When Joseph woke
up he did what the angel of the Lord had told him to do:

25 he took his wife to his home ·and, though he had not had intercourse with her, she gave birth to a son; and he named him Jesus.

The visit of the Magi

1 2 After Jesus had been born at Bethlehem in Judaea during the reign of King Herod,[a] some wise men came to
2 Jerusalem from the east. ·"Where is the infant king of the Jews?" they asked. "We saw his star as it rose[b] and have
3 come to do him homage." ·When King Herod heard this
4 he was perturbed, and so was the whole of Jerusalem. ·He called together all the chief priests and the scribes of the people, and enquired of them where the Christ was to be
5 born. ·"At Bethlehem in Judaea," they told him "for this is what the prophet wrote:

6 *And you, Bethlehem, in the land of Judah,*
you are by no means least among the leaders of Judah,
for out of you will come a leader
who will shepherd my people Israel."[c]

7 Then Herod summoned the wise men to see him privately. He asked them the exact date on which the star had ap-
8 peared, ·and sent them on to Bethlehem. "Go and find out all about the child," he said "and when you have found him, let me know, so that I too may go and do him hom-
9 age." ·Having listened to what the king had to say, they set out. And there in front of them was the star they had seen rising; it went forward and halted over the place where the
10 child was. ·The sight of the star filled them with delight,
11 and going into the house they saw the child with his mother Mary, and falling to their knees they did him homage. Then, opening their treasures, they offered him gifts
12 of gold and frankincense and myrrh.[d] ·But they were warned in a dream not to go back to Herod, and returned to their own country by a different way.

b. In a Jewish betrothal the man was already called the "husband" of the woman, and he could release himself from the engagement only by an act of repudiation, v. 19. c. "Jesus" (Hebr. Yehoshua) means "Yahweh saves." d. Is. 7:14
2 a. About 5 or 4 B.C. Herod was king of Judaea, Idumaea and Samaria from 37-4 B.C. b. "In the east" is an alternative translation, here and in v. 9. c. Mi 5:1 d. The wealth and perfumes of Arabia.

The flight into Egypt. The massacre of the Innocents

13 After they had left, the angel of the Lord appeared to Joseph in a dream and said, "Get up, take the child and his mother with you, and escape into Egypt, and stay there until I tell you, because Herod intends to search for the child and do away with him." ·So Joseph got up and, taking the child and his mother with him, left that night for Egypt, where he stayed until Herod was dead. This was to fulfill what the Lord had spoken through the prophet:

> *I called my son out of Egypt.*^e

16 Herod was furious when he realized that he had been outwitted by the wise men, and in Bethlehem and its surrounding district he had all the male children killed who were two years old or under, reckoning by the date he had been careful to ask the wise men. ·It was then that the words spoken through the prophet Jeremiah were fulfilled:

18
> *A voice was heard in Ramah,*
> *sobbing and loudly lamenting:*
> *it was Rachel weeping for her children,*
> *refusing to be comforted*
> *because they were no more.*^f

From Egypt to Nazareth

19 After Herod's death, the angel of the Lord appeared in a dream to Joseph in Egypt ·and said, "Get up, take the child and his mother with you and go back to the land of Israel, for those who wanted to kill the child are dead." ·So Joseph got up and, taking the child and his mother with him, went back to the land of Israel. ·But when he learned that Archelaus^g had succeeded his father Herod as ruler of Judaea he was afraid to go there, and being warned in a dream he left for the region of Galilee.^h ·There he settled in a town called Nazareth. In this way the words spoken through the prophets were to be fulfilled:

> *He will be called a Nazarene.*

II. THE KINGDOM OF HEAVEN PROCLAIMED

A. NARRATIVE SECTION

The preaching of John the Baptist

1 3 In due course John the Baptist appeared; he preached in the wilderness of Judaea and this was his message: 2 "Repent, for the kingdom of heaven[a] is close at hand." 3 This was the man the prophet Isaiah spoke of when he said:

> *A voice cries in the wilderness:*
> *Prepare a way for the Lord,*
> *make his paths straight.[b]*

4 This man John wore a garment made of camel-hair with a leather belt round his waist, and his food was locusts and 5 wild honey. ·Then Jerusalem and all Judaea and the whole 6 Jordan district made their way to him, ·and as they were baptized by him in the river Jordan they confessed their 7 sins. ·But when he saw a number of Pharisees and Sad- 8 ducees[c] coming for baptism he said to them, ·"Brood of vipers, who warned you to fly from the retribution that is coming? But if you are repentant, produce the appropriate 9 fruit, ·and do not presume to tell yourselves, 'We have Abraham for our father,' because, I tell you, God can 10 raise children for Abraham from these stones. ·Even now the ax is laid to the roots of the trees, so that any tree which fails to produce good fruit will be cut down and 11 thrown on the fire. ·I baptize you in water for repentance, but the one who follows me is more powerful than I am, and I am not fit to carry his sandals; he will baptize you 12 with the Holy Spirit and fire. ·His winnowing-fan is in his hand; he will clear his threshing-floor and gather his

e. Ho 11:1   f. Jr 31:15   g. Ethnarch of Judaea, 4 B.C. to A.D. 6.
h. The territory of Herod Antipas.
3 a. "kingdom of God"; Mt's phrase reflects the Jewish scruple against using the name of God.   b. Is 40:3   c. Pharisees: members of a Jewish sect known for its strict observance of the Law as it was interpreted and developed by their rabbis. Sad- ducees: conservatives who observed the written form of the Law in the scriptures.

wheat into the barn; but the chaff he will burn in a fire that will never go out."

Jesus is baptized

¹³ Then Jesus appeared: he came from Galilee to the ¹⁴ Jordan to be baptized by John. ·John tried to dissuade him. "It is I who need baptism from you" he said "and yet ¹⁵ you come to me!" ·But Jesus replied, "Leave it like this for the time being; it is fitting that we should, in this way, do all that righteousness demands." At this, John gave in to him.

¹⁶ As soon as Jesus was baptized he came up from the water, and suddenly the heavens opened and he saw the Spirit of God descending like a dove and coming down on ¹⁷ him. ·And a voice spoke from heaven, "This is my Son, the Beloved; my favor rests on him."

Temptation in the wilderness

¹ ²
4 Then Jesus was led by the Spirit out into the wilderness to be tempted by the devil. ·He fasted for forty days ³ and forty nights, after which he was very hungry, ·and the tempter came and said to him, "If you are the Son of God, ⁴ tell these stones to turn into loaves." ·But he replied, "Scripture says:

*Man does not live on bread alone
but on every word that comes from the mouth of God."ᵃ*

⁵ The devil then took him to the holy city and made him ⁶ stand on the parapet of the Temple. ·"If you are the Son of God" he said "throw yourself down; for scripture says:

*He will put you in his angels' charge,
and they will support you on their hands
in case you hurt your foot against a stone."ᵇ*

⁷ Jesus said to him, "Scripture also says:

You must not put the Lord your God to the test."ᶜ

⁸ Next, taking him to a very high mountain, the devil showed him all the kingdoms of the world and their splen- ⁹ dor. ·"I will give you all these" he said, "if you fall at my ¹⁰ feet and worship me." ·Then Jesus replied, "Be off, Satan! For scripture says:

*You must worship the Lord your God,
and serve him alone."*[d]

11 Then the devil left him, and angels appeared and looked
after him.

Return to Galilee

12 Hearing that John had been arrested he went back to
13 Galilee, •and leaving Nazareth he went and settled in
Capernaum, a lakeside town on the borders of Zebulun
14 and Naphtali. •In this way the prophecy of Isaiah was to
be fulfilled:

15   *Land of Zebulun! Land of Naphtali!*
Way of the sea on the far side of Jordan,
Galilee of the nations!
16   *The people that lived in darkness*
has seen a great light;
on those who dwell in the land and shadow of death
a light has dawned.[e]

17 From that moment Jesus began his preaching with the
message, "Repent, for the kingdom of heaven is close at
hand."

The first four disciples are called

18   As he was walking by the Sea of Galilee he saw two
brothers, Simon, who was called Peter, and his brother
Andrew; they were making a cast in the lake with their
19 net, for they were fishermen. •And he said to them, "Fol-
20 low me and I will make you fishers of men." •And they left
their nets at once and followed him.

21   Going on from there he saw another pair of brothers,
James son of Zebedee and his brother John; they were in
their boat with their father Zebedee, mending their nets,
22 and he called them. •At once, leaving the boat and their
father, they followed him.

Jesus preaches and heals the sick

23   He went round the whole of Galilee teaching in their
synagogues, proclaiming the Good News of the kingdom
and curing all kinds of diseases and sickness among the

4 **a.** Dt 8:3   **b.** Ps 91:11-12   **c.** Dt 6:16   **d.** Dt 6:13   **e.**
Is 8:23-9:1

²⁴ people. ·His fame spread throughout Syria,ᶠ and those who were suffering from diseases and painful complaints of one kind or another, the possessed, epileptics, the paralyzed,
²⁵ were all brought to him, and he cured them. ·Large crowds followed him, coming from Galilee, the Decapolis,ᵍ Jerusalem, Judaea and Transjordania.

B. THE SERMON ON THE MOUNTᵃ

The Beatitudes

¹ ⁵ Seeing the crowds, he went up the hill. There he sat
² ⁵ down and was joined by his disciples. ·Then he began to speak. This is what he taught them:

³ "How happy are the poor in spirit;
 theirs is the kingdom of heaven.
⁴ Happy *the gentle:*ᵇ
 they shall have the earth for their heritage.
⁵ Happy those who mourn:
 they shall be comforted.
⁶ Happy those who hunger and thirst for what is right:
 they shall be satisfied.
⁷ Happy the merciful:
 they shall have mercy shown them.
⁸ Happy the pure in heart:
 they shall see God.
⁹ Happy the peacemakers:
 they shall be called sons of God.
¹⁰ Happy those who are persecuted in the cause of right:
 theirs is the kingdom of heaven.

¹¹ "Happy are you when people abuse you and persecute you and speak all kinds of calumny against you on my account.
¹² Rejoice and be glad, for your reward will be great in heaven; this is how they persecuted the prophets before you.

Salt of the earth and light of the world

¹³ "You are the salt of the earth. But if salt becomes tasteless, what can make it salty again? It is good for nothing, and can only be thrown out to be trampled underfoot by men.
¹⁴ "You are the light of the world. A city built on a hill-top
¹⁵ cannot be hidden. ·No one lights a lamp to put it under a tub; they put it on the lamp-stand where it shines for every-

¹⁶ one in the house. ·In the same way your light must shine in the sight of men, so that, seeing your good works, they may give the praise to your Father in heaven.

The fulfillment of the Law

¹⁷ "Do not imagine that I have come to abolish the Law or the Prophets. I have come not to abolish but to complete ¹⁸ them. ·I tell you solemnly, till heaven and earth disappear, not one dot, not one little stroke, shall disappear from the ¹⁹ Law until its purpose is achieved. ·Therefore, the man who infringes even one of the least of these commandments and teaches others to do the same will be considered the least in the kingdom of heaven; but the man who keeps them and teaches them will be considered great in the kingdom of heaven.

The new standard higher than the old

²⁰ "For I tell you, if your virtue goes no deeper than that of the scribes and Pharisees, you will never get into the kingdom of heaven.
²¹ "You have learned how it was said to our ancestors: *You must not kill;*ᶜ and if anyone does kill he must answer for it ²² before the court. ·But I say this to you: anyone who is angry with his brother will answer for it before the court; if a man calls his brother 'Fool'ᵈ he will answer for it before the Sanhedrin;ᵉ and if a man calls him 'Renegade'ᶠ ²³ he will answer for it in hell fire. ·So then, if you are bringing your offering to the altar and there remember that your ²⁴ brother has something against you, ·leave your offering there before the altar, go and be reconciled with your brother first, and then come back and present your offer-²⁵ ing. ·Come to terms with your opponent in good time while you are still on the way to the court with him, or he may hand you over to the judge and the judge to the ²⁶ officer, and you will be thrown into prison. ·I tell you

f. I.e. Galilee and the districts listed in v. 25. g. The "ten towns," a region southeast of Galilee.
5 a. In this discourse, which occupies three ch. of this gospel, Mt has included sayings which probably originated on other occasions (cf. their parallels in Lk). b. Or "the lowly"; the word comes from the Greek version of Ps 37. c. Ex 20:13 d. Translating an Aramaic term of contempt. e. The High Court at Jerusalem. f. Apostasy was the most repulsive of all sins.

solemnly, you will not get out till you have paid the last
penny.

27 "You have learned how it was said: *You must not com-
28 mit adultery.*[g] ·But I say this to you: if a man looks at a
woman lustfully, he has already committed adultery with
29 her in his heart. ·If your right eye should cause you to
sin, tear it out and throw it away; for it will do you less
harm to lose one part of you than to have your whole
30 body thrown into hell. ·And if your right hand should
cause you to sin, cut it off and throw it away; for it will do
you less harm to lose one part of you than to have your
whole body go to hell.

31 "It has also been said: *Anyone who divorces his wife
32 must give her a writ of dismissal.*[h] ·But I say this to you:
everyone who divorces his wife, except for the case of
fornication, makes her an adulteress; and anyone who
marries a divorced woman commits adultery.

33 "Again, you have learned how it was said to our ancestors: *You must not break your oath, but must fulfill your
34 oaths to the Lord.*[i] ·But I say this to you: do not swear at
35 all, either by *heaven*, since that is God's throne; ·or by *the
earth*, since that is *his footstool*; or by Jerusalem, since
36 that is *the city of the great king*. ·Do not swear by your
own head either, since you cannot turn a single hair white
37 or black. ·All you need say is 'Yes' if you mean yes, 'No'
if you mean no; anything more than this comes from
the evil one.

38 "You have learned how it was said: *Eye for eye and tooth
39 for tooth.*[j] ·But I say this to you: offer the wicked man no
resistance. On the contrary, if anyone hits you on the right
40 cheek, offer him the other as well; ·if a man takes you to
law and would have your tunic, let him have your cloak as
41 well. ·And if anyone orders you to go one mile, go two
42 miles with him. ·Give to anyone who asks, and if anyone
wants to borrow, do not turn away.

43 "You have learned how it was said: *You must love your
44 neighbor* and hate your enemy.[k] ·But I say this to you:
love your enemies and pray for those who persecute you;
45 in this way you will be sons of your Father in heaven, for
he causes his sun to rise on bad men as well as good, and
46 his rain to fall on honest and dishonest men alike. ·For if
you love those who love you, what right have you to
claim any credit? Even the tax collectors[l] do as much, do
47 they not? ·And if you save your greetings for your

brothers, are you doing anything exceptional? Even the
48 pagans do as much, do they not? ·You must therefore be
perfect just as your heavenly Father is perfect.

Almsgiving in secret

1 6 "Be careful not to parade your good deeds before men
to attract their notice; by doing this you will lose all
2 reward from your Father in heaven. ·So when you give
alms, do not have it trumpeted before you; this is what the
hypocrites do in the synagogues and in the streets to win
men's admiration. I tell you solemnly, they have had their
3 reward. ·But when you give alms, your left hand must not
4 know what your right is doing; ·your almsgiving must be
secret, and your Father who sees all that is done in secret
will reward you.

Prayer in secret

5   "And when you pray, d _ot imitate the hypocrites: they
love to say their prayers standing up in the synagogues and
at the street corners for people to see them. I tell you
6 solemnly, they have had their reward. ·But when you pray,
*go to your private room and, when you have shut your
door, pray*ᵃ to your Father who is in that secret place, and
your Father who sees all that is done in secret will reward
you.

How to pray. The Lord's Prayer

7   "In your prayers do not babble as the pagans do, for
they think that by using many words they will make them-
8 selves heard. ·Do not be like them; your Father knows
9 what you need before you ask him. ·So you should pray
like this:

       "Our Father in heaven,
       may your name be held holy,
10   your kingdom come,
       your will be done,

g. Ex 20:14 h. Dt 24:1 i. Ex 20:7 j. Ex 21:24 k. The
quotation is from Lv 19:18; the second part of this commandment, not in the written Law, is an Aramaic way of saying
"You do not have to love your enemy." l. They were employed
by the occupying power and this earned them popular contempt.
6 a. Not a direct quotation but an allusion to the practice common in the O.T., see 2 K 4:33.

on earth as in heaven.
11 Give us today our daily bread.
12 And forgive us our debts,
as we have forgiven those who are in debt to us.
13 And do not put us to the test,
but save us from the evil one.

14 Yes, if you forgive others their failings, your heavenly
15 Father will forgive you yours; ·but if you do not forgive
others, your Father will not forgive your failings either.

Fasting in secret

16 "When you fast do not put on a gloomy look as the
hypocrites do: they pull long faces to let men know they
are fasting. I tell you solemnly, they have had their reward.
17 But when you fast, put oil on your head and wash your
18 face, ·so that no one will know you are fasting except your
Father who sees all that is done in secret; and your Father
who sees all that is done in secret will reward you.

True treasures

19 "Do not store up treasures for yourselves on earth,
where moths and woodworms destroy them and thieves
20 can break in and steal. ·But store up treasures for yourselves in heaven, where neither moth nor woodworms
21 destroy them and thieves cannot break in and steal. ·For
where your treasure is, there will your heart be also.

The eye, the lamp of the body

22 "The lamp of the body is the eye. It follows that if your
eye is sound, your whole body will be filled with light.
23 But if your eye is diseased, your whole body will be all
darkness. If then, the light inside you is darkness, what
darkness that will be!

God and money

24 "No one can be the slave of two masters: he will either
hate the first and love the second, or treat the first with
respect and the second with scorn. You cannot be the slave
both of God and of money.

Trust in Providence

25 "That is why I am telling you not to worry about your
life and what you are to eat, nor about your body and

how you are to clothe it. Surely life means more than food,
26 and the body more than clothing! ·Look at the birds in the
sky. They do not sow or reap or gather into barns; yet
your heavenly Father feeds them. Are you not worth much
27 more than they are? ·Can any of you, for all his worry-
28 ing, add one single cubit to his span of life? ·And why
worry about clothing? Think of the flowers growing in the
29 fields; they never have to work or spin; yet I assure you
that not even Solomon in all his regalia was robed like one
30 of these. ·Now if that is how God clothes the grass in the
field which is there today and thrown into the furnace
tomorrow, will he not much more look after you, you men
31 of little faith? ·So do not worry; do not say, 'What are
we to eat? What are we to drink? How are we to be
32 clothed?' ·It is the pagans who set their hearts on all these
things. Your heavenly Father knows you need them all.
33 Set your hearts on his kingdom first, and on his righteousness, and all these other things will be given you as well.
34 So do not worry about tomorrow: tomorrow will take care
of itself. Each day has enough trouble of its own.

Do not judge

½ 7 "Do not judge, and you will not be judged; ·because
the judgments you give are the judgments you will
get, and the amount you measure out is the amount you
3 will be given. ·Why do you observe the splinter in your
brother's eye and never notice the plank in your own?
4 How dare you say to your brother, 'Let me take the splinter
out of your eye,' when all the time there is a plank in your
5 own? ·Hypocrite! Take the plank out of your own eye first,
and then you will see clearly enough to take the splinter out
of your brother's eye.

Do not profane sacred things

6   "Do not give dogs what is holy;[a] and do not throw your
pearls in front of pigs, or they may trample them and then
turn on you and tear you to pieces.

7 a. The meat of animals which have been offered in sacrifice
in the Temple; the application is to the parading of holy beliefs and practices in front of those who cannot understand
them.

Effective prayer

7   "Ask, and it will be given to you; search, and you will
8 find; knock, and the door will be opened to you. ·For the
one who asks always receives; the one who searches always finds; the one who knocks will always have the door
9 opened to him. ·Is there a man among you who would
10 hand his son a stone when he asked for bread? ·Or would
11 hand him a snake when he asked for a fish? ·If you, then,
who are evil, know how to give your children what is good,
how much more will your Father in heaven give good
things to those who ask him!

The golden rule

12   "So always treat others as you would like them to treat
you; that is the meaning of the Law and the Prophets.

The two ways

13   "Enter by the narrow gate, since the road that leads to
14 perdition is wide and spacious, and many take it; ·but it is
a narrow gate and a hard road that leads to life, and only
a few find it.

False prophets

15   "Beware of false prophets[b] who come to you disguised
16 as sheep but underneath are ravenous wolves. ·You will
be able to tell them by their fruits. Can people pick grapes
17 from thorns, or figs from thistles? ·In the same way, a
sound tree produces good fruit but a rotten tree bad fruit.
18 A sound tree cannot bear bad fruit, nor a rotten tree bear
19 good fruit. ·Any tree that does not produce good fruit is
20 cut down and thrown on the fire. ·I repeat, you will be
able to tell them by their fruits.

The true disciple

21   "It is not those who say to me, 'Lord, Lord,' who will
enter the kingdom of heaven, but the person who does the
22 will of my Father in heaven. ·When the day[c] comes many
will say to me, 'Lord, Lord, did we not prophesy in your
name, cast out demons in your name, work many miracles
23 in your name?' ·Then I shall tell them to their faces: I
have never known you; *away from me, you evil men!*
24   "Therefore, everyone who listens to these words of mine
and acts on them will be like a sensible man who built his

25 house on rock. ·Rain came down, floods rose, gales blew
and hurled themselves against that house; and it did not
26 fall: it was founded on rock. ·But everyone who listens to
these words of mine and does not act on them will be like
27 a stupid man who built his house on sand. ·Rain came
down, floods rose, gales blew and struck that house, and
it fell; and what a fall it had!"

The amazement of the crowds

28   Jesus had now finished what he wanted to say, and his
29 teaching made a deep impression on the people ·because
he taught them with authority, and not like their own
scribes.[d]

III. THE KINGDOM OF HEAVEN IS PREACHED

A. NARRATIVE SECTION: TEN MIRACLES

Cure of a leper

1 O After he had come down from the mountain large
2 O crowds followed him. ·A leper now came up and bowed
low in front of him. "Sir," he said "if you want to, you can
3 cure me." ·Jesus stretched out his hand, touched him and
said, "Of course I want to! Be cured!" And his leprosy was
4 cured at once. ·Then Jesus said to him, "Mind you do not
tell anyone, but go and show yourself to the priest and
make the offering prescribed by Moses, as evidence for
them."

Cure of the centurion's servant

5   When he went into Capernaum a centurion came up
6 and pleaded with him. ·"Sir," he said "my servant is lying
7 at home paralyzed, and in great pain." ·"I will come myself
8 and cure him" said Jesus. ·The centurion replied, "Sir, I
am not worthy to have you under my roof; just give the
9 word and my servant will be cured. ·For I am under authority myself, and have soldiers under me; and I say to
one man: Go, and he goes; to another: Come here, and he
10 comes; to my servant: Do this, and he does it." ·When Jesus

b. Lying teachers of religion. c. The day of Judgment. d.
Doctors of the law, who buttressed their teaching by quotation
from the scriptures and traditions.

heard this he was astonished and said to those following
him, "I tell you solemnly, nowhere in Israel have I found
11 faith like this. •And I tell you that many will come from
east and west to take their places with Abraham and Isaac
12 and Jacob at the feast in the kingdom of heaven; •but the
subjects of the kingdom*a* will be turned out into the dark,
18 where there will be weeping and grinding of teeth." •And
to the centurion Jesus said, "Go back, then; you have believed, so let this be done for you." And the servant was
cured at that moment.

Cure of Peter's mother-in-law

14　　And going into Peter's house Jesus found Peter's
15 mother-in-law in bed with fever. •He touched her hand
and the fever left her, and she got up and began to wait
on him.

A number of cures

16　　That evening they brought him many who were possessed by devils. He cast out the spirits with a word and
17 cured all who were sick. •This was to fulfill the prophecy
of Isaiah:

> *He took our sicknesses away and carried our diseases*
> *for us.*b

Hardships of the apostolic calling

18　　When Jesus saw the great crowds all about him he gave
19 orders to leave for the other side.*c* •One of the scribes
then came up and said to him, "Master, I will follow you
20 wherever you go." •Jesus replied, "Foxes have holes and
the birds of the air have nests, but the Son of Man has
nowhere to lay his head."
21　　Another man, one of his disciples, said to him, "Sir, let
22 me go and bury my father first." •But Jesus replied, "Follow me, and leave the dead to bury their dead."

The calming of the storm

28　　Then he got into the boat followed by his disciples.
24 Without warning a storm broke over the lake, so violent
that the waves were breaking right over the boat. But he
25 was asleep. •So they went to him and woke him saying,
26 "Save us, Lord, we are going down!" •And he said to them,

"Why are you so frightened, you men of little faith?" And
with that he stood up and rebuked the winds and the sea;
27 and all was calm again. •The men were astounded and
said, "Whatever kind of man is this? Even the winds and
the sea obey him."

The demoniacs of Gadara

28 When he reached the country of the Gadarenes on the
other side, two demoniacs came toward him out of the
tombs—creatures so fierce that no one could pass that way.
29 They stood there shouting, "What do you want with us,
Son of God? Have you come here to torture us before the
30 time?"d •Now some distance away there was a large herd
31 of pigs feeding, •and the devils pleaded with Jesus, "If you
32 cast us out, send us into the herd of pigs." •And he said
to them, "Go then," and they came out and made for
the pigs; and at that the whole herd charged down the
33 cliff into the lake and perished in the water. •The swineherds ran off and made for the town, where they told
the whole story, including what had happened to the
34 demoniacs. •At this the whole town set out to meet Jesus;
and as soon as they saw him they implored him to leave
the neighborhood.

Cure of a paralytic

1 He got back in the boat, crossed the water and came
2 to his own town.a •Then some people appeared, bringing him a paralytic stretched out on a bed. Seeing their
faith, Jesus said to the paralytic, "Courage, my child, your
3 sins are forgiven." •And at this some scribes said to them-
4 selves, "This man is blaspheming." •Knowing what was in
their minds Jesus said, "Why do you have such wicked
5 thoughts in your hearts? •Now, which of these is easier:
to say, 'Your sins are forgiven,' or to say, 'Get up and
6 walk?' •But to prove to you that the Son of Man has authority on earth to forgive sins,"—he said to the paralytic
7 —"get up, and pick up your bed and go off home." •And

8 a. The Jews, natural heirs of the promises. · b. Is 53:4   c.
The E. bank of Lake Tiberias. d. The day of Judgment,
when the reign of God would banish all demons.
9 a. Capernaum, cf. 4:13.

8 the man got up and went home. ·A feeling of awe came over the crowd when they saw this, and they praised God for giving such power to men.

The call of Matthew

9   As Jesus was walking on from there he saw a man named Matthew*b* sitting by the customs house, and he said to him, "Follow me." And he got up and followed him.

Eating with sinners

10   While he was at dinner in the house it happened that a number of tax collectors and sinners*c* came to sit at
11 the table with Jesus and his disciples. ·When the Pharisees saw this, they said to his disciples, "Why does your
12 master eat with tax collectors and sinners?" ·When he heard this he replied, "It is not the healthy who need the doctor,
13 but the sick. ·Go and learn the meaning of the words: *What I want is mercy, not sacrifice.d* And indeed I did not come to call the virtuous, but sinners."

A discussion on fasting

14   Then John's*e* disciples came to him and said, "Why is it that we and the Pharisees fast, but your disciples do not?"
15 Jesus replied, "Surely the bridegroom's attendants would never think of mourning as long as the bridegroom is still with them? But the time will come for the bridegroom to
16 be taken away from them, and then they will fast. ·No one puts a piece of unshrunken cloth on to an old cloak, because the patch pulls away from the cloak and the tear
17 gets worse. ·Nor do people put new wine into old wineskins; if they do, the skins burst, the wine runs out, and the skins are lost. No; they put new wine into fresh skins and both are preserved."*f*

Cure of the woman with a hemorrhage. The official's daughter raised to life

18   While he was speaking to them, up came one of the officials, who bowed low in front of him and said, "My daughter has just died, but come and lay your hand on her
19 and her life will be saved." ·Jesus rose and, with his disciples, followed him.
20   Then from behind him came a woman, who had suf-

fered from a hemorrhage for twelve years, and she
21 touched the fringe of his cloak, ·for she said to herself,
22 "If I can only touch his cloak I shall be well again." ·Jesus
turned round and saw her; and he said to her, "Courage,
my daughter, your faith has restored you to health." And
from that moment the woman was well again.

23 When Jesus reached the official's house and saw the
flute-players, with the crowd making a commotion*g* he said,
24 "Get out of here; the little girl is not dead, she is asleep."
25 And they laughed at him. ·But when the people had been
turned out he went inside and took the little girl by the
26 hand; and she stood up. ·And the news spread all round
the countryside.

Cure of two blind men

27 As Jesus went on his way two blind men followed him
28 shouting, "Take pity on us, Son of David." ·And when
Jesus reached the house the blind men came up with him
and he said to them, "Do you believe I can do this?" They
29 said, "Sir, we do." ·Then he touched their eyes saying,
30 "Your faith deserves it, so let this be done for you." ·And
their sight returned. Then Jesus sternly warned them, "Take
31 care that no one learns about this." ·But when they had
gone, they talked about him all over the countryside.

Cure of a dumb demoniac

32 They had only just left when a man was brought to
33 him, a dumb demoniac. ·And when the devil was cast out,
the dumb man spoke and the people were amazed. "Noth-
34 ing like this has ever been seen in Israel" they said. ·But
the Pharisees said, "It is through the prince of devils that he
casts out devils."

The distress of the crowds

35 Jesus made a tour through all the towns and villages,
teaching in their synagogues, proclaiming the Good News

b. Called Levi by Mk and Lk. c. Social outcasts, made
"unclean" by breaking religious laws or following a disreputable
profession. d. Ho 6:6 e. John the Baptist. f. New devo-
tional exercises, like those which John and the Pharisees add
to the religion of the old order, will not preserve it. g. The
loud wailing of the oriental mourner.

of the kingdom and curing all kinds of diseases and sickness.

³⁶ And when he saw the crowds he felt sorry for them because they were harassed and dejected, like sheep with-
³⁷ out a shepherd. ·Then he said to his disciples, "The har-
³⁸ vest is rich but the laborers are few, ·so ask the Lord of the harvest to send laborers to his harvest."

B. THE INSTRUCTION OF THE APOSTLES

The mission of the Twelve

¹ **10** He summoned his twelve disciples, and gave them authority over unclean spirits with power to cast them out and to cure all kinds of diseases and sickness.
² These are the names of the twelve apostles: first, Simon who is called Peter, and his brother Andrew; James the
³ son of Zebedee, and his brother John; ·Philip and Barthol-omew; Thomas, and Matthew the tax collector; James the
⁴ son of Alphaeus, and Thaddaeus; ·Simon the Zealot and
⁵ Judas Iscariot, the one who was to betray him. ·These twelve Jesus sent out, instructing them as follows:

"Do not turn your steps to pagan territory, and do not
⁶ enter any Samaritan town; ·go rather to the lost sheep of
⁷ the House of Israel. ·And as you go, proclaim that the
⁸ kingdom of heaven is close at hand. ·Cure the sick, raise the dead, cleanse the lepers, cast out devils. You received
⁹ without charge, give without charge. ·Provide yourselves with no gold or silver, not even with a few coppers for your
¹⁰ purses, ·with no haversack for the journey or spare tunic or footwear or a staff, for the workman deserves his keep.
¹¹ "Whatever town or village you go into, ask for someone
¹² trustworthy and stay with him until you leave. ·As you
¹³ enter his house, salute it, ·and if the house deserves it, let your peace descend upon it; if it does not, let your peace
¹⁴ come back to you. ·And if anyone does not welcome you or listen to what you have to say, as you walk out of the
¹⁵ house or town shake the dust from your feet. ·I tell you solemnly, on the day of Judgment it will not go as hard with the land of Sodom and Gomorrah as with that town.
¹⁶ Remember, I am sending you out like sheep among wolves; so be cunning as serpents and yet as harmless as doves.

The missionaries will be persecuted[a]

17 "Beware of men: they will hand you over to sanhedrins
18 and scourge you in their synagogues. ·You will be
dragged before governors and kings for my sake, to bear
19 witness before them and the pagans. ·But when they hand
you over, do not worry about how to speak or what to say;
what you are to say will be given to you when the time
20 comes; ·because it is not you who will be speaking; the
Spirit of your Father will be speaking in you.
21 "Brother will betray brother to death, and the father his
child; children will rise against their parents and have them
22 put to death. ·You will be hated by all men on account
of my name; but the man who stands firm to the end will
23 be saved. ·If they persecute you in one town, take refuge
in the next; and if they persecute you in that, take refuge
in another. I tell you solemnly, you will not have gone
the round of the towns of Israel before the Son of Man
comes.
24 "The disciple is not superior to his teacher, nor the slave
25 to his master. ·It is enough for the disciple that he should
grow to be like his teacher, and the slave like his master.
If they have called the master of the house Beelzebul, what
will they not say of his household?

Open and fearless speech

26 "Do not be afraid of them therefore. For everything
that is now covered will be uncovered, and everything now
27 hidden will be made clear. ·What I say to you in the dark,
tell in the daylight; what you hear in whispers, proclaim
from the housetops.
28 "Do not be afraid of those who kill the body but cannot
kill the soul; fear him rather who can destroy both body
29 and soul in hell. ·Can you not buy two sparrows for a
penny? And yet not one falls to the ground without your
30 Father knowing. ·Why, every hair on your head has been
31 counted. ·So there is no need to be afraid; you are worth
more than hundreds of sparrows.
32 "So if anyone declares himself for me in the presence of
men, I will declare myself for him in the presence of my
33 Father in heaven. ·But the one who disowns me in the

10 a. The conditions described in vv. 17-39 are those of a
later time than this first mission of the Twelve.

presence of men, I will disown in the presence of my Father in heaven.

Jesus, the cause of dissension

84 "Do not suppose that I have come to bring peace to the earth: it is not peace I have come to bring, but a
85 sword. ·For I have come to set *a man against his father, a daughter against her mother, a daughter-in-law against*
86 *her mother-in-law.* ·*A man's enemies will be those of his own household.*[b]

Renouncing self to follow Jesus

87 "Anyone who prefers father or mother to me is not worthy of me. Anyone who prefers son or daughter to me
88 is not worthy of me. ·Anyone who does not take his cross
89 and follow in my footsteps is not worthy of me. ·Anyone who finds his life will lose it; anyone who loses his life for my sake will find it.

Conclusion

40 "Anyone who welcomes you welcomes me; and those who welcome me welcome the one who sent me.
41 "Anyone who welcomes a prophet because he is a prophet will have a prophet's reward; and anyone who welcomes a holy man because he is a holy man will have a holy man's reward.
42 "If anyone gives so much as a cup of cold water to one of these little ones because he is a disciple, then I tell you solemnly, he will most certainly not lose his reward."

IV. THE MYSTERY OF THE KINGDOM OF HEAVEN

A. NARRATIVE SECTION

1 **11** When Jesus had finished instructing his twelve disciples he moved on from there to teach and preach in their towns.[a]

The Baptist's question. Jesus commends him

2 Now John in his prison had heard what Christ was doing
3 and he sent his disciples to ask him, ·"Are you the one who is to come, or have we got to wait for someone else?"

4 Jesus answered, "Go back and tell John what you hear
5 and see; ·the blind see again, and the lame walk, lepers
are cleansed, and the deaf hear, and the dead are raised
to life and the Good News is proclaimed to the poor;[b]
6 and happy is the man who does not lose faith in me."

7   As the messengers were leaving, Jesus began to talk to
the people about John: "What did you go out into the
8 wilderness to see? A reed swaying in the breeze? No? ·Then
what did you go out to see? A man wearing fine clothes?
Oh no, those who wear fine clothes are to be found in
9 palaces. ·Then what did you go out for? To see a prophet?
10 Yes, I tell you, and much more than a prophet: ·he is the
one of whom scripture says:

> Look, I am going to send my messenger before you;
> he will prepare your way before you.[c]

11   "I tell you solemnly, of all the children born of women,
a greater than John the Baptist has never been seen;
yet the least in the kingdom of heaven is greater than he
12 is. ·Since John the Baptist came, up to this present time,
the kingdom of heaven has been subjected to violence and
13 the violent are taking it by storm. ·Because it was toward
John that all the prophecies of the prophets and of the
14 Law were leading; ·and he, if you will believe me, is the
15 Elijah who was to return.[d] ·If anyone has ears to hear,
let him listen!

Jesus condemns his contemporaries

16   "What description can I find for this generation? It is
like children shouting to each other as they sit in the market
place:

17   'We played the pipes for you,
             and you wouldn't dance;
           we sang dirges,
             and you wouldn't be mourners.'

18 "For John came, neither eating nor drinking, and they say,
19 'He is possessed.' ·The Son of Man came, eating and drinking, and they say, 'Look, a glutton and a drunkard, a friend

b. Mi 7:6
11 a. I.e. the Jews' towns.

of tax collectors and sinners.' Yet wisdom has been proved right by her actions."

Lament over the lake towns

20   Then he began to reproach the towns in which most of his miracles had been worked, because they refused to repent.

21   "Alas for you, Chorazin! Alas for you, Bethsaida! For if the miracles done in you had been done in Tyre and Sidon, they would have repented long ago in sackcloth and 22 ashes. ·And still, I tell you that it will not go as hard on 28 Judgment day with Tyre and Sidon as with you. ·And as for you, Capernaum, did you want to be exalted as high as heaven? *You shall be thrown down to hell.*^e For if the miracles done in you had been done in Sodom, it 24 would have been standing yet. ·And still, I tell you that it will not go as hard with the land of Sodom on Judgment day as with you."

The Good News revealed to the simple. The Father and the Son

25   At that time Jesus exclaimed, "I bless you, Father, Lord of heaven and of earth, for hiding these things from the learned and the clever and revealing them to mere chil- 26 dren. ·Yes, Father, for that is what it pleased you to do. 27 Everything has been entrusted to me by my Father; and no one knows the Son except the Father, just as no one knows the Father except the Son and those to whom the Son chooses to reveal him.

The gentle mastery of Christ

28   "Come to me, all you who labor and are overburdened, 29 and I will give you rest. ·Shoulder my yoke and learn from me, for I am gentle and humble in heart, *and you* 80 *will find rest for your souls.*^f ·Yes, my yoke is easy and my burden light."

Picking corn on the sabbath

1 **12** At that time Jesus took a walk one sabbath day through the cornfields. His disciples were hungry and 2 began to pick ears of corn and eat them. ·The Pharisees noticed it and said to him, "Look, your disciples are doing 8 something that is forbidden on the sabbath." ·But he said to them, "Have you not read what David did when he and

⁴ his followers were hungry—·how he went into the house
of God and how they ate the loaves of offering which
neither he nor his followers were allowed to eat, but which
⁵ were for the priests alone? ·Or again, have you not read
in the Law that on the sabbath day the Temple priests
⁶ break the sabbath without being blamed for it? ·Now here,
⁷ I tell you, is something greater than the Temple. ·And if
you had understood the meaning of the words: *What I
want is mercy, not sacrifice,* you would not have con-
⁸ demned the blameless. ·For the Son of Man is master of
the sabbath."

Cure of the man with a withered hand

⁹ He moved on from there and went to their synagogue,
¹⁰ and a man was there at the time who had a withered
hand. They asked him, "Is it against the law to cure a man
on the sabbath day?" hoping for something to use against
¹¹ him. ·But he said to them, "If any one of you here had
only one sheep and it fell down a hole on the sabbath day,
¹² would he not get hold of it and lift it out? ·Now a man
is far more important than a sheep, so it follows that it is
¹³ permitted to do good on the sabbath day." ·Then he said
to the man, "Stretch out your hand." He stretched it out
¹⁴ and his hand was better, as sound as the other one. ·At
this the Pharisees went out and began to plot against him,
discussing how to destroy him.

Jesus the "servant of Yahweh"

¹⁵ Jesus knew this and withdrew from the district. Many
¹⁶ followed him and he cured them all, ·but warned them
¹⁷ not to make him known. ·This was to fulfill the prophecy
of Isaiah:

¹⁸ *Here is my servant whom I have chosen,*
 my beloved, the favorite of my soul.
 I will endow him with my spirit,
 and he will proclaim the true faith to the nations.
¹⁹ *He will not brawl or shout,*
 nor will anyone hear his voice in the streets.

b. These are signs of the messianic age in the prophecies of
Isaiah. c. Ml 3:1 d. According to the last of the prophets,
Ml 3:23. e. Is 14 f. Jr 6:16

20   *He will not break the crushed reed,*
    nor put out the smouldering wick
    till he has led the truth to victory:
21   *in his name the nations will put their hope.*[a]

Jesus and Beelzebul

22   Then they brought to him a blind and dumb demoniac; and he cured him, so that the dumb man could speak 23 and see. •All the people were astounded and said, "Can 24 this be the Son of David?" •But when the Pharisees heard this they said, "The man casts out devils only through Beelzebul,[b] the prince of devils."

25   Knowing what was in their minds he said to them, "Every kingdom divided against itself is heading for ruin; and no town, no household divided against itself can stand. 26 Now if Satan casts out Satan, he is divided against him- 27 self; so how can his kingdom stand? •And if it is through Beelzebul that I cast out devils, through whom do your own experts cast them out? Let them be your judges, then. 28 But if it is through the Spirit of God that I cast devils out, then know that the kingdom of God has overtaken you.

29   "Or again, how can anyone make his way into a strong man's house and burgle his property unless he has tied up the strong man first? Only then can he burgle his house.

30   "He who is not with me is against me, and he who does 31 not gather with me scatters. •And so I tell you, every one of men's sins and blasphemies will be forgiven, but blas- 32 phemy against the Spirit will not be forgiven. •And anyone who says a word against the Son of Man will be forgiven; but let anyone speak against the Holy Spirit and he will not be forgiven either in this world or in the next.

Words betray the heart

33   "Make a tree sound and its fruit will be sound; make a tree rotten and its fruit will be rotten. For the tree can be 34 told by its fruit. •Brood of vipers, how can your speech be good when you are evil? For a man's words flow out of 35 what fills his heart. •A good man draws good things from his store of goodness; a bad man draws bad things from 36 his store of badness. •So I tell you this, that for every unfounded word men utter they will answer on Judgment 37 day, •since it is by your words you will be acquitted, and by your words condemned."

The sign of Jonah

38   Then some of the scribes and Pharisees spoke up. "Master," they said "we should like to see a sign[o] from you."

39 He replied, "It is an evil and unfaithful generation that asks for a sign! The only sign it will be given is the sign of the

40 prophet Jonah. ·For as Jonah *was in the belly of the sea-monster for three days and three nights,*[d] so will the Son of Man be in the heart of the earth for three days

41 and three nights. ·On Judgment day the men of Nineveh will stand up with this generation and condemn it, because when Jonah preached they repented; and there is some-

42 thing greater than Jonah here. ·On Judgment day the Queen of the South will rise up with this generation and condemn it, because she came from the ends of the earth to hear the wisdom of Solomon; and there is something greater than Solomon here.

The return of the unclean spirit

43   "When an unclean spirit goes out of a man it wanders through waterless country looking for a place to rest, and

44 cannot find one. ·Then it says, 'I will return to the home I came from.' But on arrival, finding it unoccupied, swept

45 and tidied, ·it then goes off and collects seven other spirits more evil than itself, and they go in and set up house there, so that the man ends up by being worse than he was before. That is what will happen to this evil generation."

The true kinsmen of Jesus

46   He was still speaking to the crowds when his mother and his brothers[e] appeared; they were standing outside and

48 were anxious to have a word with him. ·But to the man who told him this Jesus replied, "Who is my mother? Who

49 are my brothers?" ·And stretching out his hand toward his disciples he said, "Here are my mother and my brothers.

50 Anyone who does the will of my Father in heaven, he is my brother and sister and mother."

12 a. Is 42:1-4   b. "prince Baal" often contemptuously changed (e.g. 2 K 1:2f) to "Beelzebub" "Lord of the flies."   c. A miracle to prove his authority.   d. Jon 2:1   e. In Hebr. and Aramaic (and many other languages), "brothers" is the word used for cousins or even more distant relations of the same generation.

B. THE SERMON OF PARABLES

Introduction

¹ ² **13** That same day, Jesus left the house and sat by the lakeside, ·but such crowds gathered round him that he got into a boat and sat there. The people all stood on the ³ beach, ·and he told them many things in parables.

Parable of the sower

⁴ He said, "Imagine a sower going out to sow. ·As he sowed, some seeds fell on the edge of the path, and the ⁵ birds came and ate them up. ·Others fell on patches of rock where they found little soil and sprang up straight ⁶ away, because there was no depth of earth; ·but as soon as the sun came up they were scorched and, not having ⁷ any roots, they withered away. ·Others fell among thorns, ⁸ and the thorns grew up and choked them. ·Others fell on rich soil and produced their crop, some a hundredfold, ⁹ some sixty, some thirty. ·Listen, anyone who has ears!"

Why Jesus speaks in parables

¹⁰ Then the disciples went up to him and asked, "Why do ¹¹ you talk to them in parables?" ·"Because" he replied "the mysteries of the kingdom of heaven are revealed to you, ¹² but they are not revealed to them. ·For anyone who has will be given more, and he will have more than enough; but from anyone who has not, even what he has will be ¹³ taken away. ·The reason I talk to them in parables is that they look without seeing and listen without hearing or un- ¹⁴ derstanding. ·So in their case this prophecy of Isaiah is being fulfilled:

You will listen and listen again, but not understand,
see and see again, but not perceive.
¹⁵ *For the heart of this nation has grown coarse,*
their ears are dull of hearing, and they have shut their eyes,
for fear they should see with their eyes,
hear with their ears,
understand with their heart,
and be converted
and be healed by me.[a]

¹⁶ "But happy are your eyes because they see, your ears ¹⁷ because they hear! ·I tell you solemnly, many prophets

and holy men longed to see what you see, and never saw it; to hear what you hear, and never heard it.

The parable of the sower explained

18 "You, therefore, are to hear the parable of the sower.
19 When anyone hears the word of the kingdom without understanding, the evil one comes and carries off what was sown in his heart: this is the man who received the seed
20 on the edge of the path. ·The one who received it on patches of rock is the man who hears the word and wel-
21 comes it at once with joy. ·But he has no root in him, he does not last; let some trial come, or some persecution on
22 account of the word, and he falls away at once. ·The one who received the seed in thorns is the man who hears the word, but the worries of this world and the lure of riches
23 choke the word and so he produces nothing. ·And the one who received the seed in rich soil is the man who hears the word and understands it; he is the one who yields a harvest and produces now a hundredfold, now sixty, now thirty."

Parable of the darnel

24 He put another parable before them, "The kingdom of heaven may be compared to a man who sowed good seed
25 in his field. ·While everybody was asleep his enemy came,
26 sowed darnel all among the wheat, and made off. ·When the new wheat sprouted and ripened, the darnel appeared
27 as well. ·The owner's servants went to him and said, 'Sir, was it not good seed that you sowed in your field? If so,
28 where does the darnel come from?' ·'Some enemy has done this' he answered. And the servants said, 'Do you
29 want us to go and weed it out?' ·But he said, 'No, because when you weed out the darnel you might pull up
30 the wheat with it. ·Let them both grow till the harvest; and at harvest time I shall say to the reapers: First collect the darnel and tie it in bundles to be burned, then gather the wheat into my barn.' "

Parable of the mustard seed

31 He put another parable before them, "The kingdom of heaven is like a mustard seed which a man took and sowed
32 in his field. ·It is the smallest of all the seeds, but when it

13 a. Is 6:9-10

has grown it is the biggest shrub of all and becomes a tree so that the birds of the air come and shelter in its branches."

Parable of the yeast

33 He told them another parable, "The kingdom of heaven is like the yeast a woman took and mixed in with three measures of flour till it was leavened all through."

The people are taught only in parables

34 In all this Jesus spoke to the crowds in parables; indeed,
35 he would never speak to them except in parables. ·This was to fulfill the prophecy:

*I will speak to you in parables
and expound things hidden since the foundation of the
   world.*[b]

The parable of the darnel explained

36 Then, leaving the crowds, he went to the house; and his disciples came to him and said, "Explain the parable
37 about the darnel in the field to us." ·He said in reply,
38 "The sower of the good seed is the Son of Man. ·The field is the world; the good seed is the subjects of the kingdom;
39 the darnel, the subjects of the evil one; ·the enemy who sowed them, the devil; the harvest is the end of the world;
40 the reapers are the angels. ·Well then, just as the darnel is gathered up and burned in the fire, so it will be at the end
41 of time. ·The Son of Man will send his angels and they will gather out of his kingdom all things that provoke of-
42 fenses and all who do evil, ·and throw them into the blazing furnace, where there will be weeping and grinding of
43 teeth. ·Then the virtuous will shine like the sun in the kingdom of their Father.[c] Listen, anyone who has ears!

Parables of the treasure and of the pearl

44 "The kingdom of heaven is like treasure hidden in a field which someone has found; he hides it again, goes off happy, sells everything he owns and buys the field.
45 "Again, the kingdom of heaven is like a merchant look-
46 ing for fine pearls; ·when he finds one of great value he goes and sells everything he owns and buys it.

Parable of the dragnet

47 "Again, the kingdom of heaven is like a dragnet cast
48 into the sea that brings in a haul of all kinds. ·When it

is full, the fishermen haul it ashore; then, sitting down, they
collect the good ones in a basket and throw away those
49 that are no use. •This is how it will be at the end of time:
the angels will appear and separate the wicked from the
50 just •to throw them into the blazing furnace where there
will be weeping and grinding of teeth.

Conclusion

51 "Have you understood all this?" They said, "Yes." •And
52 he said to them, "Well then, every scribe who becomes a
disciple of the kingdom of heaven is like a householder
who brings out from his storeroom things both new and
old."[d]

V. THE CHURCH, FIRST-FRUITS
OF THE KINGDOM OF HEAVEN

A. NARRATIVE SECTION

A visit to Nazareth

53 When Jesus had finished these parables he left the dis-
54 trict; •and, coming to his home town,[e] he taught the people
in their synagogue in such a way that they were astonished
and said, "Where did the man get this wisdom and these
55 miraculous powers? •This is the carpenter's son, surely? Is
not his mother the woman called Mary, and his brothers
56 James and Joseph and Simon and Jude? •His sisters, too,
are they not all here with us? So where did the man get
57 it all?" •And they would not accept him. But Jesus said to
them, "A prophet is only despised in his own country and
58 in his own house," •and he did not work many miracles
there because of their lack of faith.

Herod and Jesus

1 **14** At that time Herod the tetrarch heard about the
2   reputation of Jesus, •and said to his court, "This is
John the Baptist himself; he has risen from the dead, and
that is why miraculous powers are at work in him."

b. Ps 78:2 **c.** The kingdom of the Son, v. 41, is succeeded by
the kingdom of the Father. **d.** Perhaps a saying of particular
significance to Mt, a "scribe who became a disciple." **e.** Nazareth, see 2:23.

John the Baptist beheaded

3 Now it was Herod who had arrested John, chained him up and put him in prison because of Herodias, his
4 brother Philip's*a* wife. ·For John had told him, "It is against
5 the Law for you to have her." ·He had wanted to kill him but was afraid of the people, who regarded John as a
6 prophet. ·Then, during the celebrations for Herod's birthday, the daughter of Herodias*b* danced before the com-
7 pany, and so delighted Herod ·that he promised on oath
8 to give her anything she asked. ·Prompted by her mother she said, "Give me John the Baptist's head, here, on a
9 dish." ·The king was distressed but, thinking of the oaths he had sworn and of his guests, he ordered it to be given
10,11 her, ·and sent and had John beheaded in the prison. ·The head was brought in on a dish and given to the girl who
12 took it to her mother. ·John's disciples came and took the body and buried it; then they went off to tell Jesus.

First miracle of the loaves

13 When Jesus received this news he withdrew by boat to a lonely place where they could be by themselves. But the people heard of this and, leaving the towns, went after him
14 on foot. ·So as he stepped ashore he saw a large crowd; and he took pity on them and healed their sick.
15 When evening came, the disciples went to him and said, "This is a lonely place, and the time has slipped by; so send the people away, and they can go to the villages to buy
16 themselves some food." ·Jesus replied, "There is no need for them to go: give them something to eat yourselves."
17 But they answered, "All we have with us is five loaves and
18,19 two fish." ·"Bring them here to me" he said. ·He gave orders that the people were to sit down on the grass; then he took the five loaves and the two fish, raised his eyes to heaven and said the blessing. And breaking the loaves he handed them to his disciples who gave them to the crowds.
20 They all ate as much as they wanted, and they collected
21 the scraps remaining, twelve baskets full. ·Those who ate numbered about five thousand men, to say nothing of women and children.

Jesus walks on the water and, with him, Peter

22 Directly after this he made the disciples get into the boat and go on ahead to the other side while he would send the

23 crowds away. •After sending the crowds away he went
up into the hills by himself to pray. When evening came,
24 he was there alone, •while the boat, by now far out on the
lake, was battling with a heavy sea, for there was a head-
25 wind. •In the fourth watch of the night[c] he went to-
26 ward them, walking on the lake, •and when the disciples
saw him walking on the lake they were terrified. "It is a
27 ghost" they said, and cried out in fear. •But at once Jesus
called out to them, saying, "Courage! It is I! Do not be
28 afraid." •It was Peter who answered. "Lord," he said "if it
29 is you, tell me to come to you across the water." •"Come"
said Jesus. Then Peter got out of the boat and started
30 walking toward Jesus across the water, •but as soon as
he felt the force of the wind, he took fright and began to
31 sink. "Lord! Save me!" he cried. •Jesus put out his hand at
once and held him. "Man of little faith," he said "why did
32 you doubt?" •And as they got into the boat the wind
33 dropped. •The men in the boat bowed down before him
and said, "Truly, you are the Son of God."

Cures at Gennesaret

34   Having made the crossing, they came to land at Gen-
35 nesaret. •When the local people recognized him they spread
the news through the whole neighborhood and took all
36 that were sick to him, •begging him just to let them touch
the fringe of his cloak. And all those who touched it were
completely cured.

The traditions of the Pharisees

1 **15** Pharisees and scribes from Jerusalem then came to
2 Jesus and said, •"Why do your disciples break away
from the tradition of the elders?[a] They do not wash their
3 hands when they eat food." •"And why do you" he answered "break away from the commandment of God for
4 the sake of your tradition? •For God said: *Do your duty to*[b]
your father and mother and: *Anyone who curses father or*
5 *mother must be put to death.*[c] •But you say, 'If anyone

14 a. Philip, Herod's half-brother, was still alive. b. According
to Josephus, the girl's name was Salome. c. 3 to 6 a.m.
15 a. The traditional teaching, including many additions to and
extensions of the Law. b. Often translated "honor," but the
word implies a respect expressed in practical ways, Ex 20:12.
c. Lv 20:9

says to his father or mother: Anything I have that I might
6 have used to help you is dedicated to God,' ·he is rid of
his duty to father or mother.ᵈ In this way you have made
God's word null and void by means of your tradition.
7 Hypocrites! It was you Isaiah meant when he so rightly
prophesied:

8   *This people honors me only with lip-service,*
     while their hearts are far from me.
9   *The worship they offer me is worthless;*
     the doctrines they teach are only human regulations."ᵉ

On clean and unclean

10   He called the people to him and said, "Listen, and
11 understand. ·What goes into the mouth does not make a
man unclean; it is what comes out of the mouth that makes
him unclean."
12   Then the disciples came to him and said, "Do you know
that the Pharisees were shocked when they heard what
13 you said?" ·He replied, "Any plant my heavenly Father has
14 not planted will be pulled up by the roots. ·Leave them
alone. They are blind men leading blind men; and if one
blind man leads another, both will fall into a pit."
15   At this, Peter said to him, "Explain the parable for us."
16
17 Jesus replied, "Do even you not yet understand? ·Can you
not see that whatever goes into the mouth passes through
18 the stomach and is discharged into the sewer? ·But the
things that come out of the mouth come from the heart,
19 and it is these that make a man unclean. ·For from the
heart come evil intentions: murder, adultery, fornication,
20 theft, perjury, slander. ·These are the things that make a
man unclean. But to eat with unwashed hands does not
make a man unclean."

The daughter of the Canaanite woman healed

21   Jesus left that place and withdrew to the region of Tyre
22 and Sidon. ·Then out came a Canaanite woman from that
district and started shouting, "Sir, Son of David, take pity
23 on me. My daughter is tormented by a devil." ·But he
answered her not a word. And his disciples went and
pleaded with him. "Give her what she wants," they said
24 "because she is shouting after us." ·He said in reply, "I
25 was sent only to the lost sheep of the House of Israel." ·But
the woman had come up and was kneeling at his feet.

26 "Lord," she said "help me." ·He replied, "It is not fair to
   take the children's food and throw it to the house-dogs."
27 She retorted, "Ah yes, sir; but even house-dogs can eat the
28 scraps that fall from their master's table." ·Then Jesus answered her, "Woman, you have great faith. Let your wish
   be granted." And from that moment her daughter was well
   again.

Cures near the lake

29   Jesus went on from there and reached the shores of the
   Sea of Galilee, and he went up into the hills. He sat there,
80 and large crowds came to him bringing the lame, the
   crippled, the blind, the dumb and many others; these they
81 put down at his feet, and he cured them. ·The crowds
   were astonished to see the dumb speaking, the cripples
   whole again, the lame walking and the blind with their
   sight, and they praised the God of Israel.

Second miracle of the loaves

82   But Jesus called his disciples to him and said, "I feel
   sorry for all these people; they have been with me for
   three days now and have nothing to eat. I do not want to
   send them off hungry, they might collapse on the way."
88 The disciples said to him, "Where could we get enough
84 bread in this deserted place to feed such a crowd?" ·Jesus
   said to them, "How many loaves have you?" "Seven" they
85 said "and a few small fish." ·Then he instructed the crowd
86 to sit down on the ground, ·and he took the seven loaves
   and the fish, and he gave thanks and broke them and
   handed them to the disciples who gave them to the crowds.
87 They all ate as much as they wanted, and they collected
88 what was left of the scraps, seven baskets full. ·Now four
   thousand men had eaten, to say nothing of women and
89 children. ·And when he had sent the crowds away he got
   into the boat and went to the district of Magadan.

The Pharisees ask for a sign from heaven

1 **16** The Pharisees and Sadducees came, and to test
      him they asked if he would show them a sign
2 from heaven. ·He replied, "In the evening you say, 'It will
8 be fine; there is a red sky,' ·and in the morning, 'Stormy

d. Property dedicated in this way could not be passed to another
person.   e. Is 29:13

weather today; the sky is red and overcast.' You know
how to read the face of the sky, but you cannot read the
4 signs of the times. ·It is an evil and unfaithful generation
that asks for a sign! The only sign it will be given is the
sign of Jonah." And leaving them standing there, he went
away.

The yeast of the Pharisees and Sadducees

5   The disciples, having crossed to the other shore, had
6 forgotten to take any food. ·Jesus said to them, "Keep
your eyes open, and be on your guard against the yeast of
7 the Pharisees and Sadducees." ·And they said to themselves,
8 "It is because we have not brought any bread." ·Jesus knew
it, and he said, "Men of little faith, why are you talking
9 among yourselves about having no bread? ·Do you not yet
understand? Do you not remember the five loaves for the
10 five thousand and the number of baskets you collected? ·Or
the seven loaves for the four thousand and the number of
11 baskets you collected? ·How could you fail to understand
that I was not talking about bread? What I said was: Be-
12 ware of the yeast of the Pharisees and Sadducees." ·Then
they understood that he was telling them to be on their
guard, not against the yeast for making bread, but against
the teaching of the Pharisees and Sadducees.ᵃ

Peter's profession of faith; his pre-eminence

13   When Jesus came to the region of Caesarea Philippi he
put this question to his disciples, "Who do people say
14 the Son of Man is?" ·And they said, "Some say he is John
the Baptist, some Elijah, and others Jeremiah or one of the
15 prophets." ·"But you," he said "who do you say I am?"
16 Then Simon Peter spoke up, "You are the Christ," he said
17 "the Son of the living God." ·Jesus replied, "Simon son of
Jonah, you are a happy man! Because it was not flesh
and blood that revealed this to you but my Father in
18 heaven. ·So I now say to you: You are Peterᵇ and on
this rock I will build my Church. And the gates of the
19 underworldᶜ can never hold out against it. ·I will give you
the keys of the kingdom of heaven: whatever you bind
on earth shall be considered bound in heaven; whatever
you loose on earth shall be considered loosed in heaven."ᵈ
20 Then he gave the disciples strict orders not to tell anyone
that he was the Christ.

First prophecy of the Passion

21   From that time Jesus began to make it clear to his disciples that he was destined to go to Jerusalem and suffer grievously at the hands of the elders and chief priests and scribes, to be put to death and to be raised up on the third
22   day. ·Then, taking him aside, Peter started to remonstrate with him. "Heaven preserve you, Lord;" he said "this
23   must not happen to you." ·But he turned and said to Peter, "Get behind me, Satan! You are an obstacle in my path, because the way you think is not God's way but man's."

The condition of following Christ

24   Then Jesus said to his disciples, "If anyone wants to be a follower of mine, let him renounce himself and take up
25   his cross and follow me. ·For anyone who wants to save his life will lose it; but anyone who loses his life for my
26   sake will find it. ·What, then, will a man gain if he wins the whole world and ruins his life? Or what has a man to offer in exchange for his life?
27   "For the Son of Man is going to come in the glory of his Father with his angels, and, when he does, he will re-
28   ward each one according to his behavior. ·I tell you solemnly, there are some of these standing here who will not taste death before they see the Son of Man coming with his kingdom."[e]

The transfiguration

1   **17** Six days later, Jesus took with him Peter and James and his brother John and led them up a high moun-
2   tain where they could be alone. ·There in their presence he was transfigured: his face shone like the sun and his
3   clothes became as white as the light. ·Suddenly Moses and
4   Elijah[a] appeared to them; they were talking with him. ·Then Peter spoke to Jesus. "Lord," he said "it is wonderful for

16 a. Yeast, here, is regarded as adulterating pure flour. **b.** Not, until now, a proper name: Greek *petros* (as in Engl. saltpetre) represents Aramaic *kepha*, rock. **c.** The gates symbolize the power of the underworld to hold captives. **d.** The keys have become the traditional insignia of Peter. **e.** In vv. 27-28, two different sayings have been combined because both refer to the coming of the kingdom; but the first is about Judgment day, and the second is about the destruction of Jerusalem, the sign of "the last days."
17 a. Representing the Law and the prophets.

us to be here; if you wish, I will make three tents here,
5 one for you, one for Moses and one for Elijah." ·He was
still speaking when suddenly a bright cloud covered them
with shadow, and from the cloud there came a voice which
said, "This is my Son, the Beloved; he enjoys my favor.
6 Listen to him." ·When they heard this, the disciples fell on
7 their faces, overcome with fear. ·But Jesus came up and
8 touched them. "Stand up," he said "do not be afraid." ·And
when they raised their eyes they saw no one but only Jesus.

The question about Elijah

9 As they came down from the mountain Jesus gave them
this order, "Tell no one about the vision until the Son of
10 Man has risen from the dead." ·And the disciples put this
question to him, "Why do the scribes say then that Elijah
11 has to come first?" ·"True"; he replied "Elijah is to come
12 to see that everything is once more as it should be; ·how-
ever, I tell you that Elijah has come already and they did
not recognize him but treated him as they pleased; and
13 the Son of Man will suffer similarly at their hands." ·The
disciples understood then that he had been speaking of
John the Baptist.

The epileptic demoniac

14 As they were rejoining the crowd a man came up to
15 him and went down on his knees before him. ·"Lord," he
said "take pity on my son: he is a lunatic and in a
wretched state; he is always falling into the fire or into the
16 water. ·I took him to your disciples and they were unable
17 to cure him." ·"Faithless and perverse generation!" Jesus
said in reply "How much longer must I be with you? How
much longer must I put up with you? Bring him here to
18 me." ·And when Jesus rebuked it the devil came out of
the boy who was cured from that moment.
19 Then the disciples came privately to Jesus. "Why were
20 we unable to cast it out?" they asked. ·He answered, "Because you have little faith. I tell you solemnly, if your
faith were the size of a mustard seed you could say to
this mountain, 'Move from here to there,' and it would
move; nothing would be impossible for you."

Second prophecy of the Passion

22 One day when they were together in Galilee, Jesus said
to them, "The Son of Man is going to be handed over into

23 the power of men; •they will put him to death, and on the third day he will be raised to life again." And a great sadness came over them.

The Temple tax paid by Jesus and Peter

24 When they reached Capernaum, the collectors of the half-shekel[b] came to Peter and said, "Does your master
25 not pay the half-shekel?" •"Oh yes" he replied, and went into the house. But before he could speak, Jesus said, "Simon, what is your opinion? From whom do the kings of the earth take toll or tribute? From their sons or from
26 foreigners?" •And when he replied, "From foreigners,"
27 Jesus said, "Well then, the sons are exempt. •However, so as not to offend these people, go to the lake and cast a hook; take the first fish that bites, open its mouth and there you will find a shekel; take it and give it to them for me and for you."

B. THE DISCOURSE ON THE CHURCH

Who is the greatest?

1 18 At this time the disciples came to Jesus and said,
2 "Who is the greatest in the kingdom of heaven?" •So he called a little child to him and set the child in front of
3 them. •Then he said, "I tell you solemnly, unless you change and become like little children you will never enter
4 the kingdom of heaven. •And so, the one who makes himself as little as this little child is the greatest in the kingdom of heaven.

On leading others astray

5 "Anyone who welcomes a little child like this in my
6 name welcomes me. •But anyone who is an obstacle to bring down one of these little ones who have faith in me would be better drowned in the depths of the sea with a
7 great millstone round his neck. •Alas for the world that there should be such obstacles! Obstacles indeed there must be, but alas for the man who provides them!
8 "If your hand or your foot should cause you to sin, cut it off and throw it away: it is better for you to enter into life crippled or lame, than to have two hands or two feet
9 and be thrown into eternal fire. •And if your eye should

b. A tax for the upkeep of the Temple.

cause you to sin, tear it out and throw it away: it is better for you to enter into life with one eye, than to have two eyes and be thrown into the hell of fire.

10 "See that you never despise any of these little ones, for I tell you that their angels in heaven are continually in the presence of my Father in heaven.[a]

The lost sheep

12 "Tell me. Suppose a man has a hundred sheep and one of them strays; will he not leave the ninety-nine on the 13 hillside and go in search of the stray? ·I tell you solemnly, if he finds it, it gives him more joy than do the ninety-nine 14 that did not stray at all. ·Similarly, it is never the will of your Father in heaven that one of these little ones should be lost.

Brotherly correction

15 "If your brother does something wrong, go and have it out with him alone, between your two selves. If he listens 16 to you, you have won back your brother. ·If he does not listen, take one or two others along with you: *the evidence of two or three witnesses is required to sustain any charge.* 17 But if he refuses to listen to these, report it to the community;[b] and if he refuses to listen to the community, treat him like a pagan or a tax collector.

18 "I tell you solemnly, whatever you bind on earth shall be considered bound in heaven; whatever you loose on earth shall be considered loosed in heaven.

Prayer in common

19 "I tell you solemnly once again, if two of you on earth agree to ask anything at all, it will be granted to you by 20 my Father in heaven. ·For where two or three meet in my name, I shall be there with them."

Forgiveness of injuries

21 Then Peter went up to him and said, "Lord, how often must I forgive my brother if he wrongs me? As often as 22 seven times?" ·Jesus answered, "Not seven, I tell you, but seventy-seven times.

Parable of the unforgiving debtor

23 "And so the kingdom of heaven may be compared to a king who decided to settle his accounts with his servants.

24 When the reckoning began, they brought him a man who
25 owed ten thousand talents;[c] ·but he had no means of paying, so his master gave orders that he should be sold, together with his wife and children and all his possessions, to
26 meet the debt. ·At this, the servant threw himself down at
his master's feet. 'Give me time' he said 'and I will pay
27 the whole sum.' ·And the servant's master felt so sorry for
28 him that he let him go and cancelled the debt. ·Now as
this servant went out, he happened to meet a fellow servant
who owed him one hundred denarii;[d] and he seized him by
the throat and began to throttle him. 'Pay what you owe
29 me' he said. ·His fellow servant fell at his feet and implored him, saying, 'Give me time and I will pay you.'
30 But the other would not agree; on the contrary, he had
31 him thrown into prison till he should pay the debt. ·His
fellow servants were deeply distressed when they saw what
had happened, and they went to their master and reported
32 the whole affair to him. ·Then the master sent for him.
'You wicked servant,' he said 'I cancelled all that debt
33 of yours when you appealed to me. ·Were you not bound,
then, to have pity on your fellow servant just as I had pity
34 on you?' ·And in his anger the master handed him over to
35 the torturers till he should pay all his debt. ·And that is
how my heavenly Father will deal with you unless you each
forgive your brother from your heart."

VI. THE APPROACHING ADVENT
OF THE KINGDOM OF HEAVEN

A. NARRATIVE SECTION

The question about divorce

1 19 Jesus had now finished what he wanted to say, and
he left Galilee and came into the part of Judaea
2 which is on the far side of the Jordan. ·Large crowds followed him and he healed them there.
8 Some Pharisees approached him, and to test him they
said, "Is it against the Law for a man to divorce his wife

18 a. V. 11, at the time when verse numbers were added, con-
sisted of a sentence which is not now accepted as part of the
original text. b. The community of the brothers (the Church).
c. "Millions of pounds"—about £3,000,000. d. Under £5.

⁴ on any pretext whatever?" ·He answered, "Have you not read that the creator from the beginning *made them male* ⁵ *and female* ·and that he said: *This is why a man must leave father and mother, and cling to his wife, and the two* ⁶ *become one body?* ·They are no longer two, therefore, but one body. So then, what God has united, man must not divide."

⁷ They said to him, "Then why did Moses command that a ⁸ writ of dismissal should be given in cases of divorce?" ·"It was because you were so unteachable" he said "that Moses allowed you to divorce your wives, but it was not like this ⁹ from the beginning. ·Now I say this to you: the man who divorces his wife—I am not speaking of fornication—and marries another, is guilty of adultery."

Continence

¹⁰ The disciples said to him, "If that is how things are between husband and wife, it is not advisable to marry." ¹¹ But he replied, "It is not everyone who can accept what I ¹² have said, but only those to whom it is granted. ·There are eunuchs born that way from their mother's womb, there are eunuchs made so by men and there are eunuchs who have made themselves that way for the sake of the kingdom of heaven. Let anyone accept this who can."

Jesus and the children

¹³ People brought little children to him, for him to lay his hands on them and say a prayer. The disciples turned them ¹⁴ away, ·but Jesus said, "Let the little children alone, and do not stop them coming to me; for it is to such as these ¹⁵ that the kingdom of heaven belongs." ·Then he laid his hands on them and went on his way.

The rich young man

¹⁶ And there was a man who came to him and asked, "Master, what good deed must I do to possess eternal life?" ¹⁷ Jesus said to him, "Why do you ask me about what is good? There is one alone who is good. But if you wish to enter ¹⁸ into life, keep the commandments." ·He said, "Which?" "These:" Jesus replied *"You must not kill. You must not commit adultery. You must not steal. You must not bring* ¹⁹ *false witness.* ·*Honor your father and mother,* and: *you must* ²⁰ *love your neighbor as yourself."ᵃ* ·The young man said to him, "I have kept all these. What more do I need to do?"

21 Jesus said, "If you wish to be perfect, go and sell what you
own and give the money to the poor, and you will have
22 treasure in heaven; then come, follow me." ·But when the
young man heard these words he went away sad, for he
was a man of great wealth.

The danger of riches

23   Then Jesus said to his disciples, "I tell you solemnly, it
will be hard for a rich man to enter the kingdom of heaven.
24 Yes, I tell you again, it is easier for a camel to pass through
the eye of a needle than for a rich man to enter the king-
25 dom of heaven." ·When the disciples heard this they were
26 astonished. "Who can be saved, then?" they said. ·Jesus
gazed at them. "For men" he told them "this is impossible;
for God everything is possible."

The reward of renunciation

27   Then Peter spoke. "What about us?" he said to him "We
have left everything and followed you. What are we to
28 have, then?" ·Jesus said to him, "I tell you solemnly, when
all is made new and the Son of Man sits on his throne of
glory, you will yourselves sit on twelve thrones to judge[b]
29 the twelve tribes of Israel. ·And everyone who has left
houses, brothers, sisters, father, mother, children or land
for the sake of my name will be repaid a hundred times
over, and also inherit eternal life.
30   "Many who are first will be last, and the last, first.

Parable of the vineyard laborers

1 20 "Now the kingdom of heaven is like a landowner
going out at daybreak to hire workers for his vine-
2 yard. ·He made an agreement with the workers for one
3 denarius a day, and sent them to his vineyard. ·Going
out at about the third hour he saw others standing idle in
4 the market place ·and said to them, 'You go to my vine-
5 yard too and I will give you a fair wage.' ·So they went.
At about the sixth hour and again at about the ninth hour,
6 he went out and did the same. ·Then at about the eleventh
hour he went out and found more men standing round,
and he said to them, 'Why have you been standing here
7 idle all day?' ·'Because no one has hired us' they answered. He said to them, 'You go into my vineyard too.'

19 a. Ex 20:12-16; Dt 5:16-20   **b.** I.e. to govern.

⁸ In the evening, the owner of the vineyard said to his bailiff, 'Call the workers and pay them their wages, starting with ⁹ the last arrivals and ending with the first.' ·So those who were hired at about the eleventh hour came forward and ¹⁰ received one denarius each. ·When the first came, they expected to get more, but they too received one denarius ¹¹ each. ·They took it, but grumbled at the landowner. ¹² 'The men who came last' they said 'have done only one hour, and you have treated them the same as us, though ¹³ we have done a heavy day's work in all the heat.' ·He answered one of them and said, 'My friend, I am not being unjust to you; did we not agree on one denarius? ¹⁴ Take your earnings and go. I choose to pay the last-comer ¹⁵ as much as I pay you. ·Have I no right to do what I like with my own? Why be envious because I am generous?' ¹⁶ Thus the last will be first, and the first, last."

Third prophecy of the Passion

¹⁷ Jesus was going up to Jerusalem, and on the way he ¹⁸ took the Twelve to one side and said to them, ·"Now we are going up to Jerusalem, and the Son of Man is about to be handed over to the chief priests and scribes. They will ¹⁹ condemn him to death ·and will hand him over to the pagans to be mocked and scourged and crucified; and on the third day he will rise again."

The mother of Zebedee's sons makes her request

²⁰ Then the mother of Zebedee's sons came with her sons ²¹ to make a request of him, and bowed low; ·and he said to her, "What is it you want?" She said to him, "Promise that these two sons of mine may sit one at your right hand and ²² and the other at your left in your kingdom." ·"You do not know what you are asking" Jesus answered. "Can you drink the cup that I am going to drink?" They replied, "We ²³ can." ·"Very well," he said "you shall drink my cup,ᵃ but as for seats at my right hand and my left, these are not mine to grant; they belong to those to whom these have been allotted by my Father."

Leadership with service

²⁴ When the other ten heard this they were indignant with ²⁵ the two brothers. ·But Jesus called them to him and said, "You know that among the pagans the rulers lord it over ²⁶ them, and their great men make their authority felt. ·This

is not to happen among you. No; anyone who wants to be
27 great among you must be your servant, ·and anyone who
28 wants to be first among you must be your slave, ·just as
the Son of Man came not to be served but to serve, and to
give his life as a ransom for many."

The two blind men of Jericho

29
30 As they left Jericho a large crowd followed him. ·Now
there were two blind men sitting at the side of the road.
When they heard that it was Jesus who was passing by,
31 they shouted, "Lord! Have pity on us, Son of David." ·And
the crowd scolded them and told them to keep quiet, but
they only shouted more loudly, "Lord! Have pity on us,
32 Son of David." ·Jesus stopped, called them over and said,
33 "What do you want me to do for you?" ·They said to him,
34 "Lord, let us have our sight back." ·Jesus felt pity for them
and touched their eyes, and immediately their sight returned and they followed him.

The Messiah enters Jerusalem

1 **21** When they were near Jerusalem and had come in
sight of Bethphage on the Mount of Olives, Jesus
2 sent two disciples, ·saying to them, "Go to the village facing you, and you will immediately find a tethered donkey
3 and a colt with her. Untie them and bring them to me. ·If
anyone says anything to you, you are to say, 'The Master
4 needs them and will send them back directly.' " ·This took
place to fulfill the prophecy:

5   *Say to the daughter of Zion:*
       Look, your king comes to you;
       he is humble, he rides on a donkey
       *and on a colt, the foal of a beast of burden.*ᵃ

6 So the disciples went out and did as Jesus had told them.
7 They brought the donkey and the colt, then they laid their
8 cloaks on their backs and he sat on them. ·Great crowds
of people spread their cloaks on the road, while others
were cutting branches from the trees and spreading them

20 a. Perhaps a prophecy of the martyrdom of James and John;
James was certainly put to death by Herod Agrippa about 44
A.D., Ac 12:2.
21 a. Is 62:11; Zc 9:9

⁹ in his path. ·The crowds who went in front of him and those who followed were all shouting:

"*Hosanna*ᵇ to the Son of David!
*Blessings on him who comes in the name of the Lord!*ᶜ
Hosanna in the highest heavens!"

¹⁰ And when he entered Jerusalem, the whole city was in ¹¹ turmoil. "Who is this?" people asked, ·and the crowds answered, "This is the prophet Jesus from Nazareth in Galilee."

The expulsion of the dealers from the Temple

¹² Jesus then went into the Temple and drove out all those who were selling and buying there; he upset the tables of the money changers and the chairs of those who were sell- ¹³ ing pigeons.ᵈ ·"According to scripture" he said *"my house will be called a house of prayer;*ᵉ but you are turning it ¹⁴ into a *robbers' den.*"ᶠ ·There were also blind and lame people who came to him in the Temple, and he cured them. ¹⁵ At the sight of the wonderful things he did and of the children shouting, "Hosanna to the Son of David" in the Temple, the chief priests and the scribes were indignant. ¹⁶ "Do you hear what they are saying?" they said to him. "Yes," Jesus answered "have you never read this:

By the mouths of children, babes in arms,
*you have made sure of praise?*ᵍ

¹⁷ With that he left them and went out of the city to Bethany where he spent the night.

The barren fig tree withers. Faith and prayer

¹⁸ As he was returning to the city in the early morning, he ¹⁹ felt hungry. ·Seeing a fig tree by the road, he went up to it and found nothing on it but leaves. And he said to it, "May you never bear fruit again"; and at that instant the fig tree ²⁰ withered. ·The disciples were amazed when they saw it. "What happened to the tree" they said "that it withered ²¹ there and then?" ·Jesus answered, "I tell you solemnly, if you have faith and do not doubt at all, not only will you do what I have done to the fig tree, but even if you say to this mountain, 'Get up and throw yourself into the sea,' it will ²² be done. ·And if you have faith, everything you ask for in prayer you will receive."

The authority of Jesus is questioned

23   He had gone into the Temple and was teaching, when
the chief priests and the elders of the people came to him
and said, "What authority have you for acting like this?
24 And who gave you this authority?" •"And I", replied Jesus
"will ask you a question, only one; if you tell me the
answer to it, I will then tell you my authority for acting
25 like this. •John's baptism: where did it come from: heaven
or man?" And they argued it out this way among themselves, 'If we say from heaven, he will retort, 'Then why
26 did you refuse to believe him?'; •but if we say from man,
we have the people to fear, for they all hold that John was
27 a prophet." •So their reply to Jesus was, "We do not know."
And he retorted, "Nor will I tell you my authority for acting like this.

Parable of the two sons

28   "What is your opinion? A man had two sons. He went
and said to the first, 'My boy, you go and work in the
29 vineyard today.' •He answered, 'I will not go,' but after-
30 wards thought better of it and went. •The man then went
and said the same thing to the second who answered, 'Cer-
31 tainly, sir,' but did not go. •Which of the two did the father's will?" "The first" they said. Jesus said to them, "I tell
you solemnly, tax collectors and prostitutes are making
32 their way into the kingdom of God before you. •For John
came to you, a pattern of true righteousness, but you did
not believe him, and yet the tax collectors and prostitutes
did. Even after seeing that, you refused to think better of
it and believe in him.

Parable of the wicked husbandmen

33   "Listen to another parable. There was a man, a landowner, who planted a vineyard; he fenced it round, dug a
winepress in it and built a tower; then he leased it to tenants
34 and went abroad. •When vintage time drew near he sent
35 his servants to the tenants to collect his produce. •But the
tenants seized his servants, thrashed one, killed another and
36 stoned a third. •Next he sent some more servants, this

b. Conventional shout of acclaim, like a cheer. c. Ps 118:26
d. Money changers provided Temple currency, and the traders
the animals, for making sacrificial offerings. e. Is 56:7 f. Jr
7:11 g. Ps 8:2 (LXX); Ws 10:21

time a larger number, and they dealt with them in the same
[37] way. ·Finally he sent his son to them. 'They will respect
[38] my son' he said. ·But when the tenants saw the son, they
said to each other, 'This is the heir. Come on, let us kill
[39] him and take over his inheritance.' ·So they seized him
[40] and threw him out of the vineyard and killed him. ·Now
when the owner of the vineyard comes, what will he do to
[41] those tenants?" ·They answered, "He will bring those
wretches to a wretched end and lease the vineyard to other
tenants who will deliver the produce to him when the sea-
[42] son arrives." ·Jesus said to them, "Have you never read in
the scriptures:

> It was the stone rejected by the builders
>   that became the keystone.
> This was the Lord's doing
> and it is wonderful to see?[h]

[43] I tell you, then, that the kingdom of God will be taken
from you and given to a people who will produce its fruit."
[45]   When they heard his parables, the chief priests and the
[46] scribes realized he was speaking about them, ·but though
they would have liked to arrest him they were afraid of
the crowds, who looked on him as a prophet.

Parable of the wedding feast

[1] **22** Jesus began to speak to them in parables once
[2] again, ·"The kingdom of heaven may be compared
[3] to a king who gave a feast for his son's wedding. ·He sent
his servants to call those who had been invited, but they
[4] would not come. ·Next he sent some more servants. 'Tell
those who have been invited' he said 'that I have my
banquet all prepared, my oxen and fattened cattle have
been slaughtered, everything is ready. Come to the wed-
[5] ding.' ·But they were not interested: one went off to his
[6] farm, another to his business, ·and the rest seized his
[7] servants, maltreated them and killed them. ·The king
was furious. He despatched his troops, destroyed those mur-
[8] derers and burned their town. ·Then he said to his servants,
'The wedding is ready; but as those who were invited
[9] proved to be unworthy, ·go to the crossroads in the town
[10] and invite everyone you can find to the wedding.' ·So these
servants went out on to the roads and collected together
everyone they could find, bad and good alike; and the
[11] wedding hall was filled with guests. ·When the king came

in to look at the guests he noticed one man who was not
12 wearing a wedding garment, •and said to him, 'How did
you get in here, my friend, without a wedding garment?'
13 And the man was silent. •Then the king said to the attendants, 'Bind him hand and foot and throw him out into the
dark, where there will be weeping and grinding of teeth.'
14 For many are called, but few are chosen."

On tribute to Caesar

15 Then the Pharisees went away to work out between them
·16 how to trap him in what he said. •And they sent their disciples to him, together with the Herodians,ᵃ to say, "Master,
we know that you are an honest man and teach the way
of God in an honest way, and that you are not afraid of
17 anyone, because a man's rank means nothing to you. •Tell
us your opinion, then. Is it permissible to pay taxes to
18 Caesar or not?" •But Jesus was aware of their malice and
replied, "You hypocrites! Why do you set this trap for me?
19 Let me see the money you pay the tax with." They handed
20 him a denarius, •and he said, "Whose head is this?
21 Whose name?" •"Caesar's" they replied. He then said to
them, "Very well, give back to Caesar what belongs to
22 Caesar—and to God what belongs to God." •This reply took
them by surprise, and they left him alone and went away.

The resurrection of the dead

23 That day some Sadducees—who deny that there is a resurrection—approached him and they put this question to him,
24 "Master, Moses said that if a man dies childless, his brother
is to marry the widow, his sister-in-law, to raise children
25 for his brother. •Now we had a case involving seven
brothers; the first married and then died without children,
26 leaving his wife to his brother; •the same thing happened
27 with the second and third and so on to the seventh, •and
28 then last of all the woman herself died. •Now at the resurrection to which of those seven will she be wife, since she
29 had been married to them all?" •Jesus answered them, "You
are wrong, because you understand neither the scriptures
30 nor the power of God. •For at the resurrection men and
women do not marry; no, they are like the angels in heaven.

h. Ps 118:22-23
22 a. Supporters of the ruling family, hoping to find a cause
for denouncing Jesus to the Romans.

[31] And as for the resurrection of the dead, have you never [32] read what God himself said to you: *·I am the God of Abraham, the God of Isaac and the God of Jacob?*[b] God is [33] God, not of the dead, but of the living." ·And his teaching made a deep impression on the people who heard it.

The greatest commandment of all

[34] But when the Pharisees heard that he had silenced the [35] Sadducees they got together ·and, to disconcert him, one of [36] them put a question, ·"Master, which is the greatest com- [37] mandment of the Law?" ·Jesus said, *"You must love the Lord your God with all your heart, with all your soul,* [38] *and with all your mind.* ·This is the greatest and the first [39] commandment. ·The second resembles it: *You must love* [40] *your neighbor as yourself.* ·On these two commandments hang the whole Law, and the Prophets also."

Christ not only son but also Lord of David

[41] While the Pharisees were gathered round, Jesus put to [42] them this question, ·"What is your opinion about the Christ? [43] Whose son is he?" "David's" they told him. ·"Then how is it" he said "that David, moved by the Spirit, calls him Lord, where he says:

[44]
> *The Lord said to my Lord:*
> *·Sit at my right hand*
> *and I will put your enemies*
> *under your feet?*[c]

[45] "If David can call him Lord, then how can he be his son?" [46] Not one could think of anything to say in reply, and from that day no one dared to ask him any further questions.

The scribes and Pharisees: their hypocrisy and vanity

[1] **23** Then addressing the people and his disciples Jesus [2] said, ·"The scribes and the Pharisees occupy the [3] chair of Moses. ·You must therefore do what they tell you and listen to what they say; but do not be guided by what [4] they do: since they do not practice what they preach. ·They tie up heavy burdens and lay them on men's shoulders, but [5] will they lift a finger to move them? Not they! ·Everything they do is done to attract attention, like wearing broader [6] phylacteries and longer tassels,[a] ·like wanting to take the place of honor at banquets and the front seats in the

7 synagogues, ·being greeted obsequiously in the market
squares and having people call them Rabbi.

8   "You, however, must not allow yourselves to be called
Rabbi, since you have only one Master, and you are all
9 brothers. ·You must call no one on earth your father, since
10 you have only one Father, and he is in heaven. ·Nor must
you allow yourselves to be called teachers, for you have
11 only one Teacher, the Christ. ·The greatest among you
12 must be your servant. ·Anyone who exalts himself will be
humbled, and anyone who humbles himself will be exalted.

The sevenfold indictment of the scribes and Pharisees

13   "Alas for you, scribes and Pharisees, you hypocrites! You
who shut up the kingdom of heaven in men's faces, neither
going in yourselves nor allowing others to go in[b] who want
14 to.[c]

15   "Alas for you, scribes and Pharisees, you hypocrites!
You who travel over sea and land to make a single
proselyte, and when you have him you make him twice as
fit for hell as you are.

16   "Alas for you, blind guides! You who say, 'If a man
swears by the Temple, it has no force; but if a man swears
17 by the gold of the Temple, he is bound.' ·Fools and blind!
For which is of greater worth, the gold or the Temple that
18 makes the gold sacred? ·Or else, 'If a man swears by the
altar it has no force; but if a man swears by the offering
19 that is on the altar, he is bound.' ·You blind men! For
which is of greater worth, the offering or the altar that
20 makes the offering sacred? ·Therefore, when a man swears
by the altar he is swearing by that and by everything on it.
21 And when a man swears by the Temple he is swearing by
22 that and by the One who dwells in it. ·And when a man

---

b. Ex 3:6   c. Ps 110:1
23 a. Phylacteries: containers for short texts taken from the
Law; they were worn on the arm or the forehead in obedience
to Ex 13:9,16 and Dt 6:8. The tassels were sewn to the corners
of the cloak.   b. By interpreting the Law so strictly that nobody could obey all of it.   c. Add. v. 14 "Alas for you, scribes
and Pharisees, you hypocrites! You who devour the property of
widows though you make a show of lengthy prayers. The more
severe will be the sentence you receive"; this is an interpolation
taken from Mk 12:40; Lk 20:47 and making eight maledictions
instead of the deliberate total of seven, cf. 6:9+.

swears by heaven he is swearing by the throne of God and by the One who is seated there.

23 "Alas for you, scribes and Pharisees, you hypocrites! You who pay your tithe of mint and dill and cummin*d* and have neglected the weightier matters of the Law—justice, mercy, good faith! These you should have practiced, without

24 neglecting the others. ·You blind guides! Straining out gnats and swallowing camels!

25 "Alas for you, scribes and Pharisees, you hypocrites! You who clean the outside of cup and dish and leave the inside

26 full of extortion and intemperance. ·Blind Pharisee! Clean the inside of cup and dish first so that the outside may become clean as well.

27 "Alas for you, scribes and Pharisees, you hypocrites! You who are like whitewashed tombs that look handsome on the outside, but inside are full of dead men's bones and

28 every kind of corruption. ·In the same way you appear to people from the outside like good honest men, but inside you are full of hypocrisy and lawlessness.

29 "Alas for you, scribes and Pharisees, you hypocrites! You who build the sepulchres of the prophets and decorate

30 the tombs of holy men, ·saying, 'We would never have joined in shedding the blood of the prophets, had we lived

31 in our fathers' day.' ·So! Your own evidence tells against you! You are the sons of those who murdered the

32 prophets! ·Very well then, finish off the work that your fathers began.

Their crimes and approaching punishment

33 "Serpents, brood of vipers, how can you escape being
34 condemned to hell? ·This is why, in my turn, I am sending you prophets and wise men and scribes: some you will slaughter and crucify, some you will scourge in your
35 synagogues and hunt from town to town; ·and so you will draw down on yourselves the blood of every holy man that has been shed on earth, from the blood of Abel the Holy to the blood of Zechariah son of Barachiah*e* whom you mur-
36 dered between the sanctuary and the altar. ·I tell you solemnly, all of this will recoil on this generation.

Jerusalem admonished

37 "Jerusalem, Jerusalem, you that kill the prophets and stone those who are sent to you! How often have I longed

to gather your children, as a hen gathers her chicks under
38 her wings, and you refused! ·So be it! Your house will be
39 left to you desolate, ·for, I promise, you shall not see me
any more until you say:

Blessings on him who comes in the name of the Lord![f]

B. THE SERMON ON THE END

Introduction

1 **24** Jesus left the Temple, and as he was going away his
disciples came up to draw his attention to the Temple
2 buildings. ·He said to them in reply, "You see all these? I
tell you solemnly, not a single stone here will be left on
3 another: everything will be destroyed." ·And when he was
sitting on the Mount of Olives the disciples came and asked
him privately, "Tell us, when is this going to happen, and
what will be the sign of your coming and of the end of the
world?"

The beginning of sorrows

4   And Jesus answered them, "Take care that no one de-
5 ceives you; ·because many will come using my name and
saying, 'I am the Christ,' and they will deceive many.
6 You will hear of wars and rumors of wars; do not be
alarmed, for this is something that must happen, but the
7 end will not be yet. ·For nation will fight against nation,
and kingdom against kingdom. There will be famines and
8 earthquakes here and there. ·All this is only the beginning
of the birthpangs.

9   "Then they will hand you over to be tortured and put to
death; and you will be hated by all the nations on account
10 of my name. ·And then many will fall away; men will be-
11 tray one another and hate one another. ·Many false prophets
12 will arise; they will deceive many, ·and with the increase of
13 lawlessness, love in most men will grow cold; ·but the man
who stands firm to the end will be saved.
14   "This Good News of the kingdom will be proclaimed to

d. The law of paying tithes on crops was extended to include
herbs and plants grown for flavoring. **e.** Possibly Zechariah,
the last of the prophets to be killed, according to the Jewish
scriptures (2 Ch 24:20-22). **f.** Ps 118:26

the whole world*a* as a witness to all the nations. And then the end*b* will come.

The great tribulation of Jerusalem

15 "So when you see *the disastrous abomination*, of which the prophet Daniel spoke, set up in the Holy Place (let the 16 reader understand), ·then those in Judaea must escape to 17 the mountains; ·if a man is on the housetop, he must not 18 come down to collect his belongings; ·if a man is in the 19 fields, he must not turn back to fetch his cloak. ·Alas for those with child, or with babies at the breast, when those 20 days come! ·Pray that you will not have to escape in win- 21 ter or on a sabbath. ·For then there will be *great distress such as, until now, since* the world began, there never *has* 22 *been,* nor ever will be again. ·And if that time had not been shortened, no one would have survived; but shortened that time shall be, for the sake of those who are chosen.

23 "If anyone says to you then, 'Look, here is the Christ' 24 or, 'He is there,' do not believe it; ·for false Christs and false prophets will arise and produce great signs and por- tents, enough to deceive even the chosen, if that were pos- 25 sible. ·There; I have forewarned you.

The coming of the Son of Man will be evident

26 "If, then, they say to you, 'Look, he is in the desert,' do not go there; 'Look, he is in some hiding place,' do not be- 27 lieve it; ·because the coming of the Son of Man will be like lightning striking in the east and flashing far into the west. 28 Wherever the corpse is, there will the vultures gather.

The universal significance of this coming

29 "Immediately after the distress of those days*c* the sun will be darkened, the moon will lose its brightness, the stars will fall from the sky and the powers of heaven will be 30 shaken. ·And then the sign of the Son of Man will appear in heaven; then too all the peoples of the earth will beat their breasts; and they will see the Son of Man coming on 31 the clouds of heaven with power and great glory.*d* ·And he will send his angels with a loud trumpet to gather his chosen from the four winds, from one end of heaven to the other.

The time of this coming

32 "Take the fig tree as a parable: as soon as its twigs grow supple and its leaves come out, you know that summer is

[33] near. ·So with you when you see all these things: know that
[34] he is near, at the very gates. ·I tell you solemnly, before this
generation has passed away all these things will have taken
[35] place.*e* ·Heaven and earth will pass away, but my words
[36] will never pass away. ·But as for that day and hour, nobody
knows it, neither the angels of heaven, nor the Son, no one
but the Father only.

Be on the alert

[37] "As it was in Noah's day, so will it be when the Son of
[38] Man comes. ·For in those days before the Flood people
were eating, drinking, taking wives, taking husbands, right
[39] up to the day Noah went into the ark, ·and they suspected
nothing till the Flood came and swept all away. It will be
[40] like this when the Son of Man comes. ·Then of two men in
[41] the fields one is taken, one left; ·of two women at the millstone grinding, one is taken, one left.

[42] "So stay awake, because you do not know the day when
[43] your master is coming. ·You may be quite sure of this that
if the householder had known at what time of the night the
burglar would come, he would have stayed awake and
would not have allowed anyone to break through the wall
[44] of his house. ·Therefore, you too must stand ready because
the Son of Man is coming at an hour you do not expect.

Parable of the conscientious steward

[45] "What sort of servant, then, is faithful and wise enough
for the master to place him over his household to give them
[46] their food at the proper time? ·Happy that servant if his
[47] master's arrival finds him at this employment. ·I tell you
[48] solemnly, he will place him over everything he owns. ·But
as for the dishonest servant who says to himself, 'My mas-
[49] ter is taking his time,' ·and sets about beating his fellow
[50] servants and eating and drinking with drunkards, ·his master
will come on a day he does not expect and at an hour he
[51] does not know. ·The master will cut him off and send him
to the same fate as the hypocrites, where there will be weeping and grinding of teeth.

24 a. The "inhabited world" as it was known. **b.** The fall and
destruction of Jerusalem. A prophecy of this is combined, in
this discourse, with descriptions of the "last days." **c.** Join
with v. 22. Vv. 23-28 are a digression. **d.** As foretold in
Dn 7:14. **e.** Meaning the fall and destruction of Jerusalem.

Parable of the ten bridesmaids

1 25 "Then the kingdom of heaven will be like this: Ten bridesmaids took their lamps and went to meet the **2** bridegroom. ·Five of them were foolish and five were sen- **3** sible: ·the foolish ones did take their lamps, but they **4** brought no oil, ·whereas the sensible ones took flasks of oil **5** as well as their lamps. ·The bridegroom was late, and they **6** all grew drowsy and fell asleep. ·But at midnight there was **7** a cry, 'The bridegroom is here! Go out and meet him.' ·At this, all those bridesmaids woke up and trimmed their **8** lamps, ·and the foolish ones said to the sensible ones, 'Give **9** us some of your oil: our lamps are going out.' ·But they replied, 'There may not be enough for us and for you; you had better go to those who sell it and buy some for **10** yourselves.' ·They had gone off to buy it when the bride- groom arrived. Those who were ready went in with him to **11** the wedding hall and the door was closed. ·The other brides- maids arrived later. 'Lord, Lord,' they said 'open the door **12** for us.' ·But he replied, 'I tell you solemnly, I do not know **13** you.' ·So stay awake, because you do not know either the day or the hour.

Parable of the talents

14 "It is like a man on his way abroad who summoned his **15** servants and entrusted his property to them. ·To one he gave five talents, to another two, to a third one; each in **16** proportion to his ability. Then he set out. ·The man who had received the five talents promptly went and traded with **17** them and made five more. ·The man who had received two **18** made two more in the same way. ·But the man who had re- ceived one went off and dug a hole in the ground and hid **19** his master's money. ·Now a long time after, the master of those servants came back and went through his accounts **20** with them. ·The man who had received the five talents came forward bringing five more. 'Sir,' he said 'you entrusted me with five talents; here are five more that I have made.' **21** His master said to him, 'Well done, good and faithful serv- ant; you have shown you can be faithful in small things, I will trust you with greater; come and join in your master's **22** happiness.' ·Next the man with the two talents came for- ward. 'Sir,' he said 'you entrusted me with two talents; **23** here are two more that I have made.' ·His master said to him, 'Well done, good and faithful servant; you have shown you can be faithful in small things, I will trust you with greater; come and join in your master's happiness.'

24 Last came forward the man who had the one talent. 'Sir,' said he 'I had heard you were a hard man, reaping where you have not sown and gathering where you have not scat-
25 tered; ·so I was afraid, and I went off and hid your talent in the ground. Here it is; it was yours, you have it back.'
26 But his master answered him, 'You wicked and lazy serv-ant! So you knew that I reap where I have not sown and
27 gather where I have not scattered? ·Well then, you should have deposited my money with the bankers, and on my re-
28 turn I would have recovered my capital with interest. ·So now, take the talent from him and give it to the man who
29 has the ten talents. ·For to everyone who has will be given more, and he will have more than enough; but from the
30 man who has not, even what he has will be taken away. ·As for this good-for-nothing servant, throw him out into the dark, where there will be weeping and grinding of teeth.'

The Last Judgment

31 "When the Son of Man comes in his glory, escorted by all the angels, then he will take his seat on his throne of
32 glory. ·All the nations will be assembled before him and he will separate men one from another as the shepherd
33 separates sheep from goats. ·He will place the sheep on his
34 right hand and the goats on his left. ·Then the King will say to those on his right hand, 'Come, you whom my Father has blessed, take for your heritage the kingdom prepared
35 for you since the foundation of the world. ·For I was hun-gry and you gave me food; I was thirsty and you gave me
36 drink; I was a stranger and you made me welcome; ·naked and you clothed me, sick and you visited me, in prison and
37 you came to see me.' ·Then the virtuous will say to him in reply, 'Lord, when did we see you hungry and feed you; or
38 thirsty and give you drink? ·When did we see you a stranger
39 and make you welcome; naked and clothe you; ·sick or in
40 prison and go to see you?' ·And the King will answer, 'I tell you solemnly, in so far as you did this to one of the least
41 of these brothers of mine, you did it to me.' ·Next he will say to those on his left hand, 'Go away from me, with your curse upon you, to the eternal fire prepared for the devil
42 and his angels. ·For I was hungry and you never gave me food; I was thirsty and you never gave me anything to
43 drink; ·I was a stranger and you never made me welcome,

naked and you never clothed me, sick and in prison and you
⁴⁴ never visited me.' ·Then it will be their turn to ask, 'Lord,
when did we see you hungry or thirsty, a stranger or naked,
⁴⁵ sick or in prison, and did not come to your help?' ·Then
he will answer, 'I tell you solemnly, in so far as you neglected to do this to one of the least of these, you neglected
⁴⁶ to do it to me.' ·And they will go away to eternal punishment, and the virtuous to eternal life."

VII. PASSION AND RESURRECTION

The conspiracy against Jesus

¹ 26 Jesus had now finished all he wanted to say, and he
² told his disciples, ·"It will be Passover, as you know,
in two days' time, and the Son of Man will be handed over
to be crucified."
³ Then the chief priests and the elders of the people assembled in the palace of the high priest, whose name was
⁴ Caiaphas, ·and made plans to arrest Jesus by some trick and
⁵ have him put to death. ·They said, however, "It must not be
during the festivities; there must be no disturbance among
the people."

The anointing at Bethany

⁶ Jesus was at Bethany in the house of Simon the leper,
⁷ when ·a woman came to him with an alabaster jar of the
most expensive ointment, and poured it on his head as he
⁸ was at table. ·When they saw this, the disciples were
⁹ indignant; "Why this waste?" they said. ·"This could have
been sold at a high price and the money given to the poor."
¹⁰ Jesus noticed this. "Why are you upsetting the woman?"
he said to them. "What she has done for me is one of the
¹¹ good works*a* indeed! ·You have the poor with you always,
¹² but you will not always have me. ·When she poured this
¹³ ointment on my body, she did it to prepare me for burial. ·I
tell you solemnly, wherever in all the world this Good
News is proclaimed, what she has done will be told also, in
remembrance of her."

Judas betrays Jesus

¹⁴ Then one of the Twelve, the man called Judas Iscariot,
¹⁵ went to the chief priests ·and said, "What are you prepared
¹⁶ to give me if I hand him over to you?" ·They paid him

thirty silver pieces,[b] and from that moment he looked for an opportunity to betray him.

Preparations for the Passover supper

17 Now on the first day of Unleavened Bread[c] the disciples came to Jesus to say, "Where do you want us to make the
18 preparations for you to eat the passover?" •"Go to so-and-so in the city" he replied "and say to him, 'The Master says: My time is near. It is at your house that I am keeping
19 Passover with my disciples.' " •The disciples did what Jesus told them and prepared the Passover.

The treachery of Judas foretold

20 When evening came he was at table with the twelve dis-
21 ciples. •And while they were eating he said, "I tell you sol-
22 emnly, one of you is about to betray me." •They were greatly distressed and started asking him in turn, "Not I,
23 Lord, surely?" •He answered, "Someone who has dipped
24 his hand into the dish with me, will betray me. •The Son of Man is going to his fate, as the scriptures say he will, but alas for that man by whom the Son of Man is betrayed!
25 Better for that man if he had never been born!" •Judas, who was to betray him, asked in his turn, "Not I, Rabbi, surely?" "They are your own words" answered Jesus.

The institution of the Eucharist

26 Now as they were eating,[d] Jesus took some bread, and when he had said the blessing he broke it and gave it to the disciples. "Take it and eat;" he said "this is my body."
27 Then he took a cup, and when he had returned thanks he gave it to them. "Drink all of you from this," he said
28 "for this is my blood, the blood of the covenant, which is to be poured out for many for the forgiveness of sins.
29 From now on, I tell you, I shall not drink wine until the day I drink the new wine with you in the kingdom of my Father."

26 a. As "good works," charitable deeds were reckoned superior to almsgiving. b. 30 shekels, the price fixed for a slave's life, Ex 21:32. c. Unleavened bread was normally to be eaten during the seven days which followed the Passover supper; here the writer appears to mean the first day of the whole Passover celebration. d. The Passover supper itself, for which exact rules for the blessing of bread and wine were laid down. The "eating" of v. 21 is the first course, which came before the Passover itself.

Peter's denial foretold

30 After psalms had been sung[e] they left for the Mount
31 of Olives. ·Then Jesus said to them, "You will all lose faith
in me this night,[f] for the scripture says: *I shall strike the*
32 *shepherd and the sheep of the flock will be scattered,[g]* ·but
33 after my resurrection I shall go before you to Galilee." ·At
this, Peter said, "Though all lose faith in you, I will never
34 lose faith." ·Jesus answered him, "I tell you solemnly, this
very night, before the cock crows, you will have disowned
35 me three times." ·Peter said to him, "Even if I have to die
with you, I will never disown you." And all the disciples
said the same.

Gethsemane

36 Then Jesus came with them to a small estate called
Gethsemane; and he said to his disciples, "Stay here while I
37 go over there to pray." ·He took Peter and the two sons of
Zebedee with him. And sadness came over him, and great
38 distress. ·Then he said to them, "My soul is sorrowful to
the point of death. Wait here and keep awake with me."
39 And going on a little further he fell on his face and prayed.
"My Father," he said "if it is possible, let this cup pass me
40 by. Nevertheless, let it be as you, not I, would have it." ·He
came back to the disciples and found them sleeping, and he
said to Peter, "So you had not the strength to keep awake
41 with me one hour? ·You should be awake, and praying not
to be put to the test. The spirit is willing, but the flesh is
42 weak." ·Again, a second time, he went away and prayed:
"My Father," he said "if this cup cannot pass by without
43 my drinking it, your will be done!" ·And he came back
again and found them sleeping, their eyes were so heavy.
44 Leaving them there, he went away again and prayed for the
45 third time, repeating the same words. ·Then he came back
to the disciples and said to them, "You can sleep on now
and take your rest. Now the hour has come when the Son
46 of Man is to be betrayed into the hands of sinners. ·Get up!
Let us go! My betrayer is already close at hand."

The arrest

47 He was still speaking when Judas, one of the Twelve,
appeared, and with him a large number of men armed with
swords and clubs, sent by the chief priests and elders of the
48 people. ·Now the traitor had arranged a sign with them.
"The one I kiss," he had said "he is the man. Take him in

⁴⁹ charge." ·So he went straight up to Jesus and said, "Greet-
⁵⁰ ings, Rabbi," and kissed him. ·Jesus said to him, "My
friend, do what you are here for." Then they came for-
⁵¹ ward, seized Jesus and took him in charge. ·At that, one of
the followers of Jesus grasped his sword and drew it; he
struck out at the high priest's servant, and cut off his ear.
⁵² Jesus then said, "Put your sword back, for all who draw the
⁵³ sword will die by the sword. ·Or do you think that I cannot
appeal to my Father who would promptly send more than
⁵⁴ twelve legions of angels to my defense? ·But then, how
would the scriptures be fulfilled that say this is the way it
⁵⁵ must be?" ·It was at this time that Jesus said to the crowds,
"Am I a brigand, that you had to set out to capture me
with swords and clubs? I sat teaching in the Temple day
⁵⁶ after day and you never laid hands on me." ·Now all this
happened to fulfill the prophecies in scripture. Then all the
disciples deserted him and ran away.

Jesus before the Sanhedrin

⁵⁷ The men who had arrested Jesus led him off to Caiaphas
the high priest, where the scribes and the elders were assem-
⁵⁸ bled. ·Peter followed him at a distance, and when he
reached the high priest's palace, he went in and sat down
with the attendants to see what the end would be.

⁵⁹ The chief priests and the whole Sanhedrin were looking
for evidence against Jesus, however false, on which they
⁶⁰ might pass the death-sentence. ·But they could not find any,
though several lying witnesses came forward. Eventually
⁶¹ two stepped forward ·and made a statement, "This man
said, 'I have power to destroy the Temple of God and in
⁶² three days build it up.'" ·The high priest then stood up and
said to him, "Have you no answer to that? What is this evi-
⁶³ dence these men are bringing against you?" ·But Jesus was
silent. And the high priest said to him, "I put you on oath
by the living God to tell us if you are the Christ, the Son of
⁶⁴ God." ·"The words are your own" answered Jesus. "Moreover, I tell you that from this time onward you will see the
Son of Man seated at the right hand of the Power and *com-*
⁶⁵ *ing on the clouds of heaven.*" ·At this, the high priest tore
his clothes and said, "He has blasphemed. What need of

e. The psalms of praise which end the Passover supper.
f. "be brought down": the regular expression for the losing of
faith through a difficulty or blow to it. g. Zc 13:7

witnesses have we now? There! You have just heard the
66 blasphemy. ·What is your opinion?" They answered, "He
deserves to die."
67   Then they spat in his face and hit him with their fists;
68 others said as they struck him, ·"Play the prophet, Christ!
Who hit you then?"

Peter's denials

69   Meanwhile Peter was sitting outside in the courtyard, and
a servant-girl came up to him and said, "You too were with
70 Jesus the Galilean." ·But he denied it in front of them all.
71 "I do not know what you are talking about" he said. ·When
he went out to the gateway another servant-girl saw him
and said to the people there, "This man was with Jesus the
72 Nazarene." ·And again, with an oath, he denied it, "I do not
73 know the man." ·A little later the bystanders came up and
said to Peter, "You are one of them for sure! Why, your ac-
74 cent gives you away." ·Then he started calling down curses
on himself and swearing, "I do not know the man." At that
75 moment the cock crew, ·and Peter remembered what Jesus
had said, "Before the cock crows you will have disowned
me three times." And he went outside and wept bitterly.

Jesus is taken before Pilate

1   **27** When morning came, all the chief priests and the
elders of the people met in council to bring about
2 the death of Jesus. ·They had him bound, and led him away
to hand him over to Pilate,ᵃ the governor.

The death of Judas

3   When he found that Jesus had been condemned, Judas
his betrayer was filled with remorse and took the thirty
4 silver pieces back to the chief priests and elders. ·"I have
sinned;" he said "I have betrayed innocent blood." "What
5 is that to us?" they replied "That is your concern." ·And
flinging down the silver pieces in the sanctuary he made off,
6 and went and hanged himself. ·The chief priests picked up
the silver pieces and said, "It is against the Law to put this
7 into the treasury; it is blood-money." ·So they discussed the
matter and bought the potter's field with it as a graveyard
8 for foreigners, ·and this is why the field is called the Field
9 of Blood today. ·The words of the prophet Jeremiahᵇ were
then fulfilled: *And they took the thirty silver pieces, the*
sum at which the precious One was priced by the children of

¹⁰ *Israel, ·and they gave them for the· potter's field, just as the*
    Lord directed me.

Jesus before Pilate

¹¹   Jesus, then, was brought before the governor, and the
    governor put to him this question, "Are you the king of the
¹² Jews?" Jesus replied, "It is you who say it." ·But when he
    was accused by the chief priests and the elders he refused
¹⁸ to answer at all. ·Pilate then said to him, "Do you not hear
¹⁴ how many charges they have brought against you?" ·But to
    the governor's complete amazement, he offered no reply to
    any of the charges.

¹⁵   At festival time it was the governor's practice to release
¹⁶ a prisoner for the people, anyone they chose. ·Now there
    was at that time a notorious prisoner whose name was Ba-
¹⁷ rabbas. ·So when the crowd gathered, Pilate said to them,
    "Which do you want me to release for you: Barabbas, or
¹⁸ Jesus who is called Christ?" ·For Pilate knew it was out of
    jealousy that they had handed him over.

¹⁹   Now as he was seated in the chair of judgement, his wife
    sent him a message, "Have nothing to do with that man; I
    have been upset all day by a dream I had about him."

²⁰   The chief priests and the elders, however, had persuaded
    the crowd to demand the release of Barabbas and the
²¹ execution of Jesus. ·So when the governor spoke and asked
    them, "Which of the two do you want me to release for
²² you?" they said, "Barabbas." ·"But in that case," Pilate said
    to them "what am I to do with Jesus who is called Christ?"
²³ They all said, "Let him be crucified!" ·"Why?" he asked
    "What harm has he done?" But they shouted all the louder,
²⁴ "Let him be crucified!" ·Then Pilate saw that he was mak-
    ing no impression, that in fact a riot was imminent. So he
    took some water, washed his hands in front of the crowd
    and said, "I am innocent of this man's blood. It is your
²⁵ concern." ·And the people, to a man, shouted back, "His
²⁶ blood be on us and on our children!" ·Then he released
    Barabbas for them. He ordered Jesus to be first scourged^c
    and then handed over to be crucified.

27 a. The Jews had to approach the Roman governor for confirmation and execution of any sentence of death. b. Actually
a free quotation from Zc 11:12-13. c. The normal prelude
to crucifixion.

Jesus is crowned with thorns

27   The governor's soldiers took Jesus with them into the Praetorium and collected the whole cohort round him.
28 Then they stripped him and made him wear a scarlet cloak,
29 and having twisted some thorns into a crown they put this on his head and placed a reed in his right hand. To make fun of him they knelt to him saying, "Hail, king of the
30 Jews!" ·And they spat on him and took the reed and struck
31 him on the head with it. ·And when they had finished making fun of him, they took off the cloak and dressed him in his own clothes and led him away to crucify him.

The crucifixion

32   On their way out, they came across a man from Cyrene,
33 Simon by name, and enlisted him to carry his cross. ·When they had reached a place called Golgotha,[d] that is, the place
34 of the skull, ·they gave him wine to drink mixed with gall,
35 which he tasted but refused to drink. ·When they had finished crucifying him they shared out his clothing by casting
36 lots, ·and then sat down and stayed there keeping guard over him.
37   Above his head was placed the charge against him; it
38 read: "This is Jesus, the King of the Jews." ·At the same time two robbers were crucified with him, one on the right and one on the left.

The crucified Christ is mocked

39   The passers-by jeered at him; they shook their heads
40 and said, "So you would destroy the Temple and rebuild it in three days! Then save yourself! If you are God's son,
41 come down from the cross!" ·The chief priests with the
42 scribes and elders mocked him in the same way. ·"He saved others;" they said "he cannot save himself. He is the king of Israel; let him come down from the cross now, and we will
43 believe in him. ·He puts his trust in God; now let God rescue him if he wants him. For he did say, 'I am the son
44 of God.'" ·Even the robbers who were crucified with him taunted him in the same way.

The death of Jesus

45   From the sixth hour there was darkness over all the land
46 until the ninth hour.[e] ·And about the ninth hour, Jesus cried out in a loud voice, "Eli, Eli, lama sabachthani?" that is, *"My God, my God, why have you deserted me?"*[f]

47 When some of those who stood there heard this, they said,
48 "The man is calling on Elijah," •and one of them quickly
   ran to get a sponge which he dipped in vinegar[g] and, put-
49 ting it on a reed, gave it him to drink. •"Wait!" said the rest
50 of them "and see if Elijah will come to save him." •But
   Jesus, again crying out in a loud voice, yielded up his spirit.
51   At that, the veil of the Temple[h] was torn in two from top
52 to bottom; the earth quaked; the rocks were split; •the
   tombs opened and the bodies of many holy men rose from
53 the dead, •and these, after his resurrection, came out of the
   tombs, entered the Holy City and appeared to a number of
54 people. •Meanwhile the centurion, together with the others
   guarding Jesus, had seen the earthquake and all that was
   taking place, and they were terrified and said, "In truth
   this was a son of God."
55   And many women were there, watching from a distance,
   the same women who had followed Jesus from Galilee and
56 looked after him. •Among them were Mary of Magdala,
   Mary the mother of James and Joseph, and the mother of
   Zebedee's sons.

The burial

57   When it was evening, there came a rich man of
   Arimathaea, called Joseph, who had himself become a dis-
58 ciple of Jesus. •This man went to Pilate and asked for the
   body of Jesus. Pilate thereupon ordered it to be handed
59 over. •So Joseph took the body, wrapped it in a clean shroud
60 and put it in his own new tomb which he had hewn out of
   the rock. He then rolled a large stone across the entrance
61 of the tomb and went away. •Now Mary of Magdala and
   the other Mary were there, sitting opposite the sepulchre.

The guard at the tomb

62   Next day, that is, when Preparation Day[i] was over, the
63 chief priests and the Pharisees went in a body to Pilate •and
   said to him, "Your Excellency, we recall that this impostor
   said, while he was still alive, 'After three days I shall rise

d. The Aramaic form of the name of which Calvary is the more
familiar Latin equivalent. e. From mid-day to 3 p.m. f. Ps
22:1 g. The rough wine drunk by Roman soldiers. h. There
were two curtains in the Temple; most probably this was the
inner curtain which guarded the Most Holy Place. i. The day
before the sabbath.

[64] again.' ·Therefore give the order to have the sepulchre kept secure until the third day, for fear his disciples come and steal him away and tell the people, 'He has risen from the dead.' This last piece of fraud would be worse than what [65] went before." ·"You may have your guard" said Pilate to [66] them. "Go and make all as secure as you know how." ·So they went and made the sepulchre secure, putting seals on the stone and mounting a guard.

The empty tomb. The angel's message

[1] **28** After the sabbath, and toward dawn on the first day of the week, Mary of Magdala and the other Mary [2] went to visit the sepulchre. ·And all at once there was a violent earthquake, for the angel of the Lord, descending from [3] heaven, came and rolled away the stone and sat on it. ·His [4] face was like lightning, his robe white as snow. ·The guards were so shaken, so frightened of him, that they were like [5] dead men. ·But the angel spoke; and he said to the women, "There is no need for you to be afraid. I know you are look- [6] ing for Jesus, who was crucified. ·He is not here, for he has risen, as he said he would. Come and see the place where he [7] lay, ·then go quickly and tell his disciples, 'He has risen from the dead and now he is going before you to Galilee; it [8] is there you will see him.' Now I have told you." ·Filled with awe and great joy the women came quickly away from the tomb and ran to tell the disciples.

Appearance to the women

[9] And there, coming to meet them, was Jesus. "Greetings" he said. And the women came up to him and, falling down [10] before him, clasped his feet. ·Then Jesus said to them, "Do not be afraid; go and tell my brothers that they must leave for Galilee; they will see me there."

Precautions taken by the leaders of the people

[11] While they were on their way, some of the guard went off into the city to tell the chief priests all that had hap- [12] pened. ·These held a meeting with the elders and, after some discussion, handed a considerable sum of money to [13] the soldiers ·with these instructions, "This is what you must say, 'His disciples came during the night and stole him [14] away while we were asleep.' ·And should the governor come to hear of this, we undertake to put things right with him ourselves and to see that you do not get into trouble."

¹⁵ The soldiers took the money and carried out their instructions, and to this day that is the story among the Jews.

Appearance in Galilee. The mission to the world

¹⁶   Meanwhile the eleven disciples set out for Galilee, to the
¹⁷ mountain where Jesus had arranged to meet them. ·When
they saw him they fell down before him, though some
¹⁸ hesitated. ·Jesus came up and spoke to them. He said, "All
authority in heaven and on earth has been given to me.
¹⁹ Go, therefore, make disciples of all the nations; baptize
them in the name of the Father and of the Son and of the
²⁰ Holy Spirit,ᵃ ·and teach them to observe all the commands I gave you. And know that I am with you always;
yes, to the end of time."

28 a. This formula is perhaps a reflection of the liturgical usage of the writer's own time.

THE GOSPEL ACCORDING TO

Saint Mark

I. PRELUDE TO THE PUBLIC MINISTRY
OF JESUS

The preaching of John the Baptist

¹ **1** The beginning of the Good News about Jesus Christ,
² the Son of God. ·It is written in the book of the prophet
Isaiah:

> *Look, I am going to send my messenger before you;*
> *he will prepare your way.*
³ *A voice cries in the wilderness:*
> *Prepare a way for the Lord,*
> *make his paths straight,ᵃ*

⁴ and so it was that John the Baptist appeared in the wilderness, proclaiming a baptism of repentance for the forgive-
⁵ ness of sins. ·All Judaea and all the people of Jerusalem
made their way to him, and as they were baptized by him
⁶ in the river Jordan they confessed their sins. ·John wore a
garment of camel-skin, and he lived on locusts and wild
⁷ honey. ·In the course of his preaching he said, "Someone
is following me, someone who is more powerful than I am,
and I am not fit to kneel down and undo the strap of his
⁸ sandals. ·I have baptized you with water, but he will baptize
you with the Holy Spirit."

Jesus is baptized

⁹ It was at this time that Jesus came from Nazareth in
¹⁰ Galilee and was baptized in the Jordan by John. ·No sooner
had he come up out of the water than he saw the heavens
torn apart and the Spirit, like a dove, descending on him.
¹¹ And a voice came from heaven, "You are my Son, the Beloved; my favor rests on you."

Temptation in the wilderness

¹² Immediately afterward the Spirit drove him out into the
¹³ wilderness ·and he remained there for forty days, and was

tempted by Satan. He was with the wild beasts, and the
angels looked after him.

II. THE GALILEAN MINISTRY

Jesus begins to preach

14 After John had been arrested, Jesus went into Galilee.
15 There he proclaimed the Good News from God. ·"The
time has come" he said "and the kingdom of God is close
at hand. Repent, and believe the Good News."

The first four disciples are called

16 As he was walking along by the Sea of Galilee he saw
Simon and his brother Andrew casting a net in the lake—
17 for they were fishermen. ·And Jesus said to them, "Follow
18 me and I will make you into fishers of men." ·And at once
they left their nets and followed him.
19 Going on a little farther, he saw James son of Zebedee
and his brother John; they too were in their boat, mending
20 their nets. He called them at once ·and, leaving their father
Zebedee in the boat with the men he employed, they went
after him.

Jesus teaches in Capernaum and cures a demoniac

21 They went as far as Capernaum, and as soon as the
sabbath came he went to the synagogue and began to
22 teach. ·And his teaching made a deep impression on them
because, unlike the scribes, he taught them with authority.
23 In their synagogue just then there was a man possessed
24 by an unclean spirit, and it shouted, ·"What do you want
with us, Jesus of Nazareth? Have you come to destroy us?
25 I know who you are: the Holy One of God." But Jesus
26 said sharply, "Be quiet! Come out of him!" ·And the unclean spirit threw the man into convulsions and with a
27 loud cry went out of him. ·The people were so astonished
that they started asking each other what it all meant. "Here
is a teaching that is new" they said "and with authority behind it: he gives orders even to unclean spirits and they
28 obey him." ·And his reputation rapidly spread everywhere,
through all the surrounding Galilean countryside.

1 a. Is 40:3

Cure of Simon's mother-in-law

²⁹ On leaving the synagogue, he went with James and John
³⁰ straight to the house of Simon and Andrew. ·Now Simon's
mother-in-law had gone to bed with fever, and they told
³¹ him about her straightaway. ·He went to her, took her by
the hand and helped her up. And the fever left her and
she began to wait on them.

A number of cures

³² That evening, after sunset, they brought to him all who
³³ were sick and those who were possessed by devils. ·The
³⁴ whole town came crowding round the door, ·and he cured
many who were suffering from diseases of one kind or
another; he also cast out many devils, but he would not
allow them to speak, because they knew who he was.ᵇ

Jesus quietly leaves Capernaum and travels through Galilee

³⁵ In the morning, long before dawn, he got up and left
the house, and went off to a lonely place and prayed there.
³⁶
³⁷ Simon and his companions set out in search of him, ·and
when they found him they said, "Everybody is looking for
³⁸ you." ·He answered, "Let us go elsewhere, to the neigh-
boring country towns, so that I can preach there too,
³⁹ because that is why I came." ·And he went all through
Galilee, preaching in their synagogues and casting out
devils.

Cure of a leper

⁴⁰ A leper came to him and pleaded on his knees: "If you
⁴¹ want to" he said "you can cure me." ·Feeling sorry for
him, Jesus stretched out his hand and touched him. "Of
⁴² course I want to!" he said. "Be cured!" ·And the leprosy
⁴³ left him at once and he was cured. ·Jesus immediately sent
⁴⁴ him away and sternly ordered him, ·"Mind you say nothing
to anyone, but go and show yourself to the priest, and make
the offering for your healing prescribed by Moses as evi-
⁴⁵ dence of your recovery." ·The man went away, but then
started talking about it freely and telling the story everywhere, so that Jesus could no longer go openly into any
town, but had to stay outside in places where nobody lived.
Even so, people from all around would come to him.

Cure of a paralytic

1 When he returned to Capernaum some time later, word
2 went round that he was back; ·and so many people
collected that there was no room left, even in front of the
3 door. He was preaching the word to them ·when some
people came bringing him a paralytic carried by four men,
4 but as the crowd made it impossible to get the man to him,
they stripped the roof over the place where Jesus was; and
when they had made an opening, they lowered the stretcher
5 on which the paralytic lay. ·Seeing their faith, Jesus said
6 to the paralytic, "My child, your sins are forgiven." ·Now
some scribes were sitting there, and they thought to them-
7 selves, ·"How can this man talk like that? He is blasphem-
8 ing. Who can forgive sins but God?" ·Jesus, inwardly aware
that this was what they were thinking, said to them, "Why
9 do you have these thoughts in your hearts? ·Which of these
is easier: to say to the paralytic, 'Your sins are forgiven'
or to say, 'Get up, pick up your stretcher and walk?'
10 But to prove to you that the Son of Man has authority
11 on earth to forgive sins"—he said to the paralytic—"I order you: get up, pick up your stretcher, and go off home."
12 And the man got up, picked up his stretcher at once and
walked out in front of everyone, so that they were all
astounded and praised God saying, "We have never seen
anything like this."

The call of Levi

13 He went out again to the shore of the lake;[a] and all the
14 people came to him, and he taught them. ·As he was walking on he saw Levi the son of Alphaeus, sitting by the
customs house, and he said to him, "Follow me." And he
got up and followed him.

Eating with sinners

15 When Jesus was at dinner in his house, a number of
tax collectors and sinners were also sitting at the table with
Jesus and his disciples; for there were many of them among
16 his followers. ·When the scribes of the Pharisee party saw
him eating with sinners and tax collectors, they said to his
disciples, "Why does he eat with tax collectors and sin-

b. Throughout this gospel, Jesus never explicitly claims to be
the Messiah and he forbids others to speak of the fact.
2 a. Tiberias, the "Sea of Galilee."

[17] ners?" ·When Jesus heard this he said to them, "It is not the healthy who need the doctor, but the sick. I did not come to call the virtuous, but sinners."

A discussion on fasting

[18] One day when John's disciples and the Pharisees were fasting, some people came and said to him, "Why is it that John's disciples and the disciples of the Pharisees fast, but [19] your disciples do not?" ·Jesus replied, "Surely the bridegroom's attendants would never think of fasting while the bridegroom is still with them? As long as they have the bridegroom with them, they could not think of fasting. [20] But the time will come for the bridegroom to be taken [21] away from them, and then, on that day, they will fast. ·No one sews a piece of unshrunken cloth on an old cloak; if he does, the patch pulls away from it, the new from [22] the old, and the tear gets worse. ·And nobody puts new wine into old wineskins; if he does, the wine will burst the skins, and the wine is lost and the skins too. No! New wine, fresh skins!"

Picking corn on the sabbath

[23] One sabbath day he happened to be taking a walk through the cornfields, and his disciples began to pick ears [24] of corn as they went along. ·And the Pharisees said to him, "Look, why are they doing something on the sabbath [25] day that is forbidden?" ·And he replied, "Did you never read what David did in his time of need when he and his [26] followers were hungry—·how he went into the house of God when Abiathar[b] was high priest, and ate the loaves of offering which only the priests are allowed to eat, and how he also gave some to the men with him?"

[27] And he said to them, "The sabbath was made for man, [28] not man for the sabbath; ·so the Son of Man is master even of the sabbath."

Cure of the man with a withered hand

[1] 3 He went again into a synagogue, and there was a man [2] there who had a withered hand. ·And they were watching him to see if he would cure him on the sabbath day, [3] hoping for something to use against him. ·He said to the man with the withered hand, "Stand up out in the middle!" [4] Then he said to them, "Is it against the law on the sabbath

day to do good, or to do evil; to save life, or to kill?" But
5 they said nothing. ·Then, grieved to find them so obstinate,
he looked angrily round at them, and said to the man,
"Stretch out your hand." He stretched it out and his hand
6 was better. ·The Pharisees went out and at once began to
plot with the Herodians against him, discussing how to
destroy him.

The crowds follow Jesus

7 Jesus withdrew with his disciples to the lakeside, and
great crowds from Galilee followed him. From Judaea,
8 Jerusalem, Idumaea, Transjordania and the region of Tyre
and Sidon, great numbers who had heard of all he was
9 doing came to him. ·And he asked his disciples to have a
boat ready for him because of the crowd, to keep him
10 from being crushed. ·For he had cured so many that all
who were afflicted in any way were crowding forward to
11 touch him. ·And the unclean spirits, whenever they saw
him, would fall down before him and shout, "You are the
12 Son of God!" ·But he warned them strongly not to make
him known.

The appointment of the Twelve

13 He now went up into the hills and summoned those he
14 wanted. So they came to him ·and he appointed twelve;
they were to be his companions and to be sent out to
15 preach, ·with power to cast out devils. ·And so he ap-
16 pointed the Twelve: Simon to whom he gave the name
17 Peter, ·James the son of Zebedee and John the brother
of James, to whom he gave the name Boanerges or 'Sons
18 of Thunder'; ·then Andrew, Philip, Bartholomew, Matthew, Thomas, James the son of Alphaeus, Thaddaeus,
19 Simon the Zealot ·and Judas Iscariot, the man who was
to betray him.

His relatives are concerned about Jesus

20 He went home again, and once more such a crowd
21 collected that they could not even have a meal. ·When
his relatives heard of this, they set out to take charge of
him, convinced he was out of his mind.

b. See 1 S 21:1-7. Abiathar was the better known as high priest
in David's reign, but Ahimelech is named in this source.

Allegations of the scribes

22 The scribes who had come down from Jerusalem were saying, "Beelzebul is in him" and, "It is through the prince
23 of devils that he casts devils out." ·So he called them to him and spoke to them in parables, "How can Satan cast
24 out Satan? ·If a kingdom is divided against itself, that king-
25 dom cannot last. ·And if a household is divided against
26 itself, that household can never stand. ·Now if Satan has rebelled against himself and is divided, he cannot stand
27 either—it is the end of him. ·But no one can make his way into a strong man's house and burgle his property unless he has tied up the strong man first. Only then can he burgle his house.
28 "I tell you solemnly, all men's sins will be forgiven, and
29 all their blasphemies; ·but let anyone blaspheme against the Holy Spirit and he will never have forgiveness: he is
30 guilty of an eternal sin." ·This was because they were say-ing, "An unclean spirit is in him."

The true kinsmen of Jesus

31 His mother and brothers now arrived and, standing out-
32 side, sent in a message asking for him. ·A crowd was sit-ting round him at the time the message was passed to him, "Your mother and brothers and sisters are outside asking
33 for you." ·He replied, "Who are my mother and my broth-
34 ers?" ·And looking round at those sitting in a circle about
35 him, he said, "Here are my mother and my brothers. ·Any-one who does the will of God, that person is my brother and sister and mother."

Parable of the sower

1 Again he began to teach by the lakeside, but such a
4 huge crowd gathered round him that he got into a boat on the lake and sat there. The people were all along the
2 shore, at the water's edge. ·He taught them many things in parables, and in the course of his teaching he said to
3,4 them, ·"Listen! Imagine a sower going out to sow. ·Now it happened that, as he sowed, some of the seed fell on the
5 edge of the path, and the birds came and ate it up. ·Some seed fell on rocky ground where it found little soil and sprang up straightaway, because there was no depth of
6 earth; ·and when the sun came up it was scorched and,
7 not having any roots, it withered away. ·Some seed fell

into thorns, and the thorns grew up and choked it, and it
8 produced no crop. •And some seeds fell into rich soil and,
growing tall and strong, produced crop; and yielded thirty,
9 sixty, even a hundredfold." •And he said, "Listen, anyone
who has ears to hear!"

Why Jesus speaks in parables

10   When he was alone, the Twelve, together with the others
who formed his company, asked what the parables meant.
11 He told them, "The secret of the kingdom of God is given
to you, but to those who are outside everything comes in
12 parables, •so that *they may see and see again, but not perceive; may hear and hear again, but not understand; otherwise they might be converted and be forgiven.*"[a]

The parable of the sower explained

13   He said to them, "Do you not understand this parable?
14 Then how will you understand any of the parables? •What
15 the sower is sowing is the word. •Those on the edge of the
path where the word is sown are people who have no
sooner heard it than Satan comes and carries away the
16 word that was sown in them. •Similarly, those who receive
the seed on patches of rock are people who, when first they
17 hear the word, welcome it at once with joy. •But they have
no root in them, they do not last; should some trial come,
or some persecution on account of the word, they fall
18 away at once. •Then there are others who receive the seed
19 in thorns. These have heard the word, •but the worries of
this world, the lure of riches and all the other passions
come in to choke the word, and so it produces nothing.
20 And there are those who have received the seed in rich
soil: they hear the word and accept it and yield a harvest,
thirty and sixty and a hundredfold."

Parable of the lamp

21   He also said to them, "Would you bring in a lamp to put
it under a tub or under the bed? Surely you will put it on
22 the lamp-stand? •For there is nothing hidden but it must be
disclosed, nothing kept secret except to be brought to light.
23 If anyone has ears to hear, let him listen to this."

4 a. Is 6:9-10

Parable of the measure

24 He also said to them, "Take notice of what you are
hearing. The amount you measure out is the amount you
25 will be given—and more besides; ·for the man who has
will be given more; from the man who has not, even what
he has will be taken away."

Parable of the seed growing by itself

26 He also said, "This is what the kingdom of God is like.
27 A man throws seed on the land. ·Night and day, while he
sleeps, when he is awake, the seed is sprouting and grow-
28 ing; how, he does not know. ·Of its own accord the land
produces first the shoot, then the ear, then the full grain
29 in the ear. ·And when the crop is ready, he loses no time:
he starts to reap because the harvest has come."

Parable of the mustard seed

30 He also said, "What can we say the kingdom of God is
31 like? What parable can we find for it? ·It is like a mustard
seed which at the time of its sowing in the soil is the small-
32 est of all the seeds on earth; ·yet once it is sown it grows
into the biggest shrub of them all and puts out big branches
so that the birds of the air can shelter in its shade."

The use of parables

33 Using many parables like these, he spoke the word to
them, so far as they were capable of understanding it.
34 He would not speak to them except in parables, but he
explained everything to his disciples when they were alone.

The calming of the storm

35 With the coming of evening that same day, he said to
36 them, "Let us cross over to the other side." ·And leaving
the crowd behind they took him, just as he was, in the
37 boat; and there were other boats with him. ·Then it began
to blow a gale and the waves were breaking into the boat
38 so that it was almost swamped. ·But he was in the stern,
39 his head on the cushion, asleep. ·They woke him and said
to him, "Master, do you not care? We are going down!"
And he woke up and rebuked the wind and said to the
sea, "Quiet now! Be calm!" And the wind dropped, and all
40 was calm again. ·Then he said to them, "Why are you so
41 frightened? How is it that you have no faith?" ·They were

filled with awe and said to one another, "Who can this be? Even the wind and the sea obey him."

The Gerasene demoniac

1,2 They reached the country of the Gerasenes[a] on the other side of the lake, ·and no sooner had he left the boat than a man with an unclean spirit came out from the 3 tombs toward him. ·The man lived in the tombs and no 4 one could secure him any more, even with a chain; ·because he had often been secured with fetters and chains but had snapped the chains and broken the fetters, and no 5 one had the strength to control him. ·All night and all day, among the tombs and in the mountains, he would howl 6 and gash himself with stones. ·Catching sight of Jesus from 7 a distance, he ran up and fell at his feet ·and shouted at the top of his voice, "What do you want with me, Jesus, son of the Most High God? Swear by God you will not 8 torture me!" ·—For Jesus had been saying to him, "Come 9 out of the man, unclean spirit." ·"What is your name?" Jesus asked. "My name is legion," he answered "for there 10 are many of us." ·And he begged him earnestly not to send 11 them out of the district. ·Now there was there on the 12 mountainside a great herd of pigs feeding, ·and the unclean spirits begged him, "Send us to the pigs, let us go 13 into them." ·So he gave them leave. With that, the unclean spirits came out and went into the pigs, and the herd of about two thousand pigs charged down the cliff into the 14 lake, and there they were drowned. ·The swineherds ran off and told their story in the town and in the country round about; and the people came to see what had really 15 happened. ·They came to Jesus and saw the demoniac sitting there, clothed and in his full senses—the very man who had had the legion in him before—and they were 16 afraid. ·And those who had witnessed it reported what had happened to the demoniac and what had become of 17 the pigs. ·Then they began to implore Jesus to leave the 18 neighborhood. ·As he was getting into the boat, the man who had been possessed begged to be allowed to stay with 19 him. ·Jesus would not let him but said to him, "Go home to your people and tell them all that the Lord in his mercy 20 has done for you." ·So the man went off and proceeded

5 a. "Gadarenes" in some versions.

to spread throughout the Decapolis all that Jesus had done for him. And everyone was amazed.

Cure of the woman with a hemorrhage. The daughter of Jairus raised to life

21 When Jesus had crossed again in the boat to the other side, a large crowd gathered round him and he stayed by
22 the lakeside. ·Then one of the synagogue officials came
23 up, Jairus by name, and seeing him, fell at his feet ·and pleaded with him earnestly, saying, "My little daughter is desperately sick. Do come and lay your hands on her to
24 make her better and save her life." ·Jesus went with him and a large crowd followed him; they were pressing all round him.

25 Now there was a woman who had suffered from a
26 hemorrhage for twelve years; ·after long and painful treatment under various doctors, she had spent all she had without being any the better for it, in fact, she was getting
27 worse. ·She had heard about Jesus, and she came up be-
28 hind him through the crowd and touched his cloak. ·"If I can touch even his clothes," she had told herself "I shall be
29 well again." ·And the source of the bleeding dried up in-
30 stantly, and she felt in herself that she was cured of her
31 complaint. ·Immediately aware that power had gone out from him, Jesus turned round in the crowd and said, "Who
31 touched my clothes?" ·His disciples said to him, "You see how the crowd is pressing round you and yet you say,
32 'Who touched me?'" ·But he continued to look all round
33 to see who had done it. ·Then the woman came forward, frightened and trembling[b] because she knew what had happened to her, and she fell at his feet and told him the
34 whole truth. ·"My daughter," he said "your faith has restored you to health; go in peace and be free from your complaint."

35 While he was still speaking some people arrived from the house of the synagogue official to say, "Your daughter
36 is dead: why put the Master to any further trouble?" ·But Jesus had overheard this remark of theirs and he said to
37 the official, "Do not be afraid; only have faith." ·And he allowed no one to go with him except Peter and James
38 and John the brother of James. ·So they came to the official's house and Jesus noticed all the commotion, with peo-
39 ple weeping and wailing unrestrainedly. ·He went in and said to them, "Why all this commotion and crying? The

40 child is not dead, but asleep." ·But they laughed at him. So he turned them all out and, taking with him the child's father and mother and his own companions, he went into 41 the place where the child lay. ·And taking the child by the hand he said to her, "Talitha, kum!" which means, 42 "Little girl, I tell you to get up." ·The little girl got up at once and began to walk about, for she was twelve years 43 old. At this they were overcome with astonishment, ·and he ordered them strictly not to let anyone know about it, and told them to give her something to eat.

A visit to Nazareth

1 Going from that district, he went to his home town and 2 his disciples accompanied him. ·With the coming of the sabbath he began teaching in the synagogue and most of them were astonished when they heard him. They said, "Where did the man get all this? What is this wisdom that has been granted him, and these miracles that are worked 3 through him? ·This is the carpenter, surely, the son of Mary, the brother of James and Joset and Jude and Simon? His sisters, too, are they not here with us?" And they would 4 not accept him. ·And Jesus said to them, "A prophet is only despised in his own country, among his own relations 5 and in his own house"; ·and he could work no miracle there, though he cured a few sick people by laying his 6 hands on them. ·He was amazed at their lack of faith.

The mission of the Twelve

7 He made a tour round the villages, teaching. ·Then he summoned the Twelve and began to send them out in pairs 8 giving them authority over the unclean spirits. ·And he instructed them to take nothing for the journey except a staff—no bread, no haversack, no coppers for their purses. 9 They were to wear sandals but, he added, "Do not take a 10 spare tunic." ·And he said to them, "If you enter a house 11 anywhere, stay there until you leave the district. ·And if any place does not welcome you and people refuse to listen to you, as you walk away shake off the dust from under 12 your feet as a sign to them." ·So they set off to preach 13 repentance; ·and they cast out many devils, and anointed many sick people with oil and cured them.

b. According to the Law, she was unclean, and to be touched by her would be defilement.

Herod and Jesus

¹⁴ Meanwhile King Herod had heard about him, since by now his name was well-known. Some were saying, "John the Baptist has risen from the dead, and that is why mi- ¹⁵ raculous powers are at work in him." ·Others said, "He is Elijah"; others again, "He is a prophet, like the prophets ¹⁶ we used to have." ·But when Herod heard this he said, "It is John whose head I cut off; he has risen from the dead."

John the Baptist beheaded

¹⁷ Now it was this same Herod who had sent to have John arrested, and had him chained up in prison because of Herodias, his brother Philip's wife whom he had married. ¹⁸ For John had told Herod, "It is against the law for you ¹⁹ to have your brother's wife." ·As for Herodias, she was furious with him and wanted to kill him; but she was not ²⁰ able to, ·because Herod was afraid of John, knowing him to be a good and holy man, and gave him his protection. When he had heard him speak he was greatly perplexed, and yet he liked to listen to him.

²¹ An opportunity came on Herod's birthday when he gave a banquet for the nobles of his court, for his army officers ²² and for the leading figures in Galilee. ·When the daughter of this same Herodias came in and danced, she delighted Herod and his guests; so the king said to the girl, "Ask me ²³ anything you like and I will give it you." ·And he swore her an oath, "I will give you anything you ask, even half ²⁴ my kingdom." ·She went out and said to her mother, "What shall I ask for?" She replied, "The head of John the Bap- ²⁵ tist." ·The girl hurried straight back to the king and made her request, "I want you to give me John the Baptist's head, ²⁶ here and now, on a dish." ·The king was deeply distressed but, thinking of the oaths he had sworn and of his guests, ²⁷ he was reluctant to break his word to her. ·So the king at once sent one of the bodyguard with orders to bring ²⁸ John's head. ·The man went off and beheaded him in prison; then he brought the head on a dish and gave it to ²⁹ the girl, and the girl gave it to her mother. ·When John's disciples heard about this, they came and took his body and laid it in a tomb.

First miracle of the loaves

³⁰ The apostles rejoined Jesus and told him all they had ³¹ done and taught. ·Then he said to them, "You must come

away to some lonely place all by yourselves and rest for a while"; for there were so many coming and going that the
32 apostles had no time even to eat. ·So they went off in a boat to a lonely place where they could be by themselves.
33 But people saw them going, and many could guess where; and from every town they all hurried to the place on foot
34 and reached it before them. ·So as he stepped ashore he saw a large crowd; and he took pity on them because they were like sheep without a shepherd, and he set himself to
35 teach them at some length. ·By now it was getting very late, and his disciples came up to him and said, "This is a
36 lonely place and it is getting very late; ·so send them away, and they can go to the farms and villages round about, to
37 buy themselves something to eat." ·He replied, "Give them something to eat yourselves." They answered, "Are we to go and spend two hundred denarii on bread for them to
38 eat?" ·"How many loaves have you?" he asked "Go and see." And when they had found out they said, "Five, and
39 two fish." ·Then he ordered them to get all the people to-
40 gether in groups on the green grass, ·and they sat down
41 on the ground in squares of hundreds and fifties. ·Then he took the five loaves and the two fish, raised his eyes to heaven and said the blessing; then he broke the loaves and handed them to his disciples to distribute among the peo-
42 ple. He also shared out the two fish among them all. ·They
43 all ate as much as they wanted. ·They collected twelve
44 basketfuls of scraps of bread and pieces of fish. ·Those who had eaten the loaves numbered five thousand men.

Jesus walks on the water

45 Directly after this he made his disciples get into the boat and go on ahead to Bethsaida, while he himself sent
46 the crowd away. ·After saying good-bye to them he went
47 off into the hills to pray. ·When evening came, the boat was
48 far out on the lake, and he was alone on the land. ·He could see they were worn out with rowing, for the wind was against them; and about the fourth watch of the night he came towards them, walking on the lake. He was going
49 to pass them by, ·but when they saw him walking on the
50 lake they thought it was a ghost and cried out; ·for they had all seen him and were terrified. But he at once spoke to them, and said, "Courage! It is I! Do not be afraid."
51 Then he got into the boat with them, and the wind

dropped. They were utterly and completely dumfounded,
⁵² because they had not seen what the miracle of the loaves meant; their minds were closed.

Cures at Gennesaret

⁵³ Having made the crossing, they came to land at Gen-
⁵⁴ nesaret and tied up. ·No sooner had they stepped out of
⁵⁵ the boat than people recognized him, ·and started hurry-
ing all through the countryside and brought the sick on
⁵⁶ stretchers to wherever they heard he was. ·And wherever
he went, to village, or town, or farm, they laid down the
sick in the open spaces, begging him to let them touch
even the fringe of his cloak. And all those who touched
him were cured.

The traditions of the Pharisees

¹ 7 The Pharisees and some of the scribes who had come
² from Jerusalem gathered round him, ·and they noticed
that some of his disciples were eating with unclean hands,
³ that is, without washing them. ·For the Pharisees, and the
Jews in general, follow the tradition of the elders and
never eat without washing their arms as far as the elbow;
⁴ and on returning from the market place they never eat
without first sprinkling themselves. There are also many
other observances which have been handed down to them
concerning the washing of cups and pots and bronze dishes.
⁵ So these Pharisees and scribes asked him, "Why do your
disciples not respect the tradition of the elders but eat their
⁶ food with unclean hands?" ·He answered, "It was of you
hypocrites that Isaiah so rightly prophesied in this passage
of scripture:

> *This people honors me only with lip-service,*
> *while their hearts are far from me.*
⁷ *The worship they offer me is worthless,*
> *the doctrines they teach are only human regulations.*ᵃ

⁸ You put aside the commandment of God to cling to hu-
⁹ man traditions." ·And he said to them, "How ingeniously
you get round the commandment of God in order to pre-
¹⁰ serve your own tradition! ·For Moses said: *Do your duty*
to your father and your mother, and, *Anyone who curses*
¹¹ *father or mother must be put to death.* ·But you say, 'If
a man says to his father or mother: Anything I have that
I might have used to help you is Corbanᵇ (that is, dedi-

12 cated to God), •then he is forbidden from that moment
13 to do anything for his father or mother.' •In this way you
make God's word null and void for the sake of your tradition which you have handed down. And you do many other
things like this."

On clean and unclean

14 He called the people to him again and said, "Listen to
15 me, all of you, and understand. •Nothing that goes into a
man from outside can make him unclean; it is the things
16 that come out of a man that make him unclean. •If anyone has ears to hear, let him listen to this."
17 When he had gone back into the house, away from the
18 crowd, his disciples questioned him about the parable. •He
said to them, "Do you not understand either? Can you not
see that whatever goes into a man from outside cannot
19 make him unclean, •because it does not go into his heart
but through his stomach and passes out into the sewer?"
20 (Thus he pronounced all foods clean.) •And he went on,
"It is what comes out of a man that makes him unclean.
21 For it is from within, from men's hearts, that evil inten-
22 tions emerge: fornication, theft, murder, adultery, •ava-
rice, malice, deceit, indecency, envy, slander, pride, folly.
23 All these evil things come from within and make a man
unclean."

III. JOURNEYS OUTSIDE GALILEE

The daughter of the Syrophoenician woman healed

24 He left that place and set out for the territory of Tyre.
There he went into a house and did not want anyone to
know he was there, but he could not pass unrecognized.
25 A woman whose little daughter had an unclean spirit
heard about him straightaway and came and fell at his
26 feet. •Now the woman was a pagan, by birth a Syrophoe-
nician, and she begged him to cast the devil out of her
27 daughter. •And he said to her, "The children should be
fed first, because it is not fair to take the children's food
28 and throw it to the house-dogs." •But she spoke up: "Ah
yes, sir," she replied "but the house-dogs under the table
29 can eat the children's scraps." •And he said to her, "For
saying this, you may go home happy: the devil has gone

7 a. Is 29:13   b. See note on Mt 15:6.

³⁰ out of your daughter." ·So she went off to her home and found the child lying on the bed and the devil gone.

Healing of the deaf man

³¹   Returning from the district of Tyre, he went by way of Sidon towards the Sea of Galilee, right through the De- ³² capolis region. ·And they brought him a deaf man who had an impediment in his speech; and they asked him to ³³ lay his hand on him. ·He took him aside in private, away from the crowd, put his fingers into the man's ears and ³⁴ touched his tongue with spittle. ·Then looking up to heaven he sighed; and he said to him, "Ephphatha," that is, "Be ³⁵ opened." ·And his ears were opened, and the ligament of ³⁶ his tongue was loosened and he spoke clearly. ·And Jesus ordered them to tell no one about it, but the more he in- ³⁷ sisted, the more widely they published it. ·Their admiration was unbounded. "He has done all things well," they said "he makes the deaf hear and the dumb speak."

Second miracle of the loaves

¹ 8 And now once again a great crowd had gathered, and they had nothing to eat. So he called his disciples to ² him and said to them, ·"I feel sorry for all these people; they have been with me for three days now and have ³ nothing to eat. ·If I send them off home hungry they will collapse on the way; some have come a great distance." ⁴ His disciples replied, "Where could anyone get bread to ⁵ feed these people in a deserted place like this?" ·He asked them, "How many loaves have you?" "Seven" they said. ⁶ Then he instructed the crowd to sit down on the ground, and he took the seven loaves, and after giving thanks he broke them and handed them to his disciples to distribute; ⁷ and they distributed them among the crowd. ·They had a few small fish as well, and over these he said a blessing ⁸ and ordered them to be distributed also. ·They ate as much as they wanted, and they collected seven basketfuls of the ⁹ scraps left over. ·Now there had been about four thousand ¹⁰ people. He sent them away ·and immediately, getting into the boat with his disciples, went to the region of Dal- manutha.

The Pharisees ask for a sign from heaven

¹¹   The Pharisees came up and started a discussion with him; they demanded of him a sign from heaven, to test

12 him. •And with a sigh that came straight from the heart he said, "Why does this generation demand a sign? I tell you solemnly, no sign shall be given to this generation."
13 And leaving them again and re-embarking he went away to the opposite shore.

The yeast of the Pharisees and of Herod

14 The disciples had forgotten to take any food and they
15 had only one loaf with them in the boat. •Then he gave them this warning, "Keep your eyes open; be on your guard against the yeast of the Pharisees and the yeast of Herod."
16 And they said to one another, "It is because we have no
17 bread." •And Jesus knew it, and he said to them, "Why are you talking about having no bread? Do you not yet understand? Have you no perception? Are your minds closed?
18 Have you *eyes that do not see, ears that do not hear?*[a] Or
19 do you not remember? •When I broke the five loaves among the five thousand, how many baskets full of scraps
20 did you collect?" They answered, "Twelve." •"And when I broke the seven loaves for the four thousand, how many baskets full of scraps did you collect?" And they answered,
21 "Seven." •Then he said to them, "Are you still without perception?"

Cure of a blind man at Bethsaida

22 They came to Bethsaida, and some people brought to
23 him a blind man whom they begged him to touch. •He took the blind man by the hand and led him outside the village. Then putting spittle on his eyes and laying his hands
24 on him, he asked, "Can you see anything?" •The man, who was beginning to see, replied, "I can see people; they look
25 like trees to me, but they are walking about." •Then he laid his hands on the man's eyes again and he saw clearly; he was cured, and he could see everything plainly and
26 distinctly. •And Jesus sent him home, saying, "Do not even go into the village."

Peter's profession of faith

27 Jesus and his disciples left for the villages round Caesarea Philippi. On the way he put this question to his dis-
28 ciples, "Who do people say I am?" •And they told him. "John the Baptist," they said "others Elijah; others again,

8 a. Jr 5:21; Ezk 12:2

²⁹ one of the prophets." ·"But you," he asked "who do you
   say I am?" Peter spoke up and said to him, "You are the
³⁰ Christ." ·And he gave them strict orders not to tell anyone
   about him.

First prophecy of the Passion

³¹   And he began to teach them that the Son of Man was
   destined to suffer grievously, to be rejected by the elders
   and the chief priests and the scribes, and to be put to death,
³² and after three days to rise again; ·and he said all this
   quite openly. Then, taking him aside, Peter started to re-
³³ monstrate with him. ·But, turning and seeing his disciples,
   he rebuked Peter and said to him, "Get behind me, Satan!
   Because the way you think is not God's way but man's."

The condition of following Christ

³⁴   He called the people and his disciples to him and said,
   "If anyone wants to be a follower of mine, let him renounce
³⁵ himself and take up his cross and follow me. ·For anyone
   who wants to save his life will lose it; but anyone who
   loses his life for my sake, and for the sake of the gospel,
³⁶ will save it. ·What gain, then, is it for a man to win the
³⁷ whole world and ruin his life? ·And indeed what can a
³⁸ man offer in exchange for his life? ·For if anyone in this
   adulterous and sinful generation is ashamed of me and of
   my words, the Son of Man will also be ashamed of him
   when he comes in the glory of his Father with the holy
   angels."
¹ 9 And he said to them, "I tell you solemnly, there are
     some standing here who will not taste death before
   they see the kingdom of God come with power."

The transfiguration

²   Six days later, Jesus took with him Peter and James
   and John and led them up a high mountain where they
   could be alone by themselves. There in their presence he
³ was transfigured: ·his clothes became dazzlingly white,
⁴ whiter than any earthly bleacher could make them. ·Elijah
   appeared to them with Moses; and they were talking with
⁵ Jesus. ·Then Peter spoke to Jesus: "Rabbi," he said "it is
   wonderful for us to be here; so let us make three tents,
⁶ one for you, one for Moses and one for Elijah." ·He did
⁷ not know what to say; they were so frightened. ·And a
   cloud came, covering them in shadow; and there came a

voice from the cloud, "This is my Son, the Beloved. Listen
8 to him." ·Then suddenly, when they looked round, they
saw no one with them any more but only Jesus.

The question about Elijah

9   As they came down from the mountain he warned them
to tell no one what they had seen, until after the Son of
10 Man had risen from the dead. ·They observed the warning faithfully, though among themselves they discussed
11 what "rising from the dead" could mean. ·And they put
this question to him, "Why do the scribes say that Elijah
12 has to come first?" ·"True," he said "Elijah is to come first
and to see that everything is as it should be; yet how is it
that the scriptures say about the Son of Man that he is to
13 suffer grievously and be treated with contempt? ·However,
I tell you that Elijah has come and they have treated him
as they pleased, just as the scriptures say about him."

The epileptic demoniac

14   When they rejoined the disciples they saw a large crowd
15 round them and some scribes arguing with them. ·The
moment they saw him the whole crowd were struck with
16 amazement and ran to greet him. ·"What are you arguing
17 about with them?" he asked. ·A man answered him from
the crowd, "Master, I have brought my son to you; there
18 is a spirit of dumbness in him, ·and when it takes hold of
him it throws him to the ground, and he foams at the
mouth and grinds his teeth and goes rigid. And I asked
your disciples to cast it out and they were unable to."
19 "You faithless generation" he said to them in reply. "How
much longer must I be with you? How much longer must
20 I put up with you? Bring him to me." ·They brought the
boy to him, and as soon as the spirit saw Jesus it threw
the boy into convulsions, and he fell to the ground and lay
21 writhing there, foaming at the mouth. ·Jesus asked the
father, "How long has this been happening to him?" "From
22 childhood," he replied ·"and it has often thrown him into
the fire and into the water, in order to destroy him. But
23 if you can do anything, have pity on us and help us." ·"If
you can?" retorted Jesus. "Everything is possible for any-
24 one who has faith." ·Immediately the father of the boy cried
25 out, "I do have faith. Help the little faith I have!" ·And
when Jesus saw how many people were pressing round
him, he rebuked the unclean spirit. "Deaf and dumb spirit,"

he said "I command you: come out of him and never enter
26 him again." ·Then throwing the boy into violent convulsions it came out shouting, and the boy lay there so like a
27 corpse that most of them said, "He is dead." ·But Jesus
took him by the hand and helped him up, and he was able
28 to stand. ·When he had gone indoors his disciples asked
29 him privately, "Why were we unable to cast it out?" ·"This
is the kind" he answered "that can only be driven out by
prayer."

Second prophecy of the Passion

30   After leaving that place they made their way through
31 Galilee; and he did not want anyone to know, ·because
he was instructing his disciples; he was telling them, "The
Son of Man will be delivered into the hands of men; they
will put him to death; and three days after he has been put
32 to death he will rise again." ·But they did not understand
what he said and were afraid to ask him.

Who is the greatest?

33   They came to Capernaum, and when he was in the
house he asked them, "What were you arguing about on
34 the road?" ·They said nothing because they had been argu-
35 ing which of them was the greatest. ·So he sat down, called
the Twelve to him and said, "If anyone wants to be first,
36 he must make himself last of all and servant of all." ·He
then took a little child, set him in front of them, put his
37 arms round him, and said to them, ·"Anyone who welcomes one of these little children in my name, welcomes
me; and anyone who welcomes me welcomes not me but
the one who sent me."

On using the name of Jesus

38   John said to him, "Master, we saw a man who is not
one of us casting out devils in your name; and because he
39 was not one of us we tried to stop him." ·But Jesus said,
"You must not stop him: no one who works a miracle in
40 my name is likely to speak evil of me. ·Anyone who is not
against us is for us.

Charity shown to Christ's disciples

41   "If anyone gives you a cup of water to drink just because
you belong to Christ, then I tell you solemnly, he will most
certainly not lose his reward.

On leading others astray

42 "But anyone who is an obstacle to bring down one of these little ones who have faith, would be better thrown 43 into the sea with a great millstone round his neck. •And if your hand should cause you to sin, cut it off; it is better for you to enter into life crippled, than to have two hands 45 and go to hell, into the fire that cannot be put out. •And if your foot should cause you to sin, cut it off; it is better for you to enter into life lame, than to have two feet and 47 be thrown into hell. •And if your eye should cause you to sin, tear it out; it is better for you to enter into the kingdom of God with one eye, than to have two eyes and be thrown 48 into hell •where *their worm does not die nor their fire go* 49 50 *out.*ᵃ •For everyone will be salted with fire. •Salt is a good thing, but if salt has become insipid, how can you season it again? Have salt in yourselves and be at peace with one another."

The question about divorce

1 **10** Leaving there, he came to the district of Judaea and the far side of the Jordan. And again crowds gathered round him, and again he taught them, as his 2 custom was. •Some Pharisees approached him and asked, "Is it against the law for a man to divorce his wife?" They 3 were testing him. •He answered them, "What did Moses 4 command you?" •"Moses allowed us" they said "to draw 5 up a writ of dismissal and so to divorce." •Then Jesus said to them, "It was because you were so unteachable that he 6 wrote this commandment for you. •But from the beginning 7 of creation *God made them male and female.* •*This is why* 8 *a man must leave father and mother,* •*and the two become one body.*ᵃ They are no longer two, therefore, but one 9 body. •So then, what God has united, man must not divide." 10 Back in the house the disciples questioned him again about 11 this, •and he said to them, "The man who divorces his wife 12 and marries another is guilty of adultery against her. •And if a woman divorces her husband and marries another she is guilty of adultery too."

9 a. Is 66:24
10 a. Gn 1:27; 2:24

Jesus and the children

13 People were bringing little children to him, for him
14 to touch them. The disciples turned them away, ·but when
Jesus saw this he was indignant and said to them, "Let the
little children come to me; do not stop them; for it is to such
15 as these that the kingdom of God belongs. ·I tell you solemnly, anyone who does not welcome the kingdom of God
16 like a little child will never enter it." ·Then he put his
arms round them, laid his hands on them and gave them his
blessing.

The rich young man

17 He was setting out on a journey when a man ran up,
knelt before him and put this question to him, "Good
18 master, what must I do to inherit eternal life?" ·Jesus said
to him, "Why do you call me good? No one is good but
19 God alone. ·You know the commandments: *You must not
kill; You must not commit adultery; You must not steal;
You must not bring false witness;* You must not defraud;
20 *Honor your father and mother.*" ·And he said to him,
21 "Master, I have kept all these from my earliest days." ·Jesus
looked steadily at him and loved him, and he said, "There
is one thing you lack. Go and sell everything you own and
give the money to the poor, and you will have treasure in
22 heaven; then come, follow me." ·But his face fell at these
words and he went away sad, for he was a man of great
wealth.

The danger of riches

23 Jesus looked round and said to his disciples, "How hard
it is for those who have riches to enter the kingdom of
24 God!" ·The disciples were astounded by these words, but
Jesus insisted, "My children," he said to them "how hard
25 it is to enter the kingdom of God! ·It is easier for a camel
to pass through the eye of a needle than for a rich man to
26 enter the kingdom of God." ·They were more astonished
than ever. "In that case" they said to one another "who can
27 be saved?" ·Jesus gazed at them. "For men" he said "it is
impossible, but not for God: because everything is possible
for God."

The reward of renunciation

28 Peter took this up. "What about us?" he asked him. "We
29 have left everything and followed you." ·Jesus said, "I tell

you solemnly, there is no one who has left house, brothers,
sisters, father, children or land for my sake and for the
80 sake of the gospel ·who will not be repaid a hundred times
over, houses, brothers, sisters, mothers, children and land
—not without persecutions—now in this present time and, in
the world to come, eternal life.
81   "Many who are first will be last, and the last first."

Third prophecy of the Passion

82   They were on the road, going up to Jerusalem; Jesus was
walking on ahead of them; they were in a daze, and those
who followed were apprehensive. Once more taking the
Twelve aside he began to tell them what was going to
83 happen to him: ·"Now we are going up to Jerusalem, and
the Son of Man is about to be handed over to the chief
priests and the scribes. They will condemn him to death
84 and will hand him over to the pagans, ·who will mock him
and spit at him and scourge him and put him to death; and
after three days he will rise again."

The sons of Zebedee make their request

85   James and John, the sons of Zebedee, approached him.
"Master," they said to him "we want you to do us a favor."
86 He said to them, "What is it you want me to do for you?"
87 They said to him, "Allow us to sit one at your right hand
88 and the other at your left in your glory." ·"You do not
know what you are asking" Jesus said to them. "Can you
drink the cup that I must drink, or be baptized with the
89 baptism with which I must be baptized?" ·They replied,
"We can." Jesus said to them, "The cup that I must drink
you shall drink, and with the baptism with which I must be
40 baptized you shall be baptized, ·but as for seats at my right
hand or my left, these are not mine to grant; they belong
to those to whom they have been allotted."

Leadership with service

41   When the other ten heard this they began to feel indig-
42 nant with James and John, ·so Jesus called them to him
and said to them, "You know that among the pagans their
so-called rulers lord it over them, and their great men
43 make their authority felt. ·This is not to happen among
you. No; anyone who wants to become great among you
44 must be your servant, ·and anyone who wants to be first

⁴⁵ among you must be slave to all. ·For the Son of Man himself did not come to be served but to serve, and to give his life as a ransom for many."

The blind man of Jericho

⁴⁶ They reached Jericho; and as he left Jericho with his disciples and a large crowd, Bartimaeus (that is, the son of Timaeus), a blind beggar, was sitting at the side of the ⁴⁷ road. ·When he heard that it was Jesus of Nazareth, he began to shout and to say, "Son of David, Jesus, have pity ⁴⁸ on me." ·And many of them scolded him and told him to keep quiet, but he only shouted all the louder, "Son of ⁴⁹ David, have pity on me." ·Jesus stopped and said, "Call him here." So they called the blind man. "Courage," they ⁵⁰ said "get up; he is calling you." ·So throwing off his cloak, ⁵¹ he jumped up and went to Jesus. ·Then Jesus spoke. "What do you want me to do for you?" "Rabbuni,"ᵇ the blind man ⁵² said to him "Master, let me see again." ·Jesus said to him, "Go; your faith has saved you." And immediately his sight returned and he followed him along the road.

IV. THE JERUSALEM MINISTRY

The Messiah enters Jerusalem

¹ **11** When they were approaching Jerusalem, in sight of Bethphage and Bethany, close by the Mount of Olives, ² he sent two of his disciples ·and said to them, "Go off to the village facing you, and as soon as you enter it you will find a tethered colt that no one has yet ridden. Untie it and ³ bring it here. ·If anyone says to you, 'What are you doing?' say, 'The Master needs it and will send it back here ⁴ directly.' " ·They went off and found a colt tethered near a ⁵ door in the open street. As they untied it, ·some men standing there said, "What are you doing, untying that ⁶ colt?" ·They gave the answer Jesus had told them, and the ⁷ men let them go. ·Then they took the colt to Jesus and ⁸ threw their cloaks on its back, and he sat on it. ·Many people spread their cloaks on the road, others greenery ⁹ which they had cut in the fields. ·And those who went in front and those who followed were all shouting, "*Hosanna! Blessings on him who comes in the name of the Lord!ᵃ* ¹⁰ *Blessings on the coming kingdom of our father David!* ¹¹ *Hosanna* in the highest heavens!" ·He entered Jerusalem

and went into the Temple. He looked all round him, but as it was now late, he went out to Bethany with the Twelve.

The barren fig tree

12 Next day as they were leaving Bethany, he felt hungry.
13 Seeing a fig tree in leaf some distance away, he went to see if he could find any fruit on it, but when he came up to it he found nothing but leaves; for it was not the season
14 for figs. •And he addressed the fig tree. "May no one ever eat fruit from you again" he said. And his disciples heard him say this.

The expulsion of the dealers from the Temple

15 So they reached Jerusalem and he went into the Temple and began driving out those who were selling and buying there; he upset the tables of the money changers and the
16 chairs of those who were selling pigeons. •Nor would he
17 allow anyone to carry anything through the Temple. •And he taught them and said, "Does not scripture say: *My house will be called a house of prayer for all the peoples?b*
18 But you have turned it into *a robbers' den.*"c •This came to the ears of the chief priests and the scribes, and they tried to find some way of doing away with him; they were afraid of him because the people were carried away by
19 his teaching. •And when evening came he went out of the city.

The fig tree withered. Faith and prayer

20 Next morning, as they passed by, they saw the fig tree
21 withered to the roots. •Peter remembered. "Look, Rabbi," he said to Jesus "the fig tree you cursed has withered
22 23 away." •Jesus answered, "Have faith in God. •I tell you solemnly, if anyone says to this mountain, 'Get up and throw yourself into the sea,' with no hesitation in his heart but believing that what he says will happen, it will be done for
24 him. •I tell you therefore: everything you ask and pray for, believe that you have it already, and it will be yours.
25 And when you stand in prayer, forgive whatever you have against anybody, so that your Father in heaven may forgive your failings too."

b. Aramaic: "My master."
11 a. Ps 118:25-26   b. Is 56:7   c. Jr 7:11

The authority of Jesus is questioned

27 They came to Jerusalem again, and as Jesus was walking in the Temple, the chief priests and the scribes and the
28 elders came to him, ·and they said to him, "What authority have you for acting like this? Or who gave you
29 authority to do these things?" ·Jesus said to them, "I will ask you a question, only one; answer me and I will tell you
30 my authority for acting like this. ·John's baptism: did it
31 come from heaven, or from man? Answer me that." ·And they argued it out this way among themselves: "If we say from heaven, he will say, 'Then why did you refuse to
32 believe him?' ·But dare we say from man?"—they had the people to fear, for everyone held that John was a real
33 prophet. ·So their reply to Jesus was, "We do not know." And Jesus said to them, "Nor will I tell you my authority for acting like this."

Parable of the wicked husbandmen

12 ¹ He went on to speak to them in parables. "A man planted a vineyard; he fenced it round, dug out a trough for the winepress and built a tower; then he leased
2 it to tenants and went abroad. ·When the time came, he sent a servant to the tenants to collect from them his share
3 of the produce from the vineyard. ·But they seized the man, thrashed him and sent him away empty-handed.
4 Next he sent another servant to them; him they beat about
5 the head and treated shamefully. ·And he sent another and him they killed; then a number of others, and they thrashed
6 some and killed the rest. ·He had still someone left: his beloved son. He sent him to them last of all. 'They will
7 respect my son' he said. ·But those tenants said to each other, 'This is the heir. Come on, let us kill him, and the
8 inheritance will be ours.' ·So they seized him and killed
9 him and threw him out of the vineyard. ·Now what will the owner of the vineyard do? He will come and make an
10 end of the tenants and give the vineyard to others. ·Have you not read this text of scripture:

> *It was the stone rejected by the builders*
> *that became the keystone.*
11 > *This was the Lord's doing*
> *and it is wonderful to see?*[a]

12 And they would have liked to arrest him, because they

realized that the parable was aimed at them, but they were afraid of the crowds. So they left him alone and went away.

On tribute to Caesar

18 Next they sent to him some Pharisees and some Hero-
14 dians to catch him out in what he said. ·These came and said to him, "Master, we know you are an honest man, that you are not afraid of anyone, because a man's rank means nothing to you, and that you teach the way of God in all honesty. Is it permissible to pay taxes to Caesar or
15 not? Should we pay, yes or no?" ·Seeing through their hypocrisy he said to them, "Why do you set this trap for
16 me? Hand me a denarius and let me see it." ·They handed him one and he said, "Whose head is this? Whose name?"
17 "Caesar's" they told him. ·Jesus said to them, "Give back to Caesar what belongs to Caesar—and to God what belongs to God." This reply took them completely by surprise.

The resurrection of the dead

18 Then some Sadducees—who deny that there is a resurrection—came to him and they put this question to him,
19 "Master, we have it from Moses in writing, if a man's brother dies leaving a wife but no child, the man must marry the widow to raise up children for his brother.
20 Now there were seven brothers. The first married a wife
21 and then died leaving no children. ·The second married the widow, and he too died leaving no children; with the
22 third it was the same, ·and none of the seven left any chil-
28 dren. Last of all the woman herself died. ·Now at the resurrection, when they rise again, whose wife will she be, since she had been married to all seven?"
24 Jesus said to them, "Is not the reason why you go wrong, that you understand neither the scriptures nor the power
25 of God? ·For when they rise from the dead, men and and women do not marry; no, they are like the angels in
26 heaven. ·Now about the dead rising again, have you never read in the Book of Moses, in the passage about the Bush, how God spoke to him and said: *I am the God of Abra-*
27 *ham, the God of Isaac and the God of Jacob?*[b] ·He is God, not of the dead, but of the living. You are very much mistaken."

12 a. Ps 118:22-23   b. Ex 3:6

The greatest commandment of all

28　One of the scribes who had listened to them debating and had observed how well Jesus had answered them, now came up and put a question to him, "Which is the first of
29　all the commandments?" ·Jesus replied, "This is the first:
30　*Listen, Israel, the Lord our God is the one Lord,* ·*and you must love the Lord your God with all your heart, with all your soul,* with all your mind and *with all your strength.*ᶜ
31　The second is this: *You must love your neighbor as yourself.*ᵈ There is no commandment greater than these."
32　The scribe said to him, "Well spoken, Master; what you
33　have said is true: that he is one and there is no other. ·To love him with all your heart, with all your understanding and strength, and to love your neighbor as yourself, this is far more important than any holocaust or sacrifice."
34　Jesus, seeing how wisely he had spoken, said, "You are not far from the kingdom of God." And after that no one dared to question him any more.

Christ not only son but also Lord of David

35　Later, while teaching in the Temple, Jesus said, "How can the scribes maintain that the Christ is the son of David?
36　David himself, moved by the Holy Spirit, said:

> *The Lord said to my Lord:*
> *Sit at my right hand*
> *and I will put your enemies*
> *under your feet.*ᵉ

37　David himself calls him Lord, in what way then can he be his son?" And the great majority of the people heard this with delight.

The scribes condemned by Jesus

38　In his teaching he said, "Beware of the scribes who like to walk about in long robes, to be greeted obsequiously in
39　the market squares, ·to take the front seats in the syna-
40　gogues and the places of honor at banquets; ·these are the men who swallow the property of widows, while making a show of lengthy prayers. The more severe will be the sentence they receive."

The widow's mite

41　He sat down opposite the treasury and watched the people putting money into the treasury, and many of the rich

⁴² put in a great deal. ∘A poor widow came and put in two
⁴³ small coins, the equivalent of a penny. ∘Then he called his
disciples and said to them, "I tell you solemnly, this poor
widow has put more in than all who have contributed to
⁴⁴ the treasury; ∘for they have all put in money they had
over, but she from the little she had has put in everything
she possessed, all she had to live on."

The eschatological discourse: introduction

¹ **13** As he was leaving the Temple one of his disciples
said to him, "Look at the size of those stones, Master!
² Look at the size of those buildings!" ∘And Jesus said to
him, "You see these great buildings? Not a single stone
will be left on another: everything will be destroyed."

³ And while he was sitting facing the Temple, on the
Mount of Olives, Peter, James, John and Andrew ques-
⁴ tioned him privately, ∘"Tell us, when is this going to happen, and what sign will there be that all this is about to be
fulfilled?"

The beginning of sorrows

⁵ Then Jesus began to tell them, "Take care that no one
⁶ deceives you. ∘Many will come using my name and saying,
⁷ 'I am he,' and they will deceive many. ∘When you hear
of wars and rumors of wars, do not be alarmed, this is
something that must happen, but the end will not be yet.
⁸ For nation will fight against nation, and kingdom against
kingdom. There will be earthquakes here and there; there
will be famines. This is the beginning of the birthpangs.
⁹ "Be on your guard: they will hand you over to sanhedrins; you will be beaten in synagogues; and you will
stand before governors and kings for my sake, to bear
¹⁰ witness before them, ∘since the Good News must first be
proclaimed to all the nations.
¹¹ "And when they lead you away to hand you over, do not
worry beforehand about what to say; no, say whatever is
given to you when the time comes, because it is not you
¹² who will be speaking: it will be the Holy Spirit. ∘Brother
will betray brother to death, and the father his child;
children will rise against their parents and have them put
¹³ to death. ∘You will be hated by all men on account of my

c. Dt 6:4-5   d. Lv 19:18   e. Ps 110:1

name; but the man who stands firm to the end will be saved.

The great tribulation of Jerusalem

14 "When you see *the disastrous abomination*[a] set up where it ought not to be (let the reader understand), then those 15 in Judaea must escape to the mountains; ·if a man is on the housetop, he must not come down to go into the house 16 to collect any of his belongings; ·if a man is in the fields, 17 he must not turn back to fetch his cloak. ·Alas for those with child, or with babies at the breast, when those days 18/19 come! ·Pray that this may not be in winter. ·For in those days there will be *such distress as, until now, has not been*[b] equalled since the beginning when God created the world, 20 nor ever will be again. ·And if the Lord had not shortened that time, no one would have survived; but he did shorten the time, for the sake of the elect whom he chose.

21 "And if anyone says to you then, 'Look, here is the 22 Christ' or, 'Look, he is there,' do not believe it; ·for false Christs and false prophets will arise and produce signs and 23 portents to deceive the elect, if that were possible. ·You therefore must be on your guard. I have forewarned you of everything.

The coming of the Son of Man

24 "But in those days, after that time of distress, the sun 25 will be darkened, the moon will lose its brightness, ·the stars will come falling from heaven and the powers in the 26 heavens will be shaken. ·And then they will see the Son of Man coming in the clouds, with great power and glory; 27 then too he will send the angels to gather his chosen from the four winds, from the ends of the world to the ends of heaven.

The time of this coming

28 "Take the fig tree as a parable: as soon as its twigs grow supple and its leaves come out, you know that summer is 29 near. ·So with you when you see these things happening: 30 know that he is near, at the very gates. ·I tell you solemnly, before this generation has passed away all these things will 31 have taken place. ·Heaven and earth will pass away, but my words will not pass away.

32 "But as for that day or hour, nobody knows it, neither the angels of heaven, nor the Son; no one but the Father.

Be on the alert

33   "Be on your guard, stay awake, because you never know
34 when the time will come. ·It is like a man traveling
abroad: he has gone from home, and left his servants in
charge, each with his own task; and he has told the door-
35 keeper to stay awake. ·So stay awake, because you do not
know when the master of the house is coming, evening,
36 midnight, cockcrow, dawn; ·if he comes unexpectedly, he
37 must not find you asleep. ·And what I say to you I say to
all: Stay awake!"

V. PASSION AND RESURRECTION

The conspiracy against Jesus

1 **14** It was two days before the Passover and the feast
of Unleavened Bread, and the chief priests and the
scribes were looking for a way to arrest Jesus by some trick
2 and have him put to death. ·For they said, "It must not be
during the festivities, or there will be a disturbance among
the people."

The anointing at Bethany

3   Jesus was at Bethany in the house of Simon the leper;
he was at dinner when a woman came in with an alabaster
jar of very costly ointment, pure nard. She broke the jar
4 and poured the ointment on his head. ·Some who were
there said to one another indignantly, "Why this waste of
5 ointment? ·Ointment like this could have been sold for
over three hundred denarii and the money given to the
6 poor;" and they were angry with her. ·But Jesus said,
"Leave her alone. Why are you upsetting her? What she
7 has done for me is one of the good works. ·You have the
poor with you always, and you can be kind to them when-
8 ever you wish, but you will not always have me. ·She has
done what was in her power to do: she has anointed my
9 body beforehand for its burial. ·I tell you solemnly,
wherever throughout all the world the Good News is
proclaimed, what she has done will be told also, in remembrance of her."

13 a. Dn 9:27, and ch. 11,12   b. Dn 12:1

Judas betrays Jesus

¹⁰ Judas Iscariot, one of the Twelve, approached the chief
¹¹ priests with an offer to hand Jesus over to them. ·They
were delighted to hear it, and promised to give him
money; and he looked for a way of betraying him when
the opportunity should occur.

Preparations for the Passover supper

¹² On the first day of Unleavened Bread, when the Pass-
over lamb was sacrificed, his disciples said to him, "Where
do you want us to go and make the preparations for you
¹³ to eat the passover?" ·So he sent two of his disciples, saying
to them, "Go into the city and you will meet a man carrying
¹⁴ a pitcher of water. Follow him, ·and say to the owner of
of the house which he enters, 'The Master says: Where is
my dining room in which I can eat the passover with my
¹⁵ disciples?' ·He will show you a large upper room fur-
nished with couches, all prepared. Make the preparations
¹⁶ for us there." ·The disciples set out and went to the city
and found everything as he had told them, and prepared
the Passover.

The treachery of Judas foretold

¹⁷₁₈ When evening came he arrived with the Twelve. ·And
while they were at table eating, Jesus said, "I tell you
solemnly, one of you is about to betray me, one of you
¹⁹ eating with me." ·They were distressed and asked him, one
²⁰ after another, "Not I, surely?" ·He said to them, "It is one
of the Twelve, one who is dipping into the same dish
²¹ with me. ·Yes, the Son of Man is going to his fate, as the
scriptures say he will, but alas for that man by whom the
Son of Man is betrayed! Better for that man if he had never
been born!"

The institution of the Eucharist

²² And as they were eating he took some bread, and when
he had said the blessing he broke it and gave it to them.
²³ "Take it," he said "this is my body." ·Then he took a cup,
and when he had returned thanks he gave it to them, and
²⁴ all drank from it, ·and he said to them, "This is my blood,
the blood of the covenant, which is to be poured out for
²⁵ many. ·I tell you solemnly, I shall not drink any more wine
until the day I drink the new wine in the kingdom of God."

Peter's denial foretold

26   After psalms had been sung they left for the Mount of
27 Olives. ·And Jesus said to them, "You will all lose faith, for the scripture says: *I shall strike the shepherd and the*
28 *sheep will be scattered,*[a] ·however after my resurrection
29 I shall go before you to Galilee." ·Peter said, "Even if all
30 lose faith, I will not." ·And Jesus said to him, "I tell you solemnly, this day, this very night, before the cock crows
31 twice, you will have disowned me three times." ·But he repeated still more earnestly, "If I have to die with you, I will never disown you." And they all said the same.

Gethsemane

32   They came to a small estate called Gethsemane, and
33 Jesus said to his disciples, "Stay here while I pray." ·Then he took Peter and James and John with him. And a sudden
34 fear came over him, and great distress. ·And he said to them, "My soul is sorrowful to the point of death. Wait
35 here, and keep awake." ·And going on a little farther he threw himself on the ground and prayed that, if it were
36 possible, this hour might pass him by. ·"Abba (Father)!" he said "Everything is possible for you. Take this cup away from me. But let it be as you, not I, would have it."
37 He came back and found them sleeping, and he said to Peter, "Simon, are you asleep? Had you not the strength to
38 keep awake one hour? ·You should be awake, and praying not to be put to the test. The spirit is willing, but the flesh
39 is weak." ·Again he went away and prayed, saying the
40 same words. ·And once more he came back and found them sleeping, their eyes were so heavy; and they could
41 find no answer for him. ·He came back a third time and said to them, "You can sleep on now and take your rest. It is all over. The hour has come. Now the Son of Man is
42 to be betrayed into the hands of sinners. ·Get up! Let us go! My betrayer is close at hand already."

The arrest

43   Even while he was still speaking, Judas, one of the Twelve, came up with a number of men armed with swords and clubs, sent by the chief priests and the scribes
44 and the elders. ·Now the traitor had arranged a signal with them. "The one I kiss," he had said "he is the man. Take

14 a. Zc 13:7

him in charge, and see he is well guarded when you lead
⁴⁵ him away." ·So when the traitor came, he went straight up
⁴⁶ to Jesus and said, "Rabbi!" and kissed him. ·The others
⁴⁷ seized him and took him in charge. ·Then one of the by-
standers drew his sword and struck out at the high priest's
servant, and cut off his ear.

⁴⁸   Then Jesus spoke. "Am I a brigand" he said "that you
⁴⁹ had to set out to capture me with swords and clubs? ·I was
among you teaching in the Temple day after day and you
never laid hands on me. But this is to fulfill the scriptures."
⁵⁰₅₁ And they all deserted him and ran away. ·A young
man who followed him had nothing on but a linen cloth.
⁵² They caught hold of him, ·but he left the cloth in their
hands and ran away naked.

Jesus before the Sanhedrin

⁵³   They led Jesus off to the high priest; and all the chief
priests and the elders and the scribes assembled there.
⁵⁴ Peter had followed him at a distance, right into the high
priest's palace, and was sitting with the attendants warming
himself at the fire.

⁵⁵   The chief priests and the whole Sanhedrin were looking
for evidence against Jesus on which they might pass the
⁵⁶ death-sentence. But they could not find any. ·Several, in-
deed, brought false evidence against him, but their evidence
⁵⁷ was conflicting. ·Some stood up and submitted this false
⁵⁸ evidence against him, ·"We heard him say, 'I am going
to destroy this Temple made by human hands, and in three
⁵⁹ days build another, not made by human hands.'" ·But even
⁶⁰ on this point their evidence was conflicting. ·The high
priest then stood up before the whole assembly and put
this question to Jesus, "Have you no answer to that? What
⁶¹ is this evidence these men are bringing against you?" ·But
he was silent and made no answer at all. The high
priest put a second question to him, "Are you the Christ,"
⁶² he said "the Son of the Blessed One?" ·"I am," said Jesus
"and you will see *the Son of Man seated at the right hand
of the Power* and *coming with the clouds of heaven.*"^b
⁶³ The high priest tore his robes, "What need of witnesses
⁶⁴ have we now?" he said. ·"You heard the blasphemy. What
is your finding?" And they all gave their verdict: he deserved to die.

⁶⁵   Some of them started spitting at him and, blindfolding

him, began hitting him with their fists and shouting, "Play the prophet!" And the attendants rained blows on him.

Peter's denials

66 While Peter was down below in the courtyard, one of
67 the high priest's servant-girls came up. ·She saw Peter warming himself there, stared at him and said, "You too
68 were with Jesus, the man from Nazareth." ·But he denied it. "I do not know, I do not understand, what you are talk-ing about" he said. And he went out into the forecourt.
69 The servant-girl saw him and again started telling the by-
70 standers, "This fellow is one of them." ·But again he denied it. A little later the bystanders themselves said to Peter, "You are one of them for sure! Why, you are a Galilean."
71 But he started calling down curses on himself and swear-
72 ing, "I do not know the man you speak of." ·At that mo-ment the cock crew for the second time, and Peter re-called how Jesus had said to him, "Before the cock crows twice, you will have disowned me three times." And he burst into tears.

Jesus before Pilate

1 **15** First thing in the morning, the chief priests together with the elders and scribes, in short the whole San-hedrin, had their plan ready. They had Jesus bound and took him away and handed him over to Pilate.
2 Pilate questioned him, "Are you the king of the Jews?"
3 "It is you who say it" he answered. ·And the chief priests
4 brought many accusations against him. ·Pilate questioned him again, "Have you no reply at all? See how many ac-
5 cusations they are bringing against you!" ·But, to Pilate's amazement, Jesus made no further reply.
6 At festival time Pilate used to release a prisoner for
7 them, anyone they asked for. ·Now a man called Barabbas was then in prison with the rioters who had committed
8 murder during the uprising. ·When the crowd went up and
9 began to ask Pilate the customary favor, ·Pilate answered them, "Do you want me to release for you the king of the
10 Jews?" ·For he realized it was out of jealousy that the
11 chief priests had handed Jesus over. ·The chief priests, however, had incited the crowd to demand that he should
12 release Barabbas for them instead. ·Then Pilate spoke

b. Dn 7:13; Ps 110:1

again. "But in that case," he said to them "what am I to do
13 with the man you call king of the Jews?" ·They shouted
14 back, "Crucify him!" ·"Why?" Pilate asked them "What
harm has he done?" But they shouted all the louder,
15 "Crucify him!" ·So Pilate, anxious to placate the crowd, released Barabbas for them and, having ordered Jesus to be
scourged, handed him over to be crucified.

Jesus crowned with thorns

16   The soldiers led him away to the inner part of the
palace, that is, the Praetorium, and called the whole cohort
17 together. ·They dressed him up in purple, twisted some
18 thorns into a crown and put it on him. ·And they began
19 saluting him, "Hail, king of the Jews!" ·They struck his
head with a reed and spat on him; and they went down on
20 their knees to do him homage. ·And when they had
finished making fun of him, they took off the purple and
dressed him in his own clothes.

The way of the cross

21   They led him out to crucify him. ·They enlisted a
passer-by, Simon of Cyrene, father of Alexander and
Rufus,[a] who was coming in from the country, to carry his
22 cross. ·They brought Jesus to the place called Golgotha,
which means the place of the skull.

The crucifixion

23   They offered him wine mixed with myrrh, but he re-
24 fused it. ·Then they crucified him, and shared out his
25 clothing, casting lots to decide what each should get. ·It
26 was the third hour[b] when they crucified him. ·The inscription giving the charge against him read: "The King of
27 the Jews." ·And they crucified two robbers with him, one
on his right and one on his left.

The crucified Christ is mocked

29   The passers-by jeered at him; they shook their heads
and said, "Aha! So you would destroy the Temple and re-
30 build it in three days! ·Then save yourself: come down
31 from the cross!" ·The chief priests and the scribes mocked
him among themselves in the same way. "He saved others,"
32 they said "he cannot save himself. ·Let the Christ, the king
of Israel, come down from the cross now, for us to see it

and believe." Even those who were crucified with him taunted him.

The death of Jesus

33 When the sixth hour came there was darkness over the
34 whole land until the ninth hour. ·And at the ninth hour Jesus cried out in a loud voice, "Eloi, Eloi, lama sabach-thani?" which means, *"My God, my God, why have you*
35 *deserted me?"*[c] ·When some of those who stood by heard
36 this, they said, "Listen, he is calling on Elijah." ·Some-one ran and soaked a sponge in vinegar and, putting it on a reed, gave it him to drink saying, "Wait and see if
37 Elijah will come to take him down." ·But Jesus gave a loud
38 cry and breathed his last. ·And the veil of the Temple was
39 torn in two from top to bottom. ·The centurion, who was standing in front of him, had seen how he had died, and he said, "In truth this man was a son of God."

The women on Calvary

40 There were some women watching from a distance. Among them were Mary of Magdala, Mary who was the mother of James the younger and Joset, and Salome.
41 These used to follow him and look after him when he was in Galilee. And there were many other women there who had come up to Jerusalem with him.

The burial

42 It was now evening, and since it was Preparation Day
43 (that is, the vigil of the sabbath), ·there came Joseph of Arimathaea, a prominent member of the Council, who himself lived in the hope of seeing the kingdom of God, and he boldly went to Pilate and asked for the body of
44 Jesus. ·Pilate, astonished that he should have died so soon, summoned the centurion and enquired if he was already
45 dead. ·Having been assured of this by the centurion, he
46 granted the corpse to Joseph ·who bought a shroud, took Jesus down from the cross, wrapped him in the shroud and laid him in a tomb which had been hewn out of the rock. He then rolled a stone against the entrance to the
47 tomb. ·Mary of Magdala and Mary the mother of Joset were watching and took note of where he was laid.

15 a. Alexander and Rufus were doubtless known to the Roman circle in which Mark wrote his gospel. Cf. Rm 16:13. b. 9 a.m. c. Ps 22:1

The empty tomb. The angel's message

1 16 When the Sabbath was over, Mary of Magdala, Mary the mother of James, and Salome, bought **2** spices with which to go and anoint him. ·And very early in the morning on the first day of the week they went to the tomb, just as the sun was rising.

3 They had been saying to one another, "Who will roll **4** away the stone for us from the entrance to the tomb?" ·But when they looked they could see that the stone—which was **5** very big—had already been rolled back. ·On entering the tomb they saw a young man in a white robe seated on the right-hand side, and they were struck with amazement. **6** But he said to them, "There is no need for alarm. You are looking for Jesus of Nazareth, who was crucified: he has risen, he is not here. See, here is the place where they **7** laid him. ·But you must go and tell his disciples and Peter, 'He is going before you to Galilee; it is there you will see **8** him, just as he told you.'" ·And the women came out and ran away from the tomb because they were frightened out of their wits; and they said nothing to a soul, for they were afraid . . .

Appearances of the risen Christ*

9 Having risen in the morning on the first day of the week, he appeared first to Mary of Magdala from whom he had **10** cast out seven devils. ·She then went to those who had been his companions, and who were mourning and in tears, **11** and told them. ·But they did not believe her when they heard her say that he was alive and that she had seen him. **12** After this, he showed himself under another form to two of them as they were on their way into the country. **13** These went back and told the others, who did not believe them either.

14 Lastly, he showed himself to the Eleven themselves while they were at table. He reproached them for their incredulity and obstinacy, because they had refused to be-**15** lieve those who had seen him after he had risen. ·And he said to them, "Go out to the whole world; proclaim the **16** Good News to all creation. ·He who believes and is baptized will be saved; he who does not believe will be con-**17** demned. ·These are the signs that will be associated with believers: in my name they will cast out devils; they will **18** have the gift of tongues; ·they will pick up snakes in their hands, and be unharmed should they drink deadly poison; they will lay their hands on the sick, who will recover."

19 And so the Lord Jesus, after he had spoken to them, was taken up into heaven: there at the right hand of God he 20 took his place, while they, going out, preached every-where, the Lord working with them and confirming the word by the signs that accompanied it.

16 a. Many MSS omit vv. 9-20 and this ending to the gospel may not have been written by Mark, though it is old enough.

THE GOSPEL ACCORDING TO
Saint Luke

Prologue

¹ **1** Seeing that many others have undertaken to draw up
accounts of the events that have taken place among us,
² exactly as these were handed down to us by those who
from the outset were eyewitnesses and ministers of the
³ word, ·I in my turn, after carefully going over the whole
story from the beginning, have decided to write an ordered
⁴ account for you, Theophilus, ·so that your Excellency may
learn how well founded the teaching is that you have
received.

I. THE BIRTH AND HIDDEN LIFE
OF JOHN THE BAPTIST AND OF JESUS

The birth of John the Baptist foretold

⁵ In the days of King Herod of Judaea there lived a priest
called Zechariah who belonged to the Abijah section of
the priesthood, and he had a wife, Elizabeth by name, who
⁶ was a descendant of Aaron. ·Both were worthy in the
sight of God, and scrupulously observed all the command-
⁷ ments and observances of the Lord. ·But they were child-
less: Elizabeth was barren and they were both getting on
in years.

⁸ Now it was the turn of Zechariah's section^a to serve,
⁹ and he was exercising his priestly office before God ·when
it fell to him by lot, as the ritual custom was, to enter the
¹⁰ Lord's sanctuary and burn incense there.^b ·And at the
hour of incense the whole congregation · was outside,
praying.

¹¹ Then there appeared to him the angel of the Lord,
¹² standing on the right of the altar of incense. ·The sight
¹³ disturbed Zechariah and he was overcome with fear. ·But
the angel said to him, "Zechariah, do not be afraid, your

prayer has been heard. Your wife Elizabeth is to bear you
14 a son and you must name him John.º ·He will be your
15 joy and delight and many will rejoice at his birth, ·for he
will be great in the sight of the Lord; he must drink no
wine, no strong drink.ᵈ Even from his mother's womb he
16 will be filled with the Holy Spirit, ·and he will bring back
17 many of the sons of Israel to the Lord their God. ·With
the spirit and power of Elijah, he will go before him *to
turn the hearts of fathers toward their children*ᵉ and the
disobedient back to the wisdom that the virtuous have, pre-
18 paring for the Lord a people fit for him." ·Zechariah said
to the angel, *"How can I be sure of this?'* I am an old man
19 and my wife is getting on in years." ·The angel replied, "I
am Gabriel who stand in God's presence, and I have been
20 sent to speak to you and bring you this good news. ·Listen!
Since you have not believed my words, which will come
true at their appointed time, you will be silenced and have
21 no power of speech until this has happened." ·Meanwhile
the people were waiting for Zechariah and were surprised
22 that he stayed in the sanctuary so long. ·When he came out
he could not speak to them, and they realized that he had
received a vision in the sanctuary. But he could only make
signs to them, and remained dumb.
23 When his time of service came to an end he returned
24 home. ·Some time later his wife Elizabeth conceived, and
25 for five months she kept to herself. ·"The Lord has done
this for me" she said "now that it has pleased him to take
away the humiliation I suffered among men."

The annunciation

26 In the sixth month the angel Gabriel was sent by God
27 to a town in Galilee called Nazareth, ·to a virgin betrothed
to a man named Joseph, of the House of David; and the
28 virgin's name was Mary. ·He went in and said to her, "Re-
29 joice, so highly favored! The Lord is with you." ·She was

1 a. The 24 families of the "sons of Aaron" were responsible in
rotation for service in the Temple, and in each class or family
the individual was chosen by lot. See 1 Ch 24. b. The priest
tended the brazier on the altar of incense in front of the Most
Holy Place. c. The meaning of the name is "Yahweh is
gracious." d. See Nb 6:1, where this abstinence is required in
anyone performing a vow to the Lord. e. Ml 3:23-24 f. Zechariah asks for a sign in a way reminiscent of Abram, Gn 15:8.

deeply disturbed by these words and asked herself what
30 this greeting could mean, ·but the angel said to her, "Mary,
31 do not be afraid; you have won God's favor. ·Listen!
    You are to conceive and bear a son, and you must name
32 him Jesus. ·He will be great and will be called Son of the
    Most High. The Lord God will give him the throne of his
33 ancestor David; ·he will rule over the House of Jacob for
34 ever and his reign will have no end." ·Mary said to the
    angel, "But how can this come about, since I am a virgin?"*g*
35 "The Holy Spirit will come upon you" the angel answered
    "and the power of the Most High will cover you with its
    shadow. And so the child will be holy and will be called
36 Son of God. ·Know this too: your kinswoman Elizabeth
    has, in her old age, herself conceived a son, and she whom
37 people called barren is now in her sixth month, ·*for noth-*
38 *ing is impossible to God.*"*h* ·"I am the handmaid of the
    Lord," said Mary "let what you have said be done to me."
    And the angel left her.

The visitation

39   Mary set out at that time and went as quickly as she
40 could to a town in the hill country of Judah. ·She went
41 into Zechariah's house and greeted Elizabeth. ·Now as
    soon as Elizabeth heard Mary's greeting, the child leaped
    in her womb and Elizabeth was filled with the Holy Spirit.
42 She gave a loud cry and said, "Of all women you are the
43 most blessed, and blessed is the fruit of your womb. ·Why
    should I be honored with a visit from the mother of my
44 Lord? ·For the moment your greeting reached my ears,
45 the child in my womb leaped for joy. ·Yes, blessed is she
    who believed that the promise made her by the Lord would
    be fulfilled."

The Magnificat

46   And Mary*i* said:

    "My soul proclaims the greatness of the Lord
47 and my spirit *exults in God my savior;*
48 because *he has looked upon his lowly handmaid.*
    Yes, from this day forward all generations will call me
            blessed,
49 for the Almighty has done great things for me.
    Holy is his name,

⁵⁰ and *his mercy reaches from age to age for those who fear
        him.*

⁵¹ He has shown the power of his arm,
    he has routed the proud of heart.

⁵² *He has pulled down princes* from their thrones *and exalted
        the lowly.*

⁵³ *The hungry he has filled with good things,* the rich sent
        empty away.

⁵⁴ *He has come to the help of Israel his servant, mindful of
        his mercy*

⁵⁵ —according to the promise he made to our ancestors—
    of his mercy to Abraham and to his descendants for ever."

⁵⁶   Mary stayed with Elizabeth about three months and then
    went back home.

The birth of John the Baptist and visit of the neighbors

⁵⁷   Meanwhile the time came for Elizabeth to have her
⁵⁸ child, and she gave birth to a son; ·and when her neigh-
    bors and relations heard that the Lord had shown her so
    great a kindness, they shared her joy.

The circumcision of John the Baptist

⁵⁹   Now on the eighth day they came to circumcise the
    child; they were going to callʲ him Zechariah after his
⁶⁰ father, ·but his mother spoke up. "No," she said "he is to
⁶¹ be called John." ·They said to her, "But no one in your
⁶² family has that name," ·and made signs to his father to
⁶³ find out what he wanted him called. ·The father asked for
    a writing-tablet and wrote, "His name is John." And they
⁶⁴ were all astonished. ·At that instant his power of speech
⁶⁵ returned and he spoke and praised God. ·All their neigh-
    bors were filled with awe and the whole affair was talked
⁶⁶ about throughout the hill country of Judaea. ·All those
    who heard of it treasured it in their hearts. "What will this
    child turn out to be?" they wondered. And indeed the hand
    of the Lord was with him.

g. Lit. "since I do not know man." h. Gn 8:14 i. Mary's
canticle is reminiscent of Hannah's, 1 S 2:1-10. Other quotations and allusions in the Magnificat are: 1 S 1:11; Ps
103:17; Ps 111:9; Jb 5:11 and 12:19; Ps 98:3; Ps 107:9;
Is 41:8-9. j. The name was normally given at the time of
circumcision.

The Benedictus

67   His father Zechariah was filled with the Holy Spirit and
spoke this prophecy:

68 *"Blessed be the Lord, the God of Israel,*[k]
for he has visited his people, he has come to their rescue
69 and he has raised up for us a power for salvation
in the House of his servant David,
70 even as he proclaimed,
by the mouth of his holy prophets from ancient times,
71 that he would save us from our enemies
and from the hands of all who hate us.
72 Thus he shows mercy to our ancestors,
thus *he remembers* his holy *covenant,*[l]
73 the oath he swore
to our father Abraham
74 that he would grant us, free from fear,
to be delivered from the hands of our enemies,
75 to serve him in holiness and virtue
in his presence, all our days.
76 And you, little child,
you shall be called Prophet of the Most High,
for you will go before the Lord
to prepare the way for him.
77 To give his people knowledge of salvation
through the forgiveness of their sins;
78 this by the tender mercy of our God
who from on high will bring the rising Sun to visit us,
79 to give light to *those who live
in darkness and the shadow of death,*[m]
and to guide our feet
into the way of peace."

The hidden life of John the Baptist

80   Meanwhile the child grew up and his spirit matured.
And he lived out in the wilderness until the day he appeared openly to Israel.

The birth of Jesus and visit of the shepherds

1 2 Now at this time Caesar Augustus[a] issued a decree for
2   a census of the whole world to be taken. ·This census
—the first[b]—took place while Quirinius was governor of
3 Syria, ·and everyone went to his own town to be registered.

⁴ So Joseph set out from the town of Nazareth in Galilee and traveled up to Judaea, to the town of David called ⁵ Bethlehem, since he was of David's House and line, ·in order to be registered together with Mary, his betrothed, ⁶ who was with child. ·While they were there the time came ⁷ for her to have her child, ·and she gave birth to a son, her first-born.ᵒ She wrapped him in swaddling clothes, and laid him in a manger because there was no room for them at ⁸ the inn. ·In the countryside close by there were shepherds who lived in the fields and took it in turns to watch their ⁹ flocks during the night. ·The angel of the Lord appeared to them and the glory of the Lord shone round them. They ¹⁰ were terrified, ·but the angel said, "Do not be afraid. Listen, I bring you news of great joy, a joy to be shared by ¹¹ the whole people. ·Today in the town of David a savior ¹² has been born to you; he is Christ the Lord. ·And here is a sign for you: you will find a baby wrapped in swaddling ¹³ clothes and lying in a manger." ·And suddenly with the angel there was a great throng of the heavenly host, praising God and singing:

¹⁴ "Glory to God in the highest heaven,
  and peace to men who enjoy his favor."

¹⁵ Now when the angels had gone from them into heaven, the shepherds said to one another, "Let us go to Bethlehem and see this thing that has happened which the Lord has ¹⁶ made known to us." ·So they hurried away and found Mary and Joseph, and the baby lying in the manger. ¹⁷ When they saw the child they repeated what they had been ¹⁸ told about him, ·and everyone who heard it was aston-¹⁹ ished at what the shepherds had to say. ·As for Mary, she treasured all these things and pondered them in her ²⁰ heart. ·And the shepherds went back glorifying and praising God for all they had heard and seen; it was exactly as they had been told.

The circumcision of Jesus

²¹ When the eighth day came and the child was to be circumcised, they gave him the name Jesus, the name the angel had given him before his conception.

---

k. Ps 41:13 l. Lv 26:42 m. Is 9:1
2 a. Emperor of Rome 30 B.C. to 14 A.D. b. About 8-6 B.C. c. The term does not necessarily imply younger brothers.

Jesus is presented in the Temple

22 And when the day came for them to be purified[d] as laid down by the Law of Moses, they took him up to 23 Jerusalem to present him to the Lord—observing what stands written in the Law of the Lord: *Every first-born* 24 *male must be consecrated to the Lord[e]*—and also to offer in sacrifice, in accordance with what is said in the Law of the Lord, *a pair of turtledoves or two young pigeons.[f]* 25 Now in Jerusalem there was a man named Simeon. He was an upright and devout man; he looked forward to Israel's comforting and the Holy Spirit rested on him. 26 It had been revealed to him by the Holy Spirit that he would not see death until he had set eyes on the Christ of 27 the Lord.[g] Prompted by the Spirit he came to the Temple; and when the parents brought in the child Jesus to do for 28 him what the Law required, he took him into his arms and blessed God; and he said:

The Nunc Dimittis

29 "Now, Master, you can let your servant go in peace, just as you promised;
30 because my eyes have seen the salvation
31 which you have prepared for all the nations to see,
32 a light to enlighten the pagans and the glory of your people Israel."

The prophecy of Simeon

33 As the child's father and mother stood there wondering 34 at the things that were being said about him, Simeon blessed them and said to Mary his mother, "You see this child: he is destined for the fall and for the rising of many 35 in Israel, destined to be a sign that is rejected—and a sword will pierce your own soul too—so that the secret thoughts of many may be laid bare."

The prophecy of Anna

36 There was a prophetess also, Anna the daughter of Phanuel, of the tribe of Asher. She was well on in years. Her days of girlhood over, she had been married for seven 37 years before becoming a widow. She was now eighty-four years old and never left the Temple, serving God night 38 and day with fasting and prayer. She came by just at that

moment and began to praise God; and she spoke of the
child to all who looked forward to the deliverance of
Jerusalem.[h]

The hidden life of Jesus at Nazareth

39 When they had done everything the Law of the Lord
required, they went back to Galilee, to their own town of
40 Nazareth. •Meanwhile the child grew to maturity, and
he was filled with wisdom; and God's favor was with him.

Jesus among the doctors of the Law

41 Every year his parents used to go to Jerusalem for the
42 feast of the Passover. •When he was twelve years old,
43 they went up for the feast as usual. •When they were on
their way home after the feast, the boy Jesus stayed behind
44 in Jerusalem without his parents knowing it. •They assumed
he was with the caravan, and it was only after a day's
journey that they went to look for him among their rela-
45 tions and acquaintances. •When they failed to find him
they went back to Jerusalem looking for him everywhere.
46 Three days later, they found him in the Temple, sitting
among the doctors, listening to them, and asking them ques-
47 tions; •and all those who heard him were astounded at
48 his intelligence and his replies. •They were overcome when
they saw him, and his mother said to him, "My child, why
have you done this to us? See how worried your father and
49 I have been, looking for you." •"Why were you looking for
me?" he replied "Did you not know that I must be busy
50 with my Father's affairs?" •But they did not understand
what he meant.

The hidden life at Nazareth resumed

51 He then went down with them and came to Nazareth
and lived under their authority. His mother stored up all
52 these things in her heart. •And Jesus increased in wisdom,
in stature, and in favor with God and men.

d. The mother needed to be "purified"; the child had to be "redeemed."   e. Ex 13:2   f. The offering of the poor, Lv 5:7.   g.
"The anointed one of God."   h. I.e. Israel. Jerusalem is the
holy city.

II. PRELUDE TO THE PUBLIC MINISTRY
OF JESUS

The preaching of John the Baptist

¹ In the fifteenth year of Tiberius Caesar's reign,ᵃ when Pontius Pilateᵇ was governor of Judaea, Herodᶜ tetrarch of Galilee, his brother Philipᵈ tetrarch of the lands of Ituraea and Trachonitis, Lysanias tetrarch of Abilene, ² during the pontificate of Annas and Caiaphas,ᵉ the word of God came to John son of Zechariah, in the wilderness. ³ He went through the whole Jordan district proclaiming a ⁴ baptism of repentance for the forgiveness of sins, ·as it is written in the book of the sayings of the prophet Isaiah:

> *A voice cries in the wilderness:*
> *Prepare a way for the Lord,*
> *make his paths straight.*
> ⁵ *Every valley will be filled in,*
> *every mountain and hill be laid low,*
> *winding ways will be straightened*
> *and rough roads made smooth.*
> ⁶ *And all mankind shall see the salvation of God.ᶠ*

⁷ He said, therefore, to the crowds who came to be baptized by him, "Brood of vipers, who warned you to fly from ⁸ the retribution that is coming? ·But if you are repentant, produce the appropriate fruits, and do not think of telling yourselves, 'We have Abraham for our father' because, I tell you, God can raise children for Abraham from these ⁹ stones. ·Yes, even now the ax is laid to the roots of the trees, so that any tree which fails to produce good fruit will be cut down and thrown on the fire."

¹⁰ When all the people asked him, "What must we do, ¹¹ then?" ·he answered, "If anyone has two tunics he must share with the man who has none, and the one with some- ¹² thing to eat must do the same." ·There were tax collectors too who came for baptism, and these said to him, "Master, ¹³ what must we do?" ·He said to them, "Exact no more than ¹⁴ your rate." ·Some soldiers asked him in their turn, "What about us? What must we do?" He said to them, "No intimidation! No extortion! Be content with your pay!"

¹⁵ A feeling of expectancy had grown among the people,

who were beginning to think that John might be the Christ,
16 so John declared before them all, "I baptize you with water,
but someone is coming, someone who is more powerful
than I am, and I am not fit to undo the strap of his sandals;
17 he will baptize you with the Holy Spirit and fire. ·His
winnowing-fan is in his hand to clear his threshing-floor and
to gather the wheat into his barn; but the chaff he will burn
18 in a fire that will never go out." ·As well as this, there
were many other things he said to exhort the people and
to announce the Good News to them.

John the Baptist imprisoned

19 But Herod the tetrarch, whom he criticized for his relations with his brother's wife Herodias and for all the other
20 crimes Herod had committed, ·added a further crime to
all the rest by shutting John up in prison.

Jesus is baptized

21 Now when all the people had been baptized and while
Jesus after his own baptism was at prayer, heaven opened
22 and the Holy Spirit descended on him in bodily shape, like
a dove. And a voice came from heaven, "You are my Son,
the Beloved; my favor rests on you."

The ancestry of Jesus

23 When he started to teach, Jesus was about thirty years
old, being the son, as it was thought, of Joseph son of
24 Heli, ·son of Matthat, son of Levi, son of Melchi, son of
25 Jannai, son of Joseph, ·son of Mattathias, son of Amos,
26 son of Nahum, son of Esli, son of Naggai, ·son of Maath,
son of Mattathias, son of Semein, son of Josech, son of
27 Joda, ·son of Joanan, son of Rhesa, son of Zerubbabel,
28 son of Shealtiel, son of Neri, ·son of Melchi, son of
29 Addi, son of Cosam, son of Elmadam, son of Er, ·son

3 a. By Roman dating, the 15th year of Tiberius Caesar's reign
was August 28 A.D. to August 29 A.D.; by the Syrian method,
it was Sept.-Oct. 27 A.D. to Sept.-Oct. 28 A.D. At that time,
Jesus was between 33 and 36 years old. The mistake in cal-
culating "the Christian era" results from taking Lk 3:23 as an
exact statement. b. Procurator of Judaea 26-36 A.D. c. Herod
Antipas, tetrarch of Galilee and Peraea 4 B.C. to 39 A.D. d.
Tetrarch from 4 B.C. to 34 A.D. e. Caiaphas was high priest
from 18 to 36 A.D. His father-in-law, Annas, is associated with
him here and elsewhere; he had been high priest earlier and
presumably still had great influence. f. Is 40:3-5

of Joshua, son of Eliezer, son of Jorim, son of Matthat,
30 son of Levi, ·son of Symeon, son of Judah, son of Joseph,
31 son of Jonam, son of Eliakim, ·son of Melea, son of
32 Menna, son of Mattatha, son of Nathan, son of David, ·son
of Jesse, son of Obed, son of Boaz, son of Sala, son of
33 Nahshon, ·son of Amminadab, son of Admin, son of Arni,
34 son of Hezron, son of Perez, son of Judah, ·son of Jacob,
son of Isaac, son of Abraham, son of Terah, son of Nahor,
35 son of Serug, son of Reu, son of Peleg, son of Eber, son
36 of Shelah, ·son of Cainan, son of Arphaxad, son of Shem,
37 son of Noah, son of Lamech, ·son of Methuselah, son of
Enoch, son of Jared, son of Mahalaleel, son of Cainan,
38 son of Enos, son of Seth, son of Adam, son of God.

Temptation in the wilderness

1 Filled with the Holy Spirit, Jesus left the Jordan and
2 was led by the Spirit through the wilderness, ·being
tempted there by the devil for forty days. During that
3 time he ate nothing and at the end he was hungry. ·Then
the devil said to him, "If you are the Son of God, tell this
4 stone to turn into a loaf." ·But Jesus replied, "Scripture
says: *Man does not live on bread alone.*"*a*

5 Then leading him to a height, the devil showed him in
6 a moment of time all the kingdoms of the world ·and said
to him, "I will give you all this power and the glory of
these kingdoms, for it has been committed to me and I
7 give it to anyone I choose. ·Worship me, then, and it shall
8 all be yours." ·But Jesus answered him, "Scripture says:

> *You must worship the Lord your God,*
> *and serve him alone.*"*b*

9 Then he led him to Jerusalem and made him stand on
the parapet of the Temple. "If you are the Son of God,"
10 he said to him "throw yourself down from here, ·for scripture says:

> *He will put his angels in charge of you*
> *to guard you,*

and again:

11
> *They will hold you up on their hands*
> *in case you hurt your foot against a stone.*"*c*

12 But Jesus answered him, "It has been said:

> *You must not put the Lord your God to the test.*"*d*

13 Having exhausted all these ways of tempting him, the devil left him, to return at the appointed time.

III. THE GALILEAN MINISTRY

Jesus begins to preach

14   Jesus, with the power of the Spirit in him, returned to Galilee; and his reputation spread throughout the country-
15 side. •He taught in their synagogues and everyone praised him.

Jesus at Nazareth

16   He came to Nazara, where he had been brought up, and went into the synagogue on the sabbath day as he
17 usually did. He stood up to read,^e •and they handed him the scroll of the prophet Isaiah. Unrolling the scroll he found the place where it is written:

18   *The spirit of the Lord has been given to me,*
     for he has anointed me.
     He has sent me to bring the good news to the poor,
     to proclaim liberty to captives
     and to the blind new sight,
     to set the downtrodden free,
19   *to proclaim the Lord's year of favor.*^f

20 He then rolled up the scroll, gave it back to the assistant and sat down. And all eyes in the synagogue were fixed on
21 him. •Then he began to speak to them, "This text is being
22 fulfilled today even as you listen." •And he won the approval of all, and they were astonished by the gracious words that came from his lips.

23   They said, "This is Joseph's son, surely?" •But he replied, "No doubt you will quote me the saying, 'Physician, heal yourself' and tell me, 'We have heard all that happened in Capernaum, do the same here in your own
24 countryside.'" •And he went on, "I tell you solemnly, no prophet is ever accepted in his own country.

25   "There were many widows in Israel, I can assure you, in Elijah's day, when heaven remained shut for three years and six months and a great famine raged throughout the

4 a. Dt 8:3   b. Dt 6:13   c. Ps 91:11-12   d. Dt 6:16   e. Any adult male could be permitted by the president to read the scriptures.   f. Is 61:1-2.

²⁶ land, ·but Elijah was not sent to any one of these:
he was sent *to a widow at Zarephath, a Sidonian town.*⁹
²⁷ And in the prophet Elisha's time there were many lepers
in Israel, but none of these was cured, except the Syrian,
Naaman.".

²⁸ When they heard this everyone in the synagogue was
²⁹ enraged. ·They sprang to their feet and hustled him out
of the town; and they took him up to the brow of the hill
their town was built on, intending to throw him down the
³⁰ cliff, ·but he slipped through the crowd and walked away.

Jesus teaches in Capernaum and cures a demoniac

³¹ He went down to Capernaum, a town in Galilee, and
³² taught them on the sabbath. ·And his teaching made a
deep impression on them because he spoke with authority.
³³ In the synagogue there was a man who was possessed
by the spirit of an unclean devil, and it shouted at the top
³⁴ of its voice, ·"Ha! What do you want with us, Jesus of
Nazareth? Have you come to destroy us? I know who you
³⁵ are: the Holy One of God." ·But Jesus said sharply, "Be
quiet! Come out of him!" And the devil, throwing the man
down in front of everyone, went out of him without hurt-
³⁶ ing him at all. ·Astonishment seized them and they were
all saying to one another, "What teaching! He gives orders
to unclean spirits with authority and power and they come
³⁷ out." ·And reports of him went all through the surrounding
countryside.

Cure of Simon's mother-in-law

³⁸ Leaving the synagogue he went to Simon's house. Now
Simon's mother-in-law was suffering from a high fever and
³⁹ they asked him to do something for her. ·Leaning over
her he rebuked the fever and it left her. And she immediately got up and began to wait on them.

A number of cures

⁴⁰ At sunset all those who had friends suffering from diseases of one kind or another brought them to him, and
⁴¹ laying his hands on each he cured them. ·Devils too came
out of many people, howling, "You are the Son of God."
But he rebuked them and would not allow them to speak
because they knew that he was the Christ.

Jesus quietly leaves Capernaum and travels through Judaea

42 When daylight came he left the house and made his way to a lonely place. The crowds went to look for him, and when they had caught up with him they wanted to 43 prevent him leaving them, ·but he answered, "I must proclaim the Good News of the kingdom of God to the other 44 towns too, because that is what I was sent to do." ·And he continued his preaching in the synagogues of Judaea.

The first four disciples are called

1 5 Now he was standing one day by the Lake of Gennesaret, with the crowd pressing round him listening to 2 the word of God, ·when he caught sight of two boats close to the bank. The fishermen had gone out of them and 3 were washing their nets. ·He got into one of the boats— it was Simon's—and asked him to put out a little from the shore. Then he sat down and taught the crowds from the boat.

4 When he had finished speaking he said to Simon, "Put out into deep water and pay out your nets for a catch." 5 "Master," Simon replied ·"we worked hard all night long and caught nothing, but if you say so, I will pay out the 6 nets." ·And when they had done this they netted such a 7 huge number of fish that their nets began to tear, ·so they signaled to their companions in the other boat to come and help them; when these came, they filled the two boats to sinking point.

8 When Simon Peter saw this he fell at the knees of Jesus 9 saying, "Leave me, Lord; I am a sinful man." ·For he and all his companions were completely overcome by the catch 10 they had made; ·so also were James and John, sons of Zebedee, who were Simon's partners. But Jesus said to Simon, "Do not be afraid; from now on it is men you will 11 catch." ·Then, bringing their boats back to land, they left everything and followed him.

Cure of a leper

12 Now Jesus was in one of the towns when a man appeared, covered with leprosy. Seeing Jesus he fell on his face and implored him. "Sir," he said "if you want to, 13 you can cure me." ·Jesus stretched out his hand, touched

g. 1 K 17:9.

him and said, "Of course I want to! Be cured!" And the
14 leprosy left him at once. ·He ordered him to tell no one,
"But go and show yourself to the priest and make the offering for your healing as Moses prescribed it, as evidence
for them."

15   His reputation continued to grow, and large crowds
would gather to hear him and to have their sickness cured,
16 but he would always go off to some place where he could
be alone and pray.

Cure of a paralytic

17   Now he was teaching one day, and among the audience
there were Pharisees and doctors of the Law who had
come from every village in Galilee, from Judaea and from
Jerusalem. And the Power of the Lord was behind his works
18 of healing. ·Then some men appeared, carrying on a bed
a paralyzed man whom they were trying to bring in and
19 lay down in front of him. ·But as the crowd made it impossible to find a way of getting him in, they went up on
to the flat roof and lowered him and his stretcher down
through the tiles into the middle of the gathering, in front
20 of Jesus. ·Seeing their faith he said, "My friend, your sins
21 are forgiven you." ·The scribes and the Pharisees began to
think this over. "Who is this man talking blasphemy? Who
22 can forgive sins but God alone?" ·But Jesus, aware of
their thoughts, made them this reply, "What are these
23 thoughts you have in your hearts? ·Which of these is easier:
to say, 'Your sins are forgiven you' or to say, 'Get up
24 and walk?' ·But to prove to you that the Son of Man has
authority on earth to forgive sins,"—he said to the paralyzed
man—"I order you: get up, and pick up your stretcher and
25 go home." ·And immediately before their very eyes he got
up, picked up what he had been lying on and went home
praising God.
26   They were all astounded and praised God, and were
filled with awe, saying, "We have seen strange things today."

The call of Levi

27   When he went out after this, he noticed a tax collector,
Levi by name, sitting by the customs house, and said to
28 him, "Follow me." ·And leaving everything he got up and
followed him.

Eating with sinners in Levi's house

29   In his honor Levi held a great reception in his house, and with them at table was a large gathering of tax collec-
30 tors and others. ·The Pharisees and their scribes complained to his disciples and said, "Why do you eat and drink with
31 tax collectors and sinners?" ·Jesus said to them in reply, "It is not those who are well who need the doctor, but the sick.
32 I have not come to call the virtuous, but sinners to repentance."

Discussion on fasting

33   They then said to him, "John's disciples are always fasting and saying prayers, and the disciples of the Pharisees
34 too, but yours go on eating and drinking." ·Jesus replied, "Surely you cannot make the bridegroom's attendants fast
35 while the bridegroom is still with them? ·But the time will come, the time for the bridegroom to be taken away from them; that will be the time when they will fast."
36   He also told them this parable, "No one tears a piece from a new cloak to put it on an old cloak; if he does, not only will he have torn the new one, but the piece taken from the new will not match the old.
37   "And nobody puts new wine into old skins; if he does, the new wine will burst the skins and then run out, and the
38 skins will be lost. ·No; new wine must be put into fresh
39 skins. ·And nobody who has been drinking old wine wants new. 'The old is good' he says."

Picking corn on the sabbath

1   **6** Now one sabbath he happened to be taking a walk through the cornfields, and his disciples were picking ears of corn, rubbing them in their hands and eating them.
2 Some of the Pharisees said, "Why are you doing something
3 that is forbidden on the sabbath day?" ·Jesus answered them, "So you have not read what David did when he and
4 his followers were hungry—·how he went into the house of God, took the loaves of offering and ate them and gave them to his followers, loaves which only the priests are
5 allowed to eat?" ·And he said to them, "The Son of Man is master of the sabbath."

Cure of the man with a withered hand

6   Now on another sabbath he went into the synagogue and began to teach, and a man was there whose right hand was

7 withered. ·The scribes and the Pharisees were watching
him to see if he would cure a man on the sabbath, hoping
8 to find something to use against him. ·But he knew their
thoughts; and he said to the man with the withered hand,
"Stand up! Come out into the middle." And he came out
9 and stood there. ·Then Jesus said to them, "I put it to you:
is it against the law on the sabbath to do good, or to do evil;
10 to save life, or to destroy it?" ·Then he looked round at
them all and said to the man, "Stretch out your hand." He
11 did so, and his hand was better. ·But they were furious, and
began to discuss the best way of dealing with Jesus.

The choice of the Twelve

12   Now it was about this time that he went out into the hills
to pray; and he spent the whole night in prayer to God.
13 When day came he summoned his disciples and picked out
14 twelve of them; he called them "apostles": ·Simon whom he
called Peter, and his brother Andrew; James, John, Philip,
15 Bartholomew, ·Matthew, Thomas, James son of Alphaeus,
16 Simon called the Zealot, ·Judas son of James,ᵃ and Judas
Iscariot who became a traitor.

The crowds follow Jesus

17   He then came down with them and stopped at a piece of
level ground where there was a large gathering of his disciples with a great crowd of people from all parts of Judaea
and from Jerusalem and from the coastal region of Tyre
18 and Sidon ·who had come to hear him and to be cured of
their diseases. People tormented by unclean spirits were
19 also cured, ·and everyone in the crowd was trying to touch
him because power came out of him that cured them all.

The inaugural discourse. The Beatitudes

20   Then fixing his eyes on his disciples he said:

"How happy are you who are poor: yours is the kingdom
of God.
21 Happy you who are hungry now: you shall be satisfied.
Happy you who weep now: you shall laugh.

22   "Happy are you when people hate you, drive you out,
abuse you, denounce your name as criminal, on account
23 of the Son of Man. ·Rejoice when that day comes and

dance for joy, for then your reward will be great in heaven. This was the way their ancestors treated the prophets.

The curses

24 "But alas for you who are rich: you are having your consolation now.
25 Alas for you who have your fill now: you shall go hungry. Alas for you who laugh now: you shall mourn and weep.

26 "Alas for you when the world speaks well of you! This was the way their ancestors treated the false prophets.

Love of enemies

27 "But I say this to you who are listening: Love your ene-
28 mies, do good to those who hate you, ·bless those who curse
29 you, pray for those who treat you badly. ·To the man who slaps you on one cheek, present the other cheek too; to the man who takes your cloak from you, do not refuse your
30 tunic. ·Give to everyone who asks you, and do not ask for
31 your property back from the man who robs you. ·Treat
32 others as you would like them to treat you. ·If you love those who love you, what thanks can you expect? Even
33 sinners love those who love them. ·And if you do good to those who do good to you, what thanks can you expect?
34 For even sinners do that much. ·And if you lend to those from whom you hope to receive, what thanks can you expect? Even sinners lend to sinners to, get back the same
35 amount. ·Instead, love your enemies and do good, and lend without any hope of return. You will have a great reward, and you will be sons of the Most High, for he himself is kind to the ungrateful and the wicked.

Compassion and generosity

36 "Be compassionate as your Father is compassionate.
37 Do not judge, and you will not be judged yourselves; do not condemn, and you will not be condemned yourselves;
38 grant pardon, and you will be pardoned. ·Give, and there will be gifts for you: a full measure, pressed down, shaken together, and running over, will be poured into your lap; because the amount you measure out is the amount you will be given back."

6 a. Or possibly "brother of James."

Integrity

39 He also told a parable to them, "Can one blind man
40 guide another? Surely both will fall into a pit? ·The disciple
is not superior to his teacher; the fully trained disciple will
41 always be like his teacher. ·Why do you observe the splinter
in your brother's eye and never notice the plank in your
42 own? ·How can you say to your brother, 'Brother, let me
take out the splinter that is in your eye,' when you cannot
see the plank in your own? Hypocrite! Take the plank
out of your own eye first, and then you will see clearly
enough to take out the splinter that is in your brother's eye.
43 "There is no sound tree that produces rotten fruit, nor
44 again a rotten tree that produces sound fruit. ·For every
tree can be told by its own fruit: people do not pick figs
45 from thorns, nor gather grapes from brambles. ·A good
man draws what is good from the store of goodness in his
heart; a bad man draws what is bad from the store of badness. For a man's words flow out of what fills his heart.

The true disciple

46 "Why do you call me, 'Lord, Lord' and not do what I
say?
47 "Everyone who comes to me and listens to my words and
48 acts on them—I will show you what he is like. ·He is like
the man who when he built his house dug, and dug deep,
and laid the foundations on rock; when the river was in
flood it bore down on that house but could not shake it,
49 it was so well built. ·But the one who listens and does nothing is like the man who built his house on soil, with no
foundations: as soon as the river bore down on it, it collapsed; and what a ruin that house became!"

Cure of the centurion's servant

1
2 7 When he had come to the end of all he wanted the people to hear, he went into Capernaum. ·A centurion there
had a servant, a favorite of his, who was sick and near
3 death. ·Having heard about Jesus he sent some Jewish
elders to him to ask him to come and heal his servant.
4 When they came to Jesus they pleaded earnestly with him.
5 "He deserves this of you" they said ·"because he is friendly
toward our people; in fact, he is the one who built the
6 synagogue." ·So Jesus went with them, and was not very
far from the house when the centurion sent word to him by

some friends: "Sir," he said "do not put yourself to trouble;
7 because I am not worthy to have you under my roof; •and
for this same reason I did not presume to come to you
myself; but give the word and let my servant be cured.
8 For I am under authority myself, and have soldiers under
me; and I say to one man: Go, and he goes; to another:
Come here, and he comes; to my servant: Do this, and he
9 does it." •When Jesus heard these words he was astonished
at him and, turning round, said to the crowd following
him, "I tell you, not even in Israel have I found faith like
10 this." •And when the messengers got back to the house
they found the servant in perfect health.

The son of the widow of Nain restored to life

11 Now soon afterward he went to a town called Nain,
accompanied by his disciples and a great number of people.
12 When he was near the gate of the town it happened that a
dead man was being carried out for burial, the only son of
his mother, and she was a widow. And a considerable num-
13 ber of the townspeople were with her. •When the Lord[a]
14 saw her he felt sorry for her. "Do not cry" he said. •Then
he went up and put his hand on the bier and the bearers
stood still, and he said, "Young man, I tell you to get up."
15 And the dead man sat up and began to talk, and Jesus *gave
16 him to his mother*.[b] •Everyone was filled with awe and
praised God saying, "A great prophet has appeared among
17 us; God has visited his people." •And this opinion of him
spread throughout Judaea and all over the countryside.

The Baptist's question. Jesus commends him

18 The disciples of John gave him all this news, and John,
19 summoning two of his disciples, •sent them to the Lord to
ask, "Are you the one who is to come, or must we wait for
20 someone else?" •When the men reached Jesus they said,
"John the Baptist has sent us to you, to ask, 'Are you the
one who is to come or have we to wait for someone else?'"
21 It was just then that he cured many people of diseases and
afflictions and of evil spirits, and gave the gift of sight to
22 many who were blind. •Then he gave the messengers their
answer, "Go back and tell John what you have seen and
heard: the blind see again, the lame walk, lepers are

---

7 a. For the first time in the gospel narrative Jesus is given the
title hitherto reserved for God.   b. 1 K 17:23

cleansed, and the deaf hear, the dead are raised to life, the
²³ Good News is proclaimed to the poor ·and happy is the man
who does not lose faith in me."

²⁴ When John's messengers had gone he began to talk to
²⁵ the people about John, ·"What did you go out into the wilderness to see? A reed swaying in the breeze? No? Then
what did you go out to see? A man dressed in fine clothes?
Oh no, those who go in for fine clothes and live luxuriously
²⁶ are to be found at court! ·Then what did you go out to see?
A prophet? Yes, I tell you, and much more than a prophet:
²⁷ he is the one of whom scripture says:

> *See, I am going to send my messenger before you;*
> *he will prepare the way before you.*ᵒ

²⁸ "I tell you, of all the children born of women, there is no
one greater than John; yet the least in the kingdom of God
²⁹ is greater than he is." ·All the people who heard him, and
the tax collectors too, acknowledged God's plan by accept-
³⁰ ing baptism from John; ·but by refusing baptism from him
the Pharisees and the lawyers had thwarted what God had
in mind for them.

Jesus condemns his contemporaries

³¹ "What description, then, can I find for the men of this
³² generation? What are they like? ·They are like children
shouting to one another while they sit in the market place:

> 'We played the pipes for you,
> and you wouldn't dance;
> we sang dirges,
> and you wouldn't cry."

³³ "For John the Baptist comes, not eating bread, not
³⁴ drinking wine, and you say, 'He is possessed.' ·The Son
of Man comes, eating and drinking, and you say, 'Look, a
glutton and a drunkard, a friend of tax collectors and sin-
³⁵ ners.' ·Yet Wisdom has been proved right by all her
children."

The woman who was a sinner

³⁶ One of the Pharisees invited him to a meal. When he
arrived at the Pharisee's house and took his place at table,
³⁷ a woman came in, who had a bad name in the town. She
had heard he was dining with the Pharisee and had brought

88 with her an alabaster jar of ointment. ·She waited behind
him at his feet, weeping, and her tears fell on his feet, and
she wiped them away with her hair; then she covered his
feet with kisses and anointed them with the ointment.

89　　　When the Pharisee who had invited him saw this, he said
to himself, "If this man were a prophet, he would know
who this woman is that is touching him and what a bad
40 name she has." ·Then Jesus took him up and said, "Simon,
I have something to say to you." "Speak, Master" was the
41 reply. ·"There was once a creditor who had two men in
his debt; one owed him five hundred denarii, the other
42 fifty. ·They were unable to pay, so he pardoned them
48 both. Which of them will love him more?" ·"The one who
was pardoned more, I suppose" answered Simon. Jesus
said, "You are right."

44　　　Then he turned to the woman. "Simon," he said "you
see this woman? I came into your house, and you poured no
water over my feet, but she has poured out her tears over
45 my feet and wiped them away with her hair. ·You gave
me no kiss, but she has been covering my feet with kisses
46 ever since I came in. ·You did not anoint my head with
47 oil, but she has anointed my feet with ointment. ·For this
reason I tell you that her sins, her many sins, must have
been forgiven her, or she would not have shown such great
love. It is the man who is forgiven little who shows little
48 love." ·Then he said to her, "Your sins are forgiven."
49 Those who were with him at table began to say to them-
50 selves, "Who is this man, that he even forgives sins?" ·But
he said to the woman, "Your faith has saved you; go in
peace."

The women accompanying Jesus

1 **8** Now after this he made his way through towns and
villages preaching, and proclaiming the Good News of
2 the kingdom of God. With him went the Twelve, ·as well
as certain women who had been cured of evil spirits and
ailments: Mary surnamed the Magdalene, from whom
8 seven demons had gone out, ·Joanna the wife of Herod's
steward Chuza, Susanna, and several others who provided
for them out of their own resources.

c. Ml 3:1

Parable of the sower

4   With a large crowd gathering and people from every town finding their way to him, he used this parable:

5   "A sower went out to sow his seed. As he sowed, some fell on the edge of the path and was trampled on; and the
6 birds of the air ate it up. ·Some seed fell on rock, and when it came up it withered away, having no moisture.
7 Some seed fell amongst thorns and the thorns grew with
8 it and choked it. ·And some seed fell into rich soil and grew and produced its crop a hundredfold." Saying this he cried, "Listen, anyone who has ears to hear!"

Why Jesus speaks in parables

9   His disciples asked him what this parable might mean,
10 and he said, "The mysteries of the kingdom of God are revealed to you; for the rest there are only parables, so that

> *they may see but not perceive,*
> *listen but not understand.*[a]

The parable of the sower explained

11   "This, then, is what the parable means: the seed is the
12 word of God. ·Those on the edge of the path are people who have heard it, and then the devil comes and carries away the word from their hearts in case they should believe
13 and be saved. ·Those on the rock are people who, when they first hear it, welcome the word with joy. But these have no root; they believe for a while, and in time of trial
14 they give up. ·As for the part that fell into thorns, this is people who have heard, but as they go on their way they are choked by the worries and riches and pleasures of life
15 and do not reach maturity. ·As for the part in the rich soil, this is people with a noble and generous heart who have heard the word and take it to themselves and yield a harvest through their perseverance.

Parable of the lamp

16   "No one lights a lamp to cover it with a bowl or to put it under a bed. No, he puts it on a lamp-stand so that peo-
17 ple may see the light when they come in. ·For nothing is hidden but it will be made clear, nothing secret but it will
18 be known and brought to light. ·So take care how you hear; for anyone who has will be given more; from anyone who has not, even what he thinks he has will be taken away."

The true kinsmen of Jesus

19 His mother and his brothers came looking for him, but
20 they could not get to him because of the crowd. ·He was
told, "Your mother and brothers are standing outside and
21 want to see you." ·But he said in answer, "My mother and
my brothers are those who hear the word of God and put
it into practice."

The calming of the storm

22 One day, he got into a boat with his disciples and said
to them, "Let us cross over to the other side of the lake."
23 So they put to sea, ·and as they sailed he fell asleep. When
a squall came down on the lake the boat started taking in
24 water and they found themselves in danger. ·So they went
to rouse him saying, "Master! Master! We are going
down!" Then he woke up and rebuked the wind and the
25 rough water; and they subsided and it was calm again. ·He
said to them, "Where is your faith?" They were awestruck
and astonished and said to one another, "Who can this be,
that gives orders even to winds and waves and they obey
him?"

The Gerasene demoniac

26 They came to land in the country of the Gerasenes,[b]
27 which is opposite Galilee. ·He was stepping ashore when
a man from the town who was possessed by devils came
toward him; for a long time the man had worn no clothes,
nor did he live in a house, but in the tombs.
28 Catching sight of Jesus he gave a shout, fell at his feet
and cried out at the top of his voice, "What do you want
with me, Jesus, son of the Most High God? I implore you,
29 do not torture me." ·—For Jesus had been telling the unclean spirit to come out of the man. It was a devil that
had seized on him a great many times, and then they used
to secure him with chains and fetters to restrain him, but
he would always break the fastenings, and the devil would
30 drive him out into the wilds. ·"What is your name?" Jesus
asked. "Legion" he said—because many devils had gone
31 into him. ·And these pleaded with him not to order them to
depart into the Abyss.[c]

8 a. Is 6:9 b. "Gadarenes" in some versions. c. The underworld.

³²   Now there was a large herd of pigs feeding there on the mountain, and the devils pleaded with him to let them ³³ go into these. So he gave them leave. ·The devils came out of the man and went into the pigs, and the herd charged down the cliff into the lake and were drowned.

³⁴   When the swineherds saw what had happened they ran off and told their story in the town and in the country ³⁵ round about; ·and the people went out to see what had happened. When they came to Jesus they found the man from whom the devils had gone out sitting at the feet of Jesus, clothed and in his full senses; and they were afraid. ³⁶ Those who had witnessed it told them how the man who ³⁷ had been possessed came to be healed. ·The entire population of the Gerasene territory was in a state of panic and asked Jesus to leave them. So he got into the boat and went back.

³⁸   The man from whom the devils had gone out asked to ³⁹ be allowed to stay with him, but he sent him away. ·"Go back home," he said "and report all that God has done for you." So the man went off and spread throughout the town all that Jesus had done for him.

Cure of the woman with a hemorrhage. Jairus' daughter raised to life

⁴⁰   On his return Jesus was welcomed by the crowd, for ⁴¹ they were all there waiting for him. ·And now there came a man named Jairus, who was an official of the synagogue. He fell at Jesus' feet and pleaded with him to come to his ⁴² house, ·because he had an only daughter about twelve years old, who was dying. And the crowds were almost stifling Jesus as he went.

⁴³   Now there was a woman suffering from a hemorrhage ⁴⁴ for twelve years, whom no one had been able to cure. ·She came up behind him and touched the fringe of his cloak; ⁴⁵ and the hemorrhage stopped at that instant. ·Jesus said, "Who touched me?" When they all denied that they had, Peter and his companions said, "Master, it is the crowds ⁴⁶ round you, pushing." ·But Jesus said, "Somebody touched ⁴⁷ me. I felt that power had gone out from me." ·Seeing herself discovered, the woman came forward trembling, and ⁴⁸ falling at his feet explained in front of all the ·people why she had touched him and how she had been cured at that very moment. "My daughter," he said "your faith has restored you to health; go in peace."

49 While he was still speaking, someone arrived from the
house of the synagogue official to say, "Your daughter has
50 died. Do not trouble the Master any further." ·But Jesus
had heard this, and he spoke to the man, "Do not be
51 afraid, only have faith and she will be safe." ·When he
came to the house he allowed no one to go in with him
except Peter and John and James, and the child's father
52 and mother. ·They were all weeping and mourning for
her, but Jesus said, "Stop crying; she is not dead, but
53 asleep." ·But they laughed at him, knowing she was dead.
54 But taking her by the hand he called to her, "Child, get
55 up." ·And her spirit returned and she got up at once. Then
56 he told them to give her something to eat. ·Her parents
were astonished, but he ordered them not to tell anyone
what had happened.

The mission of the Twelve

1 He called the Twelve together and gave them power
2 and authority over all devils and to cure diseases, ·and
he sent them out to proclaim the kingdom of God and to
3 heal. ·He said to them, "Take nothing for the journey:
neither staff, nor haversack, nor bread, nor money; and
4 let none of you take a spare tunic. ·Whatever house you
enter, stay there; and when you leave, let it be from there.
5 As for those who do not welcome you, when you leave
their town shake the dust from your feet as a sign to them."
6 So they set out and went from village to village proclaiming the Good News and healing everywhere.

Herod and Jesus

7 Meanwhile Herod the tetrarch had heard about all that
was going on; and he was puzzled, because some people
8 were saying that John had risen from the dead, ·others
that Elijah had reappeared, still others that one of the
9 ancient prophets had come back to life. ·But Herod said,
"John? I beheaded him. So who is this I hear such reports
about?" And he was anxious to see him.

The return of the apostles. Miracle of the loaves

10 On their return the apostles gave him an account of all
they had done. Then he took them with him and withdrew
to a town called Bethsaida where they could be by them-
11 selves. ·But the crowds got to know and they went after
him. He made them welcome and talked to them about the

kingdom of God; and he cured those who were in need of healing.

12 It was late afternoon when the Twelve came to him and said, "Send the people away, and they can go to the villages and farms round about to find lodging and food; 13 for we are in a lonely place here." ·He replied, "Give them something to eat yourselves." But they said, "We have no more than five loaves and two fish, unless we are to go 14 ourselves and buy food for all these people." ·For there were about five thousand men. But he said to his disciples, 15 "Get them to sit down in parties of about fifty." ·They did 16 so and made them all sit down. ·Then he took the five loaves and the two fish, raised his eyes to heaven, and said the blessing over them; then he broke them and handed 17 them to his disciples to distribute among the crowd. ·They all ate as much as they wanted, and when the scraps remaining were collected they filled twelve baskets.

Peter's profession of faith

18 Now one day when he was praying alone in the presence of his disciples he put this question to them, "Who 19 do the crowds say I am?" ·And they answered, "John the Baptist; others Elijah; and others say one of the ancient 20 prophets come back to life." ·"But you," he said "who do you say I am?" It was Peter who spoke up. "The Christ of 21 God" he said. ·But he gave them strict orders not to tell anyone anything about this.

First prophecy of the Passion

22 "The Son of Man" he said "is destined to suffer grievously, to be rejected by the elders and chief priests and scribes and to be put to death, and to be raised up on the third day."

The condition of following Christ

23 Then to all he said, "If anyone wants to be a follower of mine, let him renounce himself and take up his cross 24 every day and follow me. ·For anyone who wants to save his life will lose it; but anyone who loses his life for my 25 sake, that man will save it. ·What gain, then, is it for a man to have won the whole world and to have lost or 26 ruined his very self? ·For if anyone is ashamed of me and of my words, of him the Son of Man will be ashamed when

he comes in his own glory and in the glory of the Father and the holy angels.

The kingdom will come soon

27   "I tell you truly, there are some standing here who will not taste death before they see the kingdom of God."

The transfiguration

28   Now about eight days after this had been said, he took with him Peter and John and James and went up the
29 mountain to pray. ·As he prayed, the aspect of his face was changed and his clothing became brilliant as lightning.
30 Suddenly there were two men there talking to him; they
31 were Moses and Elijah ·appearing in glory, and they were speaking of his passing which he was to accomplish in
32 Jerusalem. ·Peter and his companions were heavy with sleep, but they kept awake and saw his glory and the two
33 men standing with him. ·As these were leaving him, Peter said to Jesus, "Master, it is wonderful for us to be here; so let us make three tents, one for you, one for Moses and
34 one for Elijah."—He did not know what he was saying. ·As he spoke, a cloud came and covered them with shadow; and when they went into the cloud the disciples were
35 afraid. ·And a voice came from the cloud saying, "This
36 is my Son, the Chosen One. Listen to him." ·And after the voice had spoken, Jesus was found alone. The disciples kept silence and, at that time, told no one what they had seen.

The epileptic demoniac

37   Now on the following day when they were coming down
38 from the mountain a large crowd came to meet him. ·Suddenly a man in the crowd cried out. "Master," he said "I
39 implore you to look at my son: he is my only child. ·All at once a spirit will take hold of him, and give a sudden cry and throw the boy into convulsions with foaming at the mouth; it is slow to leave him, but when it does it leaves
40 the boy worn out. ·I begged your disciples to cast it out,
41 and they could not." ·"Faithless and perverse generation!" Jesus said in reply "How much longer must I be among
42 you and put up with you? Bring your son here." ·The boy was still moving toward Jesus when the devil threw him to the ground in convulsions. But Jesus rebuked the unclean spirit and cured the boy and gave him back to his

⁴³ father, •and everyone was awestruck by the greatness of
God.

Second prophecy of the Passion

At a time when everyone was full of admiration for all
⁴⁴ he did, he said to his disciples, •"For your part, you must
have these words constantly in your mind: The Son of
Man is going to be handed over into the power of men."
⁴⁵ But they did not understand him when he said this; it was
hidden from them so that they should not see the meaning
of it, and they were afraid to ask him about what he had
just said.

Who is the greatest?

⁴⁶ An argument started between them about which of
⁴⁷ them was the greatest. •Jesus knew what thoughts were
going through their minds, and he took a little child and
⁴⁸ set him by his side •and then said to them, "Anyone who
welcomes this little child in my name welcomes me; and
anyone who welcomes me welcomes the one who sent me.
For the least among you all, that is the one who is great."

On using the name of Jesus

⁴⁹ John spoke up. "Master," he said "we saw a man casting
out devils in your name, and because he is not with us we
⁵⁰ tried to stop him." •But Jesus said to him, "You must not
stop him: anyone who is not against you is for you." •

IV. THE JOURNEY TO JERUSALEM

A Samaritan village is inhospitable

⁵¹ Now as the time drew near for him to be taken up to
⁵² heaven, he resolutely took the road for Jerusalem •and
sent messengers ahead of him. These set out, and they
went into a Samaritan village to make preparations for
⁵³ him, •but the people would not receive him because he
⁵⁴ was making for Jerusalem.ᵃ •Seeing this, the disciples
James and John said, "Lord, do you want us to call down
⁵⁵ fire from heaven to burn them up?" •But he turned and
⁵⁶ rebuked them, •and they went off to another village.

Hardships of the apostolic calling

⁵⁷ As they traveled along they met a man on the road
who said to him, "I will follow you wherever you go."

58 Jesus answered, "Foxes have holes and the birds of the air have nests, but the Son of Man has nowhere to lay his head."

59   Another to whom he said, "Follow me," replied, "Let
60 me go and bury my father first." ·But he answered, "Leave the dead to bury their dead; your duty is to go and spread the news of the kingdom of God."

61   Another said, "I will follow you, sir, but first let me go
62 and say good-bye to my people at home." ·Jesus said to him, "Once the hand is laid on the plow, no one who looks back is fit for the kingdom of God."

The mission of the seventy-two disciples

1 **10** After this the Lord appointed seventy-two others and sent them out ahead of him, in pairs, to all the towns
2 and places he himself was to visit. ·He said to them, "The harvest is rich but the laborers are few, so ask the Lord
3 of the harvest to send laborers to his harvest. ·Start off now, but remember, I am sending you out like lambs
4 among wolves. ·Carry no purse, no haversack, no sandals.
5 Salute no one on the road. ·Whatever house you go into,
6 let your first words be, 'Peace to this house!' ·And if a man of peace lives there, your peace will go and rest on
7 him; if not, it will come back to you. ·Stay in the same house, taking what food and drink they have to offer, for the laborer deserves his wages; do not move from house
8 to house. ·Whenever you go into a town where they make
9 you welcome, eat what is set before you. ·Cure those in it who are sick, and say, 'The kingdom of God is very
10 near to you.' ·But whenever you enter a town and they do not make you welcome, go out into its streets and say,
11 'We wipe off the very dust of your town that clings to our feet, and leave it with you. Yet be sure of this: the king-
12 dom of God is very near.' ·I tell you, on that day it will not go as hard with Sodom as with that town.

13   "Alas for you, Chorazin! Alas for you, Bethsaida! For if the miracles done in you had been done in Tyre and Sidon, they would have repented long ago, sitting in sack-
14 cloth and ashes. ·And still, it will not go as hard with Tyre
15 and Sidon at the Judgment as with you. ·And as for you,

9 a. The hatred of Samaritans for Jews would show itself particularly towards those who were on pilgrimage to Jerusalem.

Capernaum, did you want to be exalted high as heaven? *You shall be thrown down to hell.*ᵃ

16 "Anyone who listens to you listens to me; anyone who rejects you rejects me, and those who reject me reject the one who sent me."

True cause for the apostles to rejoice

17 The seventy-two came back rejoicing. "Lord," they said 18 "even the devils submit to us when we use your name." ·He said to them, "I watched Satan fall like lightning from 19 heaven. ·Yes, I have given you power to tread underfoot serpents and scorpions and the whole strength of the 20 enemy; nothing shall ever hurt you. ·Yet do not rejoice that the spirits submit to you; rejoice rather that your names are written in heaven."

The Good News revealed to the simple. The Father and the Son

21 It was then that, filled with joy by the Holy Spirit, he said, "I bless you, Father, Lord of heaven and of earth, for hiding these things from the learned and the clever and revealing them to mere children. Yes, Father, for that 22 is what it pleased you to do. ·Everything has been entrusted to me by my Father; and no one knows who the Son is except the Father, and who the Father is except the Son and those to whom the Son chooses to reveal him."

The privilege of the disciples

23 Then turning to his disciples he spoke to them in private, 24 "Happy the eyes that see what you see, ·for I tell you that many prophets and kings wanted to see what you see, and never saw it; to hear what you hear, and never heard it."

The great commandment

25 There was a lawyer who, to disconcert him, stood up and said to him, "Master, what must I do to inherit eternal 26 life?" ·He said to him, "What is written in the Law? What 27 do you read there?" ·He replied, *"You must love the Lord your God with all your heart, with all your soul, with all your strength, and with all your mind, and your neighbor* 28 *as yourself."*ᵇ ·"You have answered right," said Jesus "do this and life is yours."

Parable of the good Samaritan

29 But the man was anxious to justify himself and said to
30 Jesus, "And who is my neighbor?" ·Jesus replied, "A man
was once on his way down from Jerusalem to Jericho and
fell into the hands of brigands; they took all he had, beat
31 him and then made off, leaving him half dead. ·Now a
priest happened to be traveling down the same road, but
32 when he saw the man, he passed by on the other side. ·In
the same way a Levite who came to the place saw him,
33 and passed by on the other side. ·But a Samaritan traveler
who came upon him was moved with compassion when
34 he saw him. ·He went up and bandaged his wounds, pour-
ing oil and wine on them. He then lifted him on to his own
35 mount, carried him to the inn and looked after him. ·Next
day, he took out two denarii and handed them to the inn-
keeper. 'Look after him,' he said 'and on my way back
36 I will make good any extra expense you have.' ·Which
of these three, do you think, proved himself a neighbor
37 to the man who fell into the brigands' hands?" ·"The one
who took pity on him" he replied. Jesus said to him, "Go,
and do the same yourself."

Martha and Mary

38 In the course of their journey he came to a village, and
a woman named Martha welcomed him into her house.
39 She had a sister called Mary, who sat down at the Lord's
40 feet and listened to him speaking. ·Now Martha who was
distracted with all the serving said, "Lord, do you not care
that my sister is leaving me to do the serving all by myself?
41 Please tell her to help me." ·But the Lord answered: "Martha, Martha," he said "you worry and fret about so many
42 things, ·and yet few are needed, indeed only one. It is
Mary who has chosen the better part; it is not to be taken
from her."

The Lord's prayer

11 1 Now once he was in a certain place praying, and
when he had finished one of his disciples said, "Lord,
2 teach us to pray, just as John taught his disciples." ·He
said to them, "Say this when you pray:

'Father, may your name be held holy,
your kingdom come;

10 a. See Is 14:13,15. **b.** Dt 6:5 and Lv 19:18

3 give us each day our daily bread,
and forgive us our sins,
4 for we ourselves forgive each one who is in debt to us.
And do not put us to the test.' "

The importunate friend

5   He also said to them, "Suppose one of you has a friend
and goes to him in the middle of the night to say, 'My
6 friend, lend me three loaves, ·because a friend of mine on
his travels has just arrived at my house and I have nothing
7 to offer him'; ·and the man answers from inside the house,
'Do not bother me. The door is bolted now, and my children and I are in bed; I cannot get up to give it you.'
8 I tell you, if the man does not get up and give it him for
friendship's sake, persistence will be enough to make him
get up and give his friend all he wants.

Effective prayer

9   "So I say to you: Ask, and it will be given to you;
search, and you will find; knock, and the door will be
10 opened to you. ·For the one who asks always receives; the
one who searches always finds; the one who knocks will al-
11 ways have the door opened to him. ·What father among
you would hand his son a stone when he asked for bread?
12 Or hand him a snake instead of a fish? ·Or hand him a
13 scorpion if he asked for an egg? ·If you then, who are
evil, know how to give your children what is good, how
much more will the heavenly Father give the Holy Spirit
to those who ask him!".

Jesus and Beelzebul

14   He was casting out a devil and it was dumb; but when
the devil had gone out the dumb man spoke, and the people
15 were amazed. ·But some of them said, "It is through Beel-
16 zebul, the prince of devils, that he casts out devils." ·Others
17 asked him, as a test, for a sign from heaven; ·but, knowing what they were thinking, he said to them, "Every kingdom divided against itself is heading for ruin, and a house-
18 hold divided against itself collapses. ·So too with Satan:
if he is divided against himself, how can his kingdom stand?
—Since you assert that it is through Beelzebul that I cast
19 out devils. ·Now if it is through Beelzebul that I cast
out devils, through whom do your own experts cast them

20 out? Let them be your judges, then. ·But if it is through
the finger of God that I cast out devils, then know that the
21 kingdom of God has overtaken you. ·So long as a strong
man fully armed guards his own palace, his goods are un-
22 disturbed; ·but when someone stronger than he is attacks
and defeats him, the stronger man takes away all the
weapons he relied on and shares out his spoil.

No compromise

23 "He who is not with me is against me; and he who does
not gather with me scatters."

Return of the unclean spirit

24 "When an unclean spirit goes out of a man it wanders
through waterless country looking for a place to rest, and
not finding one it says, 'I will go back to the home I
25 came from.' ·But on arrival, finding it swept and tidied,
26 it then goes off and brings seven other spirits more wicked
than itself, and they go in and set up house there, so that
the man ends up by being worse than he was before."

The truly happy

27 Now as he was speaking, a woman in the crowd raised
her voice and said, "Happy the womb that bore you and
28 the breasts you sucked!" ·But he replied, "Still happier
those who hear the word of God and keep it!"

The sign of Jonah

29 The crowds got even bigger and he addressed them,
"This is a wicked generation; it is asking for a sign. The
30 only sign it will be given is the sign of Jonah. ·For just
as Jonah became a sign to the Ninevites, so will the Son
31 of Man be to this generation. ·On Judgment day the
Queen of the South will rise up with the men of this generation and condemn them, because she came from the
ends of the earth to hear the wisdom of Solomon; and
32 there is something greater than Solomon here. ·On Judgment day the men of Nineveh will stand up with this generation and condemn it, because when Jonah preached they
repented; and there is something greater than Jonah here.

The parable of the lamp repeated

33 "No one lights a lamp and puts it in some hidden place
or under a tub, but on the lamp-stand so that people may

³⁴ see the light when they come in. ·The lamp of your body is your eye. When your eye is sound, your whole body too is filled with light; but when it is diseased your body too ³⁵ will be all darkness. ·See to it then that the light inside ³⁶ you is not darkness. ·If, therefore, your whole body is filled with light, and no trace of darkness, it will be light entirely, as when the lamp shines on you with its rays."

The Pharisees and the lawyers attacked

³⁷ He had just finished speaking when a Pharisee invited him to dine at his house. He went in and sat down at the ³⁸ table. ·The Pharisee saw this and was surprised that he ³⁹ had not first washed before the meal. ·But the Lord said to him, "Oh, you Pharisees! You clean the outside of cup and plate, while inside yourselves you are filled with ⁴⁰ extortion and wickedness. ·Fools! Did not he who made ⁴¹ the outside make the inside too? ·Instead, give alms from what you have and then indeed everything will be clean ⁴² for you. ·But alas for you Pharisees! You who pay your tithe of mint and rue and all sorts of garden herbs and overlook justice and the love of God! These you should ⁴³ have practiced, without leaving the others undone. ·Alas for you Pharisees who like taking the seats of honor in the synagogues and · being greeted obsequiously in the ⁴⁴ market squares! ·Alas for you, because you are like the unmarked tombs that men walk on without knowing it!"*a*

⁴⁵ A lawyer then spoke up. "Master," he said "when you ⁴⁶ speak like this you insult us too." ·"Alas for you lawyers also," he replied "because you load on men burdens that are unendurable, burdens that you yourselves do not move a finger to lift.

⁴⁷ "Alas for you who build the tombs of the prophets, the ⁴⁸ men your ancestors killed! ·In this way you both witness what your ancestors did and approve it; they did the killing, you do the building.

⁴⁹ "And that is why the Wisdom of God said, 'I will send them prophets and apostles; some they will slaughter and ⁵⁰ persecute, ·so that this generation will have to answer for every prophet's blood that has been shed since the founda- ⁵¹ tion of the world, ·from the blood of Abel to the blood of Zechariah, who was murdered between the altar and the sanctuary.' Yes, I tell you, this generation will have to answer for it all.

⁵² "Alas for you lawyers who have taken away the key of

knowledge! You have not gone in yourselves, and have prevented others going in who wanted to."

53 When he left the house, the scribes and the Pharisees began a furious attack on him and tried to force answers
54 from him on innumerable questions, ·setting traps to catch him out in something he might say.

Open and fearless speech

1 12 Meanwhile the people had gathered in their thousands so that they were treading on one another. And he began to speak, first of all to his disciples. "Be on your guard against the yeast of the Pharisees—that is, their
2 hypocrisy. ·Everything that is now covered will be uncov-
3 ered, and everything now hidden will be made clear. ·For this reason, whatever you have said in the dark will be heard in the daylight, and what you have whispered in hidden places will be proclaimed on the housetops.
4 "To you my friends I say: Do not be afraid of those
5 who kill the body and after that can do no more. ·I will tell you whom to fear: fear him who, after he has killed, has the power to cast into hell. Yes, I tell you, fear him.
6 Can you not buy five sparrows for two pennies? And yet
7 not one is forgotten in God's sight. ·Why, every hair on your head has been counted. There is no need to be afraid: you are worth more than hundreds of sparrows.
8 "I tell you, if anyone openly declares himself for me in the presence of men, the Son of Man will declare himself
9 for him in the presence of God's angels. ·But the man who disowns me in the presence of men will be disowned in the presence of God's angels.
10 "Everyone who says a word against the Son of Man will be forgiven, but he who blasphemes against the Holy Spirit will not be forgiven.
11 "When they take you before synagogues and magistrates and authorities, do not worry about how to defend
12 yourselves or what to say, ·because when the time comes, the Holy Spirit will teach you what you must say."

On hoarding possessions

13 A man in the crowd said to him, "Master, tell my brother
14 to give me a share of our inheritance." ·"My friend," he replied "who appointed me your judge, or the arbitrator of

11 a. Thus contracting legal impurity, Nb 19:16.

¹⁵ your claims?" ·Then he said to them, "Watch, and be on your guard against avarice of any kind, for a man's life is not made secure by what he owns, even when he has more than he needs."

¹⁶ Then he told them a parable: "There was once a rich man who, having had a good harvest from his land, ¹⁷ thought to himself, 'What am I to do? I have not enough ¹⁸ room to store my crops.' ·Then he said, 'This is what I will do: I will pull down my barns and build bigger ones, ¹⁹ and store all my grain and my goods in them, ·and I will say to my soul: My soul, you have plenty of good things laid by for many years to come; take things easy, eat, ²⁰ drink, have a good time.' ·But God said to him, 'Fool! This very night the demand will be made for your soul; ²¹ and this hoard of yours, whose will it be then?' ·So it is when a man stores up treasure for himself in place of making himself rich in the sight of God."

Trust in Providence

²² Then he said to his disciples, "That is why I am telling you not to worry about your life and what you are to eat, nor about your body and how you are to clothe it. ²³ For life means more than food, and the body more than ²⁴ clothing. ·Think of the ravens. They do not sow or reap; they have no storehouses and no barns; yet God feeds them. And how much more are you worth than the birds! ²⁵ Can any of you, for all his worrying, add a single cubit ²⁶ to his span of life? ·If the smallest things, therefore, are ²⁷ outside your control, why worry about the rest? ·Think of the flowers; they never have to spin or weave; yet, I assure you, not even Solomon in all his regalia was robed ²⁸ like one of these. ·Now if that is how God clothes the grass in the field which is there today and thrown into the furnace tomorrow, how much more will he look after you, ²⁹ you men of little faith! ·But you, you must not set your hearts on things to eat and things to drink; nor must you ³⁰ worry. ·It is the pagans of this world who set their hearts on all these things. Your Father well knows you need them. ³¹ No; set your hearts on his kingdom, and these other things will be given you as well.

³² "There is no need to be afraid, little flock, for it has pleased your Father to give you the kingdom.

On almsgiving

33 "Sell your possessions and give alms. Get yourselves purses that do not wear out, treasure that will not fail you, in heaven where no thief can reach it and no moth de- **34** stroy it. ·For where your treasure is, there will your heart be also.

On being ready for the Master's return

35 "See that you are dressed for action and have your lamps **36** lit. ·Be like men waiting for their master to return from the wedding feast, ready to open the door as soon as he **37** comes and knocks. ·Happy those servants whom the master finds awake when he comes. I tell you solemnly, he will put on an apron, sit them down at table and wait on them. **38** It may be in the second watch he comes, or in the third, but **39** happy those servants if he finds them ready. ·You may be quite sure of this, that if the householder had known at what hour the burglar would come, he would not have let **40** anyone break through the wall of his house. ·You too must stand ready, because the Son of Man is coming at an hour you do not expect."

41 Peter said, "Lord, do you mean this parable for us, or **42** for everyone?" ·The Lord replied, "What sort of steward,^a then, is faithful and wise enough for the master to place him over his household to give them their allowance of **43** food at the proper time? ·Happy that servant if his mas- **44** ter's arrival finds him at this employment. ·I tell you truly, **45** he will place him over everything he owns. ·But as for the servant who says to himself, 'My master is taking his time coming,' and sets about beating the menservants and the maids, and eating and drinking and getting drunk, **46** his master will come on a day he does not expect and at an hour he does not know. The master will cut him off and send him to the same fate as the unfaithful.

47 "The servant who knows what his master wants, but has not even started to carry out those wishes, will receive very **48** many strokes of the lash. ·The one who did not know, but deserves to be beaten for what he has done, will re- ceive fewer strokes. When a man has had a great deal given him, a great deal will be demanded of him; when a

12 a. I.e. a servant or employee with authority to act as his master's deputy in his absence.

man has had a great deal given him on trust, even more will be expected of him.

Jesus and his Passion

⁴⁹ "I have come to bring fire to the earth, and how I wish ⁵⁰ it were blazing already! ·There is a baptism I must still receive, and how great is my distress till it is over!

Jesus the cause of dissension

⁵¹ "Do you suppose that I am here to bring peace on earth? ⁵² No, I tell you, but rather division. ·For from now on a household of five will be divided: three against two and ⁵³ two against three; ·the father divided against the son, son against father, mother against daughter, daughter against mother, mother-in-law against daughter-in-law, daughter-in-law against mother-in-law."

On reading the signs of the times

⁵⁴ He said again to the crowds, "When you see a cloud looming up in the west you say at once that rain is coming, ⁵⁵ and so it does. ·And when the wind is from the south you ⁵⁶ say it will be hot, and it is. ·Hypocrites! You know how to interpret the face of the earth and the sky. How is it you do not know how to interpret these times?

⁵⁷
⁵⁸ "Why not judge for yourselves what is right? ·For example: when you go to court with your opponent, try to settle with him on the way, or he may drag you before the judge and the judge hand you over to the bailiff and the ⁵⁹ bailiff have you thrown into prison. ·I tell you, you will not get out till you have paid the very last penny."

Examples inviting repentance

¹ **13** It was just about this time that some people arrived and told him about the Galileans whose blood Pilate ² had mingled with that of their sacrifices.ᵃ ·At this he said to them, "Do you suppose these Galileans who suffered like ⁸ that were greater sinners than any other Galileans? ·They were not, I tell you. No; but unless you repent you will all ⁴ perish as they did. ·Or those eighteen on whom the tower at Siloam fell and killed them? Do you suppose that they were more guilty than all the other people living in Jeru- ⁵ salem? ·They were not, I tell you. No; but unless you repent you will all perish as they did."

Parable of the barren fig tree

6 He told this parable: "A man had a fig tree planted in his vineyard, and he came looking for fruit on it but found 7 none. ·He said to the man who looked after the vineyard, 'Look here, for three years now I have been coming to look for fruit on this fig tree and finding none. Cut it 8 down: why should it be taking up the ground?' ·'Sir,' the man replied 'leave it one more year and give me time 9 to dig round it and manure it: ·it may bear fruit next year; if not, then you can cut it down.'"

Healing of the crippled woman on a sabbath

10 One sabbath day he was teaching in one of the syna-
11 gogues, ·and a woman was there who for eighteen years had been possessed by a spirit that left her enfeebled; she 12 was bent double and quite unable to stand upright. ·When Jesus saw her he called her over and said, "Woman, 13 you are rid of your infirmity" ·and he laid his hands on her. And at once she straightened up, and she glorified God.
14 But the synagogue official was indignant because Jesus had healed on the sabbath, and he addressed the people present. "There are six days" he said "when work is to be done. Come and be healed on one of those days and not 15 on the sabbath." ·But the Lord answered him. "Hypo- crites!" he said "Is there one of you who does not untie his ox or his donkey from the manger on the sabbath and 16 take it out for watering? ·And this woman, a daughter of Abraham whom Satan has held bound these eighteen years —was it not right to untie her bonds on the sabbath day?" 17 When he said this, all his adversaries were covered with confusion, and all the people were overjoyed at all the wonders he worked.

Parable of the mustard seed

18 He went on to say, "What is the kingdom of God like? 19 What shall I compare it with? ·It is like a mustard seed which a man took and threw into his garden: it grew and became a tree, and the birds of the air sheltered in its branches."

13 a. The author expects this incident, and that mentioned in v. 4, to be known to his readers; no other evidence of them re- mains.

Parable of the yeast

20 Another thing he said, "What shall I compare the king-
21 dom of God with? ·It is like the yeast a woman took and
mixed in with three measures of flour till it was leavened
all through."

The narrow door; rejection of the Jews, call of the gentiles

22 Through towns and villages he went teaching, making
23 his way to Jerusalem. ·Someone said to him, "Sir, will
24 there be only a few saved?" He said to them, ·"Try your
best to enter by the narrow door, because, I tell you, many
will try to enter and will not succeed.

25 "Once the master of the house has got up and locked
the door, you may find yourself knocking on the door,
saying, 'Lord, open to us' but he will answer, 'I do not
26 know where you come from.' ·Then you will find yourself saying, 'We once ate and drank in your company; you
27 taught in our streets' ·but he will reply, 'I do not know
where you come from. *Away from me, all you wicked
men!*ᵇ

28 "Then there will be weeping and grinding of teeth, when
you see Abraham and Isaac and Jacob and all the prophets in the kingdom of God, and yourselves turned outside.
29 And men from east and west, from north and south, will
come to take their places at the feast in the kingdom
of God.

30 "Yes, there are those now last who will be first, and
those now first who will be last."

Herod the fox

31 Just at this time some Pharisees came up. "Go away"
they said. "Leave this place, because Herod means to kill
32 you." ·He replied, "You may go and give that fox this message: Learn that today and tomorrow I cast out devils
33 and on the third dayᶜ attain my end. ·But for today and
tomorrow and the next day I must go on, since it would
not be right for a prophet to die outside Jerusalem.

Jerusalem admonished

34 "Jerusalem, Jerusalem, you that kill the prophets and
stone those who are sent to you! How often have I longed
to gather your children, as a hen gathers her brood under

85 her wings, and you refused! ·So be it! Your house will be
left to you. Yes, I promise you, you shall not see me till
the time comes when you say:

Blessings on him who comes in the name of the Lord!"[d]

Healing of a dropsical man on the sabbath

1 **14** Now on a sabbath day he had gone for a meal to
the house of one of the leading Pharisees; and they
2 watched him closely. ·There in front of him was a man
3 with dropsy, ·and Jesus addressed the lawyers and Pharisees. "Is it against the law" he asked "to cure a man on the
4 sabbath, or not?" ·But they remained silent, so he took the
5 man and cured him and sent him away. ·Then he said to
them, "Which of you here, if his son falls into a well, or his
ox, will not pull him out on a sabbath day without hesita-
6 tion?" ·And to this they could find no answer.

On choosing places at table

7 He then told the guests a parable, because he had
noticed how they picked the places of honor. He said
8 this, ·"When someone invites you to a wedding feast, do
not take your seat in the place of honor. A more distin-
9 guished person than you may have been invited, ·and the
person who invited you both may come and say, 'Give up
your place to this man.' And then, to your embarrassment,
10 you would have to go and take the lowest place. ·No;
when you are a guest, make your way to the lowest place
and sit there, so that, when your host comes, he may say,
'My friend, move up higher.' In that way, everyone with
11 you at the table will see you honored. ·For everyone who
exalts himself will be humbled, and the man who humbles
himself will be exalted."

On choosing guests to be invited

12 Then he said to his host, "When you give a lunch or a
dinner, do not ask your friends, brothers, relations or rich
neighbors, for fear they repay your courtesy by inviting
13 you in return. ·No; when you have a party, invite the poor,
14 the crippled, the lame, the blind; ·that they cannot pay you
back means that you are fortunate, because repayment will
be made to you when the virtuous rise again."

b. Ps 6:8   **c.** "after a short time."   **d.** Ps 118:26

The invited guests who made excuses

15 On hearing this, one of those gathered round the table said to him, "Happy the man who will be at the feast in the
16 kingdom of God!" ·But he said to him, "There was a man who gave a great banquet, and he invited a large number
17 of people. ·When the time for the banquet came, he sent his servant to say to those who had been invited, 'Come
18 along: everything is ready now.' ·But all alike started to make excuses. The first said, 'I have bought a piece of land and must go and see it. Please accept my apologies.'
19 Another said, 'I have bought five yoke of oxen and am on my way to try them out. Please accept my apologies.'
20 Yet another said, 'I have just got married and so am unable to come.'
21 "The servant returned and reported this to his master. Then the householder, in a rage, said to his servant, 'Go out quickly into the streets and alleys of the town and bring in here the poor, the crippled, the blind and the lame.'
22 'Sir,' said the servant 'your orders have been carried out
23 and there is still room.' ·Then the master said to his servant, 'Go to the open roads and the hedgerows and force people to come in to make sure my house is full;
24 because, I tell you, not one of those who were invited shall have a taste of my banquet.' "

Renouncing all that one holds dear

25 Great crowds accompanied him on his way and he
26 turned and spoke to them. ·"If any man comes to me without hating[a] his father, mother, wife, children, brothers, sisters, yes and his own life too, he cannot be my disciple.
27 Anyone who does not carry his cross and come after me cannot be my disciple.

Renouncing possessions

28 "And indeed, which of you here, intending to build a tower, would not first sit down and work out the cost to
29 see if he had enough to complete it? ·Otherwise, if he laid the foundation and then found himself unable to finish the work, the onlookers would all start making fun of him and
30 saying, ·'Here is a man who started to build and was un-
31 able to finish.' ·Or again, what king marching to war against another king would not first sit down and consider whether with ten thousand men he could stand up to

the other who advanced against him with twenty thousand?
82 If not, then while the other king was still a long way off, he
83 would send envoys to sue for peace. ·So in the same way,
none of you can be my disciple unless he gives up all his
possessions.

On loss of enthusiasm in a disciple

84 "Salt is a useful thing. But if the salt itself loses its taste,
85 how can it be seasoned again? ·It is good for neither soil
nor manure heap. People throw it out. Listen, anyone who
has ears to hear!"

The three parables of God's mercy

1 **15** The tax collectors and the sinners, meanwhile, were
all seeking his company to hear what he had to say,
2 and the Pharisees and the scribes complained. "This man"
3 they said "welcomes sinners and eats with them." ·So he
spoke this parable to them:

The lost sheep

4 "What man among you with a hundred sheep, losing one,
would not leave the ninety-nine in the wilderness and go
5 after the missing one till he found it? ·And when he found
6 it, would he not joyfully take it on his shoulders ·and then,
when he got home, call together his friends and neighbors? 'Rejoice with me,' he would say 'I have found my
7 sheep that was lost.' ·In the same way, I tell you, there
will be more rejoicing in heaven over one repentant sinner
than over ninety-nine virtuous men who have no need of
repentance.

The lost drachma

8 "Or again, what woman with ten drachmas would not, if
she lost one, light a lamp and sweep out the house and
9 search thoroughly till she found it? ·And then, when she
had found it, call together her friends and neighbors?
'Rejoice with me,' she would say 'I have found the
10 drachma I lost.' ·In the same way, I tell you, there is
rejoicing among the angels of God over one repentant
sinner."

14 a. Hebraism: an emphatic way of expressing a total detachment.

The lost son (the "prodigal") and the dutiful son

¹¹ ¹² He also said, "A man had two sons. ·The younger said to his father, 'Father, let me have the share of the estate that would come to me.' So the father divided the ¹³ property between them. ·A few days later, the younger son got together everything he had and left for a distant country where he squandered his money on a life of debauchery.

¹⁴ "When he had spent it all, that country experienced a ¹⁵ severe famine, and now he began to feel the pinch, ·so he hired himself out to one of the local inhabitants who put ¹⁶ him on his farm to feed the pigs. ·And he would willingly have filled his belly with the husks the pigs were eating but ¹⁷ no one offered him anything. ·Then he came to his senses and said, 'How many of my father's paid servants have more food than they want, and here am I dying of hunger! ¹⁸ I will leave this place and go to my father and say: Father, ¹⁹ I have sinned against heaven and against you; ·I no longer deserve to be called your son; treat me as one of your paid ²⁰ servants.' ·So he left the place and went back to his father.

"While he was still a long way off, his father saw him and was moved with pity. He ran to the boy, clasped him in ²¹ his arms and kissed him tenderly. ·Then his son said, 'Father, I have sinned against heaven and against you. I no ²² longer deserve to be called your son.' ·But the father said to his servants, 'Quick! Bring out the best robe and put it on him; put a ring on his finger and sandals on his feet. ²³ Bring the calf we have been fattening, and kill it; we are ²⁴ going to have a feast, a celebration, ·because this son of mine was dead and has come back to life; he was lost and is found.' And they began to celebrate.

²⁵ "Now the elder son was out in the fields, and on his way back, as he drew near the house, he could hear music and ²⁶ dancing. ·Calling one of the servants he asked what it was ²⁷ all about. ·'Your brother has come' replied the servant 'and your father has killed the calf we had fattened be- ²⁸ cause he has got him back safe and sound.' ·He was angry then and refused to go in, and his father came out to plead ²⁹ with him; ·but he answered his father, 'Look, all these years I have slaved for you and never once disobeyed your orders, yet you never offered me so much as a kid for ³⁰ me to celebrate with my friends. ·But, for this son of

yours, when he comes back after swallowing up your property—he and his women—you kill the calf we had been fattening.'

31 "The father said, 'My son, you are with me always and
32 all I have is yours. ·But it was only right we should cele-brate and rejoice, because your brother here was dead and has come to life; he was lost and is found.'"

The crafty steward

1 **16** He also said to his disciples, "There was a rich man and he had a steward who was denounced to him
2 for being wasteful with his property. ·He called for the man and said, 'What is this I hear about you? Draw me up an account of your stewardship because you are not
3 to be my steward any longer.' ·Then the steward said to himself, 'Now that my master is taking the stewardship from me, what am I to do? Dig? I am not strong enough.
4 Go begging? I should be too ashamed. ·Ah, I know what I will do to make sure that when I am dismissed from office there will be some to welcome me into their homes.'
5 "Then he called his master's debtors one by one. To the
6 first he said, 'How much do you owe my master?' ·'One hundred measures of oil' was the reply. The steward said, 'Here, take your bond; sit down straight away and write
7 fifty.' ·To another he said, 'And you, sir, how much do you owe?' 'One hundred measures of wheat' was the reply. The steward said, "Here, take your bond and write eighty.'
8 "The master praised the dishonest steward for his astute-ness.[a] For the children of this world are more astute in dealing with their own kind than are the children of light."

The right use of money

9 "And so I tell you this: use money, tainted as it is, to win you friends, and thus make sure that when it fails you,
10 they will welcome you into the tents of eternity. ·The man who can be trusted in little things can be trusted in great; the man who is dishonest in little things will be dishonest
11 in great. ·If then you cannot be trusted with money, that
12 tainted thing, who will trust you with genuine riches? ·And if you cannot be trusted with what is not yours, who will give you what is your very own?

16 a. Not for his dishonesty.

13   "No servant can be the slave of two masters: he will either hate the first and love the second, or treat the first with respect and the second with scorn. You cannot be the slave both of God and of money."

Against the Pharisees and their love of money

14   The Pharisees, who loved money, heard all this and
15 laughed at him. ·He said to them, "You are the very ones who pass yourselves off as virtuous in people's sight, but God knows your hearts. For what is thought highly of by men is loathsome in the sight of God.

The kingdom stormed

16   "Up to the time of John it was the Law and the Prophets; since then, the kingdom of God has been preached, and by violence everyone is getting in.

The Law remains

17   "It is easier for heaven and earth to disappear than for one little stroke to drop out of the Law.

Marriage indissoluble

18   "Everyone who divorces his wife and marries another is guilty of adultery, and the man who marries a woman divorced by her husband commits adultery.

The rich man and Lazarus

19   "There was a rich man who used to dress in purple and
20 fine linen and feast magnificently every day. ·And at his gate there lay a poor man called Lazarus, covered with
21 sores, ·who longed to fill himself with the scraps that fell from the rich man's table. Dogs even came and licked his
22 sores. ·Now the poor man died and was carried away by the angels to the bosom of Abraham. The rich man also died and was buried.

23   "In his torment in Hades he looked up and saw Abra-
24 ham a long way off with Lazarus in his bosom. ·So he cried out, 'Father Abraham, pity me and send Lazarus to dip the tip of his finger in water and cool my tongue, for I am
25 in agony in these flames.' ·'My son,' Abraham replied 'remember that during your life good things came your way, just as bad things came the way of Lazarus. Now he
26 is being comforted here while you are in agony. ·But that is not all: between us and you a great gulf has been fixed,

to stop anyone, if he wanted to, crossing from our side to
yours, and to stop any crossing from your side to ours.'
27 "The rich man replied, 'Father, I beg you then to send
28 Lazarus to my father's house, ·since I have five brothers,
to give them warning so that they do not come to this
29 place of torment too.' ·'They have Moses and the proph-
30 ets,' said Abraham 'let them listen to them.' ·'Ah no, father Abraham,' said the rich man 'but if someone comes
31 to them from the dead, they will repent.' ·Then Abraham
said to him, 'If they will not listen either to Moses or to
the prophets, they will not be convinced even if someone
should rise from the dead.'"

On leading others astray

1 **17** He said to his disciples, "Obstacles are sure to come,
2 but alas for the one who provides them! ·It would
be better for him to be thrown into the sea with a millstone put round his neck than that he should lead astray
3 a single one of these little ones. ·Watch yourselves!

Brotherly correction

"If your brother does something wrong, reprove him
4 and, if he is sorry, forgive him. ·And if he wrongs you
seven times a day and seven times comes back to you and
says, 'I am sorry,' you must forgive him."

The power of faith

5 The apostles said to the Lord, "Increase our faith." ·The
6 Lord replied, "Were your faith the size of a mustard seed
you could say to this mulberry tree, 'Be uprooted and
planted in the sea,' and it would obey you.

Humble service

7 "Which of you, with a servant plowing or minding
sheep, would say to him when he returned from the fields,
8 'Come and have your meal immediately'? ·Would he not
be more likely to say, 'Get my supper laid; make yourself
tidy and wait on me while I eat and drink. You can eat
9 and drink yourself afterward'? ·Must he be grateful to
10 the servant for doing what he was told? ·So with you:
when you have done all you have been told to do, say,
'We are merely servants: we have done no more than
our duty.'"

The ten lepers

11 Now on the way to Jerusalem he traveled along the
12 border between Samaria and Galilee.[a] •As he entered one
of the villages, ten lepers came to meet him. They stood
13 some way off •and called to him, "Jesus! Master! Take
14 pity on us." •When he saw them he said, "Go and show
yourselves to the priests." Now as they were going away
15 they were cleansed. •Finding himself cured, one of them
16 turned back praising God at the top of his voice •and
threw himself at the feet of Jesus and thanked him. The
17 man was a Samaritan. •This made Jesus say, "Were not
18 all ten made clean? The other nine, where are they? •It
seems that no one has come back to give praise to God,
19 except this foreigner." •And he said to the man, "Stand up
and go on your way. Your faith has saved you."

The coming of the kingdom of God

20 Asked by the Pharisees when the kingdom of God was
to come, he gave them this answer, "The coming of the
21 kingdom of God does not admit of observation •and there
will be no one to say, 'Look here! Look there!' For, you
must know, the kingdom of God is among you."

The day of the Son of Man

22 He said to the disciples, "A time will come when you will
long to see one of the days of the Son of Man and will
23 not see it. •They will say to you, 'Look there!' or, 'Look
24 here!' Make no move; do not set off in pursuit; •for as
the lightning flashing from one part of heaven lights up
the other, so will be the Son of Man when his day comes.
25 But first he must suffer grievously and be rejected by this
generation.
26 "As it was in Noah's day, so will it also be in the days
27 of the Son of Man. •People were eating and drinking,
marrying wives and husbands, right up to the day Noah
went into the ark, and the Flood came and destroyed them
28 all. •It will be the same as it was in Lot's day: people were
eating and drinking, buying and selling, planting and build-
29 ing, •but the day Lot left Sodom, God rained fire and
30 brimstone from heaven and it destroyed them all. •It will
be the same when the day comes for the Son of Man to be
revealed.
31 "When that day comes, anyone on the housetop, with his

possessions in the house, must not come down to collect
82 them, nor must anyone in the fields turn back either. •Re-
83 member Lot's wife. •Anyone who tries to preserve his life
84 will lose it; and anyone who loses it will keep it safe. •I
tell you, on that night two will be in one bed: one will be
85 taken, the other left; •two women will be grinding corn
87 together: one will be taken, the other left." •The disciples
interrupted. "Where, Lord?" they asked. He said, "Where
the body is, there too will the vultures gather."

The unscrupulous judge and the importunate widow

1 **18** Then he told them a parable about the need to pray
2 continually and never lose heart. •"There was a judge
in a certain town" he said "who had neither fear of God
3 nor respect for man. •In the same town there was a widow
who kept on coming to him and saying, 'I want justice
4 from you against my enemy!' •For a long time he refused,
but at last he said to himself, 'Maybe I have neither fear
5 of God nor respect for man, •but since she keeps pestering
me I must give this widow her just rights, or she will per-
sist in coming and worry me to death.'"
6 And the Lord said, "You notice what the unjust judge
7 has to say? •Now will not God see justice done to his
chosen who cry to him day and night even when he delays
8 to help them? •I promise you, he will see justice done to
them, and done speedily. But when the Son of Man comes,
will he find any faith on earth?"

The Pharisee and the publican

9 He spoke the following parable to some people who
prided themselves on being virtuous and despised every-
10 one else. •"Two men went up to the Temple to pray, one
11 a Pharisee, the other a tax collector. •The Pharisee stood
there and said this prayer to himself, 'I thank you, God,
that I am not grasping, unjust, adulterous like the rest of
mankind, and particularly that I am not like this tax col-
12 lector here. •I fast twice a week; I pay tithes on all I get.'
13 The tax collector stood some distance away, not daring
even to raise his eyes to heaven; but he beat his breast
14 and said, 'God, be merciful to me, a sinner.' •This man,
I tell you, went home again at rights with God; the other

17 a. Making for the Jordan valley and Jericho; from there he
goes up to Jerusalem.

did not. For everyone who exalts himself will be humbled, but the man who humbles himself will be exalted."

Jesus and the children

15   People even brought little children to him, for him to touch them; but when the disciples saw this they turned 16 them away. ·But Jesus called the children to him and said, "Let the little children come to me, and do not stop them; for it is to such as these that the kingdom of God belongs. 17 I tell you solemnly, anyone who does not welcome the kingdom of God like a little child will never enter it."

The rich aristocrat

18   A member of one of the leading families put this question to him, "Good Master, what have I to do to inherit 19 eternal life?" ·Jesus said to him, "Why do you call me 20 good? No one is good but God alone. ·You know the commandments: *You must not commit adultery; You must not kill; You must not steal; You must not bring false* 21 *witness; Honor your father and mother.*" ·He replied, "I 22 have kept all these from my earliest days till now." ·And when Jesus heard this he said, "There is still one thing you lack. Sell all that you own and distribute the money to the poor, and you will have treasure in heaven; then come, 28 follow me." ·But when he heard this he was filled with sadness, for he was very rich.

The danger of riches

24   Jesus looked at him and said, "How hard it is for those who have riches to make their way into the kingdom of 25 God! ·Yes, it is easier for a camel to pass through the eye of a needle than for a rich man to enter the kingdom of 26 God." ·"In that case" said the listeners "who can be 27 saved?" ·"Things that are impossible for men" he replied "are possible for God."

The reward of renunciation

28   Then Peter said, "What about us? We left all we had to 29 follow you." ·He said to them, "I tell you solemnly, there is no one who has left house, wife, brothers, parents or 80 children for the sake of the kingdom of God ·who will not be given repayment many times over in this present time and, in the world to come, eternal life."

Third prophecy of the Passion

31 Then taking the Twelve aside he said to them, "Now we are going up to Jerusalem, and everything that is written 32 by the prophets about the Son of Man is to come true. ·For he will be handed over to the pagans and will be mocked, 33 maltreated and spat on, ·and when they have scourged him they will put him to death; and on the third day he 34 will rise again." ·But they could make nothing of this; what he said was quite obscure to them, they had no idea what it meant.

Entering Jericho: the blind man

35 Now as he drew near to Jericho there was a blind man 36 sitting at the side of the road begging. ·When he heard 37 the crowd going past he asked what it was all about, ·and 38 they told him that Jesus the Nazarene was passing by. ·So 39 he called out, "Jesus, Son of David, have pity on me." ·The people in front scolded him and told him to keep quiet, but he shouted all the louder, "Son of David, have pity on 40 me." ·Jesus stopped and ordered them to bring the man to 41 him, and when he came up, asked him, ·"What do you want me to do for you?" "Sir," he replied "let me see 42 again." ·Jesus said to him, "Receive your sight. Your faith 43 has saved you." ·And instantly his sight returned and he followed him praising God, and all the people who saw it gave praise to God for what had happened.

Zacchaeus

1 **19** He entered Jericho and was going through the town 2 when a man whose name was Zacchaeus made his appearance; he was one of the senior tax collectors and a 3 wealthy man. ·He was anxious to see what kind of man Jesus was, but he was too short and could not see him for 4 the crowd; ·so he ran ahead and climbed a sycamore tree to catch a glimpse of Jesus who was to pass that way. 5 When Jesus reached the spot he looked up and spoke to him: "Zacchaeus, come down. Hurry, because I must stay 6 at your house today." ·And he hurried down and welcomed 7 him joyfully. ·They all complained when they saw what was happening. "He has gone to stay at a sinner's house" 8 they said. ·But Zacchaeus stood his ground and said to the Lord, "Look, sir, I am going to give half my property to the poor, and if I have cheated anybody I will pay him

⁹ back four times the amount."ᵃ ·And Jesus said to him,
"Today salvation has come to this house, because this man
¹⁰ too is a son of Abraham;ᵇ ·for the Son of Man has come
to seek out and save what was lost."

Parable of the pounds

¹¹   While the people were listening to this he went on to
tell a parable, because he was near Jerusalem and they
imagined that the kingdom of God was going to ·show it-
¹² self then and there. ·Accordingly he said, "A man of noble
birth went to a distant country to be appointed king and
¹³ afterward return.ᶜ ·He summoned ten of his servants and
gave them ten pounds. 'Do business with these' he told
¹⁴ them 'until I get back.' ·But his compatriots detested him
and sent a delegation to follow him with this message,
'We do not want this man to be our king.'
¹⁵   "Now on his return, having received his appointment as
king, he sent for those servants to whom he had given the
¹⁶ money, to find out what profit each had made. ·The first
came in and said, 'Sir, your one pound has brought in
¹⁷ ten.' ·'Well done, my good servant!' he replied 'Since
you have proved yourself faithful in a very small thing, you
¹⁸ shall have the government of ten cities.' ·Then came the
second and said, 'Sir, your one pound has made five.'
¹⁹ To this one also he said, 'And you shall be in charge of
²⁰ five cities.' ·Next came the other and said, 'Sir, here is
²¹ your pound. I put it away safely in a piece of linen ·be-
cause I was afraid of you; for you are an exacting man:
you pick up what you have not put down and reap what
²² you have not sown.' ·'You wicked servant!' he said 'Out
of your own mouth I condemn you. So you knew I was
an exacting man, picking up what I have not put down
²³ and reaping what I have not sown? ·Then why did you
not put my money in the bank? On my return I could
²⁴ have drawn it out with interest.' ·And he said to those
standing by, 'Take the pound from him and give it to the
²⁵ man who has ten pounds.' ·And they said to him, 'But,
²⁶ sir, he has ten pounds . . .' ·'I tell you, to everyone who
has will be given more; but from the man who has not,
even what he has will be taken away.
²⁷   'But as for my enemies who did not want me for their
king, bring them here and execute them in my presence.' "

V. THE JERUSALEM MINISTRY

The Messiah enters Jerusalem

28 When he had said this he went on ahead, going up to
29 Jerusalem. ·Now when he was near Bethphage and Bethany, close by the Mount of Olives as it is called, he sent
30 two of the disciples, telling them, ·"Go off to the village
opposite, and as you enter it you will find a tethered colt
31 that no one has yet ridden. Untie it and bring it here. ·If
anyone asks you, 'Why are you untying it?' you are to say
32 this, 'The Master needs it.'" ·The messengers went off
33 and found everything just as he had told them. ·As
they were untying the colt, its owner said, "Why are you
34 untying that colt?" ·and they answered, "The Master needs
it."

35 So they took the colt to Jesus, and throwing their gar-
36 ments over its back they helped Jesus on to it. ·As he
37 moved off, people spread their cloaks in the road, ·and
now, as he was approaching the downward slope of the
Mount of Olives, the whole group of disciples joyfully began to praise God at the top of their voices for all the
38 miracles they had seen. ·They cried out:

> "Blessings on the King who comes,
> in the name of the Lord!
> Peace in heaven
> and glory in the highest heavens!"

Jesus defends his disciples for acclaiming him

39 Some Pharisees in the crowd said to him, "Master, check
40 your disciples," ·but he answered, "I tell you, if these keep
silence the stones will cry out."

19 a. I.e. at the highest rate known to Jewish law (Ex 21:37) or
the rate imposed by Roman law on convicted thieves.   b. Although he belongs to a profession generally ranked with pagans.
c. Probably alluding to the journey of Archelaus to Rome in
4 B.C. to have the will of Herod the Great confirmed in his
favor. A deputation of Jews followed him there to contest
his claim.

Lament for Jerusalem

⁴¹ As he drew near and came in sight of the city he shed
⁴² tears over it ·and said, "If you in your turn had only understood on this day the message of peace! But, alas, it is
⁴³ hidden from your eyes! ·Yes, a time is coming when your enemies will raise fortifications all round you, when they
⁴⁴ will encircle you and hem you in on every side; ·they will dash you and the children inside your walls to the ground; they will leave not one stone standing on another within you—and all because you did not recognize your opportunity when God offered it!"

The expulsion of the dealers from the Temple

⁴⁵ Then he went into the Temple and began driving out
⁴⁶ those who were selling. ·"According to scripture," he said *"my house will be a house of prayer.*ᵈ But you have turned it into *a robbers' den."*ᵉ

Jesus teaches in the Temple

⁴⁷ He taught in the Temple every day. The chief priests and the scribes, with the support of the leading citizens,
⁴⁸ tried to do away with him, ·but they did not see how they could carry this out because the people as a whole hung on his words.

The Jews question the authority of Jesus

¹ **20** Now one day while he was teaching the people in the Temple and proclaiming the Good News, the chief priests and the scribes came up, together with the
² elders, ·and spoke to him. "Tell us" they said "what author-
³ ity have you for acting like this? Or who is it that gave you this authority?" ·"And I" replied Jesus "will ask you
⁴ a question. Tell me: ·John's baptism: did it come from
⁵ heaven, or from man?" ·And they argued it out this way among themselves, "If we say from heaven, he will say,
⁶ 'Why did you refuse to believe him?'; ·and if we say from man, the people will all stone us, for they are con-
⁷ vinced that John was a prophet." ·So their reply was that
⁸ they did not know where it came from. ·And Jesus said to them, "Nor will I tell you my authority for acting like this."

Parable of the wicked husbandmen

⁹ And he went on to tell the people this parable: "A man planted a vineyard and leased it to tenants, and went

10 abroad for a long while. ·When the time came, he sent a servant to the tenants to get his share of the produce of the vineyard from them. But the tenants thrashed him, and
11 sent him away empty-handed. ·But he persevered and sent a second servant; they thrashed him too and treated him
12 shamefully and sent him away empty-handed. ·He still persevered and sent a third; they wounded this one also,
13 and threw him out. ·Then the owner of the vineyard said, 'What am I to do? I will send them my dear son. Perhaps
14 they will respect him.' ·But when the tenants saw him they put their heads together. 'This is the heir,' they said
15 'let us kill him so that the inheritance will be ours.' ·So they threw him out of the vineyard and killed him.

"Now what will the owner of the vineyard do to them?
16 He will come and make an end of these tenants and give the vineyard to others." Hearing this they said, "God for-
17 bid!" ·But he looked hard at them and said, "Then what does this text in the scriptures mean:

> *It was the stone rejected by the builders*
> *that became the keystone?[a]*

18 Anyone who falls on that stone will be dashed to pieces; anyone it falls on will be crushed."
19 But for their fear of the people, the scribes and the chief priests would have liked to lay hands on him that very moment, because they realized that this parable was aimed at them.

On tribute to Caesar

20 So they waited their opportunity and sent agents to pose as men devoted to the Law, and to fasten on something he might say and so enable them to hand him over to the
21 jurisdiction and authority of the governor. ·They put to him this question, "Master, we know that you say and teach what is right; you favor no one, but teach the way
22 of God in all honesty. ·Is it permissible for us to pay taxes
23 to Caesar or not?" ·But he was aware of their cunning and
24 said, ·"Show me a denarius. Whose head and name are on
25 it?" "Caesar's" they said. ·"Well then," he said to them "give back to Caesar what belongs to Caesar—and to God what belongs to God."
26 As a result, they were unable to find fault with anything

d. Is 56:7   e. Jr 7:11
20 a. Ps 118:22

he had to say in public; his answer took them by surprise and they were silenced.

The resurrection of the dead

27 Some Sadducees—those who say that there is no resurrection—approached him and they put this question to him,
28 "Master, we have it from Moses in writing, that if a man's married brother dies childless, the man must marry the
29 widow to raise up children for his brother. ·Well then, there were seven brothers. The first, having married a
30,31 wife, died childless. ·The second ·and then the third married the widow. And the same with all seven, they died
32 leaving no children. ·Finally the woman herself died.
33 Now, at the resurrection, to which of them will she be wife since she had been married to all seven?"
34 Jesus replied, "The children of this world take wives and
35 husbands, ·but those who are judged worthy of a place in the other world and in the resurrection from the dead do
36 not marry ·because they can no longer die, for they are the same as the angels, and being children of the resur-
37 rection they are sons of God. ·And Moses himself implies that the dead rise again, in the passage about the bush where he calls the Lord *the God of Abraham, the God of*
38 *Isaac and the God of Jacob.*[b] ·Now he is God, not of the dead, but of the living; for to him all men are in fact alive."
39 Some scribes[c] then spoke up. "Well put, Master" they
40 said·—because they would not dare to ask him any more questions.

Christ, not only son but also Lord of David

41 He then said to them, "How can people maintain that
42 the Christ is son of David? ·Why, David himself says in the Book of Psalms:

> *The Lord said to my Lord:*
> *Sit at my right hand*
43 > *and I will make your enemies*
> *a footstool for you.*[d]

44 David here calls him Lord; how then can he be his son?"

The scribes condemned by Jesus

45 While all the people were listening he said to the disci-
46 ples, ·"Beware of the scribes who like to walk about in

long robes and love to be greeted obsequiously in the market squares, to take the front seats in the synagogues and
47 the places of honor at banquets, ·who swallow the property of widows, while making a show of lengthy prayers. The more severe will be the sentence they receive.''

The widow's mite

1 **21** As he looked up he saw rich people putting their
2 offerings into the treasury; ·then he happened to notice a poverty-stricken widow putting in two small coins,
3 and he said, "I tell you truly, this poor widow has put in
4 more than any of them; ·for these have all contributed money they had over, but she from the little she had has put in all she had to live on."

Discourse on the destruction of Jerusalem:[a] Introduction

5 When some were talking about the Temple, remarking how it was adorned with fine stonework and votive offer-
6 ings, he said, ·"All these things you are staring at now— the time will come when not a single stone will be left on
7 another: everything will be destroyed." ·And they put to him this question: "Master," they said "when will this happen, then, and what sign will there be that this is about to take place?"

The warning signs

8 "Take care not to be deceived," he said "because many will come using my name and saying, 'I am he' and,
9 'The time is near at hand.' Refuse to join them. ·And when you hear of wars and revolutions, do not be frightened, for this is something that must happen but the end
10 is not so soon." ·Then he said to them, "Nation will fight
11 against nation, and kingdom against kingdom. ·There will be great earthquakes and plagues and famines here and there; there will be fearful sights and great signs from heaven.
12 "But before all this happens, men will seize you and persecute you; they will hand you over to the synagogues and to imprisonment, and bring you before kings and gov-

b. Ex 3:6   c. Most scribes were Pharisees and believed in the resurrection of the dead.   d. Ps 110:1
21 a. This passage on the End Time also includes some elements of a prophecy of the destruction of Jerusalem.

¹³ ernors because of my name—and that will be your op-
¹⁴ portunity to bear witness. •Keep this carefully in mind:
¹⁵ you are not to prepare your defense, •because I myself
shall give you an eloquence and a wisdom that none of
¹⁶ your opponents will be able to resist or contradict. •You
will be betrayed even by parents and brothers, relations
¹⁷ and friends; and some of you will be put to death. •You
¹⁸ will be hated by all men on account of my name, •but not
¹⁹ a hair of your head will be lost. •Your endurance will win
you your lives.

The siege

²⁰ "When you see Jerusalem surrounded by armies, you
²¹ must realize that she will soon be laid desolate. •Then
those in Judaea must escape to the mountains, those inside
the city must leave it, and those in country districts must
²² not take refuge in it. •For this is the time of vengeance
²³ when all that scripture says[b] must be fulfilled. •Alas for
those with child, or with babies at the breast, when those
days come!

The disaster and the age of the pagans

"For great misery will descend on the land and wrath
²⁴ on this people. •They will fall by the edge of the sword
and be led captive to every pagan country; and Jerusalem
will be trampled down by the pagans until the age of the
pagans is completely over.

Cosmic disasters and the coming of the Son of Man

²⁵ "There will be signs in the sun and moon and stars; on
earth nations in agony, bewildered by the clamor of the
²⁶ ocean and its waves; •men dying of fear as they await
what menaces the world, for the powers of heaven will be
²⁷ shaken. •And then they will see the Son of Man coming in
²⁸ a cloud with power and great glory. •When these things
begin to take place, stand erect, hold your heads high,
because your liberation[c] is near at hand."

The time of this coming

²⁹ And he told them a parable, "Think of the fig tree and
³⁰ indeed every tree. •As soon as you see them bud, you
³¹ know that summer is now near. •So with you when you
see these things happening: know that the kingdom of God

82 is near. ·I tell you solemnly, before this generation has
83 passed away all will have taken place. ·Heaven and earth
will pass away, but my words will never pass away.

Be on the alert

84 "Watch yourselves, or your hearts will be coarsened
with debauchery and drunkenness and the cares of life,
85 and that day will be sprung on you suddenly, ·like a trap.
For it will come down on every living man on the face of
86 the earth. ·Stay awake, praying at all times for the strength
to survive all that is going to happen, and to stand with
confidence before the Son of Man."

The last days of Jesus

87 In the daytime he would be in the Temple teaching,
but would spend the night on the hill called the Mount of
88 Olives. ·And from early morning the people would gather
round him in the Temple to listen to him.

VI. THE PASSION

The conspiracy against Jesus: Judas betrays him

1 22 The feast of Unleavened Bread, called the Passover,
2 was now drawing near, ·and the chief priests and
the scribes were looking for some way of doing away with
him, because they mistrusted the people.

3 Then Satan entered into Judas, surnamed Iscariot, who
4 was numbered among the Twelve. ·He went to the chief
priests and the officers of the guard[a] to discuss a scheme
5 for handing Jesus over to them. ·They were delighted and
6 agreed to give him money. ·He accepted, and looked for
an opportunity to betray him to them without the people
knowing.

Preparation for the Passover supper

7 The day of Unleavened Bread came round, the day on
8 which the passover had to be sacrificed, ·and he sent Peter
and John, saying, "Go and make the preparations for us
9 to eat the passover." ·"Where do you want us to prepare
10 it?" they asked. ·"Listen," he said "as you go into the city

b. Possibly alluding to Dn 9:27.   c. Or "redemption."
22 a. The Temple police, chosen from among the Levites.

you will meet a man carrying a pitcher of water. Follow
¹¹ him into the house he enters ·and tell the owner of the
house, 'The Master has this to say to you: Where is the
dining room in which I can eat the passover with my
¹² disciples?' ·The man will show you a large upper room
furnished with couches. Make the preparations there."
¹³ They set off and found everything as he had told them, and
prepared the Passover.

The supper

¹⁴   When the hour came he took his place at table, and the
¹⁵ apostles with him. ·And he said to them, "I have longed to
¹⁶ eat this passover with you before I suffer; ·because, I tell
you, I shall not eat it again until it is fulfilled in the kingdom of God."
¹⁷   Then, taking a cup,ᵇ he gave thanks and said, "Take
¹⁸ this and share it among you, ·because from now on, I tell
you, I shall not drink wine until the kingdom of God
comes."

The institution of the Eucharist

¹⁹   Then he took some bread, and when he had given
thanks, broke it and gave it to them, saying, "This is my
body which will be given for you; do this as a memorial
²⁰ of me." ·He did the same with the cup after supper, and
said, "This cup is the new covenant in my blood which will
be poured out for you.

The treachery of Judas foretold

²¹   "And yet, here with me on the table is the hand of the
²² man who betrays me. ·The Son of Man does indeed go to
his fate even as it has been decreed, but alas for that man
²³ by whom he is betrayed!" ·And they began to ask one
another which of them it could be who was to do this
thing.

Who is the greatest?

²⁴   A dispute arose also between them about which should
²⁵ be reckoned the greatest, ·but he said to them, "Among
pagans it is the kings who lord it over them, and those who
have authority over them are given the title Benefactor.
²⁶ This must not happen with you. No; the greatest among
you must behave as if he were the youngest, the leader as
²⁷ if he were the one who serves. ·For who is the greater:

the one at table or the one who serves? The one at table, surely? Yet here am I among you as one who serves!

The reward promised to the apostles

28   "You are the men who have stood by me faithfully in
29 my trials; ·and now I confer a kingdom on you, just as
30 my Father conferred one on me: ·you will eat and drink
at my table in my kingdom, and you will sit on thrones to
judge the twelve tribes of Israel.

Peter's denial and repentance foretold

31   "Simon, Simon! Satan, you must know, has got his wish
32 to sift you all like wheat; ·but I have prayed for you, Simon, that your faith may not fail, and once you have recovered, you in your turn must strengthen your brothers."
33 "Lord," he answered "I would be ready to go to prison
34 with you, and to death." ·Jesus replied, "I tell you, Peter,
by the time the cock crows today you will have denied
three times that you know me."

A time of crisis

35   He said to them, "When I sent you out without purse or
36 haversack or sandals, were you short of anything?" ·"No"
they said. He said to them, "But now if you have a purse,
take it; if you have a haversack, do the same; if you have
37 no sword, sell your cloak and buy one, ·because I tell you
these words of scripture have to be fulfilled in me: *He
let himself be taken for a criminal.*[c] Yes, what scripture
says about me is even now reaching its fulfillment."
38 "Lord," they said "there are two swords here now." He
said to them, "That is enough!"

The Mount of Olives

39   He then left to make his way as usual to the Mount of
40 Olives, with the disciples following. ·When they reached
the place he said to them, "Pray not to be put to the test."
41   Then he withdrew from them, about a stone's throw
42 away, and knelt down and prayed. ·"Father," he said "if
you are willing, take this cup away from me. Nevertheless,
43 let your will be done, not mine." ·Then an angel appeared
44 to him, coming from heaven to give him strength. ·In his

---

b. Luke distinguishes the Passover and the cup of vv. 15-18 from the bread and the cup of vv. 19-20.   c. Is 53:12

anguish he prayed even more earnestly, and his sweat fell
to the ground like great drops of blood.

45 When he rose from prayer he went to the disciples and
46 found them sleeping for sheer grief. •"Why are you
asleep?" he said to them. "Get up and pray not to be put to
the test."

The arrest

47 He was still speaking when a number of men appeared,
and at the head of them the man called Judas, one of the
48 Twelve, who went up to Jesus to kiss him. •Jesus said,
"Judas, are you betraying the Son of Man with a kiss?"
49 His followers, seeing what was happening, said, "Lord,
50 shall we use our swords?" •And one of them struck out at
51 the high priest's servant, and cut off his right ear. •But at
this Jesus spoke. "Leave off!" he said "That will do!"
And touching the man's ear he healed him.
52 Then Jesus spoke to the chief priests and captains of
the Temple guard and elders who had come for him. "Am
I a brigand" he said "that you had to set out with swords
53 and clubs? •When I was among you in the Temple day
after day you never moved to lay hands on me. But this
is your hour; this is the reign of darkness."

Peter's denials

54 They seized him then and led him away, and they took
him to the high priest's house. Peter followed at a distance.
55 They had lit a fire in the middle of the courtyard and
56 Peter sat down among them, •and as he was sitting there
by the blaze a servant-girl saw him, peered at him, and
57 said, "This person was with him too." •But he denied it.
58 "Woman," he said "I do not know him." •Shortly afterward someone else saw him and said, "You are another of
59 them." But Peter replied, "I am not, my friend." •About
an hour later another man insisted, saying, "This fellow
60 was certainly with him. Why, he is a Galilean." •"My
friend," said Peter "I do not know what you are talking
about." At that instant, while he was still speaking, the
61 cock crew, •and the Lord turned and looked straight at
Peter, and Peter remembered what the Lord had said to
him, "Before the cock crows today, you will have dis-
62 owned me three times." •And he went outside and wept
bitterly.

Jesus mocked by the guards

63 Meanwhile the men who guarded Jesus were mocking
64 and beating him. ·They blindfolded him and questioned
him. "Play the prophet" they said. "Who hit you then?"
65 And they continued heaping insults on him.

Jesus before the Sanhedrin

66 When day broke there was a meeting of the elders of
the people, attended by the chief priests and scribes. He
67 was brought before their council, ·and they said to him,
"If you are the Christ, tell us." "If I tell you," he replied
68 "you will not believe me, ·and if I question you, you will
69 not answer. ·But from now on, the Son of Man will be
70 *seated at the right hand* of the Power *of God.*"*d* ·Then
they all said, "So you are the Son of God then?" He an-
71 swered, "It is you who say I am." ·"What need of witnesses have we now?" they said. "We have heard it for
1 ourselves from his own lips." **23** The whole assembly then
rose, and they brought him before Pilate.

Jesus before Pilate

2 They began their accusation by saying, "We found this
man inciting our people to revolt, opposing payment of the
3 tribute to Caesar, and claiming to be Christ, a king." ·Pi-
late put to him this question, "Are you the king of the
4 Jews?" "It is you who say it" he replied. ·Pilate then said
to the chief priests and the crowd, "I find no case against
5 this man." ·But they persisted, "He is inflaming the people
with his teaching all over Judaea; it has come all the way
6 from Galilee, where he started, down to here." ·When Pi-
7 late heard this, he asked if the man were a Galilean; ·and
finding that he came under Herod's jurisdiction he passed
him over to Herod who was also in Jerusalem at that time.

Jesus before Herod

8 Herod was delighted to see Jesus; he had heard about
him and had been wanting for a long time to set eyes on
him; moreover, he was hoping to see some miracle worked
9 by him. ·So he questioned him at some length; but with-
10 out getting any reply. ·Meanwhile the chief priests and
the scribes were there, violently pressing their accusations.
11 Then Herod, together with his guards, treated him with

d. Ps 110:1

contempt and made fun of him; he put a rich cloak[a] on
12 him and sent him back to Pilate. ·And though Herod and
Pilate had been enemies before, they were reconciled that
same day.

Jesus before Pilate again

13 Pilate then summoned the chief priests and the leading
14 men and the people. ·"You brought this man before me"
he said "as a political agitator. Now I have gone into the
matter myself in your presence and found no case against
the man in respect of all the charges you bring against
15 him. ·Nor has Herod either, since he has sent him back to
us. As you can see, the man has done nothing that deserves
16 death, ·so I shall have him flogged and then let him go."
18 But as one man they howled, "Away with him! Give us
19 Barabbas!" ·(This man had been thrown into prison for
causing a riot in the city and for murder.)
20 Pilate was anxious to set Jesus free and addressed them
21 again, ·but they shouted back, "Crucify him! Crucify
22 him!" ·And for the third time he spoke to them, "Why?
What harm has this man done? I have found no case
against him that deserves death, so I shall have him pun-
23 ished and then let him go." ·But they kept on shouting at
the top of their voices, demanding that he should be crucified. And their shouts were growing louder.
24 Pilate then gave his verdict: their demand was to be
25 granted. ·He released the man they asked for, who had
been imprisoned for rioting and murder, and handed Jesus
over to them to deal with as they pleased.

The way to Calvary

26 As they were leading him away they seized on a man,
Simon from Cyrene, who was coming in from the country,
and made him shoulder the cross and carry it behind Je-
27 sus. ·Large numbers of people followed him, and of
28 women too,[b] who mourned and lamented for him. ·But
Jesus turned to them and said, "Daughters of Jerusalem, do
not weep for me; weep rather for yourselves and for your
29 children. ·For the days will surely come when people will
say, 'Happy are those who are barren, the wombs that
have never borne, the breasts that have never suckled!'
30 Then they will begin to *say to the mountains, 'Fall on*
31 *us!'*; *to the hills, 'Cover us!'*[c] ·For if men use the green
32 wood like this, what will happen when it is dry?" ·Now

with him they were also leading out two other criminals to be executed.

The crucifixion

33   When they reached the place called The Skull, they crucified him there and the two criminals also, one on the 34 right, the other on the left. ·Jesus said, "Father, forgive them; they do not know what they are doing." Then they cast lots to share out his clothing.

The crucified Christ is mocked

35   ·The people stayed there watching him. As for the leaders, they jeered at him. "He saved others," they said "let him save himself if he is the Christ of God, the Chosen 36 One." ·The soldiers mocked him too, and when they ap-37 proached to offer him vinegar ·they said, "If you are the 38 king of the Jews, save yourself." ·Above him there was an inscription: "This is the King of the Jews."

The good thief

39   One of the criminals hanging there abused him. "Are you not the Christ?" he said. "Save yourself and us as 40 well." ·But the other spoke up and rebuked him. "Have you no fear of God at all?" he said. "You got the same 41 sentence as he did, ·but in our case we deserved it: we are paying for what we did. But this man has done nothing 42 wrong. ·Jesus," he said "remember me when you come 43 into your kingdom." ·"Indeed, I promise you," he replied "today you will be with me in paradise."

The death of Jesus

44   It was now about the sixth hour and, with the sun eclipsed, a darkness came over the whole land until the 45 ninth hour. ·The veil of the Temple was torn right down 46 the middle; ·and when Jesus had cried out in a loud voice, he said, "Father, *into your hands I commit my spirit.*"[d] With these words he breathed his last.

23 a. Ceremonial dress of a prince.
b. The Talmud records that noblewomen of Jerusalem used to give soothing drinks to condemned criminals. c. Ho 10:8
d. Ps 31:5

After the death

47 When the centurion saw what had taken place, he gave praise to God and said, "This was a great and good man."
48 And when all the people who had gathered for the spectacle saw what had happened, they went home beating their breasts.
49 All his friends stood at a distance; so also did the women who had accompanied him from Galilee, and they saw all this happen.

The burial

50 Then a member of the council arrived, an upright and
51 virtuous man named Joseph. ·He had not consented to what the others had planned and carried out. He came from Arimathaea, a Jewish town, and he lived in the hope
52 of seeing the kingdom of God. ·This man went to Pilate
53 and asked for the body of Jesus. ·He then took it down, wrapped it in a shroud and put him in a tomb which was
54 hewn in stone in which no one had yet been laid. ·It was Preparation Day and the sabbath was imminent.
55 Meanwhile the women who had come from Galilee with Jesus were following behind. They took note of the tomb and of the position of the body.
56 Then they returned and prepared spices and ointments. And on the sabbath day they rested, as the Law required.

VII. AFTER THE RESURRECTION

The empty tomb. The angel's message

1 **24** On the first day of the week, at the first sign of dawn, they went to the tomb with the spices they had pre-
2 pared. ·They found that the stone had been rolled away
3 from the tomb, ·but on entering discovered that the body
4 of the Lord Jesus was not there. ·As they stood there not knowing what to think, two men in brilliant clothes sud-
5 denly appeared at their side. ·Terrified, the women lowered their eyes. But the two men said to them, "Why look
6 among the dead for someone who is alive? ·He is not here; he has risen. Remember what he told you when he was
7 still in Galilee: ·that the Son of Man had to be handed over into the power of sinful men and be crucified, and

8 rise again on the third day." •And they remembered his
words.

The apostles refuse to believe the women

9 When the women returned from the tomb they told all
10 this to the Eleven and to all the others. •The women were
Mary of Magdala, Joanna, and Mary the mother of James.
11 The other women with them also told the apostles, •but
this story of theirs seemed pure nonsense, and they did not
believe them.

Peter at the tomb

12 Peter, however, went running to the tomb. He bent
down and saw the binding cloths but nothing else; he then
went back home, amazed at what had happened.

The road to Emmaus

13 That very same day, two of them were on their way to a
14 village called Emmaus, seven miles[a] from Jerusalem, •and
they were talking together about all that had happened.
15 Now as they talked this over, Jesus himself came up and
16 walked by their side; •but something prevented them from
17 recognizing him. •He said to them, "What matters are you
discussing as you walk along?" They stopped short, their
faces downcast.
18 Then one of them, called Cleopas, answered him, "You
must be the only person staying in Jerusalem who does not
know the things that have been happening there these last
19 few days." •"What things?" he asked. "All about Jesus of
Nazareth" they answered "who proved he was a great
prophet by the things he said and did in the sight of God
20 and of the whole people; •and how our chief priests and
our leaders handed him over to be sentenced to death, and
21 had him crucified. •Our own hope had been that he would
be the one to set Israel free. And this is not all: two whole
22 days have gone by since it all happened; •and some women
from our group have astounded us: they went to the tomb
23 in the early morning, •and when they did not find the body,
they came back to tell us they had seen a vision of angels
24 who declared he was alive. •Some of our friends went to
the tomb and found everything exactly as the women had
reported, but of him they saw nothing."

24 a. The identity of the village is disputed.

25 Then he said to them, "You foolish men! So slow to be-
26 lieve the full message of the prophets! ·Was it not ordained that the Christ should suffer and so enter into his
27 glory?" ·Then, starting with Moses and going through all
the prophets, he explained to them the passages throughout the scriptures that were about himself.

28 When they drew near to the village to which they were
29 going, he made as if to go on; ·but they pressed him to
stay with them. "It is nearly evening" they said "and the
30 day is almost over." So he went in to stay with them. ·Now
while he was with them at table, he took the bread and
said the blessing; then he broke it and handed it to them.
31 And their eyes were opened and they recognized him; but
32 he had vanished from their sight. ·Then they said to each
other, "Did not our hearts burn within us as he talked to us
on the road and explained the scriptures to us?"

33 They set out that instant and returned to Jerusalem.
There they found the Eleven assembled together with their
34 companions, ·who said to them, "Yes, it is true. The Lord
35 has risen and has appeared to Simon." ·Then they told
their story of what had happened on the road and how
they had recognized him at the breaking of bread.

Jesus appears to the apostles

36 They were still talking about all this when he himself
stood among them and said to them, "Peace be with you!"
37 In a state of alarm and fright, they thought they were see-
38 ing a ghost. ·But he said, "Why are you so agitated, and
39 why are these doubts rising in your hearts? ·Look at my
hands and feet; yes, it is I indeed. Touch me and see for
yourselves; a ghost has no flesh and bones as you can see I
40 have." ·And as he said this he showed them his hands and
41 feet. ·Their joy was so great that they still could not believe
it, and they stood there dumfounded; so he said to them,
42 "Have you anything here to eat?" ·And they offered him a
43 piece of grilled fish, ·which he took and ate before their
eyes.

Last instructions to the apostles

44 Then he told them, "This is what I meant when I said,
while I was still with you, that everything written about me
in the Law of Moses, in the Prophets and in the Psalms,
45 has to be fulfilled." ·He then opened their minds to under-
46 stand the scriptures, ·and he said to them, 'So you see how

it is written that the Christ would suffer and on the third
47 day rise from the dead, ·and that, in his name, repentance
for the forgiveness of sins would be preached to all the
48 nations, beginning from Jerusalem. ·You are witnesses to
this.
49 "And now I am sending down to you what the Father
has promised. Stay in the city then, until you are clothed
with the power from on high."

The ascension

50 Then he took them out as far as the outskirts of Bethany,
51 and lifting up his hands he blessed them. ·Now as he
blessed them, he withdrew from them and was carried up
52 to heaven. ·They worshiped him and then went back to
53 Jerusalem full of joy; ·and they were continually in the
Temple praising God.

INTRODUCTION TO
The Gospel and Letters of
Saint John

Date, authorship and form of the gospel

Tradition almost unanimously names John the apostle, the son of Zebedee, as the author. Before A.D. 150 the book was known and used by Ignatius of Antioch, Papias, Justin and the author of the *Odes of Solomon*, and the first explicit testimony is by Irenaeus, c. 180: "Last of all John, too, the disciple of the Lord who leaned against his breast, himself brought out a gospel while he was in Ephesus." The gospel itself has much supporting evidence, apart from its claim to be the work of an eyewitness who was a beloved disciple of the Lord: its vocabulary and style betray its semitic origin, it is familiar with Jewish customs and with the topography of Palestine, and its author is evidently a close friend of Peter.

It was published not by John himself but by his disciples after his death, and it is possible that in this gospel we have the end-stage of a slow process that has brought together not only component parts of different ages but also corrections, additions and sometimes more than one revision of the same discourse. The arrangement of the gospel is not always easy to explain, but it is clear that the author attaches special importance to the Jewish liturgical feasts which punctuate his narrative; the following analysis can be made:

> *Prologue* (1:1-18)
> I. *First week* of the messianic ministry, ending with the first miracle at Cana (1:19–2:11)
> II. *First Passover* with accompanying events, ending with the second miracle at Cana (2:12–4:54)
> III. *Sabbath "of the paralytic"* (5:1-47)
> IV. *The Passover "of the bread of life"* and its discourse (6:1-71)
> V. *The feast of Tabernacles* and the man born blind (7:1–10:21)
> VI. *The feast of Dedication* and the raising of Lazarus (10:22–11:54)

This division suggests that Christ not only fulfilled the Jewish liturgy but in doing so brought it to an end.

Special characteristics of the gospel

The fourth gospel is concerned to bring out the significance of all that Christ did and said. The things that he did were "signs," and the meaning of them, hidden at first, could be understood only after his glorification; the things he said had a deeper meaning not perceived at the time but understood only after the Spirit who spoke in the name of the risen Christ had come to "lead" his disciples "into all truth." The gospel is revelation at this stage of development.

The whole of John's thought is dominated by the mystery of the Incarnation, from the Prologue with which the book opens. Here the revelation of Christ's glory, which in the synoptic gospels is associated primarily with his return at the end of time, has a new interpretation: judgment is working here and now in the soul, and eternal life (John's counterpart to the "kingdom" of the synoptic gospels) is made to be something actually present, already in the possession of those who have faith. God's victory over evil, his salvation of the world, is already guaranteed by Christ's resurrection in glory.

The letters

The three letters are like the gospel in style and doctrine. The first, an encyclical letter to the Christian communities of 'Asia', summarizes the whole content of John's religious experience and develops themes from the gospel, for churches threatened with disintegration under the impact of the early heresies. The second letter was written to a church in answer to some who had denied the reality of the Incarnation. The third, which is probably the earliest in date, was written to settle a dispute on jurisdiction in one of the churches acknowledging John's authority.

THE GOSPEL ACCORDING TO
Saint John

PROLOGUE

1 **1** In the beginning was the Word:
the Word was with God
and the Word was God.

2 He was with God in the beginning.

3 Through him all things came to be,
not one thing had its being but through him.

4 All that came to be had life in him
and that life was the light of men,

5 a light that shines in the dark,
a light that darkness could not overpower.^a

6 A man came, sent by God.
His name was John.

7 He came as a witness,
as a witness to speak for the light,
so that everyone might believe through him.

8 He was not the light,
only a witness to speak for the light.

9 The Word was the true light
that enlightens all men;
and he was coming into the world.

10 He was in the world
that had its being through him,
and the world did not know him.

11 He came to his own domain
and his own people did not accept him.

12 But to all who did accept him
he gave power to become children of God,
to all who believe in the name of him

13 who was born not out of human stock
or urge of the flesh
or will of man
but of God himself.

14 The Word was made flesh,

he lived among us,[b]
and we saw his glory,
the glory that is his as the only Son of the Father,
full of grace and truth.

15 John appears as his witness. He proclaims:
"This is the one of whom I said:
He who comes after me
ranks before me
because he existed before me."

16 Indeed, from his fullness we have, all of us, received—
yes, grace in return for grace,

17 since, though the Law was given through Moses,
grace and truth have come through Jesus Christ.

18 No one has ever seen God;
it is the only Son, who is nearest to the Father's heart,
who has made him known.

I. THE FIRST PASSOVER

A. THE OPENING WEEK

The witness of John

19 . This is how John appeared as a witness. When the Jews[c]
sent priests and Levites from Jerusalem to ask him, "Who

20 are you?" ·he not only declared, but he declared quite

21 openly, "I am not the Christ." ·"Well then," they asked
"are you Elijah?"[d] "I am not" he said. "Are you

22 the Prophet?"[e] He answered, "No." ·So they said to him,
"Who are you? We must take back an answer to those who

23 sent us. What have you to say about yourself?" ·So John
said, "I am, as Isaiah prophesied:

> *a voice that cries in the wilderness:*
> *Make a straight way for the Lord."[f]*

1 a. Or "grasp," in the sense of "enclose" or "understand." b.
"pitched his tent among us." c. In Jn this usually indicates the
Jewish religious authorities who were hostile to Jesus; but
occasionally the Jews as a whole. d. Whose return was expected, Ml 3:23-24. e. The Prophet greater than Moses who
was expected as Messiah, on an interpretation of Dt 18:15.
f. Is 40:3

²⁴₂₅ Now these men had been sent by the Pharisees, ·and they put this further question to him, "Why are you baptizing if you are not the Christ, and not Elijah, and not the ²⁶ prophet?" ·John replied, "I baptize with water; but there ²⁷ stands among you—unknown to you—the one who is coming after me; and I am not fit to undo his sandal-strap." ²⁸ This happened at Bethany, on the far side of the Jordan, where John was baptizing.

²⁹ The next day, seeing Jesus coming toward him, John said, "Look, there is the lamb of God that takes away the ³⁰ sin of the world. ·This is the one I spoke of when I said: A man is coming after me who ranks before me because he ³¹ existed before me. ·I did not know him myself, and yet it was to reveal him to Israel that I came baptizing with wa³² ter." ·John also declared, "I saw the Spirit coming down ³³ on him from heaven like a dove and resting on him. ·I did not know him myself, but he who sent me to baptize with water had said to me, 'The man on whom you see the Spirit come down and rest is the one who is going to bap³⁴ tize with the Holy Spirit.' ·Yes, I have seen and I am the witness that he is the Chosen One of God."

The first disciples

³⁵ On the following day as John stood there again with ³⁶ two of his disciples, ·Jesus passed, and John stared hard at ³⁷ him and said, "Look, there is the lamb of God." ·Hearing ³⁸ this, the two disciples followed Jesus. ·Jesus turned round, saw them following and said, "What do you want?" They answered, "Rabbi"—which means Teacher—"where do you ³⁹ live?" ·"Come and see" he replied; so they went and saw where he lived, and stayed with him the rest of that day. It was about the tenth hour.ᵍ

⁴⁰ One of these two who became followers of Jesus after hearing what John had said was Andrew, the brother of ⁴¹ Simon Peter. ·Early next morning, Andrew met his brother and said to him, "We have found the Messiah"—which ⁴² means the Christ—·and he took Simon to Jesus. Jesus looked hard at him and said, "You are Simon son of John; you are to be called Cephas"—meaning Rock.

⁴³ The next day, after Jesus had decided to leave for Galilee, ⁴⁴ he met Philip and said, "Follow me." ·Philip came from ⁴⁵ the same town, Bethsaida, as Andrew and Peter. ·Philip found Nathanaelʰ and said to him, "We have found the one Moses wrote about in the Law, the one about whom

the prophets wrote: he is Jesus son of Joseph, from Naza-
46 reth." •"From Nazareth?" said Nathanael "Can anything
good come from that place?" "Come and see" replied
47 Philip. •When Jesus saw Nathanael coming he said of him,
"There is an Israelite who deserves the name, incapable of
48 deceit." •"How do you know me?" said Nathanael. "Before Philip came to call you," said Jesus "I saw you under
49 the fig tree." •Nathanael answered, "Rabbi, you are the
50 Son of God, you are the King of Israel." •Jesus replied,
"You believe that just because I said: I saw you under the
51 fig tree. You will see greater things than that." •And then
he added, "I tell you most solemnly, you will see heaven
laid open and, above the Son of Man, the angels of God
ascending and descending."

The wedding at Cana

1 Three days later there was a wedding at Cana in Galilee.
2 The mother of Jesus was there, •and Jesus and his dis-
3 ciples had also been invited. •When they ran out of wine,
since the wine provided for the wedding was all finished,
the mother of Jesus said to him, "They have no wine."
4 Jesus said, "Woman, why turn to me? My hour has not
5 come yet." •His mother said to the servants, *Do whatever*
6 *he tells you.*[a] •There were six stone water jars standing
there, meant for the ablutions that are customary among
7 the Jews: each could hold twenty or thirty gallons. •Jesus
said to the servants, "Fill the jars with water," and they
8 filled them to the brim. •"Draw some out now" he told
9 them "and take it to the steward." •They did this; the steward tasted the water, and it had turned into wine. Having
no idea where it came from—only the servants who had
drawn the water knew—the steward called the bridegroom
10 and said, "People generally serve the best wine first, and
keep the cheaper sort till the guests have had plenty to
drink; but you have kept the best wine till now."
11 This was the first of the signs given by Jesus: it was given
at Cana in Galilee. He let his glory be seen, and his disciples
12 believed in him. •After this he went down to Capernaum
with his mother and the brothers, but they stayed there
only a few days.

g. 4 p.m. h. Probably the Bartholomew of the other gospels.
2 a. Gn 41:55

B. THE PASSOVER

The cleansing of the Temple

13   Just before the Jewish Passover Jesus went up to Jeru-
14 salem, ·and in the Temple he found people selling cattle
and sheep and pigeons, and the money changers sitting at
15 their counters there. ·Making a whip out of some cord,
he drove them all out of the Temple, cattle and sheep as
well, scattered the money changers' coins, knocked their
16 tables over ·and said to the pigeon-sellers, "Take all this
out of here and stop turning my Father's house into a
17 market." ·Then his disciples remembered the words of
18 scripture: *Zeal for your house will devour me.*[b] ·The
Jews intervened and said, "What sign can you show us to
19 justify what you have done?" ·Jesus answered, "Destroy
20 this sanctuary, and in three days I will raise it up." ·The
Jews replied, "It has taken forty-six years to build this
sanctuary:[c] are you going to raise it up in three days?"
21 But he was speaking of the sanctuary that was his body,
22 and when Jesus rose from the dead, his disciples remembered that he had said this, and they believed the scripture
and the words he had said.
23   During his stay in Jerusalem for the Passover many believed in his name when they saw the signs that he gave,
24 but Jesus knew them all and did not trust himself to them;
25 he never needed evidence about any man; he could tell
what a man had in him.

C. THE MYSTERY OF THE SPIRIT REVEALED
TO A MASTER IN ISRAEL

The conversation with Nicodemus

1   There was one of the Pharisees called Nicodemus, a
2 **3** leading Jew, ·who came to Jesus by night and said,
"Rabbi, we know that you are a teacher who comes from
God; for no one could perform the signs that you do un-
3 less God were with him." ·Jesus answered:

> "I tell you most solemnly,
> unless a man is born from above,
> he cannot see the kingdom of God."

4 Nicodemus said, "How can a grown man be born? Can

he go back into his mother's womb and be born again?"
5 Jesus replied:

"I tell you most solemnly,
unless a man is born through water and the Spirit,
he cannot enter the kingdom of God:
6 what is born of the flesh is flesh;
what is born of the Spirit is spirit.
7 Do not be surprised when I say:
You must be born from above.
8 The wind blows wherever it pleases;
you hear its sound,
but you cannot tell where it comes from or where it is
going.
That is how it is with all who are born of the Spirit."

**9
10** "How can that be possible?" asked Nicodemus. "You,
a teacher in Israel, and you do not know these things!"
replied Jesus.

11 "I tell you most solemnly,
we speak only about what we know
and witness only to what we have seen
and yet you people reject our evidence.
12 If you do not believe me
when I speak about things in this world,
how are you going to believe me
when I speak to you about heavenly things?
13 No one has gone up to heaven
except the one who came down from heaven,
the Son of Man who is in heaven;
and the Son of Man must be lifted up
14 as Moses lifted up the serpent in the desert,
15 so that everyone who believes may have eternal life in
him.
16 Yes, God loved the world so much
that he gave his only Son,
so that everyone who believes in him may not be lost
but may have eternal life.
17 For God sent his Son into the world
not to condemn the world,
but so that through him the world might be saved.
18 No one who believes in him will be condemned;

b. Ps 69:9   c. Reconstruction work on the Temple began in
19 b.c. This is therefore the Passover of 28 a.d.

but whoever refuses to believe is condemned already,
because he has refused to believe
in the name of God's only Son.

¹⁹ On these grounds is sentence pronounced:
that though the light has come into the world
men have shown they prefer
darkness to the light
because their deeds were evil.

²⁰ And indeed, everybody who does wrong
hates the light and avoids it,
for fear his actions should be exposed;

²¹ but the man who lives by the truth
comes out into the light,
so that it may be plainly seen that what he does is done
in God."

II. JOURNEYS IN SAMARIA AND GALILEE

John bears witness for the last time

²² After this, Jesus went with his disciples into the Judaean
countryside and stayed with them there and baptized.
²³ At the same time John was baptizing at Aenon*ᵃ* near Salim,
where there was plenty of water, and people were going
²⁴ there to be baptized. This was before John had been put
in prison.

²⁵ Now some of John's disciples had opened a discussion
²⁶ with a Jew about purification, so they went to John and
said, "Rabbi, the man who was with you on the far side
of the Jordan, the man to whom you bore witness, is bap-
²⁷ tizing now; and everyone is going to him." John replied:

"A man can lay claim
only to what is given him from heaven.

²⁸ "You yourselves can bear me out: I said: I myself am
not the Christ; I am the one who has been sent in front
of him.

²⁹ "The bride is only for the bridegroom;
and yet the bridegroom's friend,
who stands there and listens,
is glad when he hears the bridegroom's voice.
This same joy I feel, and now it is complete.

³⁰ He must grow greater,
    I must grow smaller.
³¹ He who comes from above
    is above all others;
    he who is born of the earth
    is earthly himself and speaks in an earthly way.
    He who comes from heaven
³² bears witness to the things he has seen and heard,
    even if his testimony is not accepted;
³³ though all who do accept his testimony
    are attesting the truthfulness of God,
³⁴ since he whom God has sent
    speaks God's own words:
    God gives him the Spirit without reserve.
³⁵ The Father loves the Son
    and has entrusted everything to him.
³⁶ Anyone who believes in the Son has eternal life,
    but anyone who refuses to believe in the Son will never
        see life:
    the anger of God stays on him."

The savior of the world revealed to the Samaritans

¹ **4** When Jesus heard that the Pharisees had found out
    that he was making and baptizing more disciples than
² John—though in fact it was his disciples who baptized, not
³ Jesus himself—he left Judaea and went back to Galilee.
⁴ This meant that he had to cross Samaria.
⁵   On the way he came to the Samaritan town called Sychar,^a near the land that Jacob gave to his son Joseph.
⁶ Jacob's well is there and Jesus, tired by the journey,
sat straight down by the well. It was about the sixth hour.^b
⁷ When a Samaritan woman came to draw water, Jesus said
⁸ to her, "Give me a drink." ·His disciples had gone into the
⁹ town to buy food. ·The Samaritan woman said to him,
"What? You are a Jew and you ask me, a Samaritan, for
a drink?"—Jews, in fact, do not associate with Samaritans.
¹⁰ Jesus replied:

        "If you only knew what God is offering
        and who it is that is saying to you:

3 a. A tradition locates Aenon ("Springs") in the Jordan valley
7 m. from Scythopolis.
4 a. Either Shechem (Aramaic: Sichara), or Askar at the foot
of Mt Ebal. "Jacob's Well" is not mentioned in Gn. **b.** Noon.

> Give me a drink,
> you would have been the one to ask,
> and he would have given you living water."

11 "You have no bucket, sir," she answered "and the well
12 is deep: how could you get this living water? ·Are you a
greater man than our father Jacob who gave us this well
and drank from it himself with his sons and his cattle?"
13 Jesus replied:

"Whoever drinks this water
will get thirsty again;
14 but anyone who drinks the water that I shall give
will never be thirsty again:
the water that I shall give
will turn into a spring inside him, welling up to eternal
       life."

15 "Sir," said the woman "give me some of that water, so
that I may never get thirsty and never have to come here
16 again to draw water." ·"Go and call your husband" said
17 Jesus to her "and come back here." ·The woman answered, "I have no husband." He said to her, "You are
18 right to say, 'I have no husband'; ·for although you have
had five, the one you have now is not your husband. You
19 spoke the truth there." ·"I see you are a prophet, sir" said
20 the woman. ·"Our fathers worshiped on this mountain,*
while you say that Jerusalem is the place where one ought
21 to worship." ·Jesus said:

"Believe me, woman, the hour is coming
when you will worship the Father
neither on this mountain nor in Jerusalem.
22 You worship what you do not know;
we worship what we do know;
for salvation comes from the Jews.
23 But the hour will come—in fact it is here already—
when true worshipers will worship the Father in spirit and
       truth:
that is the kind of worshiper
the Father wants.
24 God is spirit,
and those who worship
must worship in spirit and truth."

25 ..The woman said to him, "I know that Messiah—that is,
  Christ—is coming; and when he comes he will tell us every-
26 thing." •"I who am speaking to you," said Jesus "I am he."
27   At this point his disciples returned, and were surprised
  to find him speaking to a woman, though none of them
  asked, "What do you want from her?" or, "Why are you
28 talking to her?" •The woman put down her water jar and
29 hurried back to the town to tell the people, •"Come and
  see a man who has told me everything I ever did; I wonder
30 if he is the Christ?" •This brought people out of the town
  and they started walking toward him.
31   Meanwhile, the disciples were urging him, "Rabbi, do
32 have something to eat"; •but he said, "I have food to eat
33 that you do not know about." •So the disciples asked one
34 another, "Has someone been bringing him food?" •But
  Jesus said:

> "My food
> is to do the will of the one who sent me,
> and to complete his work.
35 Have you not got a saying:
> Four months and then the harvest?
> Well, I tell you:
> Look around you, look at the fields;
> already they are white, ready for harvest!
36 Already •the reaper is being paid his wages,
> already he is bringing in the grain for eternal life,
> and thus sower and reaper rejoice together.
37 For here the proverb holds good:
> one sows, another reaps;
38 I sent you to reap
> a harvest you had not worked for.
> Others worked for it;
> and you have come into the rewards of their trouble."

39   Many Samaritans of that town had believed in him on
  the strength of the woman's testimony when she said, "He
40 told me all I have ever done," •so, when the Samaritans
  came up to him, they begged him to stay with them. He
41 stayed for two days, and •when he spoke to them many
42 more came to believe; •and they said to the woman, "Now
  we no longer believe because of what you told us; we have

c. Gerizim, the mountain on which the Samaritans built a rival
to the Jerusalem Temple; it was destroyed by Hyrcanus, 129 B.C.

heard him ourselves and we know that he really is the savior of the world."

The cure of the nobleman's son

⁴³⁄₄₄ When the two days were over Jesus left for Galilee. ·He himself had declared that there is no respect for a prophet ⁴⁵ in his own country, ·but on his arrival the Galileans received him well, having seen all that he had done at Jerusalem during the festival which they too had attended.

⁴⁶ He went again to Cana in Galilee, where he had changed the water into wine. Now there was a court official there ⁴⁷ whose son was ill at Capernaum ·and, hearing that Jesus had arrived in Galilee from Judaea, he went and asked him to come and cure his son as he was at the point of ⁴⁸ death. ·Jesus said, "So you will not believe unless you see ⁴⁹ signs and portents!" ·"Sir," answered the official "come ⁵⁰ down before my child dies." ·"Go home," said Jesus "your son will live." The man believed what Jesus had said ⁵¹ and started on his way; ·and while he was still on the journey back his servants met him with the news that his boy ⁵² was alive. ·He asked them when the boy had begun to recover. "The fever left him yesterday" they said "at the ⁵³ seventh hour." ·The father realized that this was exactly the time when Jesus had said, "Your son will live"; and he and all his household believed.

⁵⁴ This was the second sign given by Jesus, on his return from Judaea to Galilee.

III. THE SECOND FEAST AT JERUSALEM

The cure of a sick man at the Pool of Bethzatha

¹ ² **5** Some time after this there was a Jewish festival, and Jesus went up to Jerusalem. ·Now at the Sheep Pool in Jerusalem there is a building, called Bethzatha in He-³ brew, consisting of five porticos; ·and under these were crowds of sick people—blind, lame, paralyzed—waiting for ⁴ the water to move; ·for at intervals the angel of the Lord came down into the pool, and the water was disturbed, and the first person to enter the water after this disturbance ⁵ was cured of any ailment he suffered from. ·One man there had an illness which had lasted thirty-eight years, ⁶ and when Jesus saw him lying there and knew he had been in this condition for a long time, he said, "Do you

⁷ want to be well again?" ·"Sir," replied the sick man "I
have no one to put me into the pool when the water is disturbed; and while I am still on the way, someone else gets
⁸ there before me." ·Jesus said, "Get up, pick up your
⁹ sleeping-mat and walk." ·The man was cured at once, and
he picked up his mat and walked away.

¹⁰ Now that day happened to be the sabbath, ·so the
Jews said to the man who had been cured, "It is the sabbath; you are not allowed to carry your sleeping-mat."
¹¹ He replied, "But the man who cured me told me, 'Pick
¹² up your mat and walk.'" ·They asked, "Who is the man
¹³ who said to you, 'Pick up your mat and walk?'" ·The
man had no idea who it was, since Jesus had disappeared
¹⁴ into the crowd that filled the place. ·After a while Jesus
met him in the Temple and said, "Now you are well again,
be sure not to sin any more, or something worse may
¹⁵ happen to you." ·The man went back and told the Jews
¹⁶ that it was Jesus who had cured him. ·It was because he
did things like this on the sabbath that the Jews began to
¹⁷ persecute Jesus. ·His answer to them was, "My Father
¹⁸ goes on working, and so do I." ·But that only made the
Jews even more intent on killing him, because, not content
with breaking the sabbath, he spoke of God as his own
Father, and so made himself God's equal. .

¹⁹ To this accusation Jesus replied:

"I tell you most solemnly,
the Son can do nothing by himself;
he can do only what he sees the Father doing:
and whatever the Father does the Son does too.
²⁰ For the Father loves the Son
and shows him everything he does himself,
and he will show him even greater things than these,
works that will astonish you.
²¹ Thus, as the Father raises the dead and gives them life,
so the Son gives life to anyone he chooses;
²² for the Father judges no one;
he has entrusted all judgment to the Son,
²³ so that all may honor the Son
as they honor the Father.
Whoever refuses honor to the Son
refuses honor to the Father who sent him.
²⁴ I tell you most solemnly,
whoever listens to my words,

and believes in the one who sent me,
has eternal life;
without being brought to judgment
he has passed from death to life.
²⁵ I tell you most solemnly,
the hour will come—in fact it is here already—
when the dead will hear the voice of the Son of God,
and all who hear it will live.
²⁶ For the Father, who is the source of life,
has made the Son the source of life;
²⁷ and, because he is the Son of Man,
has appointed him supreme judge.
²⁸ Do not be surprised at this,
for the hour is coming
when the dead will leave their graves
at the sound of his voice:
²⁹ those who did good
will rise again to life;
and those who did evil, to condemnation.
³⁰ I can do nothing by myself;
I can only judge as I am told to judge,
and my judging is just,
because my aim is to do not my own will,
but the will of him who sent me.

³¹ "Were I to testify on my own behalf,
my testimony would not be valid;
³² but there is another witness who can speak on my behalf,
and I know that his testimony is valid.
³³ You sent messengers to John,
and he gave his testimony to the truth:
³⁴ not that I depend on human testimony;
no, it is for your salvation that I speak of this.
³⁵ John was a lamp alight and shining
and for a time you were content to enjoy the light that he
gave.
³⁶ But my testimony is greater than John's:
the works my Father has given me to carry out,
these same works of mine
testify that the Father has sent me.
³⁷ Besides, the Father who sent me
bears witness to me himself.
You have never heard his voice,
you have never seen his shape,

38 and his word finds no home in you
    because you do not believe
    in the one he has sent.

39 "You study the scriptures,
    believing that in them you have eternal life;
    now these same scriptures testify to me,
40 and yet you refuse to come to me for life!
41 As for human approval, this means nothing to me.
42 Besides, I know you too well:
    you have no love of God in you.
43 I have come in the name of my Father
    and you refuse to accept me;
    if someone else comes in his own name
    you will accept him.

44 How can you believe,
    since you look to one another for approval
    and are not concerned
    with the approval that comes from the one God?
45 Do not imagine that I am going to accuse you before the
         Father:
    you place your hopes on Moses,
    and Moses will be your accuser.
46 If you really believed him
    you would believe me too,
    since it was I that he was writing about;
47 but if you refuse to believe what he wrote,
    how can you believe what I say?"

IV. ANOTHER PASSOVER, THE BREAD OF LIFE

The miracle of the loaves

1 Some time after this, Jesus went off to the other side of
2 the Sea of Galilee—or of Tiberias—and a large crowd
followed him, impressed by the signs he gave by curing
3 the sick. •Jesus climbed the hillside, and sat down there
4 with his disciples. •It was shortly before the Jewish feast
of Passover.
5   Looking up, Jesus saw the crowds approaching and said
to Philip, "Where can we buy some bread for these people
6 to eat?" •He only said this to test Philip; he himself knew

⁷ exactly what he was going to do. ·Philip answered, "Two
hundred denarii would only buy enough to give them a
⁸ small piece each." ·One of his disciples, Andrew, Simon
⁹ Peter's brother, said, ·"There is a small boy here with five
barley loaves and two fish; but what is that between so
¹⁰ many?" ·Jesus said to them, "Make the people sit down."
There was plenty of grass there, and as many as five thou-
¹¹ sand men sat down. ·Then Jesus took the loaves, gave
thanks, and gave them out to all who were sitting ready;
he then did the same with the fish, giving out as much as
¹² was wanted. ·When they had eaten enough he said to the
disciples, "Pick up the pieces left over, so that nothing gets
¹³ wasted." ·So they picked them up, and filled twelve ham-
pers with scraps left over from the meal of five barley
¹⁴ loaves. ·The people, seeing this sign that he had given,
said, "This really is the prophet who is to come into the
¹⁵ world." ·Jesus, who could see they were about to come
and take him by force and make him king, escaped back
to the hills by himself.

Jesus walks on the waters

¹⁶ That evening the disciples went down to the shore of
¹⁷ the lake and ·got into a boat to make for Capernaum on
the other side of the lake. It was getting dark by now and
¹⁸ Jesus had still not rejoined them. ·The wind was strong,
¹⁹ and the sea was getting rough. ·They had rowed three or
four miles when they saw Jesus walking on the lake and
²⁰ coming towards the boat. This frightened them, ·but he
²¹ said, "It is I. Do not be afraid." ·They were for taking him
into the boat, but in no time it reached the shore at the
place they were making for.

The discourse in the synagogue at Capernaum

²² Next day, the crowd that had stayed on the other side
saw that only one boat had been there, and that Jesus
had not got into the boat with his disciples, but that the
²³ disciples had set off by themselves. ·Other boats, however,
had put in from Tiberias, near the place where the bread
²⁴ had been eaten. ·When the people saw that neither Jesus
nor his disciples were there, they got into those boats and
²⁵ crossed to Capernaum to look for Jesus. ·When they found
him on the other side, they said to him, "Rabbi, when did
²⁶ you come here?" ·Jesus answered:

"I tell you most solemnly,
you are not looking for me
because you have seen the signs
but because you had all the bread you wanted to eat.
27 Do not work for food that cannot last,
but work for food that endures to eternal life,
the kind of food the Son of Man is offering you,
for on him the Father, God himself, has set his seal."

28 Then they said to him, "What must we do if we are to
29 do the works that God wants?" ·Jesus gave them this answer, "This is working for God: you must believe in the
30 one he has sent." ·So they said, "What sign will you give
to show us that we should believe in you? What work will
31 you do? ·Our fathers had manna to eat in the desert; as
scripture says: *He gave them bread from heaven to eat.*ᵃ
32 Jesus answered:

"I tell you most solemnly,
it was not Moses who gave you bread from heaven,
it is my Father who gives you the bread from heaven,
the true bread;
33 for the bread of God
is that which comes down from heaven
and gives life to the world."

34 "Sir," they said "give us that bread always." ·Jesus an-
35 swered:

"I am the bread of life.
He who comes to me will never be hungry;
he who believes in me will never thirst.
36 But, as I have told you,
you can see me and still you do not believe.
37 All that the Father gives me will come to me,
and whoever comes to me
I shall not turn him away;
38 because I have come from heaven,
not to do my own will,
but to do the will of the one who sent me.
39 Now the will of him who sent me
is that I should lose nothing
of all that he has given to me,
and that I should raise it up on the last day.

6 a. Ex 16:4f

40　　　　Yes, it is my Father's will
　　　　　that whoever sees the Son and believes in him
　　　　　shall have eternal life,
　　　　　and that I shall raise him up on the last day."

41　　Meanwhile the Jews were complaining to each other
about him, because he had said, "I am the bread that came
42 down from heaven." ·"Surely this is Jesus son of Joseph"
they said. "We know his father and mother. How can he
43 now say, 'I have come down from heaven'?" ·Jesus said
in reply, "Stop complaining to each other.

44 "No one can come to me
　　unless he is drawn by the Father who sent me,
　　and I will raise him up at the last day.
45 It is written in the prophets:
　　They will all be taught by God,[b]
　　and to hear the teaching of the Father,
　　and learn from it,
　　is to come to me.
46 Not that anybody has seen the Father,
　　except the one who comes from God:
　　he has seen the Father.
47 I tell you most solemnly,
　　everybody who believes has eternal life.
48 I am the bread of life.
49 Your fathers ate the manna in the desert
　　and they are dead;
50 but this is the bread that comes down from heaven,
　　so that a man may eat it and not die.
51 I am the living bread which has come down from heaven.
　　Anyone who eats this bread will live for ever;
　　and the bread that I shall give
　　is my flesh, for the life of the world."

52　　Then the Jews started arguing with one another: "How
53 can this man give us his flesh to eat?" they said. ·Jesus
replied:

　　　　"I tell you most solemnly,
　　　　if you do not eat the flesh of the Son of Man
　　　　and drink his blood,
　　　　you will not have life in you.
54　　　Anyone who does eat my flesh and drink my blood
　　　　has eternal life,
　　　　and I shall raise him up on the last day.

55   For my flesh is real food
     and my blood is real drink.
56   He who eats my flesh and drinks my blood
     lives in me
     and I live in him.
57   As I, who am sent by the living Father,
     myself draw life from the Father,
     so whoever eats me will draw life from me.
58   This is the bread come down from heaven;
     not like the bread our ancestors ate:
     they are dead,
     but anyone who eats this bread will live for ever."

59   He taught this doctrine at Capernaum, in the synagogue.
60 After hearing it, many of his followers said, "This is in-
61 tolerable language. How could anyone accept it?" ·Jesus
was aware that his followers were complaining about it
62 and said, "Does this upset you? ·What if you should see
the Son of Man ascend to where he was before?

63   "It is the spirit that gives life,
        the flesh has nothing to offer.
        The words I have spoken to you are spirit
        and they are life.

64   "But there are some of you who do not believe." For
Jesus knew from the outset those who did not believe, and
65 who it was that would betray him. ·He went on, "This is
why I told you that no one could come to me unless the
66 Father allows him." ·After this, many of his disciples left
him and stopped going with him.

Peter's profession of faith

67   Then Jesus said to the Twelve, "What about you, do
68 you want to go away too?" ·Simon Peter answered,
"Lord, who shall we go to? You have the message of eter-
69 nal life, ·and we believe; we know that you are the Holy
70 One of God." ·Jesus replied, "Have I not chosen you, you
71 Twelve? Yet one of you is a devil." ·He meant Judas son
of Simon Iscariot, since this was the man, one of the
Twelve, who was going to betray him.

b. Is 54:13

V. THE FEAST OF TABERNACLES

Jesus goes up to Jerusalem for the feast and teaches there

¹ 7 After this Jesus stayed in Galilee; he could not stay in Judaea, because the Jews were out to kill him.
²³ As the Jewish feast of Tabernacles drew near, ·his brothers*ᵃ* said to him, "Why not leave this place and go to Judaea, and let your disciples*ᵇ* see the works you are
⁴ doing; ·if a man wants to be known he does not do things in secret; since you are doing all this, you should let the
⁵ whole world see." ·Not even his brothers, in fact, had faith
⁶ in him. ·Jesus answered, "The right time for me has not
⁷ come yet, but any time is the right time for you. ·The world cannot hate you, but it does hate me, because I give
⁸ evidence that its ways are evil. ·Go up to the festival yourselves: I am not going to this festival, because for me the
⁹ time is not ripe yet." ·Having said that, he stayed behind in Galilee.
¹⁰ However, after his brothers had left for the festival, he went up as well, but quite privately, without drawing atten-
¹¹ tion to himself. ·At the festival the Jews were on the
¹² look-out for him: "Where is he?" they said. ·People stood in groups whispering*ᶜ* about him. Some said, "He is a good
¹³ man"; others, "No, he is leading the people astray." ·Yet no one spoke about him openly, for fear of the Jews.
¹⁴ When the festival was half over, Jesus went to the Temple
¹⁵ and began to teach. ·The Jews were astonished and said, "How did he learn to read? He has not been taught."
¹⁶ Jesus answered them:

"My teaching is not from myself:
it comes from the one who sent me;
¹⁷ and if anyone is prepared to do his will,
he will know whether my teaching is from God
or whether my doctrine is my own.
¹⁸ When a man's doctrine is his own
he is hoping to get honor for himself;
but when he is working for the honor of one who sent
    him,
then he is sincere
and by no means an impostor.
¹⁹ Did not Moses give you the Law?

And yet not one of you keeps the Law!

20 "Why do you want to kill me?" ·The crowd replied, "You
21 are mad! Who wants to kill you?" ·Jesus answered, "One
22 work I did, and you are all surprised by it. ·Moses ordered
you to practice circumcision—not that it began with him,
it goes back to the patriarchs—and you circumcise on the
23 sabbath. ·Now if a man can be circumcised on the sabbath so that the Law of Moses is not broken, why are you
angry with me for making a man whole and complete
24 on the sabbath? ·Do not keep judging according to ap-
pearances; let your judgment be according to what is
right."

The people discuss the origin of the Messiah

25   Meanwhile some of the people of Jerusalem were saying,
26 "Isn't this the man they want to kill? ·And here he is,
speaking freely, and they have nothing to say to him! Can
it be true the authorities have made up their minds that he
27 is the Christ? ·Yet we all know where he comes from, but
when the Christ appears no one will know where he comes
from."*d*

28   Then, as Jesus taught in the Temple, he cried out:

"Yes, you know me and you know where I came from.
Yet I have not come of myself:
no, there is one who sent me and I really come from him,
and you do not know him,
29 but I know him
because I have come from him
and it was he who sent me."

30   They would have arrested him then, but because his
time had not yet come no one laid a hand on him.

Jesus foretells his approaching departure

31   There were many people in the crowds, however, who
believed in him; they were saying, "When the Christ

7 a. In the wide sense, as in Mt 12:46: relations of his own
generation. **b.** Those in Jerusalem and Judaea. **c.** Or "In
the crowds there was whispering about him." **d.** Although
the prophecy that the Messiah would be born in Bethlehem
was well known, it was commonly believed that he would
appear suddenly from some secret place.

[32] comes, will he give more signs than this man?" ·Hearing that rumors like this about him were spreading among the people, the Pharisees sent the Temple police to arrest him.
[33]   Then Jesus said:

> "I shall remain with you for only a short time now;
> then I shall go back to the one who sent me.
[34]   You will look for me and will not find me:
> where I am
> you cannot come."

[35]   The Jews then said to one another, "Where is he going that we shan't be able to find him? Is he going abroad to the people who are dispersed among the Greeks and will [36] he teach the Greeks? ·What does he mean when he says:

> 'You will look for me and will not find me:
> where I am,
> you cannot come?' "

The promise of living water

[37]   On the last day and greatest day of the festival, Jesus stood there and cried out:

> "If any man is thirsty, let him come to me!
[38]   Let the man come and drink ·who believes in me!"

As scripture says: From his breast shall flow fountains of living water.*
[39]   He was speaking of the Spirit which those who believed in him were to receive; for there was no Spirit as yet because Jesus had not yet been glorified.

Fresh discussions on the origin of the Messiah

[40]   Several people who had been listening said, "Surely he [41] must be the prophet," ·and some said, "He is the Christ," [42] but others said, "Would the Christ be from Galilee? ·Does not scripture say that the Christ must be descended from [43] David and come from the town of Bethlehem?" ·So the [44] people could not agree about him. ·Some would have liked to arrest him, but no one actually laid hands on him.
[45]   The police went back to the chief priests and Pharisees who said to them, "Why haven't you brought him?" [46] The police replied, "There has never been anybody who [47] has spoken like him." ·"So" the Pharisees answered "you

48 have been led astray as well? ·Have any of the authorities
49 believed in him? Any of the Pharisees? ·This rabble knows
50 nothing about the Law—they are damned." ·One of them,
Nicodemus—the same man who had come to Jesus earlier
51 —said to them, ·"But surely the Law does not allow us to
pass judgment on a man without giving him a hearing
52 and discovering what he is about?" ·To this they answered,
"Are you a Galilean too? Go into the matter, and see for
yourself: prophets do not come out of Galilee."

The adulterous woman*f*

53
1   They all went home, 8 and Jesus went to the Mount of
Olives.

2   At daybreak he appeared in the Temple again; and as
all the people came to him, he sat down and began to teach
them.

3   The scribes and Pharisees brought a woman along who
had been caught committing adultery; and making her
4 stand there in full view of everybody, ·they said to Jesus,
"Master, this woman was caught in the very act of com-
5 mitting adultery, ·and Moses has ordered us in the Law
to condemn women like this to death by stoning. What
6 have you to say?" ·They asked him this as a test, looking
for something to use against him. But Jesus bent down
7 and started writing on the ground with his finger. ·As they
persisted with their question, he looked up and said, "If
there is one of you who has not sinned, let him be the first
8 to throw a stone at her." ·Then he bent down and wrote
9 on the ground again. ·When they heard this they went
away one by one, beginning with the eldest, until Jesus was
left alone with the woman, who remained standing there.
10 He looked up and said, "Woman, where are they? Has
11 no one condemned you?" ·"No one, sir" she replied.
"Neither do I condemn you," said Jesus "go away, and
don't sin any more."

e. Life-giving water for Zion was a theme of the readings from
scripture on the feast of Tabernacles (Zc 14:8, Ezk 47:1f);
the liturgy included prayers for rain and the commemoration
of the miracle of Moses and the water, Ex 17.   f. The author
of this passage, 7:53-8:11, is not John; the oldest MSS do
not include it or place it elsewhere. The style is that of the
Synoptics.

Jesus, the light of the world

12   When Jesus spoke to the people again, he said:

"I am the light of the world;
anyone who follows me will not be walking in the dark;
he will have the light of life."

A discussion on the testimony of Jesus to himself

13   At this the Pharisees said to him, "You are testifying on
14 your own behalf; your testimony is not valid." ·Jesus replied:

"It is true that I am testifying on my own behalf,
but my testimony is still valid,
because I know
where I came from and where I am going;
but you do not know
where I come from or where I am going.
15   You judge by human standards;
I judge no one,
16   but if I judge,
my judgment will be sound,
because I am not alone:
the one who sent me is with me;
17   and in your Law it is written
that the testimony of two witnesses is valid.
18   I may be testifying on my own behalf,
but the Father who sent me is my witness too."

19   They asked him, "Where is your Father?" Jesus answered:

"You do not know me, nor do you know my Father;
if you did know me, you would know my Father as well."

20   He spoke these words in the Treasury, while teaching
in the Temple. No one arrested him, because his time had
not yet come.

The unbelieving Jews warned

21   Again he said to them:

"I am going away; you will look for me
and you will die in your sin.
Where I am going, you cannot come."

22   The Jews said to one another, "Will he kill himself? Is

that what he means by saying, 'Where I am going, you
23 cannot come'?" ·Jesus went on:

> "You are from below;
> I am from above.
> You are of this world;
> I am not of this world.
24   I have told you already: You will die in your sins.
> Yes, if you do not believe that I am He,
> you will die in your sins."

25 So they said to him, "Who are you?" Jesus answered:

> "What I have told you from the outset.
26   About you I have much to say
> and much to condemn;
> but the one who sent me is truthful,
> and what I have learned from him
> I declared to the world."

27 They failed to understand that he was talking to them
28 about the Father. ·So Jesus said:

> "When you have lifted up the Son of Man,
> then you will know that I am He
> and that I do nothing of myself:
> what the Father has taught me
> is what I preach;
29   he who sent me is with me,
> and has not left me to myself,
> for I always do what pleases him."

30 As he was saying this, many came to believe in him.

Jesus and Abraham

31 To the Jews who believed in him Jesus said:

> "If you make my word your home
> you will indeed be my disciples,
32   you will learn the truth
> and the truth will make you free.'"

33 They answered, "We are descended from Abraham and
we have never been the slaves of anyone; what do you
34 mean, 'You will be made free'?" ·Jesus replied:

> "I tell you most solemnly,
> everyone who commits sin is a slave.

35   Now the slave's place in the house is not assured,
      but the son's place is assured.
36   So if the Son makes you free,
      you will be free indeed.
37   I know that you are descended from Abraham;
      but in spite of that you want to kill me
      because nothing I say has penetrated into you.
38   What I, for my part, speak of
      is what I have seen with my Father;
      but you, you put into action
      the lessons learned from your father."

39   They repeated, "Our father is Abraham." Jesus said to
them:

      "If you were Abraham's children,
      you would do as Abraham did.
40   As it is, you want to kill me
      when I tell you the truth
      as I have learned it from God;
      that is not what Abraham did.
41   What you are doing is what your father does."

     "We were not born of prostitution,"[a] they went on "we
42 have one father: God." Jesus answered:

"If God were your father, you would love me,
since I have come here from God; yes, I have come from
        him;
not that I came because I chose,
no, I was sent, and by him.
43 Do you know why you cannot take in what I say?
It is because you are unable to understand my language.
44 The devil is your father,
and you prefer to do
what your father wants.

He was a murderer from the start;
he was never grounded in the truth;
there is no truth in him at all:
when he lies
he is drawing on his own store,
because he is a liar, and the father of lies.
45 But as for me, I speak the truth
and for that very reason,
you do not believe me.

46 Can one of you convict me of sin?
If I speak the truth, why do you not believe me?
47 A child of God
· listens to the words of God;
if you refuse to listen,
it is because you are not God's children."

48   The Jews replied, "Are we not right in saying that you
are a Samaritan and possessed by a devil?" Jesus answered:

49 "I am not possessed;
no, I honor my Father,
but you want to dishonor me.
50 Not that I care for my own glory,
there is someone who takes care of that and is the judge
of it.
51 I tell you most solemnly,
whoever keeps my word
will never see death."

52   The Jews said, "Now we know for certain that you are
possessed. Abraham is dead, and the prophets are dead,
and yet you say, 'Whoever keeps my word will never know
53 the taste of death.' ·Are you greater than our father Abraham, who is dead? The prophets are dead too. Who are
54 you claiming to be?" ·Jesus answered:

"If I were to seek my own glory
that would be no glory at all;
my glory is conferred by the Father,
by the one of whom you say, 'He is our God'
55 although you do not know him.
But I know him,
and if I were to say: I do not know him,
I should be a liar, as you are liars yourselves.
But I do know him, and I faithfully keep his word.
56 Your father Abraham rejoiced
to think that he would see my Day;
he saw it and was glad."

57   The Jews then said, "You are not fifty yet, and you have
58 seen Abraham!" ·Jesus replied:

8 a. By "prostitution" the prophets often mean religious in-
fidelity, cf. Ho 1:2.

> "I tell you most solemnly,
> before Abraham ever was,
> I Am."

⁵⁹ At this they picked up stones to throw at him;ᵇ but Jesus hid himself and left the Temple.

The cure of the man born blind

¹ ⁹ As he went along, he saw a man who had been blind ² from birth. ·His disciples asked him, "Rabbi, who sinned, this man or his parents, for him to have been born ³ blind?" ·"Neither he nor his parents sinned," Jesus answered "he was born blind so that the works of God might be displayed in him.

⁴ "As long as the day lasts
I must carry out the work of the one who sent me;
the night will soon be here when no one can work.
⁵ As long as I am in the world
I am the light of the world."

⁶ Having said this, he spat on the ground, made a paste with the spittle, put this over the eyes of the blind man, ⁷ and said to him, "Go and wash in the Pool of Siloam"ᵃ (a name that means "sent"). So the blind man went off and washed himself, and came away with his sight restored.
⁸ His neighbors and people who earlier had seen him begging said, "Isn't this the man who used to sit and beg?" ⁹ Some said, "Yes, it is the same one." Others said, "No, he only looks like him." The man himself said, "I am the ¹⁰ man." ·So they said to him, "Then how do your eyes come ¹¹ to be open?" ·"The man called Jesus" he answered "made a paste, daubed my eyes with it and said to me, 'Go and wash at Siloam;' so I went, and when I washed I could see." ¹² They asked, "Where is he?" "I don't know" he answered.
¹³ They brought the man who had been blind to the Phari-¹⁴ sees. ·It had been a sabbath day when Jesus made the ¹⁵ paste and opened the man's eyes, ·so when the Pharisees asked him how he had come to see, he said, "He put a ¹⁶ paste on my eyes, and I washed, and I can see." ·Then some of the Pharisees said, "This man cannot be from God: he does not keep the sabbath." Others said, "How could a sinner produce signs like this?" And there was ¹⁷ disagreement among them. ·So they spoke to the blind man again, "What have you to say about him yourself, now

that he has opened your eyes?" "He is a prophet" replied the man.

18 However, the Jews would not believe that the man had been blind and had gained his sight, without first sending 19 for his parents and ·asking them, "Is this man really your son who you say was born blind? If so, how is it that he 20 is now able to see?" ·His parents answered, "We know he 21 is our son and we know he was born blind, ·but we don't know how it is that he can see now, or who opened his eyes. He is old enough: let him speak for himself." 22 His parents spoke like this out of fear of the Jews, who had already agreed to expell from the synagogue anyone 23 who should acknowledge Jesus as the Christ. ·This was why his parents said, "He is old enough; ask him."

24 So the Jews again sent for the man and said to him, "Give glory to God![b] For our part, we know that this man 25 is a sinner." ·The man answered, "I don't know if he is a sinner; I only know that I was blind and now I can see." 26 They said to him, "What did he do to you? How did he 27 open your eyes?" ·He replied, "I have told you once and you wouldn't listen. Why do you want to hear it all again? 28 Do you want to become his disciples too?" ·At this they hurled abuse at him: "You can be his disciple," they said 29 "we are disciples of Moses: ·we know that God spoke to Moses, but as for this man, we don't know where he comes 30 from." ·The man replied, "Now here is an astonishing thing! He has opened my eyes, and you don't know where 31 he comes from! ·We know that God doesn't listen to sinners, but God does listen to men who are devout and do his 32 will. ·Ever since the world began it is unheard of for any- 33 one to open the eyes of a man who was born blind; ·if this 34 man were not from God, he couldn't do a thing." ·"Are you trying to teach us," they replied "and you a sinner through and through, since you were born!" And they drove him away.

35 Jesus heard they had driven him away, and when he found him he said to him, "Do you believe in the Son of 36 Man?" ·"Sir," the man replied "tell me who he is so that 37 I may believe in him." ·Jesus said, "You are looking at

b. Stoning was the penalty for blasphemy. Cf. 10:33.
9 a. Water from this pool was drawn during the feast of Tabernacles to symbolize the waters of blessing. b. I.e. putting the
man on oath.

³⁸ him: he is speaking to you." ·The man said, "Lord, I believe," and worshiped him.
³⁹ Jesus said:

> "It is for judgment
> that I have come into this world,
> so that those without sight may see
> and those with sight turn blind."

⁴⁰ Hearing this, some Pharisees who were present said to him,
⁴¹ "We are not blind, surely?" ·Jesus replied:

> "Blind? If you were,
> you would not be guilty,
> but since you say, 'We see,'
> your guilt remains.

The good shepherd

¹ **10** "I tell you most solemnly, anyone who does not enter the sheepfold through the gate, but gets in some
² other way is a thief and a brigand. ·The one who enters
³ through the gate is the shepherd of the flock; ·the gatekeeper lets him in, the sheep hear his voice, one by one
⁴ he calls his own sheep and leads them out. ·When he has brought out his flock, he goes ahead of them, and the
⁵ sheep follow because they know his voice. ·They never follow a stranger but run away from him: they do not recognize the voice of strangers."
⁶ Jesus told them^a this parable but they failed to understand what he meant by telling it to them.
⁷ So Jesus spoke to them again:

> "I tell you most solemnly,
> I am the gate of the sheepfold.
> ⁸ All others who have come
> are thieves and brigands;
> but the sheep took no notice of them.
> ⁹ I am the gate.
> Anyone who enters through me will be safe:
> he will go freely in and out
> and be sure of finding pasture.
> ¹⁰ The thief comes
> only to steal and kill and destroy.
> I have come
> so that they may have life
> and have it to the full.

11 I am the good shepherd:
   the good shepherd is one who lays down his life for his
            sheep.
12 The hired man, since he is not the shepherd
   and the sheep do not belong to him,
   abandons the sheep and runs away
   as soon as he sees a wolf coming,
   and then the wolf attacks and scatters the sheep;
13 this is because he is only a hired man
   and has no concern for the sheep.
14 I am the good shepherd;
   I know my own
   and my own know me,
15 just as the Father knows me
   and I know the Father;
   and I lay down my life for my sheep.
16 And there are other sheep I have
   that are not of this fold,
   and these I have to lead as well.
   They too will listen to my voice,
   and there will be only one flock,
   and one shepherd.
17 The Father loves me,
   because I lay down my life
   in order to take it up again.
18 No one takes it from me;
   I lay it down of my own free will,
   and as it is in my power to lay it down,
   so it is in my power to take it up again;
   and this is the command I have been given by my Father."

19   These words caused disagreement among the Jews.
20 Many said, "He is possessed, he is raving; why bother to
21 listen to him?" •Others said, "These are not the words of a
   man possessed by a devil: could a devil open the eyes of
   the blind?"

VI. THE FEAST OF DEDICATION

Jesus claims to be the Son of God

22   It was the time when the feast of Dedication was being
23 celebrated in Jerusalem. It was winter, •and Jesus was in

10 a. The Pharisees.

the Temple walking up and down in the Portico of Solo-
²⁴ mon. ·The Jews gathered round him and said, "How much
longer are you going to keep us in suspense? If you are
²⁵ the Christ, tell us plainly." ·Jesus replied:

"I have told you, but you do not believe.
The works I do in my Father's name are my witness;
²⁶ but you do not believe,
because you are no sheep of mine.
²⁷ The sheep that belong to me listen to my voice;
I know them and they follow me.
²⁸ I give them eternal life;
they will never be lost
and no one will ever steal them from me.
²⁹ The Father who gave them to me is greater than anyone,
and no one can steal from the Father.
³⁰ The Father and I are one."

³¹
³² The Jews fetched stones to stone him, ·so Jesus said
to them, "I have done many good works for you to see,
works from my Father; for which of these are you ston-
³³ ing me?" ·The Jews answered him, "We are not stoning
you for doing a good work but for blasphemy: you are
³⁴ only a man and you claim to be God." ·Jesus answered:

"Is it not written in your Law:
*I said, you are gods?*ᵇ
³⁵ So the Law uses the word gods
of those to whom the word of God was addressed,
and scripture cannot be rejected.
³⁶ Yet you say to someone the Father has consecrated and
sent into the world
'You are blaspheming,'
because he says, 'I am the Son of God.'
³⁷ If I am not doing my Father's work,
there is no need to believe me;
³⁸ but if I am doing it,
then even if you refuse to believe in me,
at least believe in the work I do;
then you will know for sure
that the Father is in me and I am in the Father."

³⁹ They wanted to arrest him then, but he eluded them.

Jesus withdraws to the other side of the Jordan

40   He went back again to the far side of the Jordan to stay
41 in the district where John had once been baptizing. ·Many
     people who came to him there said, "John gave no signs,
42 but all he said about this man was true"; ·and many of
     them believed in him.

The resurrection of Lazarus

1   There was a man named Lazarus who lived in the
    village of Bethany with the two sisters, Mary and
2 Martha, and he was ill.—·It was the same Mary, the sister
   of the sick man Lazarus, who anointed the Lord with
3 ointment and wiped his feet with her hair. ·The sisters
   sent this message to Jesus, "Lord, the man you love is ill."
4 On receiving the message, Jesus said, "This sickness will
   end not in death but in God's glory, and through it the Son
   of God will be glorified."

5   Jesus loved Martha and her sister and Lazarus, ·yet
6 when he heard that Lazarus was ill he stayed where he
7 was for two more days ·before saying to the disciples, "Let
8 us go to Judaea." ·The disciples said, "Rabbi, it is not long
   since the Jews wanted to stone you; are you going back
9 again?" ·Jesus replied:

    "Are there not twelve hours in the day?
     A man can walk in the daytime without stumbling
       because he has the light of this world to see by;
10   but if he walks at night he stumbles,
       because there is no light to guide him."

11   He said that and then added, "Our friend Lazarus is
12 resting, I am going to wake him." ·The disciples said to
   him, "Lord, if he is able to rest he is sure to get better."
13 The phrase Jesus used referred to the death of Lazarus,
14 but they thought that by "rest" he meant "sleep," so ·Jesus
15 put it plainly, "Lazarus is dead; ·and for your sake I am
   glad I was not there because now you will believe. But let
16 us go to him." ·Then Thomas—known as the Twin—said to
   the other disciples, "Let us go too, and die with him."
17   On arriving, Jesus found that Lazarus had been in the
18 tomb for four days already. ·Bethany is only about two
19 miles from Jerusalem, ·and many Jews had come to Martha

b. Ps 82:6

and Mary to sympathize with them over their brother.
20 When Martha heard that Jesus had come she went to meet
21 him. Mary remained sitting in the house. ·Martha said to
Jesus, "If you had been here, my brother would not have
22 died, ·but I know that, even now, whatever you ask of
23 God, he will grant you." ·"Your brother" said Jesus to her
24 "will rise again." ·Martha said, "I know he will rise again
25 at the resurrection on the last day." ·Jesus said:

"I am the resurrection.
If anyone believes in me, even though he dies he will live,
26 and whoever lives and believes in me
will never die.
Do you believe this?"

27 "Yes, Lord," she said "I believe that you are the Christ, the
Son of God, the one who was to come into this world."
28 When she had said this, she went and called her sister
Mary, saying in a low voice, "The Master is here and
29 wants to see you." ·Hearing this, Mary got up quickly and
30 went to him. ·Jesus had not yet come into the village; he
31 was still at the place where Martha had met him. ·When
the Jews who were in the house sympathizing with Mary
saw her get up so quickly and go out, they followed her,
thinking that she was going to the tomb to weep there.
32 Mary went to Jesus, and as soon as she saw him she
threw herself at his feet, saying, "Lord, if you had been
33 here, my brother would not have died." ·At the sight of her
tears, and those of the Jews who followed her, Jesus said
in great distress, with a sigh that came straight from the
34 heart, ·"Where have you put him?" They said, "Lord,
35 come and see." ·Jesus wept; ·and the Jews said, "See how
36
37 much he loved him!" ·But there were some who remarked,
"He opened the eyes of the blind man, could he not have
38 prevented this man's death?" ·Still sighing, Jesus reached
the tomb: it was a cave with a stone to close the opening.
39 Jesus said, "Take the stone away." Martha said to him,
40 "Lord, by now he will smell; this is the fourth day." ·Jesus
replied, "Have I not told you that if you believe you will
41 see the glory of God?" ·So they took away the stone. Then
Jesus lifted up his eyes and said:

"Father, I thank you for hearing my prayer.
42 I knew indeed that you always hear me,
but I speak

for the sake of all these who stand round me,
so that they may believe it was you who sent me."

43 When he had said this, he cried in a loud voice, "Lazarus,
44 here! Come out!" •The dead man came out, his feet and
hands bound with bands of stuff and a cloth round his
face. Jesus said to them, "Unbind him, let him go free."

The Jewish leaders decide on the death of Jesus

45 Many of the Jews who had come to visit Mary and had
46 seen what he did believed in him, •but some of them went
47 to tell the Pharisees what Jesus had done. •Then the chief
priests and Pharisees called a meeting. "Here is this man
working all these signs" they said "and what action are we
48 taking? •If we let him go on in this way everybody will
believe in him, and the Romans will come and destroy the
49 Holy Place and our nation." •One of them, Caiaphas, the
high priest that year, said, "You don't seem to have grasped
50 the situation at all; •you fail to see that it is better for one
man to die for the people, than for the whole nation to be
51 destroyed." •He did not speak in his own person, it was as
high priest that he made this prophecy that Jesus was to
52 die for the nation—and not for the nation only, but to
gather together in unity the scattered children of God.
53 From that day they were determined to kill him. •So
54 Jesus no longer went about openly among the Jews, but left
the district for a town called Ephraim, in the country bor-
dering on the desert, and stayed there with his disciples.

VII. THE LAST PASSOVER

A. BEFORE THE PASSION

The Passover draws near

55 The Jewish Passover drew near, and many of the country
people who had gone up to Jerusalem to purify themselves
56 looked out for Jesus, saying to one another as they stood
about in the Temple, "What do you think? Will he come to
57 the festival or not?" •The chief priests and Pharisees had
by now given their orders: anyone who knew where he
was must inform them so that they could arrest him.

The anointing at Bethany

1 **12** Six days before the Passover, Jesus went to Bethany, where Lazarus was, whom he had raised from the 2 dead. ·They gave a dinner for him there; Martha waited 3 on them and Lazarus was among those at table. ·Mary brought in a pound of very costly ointment, pure nard, and with it anointed the feet of Jesus, wiping them with her 4 hair; the house was full of the scent of the ointment. ·Then Judas Iscariot—one of his disciples, the man who was to 5 betray him—said, ·"Why wasn't this ointment sold for three 6 hundred denarii, and the money given to the poor?" ·He said this, not because he cared about the poor, but because he was a thief; he was in charge of the common fund and 7 used to help himself to the contributions. ·So Jesus said, "Leave her alone; she had to keep this scent for the day of 8 my burial. ·You have the poor with you always, you will not always have me."

9 Meanwhile a large number of Jews heard that he was there and came not only on account of Jesus but also to 10 see Lazarus whom he had raised from the dead. ·Then the 11 chief priests decided to kill Lazarus as well, ·since it was on his account that many of the Jews were leaving them and believing in Jesus.

The Messiah enters Jerusalem

12 The next day the crowds who had come up for the festi-
13 val heard that Jesus was on his way to Jerusalem. ·They took branches of palm and went out to meet him, shouting, *"Hosanna! Blessings on* the King of Israel, *who comes*
14 *in the name of the Lord."[a]* ·Jesus found a young donkey
15 and mounted it—as scripture says: ·*Do not be afraid, daughter of Zion; see, your king is coming, mounted on the colt*
16 *of a donkey.[b]* ·At the time his disciples did not understand this, but later, after Jesus had been glorified, they remembered that this had been written about him and that this
17 was in fact how they had received him. ·All who had been with him when he called Lazarus out of the tomb and raised him from the dead were telling how they had wit-
18 nessed it; ·it was because of this, too, that the crowd came out to meet him: they had heard that he had given this
19 sign. ·Then the Pharisees said to one another, "You see, there is nothing you can do; look, the whole world is running after him!"

Jesus foretells his death and subsequent glorification

20 Among those who went up to worship at the festival
21 were some Greeks.*ᵒ* ·These approached Philip, who came
from Bethsaida in Galilee, and put this request to him,
22 "Sir, we should like to see Jesus." ·Philip went to tell Andrew, and Andrew and Philip together went to tell Jesus.
23 Jesus replied to them:

"Now the hour has come
for the Son of Man to be glorified.
24 I tell you, most solemnly,
unless a wheat grain falls on the ground and dies,
it remains only a single grain;
but if it dies,
it yields a rich harvest.
25 Anyone who loves his life loses it;
anyone who hates his life in this world
will keep it for the eternal life.
26 If a man serves me, he must follow me,
wherever I am, my servant will be there too.
If anyone serves me, my Father will honor him.
27 Now my soul is troubled.
What shall I say:
Father, save me from this hour?
But it was for this very reason that I have come to this hour.
28 Father, glorify your name!"

A voice came from heaven, "I have glorified it, and I will
glorify it again."
29 People standing by, who heard this, said it was a clap of
thunder; others said, "It was an angel speaking to him."
30 Jesus answered, 'It was not for my sake that this voice
came, but for yours.

31 "Now sentence is being passed on this world;
now the prince of this world is to be overthrown.*ᵈ*
32 And when I am lifted up from the earth,
I shall draw all men to myself."

33 By these words he indicated the kind of death he would
34 die. ·The crowd answered, "The Law has taught us that the
Christ will remain for ever. How can you say, 'The Son

12 a. Ps 118:26. b. Zc 9:9f c. The "God-fearing men" of
Ac 10:2: converts who observed certain specific Mosaic observances. d. Satan.

of Man must be lifted up?' Who is this Son of Man?"
³⁵ Jesus then said:

"The light will be with you only a little longer now.
Walk while you have the light,
or the dark will overtake you;
he who walks in the dark does not know where he is going.
³⁶ While you still have the light,
believe in the light
and you will become sons of light."

Having said this, Jesus left them and kept himself hidden.

Conclusion: the unbelief of the Jews

³⁷   Though they had been present when he gave so many
³⁸ signs, they did not believe in him; ·this was to fulfill the
words of the prophet Isaiah: *Lord, who could believe
what we have heard said, and to whom has the power of*
³⁹ *the Lord been revealed?*ᵉ ·Indeed, they were unable to
⁴⁰ believe because, as Isaiah says again: ·*He has blinded their
eyes, he has hardened their heart, for fear they should see
with their eyes and understand with their heart, and turn to
me for healing.*ᶠ
⁴¹   Isaiah said this when he saw his glory,ᵍ and his words
referred to Jesus.
⁴²   · And yet there were many who did believe in him, even
among the leading men, but they did not admit it, through
fear of the Pharisees and fear of being expelled from the
⁴³ synagogue: ·they put honor from men before the honor
that comes from God.
⁴⁴   Jesus declared publicly:

"Whoever believes in me
believes not in me
but in the one who sent me,
⁴⁵ and whoever sees me,
sees the one who sent me.
⁴⁶ I, the light, have come into the world,
so that whoever believes in me
need not stay in the dark any more.
⁴⁷ If anyone hears my words and does not keep them
        faithfully,
it is not I who shall condemn him,
since I have come not to condemn the world,
but to save the world:

48 he who rejects me and refuses my words
has his judge already:
the word itself that I have spoken
will be his judge on the last day.
49 For what I have spoken does not come from myself;
no, what I was to say, what I had to speak,
was commanded by the Father who sent me,
50 and I know that his commands mean eternal life.
And therefore what the Father has told me
is what I speak."

B. THE LAST SUPPER

Jesus washes his disciples' feet

13 ¹ It was before the festival of the Passover, and Jesus knew that the hour had come for him to pass from this world to the Father. He had always loved those who were his in the world, but now he showed how perfect his love was.
² They were at supper, and the devil had already put it into the mind of Judas Iscariot son of Simon, to betray ³ him. ·Jesus knew that the Father had put everything into his hands, and that he had come from God and was return-⁴ing to God, ·and he got up from table, removed his outer garment and, taking a towel, wrapped it round his waist; ⁵ he then poured water into a basin and began to wash the disciples' feet[a] and to wipe them with the towel he was wearing.
⁶ He came to Simon Peter, who said to him, "Lord, are ⁷ you going to wash my feet?" ·Jesus answered, "At the moment you do not know what I am doing, but later you ⁸ will understand." ·"Never!" said Peter "You shall never wash my feet." Jesus replied, "If I do not wash you, you ⁹ can have nothing in common with me." ·"Then, Lord," said Simon Peter "not only my feet, but my hands and my ¹⁰ head as well!" ·Jesus said, "No one who has taken a bath needs washing, he is clean all over. You too are clean, ¹¹ though not all of you are." ·He knew who was going to betray him, that was why he said, "though not all of you are."

e. Is 53:1 f. Is 6:9f g. Isaiah's vision in the Temple, Is 6:4, interpreted as a prophetic vision of Christ's glory.
13 a. The dress and the duty are those of a slave.

12 When he had washed their feet and put on his clothes
again he went back to the table. "Do you understand" he
13 said "what I have done to you? ·You call me Master and
14 Lord, and rightly; so I am. ·If I, then, the Lord and Master, have washed your feet, you should wash each other's
15 feet. ·I have given you an example so that you may copy
what I have done to you.

16 "I tell you most solemnly,
no servant is greater than his master,
no messenger is greater than the man who sent him.

17 "Now that you know this, happiness will be yours if you
18 behave accordingly. ·I am not speaking about all of you: I
know the ones I have chosen; but what scripture says
must be fulfilled: *Someone who shares my table rebels
against me.*[b]

19 "I tell you this now, before it happens,
so that when it does happen
you may believe that I am He.
20 I tell you most solemnly,
whoever welcomes the one I send welcomes me,
and whoever welcomes me welcomes the one who sent me."

The treachery of Judas foretold

21 Having said this, Jesus was troubled in spirit and declared, "I tell you most solemnly, one of you will betray
22 me." ·The disciples looked at one another, wondering which
23 he meant. ·The disciple Jesus loved was reclining next to
24 Jesus; ·Simon Peter signed to him and said, "Ask who it
25 is he means," ·so leaning back on Jesus' breast he said,
26 "Who is it, Lord?" ·"It is the one" replied Jesus "to whom
I give the piece of bread that I shall dip in the dish." He
dipped the piece of bread and gave it to Judas son of Simon
27 Iscariot. ·At that instant, after Judas had taken the bread,
Satan entered him. Jesus then said, "What you are going
28 to do, do quickly." ·None of the others at table understood
29 the reason he said this. ·Since Judas had charge of the common fund, some of them thought Jesus was telling him,
"Buy what we need for the festival," or telling him to give
30 something to the poor. ·As soon as Judas had taken the
piece of bread he went out. Night had fallen.

³¹ When he had gone Jesus said:

"Now has the Son of Man been glorified,
and in him God has been glorified.
³² If God has been glorified in him,
God will in turn glorify him in himself,^c
and will glorify him very soon.

Farewell discourses

³³ "My little children,
I shall not be with you much longer.
You will look for me,
and, as I told the Jews,
where I am going,
you cannot come.
³⁴ I give you a new commandment:
love one another;
just as I have loved you,
you also must love one another.
³⁵ By this love you have for one another,
everyone will know that you are my disciples."

³⁶ Simon Peter said, "Lord, where are you going?" Jesus replied, "Where I am going you cannot follow me now; you ³⁷ will follow me later." ·Peter said to him, "Why can't I fol- ³⁸ low you now? I will lay down my life for you." ·"Lay down your life for me?" answered Jesus. "I tell you most solemnly, before the cock crows you will have disowned me three times.

¹ **14** "Do not let your hearts be troubled.
Trust in God still, and trust in me.
² There are many rooms in my Father's house;
if there were not, I should have told you.
I am going now to prepare a place for you,
³ and after I have gone and prepared you a place,
I shall return to take you with me;
so that where I am
you may be too.
⁴ You know the way to the place where I am going."

⁵ Thomas said, "Lord, we do not know where you are go- ⁶ ing, so how can we know the way?" ·Jesus said:

b. Ps 41:9 c. I.e. the Father will take the Son of Man to himself in glory.

"I am the Way, the Truth and the Life.
No one can come to the Father except through me.

7 If you know me, you know my Father too.
From this moment you know him and have seen him."

8 Philip said, "Lord, let us see the Father and then we shall
9 be satisfied." "Have I been with you all this time, Philip,"
said Jesus to him "and you still do not know me?

"To have seen me is to have seen the Father,
so how can you say, 'Let us see the Father'?

10 Do you not believe
that I am in the Father and the Father is in me?
The words I say to you I do not speak as from myself:
it is the Father, living in me, who is doing this work.

11 You must believe me when I say
that I am in the Father and the Father is in me;
believe it on the evidence of this work, if for no other
reason.

12 I tell you most solemnly,
whoever believes in me
will perform the same works as I do myself,
he will perform even greater works,
because I am going to the Father.

13 Whatever you ask for in my name I will do,
so that the Father may be glorified in the Son.

14 If you ask for anything in my name,
I will do it.

15 If you love me you will keep my commandments.

16 I shall ask the Father,
and he will give you another Advocate[a]
to be with you for ever,

17 that Spirit of truth
whom the world can never receive
since it neither sees nor knows him;
but you know him,
because he is with you, he is in you.

18 I will not leave you orphans;
I will come back to you.

19 In a short time the world will no longer see me;
but you will see me,
because I live and you will live.

20 On that day
you will understand that I am in my Father

and you in me and I in you.

21 Anybody who receives my commandments and keeps
them
will be one who loves me;
and anybody who loves me will be loved by my
Father,
and I shall love him and show myself to him."

22 Judas[b]—this was not Judas Iscariot—said to him, "Lord,
what is all this about? Do you intend to show yourself to
23 us and not to the world?" ·Jesus replied:

"If anyone loves me he will keep my word,
and my Father will love him,
and we shall come to him
and make our home with him.

24 Those who do not love me do not keep my words.
And my word is not my own:
it is the word of the one who sent me.

25 I have said these things to you
while still with you;

26 but the Advocate, the Holy Spirit,
whom the Father will send in my name,
will teach you everything
and remind you of all I have said to you.

27 Peace[c] I bequeath to you,
my own peace I give you,
a peace the world cannot give, this is my gift to you.
Do not let your hearts be troubled or afraid.

28 You heard me say:
I am going away, and shall return.
If you loved me you would have been glad to know
that I am going to the Father,
for the Father is greater than I.

29 I have told you this now before it happens,
so that when it does happen you may believe.

30 I shall not talk with you any longer,
because the prince of this world is on his way.
He has no power over me,

31 but the world must be brought to know that I love the
Father

14 a. Greek *parakletos*: advocate or counsellor or protector.
b. "Judas, brother of James" in Lk 6:16 and Ac 1:13; the Thaddaeus of Mt 10:3 and Mk 3:18. c. The customary Jewish
farewell.

and that I am doing exactly what the Father told me.
Come now, let us go.

The true vine

¹ **15** "I am the true vine,
and my Father is the vinedresser.
²   Every branch in me that bears no fruit
he cuts away,
and every branch that does bear fruit he prunes
to make it bear even more.
³   You are pruned already,
by means of the word that I have spoken to you.
⁴   Make your home in me, as I make mine in you.
As a branch cannot bear fruit all by itself,
but must remain part of the vine,
neither can you unless you remain in me.
⁵   I am the vine,
you are the branches.
Whoever remains in me, with me in him,
bears fruit in plenty;
for cut off from me you can do nothing.
⁶   Anyone who does not remain in me
is like a branch that has been thrown away
—he withers;
these branches are collected and thrown on the fire,
and they are burned.
⁷   If you remain in me
and my words remain in you,
you may ask what you will
and you shall get it.
⁸   It is to the glory of my Father that you should bear
much fruit,
and then you will be my disciples.
⁹   As the Father has loved me,
so I have loved you.
Remain in my love.
¹⁰   If you keep my commandments
you will remain in my love,
just as I have kept my Father's commandments
and remain in his love.
¹¹   I have told you this
so that my own joy may be in you
and your joy be complete.
¹²   This is my commandment:

love one another,
as I have loved you.

18 A man can have no greater love
than to lay down his life for his friends.

14 You are my friends,
if you do what I command you.

15 I shall not call you servants any more,
because a servant does not know
his master's business;
I call you friends,
because I have made known to you
everything I have learned from my Father.

16 You did not choose me,
no, I chose you;
and I commissioned you
to go out and to bear fruit,
fruit that will last;
and then the Father will give you
anything you ask him in my name.

17 What I command you
is to love one another.

The hostile world

18 "If the world hates you,
remember that it hated me before you.

19 If you belonged to the world,
the world would love you as its own;
but because you do not belong to the world,
because my choice withdrew you from the world,
therefore the world hates you.

20 Remember the words I said to you:
A servant is not greater than his master.
If they persecuted me,
they will persecute you too;
if they kept my word,
they will keep yours as well.

21 But it will be on my account that they will do all this,
because they do not know the one who sent me.

22 If I had not come,
if I had not spoken to them,
they would have been blameless;
but as it is they have no excuse for their sin.

23 Anyone who hates me hates my Father.

24 If I had not performed such works among them

as no one else has ever done,
they would be blameless;
but as it is, they have seen all this,
and still they hate both me and my Father.

25   But all this was only to fulfill the words written in
      their Law:
*They hated me for no reason.*ᵃ

26   When the Advocate comes,
whom I shall send to you from the Father,
the Spirit of truth who issues from the Father,
he will be my witness.

27   And you too will be witnesses,
because you have been with me from the outset.

16

1   "I have told you all this
so that your faith may not be shaken.

2   They will expell you from the synagogues,
and indeed the hour is coming
when anyone who kills you will think he is doing a
     holy duty for God.

3   They will do these things
because they have never known either the Father or
     myself.

4   But I have told you all this,
so that when the time for it comes
you may remember that I told you.

The coming of the Advocate

"I did not tell you this from the outset,
because I was with you;

5   but now I am going to the one who sent me.
Not one of you has asked, 'Where are you going?'

6   Yet you are sad at heart because I have told you this.

7   Still, I must tell you the truth:
it is for your own good that I am going
because unless I go,
the Advocate will not come to you;
but if I do go,
I will send him to you.

8   And when he comes,
he will show the world how wrong it was,
about sin,
and about who was in the right,
and about judgment:

9   about sin:
      proved by their refusal to believe in me;
10   about who was in the right:
      proved by my going to the Father
      and your seeing me no more;
11   about judgment:
      proved by the prince of this world being already
          condemned.
12   I still have many things to say to you
      but they would be too much for you now.
13   But when the Spirit of truth comes
      he will lead you to the complete truth,
      since he will not be speaking as from himself
      but will say only what he has learned;
      and he will tell you of the things to come.
14   He will glorify me,
      since all he tells you
      will be taken from what is mine.
15   Everything the Father has is mine;
      that is why I said:
      All he tells you
      will be taken from what is mine.

Jesus to return very soon

16   "In a short time you will no longer see me,
        and then a short time later you will see me again."

17   Then some of his disciples said to one another, "What
does he mean, 'In a short time you will no longer see me,
and then a short time later you will see me again' and, 'I
18 am going to the Father'? What is this 'short time'? We
19 don't know what he means." Jesus knew that they wanted
to question him, so he said, "You are asking one another
what I meant by saying: In a short time you will no longer
see me, and then a short time later you will see me again.

20   "I tell you most solemnly,
      you will be weeping and wailing
      while the world will rejoice;
      you will be sorrowful,
      but your sorrow will turn to joy.
21   A woman in childbirth suffers,
      because her time has come;

15 a. Ps 35:19

    but when she has given birth to the child she forgets
        the suffering

    in her joy that a man has been born into the world.

22   So it is with you: you are sad now,

    but I shall see you again, and your hearts will be full
        of joy,

    and that joy no one shall take from you.

23   When that day comes,

    you will not ask me any questions.

    I tell you most solemnly,

    anything you ask for from the Father

    he will grant in my name.

24   Until now you have not asked for anything in my
        name.

    Ask and you will receive,

    and so your joy will be complete.

25   I have been telling you all this in metaphors,

    the hour is coming

    when I shall no longer speak to you in metaphors;

    but tell you about the Father in plain words.

26   When that day comes

    you will ask in my name;

    and I do not say that I shall pray to the Father for
        you,

27   because the Father himself loves you

    for loving me

    and believing that I came from God.

28   I came from the Father and have come into the world

    and now I leave the world to go to the Father."

29 His disciples said, "Now you are speaking plainly and
30 not using metaphors! ·Now we see that you know everything, and do not have to wait for questions to be put into
words; because of this we believe that you came from
31 God." ·Jesus answered them:

    "Do you believe at last?

32   Listen; the time will come—in fact it has come
        already—

    when you will be scattered, each going his own way

    and leaving me alone.

    And yet I am not alone,

    because the Father is with me.

33   I have told you all this

    so that you may find peace in me.

> In the world you will have trouble,
> but be brave:
> I have conquered the world."

The priestly prayer of Christ

17 After saying this, Jesus raised his eyes to heaven and said:

1   "Father, the hour has come:
glorify your Son
so that your Son may glorify you;

2   and, through the power over all mankind[a] that you
        have given him,
let him give eternal life to all those you have en-
        trusted to him.

3   And eternal life is this:
to know you,
the only true God,
and Jesus Christ whom you have sent.

4   I have glorified you on earth
and finished the work
that you gave me to do.

5   Now, Father, it is time for you to glorify me
with that glory I had with you
before ever the world was.

6   I have made your name known
to the men you took from the world to give me.
They were yours and you gave them to me,
and they have kept your word.

7   Now at last they know
that all you have given me comes indeed from you;

8   for I have given them
the teaching you gave to me,
and they have truly accepted this, that I came from
        you,
and have believed that it was you who sent me.

9   I pray for them;
I am not praying for the world
but for those you have given me,
because they belong to you:

10   all I have is yours
and all you have is mine,
and in them I am glorified.

17 a. Lit. "all flesh."

11　　I am not in the world any longer,
　　　but they are in the world,
　　　and I am coming to you.
　　　Holy Father,
　　　keep those you have given me true to your name,
　　　so that they may be one like us.
12　　While I was with them,
　　　I kept those you had given me true to your name.
　　　I have watched over them and not one is lost
　　　except the one who chose to be lost,[b]
　　　and this was to fulfill the scriptures.
13　　But now I am coming to you
　　　and while still in the world I say these things
　　　to share my joy with them to the full.
14　　I passed your word on to them,
　　　and the world hated them,
　　　because they belong to the world
　　　no more than I belong to the world.
15　　I am not asking you to remove them from the world,
　　　but to protect them from the evil one.
16　　They do not belong to the world
　　　any more than I belong to the world.
17　　Consecrate them in the truth;
　　　your word is truth.
18　　As you sent me into the world,
　　　I have sent them into the world,
19　　and for their sake I consecrate myself
　　　so that they too may be consecrated in truth.
20　　I pray not only for these,
　　　but for those also
　　　who through their words will believe in me.
21　　May they all be one.
　　　Father, may they be one in us,
　　　as you are in me and I am in you,
　　　so that the world may believe it was you who sent me.
22　　I have given them the glory you gave to me,
　　　that they may be one as we are one.
23　　With me in them and you in me,
　　　may they be so completely one
　　　that the world will realize that it was you who sent me
　　　and that I have loved them as much as you loved me.
24　　Father,
　　　I want those you have given me
　　　to be with me where I am,

so that they may always see the glory
you have given me
because you loved me
before the foundation of the world.
25   Father, Righteous One,
the world has not known you,
but I have known you,
and these have known
that you have sent me.
26   I have made your name known to them
and will continue to make it known,
so that the love with which you loved me may be in
them,
and so that I may be in them."

C. THE PASSION

The arrest of Jesus

1 **18** After he had said all this Jesus left with his disciples
and crossed the Kedron valley. There was a garden
2 there, and he went into it with his disciples. ·Judas the
traitor knew the place well, since Jesus had often met his
3 disciples there, ·and he brought the cohort[a] to this place
together with a detachment of guards sent by the chief
priests and the Pharisees, all with lanterns and torches and
4 weapons. ·Knowing everything that was going to happen to
him, Jesus then came forward and said, "Who are you
5 looking for?" ·They answered, "Jesus the Nazarene." He
said, "I am he." Now Judas the traitor was standing among
6 them. ·When Jesus said, "I am he," they moved back and
7 fell to the ground. ·He asked them a second time, "Who
are you looking for?" They said, "Jesus the Nazarene."
8 "I have told you that I am he" replied Jesus. "If I am the
9 one you are looking for, let these others go." ·This was to
fulfill the words he had spoken, "Not one of those you gave
me have I lost."

10   Simon Peter, who carried a sword, drew it and wounded
the high priest's servant, cutting off his right ear. The
11 servant's name was Malchus. ·Jesus said to Peter, "Put your
sword back in its scabbard; am I not to drink the cup that
the Father has given me?"

b. Lit. "the son of perdition."
18 a. A detachment from the Roman garrison in Jerusalem.

Jesus before Annas and Caiaphas. Peter disowns him

12 The cohort and its captain and the Jewish guards seized
13 Jesus and bound him. ·They took him first to Annas, because Annas was the father-in-law of Caiaphas, who was
14 high priest that year. ·It was Caiaphas who had suggested
to the Jews, "It is better for one man to die for the people."
15 Simon Peter, with another disciple, followed Jesus. This
disciple, who was known to the high priest, went with Jesus
16 into the high priest's palace, ·but Peter stayed outside the
door. So the other disciple, the one known to the high priest,
went out, spoke to the woman who was keeping the door
17 and brought Peter in. ·The maid on duty at the door said
to Peter, "Aren't you another of that man's disciples?" He
18 answered, "I am not." ·Now it was cold, and the servants
and guards had lit a charcoal fire and were standing there
warming themselves; so Peter stood there too, warming
himself with the others.
19 The high priest questioned Jesus about his disciples and
20 his teaching. ·Jesus answered, "I have spoken openly for all
the world to hear; I have always taught in the synagogue
and in the Temple where all the Jews meet together: I have
21 said nothing in secret. ·But why ask me? Ask my hearers
22 what I taught: they know what I said." ·At these words, one
of the guards standing by gave Jesus a slap in the face, say-
23 ing, "Is that the way to answer the high priest?" ·Jesus replied, "If there is something wrong in what I said, point it
out; but if there is no offense in it, why do you strike me?"
24 Then Annas sent him, still bound, to Caiaphas the high
priest.
25 As Simon Peter stood there warming himself, someone
said to him, "Aren't you another of his disciples?" He de-
26 nied it saying, "I am not." ·One of the high priest's servants, a relation of the man whose ear Peter had cut off,
27 said, "Didn't I see you in the garden with him?" ·Again
Peter denied it; and at once a cock crew.

Jesus before Pilate

28 They then led Jesus from the house of Caiaphas to the
Praetorium.[b] It was now morning. They did not go into
the Praetorium themselves or they would be defiled[c] and
29 unable to eat the passover. ·So Pilate came outside to them
and said, "What charge do you bring against this man?"
30 They replied, ·"If he were not a criminal, we should not be

81 handing him over to you." ·Pilate said, "Take him yourselves, and try him by your own Law." The Jews answered,
82 "We are not allowed to put a man to death." ·This was to
   fulfill the words Jesus had spoken indicating the way he
   was going to die.

83   So Pilate went back into the Praetorium and called Jesus
84 to him, "Are you the king of the Jews?" he asked. ·Jesus
   replied, "Do you ask this of your own accord, or have
85 others spoken to you about me?" ·Pilate answered, "Am I
   a Jew? It is your own people and the chief priests who have
86 handed you over to me: what have you done?" ·Jesus replied, "Mine is not a kingdom of this world; if my kingdom were of this world, my men would have fought to
   prevent my being surrendered to the Jews. But my king-
87 dom is not of this kind." ·"So you are a king then?" said
   Pilate. "It is you who say it" answered Jesus. "Yes, I am a
   king. I was born for this, I came into the world for this: to
   bear witness to the truth; and all who are on the side of
88 truth listen to my voice." ·"Truth?" said Pilate "What is
   that?"; and with that he went out again to the Jews and
89 said, "I find no case against him. ·But according to a custom of yours I should release one prisoner at the Passover;
   would you like me, then, to release the king of the Jews?"
40 At this they shouted: "Not this man," they said "but
   Barabbas." Barabbas was a brigand.

¹₂ 19 Pilate then had Jesus taken away and scourged; ·and
      after this, the soldiers twisted some thorns into a
   crown and put it on his head, and dressed him in a pur-
8 ple robe. ·They kept coming up to him and saying, "Hail,
   king of the Jews!"; and they slapped him in the face.
4   Pilate came outside again and said to them, "Look, I am
   going to bring him out to you to let you see that I find no
5 case." ·Jesus then came out wearing the crown of thorns
6 and the purple robe. Pilate said, "Here is the man." ·When
   they saw him the chief priests and the guards shouted,
   "Crucify him! Crucify him!" Pilate said, "Take him yourselves and crucify him: I can find no case against him."
7 "We have a Law," the Jews replied "and according to that
   Law he ought to die, because he has claimed to be the Son
   of God."
⁸₉   When Pilate heard them say this his fears increased. ·Re-

b. The judicial court of the Roman procurator.   c. By entering
the house of a pagan. Cf. Lk 7:6.

entering the Praetorium, he said to Jesus, "Where do you
10 come from?" But Jesus made no answer. ·Pilate then said
to him, "Are you refusing to speak to me? Surely you know
I have power to release you and I have power to crucify
11 you?" ·"You would have no power over me" replied Jesus
"if it had not been given you from above; that is why the
one who handed me over to you has the greater guilt."

Jesus is condemned to death

12 From that moment Pilate was anxious to set him free,
but the Jews shouted, "If you set him free you are no
friend of Caesar's; anyone who makes himself king is de-
13 fying Caesar." ·Hearing these words, Pilate had Jesus
brought out, and seated himself on the chair of judgment
14 at a place called the Pavement, in Hebrew Gabbatha. ·It
was Passover Preparation Day, about the sixth hour.ᵃ
15 "Here is your king" said Pilate to the Jews. ·"Take him
away, take him away!" they said. "Crucify him!" "Do you
want me to crucify your king?" said Pilate. The chief
16 priests answered, "We have no king except Caesar." ·So in
the end Pilate handed him over to them to be crucified.

The crucifixion

17 They then took charge of Jesus, ·and carrying his own
cross he went out of the city to the place of the skull or,
18 as it was called in Hebrew, Golgotha, ·where they crucified him with two others, one on either side with Jesus in
19 the middle. ·Pilate wrote out a notice and had it fixed to
the cross; it ran: "Jesus the Nazarene, King of the Jews."
20 This notice was read by many of the Jews, because the
place where Jesus was crucified was not far from the city,
21 and the writing was in Hebrew, Latin and Greek. ·So the
Jewish chief priests said to Pilate, "You should not write
'King of the Jews,' but 'This man said: I am King of the
22 Jews.'" ·Pilate answered, "What I have written, I have
written."

Christ's garments divided

23 When the soldiers had finished crucifying Jesus they took
his clothing and divided it into four shares, one for each
soldier. His undergarment was seamless, woven in one
24 piece from neck to hem; ·so they said to one another,
"Instead of tearing it, let's throw dice to decide who is to

have it." In this way the words of scripture were fulfilled:

> They shared out my clothing among them.
> They cast lots for my clothes.[b]

This is exactly what the soldiers did.

Jesus and his mother

25   Near the cross of Jesus stood his mother and his mother's sister, Mary the wife of Clopas, and Mary of Magdala.
26 Seeing his mother and the disciple he loved standing near her, Jesus said to his mother, "Woman, this is your son."
27 Then to the disciple he said, "This is your mother." And from that moment the disciple made a place for her in his home.

The death of Jesus

28   After this, Jesus knew that everything had now been completed, and to fulfill the scripture perfectly he said:

> "I am thirsty."[c]

29   A jar full of vinegar stood there, so putting a sponge soaked in the vinegar on a hyssop stick they held it up to
30 his mouth. ·After Jesus had taken the vinegar he said, "It is accomplished;" and bowing his head he gave up his spirit.

The pierced Christ

31   It was Preparation Day, and to prevent the bodies remaining on the cross during the sabbath—since that sabbath was a day of special solemnity—the Jews asked Pilate to
32 have the legs broken[d] and the bodies taken away. ·Consequently the soldiers came and broke the legs of the first man who had been crucified with him and then of the
33 other. ·When they came to Jesus, they found he was al-
34 ready dead, and so instead of breaking his legs ·one of the soldiers pierced his side with a lance; and immediately
35 there came out blood and water. ·This is the evidence of one who saw it—trustworthy evidence, and he knows he speaks the truth—and he gives it so that you may believe as

19 a. On Preparation Day, the Passover supper was made ready for eating after sunset. The sixth hour is midday, by which time all leaven had to be removed from the house; during the feast only unleavened bread was eaten. **b.** Ps 22:18   **c.** Ps 22:15 **d.** To hasten death.

³⁶ well. ·Because all this happened to fulfill the words of scripture:

> *Not one bone of his will be broken;*[e]

³⁷ and again, in another place scripture says:

> *They will look on the one whom they have pierced.*[f]

The burial

³⁸　　After this, Joseph of Arimathaea, who was a disciple of Jesus—though a secret one because he was afraid of the Jews—asked Pilate to let him remove the body of Jesus. Pilate gave permission, so they came and took it away.
³⁹ Nicodemus came as well—the same one who had first come to Jesus at night-time—and he brought a mixture of myrrh
⁴⁰ and aloes, weighing about a hundred pounds. ·They took the body of Jesus and wrapped it with the spices in linen
⁴¹ cloths, following the Jewish burial custom. ·At the place where he had been crucified there was a garden, and in this garden a new tomb in which no one had yet been
⁴² buried. ·Since it was the Jewish Day of Preparation and the tomb was near at hand, they laid Jesus there.

VIII. THE DAY OF CHRIST'S RESURRECTION

The empty tomb

¹ 2O It was very early on the first day of the week and still dark, when Mary of Magdala came to the tomb. She saw that the stone had been moved away from the
² tomb ·and came running to Simon Peter and the other disciple, the one Jesus loved. "They have taken the Lord out of the tomb" she said "and we don't know where they have put him.".
³　So Peter set out with the other disciple to go to the
⁴ tomb. ·They ran together, but the other disciple, running
⁵ faster than Peter, reached the tomb first; ·he bent down and saw the linen cloths lying on the ground, but did not
⁶ go in. ·Simon Peter who was following now came up, went right into the tomb, saw the linen cloths on the
⁷ ground, ·and also the cloth that had been over his head; this was not with the linen cloths but rolled up in a place
⁸ by itself. ·Then the other disciple who had reached the
⁹ tomb first also went in; he saw and he believed. ·Till this

moment they had failed to understand the teaching of
10 scripture, that he must rise from the dead. •The disciples
then went home again.

The appearance to Mary of Magdala

11   Meanwhile Mary stayed outside near the tomb, weep-
12 ing. Then, still weeping, she stooped to look inside, •and
saw two angels in white sitting where the body of Jesus
13 had been, one at the head, the other at the feet. •They
said, "Woman, why are you weeping?" "They have taken
my Lord away" she replied "and I don't know where they
14 have put him." •As she said this she turned round and saw
Jesus standing there, though she did not recognize him.
15 Jesus said, "Woman, why are you weeping? Who are you
looking for?" Supposing him to be the gardener, she said,
"Sir, if you have taken him away, tell me where you have
16 put him, and I will go and remove him." •Jesus said,
"Mary!" She knew him then and said to him in Hebrew,
17 "Rabbuni!"—which means Master. •Jesus said to her, "Do
not cling to me, because I have not yet ascended to the
Father. But go and find the brothers, and tell them: I am
ascending to my Father and your Father, to my God and
18 your God." •So Mary of Magdala went and told the disciples that she had seen the Lord and that he had said
these things to her.

Appearances to the disciples

19 .   In the evening of that same day, the first day of the
week, the doors were closed in the room where the disciples were, for fear of the Jews. Jesus came and stood
20 among them. He said to them, "Peace be with you," •and
showed them his hands and his side. The disciples were
21 filled with joy when they saw the Lord, •and he said to
then again, "Peace be with you.

> "As the Father sent me,
> so am I sending you."

22 After saying this he breathed on them and said:

> "Receive the Holy Spirit.
23   For those whose sins you forgive,

e. Two texts are here combined: Ps 34:20 and Ex 12:46. The
allusion is both to God protecting the good man, and to the
ritual for preparing the Passover lamb. f. Zc 12:10

they are forgiven;
for those whose sins you retain,
they are retained."

24 Thomas, called the Twin, who was one of the Twelve,
25 was not with them when Jesus came. When the disciples
said, "We have seen the Lord," he answered, "Unless I see
the holes that the nails made in his hands and can put my
finger into the holes they made, and unless I can put my
26 hand into his side, I refuse to believe." Eight days later
the disciples were in the house again and Thomas was with
them. The doors were closed, but Jesus came in and stood
27 among them. "Peace be with you" he said. Then he spoke
to Thomas, "Put your finger here; look, here are my hands.
Give me your hand; put it into my side. Doubt no longer
28 but believe." Thomas replied, "My Lord and my God!"
29 Jesus said to him:

"You believe because you can see me.
Happy are those who have not seen and yet believe."

CONCLUSION

30 There were many other signs that Jesus worked and the
31 disciples saw, but they are not recorded in this book. These
are recorded so that you may believe that Jesus is the
Christ, the Son of God, and that believing this you may
have life through his name.

APPENDIX[a]

The appearance on the shore of Tiberias

1 **21** Later on, Jesus showed himself again to the disciples. It was by the Sea of Tiberias, and it happened
2 like this: Simon Peter, Thomas called the Twin, Nathanael from Cana in Galilee, the sons of Zebedee and two
3 more of his disciples were together. Simon Peter said,
"I'm going fishing." They replied, "We'll come with you."
They went out and got into the boat but caught nothing
that night.
4 It was light by now and there stood Jesus on the shore,
though the disciples did not realize that it was Jesus.

5 Jesus called out, "Have you caught anything, friends?"
6 And when they answered, "No," ·he said, "Throw the net out to starboard and you'll find something." So they dropped the net, and there were so many fish that they
7 could not haul it in. ·The disciple Jesus loved said to Peter, "It is the Lord." At these words "It is the Lord," Simon Peter who had practically nothing on, wrapped his cloak
8 round him and jumped into the water. ·The other disciples came on in the boat, towing the net and the fish; they were only about a hundred yards from land.

9   As soon as they came ashore they saw that there was some bread there, and a charcoal fire with fish cooking on
10 it. ·Jesus said, "Bring some of the fish you have just
11 caught." ·Simon Peter went aboard and dragged the net to the shore, full of big fish, one hundred and fifty-three of them; and in spite of there being so many the net was not
12 broken. ·Jesus said to them, "Come and have breakfast." None of the disciples was bold enough to ask, "Who are
13 you?"; they knew quite well it was the Lord. ·Jesus then stepped forward, took the bread and gave it to them, and
14 the same with the fish. ·This was the third time that Jesus showed himself to the disciples after rising from the dead.

15   After the meal Jesus said to Simon Peter, "Simon son of John, do you love me more than these others do?" He answered, "Yes Lord, you know I love you." Jesus said to
16 him, "Feed my lambs." ·A second time he said to him, "Simon son of John, do you love me?" He replied, "Yes, Lord, you know I love you." Jesus said to him, "Look after my
17 sheep." ·Then he said to him a third time, "Simon son of John, do you love me?" Peter was upset that he asked him the third time. "Do you love me?" and said, "Lord, you know everything; you know I love you." Jesus said to him, "Feed my sheep.

18   "I tell you most solemnly,
      when you were young
      you put on your own belt
      and walked where you liked;
      but when you grow old
      you will stretch out your hands,
      and somebody else will put a belt round you
      and take you where you would rather not go."

21 a. Added either by the evangelist or by a disciple of his.

INTRODUCTION TO
The Acts of the Apostles

St. Luke's Gospel and The Acts of the Apostles are the two volumes of a single work that today we should call "a history of the rise of Christianity." The two books are inseparably linked by their Prologues and by their style. From the text of Acts it is evident that the author was a Christian of the apostolic age, either a thoroughly hellenized Jew or more probably a well-educated "Greek" with a thorough knowledge of the Septuagint and of Jewish culture and traditions. No other name has ever been suggested than that of Luke, the close friend of Paul, who according to an ancient tradition was a Syrian from Antioch, a doctor and a convert from paganism.

Acts is in the form of a single continuous narrative. It begins with the birth and growth of the primitive Christian community in Jerusalem and tells of the founding of the community in Antioch by hellenist Jews and the conversion of St. Paul; it goes on to show the spread of the Church outside Palestine through the missionary travels of Paul and ends with his captivity in Rome in A.D. 61-63. The narrative can be seen to be made up of separate episodes of varying lengths, all containing a great deal of circumstantial detail and commonly joined to each other by editorial formulae.

For the later journeys of Paul, Luke appears to have his own notes; the rest of the book confirms the claim made in the Prologue of the first volume (Lk 1:1-4) that the author collected a large quantity of evidence from a variety of sources. In the editing of this, and the chronological arranging of it, a certain amount of repetition, fusion and anomalies in the order of incidents was unavoidable, but the basic reliability of the work may be seen by checking Luke's account of Paul's missionary activities with Paul's own letters, which were not among his sources. The historical worth of Acts is high, since it not only includes a major section which is an eyewitness account of the events described, but gives much detailed factual information which we should otherwise lack. Although Luke, like any other classical historian, took the freedom to reconstruct speeches which he had not himself heard, there is every evidence that he went back to true sources and treated them with respect: notice, for instance, the archaisms and semitisms left in the reported speeches of Peter and Stephen, and the remarkable distinction between the simple theological background of the earliest Christian sermons and that of Paul's later teaching. It is also to be noticed that he can include a speech which failed to convince its hearers.

Thus Acts is a principal source for much of our knowledge of life in the earliest Christian communities, of the first impact made by the Christian faith on pagan nations, of the primitive beginnings of church organization, of the early developments of Christology, of the personalities of the apostolic age. Luke is, however, not interested in presenting a formal history of the spread of Christianity. What he is interested in is: 1. The spiritual energy inside Christianity that motivates its expansion, and 2. the spiritual doctrine that he can show by object lessons with the facts at his disposal.

The Acts

OF THE APOSTLES

Prologue   *Luke*

1 In my earlier work,[a] Theophilus, I dealt with everything
2 Jesus had done and taught from the beginning ·until the
day he gave his instructions to the apostles he had chosen
3 through the Holy Spirit, and was taken up to heaven. ·He
had shown himself alive to them after his Passion by many
demonstrations: for forty days he had continued to appear
4 to them and tell them about the kingdom of God. ·When
he had been at table with them, he had told them not to
leave Jerusalem, but to wait there for what the Father had
promised. "It is" he had said "what you have heard me
5 speak about: ·John baptized with water but you, not many
days from now, will be baptized with the Holy Spirit."

The ascension

6 Now having met together,[b] they asked him, "Lord, has
the time come? Are you going to restore the kingdom to
7 Israel?" ·He replied, "It is not for you to know times or
dates that the Father has decided by his own authority,
8 but you will receive power when the Holy Spirit comes
on you, and then you will be my witnesses not only in
Jerusalem but throughout Judaea and Samaria, and indeed
to the ends of the earth."
9 As he said this he was lifted up while they looked on,
10 and a cloud took him from their sight. ·They were still
staring into the sky when suddenly two men in white were
11 standing near them ·and they said, "Why are you men
from Galilee standing here looking into the sky? Jesus
who has been taken up from you into heaven, this same
Jesus will come back in the same way as you have seen
him go there."

1 a. The gospel according to Luke.   b. This verse takes up the
narrative broken off in Lk 24:49.

I. THE JERUSALEM CHURCH

The group of apostles

¹²   So from the Mount of Olives, as it is called, they went back to Jerusalem, a short distance away, no more than a ¹³ sabbath walk; ·and when they reached the city they went to the upper room where they were staying; there were Peter and John, James and Andrew, Philip and Thomas, Bartholomew and Matthew, James son of Alphaeus and ¹⁴ Simon the Zealot, and Jude son of James.ᶜ ·All these joined in continuous prayer, together with several women, including Mary the mother of Jesus, and with his brothers.ᵈ

The election of Matthias

¹⁵   One day Peter stood up to speak to the brothersᵉ— there were about a hundred and twenty persons in the ¹⁶ congregation: ·"Brothers, the passage of scripture had to be fulfilled in which the Holy Spirit, speaking through David, foretells the fate of Judas, who offered himself as ¹⁷ a guide to the men who arrested Jesus—·after having been one of our number and actually sharing this ministry of ¹⁸ ours. ·As you know, he bought a field with the money he was paid for his crime. He fell headlong and burst open, ¹⁹ and all his entrails poured out. ·Everybody in Jerusalem heard about it and the field came to be called the Bloody ²⁰ Acre, in their language Hakeldama. ·Now in the Book of Psalms it says:

> Let his camp be reduced to ruin;
> Let there be no one to live in it.ᶠ

And again:

> Let someone else take his office.ᵍ

²¹   "We must therefore choose someone who has been with us the whole time that the Lord Jesus was traveling round ²² with us, ·someone who was with us right from the time when John was baptizing until the day when he was taken up from us—and he can act with us as a witness to his resurrection."

²³   Having nominated two candidates, Joseph known as ²⁴ Barsabbas, whose surname was Justus, and Matthias, ·they prayed, "Lord, you can read everyone's heart; show us

25 therefore which of these two you have chosen •to take
over this ministry and apostolate, which Judas abandoned
26 to go to his proper place." •They then drew lots for them,
and as the lot fell to Matthias, he was listed as one of the
twelve apostles.

Pentecost

1 When Pentecost day came round, they had all met in
2 one room, •when suddenly they heard what sounded
like a powerful wind from heaven, the noise of which filled
3 the entire house in which they were sitting; •and something appeared to them that seemed like tongues of fire;
these separated and came to rest on the head of each of
4 them. •They were all filled with the Holy Spirit, and began
to speak foreign languages as the Spirit gave them the gift
of speech.

5   Now there were devout men living in Jerusalem from
6 every nation under heaven, •and at this sound they all
assembled, each one bewildered to hear these men speak-
7 ing his own language. •They were amazed and astonished.
"Surely" they said "all these men speaking are Galileans?
8 How does it happen that each of us hears them in his own
9 native language? •Parthians, Medes and Elamites; people
from Mesopotamia, Judaea and Cappadocia, Pontus and
10 Asia, •Phrygia and Pamphylia, Egypt and the parts of
11 Libya round Cyrene; as well as visitors from Rome—Jews
and proselytes[a] alike—Cretans and Arabs; we hear them
preaching in our own language about the marvels of God."
12 Everyone was amazed and unable to explain it; they asked
13 one another what it all meant. •Some, however, laughed
it off. "They have been drinking too much new wine" they
said.

Peter's address to the crowd

14   Then Peter stood up with the Eleven and addressed them
in a loud voice:
    "Men of Judaea, and all you who live in Jerusalem,

c. "Son" (of Alphaeus, of James) is not in the Greek. This Jude
is not the Jude "brother" of Jesus, Mt 13:55 and Mk 6:3, and
brother of James (Jude 1). Nor is it likely that "James of
Alphaeus" was James brother of the Lord. d. Cousins, as in
the gospels. e. The term for Christians, usually the laity as
distinct from apostles and elders. f. Ps 69:25 g. Ps 109:8
2 a. Converts from paganism.

make no mistake about this, but listen carefully to what I
¹⁵ say. ·These men are not drunk, as you imagine; why, it is
¹⁶ only the third hour of the day.ᵇ ·On the contrary, this is
what the prophetᶜ spoke of:

¹⁷　In the days to come—it is the Lord who speaks—
　　I will pour out my spirit on all mankind.
　　Their sons and daughters shall prophesy,
　　your young men shall see visions,
　　your old men shall dream dreams.
¹⁸　Even on my slaves, men and women,
　　in those days, I will pour out my spirit.
¹⁹　I will display portents in heaven *above*
　　and *signs* on earth *below*.
²⁰　The sun will be turned into darkness
　　and the moon into blood
　　before the great Day of the Lord dawns.
²¹　All who call on the name of the Lord will be saved.

²²　"Men of Israel, listen to what I am going to say: Jesus
the Nazarene was a man commended to you by God by
the miracles and portents and signs that God worked
through him when he was among you, as you all know.
²³ This man, who was put into your power by the deliberate
intention and foreknowledge of God, you took and had
²⁴ crucified by men outside the Law.ᵈ You killed him, ·but
God raised him to life, freeing him from the pangs of
Hades; for it was impossible for him to be held in its
²⁵ power since, ·as David says of him:

　　I saw the Lord before me always,
　　for with him at my right hand nothing can shake me.
²⁶　*So my heart was glad*
　　and my tongue cried out with joy;
　　my body, too, will rest in the hope
²⁷　*that you will not abandon my soul to Hades*
　　nor allow your holy one to experience corruption.
²⁸　*You have made known the way of life to me,*
　　*you will fill me with gladness through your presence.*ᵉ

²⁹　"Brothers, no one can deny that the patriarch David
³⁰ himself is dead and buried: his tomb is still with us. ·But
since he was a prophet, and knew that God *had sworn*
him an oath *to make one of his descendants succeed him*
³¹ *on the throne,*ᶠ ·what he foresaw and spoke about was the
resurrection of the Christ: he is the one who was *not*

abandoned to Hades, and whose body did not *experience*
82 *corruption.* ·God raised this man Jesus to life, and all of
83 us are witnesses to that. ·Now raised to the heights by
. God's right hand, he has received from the Father the
Holy Spirit, who was promised, and what you see and
84 hear is the outpouring of that Spirit. ·For David himself
never went up to heaven; and yet these words are his:

> The Lord said to my Lord:
> Sit at my right hand
85 > until I make your enemies
> a footstool for you.[g]

86 "For this reason the whole House of Israel can be certain that God has made this Jesus whom you crucified
both Lord and Christ."

The first conversions

87 Hearing this, they were cut to the heart and said to
Peter and the apostles, "What must we do, brothers?"
88 "You must repent," Peter answered "and every one of you
must be baptized in the name of Jesus Christ for the forgiveness of your sins, and you will receive the gift of the
89 Holy Spirit. ·The promise that was made is for you and
your children, and for all *those who are far away, for all*
40 *those whom the Lord* our God *will call to himself.*"[h] ·He
spoke to them for a long time using many arguments, and
he urged them, "Save yourselves from this perverse gen-
41 eration." ·They were convinced by his arguments, and they
accepted what he said and were baptized. That very day
about three thousand were added to their number.

The early Christian community

42 These remained faithful to the teaching of the apostles,
to the brotherhood, to the breaking of bread and to the
prayers.
43 The many miracles and signs worked through the apostles made a deep impression on everyone.
44 The faithful all lived together and owned everything in
45 common; ·they sold their goods and possessions and shared

b. About 9 A.M.   c. Joel. See Jl 3:1-5.   d. The Romans.   e. Ps
16:8-11; quoted according to the LXX.   f. 2 S 7:12 and Ps
132:11   g. Ps 110:1   h. Is 57:19

out the proceeds among themselves according to what each one needed.

46 They went as a body to the Temple every day but met in their houses for the breaking of bread; they shared their

47 food gladly and generously; ·they praised God and were looked up to by everyone. Day by day the Lord added to their community those destined to be saved.

The cure of a lame man

1 Once, when Peter and John were going up to the Tem-

2 ple for the prayers at the ninth hour,[a] ·it happened that there was a man being carried past. He was a cripple from birth; and they used to put him down every day near the Temple entrance called the Beautiful Gate so that he could

3 beg from the people going in. ·When this man saw Peter and John on their way into the Temple he begged from

4 them. ·Both Peter and John looked straight at him and

5 said, "Look at us." ·He turned to them expectantly, hoping

6 to get something from them, ·but Peter said, "I have neither silver nor gold, but I will give you what I have: in the

7 name of Jesus Christ the Nazarene, walk!" ·Peter then took him by the hand and helped him to stand up. Instantly his

8 feet and ankles became firm, ·he jumped up, stood, and began to walk, and he went with them into the Temple,

9 walking and jumping and praising God. ·Everyone could

10 see him walking and praising God, ·and they recognized him as the man who used to sit begging at the Beautiful Gate of the Temple. They were all astonished and unable to explain what had happened to him.

Peter's address to the people

11 Everyone came running toward them in great excitement, to the Portico of Solomon, as it is called, where the

12 man was still clinging to Peter and John. ·When Peter saw the people he addressed them, "Why are you so surprised at this? Why are you staring at us as though we had made

13 this man walk by our own power or holiness? ·You are Israelites, and it is *the God of Abraham, Isaac and Jacob, the God of our ancestors, who has glorified his servant*[b] Jesus, the same Jesus you handed over and then disowned in the presence of Pilate after Pilate had decided to re-

14 lease him. ·It was you who accused the Holy One, the Just One, you who demanded the reprieve of a murderer

15 while you killed the prince of life. God, however, raised

him from the dead, and to that fact we are the witnesses;
16 and it is the name of Jesus which, through our faith in it,
has brought back the strength of this man whom you see
here and who is well known to you. It is faith in that name
that has restored this man to health, as you can all see.

17 "Now I know, brothers, that neither you nor your lead-
18 ers had any idea what you were really doing; •this was the
way God carried out what he had foretold, when he said
19 through all his prophets that his Christ would suffer. •Now
you must repent and turn to God, so that your sins may
20 be wiped out, •and so that the Lord may send the time of
comfort. Then he will send you the Christ he has predes-
21 tined, that is Jesus, •whom heaven must keep till the universal restoration comes which God proclaimed, speaking
22 through his holy prophets. •Moses, for example, said: *The
Lord God will raise up a prophet like myself for you,
from among your own brothers; you must listen to what-
23 ever he tells you.* •*The man who does not listen to that
24 prophet is to be cut off from the people.*[c] •In fact, all the
prophets that have ever spoken, from Samuel onward,
have predicted these days.

25 "You are the heirs of the prophets, the heirs of the covenant God made with our ancestors when he told Abraham:
*in your offspring all the families of the earth will be
26 blessed.*[d] •It was for you in the first place that God raised
up his servant and sent him to bless you by turning every
one of you from your wicked ways."

Peter and John before the Sanhedrin

1 **4** While they were still talking to the people the priests
came up to them, accompanied by the captain of the
2 Temple and the Sadducees.[a] •They were extremely annoyed
at their teaching the people the doctrine of the resurrection
from the dead by proclaiming the resurrection of Jesus.
3 They arrested them, but as it was already late, they held
4 them till the next day. •But many of those who had listened
to their message became believers, the total number of
whom had now risen to something like five thousand.

---

3 a. The time of evening sacrifice.　b. Ex 3:6,15 and Is 52:13
c. Dt 18:18,19　d. Gn 12:3+
4 a. The Sadducees (see note on Mt 3:7) are always repre-
sented as denying the doctrine of the resurrection, e.g. Ac 23.

⁵ The next day the rulers, elders and scribes[b] had a meet-
⁶ ing in Jerusalem ·with Annas the high priest, Caiaphas,
Jonathan, Alexander and all the members of the high-
⁷ priestly families. ·They made the prisoners stand in the
middle and began to interrogate them, "By what power,
⁸ and by whose name have you men done this?" ·Then Peter,
filled with the Holy Spirit, addressed them, "Rulers of the
⁹ people, and elders! ·If you are questioning us today about
an act of kindness to a cripple, and asking us how he was
¹⁰ healed, ·then I am glad to tell you all, and would indeed
be glad to tell the whole people of Israel, that it was by
the name of Jesus Christ the Nazarene, the one you crucified, whom God raised from the dead, by this name and
by no other that this man is able to stand up perfectly
¹¹ healthy, here in your presence, today. ·This is *the stone
rejected* by you *the builders, but which has proved to be*
¹² *the keystone.*[c] ·For of all the names in the world given
to men, this is the only one by which we can be saved."
¹³ They were astonished at the assurance shown by Peter
and John, considering they were uneducated laymen; and
¹⁴ they recognized them as associates of Jesus; ·but when they
saw the man who had been cured standing by their side,
¹⁵ they could find no answer. ·So they ordered them to stand
outside while the Sanhedrin had a private discussion.
¹⁶ "What are we going to do with these men?" they asked. "It
is obvious to everybody in Jerusalem that a miracle has
been worked through them in public, and we cannot deny
¹⁷ it. ·But to stop the whole thing spreading any further
among the people, let us caution them never to speak to
anyone in this name again."
¹⁸ So they called them in and gave them a warning on no
account to make statements or to teach in the name of
¹⁹ Jesus. ·But Peter and John retorted, "You must judge
whether in God's eyes it is right to listen to you and not to
²⁰ God. ·We cannot promise to stop proclaiming what we
²¹ have seen and heard." ·The court repeated the warnings
and then released them; they could not think of any way
to punish them, since all the people were giving glory to
²² God for what had happened. ·The man who had been
miraculously cured was over forty years old.

The apostles' prayer under persecution

²³ As soon as they were released they went to the community and told them everything the chief priests and

24 elders had said to them. ·When they heard it they lifted up their voice to God all together. "Master," they prayed "it is you who made heaven and earth and sea, and everything
25 in them; ·you it is who said through the Holy Spirit and speaking through our ancestor David, your servant:

> *Why this arrogance among the nations,*
> *these futile plots among the peoples?*
26 > *Kings on earth setting out to war,*
> *princes making an alliance,*
> *against the Lord and against his Anointed.*[d]

27   "This is what has come true: in this very city Herod and Pontius Pilate *made an alliance* with the pagan *nations* and the *peoples* of Israel, against your holy servant Jesus
28 whom you *anointed,*[e] ·but only to bring about the very thing that you in your strength and your wisdom had pre-
29 determined should happen. ·And now, Lord, take note of their threats and help your servants to proclaim your mes-
30 sage with all boldness, ·by stretching out your hand to heal and to work miracles and marvels through the name of
31 your holy servant Jesus." ·As they prayed, the house where they were assembled rocked; they were all filled with the Holy Spirit and began to proclaim the word of God boldly.

The early Christian community

32   The whole group of believers was united, heart and soul; no one claimed for his own use anything that he had, as everything they owned was held in common.
33   The apostles continued to testify to the resurrection of the Lord Jesus with great power, and they were all given great respect.
34   None of their members was ever in want, as all those who owned land or houses would sell them, and bring the
35 money from them, ·to present it to the apostles; it was then distributed to any members who might be in need.

The generosity of Barnabas

36   There was a Levite of Cypriot origin called Joseph whom the apostles surnamed Barnabas (which means "son
37 of encouragement"). ·He owned a piece of land and he

b. I.e. the Sanhedrin, explained for the non-Jewish reader.
c. Ps 118:22   d. Ps 2:1-2   e. I.e. made the Christ, the anointed Messiah.

sold it and brought the money, and presented it to the apostles.

The fraud of Ananias and Sapphira

¹₂ 5 There was another man, however, called Ananias. He and his wife, Sapphira, agreed to sell a property; ·but with his wife's connivance he kept back part of the proceeds, and brought the rest and presented it to the apostles. ⁸ "Ananias," Peter said "how can Satan have so possessed you that you should lie to the Holy Spirit and keep back ⁴ part of the money from the land? ·While you still owned the land, wasn't it yours to keep, and after you had sold it wasn't the money yours to do with as you liked? What put this scheme into your mind? It is not to men that you have ⁵ lied, but to God." ·When he heard this Ananias fell down dead. This made a profound impression on everyone ⁶ present. ·The younger men got up, wrapped the body in a sheet, carried it out and buried it.

⁷ About three hours later his wife came in, not knowing ⁸ what had taken place. ·Peter challenged her, "Tell me, was this the price you sold the land for?" "Yes," she said "that ⁹ was the price." ·Peter then said, "So you and your husband have agreed to put the Spirit of the Lord to the test! What made you do it? You hear those footsteps? They have just been to bury your husband; they will carry you out, too." ¹⁰ Instantly she dropped dead at his feet. When the young men came in they found she was dead, and they carried ¹¹ her out and buried her by the side of her husband. ·This made a profound impression on the whole Church and on all who heard it.

The general situation

^{12b} They all used to meet by common consent in the ¹³ Portico of Solomon. ·No one else ever dared to join them, ¹⁴ but the people were loud in their praise ·and the numbers of men and women who came to believe in the Lord in-^{12a} creased steadily. ·So many signs and wonders were ¹⁵ worked among the people at the hands of the apostles ·that the sick were even taken out into the streets and laid on beds and sleeping-mats in the hope that at least the shadow of Peter might fall across some of them as he went past. ¹⁶ People even came crowding in from the towns round about Jerusalem, bringing with them their sick and those tormented by unclean spirits, and all of them were cured.

The apostles' arrest and miraculous deliverance

17 Then the high priest intervened with all his supporters
from the party of the Sadducees. Prompted by jealousy,
18 they arrested the apostles and had them put in the common jail.
19 But at night the angel of the Lord opened the prison
20 gates and said as he led them out, ·"Go and stand in the
21 Temple, and tell the people all about this new Life." ·They
did as they were told; they went into the Temple at dawn
and began to preach.

A summons to appear before the Sanhedrin

When the high priest arrived, he and his supporters con-
vened the Sanhedrin—this was the full Senate of Israel—and
22 sent to the jail for them to be brought. ·But when the
officials arrived at the prison they found they were not
23 inside, so they went back and reported, ·"We found the
jail securely locked and the warders on duty at the gates,
but when we unlocked the door we found no one inside."
24 When the captain of the Temple and the chief priests heard
25 this news they wondered what this could mean. ·Then a
man arrived with fresh news. "At this very moment" he
said "the men you imprisoned are in the Temple. They are
26 standing there preaching to the people." ·The captain went
with his men and fetched them. They were afraid to use
force in case the people stoned them.
27 When they had brought them in to face the Sanhedrin,
28 the high priest demanded an explanation. ·"We gave you a
formal warning" he said "not to preach in this name, and
what have you done? You have filled Jerusalem with your
teaching, and seem determined to fix the guilt of this man's
29 death on us." ·In reply Peter and the apostles said, "Obedi-
30 ence to God comes before obedience to men; ·it was the
God of our ancestors who raised up Jesus, but it was you
31 who had him executed by hanging on a tree.[a] ·By his
own right hand God has now raised him up to be leader
and savior, to give repentance and forgiveness of sins
32 through him to Israel. ·We are witnesses to all this, we
and the Holy Spirit whom God has given to those who
33 obey him." ·This so infuriated them that they wanted to put
them to death.

5 a. The phrase recalls Dt 21:23.

Gamaliel's intervention

⁸⁴ One member of the Sanhedrin, however, a Pharisee called Gamaliel, who was a doctor of the Law and respected by the whole people,*ᵇ* stood up and asked to have ⁸⁵ the men taken outside for a time. ·Then he addressed the Sanhedrin, "Men of Israel, be careful how you deal with ⁸⁶ these people. ·There was Theudas who became notorious not so long ago. He claimed to be someone important, and he even collected about four hundred followers; but when he was killed, all his followers scattered and that was the ⁸⁷ end of them. ·And then there was Judas the Galilean, at the time of the census, who attracted crowds of supporters; ⁸⁸ but he got killed too, and all his followers dispersed. ·What I suggest, therefore, is that you leave these men alone and let them go. If this enterprise, this movement of theirs, ⁸⁹ is of human origin it will break up of its own accord; ·but if it does in fact come from God you will not only be unable to destroy them, but you might find yourselves fighting against God."

⁴⁰ His advice was accepted; ·and they had the apostles called in, gave orders for them to be flogged, warned them ⁴¹ not to speak in the name of Jesus and released them. ·And so they left the presence of the Sanhedrin glad to have had the honor of suffering humiliation for the sake of the name.

⁴² They preached every day both in the Temple and in private houses, and their proclamation of the Good News of Christ Jesus was never interrupted.

II. THE EARLIEST MISSIONS

The institution of the Seven

¹ **6** About this time, when the number of disciples was increasing, the Hellenists made a complaint against the Hebrews:*ᵃ* in the daily distribution their own widows were ² being overlooked. ·So the Twelve called a full meeting of the disciples and addressed them, "It would not be right for ⁸ us to neglect the word of God so as to give out food; ·you, brothers, must select from among yourselves seven men of good reputation, filled with the Spirit and with wisdom; we ⁴ will hand over this duty to them, ·and continue to devote

⁵ ourselves to prayer and to the service of the word." ·The whole assembly approved of this proposal and elected Stephen, a man full of faith and of the Holy Spirit, together with Philip, Prochorus, Nicanor, Timon, Parmenas, and
⁶ Nicolaus of Antioch, a convert to Judaism. ·They presented these to the apostles, who prayed and laid their hands on them.*b*

⁷ The word of the Lord continued to spread: the number of disciples in Jerusalem was greatly increased, and a large group of priests made their submission to the faith.

Stephen's arrest

⁸ Stephen was filled with grace and power and began to
⁹ work miracles and great signs among the people. ·But then certain people came forward to debate with Stephen, some from Cyrene and Alexandria who were members of the synagogue called the Synagogue of Freedmen,*c* and others
¹⁰ from Cilicia and Asia. ·They found they could not get the better of him because of his wisdom, and because it was
¹¹ the Spirit that prompted what he said. ·So they procured some men to say, "We heard him using blasphemous lan-
¹² guage against Moses and against God." ·Having in this way turned the people against him as well as the elders and scribes, they took Stephen by surprise, and arrested
¹³ him and brought him before the Sanhedrin. ·There they put up false witnesses to say, "This man is always making
¹⁴ speeches against this Holy Place and the Law. ·We have heard him say that Jesus the Nazarene is going to destroy this Place and alter the traditions that Moses handed down
¹⁵ to us." ·The members of the Sanhedrin all looked intently at Stephen, and his face appeared to them like the face of an angel.

b. Gamaliel I, a Pharisee of the school of Hillel; he was Paul's teacher.
6 a. "Hellenists": Jews from outside Palestine; they had their own synagogues in Jerusalem, where the scriptures were read in Greek. The "Hebrews" were Palestinian Jews and in their synagogues scriptures were read in Hebrew. **b.** "and they prayed and laid their hands on them"; probably meaning the apostles, handing over their duties as in v. 3. **c.** Probably the descendants of Jews carried off to Rome, 63 B.C. and sold as slaves but later released.

Stephen's speech

$\begin{smallmatrix}1\\2\end{smallmatrix}$ **7** The high priest asked, "Is this true?" ·He replied, "My brothers, my fathers, listen to what I have to say. The God of glory appeared to our ancestor Abraham, while he
3 was in Mesopotamia before settling in Haran, ·*and said to him, 'Leave your country and your family and go to the*
4 *land I will show you.'*ᵃ ·So he left Chaldaea and settled in Haran; and after his father died God made him leave Haran and come to this land where you are living today.
5 God did not give him a single square foot of this land to call his own, yet he promised to *give it to him and after*
6 *him to his descendants, childless*ᵇ though he was. ·The actual words God used when he spoke to him are that *his descendants would be exiles in a foreign land, where they would be slaves and oppressed for four hundred years.*
7 *'But I will pass judgment on the nation that enslaves them'* God said *'and after this they will leave, and wor-*
8 *ship me in this* place.'ᶜ ·Then he made the covenant of circumcision: so when his son Isaac was born he circumcised him on the eighth day. Isaac did the same for Jacob, and Jacob for the twelve patriarchs.
9 "The patriarchs were *jealous of Joseph and sold him into*
10 *slavery in Egypt.*ᵈ But *God was with him,*ᵉ ·and rescued him from all his miseries by making him wise enough to attract the attention of Pharaoh king of Egypt, who *made him governor of Egypt*ᶠ and put him in charge of the royal
11 household. ·*Then a famine came* that caused much suffering *throughout Egypt and Canaan,* and our ancestors could
12 find nothing to eat. ·When Jacob *heard that there was grain for sale in Egypt,* he sent our ancestors there on a
13 first visit, ·but it was on the second that *Joseph made himself known to his brothers,* and told Pharaoh about his
14 family. ·Joseph then sent for his father Jacob and his
15 whole family, a total of *seventy-five people.* ·Jacob went down into Egypt and after he and our ancestors had died
16 there, ·their bodies were brought back to Shechem and buried in the tomb that Abraham had bought and paid for from the sons of Hamor, the father of Shechem.
17 "As the time drew near for God to fulfill the promise he had solemnly made to Abraham, our nation in Egypt
18 *grew larger and larger,* ·until a new king came to power
19 *in Egypt who knew nothing of*ᵍ Joseph. ·*He exploited* our race, and ill-treated our ancestors, forcing them to expose

20 their babies to prevent their surviving. ·It was at this period that Moses was born, *a fine child* and favored by God. He was looked after for three months in his father's

21 house, ·and after he had been exposed, *Pharaoh's daughter*

22 adopted him and *brought him up as her own son.* ·So Moses was taught all the wisdom of the Egyptians and became a man with power both in his speech and his actions.

23   "At the age of forty he decided to visit *his countrymen,*

24 *the sons of Israel.* ·When he saw one of them being illtreated he went to his defense and rescued the man by

25 *killing the Egyptian.* ·He thought his brothers realized that through him God would liberate them, but they did not.

26 The next day, when he came across some of them fighting, he tried to reconcile them. 'Friends,' he said 'you are

27 brothers; why are you hurting each other?' ·But *the man who was attacking his fellow countryman* pushed him aside. *'And who appointed you'* he said *'to be our leader*

28 *and judge? ·Do you intend to kill me as you killed the*

29 *Egyptian yesterday?'* ·Moses fled when he heard this^h^ and *he went to stay in the land of Midian,* where he became the father of two sons.

30   "Forty years later, *in the wilderness* near Mount Sinai, *an angel appeared to him in the flames of a bush* that was

31 on fire. ·Moses was amazed by what he saw. *As he went*

32 *nearer to look at it the voice of the Lord was heard, ·'I am the God of your ancestors, the God of Abraham, Isaac and Jacob.'* Moses trembled and *did not dare to look any*

33 *more.* ·*The Lord said to him, 'Take off your shoes; the*

34 *place where you are standing is holy ground. ·I have seen the way my people are ill-treated in Egypt, I have heard their groans, and I have come down to liberate them. So come here and let me send you into Egypt.'*

35   "It was the same Moses that they had disowned when they said, *'Who appointed you to be our leader and judge?'* who was now sent to be both leader and redeemer

36 through the angel who had appeared to him in the bush. ·It was Moses who, after performing *miracles and signs in*

7 a. Gn 12:1   b. Gn 15:2   c. Gn 15:2,13,14; Ex 3:12   d. Gn 37   e. Gn 39   f. Gn 41. Other direct quotations and allusions in this paragraph are from Gn 42-50.   g. O.T. quotations from here to v. 35 are from Ex 1-3.   h. In Ex 2:15 Moses runs away because he is afraid of Pharaoh.

Egypt, led them out across the Red Sea and *through the*
37 *wilderness for forty years.* •It was Moses who told the
sons of Israel, '*God will raise up a prophet like myself*
38 *for you from among your own brothers.* •When they
held the assembly in the wilderness it was only through
Moses that our ancestors could communicate with the
angel who had spoken to him on Mount Sinai; it was he
who was entrusted with words of life to hand on to us.
39 This is the man that our ancestors refused to listen to: they
pushed him aside, *turned back to Egypt* in their thoughts,
40 and said to Aaron, '*Make some gods to be our leaders;
we do not understand what has come over this Moses who*
41 *led us out of Egypt.* •It was then that *they made a bull
calf and offered sacrifice* to the idol. They were perfectly
happy with something they had made for themselves.
42 God turned away from them and abandoned them to the
worship of the army of heaven, as scripture says in the
book of the prophets:

*Did you bring me victims and sacrifices in the wilderness
for all those forty years, you House of Israel?*
43 *No, you carried the tent of Moloch on your shoulders
and the star of the god Rephan,
those idols that you had made to adore.
So now I will exile you even farther than Babylon.*

44   "While they were in the desert our ancestors possessed
the Tent of Testimony that had been constructed according
to the instructions God gave Moses, telling him to *make an
45 exact copy of the pattern* he had been shown. •It was
handed down from one ancestor of ours to another until
Joshua brought it into the country we had conquered
from the nations which were driven out by God as we
46 advanced. Here it stayed until the time of David. •He won
God's favor and asked permission *to have a temple built
47 for* the House of *Jacob,* •though it was Solomon who
48 actually *built God's house* for him. •Even so the Most
High does not live in a house that human hands have
built: for as the prophet says:

49   *With heaven my throne
and earth my footstool,
what house could you build me,
what place could you make for my rest?*
50   *Was not all this made by my hand?*

51 "You stubborn people, with your pagan hearts and pagan ears. You are always resisting the Holy Spirit, just
52 as your ancestors used to do. ·Can you name a single prophet your ancestors never persecuted? In the past they killed those who foretold the coming of the Just One, and
53 now you have become his betrayers, his murderers. ·You who had the Law brought to you by angels are the very ones who have not kept it."
54 They were infuriated when they heard this, and ground their teeth at him. ·

The stoning of Stephen. Saul as persecutor

55 But Stephen, filled with the Holy Spirit, gazed into heaven and saw the glory of God, and Jesus standing at
56 God's right hand. ·"I can see heaven thrown open" he said "and the Son of Man standing at the right hand of
57 God." ·At this all the members of the council shouted out and stopped their ears with their hands; then they all
58 rushed at him, ·sent him out of the city and stoned him. The witnesses[q] put down their clothes at the feet of a
59 young man called Saul. ·As they were stoning him, Stephen said in invocation, "Lord Jesus, receive my spirit."
60 Then he knelt down and said aloud, "Lord, do not hold this sin against them"; and with these words he fell asleep.
1 **8** Saul entirely approved of the killing.

That day a bitter persecution started against the church in Jerusalem, and everyone[a] except the apostles fled to the country districts of Judaea and Samaria.
2 There were some devout people, however, who buried Stephen and made great mourning for him.
3 Saul then worked for the total destruction of the Church; he went from house to house arresting both men and women and sending them to prison.

Philip in Samaria

4 Those who had escaped went from place to place
5 preaching the Good News. ·One of them was Philip

i. Nb 14:33   j. Dt 18:15,18   k. Ex 32:1,23 and 32:4,6   l. The stars and planets.   m. Am 5:25-27 (LXX)   n. Ex 25:40   o. 1 K 6:2   p. Is 66:1-2   q. By the Law, the accusers had to begin the execution of the sentence.
8 a. The persecution seems to have been directed principally against the Hellenists.

who went to a Samaritan town and proclaimed the Christ
6 to them. ·The people united in welcoming the message
Philip preached, either because they had heard of the
miracles he worked or because they saw them for them-
7 selves. ·There were, for example, unclean spirits that came
shrieking out of many who were possessed, and several
8 paralytics and cripples were cured. ·As a result there was
great rejoicing in that town.

Simon the magician

9　　Now a man called Simon had already practiced magic
arts in the town and astounded the Samaritan people. He
10 had given it out that he was someone momentous, ·and
everyone believed what he said; eminent citizens and ordinary people alike had declared, "He is the divine power
11 that is called Great." ·They had only been won over to him
because of the long time he had spent working on them
12 with his magic. ·But when they believed Philip's preaching
of the Good News about the kingdom of God and the name
of Jesus Christ, they were baptized, both men and women,
13 and even Simon himself became a believer. After his
baptism Simon, who went round constantly with Philip,
was astonished when he saw the wonders and great miracles that took place.
14　　When the apostles in Jerusalem heard that Samaria had
accepted the word of God, they sent Peter and John to
15 them, ·and they went down there, and prayed for the
16 Samaritans to receive the Holy Spirit, ·for as yet he had
not come down on any of them: they had only been
17 baptized in the name of the Lord Jesus. ·Then they laid
hands on them, and they received the Holy Spirit.
18　　When Simon saw that the Spirit was given through the
imposition of hands by the apostles, he offered them some
19 money. ·"Give me the same power" he said "so that any-
20 one I lay my hands on will receive the Holy Spirit." ·Peter
answered, "May your silver be lost forever, and you with
it, for thinking that money could buy what God has given
21 for nothing! ·You have no share, no rights, in this: God
22 can see how your heart is warped. ·Repent of this wickedness of yours, and pray to the Lord; you may still be for-
23 given for thinking as you did; ·it is plain to me that you
are trapped in the bitterness of gall and the chains of sin."
24 "Pray to the Lord for me yourselves" Simon replied "so

that none of the things you have spoken about may happen to me."

25 Having given their testimony and proclaimed the word of the Lord, they went back to Jerusalem, preaching the Good News to a number of Samaritan villages.

Philip baptizes a eunuch

26 The angel of the Lord spoke to Philip saying, "Be ready to set out at noon along the road that goes from Jerusalem
27 down to Gaza, the desert road." ·So he set off on his journey. Now it happened that an Ethiopian had been on pilgrimage to Jerusalem; he was a eunuch and an officer at the court of the Kandake, or queen, of Ethiopia, and was
28 in fact her chief treasurer. ·He was now on his way home; and as he sat in his chariot he was reading the prophet
29 Isaiah. ·The Spirit said to Philip, "Go up and meet that
30 chariot." ·When Philip ran up, he heard him reading Isaiah the prophet and asked, "Do you understand what you
31 are reading?" ·"How can I" he replied "unless I have someone to guide me?" So he invited Philip to get in and
32 sit by his side. ·Now the passage of scripture he was reading was this: *Queen of Shibn (Ethiopia)*

Like a sheep that is led to the slaughter-house,
like a lamb that is dumb in front of its shearers,
like these he never opens his mouth.
33 *He has been humiliated and has no one to defend him.*
Who will ever talk about his descendants,
since his life on earth has been cut short![b]

34 The eunuch turned to Philip and said, "Tell me, is the
35 prophet referring to himself or someone else?" ·Starting, therefore, with this text of scripture Philip proceeded to explain the Good News of Jesus to him.
36 Further along the road they came to some water, and the eunuch said, "Look, there is some water here; is there
38 anything to stop me being baptized?"[c] ·He ordered the chariot to stop, then Philip and the eunuch both went down
39 into the water and Philip baptized him. ·But after they had come up out of the water again Philip was taken away by the Spirit of the Lord, and the eunuch never saw him

b. Is 53:7-8, quoted from the LXX version. c. At the time when verse numbers were introduced, there was a gloss, numbered v. 37, at this point.

⁴⁰ again but went on his way rejoicing. ·Philip found that he had reached Azotus and continued his journey proclaiming the Good News in every town as far as Caesarea.

The conversion of Saul

¹ 9 Meanwhile Saul was still breathing threats to slaughter the Lord's disciples. He had gone to the high priest ² and asked for letters addressed to the synagogues in Damascus, that would authorize him to arrest and take to Jerusalem any followers of the Way, men or women, that he could find.

³ Suddenly, while he was traveling to Damascus and just before he reached the city, there came a light from heaven ⁴ all round him. ·He fell to the ground, and then he heard a voice saying, "Saul, Saul, why are you persecuting me?" ⁵ "Who are you, Lord?" he asked, and the voice answered, ⁶ "I am Jesus, and you are persecuting me. ·Get up now and go into the city, and you will be told what you have ⁷ to do." ·The men traveling with Saul stood there speechless, for though they heard the voice they could see no one. ⁸ Saul got up from the ground, but even with his eyes wide open he could see nothing at all, and they had to lead ⁹ him into Damascus by the hand. ·For three days he was without his sight, and took neither food nor drink.

¹⁰ A disciple called Ananias who lived in Damascus had a vision in which he heard the Lord say to him, "Ananias!" ¹¹ When he replied, "Here I am, Lord," ·the Lord said, "You must go to Straight Street and ask at the house of Judas for someone called Saul, who comes from Tarsus. At this ¹² moment he is praying, ·having had a vision of a man called Ananias coming in and laying hands on him to give him back his sight."

¹³ When he heard that, Ananias said, "Lord, several people have told me about this man and all the harm he has been ¹⁴ doing to your saints in Jerusalem. ·He has only come here because he holds a warrant from the chief priests to ar- ¹⁵ rest everybody who invokes your name." ·The Lord replied, "You must go all the same, because this man is my chosen instrument to bring my name before pagans and ¹⁶ pagan kings and before the people of Israel; ·I myself will show him how much he himself must suffer for my name."

¹⁷ Then Ananias went. He entered the house, and at once laid his hands on Saul and said, "Brother Saul, I have been sent by the Lord Jesus who appeared to you on your way

here so that you may recover your sight and be filled with
18 the Holy Spirit." ·Immediately it was as though scales fell
away from Saul's eyes and he could see again. So he was
19 baptized there and then, ·and after taking some food he
regained his strength.

Saul's preaching at Damascus

After he had spent only a few days with the disciples in
20 Damascus, ·he began preaching in the synagogues. "Jesus
21 is the Son of God." ·All his hearers were amazed. "Surely"
they said "this is the man who organized the attack in Jerusalem against the people who invoke this name, and who
came here for the sole purpose of arresting them to have
22 them tried by the chief priests?" ·Saul's power increased
steadily, and he was able to throw the Jewish colony at
Damascus into complete confusion by the way he demonstrated that Jesus was the Christ.
23 Some time passed,[a] and the Jews worked out a plot to
24 kill him, ·but news of it reached Saul. To make sure of
killing him they kept watch on the gates day and night,
25 but when it was dark the disciples took him and let him
down from the top of the wall, lowering him in a basket.

Saul's visit to Jerusalem *(Galatians E, Jesus)*

26 When he got to Jerusalem he tried to join the disciples,
but they were all afraid of him: they could not believe he
27 was really a disciple. ·Barnabas, however, took charge of
him, introduced him to the apostles, and explained how the
Lord had appeared to Saul and spoken to him on his journey, and how he had preached boldly at Damascus in the
28 name of Jesus. ·Saul now started to go round with them in
Jerusalem, preaching fearlessly in the name of the Lord.
29 But after he had spoken to the Hellenists, and argued with
30 them, they became determined to kill him. ·When the
brothers knew, they took him to Caesarea, and sent him
off from there to Tarsus.

A lull

31 The churches throughout Judaea, Galilee and Samaria
were now left in peace, building themselves up, living in
the fear of the Lord, and filled with the consolation of
the Holy Spirit.

9 a. Three years, according to Ga 1:17-18.

Peter cures a paralytic at Lydda

32 Peter visited one place after another and eventually
33 came to the saints living down in Lydda. ·There he found
a man called Aeneas, a paralytic who had been bedridden
34 for eight years. ·Peter said to him, "Aeneas, Jesus Christ
cures you: get up and fold up your sleeping mat." Aeneas
35 got up immediately; ·everybody who lived in Lydda and
Sharon saw him, and they were all converted to the Lord.

Peter raises a woman to life at Jaffa

36 At Jaffa there was a woman disciple called Tabitha, or
Dorcas in Greek,[b] who never tired of doing good or
37 giving in charity. ·But the time came when she got ill and
died, and they washed her and laid her out in a room
38 upstairs. ·Lydda is not far from Jaffa, so when the disciples heard that Peter was there, they sent two men with
an urgent message for him, "Come and visit us as soon
as possible."
39 Peter went back with them straightaway, and on his arrival they took him to the upstairs room, where all the
widows stood round him in tears, showing him tunics and
other clothes Dorcas had made when she was with them.
40 Peter sent them all out of the room and knelt down and
prayed. Then he turned to the dead woman and said,
"Tabitha, stand up." She opened her eyes, looked at Peter
41 and sat up. ·Peter helped her to her feet, then he called
in the saints and widows and showed them she was alive.
42 The whole of Jaffa heard about it and many believed in
the Lord.
43 Peter stayed on some time in Jaffa, lodging with a
leather-tanner called Simon.

Peter visits a Roman centurion

1 10 One of the centurions of the Italica cohort stationed
2 in Caesarea was called Cornelius. ·He and the whole
of his household were devout and God-fearing, and he gave
generously to Jewish causes and prayed constantly to God.
3 One day at about the ninth hour he had a vision in which
he distinctly saw the angel of God come into his house and
4 call out to him, "Cornelius!" ·He stared at the vision in
terror and exclaimed, "What is it, Lord?" "Your offering
of prayers and alms" the angel answered "has been ac-
5 cepted by God. ·Now you must send someone to Jaffa and
6 fetch a man called Simon, known as Peter, ·who is lodging

⁷ with Simon the tanner whose house is by the sea." ·When the angel who said this had gone, Cornelius called two of ⁸ the slaves and a devout soldier of his staff, ·told them what had happened, and sent them off to Jaffa. *Joppa*

⁹ Next day, while they were still on their journey and had only a short distance to go before reaching Jaffa, Peter went to the housetop at about the sixth hour to pray. ¹⁰ He felt hungry and was looking forward to his meal, but ¹¹ before it was ready he fell into a trance ·and saw heaven thrown open and something like a big sheet being let down ¹² to earth by its four corners; ·it contained every possible sort of animal and bird, walking, crawling or flying ones. ¹³ A voice then said to him, "Now, Peter; kill and eat!" ¹⁴ But Peter answered, "Certainly not, Lord; I have never yet ¹⁵ eaten anything profane or unclean." ·Again, a second time, the voice spoke to him, "What God has made clean, you ¹⁶ have no right to call profane." ·This was repeated three times, and then suddenly the container was drawn up to heaven again.   *dream*

¹⁷ Peter was still worrying over the meaning of the vision he had seen, when the men sent by Cornelius arrived. They had asked where Simon's house was and they were now ¹⁸ standing at the door, ·calling out to know if the Simon ¹⁹ known as Peter was lodging there. ·Peter's mind was still on the vision and the Spirit had to tell him, "Some men ²⁰ have come to see you. ·Hurry down, and do not hesitate about going back with them; it was I who told them to ²¹ come." ·Peter went down and said to them, "I am the man ²² you are looking for; why have you come?" ·They said, "The centurion Cornelius, who is an upright and God-fearing man, highly regarded by the entire Jewish people, was directed by a holy angel to send for you and bring you to his house and to listen to what you have to say." ²³ So Peter asked them in and gave them lodging.

Next day, he was ready to go off with them, accompa-²⁴ nied by some of the brothers from Jaffa. ·They reached Caesarea the following day, and Cornelius was waiting for them. He had asked his relations and close friends to be ²⁵ there, ·and as Peter reached the house Cornelius went out ²⁶ to meet him, knelt at his feet and prostrated himself. ·But Peter helped him up. "Stand up," he said "I am only a man ²⁷ after all!" ·Talking together they went in to meet all the

b. I.e. "Gazelle."

²⁸ people assembled there, ·and Peter said to them, "You know it is forbidden for Jews to mix with people of another race and visit them, but God has made it clear to me that

²⁹ I must not call anyone profane or unclean. ·That is why I made no objection to coming when I was sent for; but

³⁰ I should like to know exactly why you sent for me." ·Cornelius replied, "Three days ago I was praying in my house at the ninth hour, when I suddenly saw a man in front of

³¹ me in shining robes. ·He said, 'Cornelius, your prayer has been heard and your alms have been accepted as a

³² sacrifice in the sight of God; ·so now you must send to Jaffa and fetch Simon known as Peter who is lodging in

³³ the house of Simon the tanner, by the sea." ·So I sent for you at once, and you have been kind enough to come. Here we all are, assembled in front of you to hear what message God has given you for us."

Peter's address in the house of Cornelius

³⁴   Then Peter addressed them: "The truth I have now come to realize" he said "is that God does not have favor-

³⁵ ites, ·but that anybody of any nationality who fears God and does what is right is acceptable to him.

³⁶   "It is true, God sent his word to the people of Israel, and it was to them that *the good news of peace was brought*ᵃ by Jesus Christ—but Jesus Christ is Lord of all

³⁷ men. ·You must have heard about the recent happenings in Judaea; about Jesus of Nazareth and how he began in

³⁸ Galilee, after John had been preaching baptism. ·*God had anointed him with the Holy Spirit*ᵇ and with power, and because God was with him, Jesus went about doing good and curing all who had fallen into the power of the devil.

³⁹ Now I, and those with me, can witness to everything he did throughout the countryside of Judaea and in Jerusalem itself: and also to the fact that they killed him by hanging

⁴⁰ him on a tree, ·yet three days afterward God raised him

⁴¹ to life and allowed him to be seen, ·not by the whole people but only by certain witnesses God had chosen beforehand. Now we are those witnesses—we have eaten and

⁴² drunk with him after his resurrection from the dead—·and he has ordered us to proclaim this to his people and to tell them that God has appointed him to judge everyone, alive

⁴³ or dead. ·It is to him that all the prophets bear this witness: that all who believe in Jesus will have their sins forgiven through his name."

Baptism of the first pagans

44 While Peter was still speaking the Holy Spirit came
45 down on all the listeners. ·Jewish believers who had accompanied Peter were all astonished that the gift of the
46 Holy Spirit should be poured out on the pagans too, ·since
they could hear them speaking strange languages and proclaiming the greatness of God. Peter himself then said,
47 "Could anyone refuse the water of baptism to these people,
now they have received the Holy Spirit just as much as we
48 have?" ·He then gave orders for them to be baptized in the
name of Jesus Christ. Afterwards they begged him to stay
on for some days.

Jerusalem: Peter justifies his conduct

1 The apostles and the brothers in Judaea heard that
2 1 1 the pagans too had accepted the word of God, ·and
when Peter came up to Jerusalem the Jews criticized him
3 and said, "So you have been visiting the uncircumcised
4 and eating with them, have you?" ·Peter in reply gave them
5 the details point by point: ·"One day, when I was in the
town of Jaffa," he began "I fell into a trance as I was praying and had a vision of something like a big sheet being
let down from heaven by its four corners. This sheet
6 reached the ground quite close to me. ·I watched it intently and saw all sorts of animals and wild beasts—every-
7 thing possible that could walk, crawl or fly. ·Then I heard
8 a voice that said to me, 'Now, Peter; kill and eat!' ·But
I answered: Certainly not, Lord; nothing profane or un-
9 clean has ever crossed my lips. ·And a second time the
voice spoke from heaven, 'What God has made clean, you
10 have no right to call profane.' ·This was repeated three
times, before the whole of it was drawn up to heaven again.
11 "Just at that moment, three men stopped outside the
house where we were staying; they had been sent from
12 Caesarea to fetch me, ·and the Spirit told me to have no
hesitation about going back with them. The six brothers
here came with me as well, and we entered the man's
13 house. ·He told us he had seen an angel standing in his
house who said, 'Send to Jaffa and fetch Simon known
14 as Peter; ·he has a message for you that will save you and
your entire household.'
15 "I had scarcely begun to speak when the Holy Spirit

10 a. Is 52:7   b. Is 61:1

came down on them in the same way as it came on us at
16 the beginning, ·and I remembered that the Lord had said,
'John baptized with water, but you will be baptized with
17 the Holy Spirit.' ·I realized then that God was giving
them the identical thing he gave to us when we believed
in the Lord Jesus Christ; and who was I to stand in God's
way?"
18   This account satisfied them, and they gave glory to God.
"God" they said "can evidently grant even the pagans the
repentance that leads to life."

Foundation of the church of Antioch   *Lebanon*

19   Those who had escaped during the persecution that happened because of Stephen traveled as far as Phoenicia
and Cyprus and Antioch,[a] but they usually proclaimed the
20 message only to Jews. ·Some of them, however, who came
from Cyprus and Cyrene, went to Antioch where they
started preaching to the Greeks, proclaiming the Good
21 News of the Lord Jesus to them as well. ·The Lord helped
them, and a great number believed and were converted
to the Lord.
22   The church in Jerusalem heard about this and they sent
23 Barnabas to Antioch. ·There he could see for himself that
God had given grace, and this pleased him, and he urged
them all to remain faithful to the Lord with heartfelt de-
24 votion; ·for he was a good man, filled with the Holy Spirit
and with faith. And a large number of people were won
over to the Lord.
25   Barnabas then left for Tarsus to look for Saul, ·and
26 when he found him he brought him to Antioch. As things
turned out they were to live together in that church a whole
year, instructing a large number of people. It was at Antioch that the disciples were first called "Christians."

Barnabas and Saul sent as deputies to Jerusalem

27   While they were there some prophets[b] came down to
28 Antioch from Jerusalem, ·and one of them whose name
was Agabus, seized by the Spirit, stood up and predicted
that a famine would spread over the whole empire. This
in fact happened before the reign of Claudius came to an
29 end.[c] ·The disciples decided to send relief, each to contribute what he could afford, to the brothers living in Ju-
30 daea. ·They did this and delivered their contributions to
the elders in the care of Barnabas and Saul.

Peter's arrest and miraculous deliverance[a]

1 2 It was about this time that King Herod started persecuting certain members of the Church. ·He beheaded
3 James the brother of John, ·and when he saw that this
4 pleased the Jews he decided to arrest Peter as well. ·This
was during the days of Unleavened Bread, and he put
Peter in prison, assigning four squads of four soldiers each
to guard him in turns. Herod meant to try Peter in public
5 after the end of Passover week. ·All the time Peter was
under guard the Church prayed to God for him unre-
mittingly.

6 On the night before Herod was to try him, Peter was
sleeping between two soldiers, fastened with double chains,
while guards kept watch at the main entrance to the prison.
7 Then suddenly the angel of the Lord stood there, and the
cell was filled with light. He tapped Peter on the side and
woke him. "Get up!" he said "Hurry!"—and the chains fell
8 from his hands. ·The angel then said, "Put on your belt
and sandals." After he had done this, the angel next said,
9 "Wrap your cloak round you and follow me." ·Peter followed him, but had no idea that what the angel did was
all happening in reality; he thought he was seeing a vision.
10 They passed through two guard posts one after the other,
and reached the iron gate leading to the city. This opened
of its own accord; they went through it and had walked
the whole length of one street when suddenly the angel
11 left him. ·It was only then that Peter came to himself.
"Now I know it is all true" he said. "The Lord really did
send his angel and has saved me from Herod and from
all that the Jewish people were so certain would happen
to me."

12 As soon as he realized this he went straight to the house
of Mary the mother of John Mark,[b] where a number of

11 a. Antioch on the Orontes, capital of Syria. b. Christian
prophets, inspired speakers, generally ranked second to the
apostles in the lists of the persons "gifted by the Spirit."
c. Claudius reigned until 54 A.D.
12 a. Herod Agrippa I was king of Judaea and Samaria, 41-44
A.D. This episode, though fitted in the book between 11:30 and
12:25, must have taken place before Barnabas and Saul
visited Jerusalem. b. Mark is mentioned in ch. 12,13 and 15:
also in Col 4 and Phm 24 and 2 Tim 4. Tradition names him
as author of the second gospel.

¹³ people had assembled and were praying. ·He knocked at the outside door and a servant called Rhoda came to answer it.
¹⁴ She recognized Peter's voice and was so overcome with joy that, instead of opening the door, she ran inside with the
¹⁵ news that Peter was standing at the main entrance. ·They said to her, "You are out of your mind," but she insisted that it was true. Then they said, "It must be his angel!"
¹⁶ Peter, meanwhile, was still knocking, so they opened the door and were amazed to see that it really was Peter him-
¹⁷ self. ·With a gesture of his hand he stopped them talking, and described to them how the Lord had led him out of prison. He added, "Tell James and the brothers." Then he left and went to another place.
¹⁸ When daylight came there was a great commotion among the soldiers, who could not imagine what had become of
¹⁹ Peter. ·Herod put out an unsuccessful search for him; he had the guards questioned, and before leaving Judaea to take up residence in Caesarea he gave orders for their execution.

The death of the persecutor

²⁰ Now Herod was on bad terms with the Tyrians and Sidonians. However, they sent a joint deputation which managed to enlist the support of Blastus, the king's chamberlain, and through him negotiated a treaty, since their country depended for its food supply on King Herod's ter-
²¹ ritory. ·A day was fixed, and Herod, wearing his robes of
²² state and enthroned on a dais, made a speech to them. ·The people acclaimed him with, "It is a god speaking, not a
²³ man!", ·and at that moment the angel of the Lord struck him down, because he had not given the glory to God. He was eaten away with worms and died.

Barnabas and Saul return to Antioch

²⁴ The word of God continued to spread and to gain fol-
²⁵ lowers. ·Barnabas and Saul completed their task and came back from Jerusalem, bringing John Mark with them.

III. THE MISSION OF BARNABAS AND PAUL
THE COUNCIL OF JERUSALEM

The mission sent out

1 13 In the church at Antioch the following were prophets and teachers: Barnabas, Simeon called Niger, and Lucius of Cyrene, Manaen, who had been brought up with 2 Herod the tetrarch, and Saul. ·One day while they were offering worship to the Lord and keeping a fast, the Holy Spirit said, "I want Barnabas and Saul set apart for the 3 work to which I have called them." ·So it was that after fasting and prayer they laid their hands on them and sent them off.

Cyprus: the magician Elymas

4 So these two, sent on their mission by the Holy Spirit, went down to Seleucia and from there sailed to Cyprus. 5 They landed at Salamis and proclaimed the word of God in the synagogues of the Jews; John acted as their assistant. 6 They traveled the whole length of the island, and at Paphos they came in contact with a Jewish magician called 7 Bar-jesus. ·This false prophet was one of the attendants of the proconsul Sergius Paulus who was an extremely intelligent man. The proconsul summoned Barnabas and Saul 8 and asked to hear the word of God, ·but Elymas Magos— as he was called in Greek—tried to stop them so as to pre- 9 vent the proconsul's conversion to the faith. ·Then Saul, 10 whose other name is Paul, looked him full in the face ·and said, "You utter fraud, you impostor, you son of the devil, you enemy of all true religion, why don't you stop twisting 11 the straightforward ways of the Lord? ·Now watch how the hand of the Lord will strike you: you will be blind, and for a time you will not see the sun." That instant, everything went misty and dark for him, and he groped about to find 12 someone to lead him by the hand. ·The proconsul, who had watched everything, became a believer, being astonished by what he had learned about the Lord..

They arrive at Antioch in Pisidia

13 Paul and his friends went by sea from Paphos to Perga in Pamphylia where John left them to go back to Jerusalem.

¹⁴ The others carried on from Perga till they reached Antioch in Pisidia. Here they went to synagogue on the sabbath ¹⁵ and took their seats. ·After the lessons from the Law and the Prophets had been read, the presidents of the synagogue sent them a message: "Brothers, if you would like to address some words of encouragement to the congregation, ¹⁶ please do so." ·Paul stood up, held up a hand for silence and began to speak:

Paul's preaching before the Jews

¹⁷ "Men of Israel, and fearers of God, listen! ·The God of our nation Israel chose our ancestors, and made our people great when they were living as foreigners in Egypt; then by ¹⁸ divine power he led them out, ·and for about forty years ¹⁹ *took care of them in the wilderness.* ·When he had destroyed *seven nations in Canaan, he put them in possession*ᵃ of their ²⁰ land ·for about four hundred and fifty years. After this he ²¹ gave them judges, down to the prophet Samuel. ·Then they demanded a king, and God gave them Saul son of Kish, a ²² man of the tribe of Benjamin. After forty years, ·he deposed him and made David their king, of whom he approved in these words, *[I have selected David son of Jesse, a man after my own heart, who will carry out my whole* ²³ *purpose.]*ᵇ ·To keep his promise, God has raised up for ²⁴ Israel one of David's descendants, Jesus, as Savior, ·whose coming was heralded by John when he proclaimed a ²⁵ baptism of repentance for the whole people of Israel. ·Before John ended his career he said, 'I am not the one you imagine me to be; that one is coming after me and I am not fit to undo his sandal.'

²⁶ "My brothers, sons of Abraham's race, and all you who fear God, this message of salvation is meant for you. ²⁷ What the people of Jerusalem and their rulers did, though they did not realize it, was in fact to fulfill the prophecies ²⁸ read on every sabbath. ·Though they found nothing to justify his death, they condemned him and asked Pilate to ²⁹ have him executed. ·When they had carried out everything that scripture foretells about him they took him down from ³⁰ the tree and buried him in a tomb. ·But God raised him ³¹ from the dead, ·and for many days he appeared to those who had accompanied him from Galilee to Jerusalem: and it is these same companions of his who are now his witnesses before our people.

³² "We have come here to tell you the Good News. It was

88 to our ancestors that God made the promise but ·it is to us, their children, that he has fulfilled it, by raising Jesus from the dead. As scripture says in the first psalm: *You are my*

84 *son: today I have become your father.* ·The fact that God raised him from the dead, never to return to corruption, is no more than what he had declared: *To you I shall give the*

85 *sure and holy things promised to David.*[c] ·This is explained by another text: *You will not allow your holy one to ex-*

86 *perience corruption.*[d] ·Now when David in his own time had served God's purposes he died; he was buried with his ancestors and has certainly *experienced corruption.*

87 The one whom God has raised up, however, has not *experienced corruption.*

88 "My brothers, I want you to realize that it is through him that forgiveness of your sins is proclaimed. Through him justification from all sins which the Law of Moses was

89 unable to justify ·is offered to every believer.

40 "So be careful—or what the prophets say will happen to you.

41 *Cast your eyes around you, mockers;*
be amazed, and perish!
For I am doing something in your own days
that you would not believe if you were to be told of it."[e]

42 As they left they were asked to preach on the same
43 theme the following sabbath. ·When the meeting broke up many Jews and devout converts joined Paul and Barnabas, and in their talks with them Paul and Barnabas urged them to remain faithful to the grace God had given them.

Paul and Barnabas preach to the pagans

44 The next sabbath almost the whole town assembled to
45 hear the word of God. ·When they saw the crowds, the Jews, prompted by jealousy, used blasphemies and con-
46 tradicted everything Paul said. ·Then Paul and Barnabas spoke out boldly. "We had to proclaim the word of God to you first, but since you have rejected it, since you do not think yourselves worthy of eternal life, we must turn to the
47 pagans. ·For this is what the Lord commanded us to do when he said:

I have made you a light for the nations,
so that my salvation may reach the ends of the earth."[f]

13 a. Dt 1:31; 7:1 **b.** 1 S 13:14 **c.** Is 55:3 **d.** Ps 16:9
e. Hab 1:5 **f.** Is 49:6, quoted freely from the LXX.

⁴⁸ It made the pagans very happy to hear this and they thanked the Lord for his message; all who were destined ⁴⁹ for eternal life became believers. ·Thus the word of the Lord spread through the whole countryside.

⁵⁰ But the Jews worked upon some of the devout women of the upper classes and the leading men of the city and persuaded them to turn against Paul and Barnabas and ⁵¹ expell them from their territory. ·So they shook the dust ⁵² from their feet in defiance and went off to Iconium; ·but the disciples were filled with joy and the Holy Spirit.

Iconium evangelized Konya

¹ **14** At Iconium they went to the Jewish synagogue, as they had at Antioch, and they spoke so effectively that a great many Jews and Greeks became believers.
² Some of the Jews, however, refused to believe, and they poisoned the minds of the pagans against the brothers.[a]
³ Accordingly Paul and Barnabas stayed on for some time, preaching fearlessly for the Lord; and the Lord supported all they said about his gift of grace, allowing signs and wonders to be performed by them.
⁴ The people in the city were divided, some supported ⁵ the Jews, others the apostles, ·but eventually with the connivance of the authorities a move was made by pagans as well as Jews to make attacks on them and to stone them. ⁶ When the apostles came to hear of this, they went off for safety to Lycaonia where, in the towns of Lystra and Derbe ⁷ and in the surrounding country, ·they preached the Good News.

Healing of a cripple

⁸ A man sat there[b] who had never walked in his life, be- ⁹ cause his feet were crippled from birth; ·and as he listened to Paul preaching, he managed to catch his eye. Seeing ¹⁰ that the man had the faith to be cured, ·Paul said in a loud voice, "Get to your feet—stand up," and the cripple jumped up and began to walk.
¹¹ When the crowd saw what Paul had done they shouted in the language of Lycaonia, "These people are gods who ¹² have come down to us disguised as men." ·They addressed Barnabas as Zeus, and since Paul was the principal speaker ¹³ they called him Hermes.[c] ·The priests of Zeus-outside-the-Gate, proposing that all the people should offer sacrifice ¹⁴ with them, brought garlanded oxen to the gates. ·When the

apostles Barnabas and Paul heard what was happening
they tore their clothes,[d] and rushed into the crowd, shout-
15 ing, •"Friends, what do you think you are doing? We are
only human beings like you. We have come with good news
to make you turn from these empty idols to the living
God who made heaven and earth and the sea and all that
16 these hold. •In the past he allowed each nation to go its own
17 way; •but even then he did not leave you without evidence
of himself in the good things he does for you: he sends you
rain from heaven, he makes your crops grow when they
18 should, he gives you food and makes you happy." •Even
this speech, however, was scarcely enough to stop the
crowd offering them sacrifice.

The mission is disrupted

19   Then some Jews arrived from Antioch and Iconium, and
turned the people against the apostles. They stoned Paul
and dragged him outside the town, thinking he was dead.
20 The disciples came crowding round him but, as they did so,
he stood up and went back to the town. The next day he
and Barnabas went off to Derbe.
21   Having preached the Good News in that town and made
a considerable number of disciples, they went back through
22 Lystra and Iconium to Antioch. •They put fresh heart into
the disciples, encouraging them to persevere in the faith.
"We all have to experience many hardships" they said
23 "before we enter the kingdom of God." •In each of these
churches they appointed elders, and with prayer and fasting they commended them to the Lord in whom they had
come to believe.
24   They passed through Pisidia and reached Pamphylia.
25 Then after proclaiming the word at Perga they went down
26 to Attalia •and from there sailed for Antioch, where they
had originally been commended to the grace of God for
the work they had now completed.
27   On their arrival they assembled the church and gave an
account of all that God had done with them, and how he
28 had opened the door of faith to the pagans. •They stayed
there with the disciples for some time.

14 a. This sentence is a parenthesis. V. 3 continues from v. 1.
b. In Lystra.   c. Mercury, the messenger or herald of the gods.
d. Conventional sign of despair.

Controversy at Antioch

1 **15** Then some men came down from Judaea[a] and taught the brothers, "Unless you have yourselves circum- **2** cised in the tradition of Moses you cannot be saved." ·This led to disagreement, and after Paul and Barnabas had had a long argument with these men it was arranged that Paul and Barnabas and others of the church should go up to Jerusalem and discuss the problem with the apostles and elders.

3 All the members of the church saw them off, and as they passed through Phoenicia and Samaria they told how the pagans had been converted, and this news was received **4** with the greatest satisfaction by the brothers. ·When they arrived in Jerusalem they were welcomed by the church and by the apostles and elders, and gave an account of all that God had done with them.

Controversy at Jerusalem

5 But certain members of the Pharisees' party who had become believers objected, insisting that the pagans should be circumcised and instructed to keep the Law of Moses. **6 7** The apostles and elders met to look into the matter, ·and after the discussion had gone on a long time, Peter stood up and addressed them.

Peter's speech

"My brothers," he said "you know perfectly well that in the early days God made his choice among you: the pagans were to learn the Good News from me and so become **8** believers. ·In fact God, who can read everyone's heart, showed his approval of them by giving the Holy Spirit to **9** them just as he had to us. ·God made no distinction be- tween them and us, since he purified their hearts by faith. **10** It would only provoke God's anger now, surely, if you im- posed on the disciples the very burden that neither we nor **11** our ancestors were strong enough to support? ·Remember, we believe that we are saved in the same way as they are: through the grace of the Lord Jesus."

12 This silenced the entire assembly, and they listened to Barnabas and Paul describing all the signs and wonders God had worked through them among the pagans.

James' speech

13 When they had finished it was James who spoke. "My
14 brothers," he said "listen to me. ·Simeon[b] has described
how God first arranged to enlist a people for his name out
15 of the pagans. ·This is entirely in harmony with the words
of the prophets, since the scriptures say:

16   *After that I shall return*
       and rebuild the fallen House of David;
       I shall rebuild it from its ruins
       and restore it.
17   *Then the rest of mankind,*
       all the pagans who are consecrated to my name,
       will look for the Lord,
18   *says the Lord who made this ·known so long ago.[c]*

19 "I rule, then, that instead of making things more difficult
20 for pagans who turn to God, ·we send them a letter telling
them merely to abstain from anything polluted by idols,[d]
from fornication,[e] from the meat of strangled animals
21 and from blood. ·For Moses has always had his preachers
in every town, and is read aloud in the synagogues every
sabbath."

The apostolic letter

22 Then the apostles and elders decided to choose delegates
to send to Antioch with Paul and Barnabas; the whole
church concurred with this. They chose Judas known as
Barsabbas and Silas,[f] both leading men in the brotherhood,
23 and gave them this letter to take with them:

"The apostles and elders, your brothers, send greetings to
the brothers of pagan birth in Antioch, Syria and Cilicia.
24 We hear that some of our members have disturbed you with
their demands and have unsettled your minds. They acted
25 without any authority from us, ·and so we have decided
unanimously to elect delegates and to send them to you
26 with Barnabas and Paul, men we highly respect ·who have
dedicated their lives to the name of our Lord Jesus Christ.

15 a. In the allusion to this incident in Ga, they are said to have
come "from James," Ga 2:12. b. Semitic form of Simon Peter's
name. c. Am 9:11,12, quoted according to the LXX. d. I.e.
which has been offered in sacrifice to false gods. e. Perhaps
all the irregular marriages listed in Lv 18. f. Silas, also mentioned in Ac 18; 1 Th, 2 Th, 2 Co, 1 P.

²⁷ Accordingly we are sending you Judas and Silas, who will confirm by word of mouth what we have written in this ²⁸ letter. ·It has been decided by the Holy Spirit and by ourselves not to saddle you with any burden beyond these ²⁹ essentials: ·you are to abstain from food sacrificed to idols, from blood, from the meat of strangled animals and from fornication. Avoid these, and you will do what is right. Farewell."

The delegates at Antioch

³⁰ The party left and went down to Antioch, where they summoned the whole community and delivered the letter. ³¹ The community read it and were delighted with the en-³² couragement it gave them. ·Judas and Silas, being themselves prophets, spoke for a long time, encouraging and ³³ strengthening the brothers. ·These two spent some time there, and then the brothers wished them peace and they ³⁵ went back to those who had sent them. ·Paul and Barnabas, however, stayed on in Antioch, and there with many others they taught and proclaimed the Good News, the word of the Lord.

IV. PAUL'S MISSIONS

Paul separates from Barnabas and recruits Silas

³⁶ On a later occasion Paul said to Barnabas, "Let us go back and visit all the towns where we preached the word of the Lord, so that we can see how the brothers are doing." ³⁷·³⁸ Barnabas suggested taking John Mark, ·but Paul was not in favor of taking along the very man who had deserted them in Pamphylia and had refused to share in their work. ³⁹ After a violent quarrel they parted company, and Bar-⁴⁰ nabas sailed off with Mark to Cyprus. ·Before Paul left, he chose Silas to accompany him and was commended by the brothers to the grace of God.

Lycaonia: Paul recruits Timothy

⁴¹ He traveled through Syria and Cilicia, consolidating the churches.

16 ¹ From there he went to Derbe, and then on to Lystra. Here there was a disciple called Timothy, whose mother was a Jewess who had become a believer; but his

2 father was a Greek. ·The brothers at Lystra and Iconium
3 spoke well of Timothy, ·and Paul, who wanted to have him
as a traveling companion, had him circumcised. This was
on account of the Jews in the locality where everyone
knew his father was a Greek.

4   As they visited one town after another, they passed on
the decisions reached by the apostles and elders in Jerusalem, with instructions to respect them.

5   So the churches grew strong in the faith, as well as growing daily in numbers.

The crossing into Asia Minor

6   They traveled through Phrygia and the Galatian country, having been told by the Holy Spirit not to preach the
7 word in Asia. ·When they reached the frontier of Mysia
they thought to cross it into Bithynia, but as the Spirit of
8 Jesus would not allow them, ·they went through Mysia and
came down to Troas.

9   One night Paul had a vision: a Macedonian appeared
and appealed to him in these words, "Come across to
10 Macedonia and help us." ·Once he had seen this vision we
lost no time in arranging a passage to Macedonia, convinced that God had called us to bring them the Good
News.

Arrival at Philippi

11 · Sailing from Troas we made a straight run for Samo-
12 thrace; the next day for Neapolis, ·and from there for
Philippi, a Roman colony and the principal city of that
particular district of Macedonia. After a few days in this
13 city ·we went along the river outside the gates as it was the
sabbath and this was a customary place for prayer.ª We
sat down and preached to the women who had come to the
14 meeting. ·One of these women was called Lydia, a devout
woman from the town of Thyatira who was in the purple-
dye trade. She listened to us, and the Lord opened her heart
15 to accept what Paul was saying. ·After she and her household had been baptized she sent us an invitation: "If you
really think me a true believer in the Lord," she said "come
and stay with us"; and she would take no refusal.

16 a. There was no synagogue in this Latin city; the Jews met
by the river for ritual ablutions.

Imprisonment of Paul and Silas

16 One day as we were going to prayer, we met a slave-girl who was a soothsayer and made a lot of money for her **17** masters by telling fortunes. ·This girl started following Paul and the rest of us and shouting, "Here are the servants of the Most High God; they have come to tell you how to be **18** saved!" ·She did this every day afterward until Paul lost his temper one day and turned round and said to the spirit, "I order you in the name of Jesus Christ to leave that woman." The spirit went out of her then and there.

19 When her masters saw that there was no hope of making any more money out of her, they seized Paul and Silas and dragged them to the law courts in the market place **20** where they charged them before the magistrates and said, "These people are causing a disturbance in our city. They **21** are Jews ·and are advocating practices which it is unlawful **22** for us as Romans to accept or follow."*b* ·The crowd joined in and showed its hostility to them, so the magistrates had **23** them stripped and ordered them to be flogged. ·They were given many lashes and then thrown into prison, and the **24** jailer was told to keep a close watch on them. ·So, following his instructions, he threw them into the inner prison and fastened their feet in the stocks.

The miraculous deliverance of Paul and Silas

25 Late that night Paul and Silas were praying and singing **26** God's praises, while the other prisoners listened. ·Suddenly there was an earthquake that shook the prison to its foundations. All the doors flew open and the chains fell **27** from all the prisoners. ·When the jailer woke and saw the doors wide open he drew his sword and was about to commit suicide, presuming that the prisoners had es- **28** caped. ·But Paul shouted at the top of his voice, "Don't do yourself any harm; we are all here."

29 The jailer called for lights, then rushed in, threw him- **30** self trembling at the feet of Paul and Silas, ·and escorted **31** them out, saying, "Sirs, what must I do to be saved?" ·They told him, "Become a believer in the Lord Jesus, and you **32** will be saved, and your household too." ·Then they preached the word of the Lord to him and to all his family. **33** Late as it was, he took them to wash their wounds, and **34** was baptized then and there with all his household. ·Afterward he took them home and gave them a meal, and the

whole family celebrated their conversion to belief in God.
35 When it was daylight the magistrates sent the officers
36 with the order: "Release those men." ·The jailer reported
the message to Paul, "The magistrates have sent an order
for your release; you can go now and be on your way."
37 "What!" Paul replied "They flog Roman citizens in public
and without trial and throw us into prison, and then think
they can push us out on the quiet! Oh no! They must come
and escort us out themselves."
38 The officers reported this to the magistrates, who were
39 horrified to hear the men were Roman citizens. ·They
40 came and begged them to leave the town. ·From the
prison they went to Lydia's house where they saw all the
brothers and gave them some encouragement; then they
left.

Thessalonika: difficulties with the Jews

1 Passing through Amphipolis and Apollonia, they
eventually reached Thessalonika, where there was a
2 Jewish synagogue. ·Paul as usual introduced himself and
for three consecutive sabbaths developed the arguments
3 from scripture for them, ·explaining and proving how it
was ordained that the Christ should suffer and rise from
the dead. "And the Christ" he said "is this Jesus whom I
4 am proclaiming to you." ·Some of them were convinced
and joined Paul and Silas, and so did a great many God-
fearing people and Greeks, as well as a number of rich
women.
5 The Jews, full of resentment, enlisted the help of a gang
from the market place, stirred up a crowd, and soon had
the whole city in an uproar. They made for Jason's house,
hoping to find them there and drag them off to the People's
6 Assembly; ·however, they only found Jason and some of
the brothers, and these they dragged before the city council,
shouting, "The people who have been turning the whole
7 world upside down have come here now; ·they have been
staying at Jason's. They have broken every one of Caesar's
edicts by claiming that there is another emperor, Jesus."
8 This accusation alarmed the citizens and the city council-
9 lors ·and they made Jason and the rest give security before
setting them free.

b. The Jews had no right to proselytize Romans.

Fresh difficulties at Beroea

10   When it was dark the brothers immediately sent Paul and Silas away to Beroea, where they visited the Jewish
11 synagogue as soon as they arrived. ·Here the Jews were more open-minded than those in Thessalonika, and they welcomed the word very readily; every day they studied
12 the scriptures to check whether it was true. ·Many Jews became believers, and so did many Greek women from the upper classes and a number of the men.
13   When the Jews of Thessalonika heard that the word of God was being preached by Paul in Beroea as well, they
14 went there to make trouble and stir up the people. ·So the brothers arranged for Paul to go immediately as far
15 as the coast, leaving Silas and Timothy behind. ·Paul's escort took him as far as Athens, and went back with instructions for Silas and Timothy to rejoin Paul as soon as they could.

Paul in Athens

16   Paul waited for them in Athens and there his whole soul was revolted at the sight of a city given over to idolatry.
17 In the synagogue he held debates with the Jews and the God-fearing, but in the market place he had debates every
18 day with anyone who would face him. ·Even a few Epicurean and Stoic philosophers argued with him. Some said, "Does this parrot know what he's talking about?" And, because he was preaching about Jesus and the resurrection, others said, "He sounds like a propagandist for some outlandish gods."[a]
19   They invited him to accompany them to the Council of the Areopagus, where they said to him, "How much of this new teaching you were speaking about are we allowed to
20 know? ·Some of the things you said seemed startling to
21 us and we would like to find out what they mean." ·The one amusement the Athenians and the foreigners living there seem to have, apart from discussing the latest ideas, is listening to lectures about them.
22   So Paul stood before the whole Council of the Areopagus and made this speech:

Paul's speech before the Council of the Areopagus

  "Men of Athens, I have seen for myself how extremely
28 scrupulous you are in all religious matters, ·because I no-

ticed, as I strolled round admiring your sacred monuments, that you had an altar inscribed: To An Unknown God. Well, the God whom I proclaim is in fact the one whom you already worship without knowing it.

24 "Since the God who made the world and everything in it is himself Lord of heaven and earth, he does not make

25 his home in shrines made by human hands. ·Nor is he dependent on anything that human hands can do for him, since he can never be in need of anything; on the contrary, it is he who gives everything—including life and breath—

26 to everyone. ·From one single stock he not only created the whole human race so that they could occupy the entire earth, but he decreed how long each nation should flourish

27 and what the boundaries of its territory should be. ·And he did this so that all nations might seek the deity and; by feeling their way toward him, succeed in finding him.

28 Yet in fact he is not far from any of us, ·since it is in him that we live, and move, and exist,[b] as indeed some of your own writers have said:

"We are all his children."[c]

29 "Since we are the children of God, we have no excuse for thinking that the deity looks like anything in gold, silver or stone that has been carved and designed by a man.

30 "God overlooked that sort of thing when men were ignorant, but now he is telling everyone everywhere that

31 they must repent, ·because he has fixed a day when the whole world will be judged, and judged in righteousness, and he has appointed a man to be the judge. And God has publicly proved this by raising this man from the dead."

32 At this mention of rising from the dead, some of them burst out laughing; others said, "We would like to hear you

33
34 talk about this again." ·After that Paul left them, ·but there were some who attached themselves to him and became believers, among them Dionysius the Areopagite and a woman called Damaris, and others besides.

Foundation of the church of Corinth

1
2 **18** After this Paul left Athens and went to Corinth, where he met a Jew called Aquila whose family

17 a. They assumed that *Anastasis* ("Resurrection") was the name of a goddess. **b.** Expression suggested by the poet Epimenides. **c.** From the *Phainomena* of Aratus.

came from Pontus. He and his wife Priscilla[a] had recently left Italy because an edict of Claudius had expelled all the
8 Jews from Rome.[b] Paul went to visit them, ·and when he found they were tentmakers, of the same trade as himself,
4 he lodged with them, and they worked together. ·Every sabbath he used to hold debates in the synagogues, trying to convert Jews as well as Greeks.
5 After Silas and Timothy had arrived from Macedonia, Paul devoted all his time to preaching, declaring to the
6 Jews that Jesus was the Christ. ·When they turned against him and started to insult him, he took his cloak and shook it out in front of them, saying, "Your blood be on your own heads; from now on I can go to the pagans with a
7 clear conscience." ·Then he left the synagogue and moved to the house next door that belonged to a worshiper of
8 God called Justus. ·Crispus, president of the synagogue, and his whole household, all became believers in the Lord. A great many Corinthians who had heard him became be-
9 lievers and were baptized. ·One night the Lord spoke to Paul in a vision, 'Do not be afraid to speak out, nor al-
10 low yourself to be silenced: ·I am with you. I have so many people on my side in this city that no one will even
11 attempt to hurt you." ·So Paul stayed there preaching the word of God among them for eighteen months.

The Jews take Paul to court

12 But while Gallio was proconsul of Achaia,[c] the Jews made a concerted attack on Paul and brought him before
18 the tribunal. ·"We accuse this man" they said "of persuad-ing people to worship God in a way that breaks the Law."
14 Before Paul could open his mouth, Gallio said to the Jews, "Listen, you Jews. If this were a misdemeanor or a crime,
15 I would not hesitate to attend to you; ·but if it is only quibbles about words and names, and about your own Law, then you must deal with it yourselves—I have no inten-tion of making legal decisions about things like that."
16
17 Then he sent them out of the court, ·and at once they all turned on Sosthenes, the synagogue president, and beat him in front of the court house. Gallio refused to take any notice at all.

Return to Antioch and departure for the third journey

18 After staying on for some time, Paul took leave of the brothers and sailed for Syria,[d] accompanied by Priscilla

and Aquila. At Cenchreae he had his hair cut off, because of a vow he had made.

19 When they reached Ephesus, he left them, but first he
20 went alone to the synagogue to debate with the Jews. ·They
21 asked him to stay longer but he declined, ·though when he left he said, "I will come back another time, God willing." Then he sailed from Ephesus.

22 He landed at Caesarea, and went up to greet the church.
23 Then he came down to Antioch ·where he spent a short time before continuing his journey through the Galatian country and then through Phrygia, encouraging all the followers.

Apollos

24 An Alexandrian Jew named Apollos now arrived in Ephesus. He was an eloquent man, with a sound knowledge
25 of the scriptures, and yet, ·though he had been given instruction in the Way of the Lord and preached with great spiritual earnestness and was accurate in all the details he taught about Jesus, he had only experienced the baptism of
26 John. ·When Priscilla and Aquila heard him speak boldly in the synagogue, they took an interest in him and gave him further instruction about the Way.

27 When Apollos thought of crossing over to Achaia, the brothers encouraged him and wrote asking the disciples to welcome him. When he arrived there he was able by God's
28 grace to help the believers considerably ·by the energetic way he refuted the Jews in public and demonstrated from the scriptures that Jesus was the Christ.

The disciples of John at Ephesus

1 **19** While Apollos was in Corinth, Paul made his way overland as far as Ephesus, where he found a number
2 of disciples. ·When he asked, "Did you receive the Holy Spirit when you became believers?" they answered, "No, we were never even told there was such a thing as a Holy
3 Spirit." ·"Then how were you baptized?" he asked. "With
4 John's baptism" they replied. ·"John's baptism" said Paul "was a baptism of repentance; but he insisted that the people should believe in the one who was to come after

18 a. Also called Prisca, Rm 16:3; 1 Co 16:19; 2 Tm 4:19. b. This edict was issued in 49 or 50. c. In 52, according to an inscription from Delphi. d. To Antioch.

⁵ him—in other words Jesus." ·When they heard this, they
⁶ were baptized in the name of the Lord Jesus, ·and the
moment Paul had laid hands on them the Holy Spirit came
down on them, and they began to speak with tongues and
⁷ to prophesy. ·There were about twelve of these men.

Foundation of the church of Ephesus

⁸ He began by going to the synagogue, where he spoke
out boldly and argued persuasively about the kingdom of
⁹ God. He did this for three months, ·till the attitude of some
of the congregation hardened into unbelief. As soon as
they began attacking the Way in front of the others, he
broke with them and took his disciples apart to hold
¹⁰ daily discussions in the lecture room of Tyrannus. ·This
went on for two years, with the result that people from
all over Asia,ᵃ both Jews and Greeks, were able to hear
the word of the Lord.

The Jewish exorcists

¹¹ So remarkable were the miracles worked by God at
¹² Paul's hands ·that handkerchiefs or aprons which had
touched him were taken to the sick, and they were cured
of their illnesses, and the evil spirits came out of them.
¹³ But some itinerant Jewish exorcists tried pronouncing
the name of the Lord Jesus over people who were possessed by evil spirits; they used to say, "I command you
¹⁴ by the Jesus whose spokesman is Paul." ·Among those
who did this were seven sons of Sceva, a Jewish chief
¹⁵ priest. ·The evil spirit replied, "Jesus I recognize, and I
¹⁶ know who Paul is, but who are you?" ·and the man with
the evil spirit hurled himself at them and overpowered first
one and then another, and handled them so violently that
¹⁷ they fled from that house naked and badly mauled. ·Every-
body in Ephesus, both Jews and Greeks, heard about this
episode; they were all greatly impressed, and the name of
the Lord Jesus came to be held in great honor.
¹⁸ Some believers, too, came forward to admit in detail
¹⁹ how they had used spells ·and a number of them who
had practiced magic collected their books and made a bon-
fire of them in public. The value of these was calculated
to be fifty thousand silver pieces.
²⁰ In this impressive way the word of the Lord spread
more and more widely and successfully.

V. A PRISONER FOR CHRIST

Paul's plans

21   When all this was over Paul made up his mind to go back
to Jerusalem through Macedonia and Achaia. "After I
have been there" he said "I must go on to see Rome as
22 well." ·So he sent two of his helpers, Timothy and Erastus,
ahead of him to Macedonia, while he remained for a time
in Asia.

Ephesus: the silversmiths' riot

23   It was during this time that a rather serious disturbance
24 broke out in connection with the Way. ·A silversmith called
Demetrius, who employed a large number of craftsmen
25 making silver shrines of Diana, ·called a general meeting of
his own men with others in the same trade. "As you men
know," he said "it is on this industry that we depend for
26 our prosperity. ·Now you must have seen and heard how,
not just in Ephesus but nearly everywhere in Asia, this man
Paul has persuaded and converted a great number of people
with his argument that gods made by hand are not gods at
27 all. ·This threatens not only to discredit our trade, but also
to reduce the sanctuary of the great goddess Diana to un-
importance. It could end up by taking away all the prestige
of a goddess venerated all over Asia, yes, and everywhere
28 in the civilized world." ·This speech roused them to fury,
and they started to shout, "Great is Diana of the Ephe-
29 sians!" ·The whole town was in an uproar and the mob
rushed to the theatre dragging along two of Paul's Mace-
30 donian traveling companions, Gaius and Aristarchus. ·Paul
wanted to make an appeal to the people, but the disciples
31 refused to let him; ·in fact, some of the Asiarchs,[b] who
were friends of his, sent messages imploring him not to
take the risk of going into the theatre.
32   By now everybody was shouting different things till the
assembly itself had no idea what was going on; most of
them did not even know why they had been summoned.
33 The Jews pushed Alexander to the front, and when some
of the crowd shouted encouragement he raised his hand

19 a. I.e. the region round Ephesus, including the seven towns
of Rv 1:11. b. Local leaders of the official state worship.

for silence in the hope of being able to explain things to
34 the people. •When they realized he was a Jew, they all
started shouting in unison, "Great is Diana of the Ephe-
35 sians!" and they kept this up for two hours. •When the
town clerk eventually succeeded in calming the crowd, he
said, "Citizens of Ephesus! Is there anybody alive who does
not know that the city of the Ephesians is the guardian of
the temple of great Diana and of her statue that fell from
36 heaven? •Nobody can contradict this and there is no need
37 for you to get excited or do anything rash. •These men you
have brought here are not guilty of any sacrilege or blas-
38 phemy against our goddess. •If Demetrius and the craftsmen he has with him want to complain about anyone,
there are the assizes and the proconsuls; let them take the
39 case to court. •And if you want to ask any more questions
40 you must raise them in the regular assembly. •We could
easily be charged with rioting for today's happenings: there
was no ground for it all, and we can give no reason for
41 this gathering." •When he had finished this speech he dismissed the assembly.

Paul leaves Ephesus 54 – 58 A.D.

1 **20** When the disturbance was over, Paul sent for the
disciples and, after speaking words of encouragement
2 to them, said good-bye and set out for Macedonia. •On
his way through those areas he said many words of encouragement to them and then made his way into Greece,
3 where he spent three months. He was leaving by ship for
Syria[a] when a plot organized against him by the Jews
4 made him decide to go back by way of Macedonia. •He
was accompanied by Sopater, son of Pyrrhus, who came
from Beroea; Aristarchus and Secundus who came from
Thessalonika; Gaius from Doberus, and Timothy, as well
5 as Tychicus and Trophimus who were from Asia. •They
6 all went on to Troas where they waited for us. •We ourselves left Philippi by ship after the days of Unleavened
Bread and met them five days later at Troas, where we
stopped for a week.

Troas: Paul raises a dead man to life

7 On the first day of the week[b] we met to break bread.
Paul was due to leave the next day, and he preached a
8 sermon that went on till the middle of the night. •A number
of lamps were lit in the upstairs room where we were as-

9 sembled, ·and as Paul went on and on, a young man called
Eutychus who was sitting on the window-sill grew drowsy
and was overcome by sleep and fell to the ground three
10 floors below. He was picked up dead. ·Paul went down
and stooped to clasp the boy to him. "There is no need to
11 worry," he said "there is still life in him." ·Then he went
back upstairs where he broke bread and ate and carried on
12 talking till he left at daybreak. ·They took the boy away
alive, and were greatly encouraged.

From Troas to Miletus

13 We were now to go on ahead by sea, so we set sail for
Assos, where we were to take Paul on board; this was what
14 he had arranged, for he wanted to go by road. ·When he
rejoined us at Assos we took him aboard and went on to
15 Mitylene. ·The next day we sailed from there and arrived
opposite Chios. The second day we touched at Samos and,
after stopping at Trogyllium, made Miletus the next day.
16 Paul had decided to pass wide of Ephesus so as to avoid
spending time in Asia, since he was anxious to be in Jerusalem, if possible, for the day of Pentecost.

Farewell to the elders of Ephesus

17 From Miletus he sent for the elders of the church of
18 Ephesus. ·When they arrived he addressed these words to
them:
"You know what my way of life has been ever since the
19 first day I set foot among you in Asia, ·how I have served
the Lord in all humility, with all the sorrows and trials that
20 came to me through the plots of the Jews. ·I have not hesitated to do anything that would be helpful to you; I have
preached to you, and instructed you both in public and in
21 your homes, ·urging both Jews and Greeks to turn to God
and to believe in our Lord Jesus.
22 "And now you see me a prisoner already in spirit; I am
on my way to Jerusalem, but have no idea what will hap-
23 pen to me there, ·except that the Holy Spirit, in town after
town, has made it clear enough that imprisonment and
24 persecution await me. ·But life to me is not a thing to waste
words on, provided that when I finish my race I have car-

20 a. Taking to Jerusalem the proceeds of the collection, Rm
15:25. b. The day was reckoned in the Jewish fashion; the
Lord's day began on the evening of Saturday and it was then
that this meeting was held.

ried out the mission the Lord Jesus gave me—and that was to bear witness to the Good News of God's grace.

25 "I now feel sure that none of you among whom I have gone about proclaiming the kingdom will ever see my face

26 again. ·And so here and now I swear that my conscience is

27 clear as far as all of you are concerned, ·for I have without faltering put before you the whole of God's purpose.

28 "Be on your guard for yourselves and for all the flock of which the Holy Spirit has made you the overseers, to feed the Church of God which he bought with his own blood.

29 I know quite well that when I have gone fierce wolves will

30 invade you and will have no mercy on the flock. ·Even from your own ranks there will be men coming forward with a travesty of the truth on their lips to induce the dis-

31 ciples to follow them. ·So be on your guard, remembering how night and day for three years I never failed to keep

32 you right, shedding tears over each one of you. ·And now I commend you to God, and to the word of his grace that has power to build you up and to give you your inheritance among all the sanctified.

33
34 "I have never asked anyone for money or clothes; ·you know for yourselves that the work I did earned enough to

35 meet my needs and those of my companions. ·I did this to show you that this is how we must exert ourselves to support the weak, remembering the words of the Lord Jesus, who himself said, 'There is more happiness in giving than in receiving.' "

36 When he had finished speaking he knelt down with them

37 all and prayed. ·By now they were all in tears; they put

38 their arms round Paul's neck and kissed him; ·what saddened them most was his saying they would never see his face again. Then they escorted him to the ship.

The journey to Jerusalem

1 **21** When we had at last torn ourselves away from them and put to sea, we set a straight course and arrived at Cos; the next day we reached Rhodes, and from there

2 went on to Patara. ·Here we found a ship bound for

3 Phoenicia, so we went on board and sailed in her. ·After sighting Cyprus and leaving it to port, we sailed to Syria and put in at Tyre, since the ship was to unload her cargo

4 there. ·We sought out the disciples and stayed there a week. Speaking in the Spirit, they kept telling Paul not to

5 go on to Jerusalem, ·but when our time was up we set off.

Together with the women and children they all escorted us
on our way till we were out of the town. When we reached
⁶ the beach, we knelt down and prayed; ·then, after saying
good-bye to each other, we went aboard and they returned
home.

⁷ The end of our voyage from Tyre came when we landed
at Ptolemais, where we greeted the brothers and stayed one
⁸ day with them. ·The next day we left and came to Caesarea.
Here we called on Philip the evangelist, one of the Seven,
⁹ and stayed with him. ·He had four virgin daughters who
¹⁰ were prophets. ·When we had been there several days a
¹¹ prophet called Agabus arrived from Judaea ·to see us. He
took Paul's girdle, and tied up his own feet and hands, and
said, "This is what the Holy Spirit says, 'The man this
girdle belongs to will be bound like this by the Jews in
¹² Jerusalem, and handed over to the pagans.'" ·When we
heard this, we and everybody there implored Paul not to go
¹³ on to Jerusalem. ·To this he replied, "What are you trying
to do—weaken my resolution by your tears? For my part, I
am ready not only to be tied up but even to die in Jerusalem
¹⁴ for the name of the Lord Jesus." ·And so, as he would not
be persuaded, we gave up the attempt, saying, "The Lord's
will be done."

Paul's arrival in Jerusalem

¹⁵ After this we packed and went on up to Jerusalem.
¹⁶ Some of the disciples from Caesarea accompanied us and
took us to the house of a Cypriot with whom we were to
lodge; he was called Mnason and had been one of the
earliest disciples.

¹⁷ On our arrival in Jerusalem the brothers gave us a very
¹⁸ warm welcome. ·The next day Paul went with us to visit
¹⁹ James, and all the elders were present. ·After greeting them
he gave a detailed account of all that God had done among
²⁰ the pagans through his ministry. ·They gave glory to God
when they heard this. "But you see, brother," they said
"how thousands of Jews have now become believers, all of
²¹ them staunch upholders of the Law, and ·they have heard
that you instruct all Jews living among the pagans to
break away from Moses, authorizing them not to circumcise their children or to follow the customary practices.
²² What is to be done? Inevitably there will be a meeting of
the whole body, since they are bound to hear that you have
²³ come. ·So do as we suggest. We have four men here who

²⁴ are under a vow; ·take these men along and be purified with them and pay all the expenses connected with the shaving of their heads.ᵃ This will let everyone know there is no truth in the reports they have heard about you and
²⁵ that you still regularly observe the Law. ·The pagans who have become believers, as we wrote when we told them our decisions, must abstain from things sacrificed to idols, from blood, from the meat of strangled animals and from fornication."

²⁶ So the next day Paul took the men along and was purified with them, and he visited the Temple to give notice of the time when the period of purification would be over and the offering would have to be presented on behalf of each of them.

Paul's arrest

²⁷ The seven days were nearly over when some Jews from Asia caught sight of him in the Temple and stirred up the
²⁸ crowd and seized him, ·shouting, "Men of Israel, help! This is the man who preaches to everyone everywhere against our people, against the Law and against this place. Now he has profaned this Holy Place by bringing Greeks
²⁹ into the Temple." ·They had, in fact, previously seen Trophimus the Ephesian in the city with him, and thought that Paul had brought him into the Temple.
³⁰ This roused the whole city; people came running from all sides; they seized Paul and dragged him out of the
³¹ Temple, and the gates were closed behind them. ·They would have killed him if a report had not reached the tribune of the cohortᵇ that there was rioting all over Jeru-
³² salem. ·He immediately called out soldiers and centurions, and charged down on the crowd, who stopped beating Paul
³³ when they saw the tribune and the soldiers. ·When the tribune came up he arrested Paul, had him bound with two chains and enquired who he was and what he had
³⁴ done. ·People in the crowd called out different things, and since the noise made it impossible for him to get any positive information, the tribune ordered Paul to be taken into
³⁵ the fortress. ·When Paul reached the steps, the crowd became so violent that he had to be carried by the soldiers;
³⁶ and indeed the whole mob was after them, shouting, "Kill him!"
³⁷ Just as Paul was being taken into the fortress, he asked the tribune if he could have a word with him. The tribune

³⁸ said, "You speak Greek, then? ·So you are not the Egyptian who started the recent revolt and led those four thousand
³⁹ cutthroats*o* out into the desert?" ·"I?" said Paul "I am a Jew and a citizen of the well-known city of Tarsus in Cilicia. Please give me permission to speak to the people."
⁴⁰ The man gave his consent and Paul, standing at the top of the steps, gestured to the people with his hand. When all was quiet again he spoke to them in Hebrew.*d*

Paul's address to the Jews of Jerusalem

¹² **22** "My brothers, my fathers, listen to what I have to say to you in my defense." ·When they realized he was speaking in Hebrew, the silence was even greater than
⁸ before. ·"I am a Jew," Paul said "and was born at Tarsus in Cilicia. I was brought up here in this city. I studied under Gamaliel and was taught the exact observance of the Law of our ancestors. In fact, I was as full of duty toward
⁴ God as you are today. ·I even persecuted this Way to the death, and sent women as well as men to prison in chains
⁵ as the high priest and the whole council of elders can testify, since they even sent me with letters to their brothers in Damascus. When I set off it was with the intention of bringing prisoners back from there to Jerusalem for punishment.
⁶ "I was on that journey and nearly at Damascus when about midday a bright light from heaven suddenly shone
⁷ round me. ·I fell to the ground and heard a voice saying,
⁸ 'Saul, Saul, why are you persecuting me?' ·I answered: Who are you, Lord? and he said to me, 'I am Jesus the
⁹ Nazarene, and you are persecuting me.' ·The people with me saw the light but did not hear his voice as he spoke to
¹⁰ me. ·I said: What am I to do, Lord? The Lord answered, 'Stand up and go into Damascus, and there you will be told
¹¹ what you have been appointed to do.' ·The light had been so dazzling that I was blind and my companions had to take me by the hand; and so I came to Damascus.
¹² "Someone called Ananias, a devout follower of the Law
¹⁸ and highly thought of by all the Jews living there, ·came to see me; he stood beside me and said, 'Brother Saul, receive

21 **a.** For the duration of a nazirite vow, the hair was not to be cut. Discharge from the vow, on fulfillment, had to be celebrated with expensive sacrifices. **b.** Commanding officer of the Roman garrison. **c.** Nationalist extremists. **d.** I.e. Aramaic.

your sight.' Instantly my sight came back and I was able
14 to see him. ·Then he said, 'The God of our ancestors has
chosen you to know his will, to see the Just One and hear
15 his own voice speaking, ·because you are to be his witness
before all mankind, testifying to what you have seen and
16 heard. ·And now why delay? It is time you were baptized
and had your sins washed away while invoking his name.'
17 "Once, after I had got back to Jerusalem, when I was
18 praying in the Temple, I fell into a trance ·and then I saw
him. 'Hurry,' he said 'leave Jerusalem at once; they will
19 not accept the testimony you are giving about me.' ·Lord,
I answered, it is because they know that I used to go from
synagogue to synagogue, imprisoning and flogging those
20 who believed in you; ·and that when the blood of your
witness*a* Stephen was being shed, I was standing by in full
agreement with his murderers, and minding their clothes.
21 Then he said to me, 'Go! I am sending you out to the
pagans far away.' "

Paul the Roman citizen

22 So far they had listened to him, but at these words they
began to shout, "Rid the earth of the man! He is not fit to
23 live!" ·They were yelling, waving their cloaks and throw-
24 ing dust into the air, ·and so the tribune had him brought
into the fortress and ordered him to be examined under the
25 lash, to find out the reason for the outcry against him. ·But
when they had strapped him down Paul said to the centurion on duty, "Is it legal for you to flog a man who is a
26 Roman citizen and has not been brought to trial?" ·When
he heard this the centurion went and told the tribune; "Do
you realize what you are doing?" he said "This man is a
27 Roman citizen." ·So the tribune came and asked him, "Tell
28 me, are you a Roman citizen?" "I am" Paul said. ·The
tribune replied, "It cost me a large sum to acquire this
29 citizenship." "But I was born to it" said Paul. ·Then those
who were about to examine him hurriedly withdrew, and
the tribune himself was alarmed when he realized that he
had put a Roman citizen in chains.

His appearance before the Sanhedrin

30 The next day, since he wanted to know what precise
charge the Jews were bringing, he freed Paul and gave
orders for a meeting of the chief priests and the entire

Sanhedrin; then he brought Paul down and stood him in front of them.

¹ **23** Paul looked steadily at the Sanhedrin and began to speak, "My brothers, to this day I have conducted ² myself before God with a perfectly clear conscience." •At this the high priest Ananias ordered his attendants to strike ³ him on the mouth. •Then Paul said to him, "God will surely strike you, you whitewashed wall! How can you sit there to judge me according to the Law, and then break ⁴ the Law by ordering a man to strike me?" •The attendants ⁵ said, "It is God's high priest you are insulting!" •Paul answered, "Brothers, I did not realize it was the high priest, for scripture says: *You must not curse a ruler of your people.*"ᵃ

⁶ Now Paul was well aware that one section was made up of Sadducees and the other of Pharisees, so he called out in the Sanhedrin, "Brothers, I am a Pharisee and the son of Pharisees. It is for our hope in the resurrection of the ⁷ dead that I am on trial." •As soon as he said this a dispute broke out between the Pharisees and Sadducees, and the ⁸ assembly was split between the two parties. •For the Sadducees say there is neither resurrection, nor angel, nor spirit, ⁹ while the Pharisees accept all three. •The shouting grew louder, and some of the scribes from the Pharisees' party stood up and protested strongly, "We find nothing wrong with this man. Suppose a spirit has spoken to him, or an ¹⁰ angel?" •Feeling was running high, and the tribune, afraid that they would tear Paul to pieces, ordered his troops to go down and haul him out and bring him into the fortress.

¹¹ Next night, the Lord appeared to him and said, "Courage! You have borne witness for me in Jerusalem, now you must do the same in Rome."

The conspiracy of the Jews against Paul

¹² When it was day, the Jews held a secret meeting at which they made a vow not to eat or drink until they had killed ¹³ Paul. •There were more than forty who took part in this ¹⁴ conspiracy, •and they went to the chief priests and elders, and told them, "We have made a solemn vow to let noth-

22 a. *Martyr:* the word had not yet acquired its restricted meaning.
23 a. Ex 22:27

¹⁵ ing pass our lips until we have killed Paul. ·Now it is up to you and the Sanhedrin together to apply to the tribune to bring him down to you, as though you meant to examine his case more closely; we, on our side, are prepared to dispose of him before he reaches you."

¹⁶ But the son of Paul's sister heard of the ambush they were laying and made his way into the fortress and told ¹⁷ Paul, ·who called one of the centurions and said, "Take this young man to the tribune; he has something to tell ¹⁸ him." ·So the man took him to the tribune, and reported, "The prisoner Paul summoned me and requested me to bring this young man to you; he has something to tell you." ¹⁹ Then the tribune took him by the hand and drew him aside ²⁰ and asked, "What is it you have to tell me?" ·He replied, "The Jews have made a plan to ask you to take Paul down to the Sanhedrin tomorrow, as though they meant to in- ²¹ quire more closely into his case. ·Do not let them persuade you. There are more than forty of them lying in wait for him, and they have vowed not to eat or drink until they have got rid of him. They are ready now and only waiting ²² for your order to be given." ·The tribune let the young man go with this caution, "Tell no one that you have given me this information."

Paul transferred to Caesarea

²³ Then he summoned two of the centurions and said, "Get two hundred soldiers ready to leave for Caesarea by the third hour of the night with seventy cavalry and two hun- ²⁴ dred auxiliaries; ·provide horses for Paul, and deliver him ²⁵ unharmed to Felix the governor."ᵇ ·He also wrote a letter ²⁶ in these terms: ·"Claudius Lysias to his Excellency the ²⁷ governor Felix, greetings. ·This man had been seized by the Jews and would have been murdered by them but I came on the scene with my troops and got him away, hav- ²⁸ ing discovered that he was a Roman citizen. ·Wanting to find out what charge they were making against him, I ²⁹ brought him before their Sanhedrin. ·I found that the ac- cusation concerned disputed points of their Law, but that ³⁰ there was no charge deserving death or imprisonment. ·My information is that there is a conspiracy against the man, so I hasten to send him to you, and have notified his ac- cusers that they must state their case against him in your presence."

⁸¹ The soldiers carried out their orders; they took Paul and
⁸² escorted him by night to Antipatris. ·Next day they left the
mounted escort to go on with him and returned to the
⁸³ fortress. ·On arriving at Caesarea the escort delivered the
⁸⁴ letter to the governor and handed Paul over to him. ·The
governor read the letter and asked him what province he
came from. Learning that he was from Cilicia he said,
⁸⁵ "I will hear your case as soon as your accusers are here
too." Then he ordered him to be held in Herod's praetorium.

The case before Felix

¹ **24** Five days later the high priest Ananias came down
with some of the elders and an advocate named
Tertullus, and they laid information against Paul before the
² governor. ·Paul was called, and Tertullus opened for the
prosecution, "Your Excellency, Felix, the unbroken peace
we enjoy and the reforms this nation owes to your foresight
³ are matters we accept, always and everywhere, with all
⁴ gratitude. ·I do not want to take up too much of your time,
⁵ but I beg you to give us a brief hearing. ·The plain truth is
that we find this man a perfect pest; he stirs up trouble
among Jews the world over, and is a ringleader of the
⁶ Nazarene sect. ·He has even attempted to profane the
Temple. We placed him under arrest, intending to judge him
⁷ according to our Law, ·but the tribune Lysias intervened
⁸ and took him out of our hands by force, ·ordering his accusers to appear before you; if you ask himᵃ you can find
out for yourself the truth of all our accusations against this
⁹ man." ·The Jews supported him, asserting that these were
the facts.
¹⁰ When the governor motioned him to speak, Paul answered:

Paul's speech before the Roman governor

"I know that you have administered justice over this
nation for many years, and I can therefore speak with con-
¹¹ fidence in my defense. ·As you can verify for yourself, it
is no more than twelve days since I went up to Jerusalem
¹² on pilgrimage, ·and it is not true that they ever found me
arguing with anyone or stirring up the mob, either in the
¹³ Temple, in the synagogues, or about the town; ·neither can

b. Antoninus Felix, procurator of Judaea from 52 to 59-60.
24 a. Lysias.

they prove any of the accusations they are making against me now.

14 "What I do admit to you is this: it is according to the Way which they describe as a sect that I worship the God of my ancestors, retaining my belief in all points of the 15 Law and in what is written in the prophets; ·and I hold the same hope in God as they do that there will be a resurrec- 16 tion of good men and bad men alike. ·In these things, I, as much as they, do my best to keep a clear conscience at all times before God and man.

17 "After several years I came to bring alms to my nation 18 and to make offerings; ·it was in connection with these that they found me in the Temple; I had been purified, and 19 there was no crowd involved, and no disturbance. ·But some Jews from Asia . . . —these are the ones who should have appeared before you and accused me of whatever they had 20 against me. ·At least let those who are present say what crime they found me guilty of when I stood before the 21 Sanhedrin, ·unless it were to do with this single outburst, when I stood up among them and called out: It is about the resurrection of the dead that I am on trial before you to-day."

Paul's captivity at Caesarea

22 At this, Felix, who knew more about the Way than most people, adjourned the case, saying, "When Lysias the trib- 23 une has come down I will go into your case." ·He then gave orders to the centurion that Paul should be kept un-der arrest but free from restriction, and that none of his own people should be prevented from seeing to his needs.

24 Some days later Felix came with his wife Drusilla who was a Jewess.[b] He sent for Paul and gave him a hearing on 25 the subject of faith in Christ Jesus. ·But when he began to treat of righteousness, self-control and the coming Judg-ment, Felix took fright and said, "You may go for the 26 present; I will send for you when I find it convenient." ·At the same time he had hopes of receiving money from Paul, and for this reason he sent for him frequently and had talks with him.

27 When the two years[c] came to an end, Felix was succeeded by Porcius Festus and, being anxious to gain favor with the Jews, Felix left Paul in custody.

Paul appeals to Caesar

¹ ² **25** Three days after his arrival in the province, Festus went up to Jerusalem from Caesarea. ·The chief priests and leaders of the Jews informed him of the case ³ against Paul, urgently ·asking him to support them rather than Paul, and to have him transferred to Jerusalem. They were, in fact, preparing an ambush to murder him ⁴ on the way. ·But Festus replied that Paul would remain in custody in Caesarea, and that he would be going back there ⁵ shortly himself. ·"Let your authorities come down with me" he said "and if there is anything wrong about the man, they can bring a charge against him."

⁶ After staying with them for eight or ten days at the most, he went down to Caesarea and the next day he took his ⁷ seat on the tribunal and had Paul brought in. ·As soon as Paul appeared, the Jews who had come down from Jerusalem surrounded him, making many serious accusations ⁸ which they were unable to substantiate. ·Paul's defense was this, "I have committed no offense whatever against either ⁹ Jewish law, or the Temple, or Caesar." ·Festus was anxious to gain favor with the Jews, so he said to Paul, "Are you willing to go up to Jerusalem and be tried on these ¹⁰ charges before me there?" ·But Paul replied, "I am standing before the tribunal of Caesar and this is where I should be tried. I have done the Jews no wrong, as you very well ¹¹ know. ·If I am guilty of committing any capital crime, I do not ask to be spared the death penalty. But if there is no substance in the accusations these persons bring against me, no one has a right to surrender me to them. I appeal ¹² to Caesar." ·Then Festus conferred with his advisers and replied, "You have appealed to Caesar; to Caesar you shall go."

Paul appears before King Agrippa

¹³ Some days later King Agrippa and Bernice*ᵃ* arrived in ¹⁴ Caesarea and paid their respects to Festus. ·Their visit lasted several days, and Festus put Paul's case before the king. "There is a man here" he said "whom Felix left be-

b. Youngest daughter of Herod Agrippa. **c.** The maximum length of protective custody; Felix was breaking the law by continuing to detain Paul.
25 a. Agrippa, Bernice and Drusilla (24:24) were children of Herod Agrippa I.

¹⁵ hind in custody, ·and while I was in Jerusalem the chief priests and elders of the Jews laid information against him, ¹⁶ demanding his condemnation. ·But I told them that Romans are not in the habit of surrendering any man, until the accused confronts his accusers and is given an opportunity to defend himself against the charge. ·So they came here with me, and I wasted no time but took my seat on the tribunal the very next day and had the man brought in. ¹⁸ When confronted with him, his accusers did not charge ¹⁹ him with any of the crimes I had expected; ·but they had some argument or other with him about their own religion and about a dead man called Jesus whom Paul alleged to ²⁰ be alive. ·Not feeling qualified to deal with questions of this sort, I asked him if he would be willing to go to Jeru- ²¹ salem to be tried there on this issue. ·But Paul put in an appeal for his case to be reserved for the judgment of the august emperor, so I ordered him to be remanded until I ²² could send him to Caesar." ·Agrippa said to Festus, "I should like to hear the man myself." "Tomorrow" he answered "you shall hear him."

²³ So the next day Agrippa and Bernice arrived in great state and entered the audience chamber attended by the tribunes and the city notables; and Festus ordered Paul to ²⁴ be brought in. ·Then Festus said, "King Agrippa, and all here present with us, you see before you the man about whom the whole Jewish community has petitioned me, both in Jerusalem and here, loudly protesting that he ought ²⁵ not to be allowed to remain alive. ·For my own part I am satisfied that he has committed no capital crime, but when he himself appealed to the august emperor I decided to ²⁶ send him. ·But I have nothing definite that I can write to his Imperial Majesty about him; that is why I have produced him before you all, and before you in particular, King Agrippa, so that after the examination I may have ²⁷ something to write. ·It seems to me pointless to send a prisoner without indicating the charges against him."

¹ **26** Then Agrippa said to Paul, "You have leave to speak on your own behalf". And Paul held up his hand and began his defense:

Paul's speech before King Agrippa

² "I consider myself fortunate, King Agrippa, in that it is before you I am to answer today all the charges made

8 against me by the Jews, ·the more so because you are an expert in matters of custom and controversy among the Jews. So I beg you to listen to me patiently.

4 "My manner of life from my youth, a life spent from the beginning among my own people and in Jerusalem, is 5 common knowledge among the Jews. ·They have known me for a long time and could testify, if they would, that I followed the strictest party in our religion and lived as a 6 Pharisee. ·And now it is for my hope in the promise made 7 by God to our ancestors that I am on trial, ·the promise that our twelve tribes, constant in worship night and day, hope to attain. For that hope, Sire, I am actually put on 8 trial by Jews! ·Why does it seem incredible to you that God should raise the dead?

9 "As for me, I once thought it was my duty to use every 10 means to oppose the name of Jesus the Nazarene. ·This I did in Jerusalem; I myself threw many of the saints into prison, acting on authority from the chief priests, and when they were sentenced to death I cast my vote against 11 them. ·I often went round the synagogues inflicting penalties, trying in this way to force them to renounce their faith; my fury against them was so extreme that I even pursued them into foreign cities.

12 "On one such expedition I was going to Damascus, armed with full powers and a commission from the chief 18 priests, ·and at midday as I was on my way, your Majesty, I saw a light brighter than the sun come down from heaven. 14 It shone brilliantly round me and my fellow travelers. ·We all fell to the ground, and I heard a voice saying to me in Hebrew, 'Saul, Saul, why are you persecuting me? It is 15 hard for you, kicking like this against the goad.'*a* ·Then I said: Who are you, Lord? And the Lord answered, 'I am 16 Jesus, and you are persecuting me. ·But get up and stand on your feet, for I have appeared to you for this reason: to appoint you as my servant and as witness of this vision in which you have seen me, and of others in which I shall 17 appear to you. ·*I shall deliver you* from the people and 18 *from the pagans, to whom I am sending you* ·*to open their eyes,* so that they may turn *from darkness to light,*b from the dominion of Satan to God, and receive, through faith

26 a. Greek proverbial expression for useless resistance.
b. Quotations from Jr 1; Is 42; Is 9.

in me, forgiveness of their sins and a share in the inheritance of the sanctified.'

19 "After that, King Agrippa, I could not disobey the heav-
20 enly vision. ·On the contrary I started preaching, first to the people of Damascus, then to those of Jerusalem and all the countryside of Judaea, and also to the pagans, urging them to repent and turn to God, proving their change of
21 heart by their deeds. ·This was why the Jews laid hands on
22 me in the Temple and tried to do away with me. ·But I was blessed with God's help, and so I have stood firm to this day, testifying to great and small alike, saying nothing more than what the prophets and Moses himself said would hap-
23 pen: ·that the Christ was to suffer and that, as the first to rise from the dead, he was to proclaim that light now shone for our people and for the pagans too."

His hearers' reactions

24 He had reached this point in his defense when Festus shouted out, "Paul, you are out of your mind; all that learn-
25 ing of yours is driving you mad." ·"Festus, your Excellency," answered Paul "I am not mad: I am speaking
26 nothing but the sober truth. ·The king understands these matters, and to him I now speak with assurance, confident that nothing of all this is lost on him; after all, these things
27 were not done in a corner. ·King Agrippa, do you believe
28 in the prophets? I know you do." ·At this Agrippa said to Paul, "A little more, and your arguments would make a
29 Christian of me." ·"Little or more," Paul replied "I wish before God that not only you but all who have heard me today would come to be as I am—except for these chains."
30 At this the king rose to his feet, with the governor and
31 Bernice and those who sat there with them. ·When they had retired they talked together and agreed, "This man is
32 doing nothing that deserves death or imprisonment." ·And Agrippa remarked to Festus, "The man could have been set free if he had not appealed to Caesar."

The departure for Rome

1 **27** When it had been decided that we should sail for Italy, Paul and some other prisoners were handed over to a centurion called Julius, of the Augustan cohort.
2 We boarded a vessel from Adramyttium bound for ports on the Asiatic coast, and put to sea; we had Aristarchus
3 with us, a Macedonian of Thessalonika. ·Next day we put

in at Sidon, and Julius was considerate enough to allow
Paul to go to his friends to be looked after.

4 From there we put to sea again, but as the winds were
5 against us we sailed under the lee of Cyprus, ·then across
the open sea off Cilicia and Pamphylia, taking a fortnight
6 to reach Myra in Lycia. ·There the centurion found an
Alexandrian ship leaving for Italy and put us aboard.
7 For some days we made little headway, and we had difficulty in making Cnidus. The wind would not allow us to
touch there, so we sailed under the lee of Crete off Cape
8 Salmone ·and struggled along the coast until we came to a
place called Fair Havens, near the town of Lasea.

Storm and shipwreck

9 A great deal of time had been lost, and navigation was
already hazardous since it was now well after the time of
10 the Fast,⁶ so Paul gave them this warning, ·"Friends, I can
see this voyage will be dangerous and that we run the risk
of losing not only the cargo and the ship but also our lives
11 as well." ·But the centurion took more notice of the captain and the ship's owner than of what Paul was saying;
12 and since the harbor was unsuitable for wintering, the
majority were for putting out from there in the hope of
wintering at Phoenix—a harbor in Crete, facing southwest
and northwest.
13 A southerly breeze sprang up and, thinking their objec-
tive as good as reached, they weighed anchor and began to
14 sail past Crete, close inshore. ·But it was not long before a
hurricane, the "northeaster" as they call it, burst on them
15 from across the island. ·The ship was caught and could not
be turned head-on to the wind, so we had to give way to it
16 and let ourselves be driven. ·We ran under the lee of the
small island called Cauda and managed with some difficulty
17 to bring the ship's boat under control. ·They hoisted it
aboard and with the help of tackle bound cables round the
ship; then, afraid of running aground on the Syrtis banks,
they floated out the sea-anchor and so let themselves drift.
18 As we were making very heavy weather of it, the next day
19 they began to jettison the cargo, ·and the third day they
20 threw the ship's gear overboard with their own hands. ·For
a number of days both the sun and the stars were invisible

27 a. "the Fast," the feast of Atonement, was kept about the
time of the autumn equinox; winter was coming on.

and the storm raged unabated until at last we gave up all hope of surviving.

21 Then, when they had been without food for a long time, Paul stood up among the men. "Friends," he said "if you had listened to me and not put out from Crete, you would
22 have spared yourselves all this damage and loss. ·But now I ask you not to give way to despair. There will be no loss of
23 life at all, only of the ship. ·Last night there was standing beside me an angel of the God to whom I belong and whom
24 I serve, ·and he said, 'Do not be afraid, Paul. You are destined to appear before Caesar, and for this reason God
25 grants you the safety of all who are sailing with you.' ·So take courage, friends; I trust in God that things will turn
26 out just as I was told; ·but we are to be stranded on some island."

27 On the fourteenth night we were being driven one way and another in the Adriatic,*b* when about midnight the
28 crew sensed that land of some sort was near. ·They took soundings and found twenty fathoms; after a short interval
29 they sounded again and found fifteen fathoms. ·Then, afraid that we might run aground somewhere on a reef, they dropped four anchors from the stern and prayed for day-
30 light. ·When some of the crew tried to escape from the ship and lowered the ship's boat into the sea as though to lay
31 out anchors from the bows, ·Paul said to the centurion and his men, "Unless those men stay on board you cannot hope
32 to be saved." ·So the soldiers cut the boat's ropes and let it drop away.

33 Just before daybreak Paul urged them all to have some-thing to eat. "For fourteen days" he said "you have been
34 in suspense, going hungry and eating nothing. ·Let me per-suade you to have something to eat; your safety is not in
35 doubt. Not a hair of your heads will be lost." ·With these words he took some bread, gave thanks to God in front of
36 them all, broke it and began to eat. ·Then they all plucked
37 up courage and took something to eat themselves. ·We were in all two hundred and seventy-six souls on board
38 that ship. ·When they had eaten what they wanted they lightened the ship by throwing the corn overboard into the sea.

39 When day came they did not recognize the land, but they could make out a kind of bay with a beach; they planned to run the ship aground on this if they could.
40 They slipped the anchors and left them to the sea, and at

the same time loosened the lashings of the rudders; then, hoisting the foresail to the wind, they headed for the beach.

41 But the cross-currents carried them into a shoal and the vessel ran aground. The bows were wedged in and stuck fast, while the stern began to break up with the pounding of the waves.

42 The soldiers planned to kill the prisoners for fear that 43 any should swim off and escape. •But the centurion was determined to bring Paul safely through, and would not let them do what they intended. He gave orders that those who could swim should jump overboard first and so get ashore, 44 and the rest follow either on planks or on pieces of wreckage. In this way all came safe and sound to land.

Waiting in Malta

1 28 Once we had come safely through, we discovered 2 that the island was called Malta. •The inhabitants treated us with unusual kindness. They made us all welcome, and they lit a huge fire because it had started to rain 3 and the weather was cold. •Paul had collected a bundle of sticks and was putting them on the fire when a viper 4 brought out by the heat attached itself to his hand. •When the natives saw the creature hanging from his hand they said to one another, "That man must be a murderer; he may have escaped the sea, but divine vengeance would not 5 let him live." •However, he shook the creature off into the 6 fire and came to no harm, •although they were expecting him at any moment to swell up or drop dead on the spot. After they had waited a long time without seeing anything out of the ordinary happen to him, they changed their minds and began to say he was a god.

7 In that neighborhood there were estates belonging to the prefect of the island, whose name was Publius. He received 8 us and entertained us hospitably for three days. •It so happened that Publius' father was in bed, suffering from feverish attacks and dysentery. Paul went in to see him, and after a prayer he laid his hands on the man and healed him. 9 When this happened, the other sick people on the island 10 came as well and were cured; •they honored us with many marks of respect, and when we sailed they put on board the provisions we needed.

b. The term includes the seas between Greece, Italy and Africa.

From Malta to Rome

11 At the end of three months we set sail in a ship that had wintered in the island; she came from Alexandria and her
12 figurehead was the Twins. ·We put in at Syracuse and spent
13 three days there; ·from there we followed the coast up to Rhegium. After one day there a south wind sprang up and
14 on the second day we made Puteoli,ᵃ ·where we found some brothers and were much rewarded by staying a week with them. And so we came to Rome.
15 When the brothers there heard of our arrival they came to meet us, as far as the Forum of Appius and the Three Taverns. When Paul saw them he thanked God and took
16 courage. ·On our arrival in Rome Paul was allowed to stay in lodgings of his own with the soldier who guarded him.

Paul makes contact with the Roman Jews

17 After three days he called together the leading Jews. When they had assembled, he said to them, "Brothers, although I have done nothing against our people or the customs of our ancestors, I was arrested in Jerusalem and
18 handed over to the Romans. ·They examined me and would have set me free, since they found me guilty of noth-
19 ing involving the death penalty; ·but the Jews lodged an objection, and I was forced to appeal to Caesar, not that I
20 had any accusation to make against my own nation. ·That is why I have asked to see you and talk to you, for it is on account of the hope of Israel that I wear this chain."
21 They answered, "We have received no letters from Judaea about you, nor has any countryman of yours arrived here with any report or story of anything to your discredit.
22 We think it would be as well to hear your own account of your position; all we know about this sect is that opinion everywhere condemns it."

Paul's declaration to the Roman Jews

23 So they arranged a day with him and a large number of them visited him at his lodgings. He put his case to them, testifying to the kingdom of God and trying to persuade them about Jesus, arguing from the Law of Moses and the prophets. This went on from early morning until evening,
24 and some were convinced by what he said, while the rest
25 were skeptical. ·So they disagreed among themselves and, as they went away, Paul had one last thing to say to them,

'How aptly the Holy Spirit spoke when he told your ancestors through the prophet Isaiah:

26 *Go to this nation and say:*
You will hear and hear again but not understand,
see and see again, but not perceive.
27 *For the heart of this nation has grown coarse,*
their ears are dull of hearing and they have shut their eyes,
for fear they should see with their eyes,
hear with their ears,
understand with their heart,
and be converted
and be healed by me.[b]

28 "Understand, then, that this salvation of God has been
sent to the pagans; they will listen to it."

Epilogue

30 Paul spent the whole of the two years[c] in his own
rented lodging. He welcomed all who came to visit him,
31 proclaiming the kingdom of God and teaching the truth
about the Lord Jesus Christ with complete freedom and
without hindrance from anyone.

28 a. Pozzuoli, on the Gulf of Naples.   b. Is 6:9-10   c. See
note on 24:27.

Eusebius le 6 - reign of Nero.

Eusebius

INTRODUCTION TO
The Letters of Saint Paul

Paul was born about A.D. 10, of a Jewish family living among "the Greeks" at Tarsus, a Roman municipality in Cilicia. He was educated as a Pharisee in Jerusalem. He was converted to belief in Christ about A.D. 34, and many particulars of his life as an apostle can be found in his letters and in Acts. The letters may be dated from A.D. 50-65. Paul was imprisoned in Rome, A.D. 61-63, and set free for want of evidence; a second imprisonment in Rome ended, according to a very ancient tradition, in martyrdom by execution, probably in the year 67.

Paul's letters show him as a man of sensitive temperament and warm emotions, completely dedicated to the spreading of the "Good News" that Christ by his death and resurrection was proved to be the one universal savior of Jew and "Greek" alike. Crises and controversies led him to explain the message of the gospel in ways adapted to the needs of his readers and so to bring into play his remarkable powers of theological analysis and his grasp of profundities. His letters, in a fluent Greek which was his second mother-tongue, were generally a response to a particular situation in a particular church, and although some passages in them were obviously written after long and careful thought, more often the style suggests spontaneity and urgency. The letters were usually dictated, and then signed by Paul with a short personal greeting.

The order in which the letters are printed in this Bible is the traditional one which arranges them in order of diminishing length. If they are read in the order in which they were written, the development in Paul's theological thinking can be seen as he finds expression for further depths and implications in the gospel.

1 and 2 Thessalonians. A.D. 50-51

1 Thessalonians was written from Corinth, when Paul's companion Timothy had come back from a second visit to Thessalonika and reported to Paul on the state of the church there. Besides a series of practical recommendations, it includes Paul's

teaching on death and the "second coming" of Christ, expressed in the terms of contemporary apocalyptic writing.

2 Thessalonians, written about a year later, shows that Paul's thought on the same subject had deepened. Parts of the two letters show some close correspondences, and some critics have doubted the authenticity of 2 Thessalonians. However, the earliest authorities accepted them as both by Paul.

1 and 2 Corinthians. A.D. 57

Corinth, a great and populous port, was a magnet to every sort of philosophy and religion and was also a notorious center of immorality. Paul's converts in the city were particularly in need of instruction and guidance, both about the Good News itself and about the Christian life which it implied. Paul appears to have written four letters to the church in Corinth, of which we now have only two.

His first letter to Corinth has not survived, and the earliest we have was written from Ephesus sometime near Easter, 57. Shortly afterwards, Paul had to pay a brief visit to Corinth in which he had to take painful disciplinary measures, and when later he sent a representative to Corinth instead of going himself, the Corinthians did not accept his authority, and Paul wrote a third letter which was very severe. In Macedonia, towards the end of 57, Paul heard from Titus that the "severe letter" had had the desired effect, and then he wrote the letter which we know as 2 Corinthians.

However, 2 Corinthians is not a single consistent letter; it has been suggested that it includes part of the lost first letter (2 Co 6:14-7:1) and part of the "severe letter" (2 Co 10-13).

The two letters to the Corinthians contain much information about urgent problems that faced the church and the important decisions which were made to meet them: questions of morality, about the liturgy and the holding of assemblies, the recognition of spiritual gifts and the avoidance of contamination from pagan religions. It was Paul's religious genius to turn what might have remained textbook cases of conscience into the means of exploring the profound doctrines of Christian liberty, the sanctification of the body, the supremacy of love, and union with Christ.

Galatians. Romans. A.D. 57-58

These two letters analyze the same problem, but while Galatians is Paul's immediate response to a particular situation, Romans is more like a systematic treatise and gives a methodical arrangement to all the new ideas that had emerged from the argument.

Paul had not himself founded the church at Rome. It was a mixed community in which there was a danger that Jewish and non-Jewish converts might look down on each other, and Paul, before visiting the church, sent this considered examination of how Judaism and Christianity were related to one another, using the ideas which he had developed in the Galatian crisis and further refining them. In both these letters we can see Paul correcting the unbalance of the Greek outlook which relied too exclusively on human reason, just as in earlier letters he had corrected the unbalance of the Jewish outlook which relied too heavily on the Law.

Philippians. A.D. 56-57

This is a letter without a lot of doctrinal exposition in it, giving some news to his converts at Philippi and warning them of some enemies who had worked against Paul elsewhere and might turn to them next. At the time of writing, Paul was under arrest, but it is unlikely that this letter was written from Rome during his imprisonment there in 61-63 and it may have been written from Ephesus.

Ephesians. Colossians. Philemon. A.D. 61-63

All three letters are closely related and were written while Paul was under arrest in Rome. It appears that the relation between Ephesians and Colossians is like that between Romans and Galatians. The news of a crisis at Colossae led Paul to write a letter to the Christians there against the growing belief and trust in celestial and cosmic powers. Paul accepts these powers as the angels of Jewish tradition, but he shows that in the great scheme of salvation they have only a preparatory and subordinate part and now there is a new order in which Christ is all. About the same time, he wrote a fuller and more systematic treatment of the same ideas and this is the letter that we know as "Ephesians" though it was probably written for circulation through all the churches.

Some critics have questioned the authorship of both these letters, and particularly of Ephesians, since it seems to borrow ideas from Colossians and not always to digest them smoothly. But we know nothing of any other person capable of writing them; in parts of them, Paul is at his most personal and characteristic, and they represent a further reconsideration of themes which he had already explored in his earlier letters.

The short letter to Philemon is a personal message which was written in Paul's own handwriting.

1 Timothy. Titus. 2 Timothy. A.D. 65

These are letters of advice and instruction to two of Paul's most loyal followers in their work of organizing and leading the communities to which he had sent them. It is possible that 1 Timothy and Titus were written from Macedonia about A.D. 65, but by the time he wrote 2 Timothy, Paul was a prisoner in Rome awaiting death. From the details of his recent movements given in this letter, this must have been a second imprisonment, and not that of 61-63.

Hebrews. A.D. 67

The question who wrote this letter to Jewish Christians has been a subject of debate from the earliest times. It is ranked with Paul's letters in importance, its doctrine has Pauline overtones, and it was written from Italy, perhaps from Rome; but while there may be a strong presumption that its author had come under the influence of Paul, the letter can hardly be attributed to Paul himself.

It is a sustained argument from Old Testament texts, to keep its readers firm under persecution. The theme is that the ineffectual sacrifices of the levitical priests are replaced by the one uniquely efficacious sacrifice of Christ, and that his priesthood is of an altogether higher order than that of the Jewish priests, derived from Aaron.

Romans

THE LETTER OF PAUL
TO THE CHURCH IN ROME

Address

¹ From Paul, a servant of Christ Jesus who has been called to be an apostle, and specially chosen to preach ² the Good News that God ·promised long ago through his prophets in the scriptures.

³ This news is about the Son of God who, according to the ⁴ human nature he took, was a descendant of David: ·it is about Jesus Christ our Lord who, in the order of the spirit, the spirit of holiness that was in him, was proclaimed Son of God in all his power through his resurrection from the ⁵ dead. ·Through him we received grace and our apostolic mission to preach the obedience of faith to all pagan nations ⁶ in honor of his name. ·You are one of these nations, and ⁷ by his call belong to Jesus Christ. ·To you all, then, who are God's beloved in Rome, called to be saints, may God our Father and the Lord Jesus Christ send grace and peace.

Thanksgiving and prayer

⁸ First I thank my God through Jesus Christ for all of you and for the way in which your faith is spoken of all over ⁹ the world. ·The God I worship spiritually by preaching the Good News of his Son knows that I never fail to mention ¹⁰ you in my prayers, ·and to ask to be allowed at long last the ¹¹ opportunity to visit you, if he so wills. ·For I am longing to see you either to strengthen you by sharing a spiritual gift ¹² with you, ·or what is better, to find encouragement ¹³ among you from our common faith. ·I want you to know, brothers, that I have often planned to visit you—though until now I have always been prevented—in the hope that I might work as fruitfully among you as I have done ¹⁴ among the other pagans. ·I owe a duty to Greeks[a] just as much as to barbarians, to the educated just as much as to

15 the uneducated, ·and it is this that makes me want to bring the Good News to you too in Rome.

SALVATION BY FAITH
I. JUSTIFICATION

The theme stated

16 For I am not ashamed of the Good News: it is the power of God saving all who have faith—Jews first, but Greeks as
17 well—·since this is what reveals the justice of God to us: it shows how faith leads to faith, or as scripture says: *The upright man finds life through faith.*[b]

A. GOD'S ANGER AGAINST PAGAN AND JEW

God's anger against the pagans

18 The anger of God is being revealed from heaven against all the impiety and depravity of men who keep truth im-
19 prisoned in their wickedness. ·For what can be known about God is perfectly plain to them since God himself has made
20 it plain. ·Ever since God created the world his everlasting power and deity—however invisible—have been there for the mind to see in the things he has made. That is why such
21 people are without excuse: ·they knew God and yet refused to honor him as God or to thank him; instead, they made nonsense out of logic and their empty minds were darkened.
22 The more they called themselves philosophers, the more
23 stupid they grew, ·until *they exchanged the glory*[c] of the immortal God for a worthless imitation, *for the image* of
24 mortal man, of birds, of quadrupeds and reptiles. ·That is why God left them to their filthy enjoyments and the prac-
25 tices with which they dishonor their own bodies, ·since they have given up divine truth for a lie and have worshiped and served creatures instead of the creator, who is blessed for ever. Amen!
26 That is why God has abandoned them to degrading passions: why their women have turned from natural inter-

1 a. When contrasted with "barbarians" (as here), "Greeks" means the inhabitants of the hellenic world, including the Romans; when contrasted with "Jews," it means the pagans in general. b. Hab 2:4 c. Ps 106:20

27 course to unnatural practices ·and why their menfolk have given up natural intercourse to be consumed with passion for each other, men doing shameless things with men and getting an appropriate reward for their perversion.

28 In other words, since they refused to see it was rational to acknowledge God, God has left them to their own irra-

29 tional ideas and to their monstrous behavior. ·And so they are steeped in all sorts of depravity, rottenness, greed and malice, and addicted to envy, murder, wrangling, treachery

30 and spite. ·Libellers, slanderers, enemies of God, rude, arrogant and boastful, enterprising in sin, rebellious to

31
32 parents, ·without brains, honor, love or pity. ·They know what God's verdict is: that those who behave like this deserve to die—and yet they do it; and what is worse, encourage others to do the same.

The Jews are not exempt from God's anger

1 2 So no matter who you are, if you pass judgment you have no excuse. In judging others you condemn yourself, since you behave no differently from those you judge.

2 We know that God condemns that sort of behavior im-

3 partially: ·and when you judge those who behave like this while you are doing exactly the same, do you think you will

4 escape God's judgment? ·Or are you abusing his abundant goodness, patience and toleration, not realizing that this

5 goodness of God is meant to lead you to repentance? ·Your stubborn refusal to repent is only adding to the anger God will have toward you on that day of anger when his just

6 judgments will be made known. ·*He will repay each one*

7 *as his works deserve.*ᵃ ·For those who sought renown and honor and immortality by always doing good there will be

8 eternal life; ·for the unsubmissive who refused to take truth for their guide and took depravity instead, there will

9 be anger and fury. ·Pain and suffering will come to every human being who employs himself in evil—Jews first, but

10 Greeks as well; ·renown, honor and peace will come to everyone who does good—Jews first, but Greeks as well.

11 God has no favorites.

The Law will not save them

12 Sinners who were not subject to the Law will perish all the same, without that Law; sinners who were under the

13 Law will have that Law to judge them. ·It is not listening to the Law but keeping it that will make people holy in the

14 sight of God. ·For instance, pagans who never heard of the Law but are led by reason to do what the Law commands, may not actually "possess" the Law, but they can be said
15 to "be" the Law. ·They can point to the substance of the Law engraved on their hearts—they can call a witness, that is, their own conscience—they have accusation and de-
16 fense, that is, their own inner mental dialogue.[b] · . . . on the day when, according to the Good News I preach, God, through Jesus Christ, judges the secrets of mankind.

17   If you call yourself a Jew, if you really trust in the Law
18 and are proud of your God, ·if you know God's will
19 through the Law and can tell what is right, ·if you are convinced you can guide the blind and be a beacon to
20 those in the dark, ·if you can teach the ignorant and instruct the unlearned because your Law embodies all knowledge
21 and truth, ·then why not teach yourself as well as
22 others? You preach against stealing, yet you steal; ·you forbid adultery, yet you commit adultery; you despise idols,
23 yet you rob their temples. ·By boasting about the Law and
24 then disobeying it, you bring God into contempt. ·As scripture says: *It is your fault that the name of God is blasphemed among the pagans.*

Circumcision will not save them

25   It is a good thing to be circumcised if you keep the Law; but if you break the Law, you might as well have stayed
26 uncircumcised. ·If a man who is not circumcised obeys the commandments of the Law, surely that makes up for not
27 being circumcised? ·More than that, the man who keeps the Law, even though he has not been physically circumcised, is a living condemnation of the way you disobey the Law in spite of being circumcised and having it all written down.
28 To be a Jew is not just to look like a Jew, and circumcision
29 is more than a physical operation. ·The real Jew is the one who is inwardly a Jew, and the real circumcision is in the heart—something not of the letter but of the spirit. A Jew like that may not be praised by man, but he will be praised by God.

God's promises will not save them

1   **3**   Well then, is a Jew any better off? Is there any advan-
2   tage in being circumcised? ·A great advantage in every

---

2 a. Ps 6:12   b. This verse follows on from v. 13.

way. First, the Jews are the people to whom God's message
8 was entrusted. ·What if some of them were unfaithful?
4 Will their lack of fidelity cancel God's fidelity? ·That would
be absurd. God will always be true even though *everyone*
proves to be *false;*[a] so scripture says: *In all you say your
justice shows, and when you are judged you win your*
5 *case.*[b] ·But if our lack of holiness makes God demonstrate
his integrity, how can we say God is unjust when—to use a
6 human analogy—he gets angry with us in return? ·That
would be absurd, it would mean God could never judge
7 the world. ·You might as well say that since my un-
truthfulness makes God demonstrate his truthfulness and
thus gives him glory, I should not be judged to be a sinner
8 at all. ·That would be the same as saying: Do evil as a
means to good. Some slanderers have accused us of teaching this, but they are justly condemned.

All are guilty

9   Well: are we any better off? Not at all: as we said before,
10 Jews and Greeks are all under sin's dominion. ·As scripture
says:

> *There is not a good man left, no, not one;*
11 > *there is not one who understands,*
> *not one who looks for God.*
12 > *All have turned aside, tainted all alike;*
> *there is not one good man left, not a single one.*
13 > *Their throats are yawning graves;*
> *their tongues are full of deceit.*
> *Vipers' venom is on their lips,*
14 > *bitter curses fill their mouths.*
15 > *Their feet are swift when blood is to be shed,*
16 > *wherever they go there is havoc and ruin.*
17 > *They know nothing of the way of peace,*
18 > *there is no fear of God before their eyes.*[c]

19   Now all this that the Law says is said, as we know, for the
benefit of those who are subject to the Law, but it is meant
to silence everyone and to lay the whole world open to
20 God's judgment; ·and this is because *no one can be justified in the sight*[d] of God by keeping the Law: all that law
does is to tell us what is sinful.

B. FAITH AND THE JUSTICE OF GOD

The revelation of God's justice

21 God's justice that was made known through the Law and
22 the Prophets has now been revealed outside the Law, ·since
it is the same justice of God that comes through faith to
everyone, Jew and pagan alike, who believes in Jesus Christ.
23 Both Jew and pagan sinned and forfeited God's glory,
24 and both are justified through the free gift of his grace by
25 being redeemed in Christ Jesus ·who was appointed by God
to sacrifice his life so as to win reconciliation through
faith. In this way God makes his justice known; first, for
the past, when sins went unpunished because he held his
26 hand, ·then, for the present age, by showing positively
that he is just, and that he justifies everyone who believes
in Jesus.

What faith does

27 So what becomes of our boasts? There is no room for
them. What sort of law excludes them? The sort of law that
tells us what to do? On the contrary, it is the law of faith,
28 since, as we see it, a man is justified by faith and not by
29 doing something the Law tells him to do. ·Is God the God
of Jews alone and not of the pagans too? Of the pagans too,
30 most certainly, ·since there is only one God, and he is the
one who will justify the circumcised because of their faith
31 and justify the uncircumcised through their faith. ·Do we
mean that faith makes the Law pointless? Not at all: we
are giving the Law its true value.

C. THE EXAMPLE OF ABRAHAM

Abraham justified by faith

1 **4** Apply this to Abraham, the ancestor from whom we
2   are all descended. ·If Abraham was justified as a reward for doing something, he would really have had some-
3 thing to boast about, though not in God's sight ·because
scripture says: *Abraham put his faith in God, and this*
4 *faith was considered as justifying him.*[a] ·If a man has work

3 a. Ps 116:11 b. Ps 51:4 (LXX) c. Quotations from Ps 14,
Ps 5, Ps 140, Ps 10, Is 59, Ps 36. d. Ps 143:2
4 a. Gn 15:6

to show, his wages are not considered as a favor but as
5 his due; ·but when a man has nothing to show except faith
in the one who justifies sinners, then his faith is considered
6 as justifying him. ·And David says the same: a man is
happy if God considers him righteous, irrespective of good
deeds:

7 *Happy those whose crimes are forgiven,*
whose sins are blotted out;
8 *happy the man whom the Lord considers sinless.*[b]

Justified before circumcision

9 Is this happiness meant only for the circumcised, or is it
meant for others as well? Think of Abraham again: *his*
10 *faith,* we say, *was considered as justifying him,* ·but when
was this done? When he was already circumcised or before
he had been circumcised? It was before he had been cir-
11 cumcised, not after; ·and when he was *circumcised* later it
was only *as a sign* and guarantee that the faith he had before his circumcision justified him. In this way Abraham
became the ancestor of all uncircumcised believers, so that
12 they too might be considered righteous; ·and ancestor, also,
of those who though circumcised do not rely on that fact
alone, but follow our ancestor Abraham along the path
of faith he trod before he had been circumcised.

Not justified by obedience to the Law

13 The promise of inheriting the world was not made to
Abraham and his descendants on account of any law but
on account of the righteousness which consists in faith.
14 If the world is only to be inherited by those who submit to
the Law, then faith is pointless and the promise worth
15 nothing. ·Law involves the possibility of punishment for
breaking the law—only where there is no law can that be
16 avoided. ·That is why what fulfills the promise depends
on faith, so that it may be a free gift and be available to all
of Abraham's descendants, not only those who belong to
the Law but also those who belong to the faith of Abraham
17 who is the father of all of us. ·As scripture says: *I have*
made you the ancestor of many nations[c]—Abraham is our
father in the eyes of God, in whom he put his faith, and
who brings the dead to life and calls into being what does
not exist.

Abraham's faith, a model of Christian faith

18   Though it seemed Abraham's hope could not be fulfilled, he hoped and he believed, and through doing so he did become *the father of many nations* exactly as he had been promised: *Your descendants will be as many as the stars.*[d]
19 Even the thought that his body was past fatherhood—he was about a hundred years old—and Sarah too old to be-
20 come a mother, did not shake his belief. ·Since God had promised it, Abraham refused either to deny it or even to doubt it, but drew strength from faith and gave glory to
21 God, ·convinced that God had power to do what he had
22 promised. ·This is the faith that was *"considered as justify-*
23 *ing him."* ·Scripture however does not refer only to him but to us as well when it says that his faith was thus "con-
24 sidered"; ·our faith too will be "considered" if we believe
25 in him who raised Jesus our Lord from the dead, ·Jesus who was *put to death for our sins*[e] and raised to life to justify us.

II. SALVATION

Faith guarantees salvation

1   So far then we have seen that, through our Lord Jesus Christ, by faith we are judged righteous and at peace
2 with God, ·since it is by faith and through Jesus that we have entered this state of grace in which we can boast
3 about looking forward to God's glory. ·But that is not all we can boast about; we can boast about our sufferings.
4 These sufferings bring patience, as we know, ·and patience
5 brings perseverance, and perseverance brings hope, ·and this hope is not deceptive, because the love of God has been poured into our hearts by the Holy Spirit which has been
6 given us. ·We were still helpless when at his appointed
7 moment Christ died for sinful men. ·It is not easy to die even for a good man—though of course for someone really
8 worthy, a man might be prepared to die—·but what proves that God loves us is that Christ died for us while we were
9 still sinners. ·Having died to make us righteous, is it likely that he would now fail to save us from God's anger?

b. Ps 32:1-2   c. Gn 17:5 (the same chapter to which allusion is made in 4:11, above).   d. Gn 15:5   e. Is 53:5,6

10 When we were reconciled to God by the death of his Son, we were still enemies; now that we have been reconciled, surely we may count on being saved by the life of his Son?

11 Not merely because we have been reconciled but because we are filled with joyful trust in God, through our Lord Jesus Christ, through whom we have already gained our reconciliation.

A. DELIVERANCE FROM SIN AND DEATH AND LAW

Adam and Jesus Christ

12 Well then, sin *entered the world* through one man, and through sin death, and thus death has spread through the

13 whole human race because everyone has sinned. ·Sin existed in the world long before the Law was given. There was no law and so no one could be accused of the sin of

14 "law-breaking," ·yet death reigned over all from Adam to Moses, even though their sin, unlike that of Adam, was not a matter of breaking a law.

15 Adam prefigured the One to come, ·but the gift itself considerably outweighed the fall. If it is certain that through one man's fall so many died, it is even more certain that divine grace, coming through the one man, Jesus Christ,

16 came to so many as an abundant free gift. ·The results of the gift also outweigh the results of one man's sin: for after one single fall came judgment with a verdict of condemnation, now after many falls comes grace with its ver-

17 dict of acquittal. ·If it is certain that death reigned over everyone as the consequence of one man's fall, it is even more certain that one man, Jesus Christ, will cause everyone to reign in life who receives the free gift that he does

18 not deserve, of being made righteous. ·Again, as one man's fall brought condemnation on everyone, so the good act of

19 one man brings everyone life and makes them justified. ·As by one man's disobedience many were made sinners, so by

20 one man's obedience many will be made righteous. ·When law came, it was to multiply the opportunities of falling, but however great the number of sins committed, grace

21 was even greater; ·and so, just as sin reigned wherever there was death, so grace will reign to bring eternal life thanks to the righteousness that comes through Jesus Christ our Lord.

Baptism

1 Does it follow that we should remain in sin so as to let
2 grace have greater scope? ·Of course not. We are dead
3 to sin, so how can we continue to live in it? ·You have been
taught that when we were baptized in Christ Jesus we were
4 baptized in his death; ·in other words, when we were baptized we went into the tomb with him and joined him in
death, so that as Christ was raised from the dead by the
Father's glory, we too might live a new life.
5 If in union with Christ we have imitated his death, we
6 shall also imitate him in his resurrection. ·We must realize
that our former selves have been crucified with him to destroy this sinful body and to free us from the slavery of sin.
7 When a man dies, of course, he has finished with sin.
8 But we believe that having died with Christ we shall re-
9 turn to life with him: ·Christ, as we know, having been
raised from the dead will never die again. Death has no
10 power over him any more. ·When he died, he died, once
11 for all, to sin, so his life now is life with God; ·and in that
way, you too must consider yourselves to be dead to sin but
alive for God in Christ Jesus.

Holiness, not sin, to be the master

12 That is why you must not let sin reign in your mortal
bodies or command your obedience to bodily passions,
13 why you must not let any part of your body turn into an
unholy weapon fighting on the side of sin; you should,
instead, offer yourselves to God, and consider yourselves
dead men brought back to life; you should make every
part of your body into a weapon fighting on the side of God;
14 and then sin will no longer dominate your life, since you
are living by grace and not by law.

The Christian is freed from the slavery of sin

15 Does the fact that we are living by grace and not by law
16 mean that we are free to sin? Of course not. ·You know
that if you agree to serve and obey a master you become
his slaves. You cannot be slaves of sin that leads to death
and at the same time slaves of obedience that leads to right-
17 eousness. ·You were once slaves of sin, but thank God you
submitted without reservation to the creed you were taught.
18 You may have been freed from the slavery of sin, but only
19 to become "slaves" of righteousness. ·If I may use human

terms to help your natural weakness: as once you put your bodies at the service of vice and immorality, so now you must put them at the service of righteousness for your sanctification.

The reward of sin and the reward of holiness

20 When you were slaves of sin, you felt no obligation to 21 righteousness, ·and what did you get from this? Nothing but experiences that now make you blush, since that sort 22 of behavior ends in death. ·Now, however, you have been set free from sin, you have been made slaves of God, and you get a reward leading to your sanctification and ending 23 in eternal life. ·For the wage paid by sin is death; the present given by God is eternal life in Christ Jesus our Lord.

The Christian is not bound by the Law

1 **7** Brothers, those of you who have studied law will know 2 that laws affect a person only during his lifetime. ·A married woman, for instance, has legal obligations to her husband while he is alive, but all these obligations come to 3 an end if the husband dies. ·So if she gives herself to another man while her husband is still alive, she is legally an adulteress; but after her husband is dead her legal obligations come to an end, and she can marry someone 4 else without becoming an adulteress. ·That is why you, my brothers, who through the body of Christ are now dead to the Law, can now give yourselves to another husband, to him who rose from the dead to make us productive for 5 God. ·Before our conversion[a] our sinful passions, quite unsubdued by the Law, fertilized our bodies to make them 6 give birth to death. ·But now we are rid of the Law, freed by death from our imprisonment, free to serve in the new spiritual way and not the old way of a written law.

The function of the Law

7 Does it follow that the Law itself is sin? Of course not. What I mean is that I should not have known what sin was except for the Law. I should not for instance have known what it means to covet if the Law had not said *You shall* 8 *not covet.* ·But it was this commandment that sin took advantage of to produce all kinds of covetousness in me, for when there is no Law, sin is dead.

9 Once, when there was no Law, I[b] was alive; but when 10 the commandment came, sin came to life ·and I died: the

commandment was meant to lead me to life but it turned
11 out to mean death for me, ·because sin took advantage of
the commandment to mislead me, and so sin, through that
commandment, killed me.

12 The Law is sacred, and what it commands is sacred, just
13 and good. ·Does that mean that something good killed me?
Of course not. But sin, to show itself in its true colors,
used that good thing to kill me; and thus sin, thanks to the
commandment, was able to exercise all its sinful power.

The inward struggle

14 The Law, of course, as we all know, is spiritual; but I
15 am unspiritual; I have been sold as a slave to sin. ·I cannot
understand my own behavior. I fail to carry out the things
I want to do, and I find myself doing the very things I hate.
16 When I act against my own will, that means I have a self
17 that acknowledges that the Law is good, ·and so the thing
behaving in that way is not my self but sin living in me.
18 The fact is, I know of nothing good living in me—living,
that is, in my unspiritual self—for though the will to do
19 what is good is in me, the performance is not, ·with the
result that instead of doing the good things I want to do, I
20 carry out the sinful things I do not want. ·When I act
against my will, then, it is not my true self doing it, but sin
which lives in me.

21 In fact, this seems to be the rule, that every single time I
want to do good it is something evil that comes to hand.
22
23 In my inmost self I dearly love God's Law, but ·I can see
that my body follows a different law that battles against
the law which my reason dictates. This is what makes me a
prisoner of that law of sin which lives inside my body.

24 What a wretched man I am! Who will rescue me from
25 this body doomed to death? ·Thanks be to God through
Jesus Christ our Lord!

In short, it is I who with my reason serve the Law of God,
and no less I who serve in my unspiritual self the law of
sin.

7 a. "While we were in the flesh.". b. Rhetorical figure; Paul
speaks in the person of mankind.

B. THE CHRISTIAN'S SPIRITUAL LIFE

The life of the spirit

¹ ² **8** The reason, therefore, why those who are in Christ Jesus are not condemned, ·is that the law of the spirit of life in Christ Jesus has set you free from the law of sin and ³ death. ·God has done what the Law, because of our un-spiritual nature,ᵃ was unable to do. God dealt with sin by sending his own Son in a body as physical as any sinful ⁴ body, and in that body God condemned sin. ·He did this in order that the Law's just demands might be satisfied in us, who behave not as our unspiritual nature but as the spirit dictates.

⁵ The unspiritual are interested only in what is unspiritual, ⁶ but the spiritual are interested in spiritual things. ·It is death to limit oneself to what is unspiritual; life and peace ⁷ can only come with concern for the spiritual. ·That is be-cause to limit oneself to what is unspiritual is to be at enmity with God: such a limitation never could and never ⁸ does submit to God's law. ·People who are interested only ⁹ in unspiritual things can never be pleasing to God. ·Your interests, however, are not in the unspiritual, but in the spiritual, since the Spirit of God has made his home in you. In fact, unless you possessed the Spirit of Christ you ¹⁰ would not belong to him. ·Though your body may be dead it is because of sin, but if Christ is in you then your spirit ¹¹ is life itself because you have been justified; ·and if the Spirit of him who raised Jesus from the dead is living in you, then he who raised Jesus from the dead will give life to your own mortal bodies through his Spirit living in you.

¹² So then, my brothers, there is no necessity for us to obey ¹³ our unspiritual selves or to live unspiritual lives. ·If you do live in that way, you are doomed to die; but if by the Spirit you put an end to the misdeeds of the body you will live.

Children of God

¹⁴ ¹⁵ Everyone moved by the Spirit is a son of God. ·The spirit you received is not the spirit of slaves bringing fear into your lives again; it is the spirit of sons, and it makes ¹⁶ us cry out, "Abba, Father!"ᵇ ·The Spirit himself and our ¹⁷ spirit bear united witness that we are children of God. ·And

if we are children we are heirs as well: heirs of God and coheirs with Christ, sharing his sufferings so as to share his glory.

Glory as our destiny

18 I think that what we suffer in this life can never be compared to the glory, as yet unrevealed, which is waiting
19 for us. ·The whole creation is eagerly waiting for God to
20 reveal his sons. ·It was not for any fault on the part of creation that it was made unable to attain its purpose, it was made so by God; but creation still retains the hope
21 of being freed, like us, from its slavery to decadence, to enjoy the same freedom and glory as the children of God.
22 From the beginning till now the entire creation, as we know,
23 has been groaning in one great act of giving birth; ·and not only creation, but all of us who possess the first-fruits of the Spirit, we too groan inwardly as we wait for our
24 bodies to be set free. ·For we must be content to hope that we shall be saved—our salvation is not in sight, we should
25 not have to be hoping for it if it were—·but, as I say, we must hope to be saved since we are not saved yet—it is something we must wait for with patience.
26 The Spirit too comes to help us in our weakness. For when we cannot choose words in order to pray properly, the Spirit himself expresses our plea in a way that could
27 never be put into words, ·and God who knows everything in our hearts knows perfectly well what he means, and that the pleas of the saints expressed by the Spirit are according to the mind of God.

God has called us to share his glory

28 We know that by turning everything to their good God co-operates with all those who love him, with all those that
29 he has called according to his purpose. ·They are the ones he chose specially long ago and intended to become true images of his Son, so that his Son might be the eldest of
30 many brothers. ·He called those he intended for this; those he called he justified, and with those he justified he shared his glory.

A hymn to God's love

31 After saying this, what can we add? With God on our
32 side who can be against us? ·Since God did not spare his

8 a. "flesh."   b. The prayer of Christ in Gethsemane.

own Son, but gave him up to benefit us all, we may be certain, after such a gift, that he will not refuse anything he
33 can give. •Could anyone accuse those that God has chosen?
34 When God acquits, •could anyone condemn? Could Christ Jesus? No! He not only died for us—he rose from the dead, and there at God's right hand he stands and pleads for us.
35 Nothing therefore can come between us and the love of Christ, even if we are troubled or worried, or being persecuted, or lacking food or clothes, or being threatened or
36 even attacked. •As scripture promised: *For your sake we are being massacred daily, and reckoned as sheep for the*
37 *slaughter.*[o] •These are the trials through which we triumph, by the power of him who loved us.
38 For I am certain of this: neither death nor life, no angel, no prince, nothing that exists, nothing still to come, not
39 any power, •or height or depth,[d] nor any created thing, can ever come between us and the love of God made visible in Christ Jesus our Lord.

C. THE PLACE OF ISRAEL

The privileges of Israel

1 9 What I want to say now is no pretence; I say it in union with Christ—it is the truth—my conscience in union with
2 the Holy Spirit assures me of it too. •What I want to say is this: my sorrow is so great, my mental anguish so end-
3 less, •I would willingly be condemned[a] and be cut off from Christ if it could help my brothers of Israel, my own flesh
4 and blood. •They were adopted as sons, they were given the glory and the covenants; the Law and the ritual were drawn up for them, and the promises were made to them.
5 They are descended from the patriarchs and from their flesh and blood came Christ who is above all, God for ever blessed! Amen.

God has kept his promise

6 Does this mean that God has failed to keep his promise? Of course not. Not all those who descend from Israel is
7 Israel; •not all the descendants of Abraham are his true children. Remember: *It is through Isaac that your name*
8 *will be carried on,*[b] •which means that it is not physical descent that decides who are the children of God; it is only the children of the promise who will count as the true
9 descendants. •The actual words in which the promise was

made were: *I shall visit you* at such and such a time, *and*
10 *Sarah will have a son.*ᶜ ·Even more to the point is what
was said to Rebecca when she was pregnant by our an-
11 cestor Isaac, ·but before her twin children were born and
before either had done good or evil. In order to stress that
12 God's choice is free, ·since it depends on the one who calls,
not on human merit, Rebecca was told: *the elder shall*
13 *serve the younger,*ᵈ ·or as scripture says elsewhere: *I*
*showed my love for Jacob and my hatred for Esau.*ᵉ

God is not unjust

14
15 Does it follow that God is unjust? Of course not. ·Take
what God said to Moses: *I have mercy on whom I will, and*
16 *I show pity to whom I please.*ᶠ ·In other words, the only
thing that counts is not what human beings want or try to
17 do, but the mercy of God. ·For in scripture he says to
Pharaoh: *It was for this I raised you up, to use you as a*
means of showing my power and to make my name known
18 *throughout the world.*ᵍ ·In other words, when God wants
to show mercy he does, and when he wants to harden
someone's heart he does so.
19 You will ask me, "In that case, how can God ever blame
20 anyone, since no one can oppose his will?" ·But what right
have you, a human being, to cross-examine God? *The pot*
has no right to say to the potter: Why did you make me
21 *this shape?*ʰ ·Surely a potter can do what he likes with the
clay? It is surely for him to decide whether he will use a
particular lump of clay to make a special pot or an ordinary
one?
22 Or else imagine that although God is ready to show his
anger and display his power, yet he patiently puts up with
the people who make him angry, however much they de-
23 serve to be destroyed. ·He puts up with them for the sake
of those other people, to whom he wants to be merciful,
to whom he wants to reveal the richness of his glory, people
24 he had prepared for this glory long ago. ·Well, we are those
people; whether we were Jews or pagans we are the ones
he has called.

c. Ps 44:11   d. "powers," "heights" and "depths" are probably
cosmic forces hostile to mankind.
9 a. *Anathema,* cursed and excommunicated.   b. Gn 21:12
c. Gn 18:10   d. Gn 25:23   e. Ml 1:2-3   f. Ex 33:19   g. Ex
9:16   h. Is 29:16

All has been foretold in the Old Testament

25　　That is exactly what God says in Hosea: *I shall say to a people that was not mine, "You are my people," and to a*
26　*nation I never loved, "I love you."* •*Instead of being told, "You are no people of mine," they will now be called the*
27　*sons of the living God.*[j] •Referring to Israel Isaiah had this to say: *Though Israel should have as many descendants as there are grains of sand on the seashore, only a remnant*
28　*will be saved,* •*for without hesitation or delay the Lord will*
29　*execute his sentence on the earth.*[j] •As Isaiah foretold: *Had the Lord of hosts not left us some descendants we should now be like Sodom, we should be like Gomorrah.*[k]
30　　From this it follows that the pagans who were not looking for righteousness found it all the same, a righteousness
31　that comes of faith, •while Israel, looking for a righteousness derived from law failed to do what that law required.
32　Why did they fail? Because they relied on good deeds instead of trusting in faith. In other words, they *stumbled*
33　*over the stumbling-stone*[l] •mentioned in scripture: *See how I lay in Zion a stone to stumble over, a rock to trip men up —only those who believe in him will have no cause for shame.*[m]

Israel fails to see that it is God who makes us holy

1　**10** Brothers, I have the very warmest love for the Jews,
2　and I pray to God for them to be saved. •I can swear
3　to their fervor for God, but their zeal is misguided. •Failing to recognize the righteousness that comes from God, they try to promote their own idea of it, instead of submit-
4　ting to the righteousness of God. •But now the Law has come to an end with Christ, and everyone who has faith may be justified.

The testimony of Moses

5　　When Moses refers to being justified by the Law, he writes: *those who keep the Law will draw life from it.*[a]
6　But the righteousness that comes from faith says this: Do not tell yourself you have to bring Christ down—as in the
7　text: *Who will go up to heaven?*[b] •or that you have to bring Christ back from the dead—as in the text: *Who will go*
8　*down to the underworld?* •On the positive side it says: *The word,* that is the faith we proclaim, *is very near to you, it*
9　*is on your lips and in your heart.* •If your lips confess that Jesus is Lord and if you believe in your heart that God

10 raised him from the dead, then you will be saved. ·By believing from the heart you are made righteous; by confess-
11 ing with your lips you are saved. ·When scripture says:
those who believe in him will have no cause for shame,[c]
12 it makes no distinction between Jew and Greek: all belong
to the same Lord who is rich enough, however many ask
13 his help, ·*for everyone who calls on the name of the Lord
will be saved.*[d]

Israel has no excuse

14 But they will not ask his help unless they believe in him,
and they will not believe in him unless they have heard of
him, and they will not hear of him unless they get a
15 preacher, ·and they will never have a preacher unless one
is sent, but as scripture says: *The footsteps of those who
16 bring good news is a welcome sound.*[e] ·Not everyone, of
course, listens to the Good News. As Isaiah says: *Lord,
17 how many believed what we proclaimed?*[f] ·So faith comes
from what is preached, and what is preached comes from
the word of Christ.
18 Let me put the question: is it possible that they did not
hear? Indeed they did; in the words of the psalm, *their
voice has gone out through all the earth, and their message
19 to the ends of the world.*[g] ·A second question: is it possible
that Israel did not understand? Moses answered this long
ago: *I will make you jealous of people who are not even a
nation; I will make you angry with an irreligious people.*[h]
20 Isaiah said more clearly: *I have been found by those who
did not seek me, and have revealed myself to those who
21 did not consult me;*[i] ·and referring to Israel he goes on:
*Each day I stretched out my hand to a disobedient and
rebellious people.*

The remnant of Israel

1 11 Let me put a further question then: is it possible that
God has rejected his people?[a] Of course not. I, an
Israelite, descended from Abraham through the tribe of
2 Benjamin, ·could never agree that God had rejected his

i. Ho 2:25 and 2:1 j. Is 10:22-23 k. Is 1:9 l. Is 8:14
m. Is 28:16
10 a. Lv 18:5 b. This quotation, and the two following, are a
free rendering of Dt 30:12-14. c. Is 28:16 d. Jl 3:5 e. Is
52:7 f. Is 53:1 g. Ps 19:4 h. Dt 32:21 i. Is 65:1,2
11 a. Ps 94:14

people, the people he chose specially long ago. Do you remember what scripture says of Elijah—how he complained
3 to God about Israel's behavior? *Lord, they have killed
your prophets and broken down your altars. I, and I only,
4 remain, and they want to kill me.*[b] *What did God say to
that? *I have kept for myself seven thousand men who have
5 not bent the knee to Baal.*[c] *Today the same thing has hap-
6 pened: there is a remnant, chosen by grace. *By grace, you
notice, nothing therefore to do with good deeds, or grace
would not be grace at all!

7   What follows? It was not Israel as a whole that found
what it was seeking, but only the chosen few. The rest
8 were not allowed to see the truth; *as scripture says: *God
has given them a sluggish spirit, unseeing eyes and inatten-
9 tive ears, and they are still like that today.*[d] *And David
says: *May their own table prove a trap for them, a snare
10 and a pitfall—let that be their punishment; *may their eyes
be struck incurably blind, their backs bend for ever.*[e]

The Jews to be restored in the future

11   Let me put another question then: have the Jews fallen
for ever, or have they just stumbled? Obviously they have
not fallen for ever: their fall, though, has saved the pagans
12 in a way the Jews may now well emulate. *Think of the
extent to which the world, the pagan world, has benefited
from their fall and defection—then think how much more
13 it will benefit from the conversion of them all. *Let me tell
you pagans[f] this: I have been sent to the pagans as their
14 apostle, and I am proud of being sent, *but the purpose of
it is to make my own people envious of you, and in this
15 way save some of them. *Since their rejection meant the
reconciliation of the world, do you know what their ad-
mission will mean? Nothing less than a resurrection from
the dead!

The Jews are still the chosen people

16   A whole batch of bread is made holy if the first handful
of dough is made holy; all the branches are holy if the root
17 is holy. *No doubt some of the branches have been cut off,
and, like shoots of wild olive, you have been grafted
among the rest to share with them the rich sap provided by
18 the olive tree itself, *but still, even if you think yourself
superior to the other branches, remember that you do not
19 support the root; it is the root that supports you. *You will

say, "Those branches were cut off on purpose to let me be
20 grafted in!" True, ·they were cut off, but through their unbelief; if you still hold firm, it is only thanks to your faith.
Rather than making you ·proud, that ·should make ·you
21 afraid. ·God did not spare the natural branches, and he is
22 not likely to spare you. ·Do not forget that God can be
severe as well as kind: he is severe to those who fell, and
he is kind to you, but only for as long as he chooses to be,
23 otherwise you will find yourself cut off too, ·and the Jews,
if they give up their unbelief, grafted back in your place.
24 God is perfectly able to graft them back again; ·after all, if
you were cut from your natural wild olive to be grafted
unnaturally on to a cultivated olive, it will be much easier
for them, the natural branches, to be grafted back on the
tree they came from.

The conversion of the Jews

25　There is a hidden reason for all this, brothers, of which
I do not want you to be ignorant, in case you think you
know more than you do. One section of Israel has become
blind, but this will last only until the whole pagan world
26 has entered, ·and then after this the rest of Israel will be
saved as well. As scripture says: *The liberator will come*
27 *from Zion, he will banish godlessness from Jacob. ·And
this is the covenant I will make with them when I take their
sins away.*[g]
28　The Jews are enemies of God only with regard to the
Good News, and enemies only for your sake; but as the
chosen people, they are still loved by God, loved for the
29 sake of their ancestors. ·God never takes back his gifts or
revokes his choice.
30　Just as you changed from being disobedient to God, and
31 now enjoy mercy because of their disobedience, ·so those
who are disobedient now—and only because of the mercy
32 shown to you—will also enjoy mercy eventually. ·God has
imprisoned all men in their own disobedience only to show
mercy to all mankind.

A hymn to God's mercy and wisdom

33　How rich are the depths of God—how deep his wisdom
and knowledge—and how impossible to penetrate his mo-

---

b. 1 K 19:10,14　c. 1 K 19:18　d. Is 29:10　e. Ps 69:22f
f. Converts from paganism.　g. Is 27:9

34 tives or understand his methods! *·Who could ever know the mind of the Lord? Who could ever be his counsellor?*
35 *Who could ever give him anything or lend him anything?ʰ*
36 All that exists comes from him; all is by him and for him. To him be glory for ever! Amen.

EXHORTATION

Spiritual worship

1 **12** Think of God's mercy, my brothers, and worship him, I beg you, in a way that is worthy of thinking beings, by offering your living bodies as a holy sacrifice,
2 truly pleasing to God. ·Do not model yourselves on the behavior of the world around you, but let your behavior change, modeled by your new mind. This is the only way to discover the will of God and know what is good, what it is that God wants, what is the perfect thing to do.

Humility and charity

3 In the light of the grace I have received I want to urge each one among you not to exaggerate his real importance. Each of you must judge himself soberly by the standard of
4 the faith God has given him. ·Just as each of our bodies has several parts and each part has a separate function,
5 so all of us, in union with Christ, form one body, and as
6 parts of it we belong to each other. ·Our gifts differ according to the grace given us. If your gift is prophecy, then
7 use it as your faith suggests; ·if administration, then use it for administration; if teaching, then use it for teaching.
8 Let the preachers deliver sermons, the almsgivers give freely, the officials be diligent, and those who do works of mercy do them cheerfully.
9 Do not let your love be a pretense, but sincerely prefer
10 good to evil. ·Love each other as much as brothers should,
11 and have a profound respect for each other. ·Work for the Lord with untiring effort and with great earnestness of
12 spirit. ·If you have hope, this will make you cheerful. Do
13 not give up if trials come; and keep on praying. ·If any of the saints are in need you must share with them; and you should make hospitality your special care.

Charity to everyone, including enemies

14 Bless those who persecute you: never curse them, bless

15 them. ·Rejoice with those who rejoice and be sad with
16 those in sorrow. ·Treat everyone with equal kindness;
never be condescending but make real friends with the
poor. Do not allow yourself to become self-satisfied.
17 Never repay evil with evil but let everyone see that you
18 are interested only in the highest ideals. ·Do all you can
19 to live at peace with everyone. ·Never try to get revenge;
leave that, my friends, to God's anger. As scripture says:
Vengeance is mine—I will pay them back,[a] the Lord prom-
20 ises. ·But there is more: *If your enemy is hungry, you
should give him food, and if he is thirsty, let him drink.*
21 *Thus you heap red-hot coals on his head.*[b] ·Resist evil and
conquer it with good.

Submission to civil authority

1 **13** You must all obey the governing authorities. Since
all government comes from God, the civil authori-
2 ties were appointed by God, ·and so anyone who resists
authority is rebelling against God's decision, and such an
3 act is bound to be punished. ·Good behavior is not afraid
of magistrates; only criminals have anything to fear. If
you want to live without being afraid of authority, you
must live honestly and authority may even honor you.
4 The state is there to serve God for your benefit. If you
break the law, however, you may well have fear: the bearing of the sword has its significance. The authorities are
there to serve God: they carry out God's revenge by pun-
5 ishing wrongdoers. ·You must obey, therefore, not only
because you are afraid of being punished, but also for con-
6 science' sake. ·This is also the reason why you must pay
taxes, since all government officials are God's officers. They
7 serve God by collecting taxes. ·Pay every government official what he has a right to ask—whether it be direct tax
or indirect, fear or honor.

Love and law

8 Avoid getting into debt, except the debt of mutual love.
If you love your fellow men you have carried out your
9 obligations. ·All the commandments: *You shall not commit adultery, you shall not kill, you shall not steal, you
shall not covet,*[a] and so on, are summed up in this single

h. Is 40:13
12 a. Dt 32:35   b. Pr 25:21-22
13 a. From the Commandments in Ex 20 and Dt 17.

command: *You must love your neighbor as yourself.*[b]
¹⁰ Love is the one thing that cannot hurt your neighbor; that is why it is the answer to every one of the commandments.

Children of the light

¹¹ Besides, you know "the time" has come: you must wake up now: our salvation is even nearer than it was when we ¹² were converted. ·The night is almost over, it will be daylight soon—let us give up all the things we prefer to do under cover of the dark; let us arm ourselves and appear ¹³ in the light. ·Let us live decently as people do in the daytime: no drunken orgies, no promiscuity or licentiousness, ¹⁴ and no wrangling or jealousy. ·Let your armor be the Lord Jesus Christ; forget about satisfying your bodies with all their cravings.

Charity towards the scrupulous

¹ **14** If a person's faith is not strong enough, welcome him ² all the same without starting an argument. ·People range from those who believe they may eat any sort of meat to those whose faith is so weak they dare not eat ³ anything except vegetables. ·Meat-eaters must not despise the scrupulous. On the other hand, the scrupulous must not condemn those who feel free to eat anything they ⁴ choose, since God has welcomed them. ·It is not for you to condemn someone else's servant: whether he stands or falls it is his own master's business; he will stand, you may be sure, because the Lord has power to make him stand. ⁵ If one man keeps certain days as holier than others, and another considers all days to be equally holy, each must ⁶ be left free to hold his own opinion. ·The one who observes special days does so in honor of the Lord. The one who eats meat also does so in honor of the Lord, since he gives thanks to God; but then the man who abstains does that too in honor of the Lord, and so he also ⁷ gives God thanks. ·The life and death of each of us has ⁸ its influence on others; ·if we live, we live for the Lord; and if we die, we die for the Lord, so that alive or dead ⁹ we belong to the Lord. ·This explains why Christ both died and came to life, it was so that he might be Lord ¹⁰ both of the dead and of the living. ·This is also why you should never pass judgment on a brother or treat him with contempt, as some of you have done. We shall all have to

11 stand before the judgment seat of God; •as scripture says:
   By my life—it is the Lord who speaks—every knee shall
12 *bend before me, and every tongue shall praise God.*[a] •It is
   to God, therefore, that each of us must give an account of
   himself.
13   Far from passing judgment on each other, therefore,
   you should make up your mind never to be the cause of
14 your brother tripping or falling. •Now I am perfectly well
   aware, of course, and I speak for the Lord Jesus, that no
   food is unclean in itself; however, if someone thinks that a
15 particular food is unclean, then it is unclean for him. •And
   indeed if your attitude to food is upsetting your brother,
   then you are hardly being guided by charity. You are certainly not free to eat what you like if that means the downfall of someone for whom Christ died.
16   In short, you must not compromise your privilege,
17 because the kingdom of God does not mean eating or
   drinking this or that, it means righteousness and peace and
18 joy brought by the Holy Spirit. •If you serve Christ in this
19 way you will please God and be respected by men. •So
   let us adopt any custom that leads to peace and our mutual
20 improvement; •do not wreck God's work over a question
   of food. Of course all food is clean, but it becomes evil
21 if by eating it you make somebody else fall away. •In such
   cases the best course is to abstain from meat and wine and
   anything else that would make your brother trip or fall or
   weaken in any way.
22   Hold on to your own belief, as between yourself and
   God—and consider the man fortunate who can make his
23 decision without going against his conscience. •But anybody who eats in a state of doubt is condemned, because
   he is not in good faith; and every act done in bad faith
   is a sin.
1 **15** We who are strong have a duty to put up with the
   qualms of the weak without thinking of ourselves.
2 Each of us should think of his neighbors and help them
3 to become stronger Christians. •Christ did not think of
   himself: the words of scripture—*the insults of those who*
4 *insult you fall on me*[a]—apply to him. •And indeed everything that was written long ago in the scriptures was meant

   b. Lv 19:18
   14 a. Is 45:23
   15 a. Ps 69:9

to teach us something about hope from the examples scripture gives of how people who did not give up were helped
⁵ by God. ·And may he who helps us when we refuse to give up, help you all to be tolerant with each other, following the example of Christ Jesus, ·so that united in mind
⁶ and voice you may give glory to the God and Father of our Lord Jesus Christ.

An appeal for unity

⁷ It can only be to God's glory, then, for you to treat each other in the same friendly way as Christ treated you.
⁸ The reason Christ became the servant of circumcised Jews was not only so that God could faithfully carry out the
⁹ promises made to the patriarchs, ·it was also to get the pagans to give glory to God for his mercy, as scripture says in one place: *For this I shall praise you among the*
¹⁰ *pagans and sing to your name.*[b] ·And in another place:
¹¹ *Rejoice, pagans, with his people,*[c] ·and in a third place: *Let all the pagans praise the Lord, let all the peoples sing*
¹² *his praises.*[d] ·Isaiah too has this to say: *The root of Jesse will appear, rising up to rule the pagans, and in him the pagans will put their hope.*[e]
¹³ May the God of hope bring you such joy and peace in your faith that the power of the Holy Spirit will remove all bounds to hope.

EPILOGUE

Paul's ministry

¹⁴ It is not because I have any doubts about you, my brothers; on the contrary I am quite certain that you are full of good intentions, perfectly well instructed and able to advise
¹⁵ each other. ·The reason why I have written to you, and put some things rather strongly, is to refresh your mem-
¹⁶ ories, since God has given me this special position. ·He has appointed me as a priest of Jesus Christ, and I am to carry out my priestly duty by bringing the Good News from God to the pagans, and so make them acceptable as an offering, made holy by the Holy Spirit.
¹⁷ I think I have some reason to be proud of what I, in union with Christ Jesus, have been able to do for God.

18 What I am presuming to speak of, of course, is only what Christ himself has done to win the allegiance of the pagans, 19 using what I have said and done ·by the power of signs and wonders, by the power of the Holy Spirit. Thus, all the way along, from Jerusalem to Illyricum,[f] I have preached Christ's Good News to the utmost of my capacity. 20 I have always, however, made it an unbroken rule never to preach where Christ's name has already been heard. The reason for that was that I had no wish to build on other men's foundations; ·on the contrary, my chief con- 21 cern has been to fulfill the text: *Those who have never been told about him will see him, and those who have never heard about him will understand.*[g]

Paul's plans

22 That is the reason why I have been kept from visiting 23 you so long, ·though for many years I have been longing to pay you a visit. Now, however, having no more work 24 to do here, ·I hope to see you on my way to Spain and, after enjoying a little of your company, to complete the 25 rest of the journey with your good wishes. ·First, however, I must take a present of money to the saints in Jerusalem, 26 since Macedonia and Achaia have decided to send a gen- erous contribution to the poor among the saints at Jeru- 27 salem. ·A generous contribution as it should be, since it is really repaying a debt: the pagans who share the spiritual possessions of these poor people have a duty to help them 28 with temporal possessions. ·So when I have done this and officially handed over what has been raised, I shall set out 29 for Spain and visit you on the way. ·I know that when I reach you I shall arrive with rich blessings from Christ. 30 But I beg you, brothers, by our Lord Jesus Christ and the love of the Spirit, to help me through my dangers by 31 praying to God for me. ·Pray that I may escape the un- believers in Judaea, and that the aid I carry to Jerusalem 32 may be accepted by the saints. ·Then, if God wills, I shall be feeling very happy when I come to enjoy a period of 33 rest among you. ·May the God of peace be with you all! Amen.

b. Ps 18:50 c. Dt 32:43 (LXX) d. Ps 117:1 e. Is 11:10; 11:1 f. The two extremes of Paul's missionary journeys. g. Is 52:15

Greetings and good wishes

1 **16** I commend to you our sister Phoebe,[a] a deaconess
2 of the church at Cenchreae. ·Give her, in union with
the Lord, a welcome worthy of saints, and help her with
anything she needs: she has looked after a great many
people, myself included.

3 My greetings to Prisca and Aquila, my fellow workers
4 in Christ Jesus, ·who risked death to save my life:[b] I am
not the only one to owe them a debt of gratitude, all the
5 churches among the pagans do as well. ·My greetings also
to the church that meets at their house.

6 Greetings to my friend Epaenetus, the first of Asia's
gifts to Christ; greetings to Mary who worked so hard for
7 you; ·to those outstanding apostles Andronicus and Junias,
my compatriots and fellow prisoners who became Chris-
8 tians before me; ·to Ampliatus, my friend in the Lord;
9 to Urban, my fellow worker in Christ; to my friend
10 Stachys; ·to Apelles who has gone through so much for
Christ; to everyone who belongs to the household of Aris-
11 tobulus; ·to my compatriot Herodion; to those in the
12 household of Narcissus who belong to the Lord; ·to Try-
phaena and Tryphosa, who work hard for the Lord; to
13 my friend Persis who has done so much for the Lord; ·to
Rufus, a chosen servant of the Lord, and to his mother
14 who has been a mother to me too. ·Greetings to Asyn-
critus, Phlegon, Hermes, Patrobas, Hermas, and all the
15 brothers who are with them; ·to Philologus and Julia,
Nereus and his sister, and Olympas and all the saints who
16 are with them. ·Greet each other with a holy kiss. All the
churches of Christ send greetings.

A warning and first postscript

17 I implore you, brothers, be on your guard against anybody who encourages trouble or puts difficulties in the way
18 of the doctrine you have been taught. Avoid them. ·People
like that are not slaves of Jesus Christ, they are slaves of
their own appetites, confusing the simple-minded with their
19 pious and persuasive arguments. ·Your fidelity to Christ,
anyway, is famous everywhere, and that makes me very
happy about you. I only hope that you are also wise in
20 what is good, and innocent of what is bad. ·The God of
peace will soon crush Satan beneath your feet. The grace
of our Lord Jesus Christ be with you.

Last greetings and second postscript

21 Timothy, who is working with me, sends his greetings;
22 so do my compatriots, Lucius, Jason and Sosipater. ·I,
Tertius, who wrote out this letter, greet you in the Lord.
23 Greetings from Gaius, who is entertaining me and from
the whole church that meets in his house. Erastus, the city
treasurer, sends his greetings; so does our brother Quartus.

Doxology

25 Glory to him who is able to give you the strength to live
according to the Good News I preach, and in which I
proclaim Jesus Christ, the revelation of a mystery kept
26 secret for endless ages, ·but now so clear that it must be
broadcast to pagans everywhere to bring them to the obedience of faith. This is only what scripture has predicted,
and it is all part of the way the eternal God wants things
27 to be. ·He alone is wisdom; give glory therefore to him
through Jesus Christ for ever and ever. Amen.

16 a. Probably the bearer of the letter.   b. Probably in Ephesus,
either at the time of the riot described in Ac 19 or during Paul's
imprisonment there.

1 Corinthians

THE FIRST LETTER OF PAUL TO THE CHURCH AT CORINTH

INTRODUCTION

Address and greetings. Thanksgiving

¹ ² I, Paul, appointed by God to be an apostle, together with brother Sosthenes, send greetings ·to the church of God in Corinth, to the holy people of Jesus Christ, who are called to take their place among all the saints everywhere who pray to our Lord Jesus Christ; for he is their ⁸ Lord no less than ours. ·May God our Father and the Lord Jesus Christ send you grace and peace.

⁴ I never stop thanking God for all the graces you have ⁵ received through Jesus Christ. ·I thank him that you have been enriched in so many ways, especially in your teachers ⁶ and preachers; ·the witness to Christ has indeed been ⁷ strong among you ·so that you will not be without any of the gifts of the Spirit while you are waiting for our Lord ⁸ Jesus Christ to be revealed; ·and he will keep you steady and without blame until the last day, the day of our Lord ⁰ Jesus Christ, ·because God by calling you has joined you to his Son, Jesus Christ; and God is faithful.

I. DIVISIONS AND SCANDALS

A. FACTIONS IN THE CORINTHIAN CHURCH

Dissensions among the faithful

¹⁰ All the same, I do appeal to you, brothers, for the sake of our Lord Jesus Christ, to make up the differences between you, and instead of disagreeing among yourselves, ¹¹ to be united again in your belief and practice. ·From what Chloe's people have been telling me, my dear brothers, it

12 is clear that there are serious differences among you. ·What I mean are all these slogans that you have, like: "I am for Paul," "I am for Apollos," "I am for Cephas,"ª "I am for
13 Christ." ·Has Christ been parceled out? Was it Paul that was crucified for you? Were you baptized in the name of
14 Paul? ·I am thankful that I never baptized any of you
15 after Crispus and Gaius ·so none of you can say he was
16 baptized in my name. ·Then there was the family of Stephanas, of course, that I baptized too, but no one else as far as I can remember.

The true wisdom and the false

17 For Christ did not send me to baptize, but to preach the Good News, and not to preach that in the terms of philosophyᵇ in which the crucifixion of Christ cannot be
18 expressed. ·The language of the cross may be illogical to those who are not on the way to salvation, but those of
19 us who are on the way see it as God's power to save. ·As scripture says: *I shall destroy the wisdom of the wise and*
20 *bring to nothing all the learning of the learned.* ·*Where are the philosophers now? Where are the scribes?*ᶜ Where are any of our thinkers today? Do you see now how God
21 has shown up the foolishness of human wisdom? ·If it was God's wisdom that human wisdom should not know God, it was because God wanted to save those who have faith through the foolishness of the message that we preach.
22 And so, while the Jews demand miracles and the Greeks
23 look for wisdom, ·here are we preaching a crucified Christ; to the Jews an obstacle that they cannot get over, to the
24 pagans madness; ·but to those who have been called, whether they are Jews or Greeks, a Christ who is the
25 power and the wisdom of God. ·For God's foolishness is wiser than human wisdom, and God's weakness is stronger than human strength.
26 Take yourselves for instance, brothers, at the time when you were called: how many of you were wise in the ordinary sense of the word, how many were influential people,
27 or came from noble families? ·No, it was to shame the wise that God chose what is foolish by human reckoning, and to shame what is strong that he chose what is weak

1 a. Peter. b. "wisdom," the term used by Paul for the human wisdom of philosophy and rhetoric. c. Quotations from Is 29: 14, Ps 33:10 and Is 33:18 (LXX).

²⁸ by human reckoning; ·those whom the world thinks common and contemptible are the ones that God has chosen —those who are nothing at all to show up those who are ²⁹ everything. ·The human race has nothing to boast about ³⁰ to God, ·but you God has made members of Christ Jesus and by God's doing he has become our wisdom, and our ³¹ virtue, and our holiness, and our freedom. ·As scripture says: *if anyone wants to boast, let him boast about the Lord.*ᵈ

¹ **2** As for me, brothers, when I came to you, it was not with any show of oratory or philosophy, but simply to ² tell you what God had guaranteed. ·During my stay with you, the only knowledge I claimed to have was about ³ Jesus, and only about him as the crucified Christ. ·Far from relying on any power of my own, I came among you ⁴ in great "fear and trembling"ᵃ ·and in my speeches and the sermons that I gave, there were none of the arguments that belong to philosophy; only a demonstration of the ⁵ power of the Spirit. ·And I did this so that your faith should not depend on human philosophy but on the power of God.

⁶ But still we have a wisdom to offer those who have reached maturity: not a philosophy of our age, it is true, still less of the masters of our age, which are coming to ⁷ their end. ·The hidden wisdom of God which we teach in our mysteries is the wisdom that God predestined to be ⁸ for our glory before the ages began. ·It is a wisdom that none of the masters of this age have ever known, or they ⁹ would not have crucified the Lord of Glory; ·we teach what scripture calls: *the things that no eye has seen and no ear has heard, things beyond the mind of man, all that God has prepared for those who love him.*ᵇ

¹⁰ These are the very things that God has revealed to us through the Spirit, for the Spirit reaches the depths of ¹¹ everything, even the depths of God. ·After all, the depths of a man can only be known by his own spirit, not by any other man, and in the same way the depths of God can ¹² only be known by the Spirit of God. ·Now instead of the spirit of the world, we have received the Spirit that comes from God, to teach us to understand the gifts that he has ¹³ given us. ·Therefore we teach, not in the way in which philosophy is taught, but in the way that the Spirit teaches ¹⁴ us: we teach spiritual things spiritually. ·An unspiritual person is one who does not accept anything of the Spirit

of God: he sees it all as nonsense; it is beyond his understanding because it can only be understood by means of
15 the Spirit. ·A spiritual man, on the other hand, is able to judge the value of everything, and his own value is not to
16 be judged by other men. ·As scripture says: *Who can know the mind of the Lord, so who can teach him?*[o] But we are those who have the mind of Christ.

1 **3** Brothers, I myself was unable to speak to you as people of the Spirit: I treated you as sensual men, still
2 infants in Christ. ·What I fed you with was milk, not solid food, for you were not ready for it; and indeed, you are
3 still not ready for it ·since you are still unspiritual. Isn't that obvious from all the jealousy and wrangling that there is among you, from the way that you go on behaving like
4 ordinary people? ·What could be more unspiritual than your slogans, "I am for Paul" and "I am for Apollos?"

The place of the Christian preacher

5 After all, what is Apollos and what is Paul? They are servants who brought the faith to you. Even the different ways in which they brought it were assigned to them by the
6 Lord. ·I did the planting, Apollos did the watering, but
7 God made things grow. ·Neither the planter nor the wa-
8 terer matters: only God, who makes things grow. ·It is all one who does the planting and who does the watering, and each will duly be paid according to his share in the work.
9 We are fellow workers with God; you are God's farm, God's building.
10 By the grace God gave me, I succeeded as an architect and laid the foundations, on which someone else is doing the building. Everyone doing the building must work care-
11 fully. ·For the foundation, nobody can lay any other than the one which has already been laid, that is Jesus Christ.
12 On this foundation you can build in gold, silver and jewels,
13 or in wood, grass and straw, ·but whatever the material, the work of each builder is going to be clearly revealed when the day comes. That day will begin with fire, and the
14 fire will test the quality of each man's work. ·If his struc-
15 ture stands up to it, he will get his wages; ·if it is burned

d. Jr 9:22-23
2 a. A scriptural cliché frequently used by Paul. b. A free combination of Is 64:3 and Jr 3:16. c. Is 40:13

down, he will be the loser, and though he is saved himself,
it will be as one who has gone through fire.

16 Didn't you realize that you were God's temple and that
17 the Spirit of God was living among you? ·If anybody
should destroy the temple of God, God will destroy him,
because the temple of God is sacred; and you are that
temple.

Conclusions

18 Make no mistake about it: if any one of you thinks of
himself as wise, in the ordinary sense of the word, then
he must learn to be a fool before he really can be wise.
19 Why? Because the wisdom of this world is foolishness to
God. As scripture says: *The Lord knows wise men's*
20 *thoughts: he knows how useless they are:*[a] ·or again: *God*
21 *is not convinced by the arguments of the wise.*[b] ·So there
22 is nothing to boast about in anything human: ·Paul, Apollos, Cephas, the world, life and death, the present and the
23 future, are all your servants; ·but you belong to Christ
and Christ belongs to God.

1,2 4 People must think of us as Christ's servants, stewards
entrusted with the mysteries of God. ·What is expected
of stewards is that each one should be found worthy of his
3 trust. ·Not that it makes the slightest difference to me
whether you, or indeed any human tribunal, find me
worthy or not. I will not even pass judgment on myself.
4 True, my conscience does not reproach me at all, but that
does not prove that I am acquitted: the Lord alone is my
5 judge. ·There must be no passing of premature judgment.
Leave that until the Lord comes: he will light up all that
is hidden in the dark and reveal the secret intentions of
men's hearts. Then will be the time for each one to have
whatever praise he deserves, from God.

6 Now in everything I have said here, brothers, I have
taken Apollos and myself as an example (remember the
maxim: "Keep to what is written"); it is not for you, so
full of your own importance, to go taking sides for one
7 man against another. ·In any case, brother, has anybody
given you some special right? What do you have that was
not given to you? And if it was given, how can you boast
8 as though it were not? ·Is it that you have everything you
want—that you are rich already, in possession of your kingdom, with us left outside? Indeed I wish you were really
9 kings, and we could be kings with you! ·But instead, it

seems to me, God has put us apostles at the end of his parade, with the men sentenced to death; it is true—we have been put on show in front of the whole universe, 10 angels as well as men. •Here we are, fools for the sake of Christ, while you are the learned men in Christ; we have no power, but you are influential; you are celebrities, we 11 are nobodies. •To this day, we go without food and drink 12 and clothes; we are beaten and have no homes; •we work for our living with our own hands. When we are cursed, we answer with a blessing; when we are hounded, we put 13 up with it; •we are insulted and we answer politely. We are treated as the offal of the world, still to this day, the scum of the earth.

An appeal

14 I am saying all this not just to make you ashamed but 15 to bring you, as my dearest children, to your senses. •You might have thousands of guardians in Christ, but not more than one father and it was I who begot you in Christ Jesus 16 by preaching the Good News. •That is why I beg you to 17 copy me •and why I have sent you Timothy, my dear and faithful son in the Lord: he will remind you of the way that I live in Christ, as I teach it everywhere in all the churches.

18 When it seemed that I was not coming to visit you, 19 some of you became self-important, •but I will be visiting you soon, the Lord willing, and then I shall want to know not what these self-important people have to say, but what 20 they can do, •since the kingdom of God is not just words, 21 it is power. •It is for you to decide: do I come with a stick in my hand or in a spirit of love and goodwill?

B. INCEST IN CORINTH

1 **5** I have been told as an undoubted fact that one of you is living with his father's wife.[a] This is a case of sexual immorality among you that must be unparalleled even 2 among pagans. •How can you be so proud of yourselves? You should be in mourning. A man who does a thing like that ought to have been expelled from the community.

---

3 a. Jb 5:13   b. Ps 94:11
5 a. Stepmother. Lv 18:8 forbids sexual relations with "your father's wife."

³ Though I am far away in body, I am with you in spirit, and have already condemned the man who did this thing ⁴ as if I were actually present. •When you are assembled together in the name of the Lord Jesus, and I am spiritually present with you, then with the power of our Lord Jesus ⁵ he is to be handed over to Satan so that his sensual body may be destroyed and his spirit saved on the day of the Lord.

⁶ The pride that you take in yourselves is hardly to your credit. You must know how even a small amount of yeast ⁷ is enough to leaven all the dough, •so get rid of all the old yeast, and make yourselves into a completely new batch of bread, unleavened as you are meant to be. Christ, ⁸ our passover, has been sacrificed; •let us celebrate the feast, then, by getting rid of all the old yeast of evil and wickedness, having only the unleavened bread of sincerity and truth.^b

⁹ When I wrote in my letter to you not to associate with ¹⁰ people living immoral lives, •I was not meaning to include all the people in the world who are sexually immoral, any more than I meant to include all usurers and swindlers or idol-worshipers. To do that, you would have to withdraw ¹¹ from the world altogether. •What I wrote was that you should not associate with a brother Christian who is leading an immoral life, or is a usurer, or idolatrous, or a slanderer, or a drunkard, or is dishonest; you should not ¹² even eat a meal with people like that. •It is not my business to pass judgment on those outside. Of those who are in- ¹³ side, you can surely be the judges. •But of those who are outside, God is the judge.

You must drive out this evil-doer from among you.^c

C. RECOURSE TO THE PAGAN COURTS

¹ **6** How dare one of your members take up a complaint against another in the lawcourts of the unjust^a instead ² of before the saints? •As you know, it is the saints who are to "judge the world"; and if the world is to be judged ³ by you, how can you be unfit to judge trifling cases? •Since we are also to judge angels, it follows that we can judge ⁴ matters of everyday life; •but when you have had cases of that kind, the people you appointed to try them were not ⁵ even respected in the Church. •You should be ashamed: is there really not one reliable man among you to settle

6 differences between brothers ·and so one brother brings a
7 court case against another in front of unbelievers? ·It is
bad enough for you to have lawsuits at all against one
another: oughtn't you to let yourselves be wronged, and
8 let yourselves be cheated? ·But you are doing the wrong-
ing and the cheating, and to your own brothers.

9   You know perfectly well that people who do wrong will
not inherit the kingdom of God: people of immoral lives,
10 idolaters, adulterers, catamites, sodomites, ·thieves, usu-
rers, drunkards, slanderers and swindlers will never inherit
11 the kingdom of God. ·These are the sort of people some
of you were once, but now you have been washed clean,
and sanctified, and justified through the name of the Lord
Jesus Christ and through the Spirit of our God.

D. FORNICATION

12   "For me there are no forbidden things";[b] maybe, but
not everything does good. I agree there are no forbidden
things for me, but I am not going to let anything dominate
13 me. ·Food is only meant for the stomach, and the stomach
for food; yes, and God is going to do away with both of
them. But the body—this is not meant for fornication; it is
14 for the Lord, and the Lord for the body. ·God, who raised
the Lord from the dead, will by his power raise us up too.
15   You know, surely, that your bodies are members making up the body of Christ; do you think I can take parts of
Christ's body and join them to the body of a prostitute?
16 Never! ·As you know, a man who goes with a prostitute
is one body with her, since *the two*, as it is said, *become*
17 *one flesh.* ·But anyone who is joined to the Lord is one
spirit with him.
18   Keep away from fornication. All the other sins are committed outside the body; but to fornicate is to sin against
19 your own body. ·Your body, you know, is the temple of
the Holy Spirit, who is in you since you received him from
20 God. You are not your own property; ·you have been

b. See note a to Jn 19, on the Passover practice.   c. Dt 13:6
6 a. The pagan magistrates of Corinth.   b. Probably one of
Paul's own sayings which has been misapplied by false teachers: this section of the letter is directed against the libertines,
who had been teaching that sexual intercourse was as necessary for the body as food and drink.

bought and paid for. That is why you should use your body for the glory of God.

II. ANSWERS TO VARIOUS QUESTIONS

A. MARRIAGE AND VIRGINITY

1,2 7 Now for the questions about which you wrote. Yes, it is a good thing for a man not to touch a woman; •but since sex is always a danger, let each man have his own 3 wife and each woman her own husband. •The husband must give his wife what she has the right to expect, and so 4 too the wife to the husband. •The wife has no rights over her own body; it is the husband who has them. In the same way, the husband has no rights over his body; the wife has 5 them. •Do not refuse each other except by mutual consent, and then only for an agreed time, to leave yourselves free for prayer; then come together again in case Satan should 6 take advantage of your weakness to tempt you. •This is a 7 suggestion, not a rule: •I should like everyone to be like me, but everybody has his own particular gifts from God, one with a gift for one thing and another with a gift for the opposite.

8 There is something I want to add for the sake of widows and those who are not married: it is a good thing for them 9 to stay as they are, like me, •but if they cannot control the sexual urges, they should get married, since it is better to be married than to be tortured.

10 For the married I have something to say, and this is not from me but from the Lord: a wife must not leave her hus-11 band—or if she does leave him, she must either remain unmarried or else make it up with her husband—nor must a husband send his wife away.

12 The rest is from me and not from the Lord. If a brother has a wife who is an unbeliever, and she is content to live 13 with him, he must not send her away; •and if a woman has an unbeliever for her husband, and he is content to live 14 with her, she must not leave him. •This is because the unbelieving husband is made one with the saints through his wife, and the unbelieving wife is made one with the saints through her husband. If this were not so, your children 15 would be unclean, whereas in fact they are holy. •However, if the unbelieving partner does not consent, they may sepa-

rate; in these circumstances, the brother or sister is not tied:
16 God has called you to a life of peace. ·If you are a wife, it
may be your part to save your husband, for all you know;
if a husband, for all you know, it may be your part to save
your wife.
17   For the rest, what each one has is what the Lord has
given him and he should continue as he was when God's
call reached him. This is the ruling that I give in all the
18 churches. ·If anyone had already been circumcised at the
time of his call, he need not disguise it, and anyone who
was uncircumcised at the time of his call need not be cir-
19 cumcised; ·because to be circumcised or uncircumcised
means nothing: what does matter is to keep the command-
20 ments of God. ·Let everyone stay as he was at the time of
21 his call. ·If, when you were called, you were a slave, do not
let this bother you; but if you should have the chance of
22 being free, accept it. ·A slave, when he is called in the
Lord, becomes the Lord's freedman, and a freeman called
23 in the Lord becomes Christ's slave. ·You have all been
24 bought and paid for; do not be slaves of other men. ·Each
one of you, my brothers, should stay as he was before God
at the time of his call.
25   About remaining celibate, I have no directions from the
Lord but give my own opinion as one who, by the Lord's
26 mercy, has stayed faithful. ·Well then, I believe that in these
present times of stress this is right: that it is good for a
27 man to stay as he is. ·If you are tied to a wife, do not look
for freedom; if you are free of a wife, then do not look for
28 one. ·But if you marry, it is no sin, and it is not a sin for a
young girl to get married. They will have their troubles,
though, in their married life, and I should like to spare you
that.
29   Brothers, this is what I mean: our time is growing short.
Those who have wives should live as though they had none,
30 and those who mourn should live as though they had nothing to mourn for; those who are enjoying life should live
as though there were nothing to laugh about; those whose
life is buying things should live as though they had nothing
31 of their own; ·and those who have to deal with the world
should not become engrossed in it. I say this because the
world as we know it is passing away.
32   I would like to see you free from all worry. An unmarried
man can devote himself to the Lord's affairs, all he need
33 worry about is pleasing the Lord; ·but a married man has

to bother about the world's affairs and devote himself to
³⁴ pleasing his wife: ·he is torn two ways. In the same way an
unmarried woman, like a young girl, can devote herself to
the Lord's affairs; all she need worry about is being holy in
body and spirit. The married woman, on the other hand,
has to worry about the world's affairs and devote herself to
³⁵ pleasing her husband. ·I say this only to help you, not to
put a halter round your necks, but simply to make sure that
everything is as it should be, and that you give your un-
divided attention to the Lord.

³⁶ Still, if there is anyone who feels that it would not be
fair to his daughter to let her grow too old for marriage,
and that he should do something about it, he is free to do
³⁷ as he likes: he is not sinning if there is a marriage. ·On the
other hand, if someone has firmly made his mind up, without any compulsion and in complete freedom of choice,
to keep his daughter as she is, he will be doing a good
³⁸ thing. ·In other words, the man who sees that his daughter
is married has done a good thing but the man who keeps his
daughter unmarried has done something even better.ᵃ

³⁹ A wife is tied as long as her husband is alive. But if the
husband dies, she is free to marry anybody she likes, only
⁴⁰ it must be in the Lord. ·She would be happier, in my opinion, if she stayed as she is—and I too have the Spirit of
God, I think.

B. FOOD OFFERED TO IDOLS

General principles

¹ 8 Now about food sacrificed to idols. "We all have
knowledge"; yes, that is so, but knowledge gives self-
² importance—it is love that makes the building grow. ·A
man may imagine he understands something, but still not
³ understand anything in the way that he ought to. ·But any
⁴ man who loves God is known by him. ·Well then, about
eating food sacrificed to idols:ᵃ we know that idols do not
really exist in the world and that there is no god but the
⁵ One. ·And even if there were things called gods, either in
the sky or on earth—where there certainly seem to be
⁶ "gods" and "lords" in plenty—·still for us there is one God,
the Father, from whom all things come and for whom we
exist; and there is one Lord, Jesus Christ, through whom
all things come and through whom we exist.

The claims of love

7   Some people, however, do not have this knowledge. There are some who have been so long used to idols that they eat this food as though it really had been sacrificed to the idol, and their conscience, being weak, is defiled by

8 it. ·Food, of course, cannot bring us in touch with God: we lose nothing if we refuse to eat, we gain nothing if we

9 eat. ·Only be careful that you do not make use of this

10 freedom in a way that proves a pitfall for the weak. ·Suppose someone sees you, a man who understands, eating in some temple of an idol; his own conscience, even if it is weak, may encourage him to eat food which has been

11 offered to idols. ·In this way your knowledge could become the ruin of someone weak, of a brother for whom

12 Christ died. ·By sinning in this way against your brothers, and injuring their weak consciences, it would be Christ

13 against whom you sinned. ·That is why, since food can be the occasion of my brother's downfall, I shall never eat meat again in case I am the cause of a brother's downfall.

Paul invokes his own example

1 9 I, personally, am free: I am an apostle and I have seen

2   Jesus our Lord. You are all my work in the Lord. ·Even if I were not an apostle to others, I should still be an apostle

3 to you who are the seal of my apostolate in the Lord. ·My

4 answer to those who want to interrogate me is this: ·Have

5 we not every right to eat and drink?[a] ·And the right to take a Christian woman round with us, like all the other apos-

6 tles and the brothers of the Lord and Cephas? ·Are Barnabas and I the only ones who are not allowed to stop

7 working? ·Nobody ever paid money to stay in the army, and nobody ever planted a vineyard and refused to eat the fruit of it. Who has there ever been that kept a flock and did not feed on the milk from his flock?

8   These may be only human comparisons, but does not the

7 a. "daughter" is not the only possible word; this passage has been read as alluding to the practice of a man and a woman living together under vows of chastity; a practice for which there is evidence of a later date.
8 a. At feasts and public ceremonies, portions of the food were "sacrificed" and went to the gods, the priests and the donors; the whole of the food was regarded as dedicated, whether it was eaten at a ceremonial meal or part of it sold in the markets.
9 a. At the expense of the Christian congregations.

⁹ Law itself say the same thing? ·It is written in the Law of
Moses: *You must not put a muzzle on the ox when it is
treading out the corn.*ᵇ Is it about oxen that God is con-
¹⁰ cerned, ·or is there not an obvious reference to ourselves?
Clearly this was written for our sake to show that the
plowman ought to plow in expectation, and the thresher
¹¹ to thresh in the expectation of getting his share. ·If we have
sown spiritual things for you, why should you be surprised
¹² if we harvest your material things? ·Others are allowed
these rights over you and our right is surely greater? In
fact we have never exercised this right. On the contrary
we have put up with anything rather than obstruct the
¹⁸ Good News of Christ in any way. ·Remember that the
ministers serving in the Temple get their food from the
Temple and those serving at the altar can claim their share
¹⁴ from the altar itself. ·In the same sort of way the Lord directed that those who preach the gospel should get their
living from the gospel.
¹⁵   However, I have not exercised any of these rights, and I
am not writing all this to secure this treatment for myself.
I would rather die than let anyone take away something
¹⁶ that I can boast of. ·Not that I do boast of preaching the
gospel, since it is a duty which has been laid on me; I
¹⁷ should be punished if I did not preach it! ·If I had chosen
this work myself, I might have been paid for it, but as I
have not, it is a responsibility which has been put into my
¹⁸ hands. ·Do you know what my reward is? It is this: in my
preaching, to be able to offer the Good News free, and not
insist on the rights which the gospel gives me.
¹⁹   So though I am not a slave of any man I have made
myself the slave of everyone so as to win as many as I could.
²⁰ I made myself a Jew to the Jews, to win the Jews; that is,
I who am not a subject of the Law made myself a subject
of the Law to those who are the subjects of the Law, to win
²¹ those who are subject to the Law. ·To those who have no
Law, I was free of the Law myself (though not free from
God's law, being under the law of Christ) to win those who
²² have no Law. ·For the weak I made myself weak. I made
myself all things to all men in order to save some at any
²³ cost; ·and I still do this, for the sake of the gospel, to have a
share in its blessings.
²⁴   All the runners at the stadium are trying to win, but
only one of them gets the prize. You must run in the same
²⁵ way, meaning to win. ·All the fighters at the games go into

strict training; they do this just to win a wreath that will
wither away, but we do it for a wreath that will never
26 wither. ·That is how I run, intent on winning; that is how I
27 fight, not beating the air. ·I treat my body hard and make
it obey me, for, having been an announcer myself, I should
not want to be disqualified.

A warning, and the lessons of Israel's history

1 **10** I want to remind you, brothers, how our fathers were
all guided by a cloud above them and how they all
2 passed through the sea. ·They were all baptized into Moses
3 in this cloud and in this sea; ·all ate the same spiritual
4 food ·and all drank the same spiritual drink, since they all
drank from the spiritual rock that followed them as they
5 went, and that rock was Christ. ·In spite of this, most of
them failed to please God and their corpses littered the
desert.
6   These things all happened as warnings[a] for us, not to
have the wicked lusts for forbidden things that they had.
7 Do not become idolaters as some of them did, for scripture
says: *After sitting down to eat and drink, the people got
8 up to amuse themselves.*[b] ·We must never fall into sexual
immorality: some of them did, and twenty-three thousand
9 met their downfall in one day. ·We are not to put the Lord
to the test: some of them did, and they were killed by
10 snakes. ·You must never complain: some of them did, and
they were killed by the Destroyer.
11   All this happened to them as a warning, and it was written down to be a lesson for us who are living at the end of
12 the age. ·The man who thinks he is safe must be careful
13 that he does not fall. ·The trials that you have had to bear
are no more than people normally have. You can trust God
not to let you be tried beyond your strength, and with any
trial he will give you a way out of it and the strength to
bear it.

Sacrificial feasts. No compromise with idolatry

14   This is the reason, my dear brothers, why you must keep
15 clear of idolatry. ·I say to you as sensible people: judge for
16 yourselves what I am saying. ·The blessing-cup that we bless

b. Dt 25:4
10 a. Lit. "types"; events prefiguring in the history of Israel the
spiritual realities of the messianic age.   b. Ex 32:6

is a communion with the blood of Christ, and the bread that we break is a communion with the body of Christ. [17] The fact that there is only one loaf means that, though there are many of us, we form a single body because we [18] all have a share in this one loaf. ·Look at the other Israel, the race, where those who eat the sacrifices are in commun- [19] ion with the altar. ·Does this mean that the food sacrificed [20] to idols has a real value, or that the idol itself is real? ·Not at all. It simply means that the sacrifices that they offer *they sacrifice to demons who are not God.*[o] I have no de- [21] sire to see you in communion with demons. ·You cannot drink the cup of the Lord and the cup of demons. You cannot take your share at the table of the Lord and at the [22] table of demons. ·Do we want to make the Lord angry; are we stronger than he is?

Food sacrificed to idols. Practical solutions

[23] "For me there are no forbidden things," but not every-thing does good. True, there are no forbidden things, but [24] it is not everything that helps the building to grow. ·No-body should be looking for his own advantage, but every-[25] body for the other man's. ·Do not hesitate to eat anything that is sold in butchers' shops: there is no need to raise [26] questions of conscience; ·for *the earth and everything that* [27] *is in it belong to the Lord.*[d] ·If an unbeliever invites you to his house, go if you want to, and eat whatever is put in front of you, without asking questions just to satisfy con-[28] science. ·But if someone says to you, "This food was of-fered in sacrifice," then, out of consideration for the man that told you, you should not eat it, for the sake of his [29] scruples; ·his scruples, you see, not your own. Why should [30] my freedom depend on somebody else's conscience? ·If I take my share with thankfulness, why should I be blamed for food for which I have thanked God?

Conclusion

[31] Whatever you eat, whatever you drink, whatever you do [32] at all, do it for the glory of God. ·Never do anything offen-sive to anyone—to Jews or Greeks or to the Church of God; [33] just as I try to be helpful to everyone at all times, not anx-ious for my own advantage but for the advantage of every-body else, so that they may be saved.

[1] **11** Take me for your model, as I take Christ.

C. DECORUM IN PUBLIC WORSHIP

Women's behavior at services

2   You have done well in remembering me so constantly
and in maintaining the traditions just as I passed them on
3 to you. However, what I want you to understand is that
Christ is the head of every man, man is the head of woman,
4 and God is the head of Christ. For a man to pray or
prophesy with his head covered is a sign of disrespect to
5 his head.[a] For a woman, however, it is a sign of disrespect
to her head[b] if she prays or prophesies unveiled; she might
6 as well have her hair shaved off. In fact, a woman who
will not wear a veil ought to have her hair cut off. If a
woman is ashamed to have her hair cut off or shaved, she
ought to wear a veil.
7   A man should certainly not cover his head, since he is
the image of God and reflects God's glory; but woman is
8 the reflection of man's glory. For man did not come from
9 woman; no, woman came from man; and man was not
created for the sake of woman, but woman was created
10 for the sake of man. That is the argument for women's
covering their heads with a symbol of the authority over
11 them, out of respect for the angels.[c] However, though
woman cannot do without man, neither can man do with-
12 out woman, in the Lord; woman may come from man, but
man is born of woman—both come from God.
13   Ask yourselves if it is fitting for a woman to pray to God
14 without a veil; and whether nature itself does not tell you
15 that long hair on a man is nothing to be admired, while a
woman, who was given her hair as a covering, thinks long
hair her glory?
16   To anyone who might still want to argue: it is not the
custom with us, nor in the churches of God.

The Lord's Supper

17   Now that I am on the subject of instructions, I cannot
say that you have done well in holding meetings that do
18 you more harm than good. In the first place, I hear that

c. Dt 32:17   d. Ps 24:1
11 a. His leader, a Greek pun.   b. Her husband, who is her
head; she is claiming equality.   c. The guardians of due order
in public worship.

when you all come together as a community, there are
19 separate factions among you, and I half believe it—since
there must no doubt be separate groups among you, to dis-
20 tinguish those who are to be trusted. ·The point is, when
you hold these meetings, it is not the Lord's Supper[d] that
21 you are eating, ·since when the time comes to eat, everyone
is in such a hurry to start his own supper that one person
22 goes hungry while another is getting drunk. ·Surely you
have homes for eating and drinking in? Surely you have
enough respect for the community of God not to make
poor people embarrassed? What am I to say to you? Congratulate you? I cannot congratulate you on this.
23   For this is what I received from the Lord, and in turn
passed on to you: that on the same night that he was be-
24 trayed, the Lord Jesus took some bread, ·and thanked God
for it and broke it, and he said, "This is my body, which
25 is for you; do this as a memorial of me." ·In the same way
he took the cup after supper, and said, "This cup is the new
covenant in my blood. Whenever you drink it, do this as a
26 memorial of me." ·Until the Lord comes, therefore, every
time you eat this bread and drink this cup, you are pro-
27 claiming his death, ·and so anyone who eats the bread or
drinks without recognizing the Body is eating and drinking
unworthily towards the body and blood of the Lord.
28   Everyone is to recollect himself before eating this bread
29 and drinking this cup; ·because a person who eats and
drinks without recognising the Body is eating and drinking
30 his own condemnation. ·In fact that is why many of you
31 are weak and ill and some of you have died. ·If only we
recollected ourselves, we should not be punished like that.
32 But when the Lord does punish us like that, it is to correct
us and stop us from being condemned with the world.
33   So to sum up, my dear brothers, when you meet for the
34 Meal, wait for one another. ·Anyone who is hungry should
eat at home, and then your meeting will not bring your
condemnation. The other matters I shall adjust when I
come.

Spiritual gifts

1 **12** Now my dear brothers, I want to clear up a wrong
2   impression about spiritual gifts. ·You remember that,
when you were pagans, whenever you felt irresistibly drawn,
3 it was toward dumb idols? ·It is for that reason that I want
you to understand that on the one hand no one can be

speaking under the influence of the Holy Spirit and say, "Curse Jesus," and on the other hand, no one can say, "Jesus is Lord" unless he is under the influence of the Holy Spirit.

The variety and the unity of gifts.

⁴ There is a variety of gifts but always the same Spirit; ⁵ there are all sorts of service to be done, but always to the ⁶ same Lord; ·working in all sorts of different ways in different people, it is the same God who is working in all ⁷ of them. ·The particular way in which the Spirit is given to ⁸ each person is for a good purpose. ·One may have the gift of preaching with wisdom given him by the Spirit; another may have the gift of preaching instruction given him by ⁹ the same Spirit; ·and another gift of faith given by the same Spirit; another again the gift of healing, through this ¹⁰ one Spirit; ·one, the power of miracles; another, prophecy; another the gift of recognizing spirits; another the gift of ¹¹ tongues and another the ability to interpret them. ·All these are the work of one and the same Spirit, who distributes different gifts to different people just as he chooses.

The analogy of the body

¹² Just as a human body, though it is made up of many parts, is a single unit because all these parts, though many, ¹³ make one body, so it is with Christ. ·In the one Spirit we were all baptized, Jews as well as Greeks, slaves as well as citizens, and one Spirit was given to us all to drink.

¹⁴ Nor is the body to be identified with any one of its many ¹⁵ parts. ·If the foot were to say, "I am not a hand and so I do not belong to the body," would that mean that it ¹⁶ stopped being part of the body? ·If the ear were to say, "I am not an eye, and so I do not belong to the body," would ¹⁷ that mean that it was not a part of the body? ·If your whole body was just one eye, how would you hear anything? If it was just one ear, how would you smell anything?

¹⁸ Instead of that, God put all the separate parts into the ¹⁹ body on purpose. ·If all the parts were the same, how could ²⁰ it be a body? ·As it is, the parts are many but the body is ²¹ one. ·The eye cannot say to the hand, "I do not need you," nor can the head say to the feet, "I do not need you."

d. The *agapē*, or love feast, preceding the liturgical meal.

²²   What is more, it is precisely the parts of the body that seem to be the weakest which are the indispensable ones; ²³ and it is the least honorable parts of the body that we clothe with the greatest care. So our more improper parts ²⁴ get decorated ·in a way that our more proper parts do not need. God has arranged the body so that more dignity is ²⁵ given to the parts which are without it, ·and so that there may not be disagreements inside the body, but that each ²⁶ part may be equally concerned for all the others. ·If one part is hurt, all parts are hurt with it. If one part is given special honor, all parts enjoy it.

²⁷   Now you together are Christ's body; but each of you is ²⁸ a different part of it. ·In the Church, God has given the first place to apostles, the second to prophets, the third to teachers; after them, miracles, and after them the gift of healing; helpers, good leaders, those with many languages. ²⁹ Are all of them apostles, or all of them prophets, or all of ³⁰ them teachers? Do they all have the gift of miracles, ·or all have the gift of healing? Do all speak strange languages, and all interpret them?

The order of importance in spiritual gifts. Love

³¹   Be ambitious for the higher gifts. And I am going to show you a way that is better than any of them.

¹ **13** If I have all the eloquence of men or of angels, but speak without love, I am simply a gong booming or ² a cymbal clashing. ·If I have the gift of prophecy, understanding all the mysteries there are, and knowing everything, and if I have faith in all its fullness, to move moun- ³ tains, but without love, then I am nothing at all. ·If I give away all that I possess, piece by piece, and if I even let them take my body to burn it, but am without love, it will do me no good whatever.

⁴   Love is always patient and kind; it is never jealous; love ⁵ is never boastful or conceited; ·it is never rude or selfish; ⁶ it does not take offense, and is not resentful. ·Love takes no pleasure in other people's sins but delights in the truth; ⁷ it is always ready to excuse, to trust, to hope, and to endure whatever comes.

⁸   Love does not come to an end. But if there are gifts of prophecy, the time will come when they must fail; or the gift of languages, it will not continue for ever; and knowl- edge—for this, too, the time will come when it must fail. ⁹ For our knowledge is imperfect and our prophesying is

10 imperfect; ·but once perfection comes, all imperfect things
11 will disappear. ·When I was a child, I used to talk like a
child, and think like a child, and argue like a child, but
now I am a man, all childish ways are put behind me.
12 Now we are seeing a dim reflection in a mirror; but then
we shall be seeing face to face. The knowledge that I have
now is imperfect; but then I shall know as fully as I am
known.
13.   In short, there are three things that last: faith, hope and
love; and the greatest of these is love.

**Spiritual gifts: their respective importance in the
community**

1 **14** You must want love more than anything else; but
still hope for the spiritual gifts as well, especially
2 prophecy. ·Anybody with the gift of tongues speaks to
God, but not to other people; because nobody understands
3 him when he talks in the spirit about mysterious things. ·On
the other hand, the man who prophesies does talk to other
people, to their improvement, their encouragement and
4 their consolation. ·The one with the gift of tongues talks
for his own benefit, but the man who prophesies does so
5 for the benefit of the community. ·While I should like you
all to have the gift of tongues, I would much rather you
could prophesy, since the man who prophesies is of greater
importance than the man with the gift of tongues, unless
of course the latter offers an interpretation so that the
church may get some benefit.
6   Now suppose, my dear brothers, I am someone with the
gift of tongues, and I come to visit you, what use shall I
be if all my talking reveals nothing new, tells you nothing,
7 and neither inspires you nor instructs you? ·Think of a
musical instrument, a flute or a harp: if one note on it
cannot be distinguished from another, how can you tell
8 what tune is being played? ·Or if no one can be sure which
call the trumpet has sounded, who will be ready for the
9 attack? ·It is the same with you: if your tongue does not
produce intelligible speech, how can anyone know what
10 you are saying? You will be talking to the air. ·There are
any number of different languages in the world, and not
11 one of them is meaningless, ·but if I am ignorant of what
the sounds mean, I am a savage to the man who is speak-
12 ing, and he is a savage to me. ·It is the same in your own

case: since you aspire to spiritual gifts, concentrate on those which will grow to benefit the community.

13 That is why anybody who has the gift of tongues must 14 pray for the power of interpreting them. ·For if I use this gift in my prayers, my spirit may be praying but my mind 15 is left barren. ·What is the answer to that? Surely I should pray not only with the spirit but with the mind as well? And sing praises not only with the spirit but with the mind 16 as well? ·Any uninitiated person will never be able to say Amen to your thanksgiving, if you only bless God with the 17 spirit, for he will have no idea what you are saying. ·However well you make your thanksgiving, the other gets no 18 benefit from it. ·I thank God that I have a greater gift of 19 tongues than all of you, ·but when I am in the presence of the community I would rather say five words that mean something than ten thousand words in a tongue.

20 Brothers, you are not to be childish in your outlook. You can be babies as far as wickedness is concerned, but 21 mentally you must be adult. ·In the written Law it says: *Through men speaking strange languages and through the lips of foreigners, I shall talk to the nation, and still* 22 *they will not listen to me, says the Lord.*[a] ·You see then, that the strange languages are meant to be a sign not for believers but for unbelievers, while on the other hand, 23 prophecy is a sign not for unbelievers but for believers. ·So that any uninitiated people or unbelievers, coming into a meeting of the whole church where everybody was speak-24 ing in tongues, would say you were all mad; ·but if you were all prophesying and an unbeliever or uninitiated person came in, he would find himself analyzed and judged by 25 everyone speaking; ·he would find his secret thoughts laid bare, and then fall on his face and worship God, declaring that *God is among you indeed.*[b]

Regulating spiritual gifts

26 So, my dear brothers, what conclusion is to be drawn? At all your meetings, let everyone be ready with a psalm or a sermon or a revelation, or ready to use his gift of tongues or to give an interpretation; but it must always 27 be for the common good. ·If there are people present with the gift of tongues, let only two or three, at the most, be allowed to use it, and only one at a time, and there must 28 be someone to interpret. ·If there is no interpreter present, they must keep quiet in church and speak only to them-

29 selves and to God. ·As for prophets, let two or three of
30 them speak, and the others attend to them. ·If one of the
listeners receives a revelation, then the man who is already
31 speaking should stop. ·For you can all prophesy in turn,
so that everybody will learn something and everybody will
32 be encouraged. ·Prophets can always control their prophetic
33 spirits, ·since God is not a God of disorder but of peace.
34   As in all the churches of the saints, ·women are to remain quiet at meetings since they have no permission to
speak; they must keep in the background as the Law itself
35 lays it down. ·If they have any questions to ask, they should
ask their husbands at home: it does not seem right for a
woman to raise her voice at meetings.

36   Do you think the word of God came out of yourselves?
37 Or that it has come only to you? ·Anyone who claims to be
a prophet or inspired ought to recognize that what I am
38 writing to you is a command from the Lord. ·Unless he
recognizes this, you should not recognize him.

39   And so, my dear brothers, by all means be ambitious to
40 prophesy, do not suppress the gift of tongues, ·but let
everything be done with propriety and in order.

III. THE RESURRECTION OF THE DEAD

The fact of the resurrection

1 **15** Brothers, I want to remind you of the gospel I
preached to you, the gospel that you received and in
2 which you are firmly established; ·because the gospel will
save you only if you keep believing exactly what I preached
to you—believing anything else will not lead to anything.
3   Well then, in the first place, I taught you what I had been
taught myself, namely that Christ died for our sins, in
4 accordance with the scriptures; ·that he was buried; and
that he was raised to life on the third day, in accordance
5 with the scriptures; ·that he appeared first to Cephas and
6 secondly to the Twelve. ·Next he appeared to more than
five hundred of the brothers at the same time, most of whom
7 are still alive, though some have died; ·then he appeared to
8 James, and then to all the apostles; ·and last of all he appeared to me too; it was as though I was born when no
one expected it.

14 a. A free version of Is 28:11-12.   b. Is 45:14

⁹ I am the least of the apostles; in fact, since I persecuted the Church of God, I hardly deserve the name apostle; ¹⁰ but by God's grace that is what I am, and the grace that he gave me has not been fruitless. On the contrary, I, or rather the grace of God that is with me, have worked harder than any of the others; ·but what matters is that I preach what they preach, and this is what you all believed.

¹² Now if Christ raised from the dead is what has been preached, how can some of you be saying that there is no resurrection of the dead? ·If there is no resurrection of the dead, Christ himself cannot have been raised, ·and if Christ has not been raised then our preaching is useless and your believing it is useless; ·indeed, we are shown up as witnesses who have committed perjury before God, because we swore in evidence before God that he had raised Christ to life. ¹⁶ For if the dead are not raised, Christ has not been raised, ¹⁷ and if Christ has not been raised, you are still in your sins. ¹⁸ And what is more serious, all who have died in Christ have ¹⁹ perished. ·If our hope in Christ has been for this life only, we are the most unfortunate of all people.

²⁰ But Christ has in fact been raised from the dead, the ²¹ first-fruits of all who have fallen asleep. ·Death came through one man and in the same way the resurrection ²² of the dead has come through one man. ·Just as all men die in Adam, so all men will be brought to life in Christ; ²³ but all of them in their proper order: Christ as the first-fruits and then, after the coming of Christ, those who be- ²⁴ long to him. ·After that will come the end, when he hands over the kingdom to God the Father, having done away ²⁵ with every sovereignty, authority and power. ·For he must ²⁶ be king *until he has put all his enemies under his feet*ᵃ ·and the last of the enemies to be destroyed is death, for every- ²⁷ thing is to be *put under his feet*. ·—Though when it is said that *everything is subjected*, this clearly cannot include the ²⁸ One who subjected everything to him. ·And when everything is subjected to him, then the Son himself will be subject in his turn to the One who subjected all things to him, so that God may be all in all.

²⁹ If this were not true, what do people hope to gain by being baptized for the dead? If the dead are not ever going ³⁰ to be raised, why be baptized on their behalf? ·What about ³¹ ourselves? Why are we living under a constant threat? ·I face death every day, brothers, and I can swear it by the ³² pride that I take in you in Christ Jesus our Lord. ·If my

motives were only human ones, what good would it do me
88 to fight the wild animals at Ephesus? •You say: *Let us eat and drink today; tomorrow we shall be dead.*[b] You must stop being led astray: "Bad friends ruin the noblest peo-
84 ple."[c] •Come to your senses, behave properly, and leave sin alone; there are some of you who seem not to know God at all; you should be ashamed.

The manner of the resurrection

85   Someone may ask, "How are dead people raised, and what sort of body do they have when they come back?"
86 They are stupid questions. Whatever you sow in the ground
87 has to die before it is given new life •and the thing that you sow is not what is going to come; you sow a bare grain, say
88 of wheat or something like that, •and then God gives it the sort of body that he has chosen: each sort of seed gets its own sort of body.
89   Everything that is flesh is not the same flesh: there is human flesh, animals' flesh, the flesh of birds and the flesh of
40 fish. •Then there are heavenly bodies and there are earthly bodies; but the heavenly bodies have a beauty of their own
41 and the earthly bodies a different one. •The sun has its brightness, the moon a different brightness, and the stars a different brightness, and the stars differ from each other in
42 brightness. •It is the same with the resurrection of the dead: the thing that is sown is perishable but what is raised is
43 imperishable; •the thing that is sown is contemptible but what is raised is glorious; the thing that is sown is weak
44 but what is raised is powerful; •when it is sown it embodies the soul, when it is raised it embodies the spirit.
    If the soul has its own embodiment, so does the spirit
45 have its own embodiment. •The first *man*, Adam, as scripture says, *became a living soul*; but the last Adam has
46 become a life-giving spirit. •That is, first the one with the soul, not the spirit, and after that, the one with the spirit.
47 The first man, being from the earth, is earthly by nature;
48 the second man is from heaven. •As this earthly man was, so are we on earth; and as the heavenly man is, so are we
49 in heaven. •And we, who have been modeled on the earthly man, will be modeled on the heavenly man.
50   Or else, brothers, put it this way: flesh and blood cannot

15 a. Ps 110:1   b. Is 22:13   c. This quotation from Menander's *Thais* may have become a proverb.

inherit the kingdom of God: and the perishable cannot in-
51 herit what lasts for ever. ·I will tell you something that has
been secret: that we are not all going to die, but we shall all
52 be changed. ·This will be instantaneous, in the twinkling of
an eye, when the last trumpet sounds. It will sound, and the
dead will be raised, imperishable, and we shall be changed
53 as well, ·because our present perishable nature must put on
imperishability and this mortal nature must put on immortality.

A hymn of triumph. Conclusion

54 When this perishable nature has put on imperishability,
and when this mortal nature has put on immortality, then
the words of scripture will come true: *Death is swallowed*
55 *up in victory.* ·*Death, where is your victory? Death, where*
56 *is your sting?ᵈ* ·Now the sting of death is sin, and sin gets its
57 power from the Law. ·So let us thank God for giving us the
victory through our Lord Jesus Christ.
58 Never give in then, my dear brothers, never admit defeat;
keep on working at the Lord's work always, knowing that,
in the Lord, you cannot be laboring in vain.

CONCLUSION

Commendations. Greetings

1 **16** Now about the collection made for the saints: you
are to do as I told the churches in Galatia to do.
2 Every Sunday, each one of you must put aside what he can
afford, so that collections need not be made after I have
3 come. ·When I am with you, I will send your offering to
Jerusalem by the hand of whatever men you give letters
4 of reference to; ·if it seems worth while for me to go too,
they can travel with me.
5 I shall be coming to you after I have passed through
Macedonia—and I am doing no more than pass through
6 Macedonia—·and I may be staying with you, perhaps even
passing the winter, to make sure that it is you who send me
7 on my way wherever my travels take me. ·As you see, I do
not want to make it only a passing visit to you and I hope
8 to spend some time with you, the Lord permitting. ·In any
9 case I shall be staying at Ephesus until Pentecost ·because
a big and important door has opened for my work and
there is a great deal of opposition.

¹⁰ If Timothy comes, show him that he has nothing to be
¹¹ afraid of in you: like me, he is doing the Lord's work, •and
nobody is to be scornful of him. Send him happily on his
way to come back to me; the brothers and I are waiting for
¹² him. •As for our brother Apollos, I begged him to come to
you with the brothers but he was quite firm that he did not
want to go yet and he will come as soon as he can.

¹³ Be awake to all the dangers; stay firm in the faith; be
¹⁴ brave and be strong. •Let everything you do be done in
love.

¹⁵ There is something else to ask you, brothers. You know
how the Stephanas family, who were the first-fruits of
¹⁶ Achaia, have really worked hard to help the saints. •Well,
I want you in your turn to put yourselves at the service of
people like this, and anyone who helps and works with
¹⁷ them. •I am delighted that Stephanas, Fortunatus and
Achaicus have arrived; they make up for your absence.
¹⁸ They have settled my mind, and yours too; I hope you
appreciate men like this.

¹⁹ All the churches of Asia send you greetings. Aquila and
Prisca, with the church that meets at their house, send you
²⁰ their warmest wishes, in the Lord. •All the brothers send
you their greetings. Greet one another with a holy kiss.
²¹ This greeting is in my own hand—Paul.
²² If anyone does not love the Lord, a curse on him.
"Maran atha."ᵃ
²³ The grace of the Lord Jesus be with you.
²⁴ My love is with you all in Christ Jesus.

d. A free version; see Ho 13:14.
16 a. Aramaic. "The Lord is coming," or "Lord, come."

2 Corinthians

THE SECOND LETTER OF PAUL
TO THE CHURCH AT CORINTH

INTRODUCTION

Address and greetings. Thanksgiving

¹ **1** From Paul, appointed by God to be an apostle of Christ
Jesus, and from Timothy, one of the brothers, to the
church of God at Corinth and to all the saints in the whole
² of Achaia. ·Grace and peace to you from God our Father
and the Lord Jesus Christ.

³ Blessed be the God and Father of our Lord Jesus Christ,
⁴ a gentle Father and the God of all consolation, ·who comforts us in all our sorrows, so that we can offer others, in
their sorrows, the consolation that we have received from
⁵ God ourselves. ·Indeed, as the sufferings of Christ over-
flow to us, so, through Christ, does our consolation over-
⁶ flow. ·When we are made to suffer, it is for your consolation and salvation. When, instead, we are comforted, this
should be a consolation to you, supporting you in patiently
⁷ bearing the same sufferings as we bear. ·And our hope
for you is confident, since we know that, sharing our sufferings, you will also share our consolations.

⁸ For we should like you to realize, brothers, that the
things we had to undergo in Asia were more of a burden
than we could carry, so that we despaired of coming
⁹ through alive. ·Yes, we were carrying our own death warrant with us, and it has taught us not to rely on ourselves
¹⁰ but only on God, who raises the dead to life. ·And he
saved us from dying, as he will save us again; yes, that
is our firm hope in him, that in the future he will save us
¹¹ again. ·You must all join in the prayers for us: the more
people there are asking for help for us, the more will be
giving thanks when it is granted to us.

I. SOME RECENT EVENTS REVIEWED

Why Paul changed his plans

12 There is one thing we are proud of, and our conscience tells us it is true: that we have always treated everybody, and especially you, with the reverence and sincerity which come from God, and by the grace of God we have done 13 this without ulterior motives. ·There are no hidden meanings in our letters besides what you can read for yourselves 14 and understand. ·And I hope that, although you do not know us very well yet, you will have come to recognize, when the day of our Lord Jesus comes, that you can be as proud of us as we are of you.

15 Because I was so sure of this, I had meant to come to 16 you first, so that you would benefit doubly; ·staying with you before going to Macedonia and coming back to you again on the way back from Macedonia, for you to see 17 me on my way to Judaea. ·Do you think I was not sure of my own intentions when I planned this? Do you really think that when I am making my plans, my motives are ordinary human ones, and that I say Yes, yes, and No, no, 18 at the same time? ·I swear by God's truth, there is no Yes 19 and No about what we say to you. ·The Son of God, the Christ Jesus that we proclaimed among you—I mean Silvanus and Timothy and I—was never Yes and No: with 20 him it was always Yes, ·and however many the promises God made, the Yes to them all is in him. That is why it is "through him" that we answer Amen to the praise of God. 21 Remember it is God himself who assures us all, and you, 22 of our standing in Christ, and has anointed us, ·marking us with his seal and giving us the pledge, the Spirit, that we carry in our hearts.

23 By my life, I call God to witness that the reason why I did not come to Corinth after all was to spare your feel-24 ings. ·We are not dictators over your faith, but are fellow workers with you for your happiness; in the faith you are 1 steady enough. 2 Well then, I made up my mind not to pay 2 you a second distressing visit. ·I may have hurt you, but if so I have hurt the only people who could give me any 8 pleasure. ·I wrote as I did to make sure that, when I came, I should not be distressed by the very people who

should have made me happy. I am sure you all know that
⁴ I could never be happy unless you were. ·When I wrote
to you, in deep distress and anguish of mind, and in tears,
it was not to make you feel hurt but to let you know how
much love I have for you.
⁵   Someone has been the cause of pain; and the cause of
pain not to me, but to some degree—not to overstate it—
⁶ to all of you. ·The punishment already imposed by the
⁷ majority on the man in question is enough; ·and the best
thing now is to give him your forgiveness and encourage-
⁸ ment, or he might break down from so much misery. ·So
I am asking you to give some definite proof of your love
⁹ for him. ·What I really wrote for, after all, was to test
¹⁰ you and see whether you are completely obedient. ·Any-
body that you forgive, I forgive; and as for my forgiving
anything—if there has been anything to be forgiven, I have
¹¹ forgiven it for your sake in the presence of Christ. ·And
so we will not be outwitted by Satan—we know well enough
what his intentions are.

From Troas to Macedonia. The apostolate: its importance

¹²   When I went up to Troas to preach the Good News of
Christ, and the door was wide open for my work there in
¹³ the Lord, ·I was so continually uneasy in mind at not
meeting brother Titus there, I said good-bye to them and
went on to Macedonia.
¹⁴   Thanks be to God who, wherever he goes, makes us,
in Christ, partners of his triumph,*a* and through us is
spreading the knowledge of himself, like a sweet smell,
¹⁵ everywhere. ·We are Christ's incense to God for those
¹⁶ who are being saved and for those who are not; ·for the
last, the smell of death that leads to death, for the first the
sweet smell of life that leads to life. And who could be quali-
¹⁷ fied for work like this? ·At least we do not go round offering the word of God for sale, as many other people do.
In Christ, we speak as men of sincerity, as envoys of God
and in God's presence.
¹ **3** Does this sound like a new attempt to commend ourselves to you? Unlike other people, we need no letters
² of recommendation either to you or from you, ·because
you are yourselves our letter, written in our hearts, that
³ anybody can see and read, ·and it is plain that you are a
letter from Christ, drawn up by us, and written not with

ink but with the Spirit of the living God, not on stone tablets but on the tablets of your living hearts.
4 Before God, we are confident of this through Christ:
5 not that we are qualified in ourselves to claim anything as our own work: all our qualifications come from God.
6 He is the one who has given us the qualifications to be the administrators of this new covenant, which is not a covenant of written letters but of the Spirit: the written letters
7 bring death, but the Spirit gives life. ·Now if the administering of death, in the written letters engraved on stones, was accompanied by such a brightness that the Israelites could not bear looking at the face of Moses, though it
8 was a brightness that faded, ·then how much greater will be the brightness that surrounds the administering of the
9 Spirit! ·For if there was any splendor in administering condemnation, there must be very much greater splendor
10 in administering justification. ·In fact, compared with this greater splendor, the thing that used to have such splen-
11 dor now seems to have none; ·and if what was so temporary had any splendor, there must be much more in what is going to last for ever.
12
13 ·Having this hope, we can be quite confident; ·not like Moses, who put a veil over his face so that the Israelites
14 would not notice the ending of what had to fade.[a] ·And anyway, their minds had been dulled; indeed, to this very day, that same veil is still there when the old covenant is being read, a veil never lifted, since Christ alone can re-
15 move it. ·Yes, even today, whenever Moses is read, the
16 veil is over their minds. ·It will not be removed until they
17 turn to the Lord. ·Now this Lord is the Spirit, and where
18 the Spirit of the Lord is, there is freedom. ·And we, with our unveiled faces reflecting like mirrors the brightness of the Lord, all grow brighter and brighter as we are turned into the image that we reflect; this is the work of the Lord who is Spirit.
1 **4** Since we have by an act of mercy been entrusted with this work of administration, there is no weakening on
2 our part. ·On the contrary, we will have none of the reticence of those who are ashamed, no deceitfulness or watering down the word of God; but the way we commend

2 a. Like a victorious general making his ceremonial entry into Rome.
3 a. See Ex 34:33.

ourselves to every human being with a conscience is by
8 stating the truth openly in the sight of God. ·If our gospel
does not penetrate the veil, then the veil is on those who
4 are not on the way to salvation; ·the unbelievers whose
minds the god of this world has blinded, to stop them
seeing the light shed by the Good News of the glory of
5 Christ, who is the image of God. ·For it is not ourselves
that we are preaching, but Christ Jesus as the Lord, and
6 ourselves as your servants for Jesus' sake. ·It is the
same God that said, "Let there be light shining out of darkness,"
who has shone in our minds to radiate the light of the
knowledge of God's glory, the glory on the face of Christ.

The trials and hopes of the apostolate

7 　We are only the earthenware jars that hold this treasure, to make it clear that such an overwhelming power
8 comes from God and not from us. ·We are in difficulties
on all sides, but never cornered; we see no answer to our
9 problems, but never despair; ·we have been persecuted,
10 but never deserted; knocked down, but never killed; ·al-
ways, wherever we may be, we carry with us in our body
the death of Jesus, so that the life of Jesus, too, may always
11 be seen in our body. ·Indeed, while we are still alive, we
are consigned to our death every day, for the sake of Jesus,
so that in our mortal flesh the life of Jesus, too, may be
12 openly shown. ·So death is at work in us, but life in you.
13 　But as we have the same spirit of faith that is mentioned in scripture—*I believed, and therefore I spoke*[a]—we
14 too believe and therefore we too speak, ·knowing that he
who raised the Lord Jesus to life will raise us with Jesus
15 in our turn, and put us by his side and you with us. ·You
see, all this is for your benefit, so that the more grace is
multiplied among people, the more thanksgiving there will
be, to the glory of God.
16 　That is why there is no weakening on our part, and instead, though this outer man of ours may be falling into
17 decay, the inner man is renewed day by day. ·Yes, the
troubles which are soon over, though they weigh little,
train us for the carrying of a weight of eternal glory which
18 is out of all proportion to them. ·And so we have no eyes
for things that are visible, but only for things that are invisible; for visible things last only for a time, and the invisible things are eternal.

1 For we know that when the tent that we live in on
  5 earth is folded up, there is a house built by God for
  us, an everlasting home not made by human hands, in the
2 heavens. ·In this present state, it is true, we groan as we
  wait with longing to put on our heavenly home over the
3 other; ·we should like to be found wearing clothes and
4 not without them. ·Yes, we groan and find it a burden
  being still in this tent, not that we want to strip it off, but
  to put the second garment over it and to have what must
5 die taken up into life. ·This is the purpose for which God
  made us, and he has given us the pledge of the Spirit.
6 We are always full of confidence, then, when we remember that to live in the body means to be exiled from
7 the Lord, ·going as we do by faith and not by sight·—we
8 are full of confidence, I say, and actually want to be exiled from the body and make our home with the Lord.
9 Whether we are living in the body or exiled from it, we
10 are intent on pleasing him. ·For all the truth about us
  will be brought out in the law court of Christ, and each of
  us will get what he deserves for the things he did in the
  body, good or bad.

The apostolate in action

11 And so it is with the fear of the Lord in mind that we
  try to win people over. God knows us for what we really
  are, and I hope that in your consciences you know us too.
12 This is not another attempt to commend ourselves to you:
  we are simply giving you reasons to be proud of us, so
  that you will have an answer ready for the people who can
13 boast more about what they seem than what they are. ·If
  we seemed out of our senses, it was for God; but if we are
14 being reasonable now, it is for your sake. ·And this is
  because the love of Christ overwhelms us when we reflect
  that if one man has died for all, then all men should be
15 dead; ·and the reason he died for all was so that living
  men should live no longer for themselves, but for him who
  died and was raised to life for them.
16 From now onward, therefore, we do not judge anyone
  by the standards of the flesh. Even if we did once know
  Christ in the flesh, that is not how we know him now.
17 And for anyone who is in Christ, there is a new creation;
  the old creation has gone, and now the new one is here.

4 a. Ps 116:10

¹⁸ It is all God's work. It was God who reconciled us to himself through Christ and gave us the work of handing on
¹⁹ this reconciliation. ·In other words, God in Christ was reconciling the world to himself, not holding men's faults against them, and he has entrusted to us the news that
²⁰ they are reconciled. ·So we are ambassadors for Christ; it is as though God were appealing through us, and the appeal that we make in Christ's name is: be reconciled to
²¹ God. ·For our sake God made the sinless one into sin, so
¹ that in him we might become the goodness of God. 6 As his fellow workers, we beg you once again not to neglect
² the grace of God that you have received. ·For he says: *At the favorable time, I have listened to you; on the day of salvation I came to your help.ᵃ* Well, now is the favorable time; this is the day of salvation.
³   We do nothing that people might object to, so as not to
⁴ bring discredit on our function as God's servants. ·Instead, we prove we are servants of God by great fortitude in
⁵ times of suffering: in times of hardship and distress; ·when we are flogged, or sent to prison, or mobbed; laboring,
⁶ sleepless, starving. ·We prove we are God's servants by our purity, knowledge, patience and kindness; by a spirit
⁷ of holiness, by a love free from affectation; ·by the word of truth and by the power of God; by being armed with the weapons of righteousness in the right hand and in the
⁸ left, ·prepared for honor or disgrace, for blame or praise;
⁹ taken for impostors while we are genuine; ·obscure yet famous; said to be dying and here are we alive; rumored
¹⁰ to be executed before we are sentenced; ·thought most miserable and yet we are always rejoicing; taken for paupers though we make others rich, for people having nothing though we have everything.

Paul opens his heart. A warning

¹¹   Corinthians, we have spoken to you very frankly; our
¹² mind has been opened in front of you. ·Any constraint that you feel is not on our side; the constraint is in your
¹³ own selves. ·I speak as if to children of mine: as a fair exchange, open your minds in the same way.
¹⁴   Do not harness yourselves in an uneven team with unbelievers. Virtue is no companion for crime. Light and
¹⁵ darkness have nothing in common. ·Christ is not the ally of Beliar, nor has a believer anything to share with an
¹⁶ unbeliever. ·The temple of God has no common ground

with idols, and that is what we are—the temple of the living God. We have God's word for it: *I will make my home among them and live with them; I will be their God and* 17 *they shall be my people.*[b] ·Then *come away from them and keep aloof, says the Lord. Touch nothing that is un-* 18 *clean,*[c] *and I will welcome you ·and be your father, and you shall be my sons and daughters, says the Almighty Lord.*[d]

1 With promises like these made to us, dear brothers, let us wash off all that can soil either body or spirit, to reach perfection of holiness in the fear of God.

2 Keep a place for us in your hearts. We have not injured 3 anyone, or ruined anyone, or exploited anyone. ·I am not saying this to put any blame on you; as I have already told you, you are in our hearts—together we live or together we 4 die. ·I have the very greatest confidence in you, and I am so proud of you that in all our trouble I am filled with consolation and my joy is overflowing.

Paul in Macedonia; he is joined by Titus

5 Even after we had come to Macedonia, however, there was no rest for this body of ours. Far from it; we found trouble on all sides: quarrels outside, misgivings inside. 6 But God comforts the miserable, and he comforted us, 7 by the arrival of Titus, ·and not only by his arrival but also by the comfort which he had gained from you. He has told us all about how you want to see me, how sorry you were, and how concerned for me, and so I am happier now than I was before. 8 But to tell the truth, even if I distressed you by my letter, I do not regret it. I did regret it before, and I see that that 9 letter did distress you, at least for a time; ·but I am happy now—not because I made you suffer, but because your suffering led to your repentance. Yours has been a kind of suffering that God approves, and so you have come to no 10 kind of harm from us. ·To suffer in God's way means changing for the better and leaves no regrets, but to suffer 11 as the world knows suffering brings death. ·Just look at what suffering in God's way has brought you: what keenness, what explanations, what indignation, what alarm! Yes, and what aching to see me, what concern for me, and what justice done! In every way you have shown yourselves

6 a. Is 49:8   b. Lv 26:11-12   c. Is 52:11   d. Is 43:6

¹² blameless in this affair. ·So then, though I wrote the letter to you, it was not written for the sake either of the offender or of the one offended; it was to make you realize, in the
¹³ sight of God, your own concern for us. ·That is what we have found so encouraging.

With this encouragement, too, we had the even greater happiness of finding Titus so happy; thanks to you all, he
¹⁴ has no more worries; ·I had rather boasted to him about you, and now I have not been made to look foolish; in fact, our boasting to Titus has proved to be as true as any-
¹⁵ thing that we ever said to you. ·His own personal affection for you is all the greater when he remembers how willing you have all been, and with what deep respect you wel-
¹⁶ comed him. ·I am very happy knowing that I can rely on you so completely.

II. ORGANIZATION OF THE COLLECTION

Why the Corinthians should be generous

¹ Now here, brothers, is the news of the grace of God
² which was given in the churches in Macedonia; ·and of how, throughout great trials by suffering, their constant cheerfulness and their intense poverty have overflowed in
³ a wealth of generosity. ·I can swear that they gave not only as much as they could afford, but far more, and quite
⁴ spontaneously, ·begging and begging us for the favor of
⁵ sharing in this service to the saints ·and, what was quite unexpected, they offered their own selves first to God and, under God, to us.
⁶ Because of this, we have asked Titus, since he has al-ready made a beginning, to bring this work of mercy to
⁷ the same point of success among you. ·You always have the most of everything—of faith, of eloquence, of under-standing, of keenness for any cause, and the biggest share of our affection—so we expect you to put the most into this
⁸ work of mercy too. ·It is not an order that I am giving you; I am just testing the genuineness of your love against
⁹ the keenness of others. ·Remember how generous the Lord Jesus was: he was rich, but he became poor for your sake,
¹⁰ to make you rich out of his poverty. ·As I say, I am only making a suggestion; it is only fair to you, since you were the first, a year ago, not only in taking action but even in

11 deciding to. ·So now finish the work and let the results be worthy, as far as you can afford it, of the decision you
12 made so promptly. ·As long as the readiness is there, a man is acceptable with whatever he can afford; never mind
13 what is beyond his means. ·This does not mean that to give relief to others you ought to make things difficult for
14 yourselves: it is a question of balancing ·what happens to be your surplus now against their present need, and one day they may have something to spare that will supply
15 your own need. That is how we strike a balance: ·as scripture says: *The man who gathered much had none too much, the man who gathered little did not go short.*[a]

The delegates recommended to the Corinthians

16 I thank God for putting into Titus' heart the same con-
17 cern for you that I have myself. ·He did what we asked him; indeed he is more concerned than ever, and is visit-
18 ing you on his own initiative. ·As his companion we are sending the brother who is famous in all the churches for
19 spreading the gospel. ·More than that, he happens to be the same brother who has been elected by the churches to be our companion on this errand of mercy that, for the glory of God, we have undertaken to satisfy our impatience
20 to help. ·We hope that in this way there will be no accusa-
21 tions made about our administering such a large fund; ·for *we are trying to do right* not only *in the sight of God* but
22 *also* in the sight of *men.*[b] ·To accompany these, we are sending a third brother, of whose keenness we have often had proof in many different ways, and who is particularly keen about this, because he has great confidence in you.
23 Titus, perhaps I should add, is my own colleague and fellow worker in your interests; the other two brothers, who are delegates of the churches, are a real glory to Christ.
24 So then, in front of all the churches, give them a proof of your love, and prove to them that we are right to be proud of you.

1 **9** There is really no need for me to write to you on the
2 subject of offering your services to the saints, ·since I know how anxious you are to help; in fact, I boast about you to the Macedonians, telling them, "Achaia has been ready since last year." So your zeal has been a spur to
3 many more. ·I am sending the brothers all the same, to

8 a. Ex 16:18   b. Pr 3:4 (LXX)

make sure that our boasting about you does not prove to have been empty this time, and that you really are ready
⁴ as I said you would be. ·If some of the Macedonians who are coming with me found you unprepared, we should be humiliated—to say nothing of yourselves—after being so
⁵ confident. ·That is why I have thought it necessary to ask these brothers to go on to you ahead of us, and make sure in advance that the gift you promised is all ready, and that it all comes as a gift out of your generosity and not by being extorted from you.

Blessings to be expected from the collection

⁶ Do not forget: thin sowing means thin reaping; the more
⁷ you sow, the more you reap. ·Each one should give what he has decided in his own mind, not grudgingly or because
⁸ he is made to, for *God loves a cheerful giver.*ᵃ ·And there is no limit to the blessings which God can send you—he will make sure that you will always have all you need for yourselves in every possible circumstance, and still have
⁹ something to spare for all sorts of good works. ·As scripture says: *He was free in almsgiving, and gave to the poor: his good deeds will never be forgotten.*ᵇ
¹⁰ The one who provides *seed for the sower and bread for food* will provide you with all the seed you want and make
¹¹ *the harvest of your good deeds* a larger one, ·and, made richer in every way, you will be able to do all the generous things which, through us, are the cause of thanksgiving to
¹² God. ·For doing this holy service is not only supplying all the needs of the saints, but it is also increasing the amount
¹³ of thanksgiving that God receives. ·By offering this service, you show them what you are, and that makes them give glory to God for the way you accept and profess the gospel of Christ, and for your sympathetic generosity to
¹⁴ them and to all. ·And their prayers for you, too, show how they are drawn to you on account of all the grace that God
¹⁵ has given you. ·Thanks be to God for his inexpressible gift!

III. PAUL'S APOLOGIA

Paul's reply to accusations of weakness

¹ **10** This is a personal matter; this is Paul himself appealing to you by the gentleness and patience of

Christ—I, the man who is so humble when he is facing
2 you, but bullies you when he is at a distance. ·I only ask
that I do not have to bully you when I come, with all the
confident assurance I mean to show when I come face to
face with people I could name who think we go by ordi-
3 nary human motives. ·We live in the flesh, of course, but
4 the muscles that we fight with are not flesh. ·Our war is
not fought with weapons of flesh, yet they are strong
enough, in God's cause, to demolish fortresses. We de-
5 molish sophistries, ·and the arrogance that tries to resist
the knowledge of God; every thought is our prisoner, cap-
6 tured to be brought into obedience to Christ. ·Once you
have given your complete obedience, we are prepared to
punish any disobedience.

7   Face plain facts. Anybody who is convinced that he
belongs to Christ must go on to reflect that we all belong
8 to Christ no less than he does. ·Maybe I do boast rather
too much about our authority, but the Lord gave it to me
for building you up and not for pulling you down, and I
9 shall not be ashamed of it. ·I do not want you to think of
10 me as someone who only frightens you by letter. ·Some-
one said, "He writes powerful and strongly-worded letters
but when he is with you you see only half a man and no
11 preacher at all." ·The man who said that can remember
this: whatever we are like in the words of our letters when
we are absent, that is what we shall be like in our actions
when we are present.

His reply to the accusation of ambition

12   We are not being so bold as to rank ourselves, or invite
comparison, with certain people who write their own references. Measuring themselves against themselves, and
comparing themselves to themselves, they are simply fool-
13 ish. ·We, on the other hand, are not going to boast without
a standard to measure against: taking for our measure the
yardstick which God gave us to measure with, which is
14 long enough to reach to you. ·We are not stretching further than we ought; otherwise we should not have reached
you, as we did come all the way to you with the gospel
15 of Christ. ·So we are not boasting without any measure,
about work that was done by other people; in fact, we trust
that, as your faith grows, we shall get taller and taller.

9 a. Pr 22:8 (LXX)   b. Ps 112:9

¹⁶ when judged by our own standard. •I mean, we shall be carrying the gospel to places far beyond you, without encroaching on anyone else's field, not boasting of the work
¹⁷ already done. •*If anyone wants to boast, let him boast of*
¹⁸ *the Lord.*^a •It is not the man who commends himself that can be accepted, but the man who is commended by the Lord.

Paul is driven to sound his own praises

¹ I only wish you were able to tolerate a little foolishness from me. But of course: you are tolerant to-
² wards me. •You see, the jealousy that I feel for you is God's own jealousy: I arranged for you to marry Christ so that I might give you away as a chaste virgin to this
³ one husband. •But the serpent, with his cunning, seduced Eve, and I am afraid that in the same way your ideas may get corrupted and turned away from simple devotion to
⁴ Christ. •Because any newcomer has only to proclaim a new Jesus, different from the one that we preached, or you have only to receive a new spirit, different from the one you have already received, or a new gospel, different from the one you have already accepted—and you welcome
⁵ it with open arms. •As far as I can tell, these arch-apostles
⁶ have nothing more than I have. •I may not be a polished speechmaker, but as for knowledge, that is a different matter; surely we have made this plain, speaking on every subject in front of all of you.
⁷ Or was I wrong, lowering myself so as to lift you high, by preaching the gospel of God to you and taking no fee
⁸ for it? •I was robbing other churches living on them so
⁹ that I could serve you. •When I was with you and ran out of money, I was no burden to anyone; the brothers who came from Macedonia provided me with everything I wanted. I was very careful, and I always shall be, not to
¹⁰ be a burden to you in any way, •and by Christ's truth in me, this cause of boasting will never be taken from me
¹¹ in the regions of Achaia. •Would I do that if I did not
¹² love you? God knows I do. •I intend to go on doing what I am doing now—leaving no opportunity for those people who are looking for an opportunity to claim equality with
¹³ us in what they boast of. •These people are counterfeit apostles, they are dishonest workmen disguised as apostles
¹⁴ of Christ. •There is nothing unexpected about that; if Satan
¹⁵ himself goes disguised as an angel of light, •there is no

need to be surprised when his servants, too, disguise themselves as the servants of righteousness. They will come to the end that they deserve.

16 As I said before, let no one take me for a fool; but if you must, then treat me as a fool and let me do a little 17 boasting of my own. ·What I am going to say now is not prompted by the Lord, but said as if in a fit of folly, in the 18 certainty that I have something to boast about. ·So many others have been boasting of their worldly achievements, 19 that I will boast myself. ·You are all wise men and can 20 cheerfully tolerate fools, ·yes, even to tolerating somebody who makes slaves of you, makes you feed him, imposes 21 on you, orders you about and slaps you in the face. ·I hope you are ashamed of us for being weak with you instead!

But if anyone wants some brazen speaking—I am still talking as a fool—then I can be as brazen as any of them, 22 and about the same things. ·Hebrews, are they? So am I. Israelites? So am I. Descendants of Abraham? So am I. 23 The servants of Christ? I must be mad to say this, but so am I, and more than they: more, because I have worked harder, I have been sent to prison more often, and whipped 24 so many times more, often almost to death. ·Five times I 25 had the thirty-nine lashes from the Jews; ·three times I have been beaten with sticks; once I was stoned; three times I have been shipwrecked and once adrift in the open 26 sea for a night and a day. ·Constantly traveling, I have been in danger from rivers and in danger from brigands, in danger from my own people and in danger from pagans; in danger in the towns, in danger in the open country, 27 danger at sea and danger from so-called brothers. ·I have worked and labored, often without sleep; I have been hungry and thirsty and often starving; I have been in the 28 cold without clothes. ·And, to leave out much more, there is my daily preoccupation: my anxiety for all the churches. 29 When any man has had scruples, I have had scruples with him; when any man is made to fall, I am tortured.

30 If I am to boast, then let me boast of my own feebleness. 31 The God and Father of the Lord Jesus—bless him for ever 32 —knows that I am not lying. ·When I was in Damascus, the ethnarch of King Aretas put guards round the city to 33 catch me, ·and I had to be let down over the wall in a hamper, through a window, in order to escape.

10 a. Jr 9:23

1 **12** Must I go on boasting, though there is nothing to be gained by it? But I will move on to the visions and 2 revelations I have had from the Lord. ·I know a man in Christ who, fourteen years ago, was caught up—whether still in the body or out of the body, I do not know; God 3 knows—right into the third heaven.*ᵃ* ·I do know, however, that this same person—whether in the body or out of the 4 body, I do not know; God knows—·was caught up into paradise and heard things which must not and cannot be put 5 into human language. ·I will boast about a man like that, but not about anything of my own except my weaknesses. 6 If I should decide to boast, I should not be made to look foolish, because I should only be speaking the truth; but I am not going to, in case anyone should begin to think I am better than he can actually see and hear me to be.

7 In view of the extraordinary nature of these revelations, to stop me from getting too proud I was given a thorn in the flesh, an angel of Satan to beat me and stop me from 8 getting too proud! ·About this thing, I have pleaded with 9 the Lord three times for it to leave me, ·but he has said, "My grace is enough for you: my power is at its best in weakness." So I shall be very happy to make my weaknesses my special boast so that the power of Christ may 10 stay over me, ·and that is why I am quite content with my weaknesses, and with insults, hardships, persecutions, and the agonies I go through for Christ's sake. For it is when I am weak that I am strong.

11 I have been talking like a fool, but you forced me to do it: you are the ones who should have been commending me. Though I am a nobody, there is not a thing these arch-12 apostles have that I do not have as well. ·You have seen done among you all the things that mark the true apostle, unfailingly produced: the signs, the marvels, the miracles. 13 Is there anything of which you have had less than the other churches have had, except that I have not myself been a burden on you? For this unfairness, please forgive me. 14 I am all prepared now to come to you for the third time, and I am not going to be a burden on you: it is you I want, not your possessions. Children are not expected to 15 save up for their parents, but parents for children. ·I am perfectly willing to spend what I have, and to be expended, in the interests of your souls. Because I love you more, must I be loved the less? 16 All very well, you say: I personally put no pressure on

you, but like the cunning fellow that I am, I took you in by
17 a trick. ·So we exploited you, did we, through one of the
18 men that I have sent to you? ·Well, Titus went at my urging,
and I sent the brother that came with him. Can Titus have
exploited you? You know that he and I have always been
guided by the same spirit and trodden in the same tracks.

Paul's fears and anxieties

19   All this time you have been thinking that our defense is
addressed to you, but it is before God that we, in Christ,
are speaking; and it is all, my dear brothers, for your
20 benefit. ·What I am afraid of is that when I come I may
find you different from what I want you to be, and you may
find that I am not as you would like me to be; and then
there will be wrangling, jealousy, and tempers roused, in-
trigues and backbiting and gossip, obstinacies and disorder.
21 I am afraid that on my next visit, my God may make me
ashamed on your account and I shall be grieving over all
those who sinned before and have still not repented of the
impurities, fornication and debauchery they committed.
1 **13** This will be the third time I have come to you. *The
evidence of three, or at least two, witnesses is neces-*
2 *sary to sustain the charge.*[a] ·I gave warning when I was
with you the second time and I give warning now, too,
before I come, to those who sinned before and to any
others, that when I come again, I shall have no mercy.
3 You want proof, you say, that it is Christ speaking in me:
you have known him not as a weakling, but as a power
4 among you? ·Yes, but he was crucified through weakness,
and still he lives now through the power of God. So then,
we are weak, as he was, but we shall live with him, through
the power of God, for your benefit.
5   Examine yourselves to make sure you are in the faith;
test yourselves. Do you acknowledge that Jesus Christ is
6 really in you? If not, you have failed the test, ·but we, as
7 I hope you will come to see, have not failed it. ·We pray
to God that you will do nothing wrong: not that we want
to appear as the ones who have been successful—we would
8 rather that you did well even though we failed. ·We have
9 no power to resist the truth; only to further it. ·We are
only too glad to be weak provided you are strong. What

12 a. I.e. the highest heaven.
13 a. Dt 19:15

Galatians

THE LETTER OF PAUL
TO THE CHURCH IN GALATIA

Address

¹⁄₂ **1** From Paul to the churches of Galatia, and from all the brothers who are here with me, an apostle who does not owe his authority to men or his appointment to any human being but who has been appointed by Jesus Christ and ³ by God the Father who raised Jesus from the dead. ·We wish you the grace and peace of God our Father and of the ⁴ Lord Jesus Christ, ·who in order to rescue us from this present wicked world sacrificed himself for our sins, in ac- ⁵ cordance with the will of God our Father, ·to whom be glory for ever and ever. Amen.

A warning

⁶ I am astonished at the promptness with which you have turned away from the one who called you and have de- ⁷ cided to follow a different version of the Good News. ·Not that there can be more than one Good News; it is merely that some troublemakers among you want to change the ⁸ Good News of Christ; ·and let me warn you that if anyone preaches a version of the Good News different from the one we have already preached to you, whether it be ourselves or an angel from heaven, he is to be condemned. ⁹ I am only repeating what we told you before: if anyone preaches a version of the Good News different from the ¹⁰ one you have already heard, he is to be condemned. ·So now whom am I trying to please—man, or God? Would you say it is men's approval I am looking for?ᵃ If I still wanted that, I should not be what I am—a servant of Christ.

1 a. Probably a rejoinder to an accusation by the judaizers that Paul was trying to make the pagans' conversion easy by not insisting on circumcision.

I. PAUL'S APOLOGIA

God's call

¹¹ The fact is, brothers, and I want you to realize this, the ¹² Good News I preached is not a human message ·that I was given by men, it is something I learned only through a ¹³ revelation of Jesus Christ. ·You must have heard of my career as a practicing Jew, how merciless I was in persecuting the Church of God, how much damage I did to it, ¹⁴ how I stood out among other Jews of my generation, and how enthusiastic I was for the traditions of my ancestors. ¹⁵ Then God, who had specially *chosen* me while I was *still in my mother's womb,*[b] called me through his grace and ¹⁶ chose ·to reveal his Son in me, so that I might preach the Good News about him to the pagans. I did not stop to discuss ¹⁷ this with any human being, ·nor did I go up to Jerusalem to see those who were already apostles before me, but I went off to Arabia[c] at once and later went straight ¹⁸ back from there to Damascus. ·Even when after three years I went up to Jerusalem to visit Cephas and stayed with him ¹⁹ for fifteen days, ·I did not see any of the other apostles; ²⁰ I only saw James, the brother of the Lord, ·and I swear before God that what I have just written is the literal truth. ²¹ After that I went to Syria and Cilicia, ·and was still not ²² known by sight to the churches of Christ in Judaea, ·who ²³ had heard nothing except that their one-time persecutor was now preaching the faith he had previously tried to ²⁴ destroy; ·and they gave glory to God for me.

The meeting at Jerusalem

¹ 2 It was not till fourteen years had passed that I went up to Jerusalem again. I went with Barnabas and took ² Titus with me. ·I went there as the result of a revelation, and privately I laid before the leading men the Good News as I proclaim it among the pagans; I did so for fear the course I was adopting or had already adopted would not ³ be allowed. ·And what happened? Even though Titus who had come with me is a Greek, he was not obliged to be cir- ⁴ cumcised. ·The question came up only because some who do not really belong to the brotherhood have furtively crept in to spy on the liberty we enjoy in Christ Jesus, and ⁵ want to reduce us all to slavery. ·I was so determined to

safeguard for you the true meaning of the Good News,
that I refused even out of deference to yield to such people
6 for one moment. •As a result, these people who are acknowledged leaders—not that their importance matters to me, since God has no favorites—these leaders, as I say, had
7 nothing to add to the Good News as I preach it. •On the contrary, they recognized that I had been commissioned to preach the Good News to the uncircumcised just as Peter had been commissioned to preach it to the circum-
8 cised. •The same person whose action had made Peter the apostle of the circumcised had given me a similar mis-
9 sion to the pagans. •So, James, Cephas and John, these leaders, these pillars, shook hands with Barnabas and me as a sign of partnership: we were to go to the pagans and
10 they to the circumcised.*a* •The only thing they insisted on was that we should remember to help the poor, as indeed I was anxious to do.

Peter and Paul at Antioch

11 When Cephas came to Antioch, however, I opposed him
12 to his face, since he was manifestly in the wrong. •His custom had been to eat with the pagans,*b* but after certain friends of James arrived he stopped doing this and kept away from them altogether for fear of the group that in-
13 sisted on circumcision. •The other Jews joined him in this pretense, and even Barnabas felt himself obliged to copy their behavior.
14 When I saw they were not respecting the true meaning of the Good News, I said to Cephas in front of everyone, "In spite of being a Jew, you live like the pagans and not like the Jews, so you have no right to make the pagans copy Jewish ways."

The Good News as proclaimed by Paul

15 "Though we were born Jews and not pagan sinners,
16 we acknowledge that what makes a man righteous is not obedience to the Law, but faith in Jesus Christ. We had to

b. Is 49:1 c. Probably the kingdom of the Nabataean Arabs, to the S. of Damascus.
2 a. The distinction is geographical rather than racial; when Paul went among the Gentiles the resident Jews were his first concern. b. Converts from paganism.

become believers in Christ Jesus no less than you had, and now we hold that faith in Christ rather than fidelity to the Law is what justifies us, and that *no one can be justified*[o]
17 by keeping the Law. ·Now if we were to admit that the result of looking to Christ to justify us is to make us sinners like the rest, it would follow that Christ had induced us to
18 sin, which would be absurd. ·If I were to return to a position I had already abandoned, I should be admitting I had
19 done something wrong. ·In other words, through the Law I am dead to the Law, so that now I can live for God. I
20 have been crucified with Christ, ·and I live now not with my own life but with the life of Christ who lives in me. The life I now live in this body I live in faith: faith in the Son of God who loved me and who sacrificed himself for
21 my sake. ·I cannot bring myself to give up God's gift: if the Law can justify us, there is no point in the death of Christ."

II. DOCTRINAL MATTERS

Justification by faith

1 **3** Are you people in Galatia mad? Has someone put a spell on you, in spite of the plain explanation you have
2 had of the crucifixion of Jesus Christ? ·Let me ask you one question: was it because you practiced the Law that you received the Spirit, or because you believed what was
3 preached to you? ·Are you foolish enough to end in out-
4 ward observances what you began in the Spirit? ·Have all the favors you received been wasted? And if this were so,
5 they would most certainly have been wasted. ·Does God give you the Spirit so freely and work miracles among you because you practice the Law, or because you believed what was preached to you?
6 Take Abraham for example: *he put his faith in God,*
7 *and this faith was considered as justifying him.*[a] ·Don't you see that it is those who rely on faith who are the sons of
8 Abraham? ·Scripture foresaw that God was going to use faith to justify the pagans, and proclaimed the Good News long ago when Abraham was told: *In you all the pagans*
9 *will be blessed.*[b] ·Those therefore who rely on faith receive the same blessing as Abraham, the man of faith.

The curse brought by the Law

10 ·· On the other hand, those who rely on the keeping of the Law are under a curse, since scripture says: *Cursed be everyone who does not persevere in observing everything*
11 *prescribed in the book of the Law.*ᶜ ·The Law will not justify anyone in the sight of God, because we are told:
12 *the righteous man finds life through faith.*ᵈ ·The Law is not even based on faith, since we are told: *The man who practices these precepts finds life through practicing them.*ᵉ
13 Christ redeemed us from the curse of the Law by being cursed for our sake, since scripture says: *Cursed be*
14 *everyone who is hanged on a tree.*ᶠ ·This was done so that in Christ Jesus the blessing of Abraham might include the pagans, and so that through faith we might receive the promised Spirit.

The Law did not cancel the promise

15 · Compare this, brothers, with what happens in ordinary life. If a will has been drawn up in due form, no one is
16 allowed to disregard it or add to it. ·Now the promises were addressed to Abraham *and to his descendants*—notice, in passing, that scripture does not use a plural word as if there were several descendants, it uses the singular: to his
17 posterity, which is Christ. ·But my point is this: once God had expressed his will in due form, no law that came four hundred and thirty years later could cancel that and make
18 the promise meaningless. ·If you inherit something as a legal right, it does not come to you as the result of a promise, and it was precisely in the form of a promise that God made his gift to Abraham.

The purpose of the Law

19 What then was the purpose of adding the Law? This was done to specify crimes, until the posterity came to whom the promise was addressed. The Law was promul-
20 gated by angels,ᵍ assisted by an intermediary. ·Now there can only be an intermediary between two parties, yet God
21 is one. ·Does this mean that there is opposition between

c. Ps 143:2
3 a. Gn 15:6 b. Gn 12:3 c. Dt 27:26 d. Hab 2:4 e. Lv 18:5 f. Dt 21:23 g. In Jewish tradition angels were present at Sinai; the "intermediary" is Moses.

the Law and the promises of God? Of course not. We could have been justified by the Law if the Law we were
22 given had been capable of giving life, ·but it is not: scripture makes no exceptions when it says that sin is master everywhere. In this way the promise can only be given through faith in Jesus Christ and can only be given to those who have this faith.

The coming of faith

23 Before faith came, we were allowed no freedom by the Law; we were being looked after till faith was revealed.
24 The Law was to be our guardian until the Christ came
25 and we could be justified by faith. ·Now that that time has
26 come we are no longer under that guardian, ·and you are,
27 all of you, sons of God through faith in Christ Jesus. ·All baptized in Christ, you have all clothed yourselves in Christ,
28 and there are no more distinctions between Jew and Greek, slave and free, male and female, but all of you are
29 one in Christ Jesus. ·Merely by belonging to Christ you are the posterity of Abraham, the heirs he was promised.

Sons of God

1 **4** Let me put this another way: an heir, even if he has actually inherited everything, is no different from a
2 slave for as long as he remains a child. ·He is under the control of guardians and administrators until he reaches
3 the age fixed by his father. ·Now before we came of age we were as good as slaves to the elemental principles of this
4 world,ᵃ ·but when the appointed time came, God sent his
5 Son, born of a woman, born a subject of the Law, ·to redeem the subjects of the Law and to enable us to be
6 adopted as sons. ·The proof that you are sons is that God has sent the Spirit of his Son into our hearts: the Spirit
7 that cries, "Abba, Father," ·and it is this that makes you a son, you are not a slave any more; and if God has made you son, then he has made you heir.
8 Once you were ignorant of God, and enslaved to "gods"
9 who are not really gods at all; ·but now that you have come to acknowledge God—or rather, now that God has acknowledged you—how can you want to go back to elemental things like these, that can do nothing and give noth-
10 ing, and be their slaves? ·You and your special days and
11 months and seasons and years! ·You make me feel I have wasted my time with you.

A personal appeal

12 Brothers, all I ask is that you should copy me as I copied you. You have never treated me in an unfriendly way be-
13 fore; ·even at the beginning, when that illness gave me the
14 opportunity to preach the Good News to you, ·you never showed the least sign of being revolted or disgusted by my disease that was such a trial to you; instead you welcomed me as an angel of God, as if I were Christ Jesus himself.
15 What has become of this enthusiasm you had? I swear that you would even have gone so far as to pluck out your eyes
16 and give them to me. ·Is it telling you the truth that has
17 made me your enemy? ·The blame lies in the way they have tried to win you over: by separating you from me,
18 they want to win you over to themselves. ·It is always a good thing to win people over—and I do not have to be
19 there with you—but it must be for a good purpose, ·my children! I must go through the pain of giving birth to you
20 all over again, until Christ is formed in you. ·I wish I were with you now so that I could know exactly what to say; as it is, I have no idea what to do for the best.

The two covenants: Hagar and Sarah

21 You want to be subject to the Law? Then listen to what
22 the Law says. ·It says, if you remember, that Abraham had two sons, one by the slave-girl, and one by his free-born
23 wife. ·The child of the slave-girl was born in the ordinary way; the child of the free woman was born as the result of
24 a promise. ·This can be regarded as an allegory: the women stand for the two covenants. The first who comes from Mount Sinai, and whose children are slaves, is Hagar—
25 since Sinai is in Arabia—and she corresponds to the present
26 Jerusalem that is a slave like her children. ·The Jeru-
27 salem above, however, is free and is our mother; ·since scripture says: *Shout for joy, you barren women who bore no children! Break into shouts of joy and gladness, you who were never in labor. For there are more sons of the*
28 *forsaken one than sons of the wedded wife.*[b] ·Now you,
29 my brothers, like Isaac, are children of the promise, ·and as at that time the child born in the ordinary way perse-
30 cuted the child born in the Spirit's way, so also now. ·Does

4 a. The principles that make up the physical universe; Paul has related the Law to "outward observances," 3:3   b. Is 54:1

not scripture say: *Drive away that slave-girl and her son;
this slave-girl's son is not to share the inheritance with the*
³¹ *son*ᵒ *of the free woman?* ·So, my brothers, we are the children, not of the slave-girl, but of the free-born wife.

III. EXHORTATION

Christian liberty

¹ When Christ freed us, he meant us to remain free.
Stand firm, therefore, and do not submit again to the
² yoke of slavery. ·It is I, Paul, who tell you this: if you
allow yourselves to be circumcised, Christ will be of no
³ benefit to you at all. ·With all solemnity I repeat my warning: Everyone who accepts circumcision is obliged to
⁴ keep the whole Law. ·But if you do look to the Law to
make you justified, then you have separated yourselves
⁵ from Christ, and have fallen from grace. ·Christians are
told by the Spirit to look to faith for those rewards that
⁶ righteousness hopes for, ·since in Christ Jesus whether you
are circumcised or not makes no difference—what matters
is faith that expresses itself in love.

⁷ You began your race well: who made you less anxious
⁸ to obey the truth? ·You were not prompted by him who
⁹ called you! ·The yeast seems to be spreading through the
¹⁰ whole batch of you. ·I feel sure that, united in the Lord,
you will agree with me, and anybody who troubles you in
¹¹ future will be condemned, no matter who he is. ·As for
me, my brothers, if I still preach circumcision,ᵃ why am
I still persecuted? If I did that now, would there be any
¹² scandal of the cross? ·Tell those who are disturbing you
I would like to see the knife slip.

Liberty and charity

¹³ My brothers, you were called, as you know, to liberty;
but be careful, or this liberty will provide an opening for
self-indulgence. Serve one another, rather, in works of love,
¹⁴ since the whole of the Law is summarized in a single com-
¹⁵ mand: *Love your neighbor as yourself.*ᵇ ·If you go snap-
ping at each other and tearing each other to pieces, you
had better watch or you will destroy the whole community.
¹⁶ Let me put it like this: if you are guided by the Spirit
you will be in no danger of yielding to self-indulgence,

¹⁷ since self-indulgence is the opposite of the Spirit, the Spirit is totally against such a thing, and it is precisely because the two are so opposed that you do not always carry out
¹⁸ your good intentions. ·If you are led by the Spirit, no law
¹⁹ can touch you. ·When self-indulgence is at work the results are obvious: fornication, gross indecency and sexual
²⁰ irresponsibility; ·idolatry and sorcery; feuds and wrangling, jealousy, bad temper and quarrels; disagreements, factions,
²¹ envy; drunkenness, orgies and similar things. I warn you now, as I warned you before: those who behave like this
²² will not inherit the kingdom of God. ·What the Spirit brings is very different: love, joy, peace, patience, kindness,
²³ goodness, trustfulness, ·gentleness and self-control. There
²⁴ can be no law against things like that, of course. ·You cannot belong to Christ Jesus unless you crucify all self-indulgent passions and desires.
²⁵ Since the Spirit is our life, let us be directed by the
²⁶ Spirit. ·We must stop being conceited, provocative and envious.

On kindness and perseverance

¹ Brothers, if one of you misbehaves, the more spiritual of you who set him right should do so in a spirit of gentleness, not forgetting that you may be tempted your-
² selves. ·You should carry each other's troubles and fulfill
³ the law of Christ. ·It is the people who are not important
⁴ who often make the mistake of thinking that they are. ·Let each of you examine his own conduct; if you find anything to boast about, it will at least be something of your own,
⁵ not just something better than your neighbour has. ·Everyone has his own burden to carry.
⁶ People under instruction should always contribute something to the support of the man who is instructing them.
⁷ Don't delude yourself into thinking God can be cheated:
⁸ where a man sows, there he reaps: ·if he sows in the field of self-indulgence he will get a harvest of corruption out of it; if he sows in the field of the Spirit he will get from it
⁹ a harvest of eternal life. ·We must never get tired of doing good because if we don't give up the struggle we shall get
¹⁰ our harvest at the proper time. ·While we have the chance,

c. Gn 21:10
5 a. As Paul's enemies were apparently claiming. b. Lv 19:18

we must do good to all, and especially to our brothers in the faith.

Epilogue

11 Take good note of what I am adding in my own hand-
12 writing and in large letters. ·It is only self-interest that makes them want to force circumcision on you—they want
13 to escape persecution for the cross of Christ—·they accept circumcision but do not keep the Law themselves; they only want you to be circumcised so that they can boast of
14 the fact. ·As for me, the only thing I can boast about is the cross of our Lord Jesus Christ, through whom the
15 world is crucified to me, and I to the world. ·It does not matter if a person is circumcised or not; what matters is
16 for him to become an altogether new creature. ·Peace and mercy to all who follow this rule, who form the Israel of God.
17 I want no more trouble from anybody after this; the
18 marks on my body are those of Jesus. ·The grace of our Lord Jesus Christ be with your spirit, my brothers. Amen.

Ephesians

THE LETTER OF PAUL
TO THE CHURCH AT EPHESUS

Address and greetings

1 ¹ From Paul, appointed by God to be an apostle of Christ
Jesus, to the saints who are faithful to Christ Jesus:
² Grace and peace to you from God our Father and from
the Lord Jesus Christ.

I. THE MYSTERY OF SALVATION
AND OF THE CHURCH

God's plan of salvation

³ Blessed be God the Father of our Lord Jesus Christ,
who has blessed us with all the spiritual blessings of heaven
in Christ.
⁴ Before the world was made, he chose us, chose us in Christ,
to be holy and spotless, and to live through love in his
presence,
⁵ determining that we should become his adopted sons,
through Jesus Christ
for his own kind purposes,
⁶ to make us praise the glory of his grace,
his free gift to us in the Beloved,
⁷ in whom, through his blood, we gain our freedom, the
forgiveness of our sins.
Such is the richness of the grace
⁸ which he has showered on us
in all wisdom and insight.
⁹ He has let us know the mystery of his purpose,
the hidden plan he so kindly made in Christ from the beginning
¹⁰ to act upon when the times had run their course to the end:

that he would bring everything together under Christ, as
       head,
everything in the heavens and everything on earth.

11 And it is in him that we were claimed as God's own,
chosen from the beginning,
under the predetermined plan of the one who guides all
       things
as he decides by his own will;

12 chosen to be,
for his greater glory,
the people who would put their hopes in Christ before he
       came.

13 Now you too, in him,
have heard the message of the truth and the good news of
       your salvation,
and have believed it;
and you too have been stamped with the seal of the Holy
       Spirit of the Promise,

14 the pledge of our inheritance
which brings freedom for those whom God has taken for
       his own,
to make his glory praised.

The triumph and the supremacy of Christ

15 That will explain why I, having once heard about your
faith in the Lord Jesus, and the love that you show towards
16 all the saints, ·have never failed to remember you in my
17 prayers and to thank God for you. ·May the God of our
Lord Jesus Christ, the Father of glory, give you a spirit of
wisdom and perception of what is revealed, to bring you
18 to full knowledge of him. ·May he enlighten the eyes of
your mind so that you can see what hope his call holds
for you, what rich glories he has promised the saints will
19 inherit ·and how infinitely great is the power that he has
exercised for us believers. This you can tell from the
20 strength of his power ·at work in Christ, when he used it
to raise him from the dead and to make him sit at his right
21 hand, in heaven, ·far above every Sovereignty, Authority,
Power, or Domination,[a] or any other name that can be
named, not only in this age but also in the age to come.
22 *He has put all things under his feet,*[b] and made him, as the
23 ruler of everything, the head of the Church; ·which is his
body, the fullness of him who fills the whole creation.

Salvation in Christ a free gift

1 2 And you were dead, through the crimes and the sins
2 in which you used to live when you were following the
way of this world, obeying the ruler who governs the air,[a]
3 the spirit who is at work in the rebellious. ·We all were
among them too in the past, living sensual lives, ruled entirely by our own physical desires and our own ideas; so
that by nature we were as much under God's anger as the
4 rest of the world. ·But God loved us with so much love
5 that he was generous with his mercy: ·when we were dead
through our sins, he brought us to life with Christ—it is
6 through grace that you have been saved—·and raised us
up with him and gave us a place with him in heaven, in
Christ Jesus.

7 This was to show for all ages to come, through his goodness toward us in Christ Jesus, how infinitely rich he is
8 in grace. ·Because it is by grace that you have been saved,
through faith; not by anything of your own, but by a gift
9 from God; ·not by anything that you have done, so that
10 nobody can claim the credit. ·We are God's work of art,
created in Christ Jesus to live the good life as from the
beginning he had meant us to live it.

Reconciliation of the Jews and the pagans with each other and with God

11 Do not forget, then, that there was a time when you
who were pagans physically, termed the Uncircumcised by
those who speak of themselves as the Circumcision by rea-
12 son of a physical operation, ·do not forget, I say, that you
had no Christ and were excluded from membership of
Israel, aliens with no part in the covenants with their Promise; you were immersed in this world, without hope and
13 without God. ·But now in Christ Jesus, you that used to
be so far apart from us have been brought very close, by
14 the blood of Christ. ·For he is the peace between us, and
has made the two into one and broken down the barrier
which used to keep them apart, actually destroying in his
15 own person the hostility ·caused by the rules and decrees
of the Law. This was to create one single New Man in

1 a. Orders of the angelic hierarchy in Jewish literature. **b.** Ps
8:6
2 a. Satan.

himself out of the two of them and by restoring peace
16 through the cross, to unite them both in a single Body and
reconcile them with God. In his own person he killed the
17 hostility. ·Later he came to bring the good news of peace,
peace to you who were far away and peace to those who
18 *were near at hand.*[b] ·Through him, both of us have in the
one Spirit our way to come to the Father.

19 So you are no longer aliens or foreign visitors: you are
citizens like all the saints, and part of God's household.
20 You are part of a building that has the apostles and
prophets[c] for its foundations, and Christ Jesus himself for
21 its main cornerstone. ·As every structure is aligned on him,
22 all grow into one holy temple in the Lord; ·and you too,
in him, are being built into a house where God lives, in
the Spirit.

Paul, a servant of the mystery

1 **3** So I, Paul, a prisoner of Christ Jesus for the sake of
2 you pagans. . . . ·You have probably heard how I have
been entrusted by God with the grace he meant for you,
3 and that it was by a revelation that I was given the knowledge of the mystery, as I have just described it very shortly.
4 If you read my words, you will have some idea of the
5 depths that I see in the mystery of Christ. ·This mystery
that has now been revealed through the Spirit to his holy
apostles and prophets was unknown to any men in past
6 generations; ·it means that pagans now share the same
inheritance, that they are parts of the same body, and that
the same promise has been made to them, in Christ Jesus,
7 through the gospel. ·I have been made the servant of that
gospel by a gift of grace from God who gave it to me by
8 his own power. ·I, who am less than the least of all the
saints, have been entrusted with this special grace, not only
of proclaiming to the pagans the infinite treasure of Christ
9 but also of explaining how the mystery is to be dispensed.
Through all the ages, this has been kept hidden in God,
10 the creator of everything. Why? ·So that the Sovereignties
and Powers should learn only now, through the Church,
11 how comprehensive God's wisdom really is, ·exactly according to the plan which he had had from all eternity in
12 Christ Jesus our Lord. ·This is why we are bold enough to
approach God in complete confidence, through our faith
13 in him; ·so, I beg you, never lose confidence just because

of the trials that I go through on your account: they are your glory.

Paul's prayer

14 This, then, is what I pray, kneeling before the Father,
15 from whom every family,[a] whether spiritual or natural, takes its name:
16 Out of his infinite glory, may he give you the power
17 through his Spirit for your hidden self to grow strong, ·so that Christ may live in your hearts through faith, and then,
18 planted in love and built on love, ·you will with all the saints have strength to grasp the breadth and the length,
19 the height and the depth; ·until, knowing the love of Christ, which is beyond all knowledge, you are filled with the utter fullness of God.
20 Glory be to him whose power, working in us, can do
21 infinitely more than we can ask or imagine; ·glory be to him from generation to generation in the Church and in Christ Jesus for ever and ever. Amen.

II. EXHORTATION

A call to unity

1,2 **4** I, the prisoner in the Lord, implore you therefore to lead a life worthy of your vocation. ·Bear with one another charitably, in complete selflessness, gentleness and
3 patience. ·Do all you can to preserve the unity of the
4 Spirit by the peace that binds you together. ·There is one Body, one Spirit, just as you were all called into one
5 and the same hope when you were called. ·There is one
6 Lord, one faith, one baptism, ·and one God who is Father of all, over all, through all and within all.
7 Each one of us, however, has been given his own share
8 of grace, given as Christ allotted it. ·It was said that he would:

When he ascended to the height, he captured prisoners, he gave gifts to men.[a]

b. Is 57:19   c. The N.T. prophets.
3 a. A pun on the words "Father" and "family" (clan or tribe) is lost in translation; traces of it survive in *paternity* and *patriotism*.
4 a. Ps 68:18

⁹ When it says, "he ascended," what can it mean if not that he descended right down to the lower regions of the
¹⁰ earth? ·The one who rose higher than all the heavens to fill all things is none other than the one who descended.
¹¹ And to some, his gift was that they should be apostles; to some, prophets; to some, evangelists; to some, pastors and
¹² teachers; ·so that the saints together make a unity in the
¹³ work of service, building up the body of Christ. ·In this way we are all to come to unity in our faith and in our knowledge of the Son of God, until we become the perfect Man, fully mature with the fullness of Christ himself.
¹⁴ Then we shall not be children any longer, or tossed one way and another and carried along by every wind of doctrine, at the mercy of all the tricks men play and their
¹⁵ cleverness in practicing deceit. ·If we live by the truth and in love, we shall grow in all ways into Christ, who is the
¹⁶ head ·by whom the whole body is fitted and joined together, every joint adding its own strength, for each separate part to work according to its function. So the body grows until it has built itself up, in love.

The new life in Christ

¹⁷ In particular, I want to urge you in the name of the Lord, not to go on living the aimless kind of life that
¹⁸ pagans live. ·Intellectually they are in the dark, and they are estranged from the life of God, without knowledge
¹⁹ because they have shut their hearts to it. ·Their sense of right and wrong once dulled, they have abandoned themselves to sexuality and eagerly pursue a career of indecency
²⁰ of every kind. ·Now that is hardly the way you have
²¹ learned from Christ, ·unless you failed to hear him properly when you were taught what the truth is in Jesus.
²² You must give up your old way of life; you must put aside your old self, which gets corrupted by following il-
²³ lusory desires. ·Your mind must be renewed by a spiri-
²⁴ tual revolution ·so that you can put on the new self that has been created in God's way, in the goodness and holiness of the truth.
²⁵ So from now on, there must be no more lies: *You must speak the truth to one another,*ᵇ since we are all
²⁶ parts of one another. ·*Even if you are angry, you must*
²⁷ *not sin:*ᶜ never let the sun set on your anger ·or else
²⁸ you will give the devil a foothold. ·Anyone who was a

thief must stop stealing; he should try to find some useful manual work instead, and be able to do some good by
²⁹ helping others that are in need. ·Guard against foul talk; let your words be for the improvement of others, as oc-
³⁰ casion offers, and do good to your listeners, ·otherwise you will only be grieving the Holy Spirit of God who has marked you with his seal for you to be set free when the
³¹ day comes. ·Never have grudges against others, or lose your temper, or raise your voice to anybody, or call each
³² other names, or allow any sort of spitefulness. ·Be friends with one another, and kind, forgiving each other as readily as God forgave you in Christ.

¹ ⁵ Try, then, to imitate God, as children of his that he
² loves, ·and follow Christ by loving as he loved you, giving himself up in our place *as a fragrant offering and*
³ *a sacrifice to God.ᵃ* ·Among you there must be not even a mention of fornication or impurity in any of its forms,
⁴ or promiscuity: this would hardly become the saints! ·There must be no coarseness, or salacious talk and jokes— all this is wrong for you; raise your voices in thanksgiving
⁵ instead. ·For you can be quite certain that nobody who actually indulges in fornication or impurity or promiscuity —which is worshiping a false god—can inherit anything
⁶ of the kingdom of God. ·Do not let anyone deceive you with empty arguments: it is for this loose living that God's
⁷ anger comes down on those who rebel against him. ·Make
⁸ sure that you are not included with them. ·You were darkness once, but now you are light in the Lord; be like
⁹ children of light, ·for the effects of the light are seen in
¹⁰ complete goodness and right living and truth. ·Try to dis-
¹¹ cover what the Lord wants of you, ·having nothing to do with the futile works of darkness but exposing them by
¹² contrast. ·The things which are done in secret are things
¹³ that people are ashamed even to speak of; ·but anything
¹⁴ exposed by the light will be illuminated ·and anything illuminated turns into light. That is why it is said:ᵇ

> Wake up from your sleep,
> rise from the dead,
> and Christ will shine on you.

b. Zc 8:16   c. Ps 4:4 (LXX)
5 a. Ex 29:18   b. Presumably a quotation from a Christian hymn.

¹⁵ So be very careful about the sort of lives you lead, like
¹⁶ intelligent and not like senseless people. ·This may be a
¹⁷ wicked age, but your lives should redeem it. ·And do not
be thoughtless but recognize what is the will of the Lord.
¹⁸ Do not drug yourselves with wine, this is simply dissipa-
¹⁹ tion; be filled with the Spirit. ·Sing the words and tunes
of the Psalms and hymns when you are together, and go
²⁰ on singing and chanting to the Lord in your hearts, ·so
that always and everywhere you are giving thanks to God
who is our Father in the name of our Lord Jesus Christ.

The morals of the home

²¹
²²   Give way to one another in obedience to Christ. ·Wives
should regard their husbands as they regard the Lord,
²³ since as Christ is head of the Church and saves the whole
²⁴ body, so is a husband the head of his wife; ·and as the
Church submits to Christ, so should wives to their hus-
²⁵ bands, in everything. ·Husbands should love their wives
just as Christ loved the Church and sacrificed himself for
²⁶ her ·to make her holy. He made her clean by washing her
²⁷ in water with a form of words, ·so that when he took her
to himself she would be glorious, with no speck or wrinkle
²⁸ or anything like that, but holy and faultless. ·In the same
way, husbands must love their wives as they love their own
bodies; for a man to love his wife is for him to love him-
²⁹ self. ·A man never hates his own body, but he feeds it and
looks after it; and that is the way Christ treats the Church,
³⁰
³¹ because it is his body—and we are its living parts. ·*For
this reason, a man must leave his father and mother and
be joined to his wife, and the two will become one body.*ᶜ
³² This mystery has many implications; but I am saying it
³³ applies to Christ and the Church. ·To sum up; you too,
each one of you, must love his wife as he loves himself;
and let every wife respect her husband.

¹ **6** Children, be obedient to your parents in the Lord—
² that is your duty. ·The first commandment that has a
promise attached to it is: *Honor your father and mother,*
³ and the promise is: *and you will prosper and have a long*
⁴ *life in the land.*ᵃ ·And parents, never drive your children
to resentment but in bringing them up correct them and
guide them as the Lord does.
⁵   Slaves, be obedient to the men who are called your
masters in this world, with deep respect and sincere loyalty,

⁶ as you are obedient to Christ: ·not only when you are under their eye, as if you had only to please men, but because you are slaves of Christ and wholeheartedly do the
⁷ will of God. ·Work hard and willingly, but do it for the
·⁸ sake of the Lord and not for the sake of men. ·You can be sure that everyone, whether a slave or a free man, will be properly rewarded by the Lord for whatever work he
⁹ has done well. ·And those of you who are employers, treat your slaves in the same spirit; do without threats, remembering that they and you have the same Master in heaven and he is not impressed by one person more than by another.

The spiritual war

¹⁰ Finally, grow strong in the Lord, with the strength of
¹¹ his power. ·Put God's armor on so as to be able to resist
¹² the devil's tactics. ·For it is not against human enemies that we have to struggle, but against the Sovereignties and the Powers who originate the darkness in this world,
¹³ the spiritual army of evil in the heavens. ·That is why you must rely on God's armor, or you will not be able to put up any resistance when the worst happens, or have enough resources to hold your ground.
¹⁴ So stand your ground, with *truth buckled round your*
¹⁵ *waist,* and *integrity for a breastplate,*[b] ·wearing for shoes on your feet *the eagerness to spread the gospel of peace*[c]
¹⁶ and always carrying the shield of faith so that you can use
¹⁷ it to put out the burning arrows of the evil one. ·And then you must accept *salvation from God to be your helmet* and receive the word of God from the Spirit to use as a sword.
¹⁸ Pray all the time, asking for what you need, praying in the Spirit on every possible occasion. Never get tired of
¹⁹ staying awake to pray for all the saints; ·and pray for me to be given an opportunity to open my mouth and speak
²⁰ without fear and give out the mystery of the gospel ·of which I am an ambassador in chains; pray that in proclaiming it I may speak as boldly as I ought to.

c. Gn 2:24
6 a. Ex 20:12   b. Is 59:17   c. Is 40:9

Philippians

THE LETTER OF PAUL
TO THE CHURCH AT PHILIPPI

Address

1 ¹ From Paul and Timothy, servants of Christ Jesus, to all the saints in Christ Jesus, together with their presid- ² ing elders and deacons. ·We wish you the grace and peace of God our Father and of the Lord Jesus Christ.

Thanksgiving and prayer

³ I thank my God whenever I think of you; and ·every
⁵ time I pray for all of you, I pray with joy, ·remembering how you have helped to spread the Good News from the
⁶ day you first heard it right up to the present. ·I am quite certain that the One who began this good work in you will see that it is finished when the Day of Christ Jesus comes.
⁷ It is only natural that I should feel like this towards you all, since you have shared the privileges which have been mine: both my chains and my work defending and establishing
⁸ the gospel. You have a permanent place in my heart, ·and God knows how much I miss you all, loving you as Christ
⁹ Jesus loves you. ·My prayer is that your love for each other may increase more and more and never stop improving
¹⁰ your knowledge and deepening your perception ·so that you can always recognize what is best. This will help you to become pure and blameless, and prepare you for the
¹¹ Day of Christ, ·when you will reach the perfect good- ness which Jesus Christ produces in us for the glory and praise of God.

Paul's own circumstances

¹² I am glad to tell you, brothers, that the things that hap- pen to me have actually been a help to the Good News.
¹³ My chains, in Christ, have become famous not only all
¹⁴ over the Praetorium but everywhere, ·and most of the

brothers have taken courage in the Lord from these chains
of mine and are getting more and more daring in announc-
15 ing the Message without any fear. ·It is true that some of
them are doing it just out of rivalry and competition, but
16 the rest preach Christ with the right intention, ·out of
nothing but love, as they know that this is my invariable
17 way of defending the gospel. ·The others, who proclaim
Christ for jealous or selfish motives, do not mind if they
18 make my chains heavier to bear. ·But does it matter?
Whether from dishonest motives or in sincerity, Christ is
19 proclaimed; and that makes me happy; ·and I shall continue being happy, because I know *this will help to
save me,*ᵃ thanks to your prayers and to the help which
20 will be given to me by the Spirit of Jesus. ·My one hope
and trust is that I shall never have to admit defeat, but
that now as always I shall have the courage for Christ to
be glorified in my body, whether by my life or by my
21 death. ·Life to me, of course, is Christ, but then death
22 would bring me something more; ·but then again, if living
in this body means doing work which is having good
23 results—I do not know what I should choose. ·I am caught
in this dilemma: I want to be gone and be with Christ,
24 which would be very much the better, ·but for me to stay
alive in this body is a more urgent need for your sake.
25 This weighs with me so much that I feel sure I shall survive
and stay with you all, and help you to progress in the faith
26 and even increase your joy in it; ·and so you will have
another reason to give praise to Christ Jesus on my account when I am with you again.

Fight for the faith

27 Avoid anything in your everyday lives that would be
unworthy of the gospel of Christ, so that, whether I come
to you and see for myself, or stay at a distance and only
hear about you, I shall know that you are unanimous in
meeting the attack with firm resistance, united by your
28 love for the faith of the gospel ·and quite unshaken by
your enemies. This would be the sure sign that they will
lose and you will be saved. It would be a sign from God
29 that he has given you the privilege not only of believing
30 in Christ, but of suffering for him as well. ·You and I are
together in the same fight as you saw me fighting before
and, as you will have heard, I am fighting still.

Preserve unity in humility

1 2 If our life in Christ means anything to you, if love can persuade at all, or the Spirit that we have in common,
2 or any tenderness and sympathy, •then be united in your convictions and united in your love, with a common purpose and a common mind. That is the one thing which
3 would make me completely happy. •There must be no competition among you, no conceit; but everybody is to be self-effacing. Always consider the other person to be better
4 than yourself, •so that nobody thinks of his own interests first but everybody thinks of other people's interests in-
5 stead. •In your minds you must be the same as Christ Jesus:[a]

6   His state was divine,
          yet he did not cling
          to his equality with God
7   but emptied himself
          to assume the condition of a slave,
          and became as men are;
          and being as all men are,
8   he was humbler yet,
          even to accepting death,
          death on a cross.
9   But God raised him high
          and gave him the name
          which is above all other names
10   so that *all beings*
          in the heavens, on earth and in the underworld,
          should bend the knee[b] at the name of Jesus
11   and that every tongue should acclaim
          Jesus Christ as Lord,
          to the glory of God the Father.

Work for salvation

12 So then, my dear friends, continue to do as I tell you, as you always have; not only as you did when I was there with you, but even more now that I am no longer there;
13 and work for your salvation "in fear and trembling." •It is God, for his own loving purpose, who puts both the will

1 a. Jb 13:16 (LXX)
2 a. Vv. 6-11 are a hymn, though whether composed or only quoted by Paul is uncertain.   b. Is 45:23

¹⁴ and the action into you. ·Do all that has to be done without
¹⁵ complaining or arguing ·and then you will be innocent
and genuine, *perfect children of God among a deceitful
and underhand brood,*ᶜ and you will shine in the world
¹⁶ like bright stars ·because you are offering it the word of
life. This would give me something to be proud of for
the Day of Christ, and would mean that I had not run in
¹⁷ the race and exhausted myself for nothing. ·And then, if
my blood has to be shed as part of your own sacrifice and
offering—which is your faithᵈ—I shall still be happy and
¹⁸ rejoice with all of you, ·and you must be just as happy
and rejoice with me.

The mission of Timothy and Epaphroditus

¹⁹ I hope, in the Lord Jesus, to send Timothy to you
²⁰ soon, and I shall be reassured by having news of you. ·I
have nobody else like him here, as wholeheartedly con-
²¹ cerned for your welfare: ·all the rest seem more interested
²² in themselves than in Jesus Christ. ·But you know how he
has proved himself by working with me on behalf of the
²³ Good News like a son helping his father. ·That is why he
is the one that I am hoping to send you, as soon as I know
²⁴ something definite about my fate. ·But I continue to trust,
in the Lord, that I shall be coming soon myself.
²⁵ It is essential, I think, to send brother Epaphroditus back
to you. He was sent as your representative to help me
when I needed someone to be my companion in working
²⁶ and battling, ·but he misses you all and is worried because
²⁷ you heard about his illness. ·It is true that he has been
ill, and almost died, but God took pity on him, and on
me as well as him, and spared me what would have been
²⁸ one grief on top of another. ·So I shall send him back
as promptly as I can; you will be happy to see him again,
²⁹ and that will make me less sorry. ·Give him a most hearty
welcome, in the Lord; people like him are to be honored.
³⁰ It was for Christ's work that he came so near to dying,
and he risked his life to give me the help that you were
³ not able to give me yourselves.
¹ **3** Finally, my brothers, rejoice in the Lord.ᵃ

The true way of Christian salvation

It is no trouble to me to repeat what I have already
written to you, and as far as you are concerned, it will

2 make for safety. ·Beware of dogs! Watch out for the people who are making mischief. Watch out for the cut-
3 ters.[b] ·We are the real people of the circumcision, we who worship in accordance with the Spirit of God; we have our own glory from Christ Jesus without having to rely on
4 a physical operation. ·If it came to relying on physical evidence, I should be fully qualified myself. Take any man who thinks he can rely on what is physical: I am even
5 better qualified. ·I was born of the race of Israel and of the tribe of Benjamin, a Hebrew born of Hebrew parents, and I was circumcised when I was eight days old. As for
6 the Law, I was a Pharisee; ·as for working for religion, I was a persecutor of the Church; as far as the Law can
7 make you perfect, I was faultless. ·But because of Christ, I have come to consider all these advantages that I had as
8 disadvantages. ·Not only that, but I believe nothing can happen that will outweigh the supreme advantage of know-ing Christ Jesus my Lord. For him I have accepted the loss of everything, and I look on everything as so much
9 rubbish if only I can have Christ ·and be given a place in him. I am no longer trying for perfection by my own efforts, the perfection that comes from the Law, but I want only the perfection that comes through faith in
10 Christ, and is from God and based on faith. ·All I want is to know Christ and the power of his resurrection and to share his sufferings by reproducing the pattern of his death.
11 That is the way I can hope to take my place in the resur-
12 rection of the dead. ·Not that I have become perfect yet: I have not yet won, but I am still running, trying to cap-
13 ture the prize for which Christ Jesus captured me. ·I can assure you my brothers, I am far from thinking that I have already won. All I can say is that I forget the past and I
14 strain ahead for what is still to come; ·I am racing for the finish, for the prize to which God calls us upward to
15 receive in Christ Jesus. ·We who are called "perfect" must all think in this way. If there is some point on which you see things differently, God will make it clear to you;

c. Dt 32:5   d. Libations were common to Greek and Jewish sacrifices.
3 a. Paul's conclusion is interrupted by a long postscript.
b. A contemptuous reference to the circumcisers comparing circumcision with self-inflicted gashes in pagan cults.

¹⁶ meanwhile, let us go forward on the road that has brought us to where we are.

¹⁷ My brothers, be united in following my rule of life. Take as your models everybody who is already doing this ¹⁸ and study them as you used to study us. ·I have told you often, and I repeat it today with tears, there are many who are behaving as the enemies of the cross of Christ. ¹⁹ They are destined to be lost. They make foods into their god and they are proudest of something they ought to think shameful; the things they think important are earthly ²⁰ things. ·For us, our homeland is in heaven, and from heaven comes the savior we are waiting for, the Lord ²¹ Jesus Christ, ·and he will transfigure these wretched bodies of ours into copies of his glorious body. He will do that by the same power with which he can subdue the whole universe.

¹ **4** So then, my brothers and dear friends, do not give way but remain faithful in the Lord. I miss you very much, dear friends; you are my joy and my crown.

Last advice

² I appeal to Evodia and I appeal to Syntyche to come ³ to agreement with each other, in the Lord; ·and I ask you, Syzygus,^a to be truly a "companion" and to help them in this. These women were a help to me when I was fighting to defend the Good News—and so, at the same time, were Clement and the others who worked with me. Their names are written in the book of life.

⁴ I want you to be happy, always happy in the Lord; I ⁵ repeat, what I want is your happiness. ·Let your tolerance ⁶ be evident to everyone: the Lord is very near. ·There is no need to worry; but if there is anything you need, pray for it, asking God for it with prayer and thanksgiving, ⁷ and that peace of God, which is so much greater than we can understand, will guard your hearts and your thoughts, ⁸ in Christ Jesus. ·Finally, brothers, fill your minds with everything that is true, everything that is noble, everything that is good and pure, everything that we love and honor, and everything that can be thought virtuous or worthy of ⁹ praise. ·Keep doing all the things that you learned from me and have been taught by me and have heard or seen that I do. Then the God of peace will be with you.

Thanks for help received

10 It is a great joy to me, in the Lord, that at last you have shown some concern for me again; though of course you were concerned before, and only lacked an opportunity.
11 I am not talking about shortage of money: I have learned
12 to manage on whatever I have, ·I know how to be poor and I know how to be rich too. I have been through my initiation and now I am ready for anything anywhere: full
13 stomach or empty stomach, poverty or plenty. ·There is nothing I cannot master with the help of the One who
14 gives me strength. ·All the same, it was good of you to
15 share with me in my hardships. ·In the early days of the Good News, as you people of Philippi well know, when I left Macedonia, no other church helped me with gifts of
16 money. You were the only ones; ·and twice since my stay
17 in Thessalonika you have sent me what I needed. ·It is not your gift that I value; what is valuable to me is the interest
18 that is mounting up in your account. ·Now for the time being I have everything that I need and more: I am fully provided now that I have received from Epaphroditus the offering that you sent, *a sweet fragrance*—the sacrifice
19 that God accepts and finds pleasing. ·In return my God will fulfill all your needs, in Christ Jesus, as lavishly as only
20 God can. ·Glory to God, our Father, for ever and ever. Amen.

Greetings and final wish

21 My greetings to every one of the saints in Christ Jesus.
22 The brothers who are with me send their greetings. ·All the saints send their greetings, especially those of the im-
23 perial household.[b] ·May the grace of the Lord Jesus Christ be with your spirit.

4 a. "Companion" is the meaning of the proper name Syzygus.
b. I.e. in the service of the emperor.

Colossians

THE LETTER OF PAUL
TO THE CHURCH AT COLOSSAE

Preface

Address

¹ ² From Paul, appointed by God to be an apostle of Christ Jesus, and from our brother Timothy ·to the saints in Colossae, our faithful brothers in Christ: Grace and peace to you from God our Father.

Thanksgiving and prayer

³ We have never failed to remember you in our prayers and to give thanks for you to God, the Father of our Lord ⁴ Jesus Christ, ·ever since we heard about your faith in Christ Jesus and the love that you show toward all the ⁵ saints ·because of the hope which is stored up for you in heaven. It is only recently that you heard of this, when it was announced in the message of the truth. The Good ⁶ News ·which has reached you is spreading all over the world and producing the same results as it has among you ever since the day when you heard about God's ⁷ grace and understood what this really is. ·Epaphras, who taught you, is one of our closest fellow workers and a ⁸ faithful deputy for us as Christ's servant, ·and it was he who told us all about your love in the Spirit.

⁹ That will explain why, ever since the day he told us, we have never failed to pray for you, and what we ask God is that through perfect wisdom and spiritual understanding ¹⁰ you should reach the fullest knowledge of his will. ·So you will be able to lead the kind of life which the Lord expects of you, a life acceptable to him in all its aspects; showing the results in all the good actions you do and increasing ¹¹ your knowledge of God. ·You will have in you the strength, based on his own glorious power, never to give ¹² in, but to bear anything joyfully, ·thanking the Father

who has made it possible for you to join the saints and
with them to inherit the light.

¹³ Because that is what he has done: he has taken us out
of the power of darkness and created a place for us in
¹⁴ the kingdom of the Son that he loves, ·and in him, we
gain our freedom, the forgiveness of our sins.

I. FORMAL INSTRUCTION

Christ is the head of all creation

¹⁵ He is the image of the unseen God
and the first-born of all creation,
¹⁶ for in him were created
all things in heaven and on earth:
everything visible and everything invisible,
Thrones, Dominations, Sovereignties, Powers—
all things were created through him and for him.
¹⁷ Before anything was created, he existed,
and he holds all things in unity.
¹⁸ Now the Church is his body,
he is its head.

As he is the Beginning,
he was first to be born from the dead,
so that he should be first in every way;
¹⁹ because God wanted all perfection
to be found in him
²⁰ and all things to be reconciled through him and for him,
everything in heaven and everything on earth,
when he made peace
by his death on the cross.

The Colossians have their share in salvation

²¹ Not long ago, you were foreigners and enemies, in the
way that you used to think and the evil things that you did;
²² but now he has reconciled you, by his death and in that
mortal body. Now you are able to appear before him holy,
²³ pure and blameless—·as long as you persevere and stand
firm on the solid base of the faith, never letting yourselves drift away from the hope promised by the Good
News, which you have heard, which has been preached
to the whole human race, and of which I, Paul, have become the servant.

Paul's labors in the service of the pagans

24   It makes me happy to suffer for you, as I am suffering now, and in my own body to do what I can to make up all that has still to be undergone by Christ for the sake 25 of his body, the Church. ·I became the servant of the Church when God made me responsible for delivering 26 God's message to you, ·the message which was a mystery hidden for generations and centuries and has now been 27 revealed to his saints. ·It was God's purpose to reveal it to them and to show all the rich glory of this mystery to pagans. The mystery is Christ among you, your hope of 28 glory: ·this is the Christ we proclaim, this is the wisdom in which we thoroughly train everyone and instruct every- 29 one, to make them all perfect in Christ. ·It is for this I struggle wearily on, helped only by his power driving me irresistibly.

Paul's concern for the Colossians' faith

1 2 Yes, I want you to know that I do have to struggle hard for you, and for those in Laodicea, and for so 2 many others who have never seen me face to face. ·It is all to bind you together in love and to stir your minds, so that your understanding may come to full development, 3 until you really know God's secret ·in which all the jewels of wisdom and knowledge are hidden.

4   I say this to make sure that no one deceives you with 5 specious arguments. ·I may be absent in body, but in spirit I am there among you, delighted to find you all in harmony and to see how firm your faith in Christ is.

II. A WARNING AGAINST SOME ERRORS

Live according to the true faith in Christ, not according to false teaching

6   You must live your whole life according to the Christ 7 you have received—Jesus the Lord; ·you must be rooted in him and built on him and held firm by the faith you have been taught, and full of thanksgiving.

8 · Make sure that no one traps you and deprives you of your freedom by some secondhand, empty, rational philosophy based on the principles of this world instead of on Christ.

Christ alone is the true head of men and angels

9 In his body lives the fullness of divinity, and in him you
10 too find your own fulfillment, ·in the one who is the head of every Sovereignty and Power.[a]

11 In him you have been circumcised, with a circumcision not performed by human hand, but by the complete stripping of your body of flesh. This is circumcision according
12 to Christ. ·You have been buried with him, when you were baptized; and by baptism, too, you have been raised up with him through your belief in the power of God
13 who raised him from the dead. ·You were dead, because you were sinners and had not been circumcised: he[b] has brought you to life with him, he has forgiven us all our sins.

14 He has overridden the Law, and canceled every record of the debt that we had to pay; he has done away with
15 it by nailing it to the cross;[c] ·and so he got rid of the Sovereignties and the Powers, and paraded them in public, behind him in his triumphal procession.[d]

Against the false asceticism based on "the principles of this world"

16 From now onward, never let anyone else decide what you should eat or drink, or whether you are to observe
17 annual festivals, New Moons or sabbaths. ·These were only pale reflections of what was coming: the reality is Christ.
18 Do not be taken in by people who like groveling to angels and worshiping them; people like that are always going on about some vision they have had, inflating themselves
19 to a false importance with their worldly outlook. ·A man of this sort is not united to the head, and it is the head that adds strength and holds the whole body together, with all its joints and sinews—and this is the only way in which it can reach its full growth in God.
20 If you have really died with Christ to the principles of this world, why do you still let rules dictate to you, as
21 though you were still living in the world? ·"It is forbidden to pick up this, it is forbidden to taste that, it is forbidden
22 to touch something else"; ·all these prohibitions are only

2 a. I.e. over the highest orders of angels.   b. God the Father.
c. Destroying our death warrant.   d. The tradition was that the Law was brought down to Moses by angels.

concerned with things that perish by their very use—an
28 example of *human doctrines and regulations!*[e] ·It may be
argued that true wisdom is to be found in these, with their
self-imposed devotions, their self-abasement, and their
severe treatment of the body; but once the flesh starts to
protest, they are no use at all.

Life-giving union with the glorified Christ

1 **3** Since you have been brought back to true life with
Christ, you must look for the things that are in heaven,
2 where Christ is, sitting at God's right hand. ·Let your
thoughts be on heavenly things, not on the things that are
3 on the earth, ·because you have died, and now the life you
4 have is hidden with Christ in God. ·But when Christ is revealed—and he is your life—you too will be revealed in all
your glory with him.

III. EXHORTATION

General rules of Christian behavior

5 That is why you must kill everything in you that belongs
only to earthly life: fornication, impurity, guilty passion,
evil desires and especially greed, which is the same thing
6 as worshiping a false god; ·all this is the sort of behavior
7 that makes God angry. ·And it is the way in which you
used to live when you were surrounded by people doing
8 the same thing, ·but now you, of all people, must give all
these things up: getting angry, being bad-tempered, spite-
9 fulness, abusive language and dirty talk; ·and never tell
each other lies. You have stripped off your old behavior
10 with your old self, ·and you have put on a new self which
will progress toward true knowledge the more it is re-
11 newed in the image of its creator; ·and in that image there
is no room for distinction between Greek and Jew, between the circumcised or the uncircumcised, or between
barbarian and Scythian, slave and free man. There is only
Christ: he is everything and he is in everything.
12 You are God's chosen race, his saints; he loves you, and
you should be clothed in sincere compassion, in kindness
18 and humility, gentleness and patience. ·Bear with one another; forgive each other as soon as a quarrel begins. The
14 Lord has forgiven you; now you must do the same. ·Over

all these clothes, to keep them together and complete them,
15 put on love. ·And may the peace of Christ reign in your
hearts, because it is for this that you were called together
as parts of one body. Always be thankful.
16   Let the message of Christ, in all its richness, find a home
with you. Teach each other, and advise each other, in all
wisdom. With gratitude in your hearts sing psalms and
17 hymns and inspired songs to God; ·and never say or do
anything except in the name of the Lord Jesus, giving
thanks to God the Father through him.

The morals of the home and household

18   Wives, give way to your husbands, as you should in the
19 Lord. ·Husbands, love your wives and treat them with
20 gentleness. ·Children, be obedient to your parents always,
21 because that is what will please the Lord. ·Parents, never
drive your children to resentment or you will make them
feel frustrated.
22   Slaves, be obedient to the men who are called your
masters in this world; not only when you are under their
eye, as if you had only to please men, but wholeheartedly,
23 out of respect for the Master. ·Whatever your work is,
put your heart into it as if it were for the Lord and not
24 for men, ·knowing that the Lord will repay you by making
you his heirs. It is Christ the Lord that you are serving;
25 anyone who does wrong will be repaid in kind and he does
1 not favor one person more than another. 4 Masters, make
sure that your slaves are given what is just and fair, knowing that you too have a Master in heaven.

The apostolic spirit

2   Be persevering in your prayers and be thankful as you
3 stay awake to pray. ·Pray for us especially, asking God
to show us opportunities for announcing the message and
proclaiming the mystery of Christ, for the sake of which
4 I am in chains; ·pray that I may proclaim it as clearly as
I ought.
5   Be tactful with those who are not Christians and be sure
6 you make the best use of your time with them. ·Talk to
them agreeably and with a flavor of wit, and try to fit
your answers to the needs of each one.

e. Is 29:13

Personal news

7 Tychicus will tell you all the news about me. He is a brother I love very much, and a loyal helper and com-
8 panion in the service of the Lord. ·I am sending him to you precisely for this purpose: to give you news about us
9 and to reassure you. ·With him I am sending Onesimus, that dear and faithful brother who is a fellow citizen of yours. They will tell you everything that is happening here.

Greetings and final wishes

10 Aristarchus, who is here in prison with me, sends his greetings, and so does Mark, the cousin of Barnabas—you were sent some instructions about him; if he comes to you,
11 give him a warm welcome—·and Jesus Justus adds his greetings. Of all those who have come over from the Circumcision, these are the only ones actually working with me for the kingdom of God. They have been a great com-
12 fort to me. ·Epaphras, your fellow citizen, sends his greetings; this servant of Christ Jesus never stops battling for you, praying that you will never lapse but always hold
13 perfectly and securely to the will of God. ·I can testify for him that he works hard for you, as well as for those at
14 Laodicea and Hierapolis. ·Greetings from my dear friend Luke, the doctor, and also from Demas.
15 Please give my greetings to the brothers at Laodicea and to Nympha and the church which meets in her house.
16 After this letter has been read among you, send it on to be read in the church of the Laodiceans; and get the letter
17 from Laodicea for you to read yourselves. ·Give Archippus this message, "Remember the service that the Lord wants you to do, and try to carry it out."
18 Here is a greeting in my own handwriting—PAUL. Remember the chains I wear. Grace be with you.

1 Thessalonians

THE FIRST LETTER OF PAUL TO THE CHURCH IN THESSALONIKA

Address

1 ¹ From Paul, Silvanus and Timothy, to the Church in Thessalonika which is in God the Father and the Lord Jesus Christ; wishing you grace and peace.

Thanksgiving and congratulations

² We always mention you in our prayers and thank God ³ for you all, ·and constantly remember before God our Father how you have shown your faith in action, worked for love and persevered through hope, in our Lord Jesus Christ.

⁴ We know, brothers, that God loves you and that you ⁵ have been chosen, ·because when we brought the Good News to you, it came to you not only as words, but as power and as the Holy Spirit and as utter conviction. And you observed the sort of life we lived when we were with ⁶ you, which was for your instruction, ·and you were led to become imitators of us, and of the Lord; and it was with the joy of the Holy Spirit that you took to the gospel, ⁷ in spite of the great opposition all round you. ·This has made you the great example to all believers in Macedonia ⁸ and Achaia ·since it was from you that the word of the Lord started to spread—and not only throughout Macedonia and Achaia, for the news of your faith in God has spread everywhere. We do not need to tell other people ⁹ about it: ·other people tell us how we started the work among you, how you broke with idolatry when you were converted to God and became servants of the real, living ¹⁰ God; ·and how you are now waiting for Jesus, his Son, whom he raised from the dead, to come from heaven to save us from the retribution which is coming.

Paul's example in Thessalonika

1 2 You know yourselves, my brothers, that our visit to you has not proved ineffectual.

2 We had, as you know, been given rough treatment and been grossly insulted at Philippi, and it was our God who gave us the courage to proclaim his Good News to you

3 in the face of great opposition. ·We have not taken to preaching because we are deluded, or immoral, or trying

4 to deceive anyone; ·it was God who decided that we were fit to be entrusted with the Good News, and when we are speaking, we are not trying to please men but God, *who*

5 *can read* our *inmost thoughts.*ᵃ ·You know very well, and we can swear it before God, that never at any time have our speeches been simply flattery, or a cover for trying to

6 get money; ·nor have we ever looked for any special

7 honor from men, either from you or anybody else, ·when we could have imposed ourselves on you with full weight, as apostles of Christ.

Instead, we were unassuming. Like a mother feeding

8 and looking after her own children, ·we felt so devoted and protective toward you, and had come to love you so much, that we were eager to hand over to you not only the

9 Good News but our whole lives as well. ·Let me remind you, brothers, how hard we used to·work, slaving night and day so as not to be a burden on any one of you while we

10 were proclaiming God's Good News to you. ·You are witnesses, and so is God, that our treatment of you, since you

11 became believers, has been impeccably right and fair. ·You can remember how we treated every one of you as a father

12 treats his children, ·teaching you what was right, encouraging you and appealing to you to live a life worthy of God, who is calling you to share the glory of his kingdom.

The faith and the patience of the Thessalonians

13 Another reason why we constantly thank God for you is that as soon as you heard the message that we brought you as God's message, you accepted it for what it really is, God's message and not some human thinking; and it is

14 still a living power among you who believe it. ·For you, my brothers, have been like the churches of God in Christ Jesus which are in Judaea, in suffering the same treatment from your own countrymen as they have suffered from

15 the Jews, ·the people who put the Lord Jesus to death,

and the prophets too. And now they have been persecuting us, and acting in a way that cannot please God and makes
16 them the enemies of the whole human race, ·because they are hindering us from preaching to the pagans and trying to save them. They never stop trying *to finish off the sins they have begun,*[b] but retribution is overtaking them at last.

Paul's anxiety

17 A short time after we had been separated from you—in body but never in thought, brothers—we had an especially strong desire and longing to see you face to face again,
18 and we tried hard to come and visit you; I, Paul, tried
19 more than once, but Satan prevented us. ·What do you think is our pride and our joy? You are; and you will be *the crown* of which we shall be *proudest* in the presence
20 of our Lord Jesus when he comes; ·you are our pride and our joy.

Timothy's mission to Thessalonika

1 3 When we could not bear the waiting any longer, we decided it would be best to be left without a companion
2 at Athens, and ·sent our brother Timothy, who is God's helper in spreading the Good News of Christ, to keep you
3 firm and strong in the faith ·and prevent any of you from being unsettled by the present troubles. As you know, these
4 are bound to come our way: ·when we were with you, we warned you that we must expect to have persecutions to bear, and that is what has happened now, as you have
5 found out. ·That is why, when I could not stand waiting any longer, I sent to assure myself of your faith: I was afraid the Tempter[a] might have tried you too hard, and all our work might have been wasted.

Paul thanks God for good reports of the Thessalonians

6 However, Timothy is now back from you and he has given us good news of your faith and your love, telling us that you always remember us with pleasure and want to
7 see us quite as much as we want to see you. ·And so, brothers, your faith has been a great comfort to us in the

2 a. Jr 11:20　b. 2 M 6:14
3 a. I.e. "the one who puts you to the test."

⁸ middle of our own troubles and sorrows; ·now we can breathe again, as you are still holding firm in the Lord. ⁹ How can we thank God enough for you, for all the joy ¹⁰ we feel before our God on your account? ·We are earnestly praying night and day to be able to see you face to face again and make up any shortcomings in your faith. ¹¹ May God our Father himself, and our Lord Jesus Christ, ¹² make it easy for us to come to you. ·May the Lord be generous in increasing your love and make you love one another and the whole human race as much as we love ¹³ you. ·And may he so confirm your hearts in holiness that you may be blameless in the sight of our God and Father when our Lord Jesus Christ comes *with all his saints*.

Live in holiness and charity

¹ **4** Finally, brothers, we urge you and appeal to you in the Lord Jesus to make more and more progress in the kind of life that you are meant to live: the life that God wants, as you learned from us, and as you are already living it. ² You have not forgotten the instructions we gave you on the authority of the Lord Jesus. ³ What God wants is for you all to be holy. He wants ⁴ you to keep away from fornication, ·and each one of you to know how to use the body that belongs to him*ᵃ* in a way ⁵ that is holy and honorable, ·not giving way to selfish lust ⁶ like *the pagans who do not know God.ᵇ* ·He wants nobody at all ever to sin by taking advantage of a brother in these matters; the Lord always punishes sins of that sort, as we ⁷ told you before and assured you. ·We have been called by ⁸ God to be holy, not to be immoral; ·in other words, anyone who objects is not objecting to a human authority, but to God, *who gives you his* Holy *Spirit.ᶜ* ⁹ As for loving our brothers, there is no need for anyone to write to you about that, since you have learned from ¹⁰ God yourselves to love one another, ·and in fact this is what you are doing with all the brothers throughout the whole of Macedonia. However, we do urge you, brothers, ¹¹ to go on making even greater progress ·and to make a point of living quietly, attending to your own business and ¹² earning your living, just as we told you to, ·so that you are seen to be respectable by those outside the Church, though you do not have to depend on them.

The dead and the living at the time of the Lord's coming

¹³ We want you to be quite certain, brothers, about those who have died,^d to make sure that you do not grieve about ¹⁴ them, like the other people who have no hope. •We believe that Jesus died and rose again, and that it will be the same for those who have died in Jesus: God will bring ¹⁵ them with him. •We can tell you this from the Lord's own teaching, that any of us who are left alive until the Lord's coming will not have any advantage over those who have ¹⁶ died. •At the trumpet of God, the voice of the archangel will call out the command and the Lord himself will come down from heaven; those who have died in Christ will be ¹⁷ the first to rise, •and then those of us who are still alive will be taken up in the clouds, together with them, to meet the Lord in the air. So we shall stay with the Lord for ever. ¹⁸ With such thoughts as these you should comfort one another.

Watchfulness while awaiting the coming of the Lord

¹ **5** You will not be expecting us to write anything to you, ² brothers, about "times and seasons," •since you know very well that the Day of the Lord is going to come like a ³ thief in the night. •It is when people are saying, "How quiet and peaceful it is" that the worst suddenly happens, as suddenly as labor pains come on a pregnant woman; and there will be no way for anybody to evade it.

⁴ But it is not as if you live in the dark, my brothers, for ⁵ that Day to overtake you like a thief. •No, you are all sons of light and sons of the day: we do not belong to the ⁶ night or to darkness, •so we should not go on sleeping, as everyone else does, but stay wide awake and sober. ⁷ Night is the time for sleepers to sleep and drunkards to ⁸ be drunk, •but we belong to the day and we should be sober; let us put on faith and love for a *breastplate*, and ⁹ the hope of *salvation* for a *helmet*. •God never meant us to experience the Retribution, but to win salvation through ¹⁰ our Lord Jesus Christ, •who died for us so that, alive or ¹¹ dead, we should still live united to him. •So give encouragement to each other, and keep strengthening one another, as you do already.

4 a. Lit. "the vessel that is his": either his own body or his wife's. b. Jr 10:25; Ps 79:6   c. Ezk 37:14   d. Lit. "those who are sleeping."

Some demands made by life in community

12 We appeal to you, my brothers, to be considerate to those who are working amongst you and are above you
13 in the Lord as your teachers. ·Have the greatest respect and affection for them because of their work.

14 Be at peace among yourselves. ·And this is what we ask you to do, brothers: warn the idlers, give courage to those who are apprehensive, care for the weak and be pa-
15 tient with everyone. ·Make sure that people do not try to take revenge; you must all think of what is best for each
16,17 other and for the community. ·Be happy at all times; ·pray
18 constantly; ·and for all things give thanks to God, because this is what God expects you to do in Christ Jesus.

19,20 Never try to suppress the Spirit ·or treat the gift of
21 prophecy with contempt; ·think before you do anything
22 —hold on to what is good ·and *avoid every* form of *evil*.

Closing prayer and farewell

23 May the God of peace make you perfect and holy; and may you all be kept safe and blameless, spirit, soul and
24 body, for the coming of our Lord Jesus Christ. ·God has called you and he will not fail you.

25 Pray for us, my brothers.

26,27 Greet all the brothers with the holy kiss. ·My orders, in the Lord's name, are that this letter is to be read to all the brothers.

28 The grace of our Lord Jesus Christ be with you.

2 Thessalonians

THE SECOND LETTER OF PAUL TO THE CHURCH IN THESSALONIKA

Address

1 ¹ From Paul, Silvanus and Timothy, to the Church in Thessalonika which is in God our Father and the Lord ² Jesus Christ; ·wishing you grace and peace from God the Father and the Lord Jesus Christ.

Thanksgiving and encouragement. The Last Judgment

³ We feel we must be continually thanking God for you, brothers; quite rightly, because your faith is growing so wonderfully and the love that you have for one another ⁴ never stops increasing; ·and among the churches of God we can take special pride in you for your constancy and faith under all the persecutions and troubles you have to ⁵ bear. ·It all shows that God's judgment is just, and the purpose of it is that you may be found worthy of the kingdom of God; it is for the sake of this that you are suffering now.

⁶ God will very rightly repay with injury those who are ⁷ injuring you, ·and reward you, who are suffering now, with the same peace as he will give us, when the Lord Jesus appears from heaven with the angels of his power. ⁸ He will come *in flaming fire* to impose the penalty on *all who do not acknowledge God*[a] and *refuse to accept* the ⁹ Good News of our Lord Jesus. ·It will be their punishment to be lost eternally, excluded *from the presence of the Lord* ¹⁰ *and from the glory of his strength* ·*on that day* when he comes *to be glorified among his saints* and *seen in his*

1 a. God's *coming in fire* is quoted from Is 66:15; the penalty on *those who do not acknowledge him* is a quotation from Jr 10:25.

glory[b] by all who believe in him; and you are believers, through our witness.

11 Knowing this, we pray continually that our God will make you worthy of his call, and by his power fulfill all your desires for goodness and complete all that you have 12 been doing through faith; ·because in this way *the name* of our Lord Jesus Christ *will be glorified* in you and you in him, by the grace of our God and the Lord Jesus Christ.

The coming of the Lord and the prelude to it

1 To turn now, brothers, to the coming of our Lord Jesus Christ and how we shall all be gathered round him: 2 please do not get excited too soon or alarmed by any prediction or rumor or any letter claiming to come from us, implying that the Day of the Lord has already arrived. 3 Never let anyone deceive you in this way.

It cannot happen until the Great Revolt has taken place 4 and the Rebel, the Lost One, has appeared. ·This is the Enemy, the one who claims to be so much *greater than all* that men call "god," so much greater than anything that is worshiped, that *he enthrones himself* in *God's* sanctuary 5 and claims that he is God. ·Surely you remember me telling 6 you about this when I was with you? ·And you know, too, what is still holding him back from appearing before his 7 appointed time. ·Rebellion is at its work already, but in secret, and the one who is holding it back has first to be 8 removed ·before the Rebel appears openly. The Lord *will kill him with the breath of his mouth*[a] and will annihilate him with his glorious appearance at his coming.

9 But when the Rebel comes, Satan will set to work: there will be all kinds of miracles and a deceptive show of signs 10 and portents, ·and everything evil that can deceive those who are bound for destruction because they would not grasp the love of the truth which could have saved them. 11 The reason why God is sending a power to delude them 12 and make them believe what is untrue ·is to condemn all who refused to believe in the truth and chose wickedness instead.

Encouragement to persevere

13 But we feel that we must be continually thanking God for you, brothers whom the Lord loves, because God chose you from the beginning to be saved by the sanctifying 14 Spirit and by faith in the truth. ·Through the Good News

that we brought he called you to this so that you should
15 share the glory of our Lord Jesus Christ. ·Stand firm, then,
brothers, and keep the traditions that we taught you,
16 whether by word of mouth or by letter. ·May our Lord
Jesus Christ himself, and God our Father who has given
us his love and, through his grace, such inexhaustible com-
17 fort and such sure hope, ·comfort you and strengthen you
in everything good that you do or say.

1 **3** Finally, brothers, pray for us; pray that the Lord's message may spread quickly, and be received with honour
2 as it was among you; ·and pray that we may be preserved
from the interference of bigoted and evil people, for faith
8 is not given to everyone. ·But the Lord is faithful, and he
will give you strength and guard you from the evil one,
4 and we, in the Lord, have every confidence that you are
5 doing and will go on doing all that we tell you. ·May the
Lord turn your hearts toward the love of God and the
fortitude of Christ.

Against idleness and disunity

6   In the name of the Lord Jesus Christ, we urge you,
brothers, to keep away from any of the brothers who refuses to work or to live according to the tradition we passed
on to you.
7   You know how you are supposed to imitate us: now we
8 were not idle when we were with you, ·nor did we ever
have our meals at anyone's table without paying for them;
no, we worked night and day, slaving and straining, so as
9 not to be a burden on any of you. ·This was not because
we had no right to be, but in order to make ourselves an
example for you to follow.
10   We gave you a rule when we were with you: not to let
11 anyone have any food if he refused to do any work. ·Now
we hear that there are some of you who are living in idle-
ness, doing no work themselves but interfering with every-
12 one else's. ·In the Lord Jesus Christ, we order and call on
people of this kind to go on quietly working and earning
the food that they eat.
13   My brothers, never grow tired of doing what is right.
14 If anyone refuses to obey what I have written in this letter,
take note of him and have nothing to do with him, so that

b. Quotations from Is 2:10-17; 49:3; 66:5.
2 a. Is 11:4

1 Timothy

THE FIRST LETTER
FROM PAUL TO TIMOTHY

Address

¹ From Paul, apostle of Christ Jesus appointed by the command of God our savior and of Christ Jesus our ² hope, ·to Timothy, true child of mine in the faith; wishing you grace, mercy and peace from God the Father and from Christ Jesus our Lord.

Suppress the false teachers

³ As I asked you when I was leaving for Macedonia, please stay at Ephesus, to insist that certain people stop ⁴ teaching strange doctrines ·and taking notice of myths and endless genealogies; these things are only likely to raise irrelevant doubts instead of furthering the designs of God ⁵ which are revealed in faith. ·The only purpose of this instruction is that there should be love, coming out of a pure ⁶ heart, a clear conscience and a sincere faith. ·There are some people who have gone off the straight course and ⁷ taken a road that leads to empty speculation; ·they claim to be doctors of the Law but they understand neither the arguments they are using nor the opinions they are upholding.

The purpose of the Law

⁸ We know, of course, that the Law is good, but only ⁹ provided it is treated like any law, ·in the understanding that laws are not framed for people who are good. On the contrary, they are for criminals and revolutionaries, for the irreligious and the wicked, for the sacrilegious and the irreverent; they are for people who kill their fathers or moth- ¹⁰ ers and for murderers, ·for those who are immoral with women or with boys or with men, for liars and for perjurers—and for everything else that is contrary to the sound

11 teaching ·that goes with the Good News of the glory of the
blessed God, the gospel that was entrusted to me.

Paul on his own calling

12   I thank Christ Jesus our Lord, who has given me
strength, and who judged me faithful enough to call me
13 into his service ·even though I used to be a blasphemer
and did all I could to injure and discredit the faith. Mercy,
however, was shown me, because until I became a believer
14 I had been acting in ignorance; ·and the grace of our Lord
filled me with faith and with the love that is in Christ Jesus.
15 Here is a saying that you can rely on and nobody should
doubt: that Christ Jesus came into the world to save sin-
16 ners. I myself am the greatest of them; ·and if mercy has
been shown to me, it is because Jesus Christ meant to make
me the greatest evidence of his inexhaustible patience for
all the other people who would later have to trust in him
17 to come to eternal life. ·To the eternal King, the undying,
invisible and only God, be honor and glory for ever and
ever. Amen.

Timothy's responsibility

18   Timothy, my son, these are the instructions that I am
giving you: I ask you to remember the words once spoken
over you by the prophets, and taking them to heart to fight
19 like a good soldier ·with faith and a good conscience for
your weapons. Some people have put conscience aside and
20 wrecked their faith in consequence. ·I mean men like
Hymenaeus and Alexander, whom I have handed over to
Satan to teach them not to be blasphemous.

Liturgical prayer

1 2 My advice is that, first of all, there should be prayers offered for everyone—petitions, intercessions and thanks-
2 giving—·and especially for kings and others in authority,
so that we may be able to live religious and reverent lives
3 in peace and quiet. ·To do this is right, and will please
4 God our savior: ·he wants everyone to be saved and
5 reach full knowledge of the truth. ·For there is only one
God, and there is only one mediator between God and
6 mankind, himself a man, Christ Jesus, ·who sacrificed himself as a ransom for them all. He is the evidence of this,
7 sent at the appointed time, and ·I have been named a

herald and apostle of it and—I am telling the truth and no lie—a teacher of the faith and the truth to the pagans.

8 In every place, then, I want the men to lift their hands up reverently in prayer, with no anger or argument.

Women in the assembly

9 Similarly, I direct that women are to wear suitable clothes and to be dressed quietly and modestly, without braided hair or gold and jewellery or expensive clothes;
10 their adornment is ·to do the sort of good works that are
11 proper for women who profess to be religious. ·During
12 instruction, a woman should be quiet and respectful. ·I am not giving permission for a woman to teach or to tell a
13 man what to do. A woman ought not to speak, ·because
14 Adam was formed first and Eve afterwards, ·and it was not Adam who was led astray but the woman who was
15 led astray and fell into sin. ·Nevertheless, she will be saved by childbearing, provided she lives a modest life and is constant in faith and love and holiness.

The elder-in-charge

1 3 Here is a saying that you can rely on: To want to be a
2 presiding elder[a] is to want to do a noble work. ·That is why the president must have an impeccable character. He must not have been married more than once, and he must be temperate, discreet and courteous, hospitable and
8 a good teacher; ·not a heavy drinker, nor hot-tempered, but kind and peaceable. He must not be a lover of money.
4 He must be a man who manages his own family well and brings his children up to obey him and be well-behaved:
5 how can any man who does not understand how to manage his own family have responsibility for the church of God?
6 He should not be a new convert, in case pride might turn his head and then he might be condemned as the devil was
7 condemned. ·It is also necessary that people outside the Church should speak well of him, so that he never gets a bad reputation and falls into the devil's trap.

Deacons

8 In the same way, deacons must be respectable men whose word can be trusted, moderate in the amount of

3 a. The word *episcopos* used here by Paul had not yet acquired the same meaning as "bishop."

wine they drink and with no squalid greed for money.
⁹ They must be conscientious believers in the mystery of the
¹⁰ faith. ·They are to be examined first, and only admitted to
¹¹ serve as deacons if there is nothing against them. ·In the
same way, the women must be respectable, not gossips but
¹² sober and quite reliable. ·Deacons must not have been
married more than once, and must be men who manage
¹³ their children and families well. ·Those of them who carry
out their duties well as deacons will earn a high standing
for themselves and be rewarded with great assurance in
their work for the faith in Christ Jesus.

The Church and the mystery of the spiritual life

¹⁴ At the moment of writing to you, I am hoping that I
¹⁵ may be with you soon; ·but in case I should be delayed,
I wanted you to know how people ought to behave in God's
family—that is, in the Church of the living God, which
¹⁶ upholds the truth and keeps it safe. ·Without any doubt,
the mystery of our religion is very deep indeed:

> He was made visible in the flesh,
> attested by the Spirit,
> seen by angels,
> proclaimed to the pagans,
> believed in by the world,
> taken up in glory.

False teachers

¹ **4** The Spirit has explicitly said that during the last times
there will be some who will desert the faith and choose
to listen to deceitful spirits and doctrines that come from
² the devils; ·and the cause of this is the lies told by hypocrites whose consciences are branded as though with a red-
³ hot iron:ᵃ ·they will say marriage is forbidden, and lay
down rules about abstaining from foods which God created
to be accepted with thanksgiving by all who believe and
⁴ who know the truth.ᵇ ·Everything God has created is
good, and no food is to be rejected, provided grace is said
⁵ for it: ·the word of God and the prayer make it holy.
⁶ If you put all this to the brothers, you will be a good
servant of Christ Jesus and show that you have really di-
gested the teaching of the faith and the good doctrine which
⁷ you have always followed. ·Have nothing to do with god-
less myths and old wives' tales. Train yourself spiritually.

8 "Physical exercises are useful enough, but the usefulness
of spirituality is unlimited, since it holds out the reward of
9 life here and now and of the future life as well"; ·that is a
saying that you can rely on and nobody should doubt it.
10 I mean that the point of all our toiling and battling is that
we have put our trust in the living God and he is the savior
of the whole human race but particularly of all believers.
11 This is what you are to enforce in your teaching.
12 Do not let people disregard you because you are young,
but be an example to all the believers in the way you speak
and behave, and in your love, your faith and your purity.
13 Make use of the time until I arrive by reading to the peo-
14 ple, preaching and teaching. ·You have in you a spiritual
gift which was given to you when the prophets spoke and
the body of elders laid their hands on you; do not let it lie
15 unused. ·Think hard about all this, and put it into practice,
and everyone will be able to see how you are advancing.
16 Take great care about what you do and what you teach;
always do this, and in this way you will save both yourself
and those who listen to you.

Pastoral practice

1 Do not speak harshly to a man older than yourself, but
5 advise him as you would your own father; treat the
2 younger men as brothers ·and older women as you would
your mother. Always treat young women with propriety,
as if they were sisters.

Widows

8 Be considerate to widows; I mean those who are truly
4 widows. ·If a widow has children or grandchildren, they
are to learn first of all to do their duty to their own families
and repay their debt to their parents, because this is what
5 pleases God. ·But a woman who is really widowed and
left without anybody can give herself up to God and consecrate all her days and nights to petitions and prayer.
6 The one who thinks only of pleasure is already dead while
7 she is still alive: ·remind them of all this, too, so that their
8 lives may be blameless. ·Anyone who does not look after

4 a. Like runaway slaves. b. The rejection of marriage was
to be one of the hallmarks of Gnosticism; dietary regulations
were more specifically Jewish.

his own relations, especially if they are living with him, has rejected the faith and is worse than an unbeliever.

9 Enrollment as a widow is permissible only for a woman
10 at least sixty years old who has had only one husband. •She must be a woman known for her good works and for the way in which she has brought up her children, shown hospitality to strangers and washed the saints' feet, helped people who are in trouble and been active in all kinds of
11 good work. •Do not accept young widows because if their natural desires get stronger than their dedication to Christ,
12 they want to marry again, •and then people condemn them
13 for being unfaithful to their original promise. •Besides, they learn how to be idle and go round from house to house; and then, not merely idle, they learn to be gossips and meddlers in other people's affairs, and to chatter when
14 they would be better keeping quiet. •I think it is best for young widows to marry again and have children and a home to look after, and not give the enemy any chance
15 to raise a scandal about them; •there are already some
16 who have left us to follow Satan. •If a Christian woman has widowed relatives, she should support them and not make the Church bear the expense but enable it to support those who are genuinely widows.

The elders

17 The elders who do their work well while they are in charge are to be given double consideration, especially
18 those who are assiduous in preaching and teaching. •As scripture says: *You must not muzzle an ox when it is treading out the corn;*[a] and again: *The worker deserves*
19 *his pay.*[b] •Never accept any accusation brought against an elder unless it is supported *by two or three witnesses.*
20 If any of them are at fault, reprimand them publicly, as a
21 warning to the rest. •Before God, and before Jesus Christ and the angels he has chosen, I put it to you as a duty to keep these rules impartially and never to be influenced by
22 favoritism. •Do not be too quick to lay hands on any man, and never make yourself an accomplice in anybody else's sin; keep yourself pure.
23 You should give up drinking only water and have a little wine for the sake of your digestion and the frequent bouts of illness that you have.
24 The faults of some people are obvious long before anyone makes any complaint about them, while others have

²⁵ faults that are not discovered until afterward. ·In the same way, the good that people do can be obvious; but even when it is not, it cannot be hidden for ever.

Slaves

¹ **6** All slaves "under the yoke" must have unqualified respect for their masters, so that the name of God and ² our teaching are not brought into disrepute. ·Slaves whose masters are believers are not to think any the less of them because they are brothers; on the contrary, they should serve them all the better, since those who have the benefit of their services are believers and dear to God.

The true teacher and the false teacher

This is what you are to teach them to believe and per-
³ suade them to do. ·Anyone who teaches anything different, and does not keep to the sound teaching which is that of our Lord Jesus Christ, the doctrine which is in ac-
⁴ cordance with true religion, ·is simply ignorant and must be full of self-conceit—with a craze for questioning everything and arguing about words. All that can come of this is jealousy, contention, abuse and wicked mistrust of
⁵ one another; ·and unending disputes by people who are neither rational nor informed and imagine that religion
⁶ is a way of making a profit. ·Religion, of course, does bring large profits, but only to those who are content with
⁷ what they have. ·We brought nothing into the world, and
⁸ we can take nothing out of it; ·but as long as we have
⁹ food and clothing, let us be content with that. ·People who long to be rich are a prey to temptation; they get trapped into all sorts of foolish and dangerous ambitions which eventually plunge them into ruin and destruction.
¹⁰ "The love of money is the root of all evils" and there are some who, pursuing it, have wandered away from the faith, and so given their souls any number of fatal wounds.

Timothy's vocation recalled

¹¹ But, as a man dedicated to God, you must avoid all that. You must aim to be saintly and religious, filled with
¹² faith and love, patient and gentle. ·Fight the good fight of the faith and win for yourself the eternal life to which you

5 a. Dt 25:4   b. Not traceable in the O.T.; but this is also to be found in Lk 10:7 where, again, it may be a quotation.

were called when you made your profession and spoke up
¹³ for the truth in front of many witnesses. ·Now, before
God the source of all life and before Jesus Christ, who
spoke up as a witness for the truth in front of Pontius
¹⁴ Pilate, I put to you the duty ·of doing all that you have
been told, with no faults or failures, until the Appearing
of our Lord Jesus Christ,

¹⁵   who at the due time will be revealed
       by God, the blessed and only Ruler of all,
       the King of kings and the Lord of lords,
¹⁶   who alone is immortal,
       whose home is in inaccessible light,
       whom no man has seen and no man is able to see:
       to him be honor and everlasting power. Amen.

Rich Christians

¹⁷   Warn those who are rich in this world's goods that
they are not to look down on other people; and not to set
their hopes on money, which is untrustworthy, but on God
who, out of his riches, gives us all that we need for our
¹⁸ happiness. ·Tell them that they are to do good, and be
rich in good works, to be generous and willing to share—
¹⁹ this is the way they can save up a good capital sum for
the future if they want to make sure of the only life that
is real.

Final warning and conclusion

²⁰   My dear Timothy, take great care of all that has
been entrusted to you. Have nothing to do with the pointless philosophical discussions and antagonistic beliefs of
²¹ the "knowledge" which is not knowledge at all; ·by adopting this, some have gone right away from the faith. Grace
be with you.

2 Timothy

THE SECOND LETTER FROM PAUL TO TIMOTHY

Greeting and thanksgiving

1 **1** From Paul, appointed by God to be an apostle of Christ Jesus in his design to promise life in Christ 2 Jesus; ·to Timothy, dear child of mine, wishing you grace, mercy and peace from God the Father and from Christ Jesus our Lord.

3 Night and day I thank God, keeping my conscience clear and remembering my duty to him as my ancestors did, and always I remember you in my prayers; I remem- 4 ber your tears ·and long to see you again to complete my 5 happiness. ·Then I am reminded of the sincere faith which you have; it came first to live in your grandmother Lois, and your mother Eunice, and I have no doubt that it is the same faith in you as well.

The gifts that Timothy has received

6 That is why I am reminding you now to fan into a flame the gift that God gave you when I laid my hands 7 on you. ·God's gift was not a spirit of timidity, but the 8 Spirit of power, and love, and self-control. ·So you are never to be ashamed of witnessing to the Lord, or ashamed of me for being his prisoner; but with me, bear the hardships for the sake of the Good News, relying on the power 9 of God ·who has saved us and called us to be holy— not because of anything we ourselves have done but for his own purpose and by his own grace. ·This grace had already been granted to us, in Christ Jesus, before the 10 beginning of time, ·but it has only been revealed by the Appearing of our savior Christ Jesus. He abolished death, and he has proclaimed life and immortality through 11 the Good News; ·and I have been named its herald, its apostle and its teacher.

¹² It is only on account of this that I am experiencing fresh hardships here now;ᵃ but I have not lost confidence, because I know who it is that I have put my trust in, and I have no doubt at all that he is able to take care of all that I have entrusted to him until that Day.

¹³ Keep as your pattern the sound teaching you have heard from me, in the faith and love that are in Christ
¹⁴ Jesus. ·You have been trusted to look after something precious; guard it with the help of the Holy Spirit who lives in us.

¹⁵ As you know, Phygelus and Hermogenes and all the others from Asia refuse to have anything more to do with
¹⁶ me. ·I hope the Lord will be kind to all the family of Onesiphorus, because he has often been a comfort to me
¹⁷ and has never been ashamed of my chains. ·On the contrary, as soon as he reached Rome, he really searched
¹⁸ hard for me and found out where I was. ·May it be the Lord's will that he shall find the Lord's mercy on that Day. You know better than anyone else how much he helped me at Ephesus.

How Timothy should face hardships

¹ ² Accept the strength, my dear son, that comes from the grace of Christ Jesus. ·You have heard everything that I teach in public; hand it on to reliable people so that they in turn will be able to teach others.
³ Put up with your share of difficulties, like a good soldier
⁴ of Christ Jesus. ·In the army, no soldier gets himself mixed up in civilian life, because he must be at the disposal of
⁵ the man who enlisted him; ·or take an athlete—he cannot win any crown unless he has kept all the rules of the con-
⁶ test; ·and again, it is the working farmer who has the
⁷ first claim on any crop that is harvested. ·Think over what I have said, and the Lord will show you how to understand it all.

⁸ Remember the Good News that I carry, "Jesus Christ risen from the dead, sprung from the race of David";
⁹ it is on account of this that I have my own hardships to bear, even to being chained like a criminal—but they
¹⁰ cannot chain up God's news. ·So I bear it all for the sake of those who are chosen, so that in the end they may have the salvation that is in Christ Jesus and the eternal glory that comes with it.

11 Here is a saying that you can rely on:

If we have died with him, then we shall live with him.
12 If we hold firm, then we shall reign with him.
If we disown him, then he will disown us.
13 We may be unfaithful, but he is always faithful,
for he cannot disown his own self.

The struggle against the immediate danger from false teachers

14   Remind them of this; and tell them in the name of God that there is to be no wrangling about words: all that this ever achieves is the destruction of those who are lis-
15 tening. ·Do all you can to present yourself in front of God as a man who has come through his trials, and a man who has no cause to be ashamed of his life's work and has kept a straight course with the message of the truth.
16 Have nothing to do with pointless philosophical discussions—they only lead further and further away from true
17 religion. ·Talk of this kind corrodes like gangrene, as in
18 the case of Hymenaeus and Philetus, ·the men who have gone right away from the truth and claim that the resurrection has already taken place. Some people's faith cannot stand up to them.
19   However, God's solid foundation stone is still in position, and this is the inscription on it: *"The Lord knows those who are his own"*[a] and *"All who call on the name of the Lord*[b] must avoid sin."
20   Not all the dishes in a large house are made of gold and silver; some are made of wood or earthenware: some are kept for special occasions and others are for ordinary
21 purposes. ·Now, to avoid these faults that I am speaking about is the way for anyone to become a vessel for special occasions, fit for the Master himself to use, and kept ready for any good work.
22   Instead of giving in to your impulses like a young man, fasten your attention on holiness, faith, love and peace, in union with all those who call on the Lord with pure minds.
23 Avoid these futile and silly speculations, understanding
24 that they only give rise to quarrels; ·and a servant of the Lord is not to engage in quarrels, but has to be kind
25 to everyone, a good teacher, and patient. ·He has to be

1 a. The second imprisonment at Rome.
2 a. Nb 16:5,26   b. Is 26:13

gentle when he corrects people who dispute what he says, never forgetting that God may give them a change of
26 mind so that they recognize the truth and ·come to their senses, once out of the trap where the devil caught them and kept them enslaved.

The dangers of the last days

1 **3** You may be quite sure that in the last days there are
2 **3** going to be some difficult times. ·People will be self-centered and grasping; boastful, arrogant and rude; dis-
8 obedient to their parents, ungrateful, irreligious; ·heartless and unappeasable; they will be slanderers, profligates,
4 savages and enemies of everything that is good; ·they will be treacherous and reckless and demented by pride, pre-
5 ferring their own pleasure to God. ·They will keep up the outward appearance of religion but will have rejected the inner power of it. Have nothing to do with people like that.
6 Of the same kind, too, are those men who insinuate themselves into families in order to get influence over silly women who are obsessed with their sins and follow one
7 craze after another ·in the attempt to educate themselves,
8 but can never come to knowledge of the truth. ·Men like this defy the truth just as Jannes and Jambres defied Moses:*a* their minds are corrupt and their faith spurious.
9 But they will not be able to go on any longer: their foolishness, like that of the other two, must become obvious to everybody.
10 You know, though, what I have taught, how I have lived, what I have aimed at; you know my faith, my
11 patience and my love; my constancy ·and the persecutions and hardships that came to me in places like Antioch, Iconium and Lystra—all the persecutions I have endured; and the Lord has rescued me from every one of them.
12 You are well aware, then, that anybody who tries to live in
13 devotion to Christ is certain to be attacked; ·while these wicked impostors will go from bad to worse, deceiving others and deceived themselves.
14 You must keep to what you have been taught and
15 know to be true; remember who your teachers were, ·and how, ever since you were a child, you have known the holy scriptures—from these you can learn the wisdom that
16 leads to salvation through faith in Christ Jesus. ·All scripture is inspired by God and can profitably be used for

teaching, for refuting error, for guiding people's lives and
17 teaching them to be holy. •This is how the man who is dedicated to God becomes fully equipped and ready for any good work.

A solemn charge

1 **4** Before God and before Christ Jesus who is to be judge of the living and the dead, I put this duty to you, in the
2 name of his Appearing and of his kingdom: •proclaim the message and, welcome or unwelcome, insist on it. Refute falsehood, correct error, call to obedience—but do
3 all with patience and with the intention of teaching. •The time is sure to come when, far from being content with sound teaching, people will be avid for the latest novelty and collect themselves a whole series of teachers according
4 to their own tastes; •and then, instead of listening to the
5 truth, they will turn to myths. •Be careful always to choose the right course; be brave under trials; make the preaching of the Good News your life's work, in thoroughgoing service.

Paul in the evening of his life

6 As for me, my life is already being poured away as a
7 libation, and the time has come for me to be gone. •I have fought the good fight to the end; I have run the
8 race to the finish; I have kept the faith; •all there is to come now is the crown of righteousness reserved for me, which the Lord, the righteous judge, will give to me on that Day; and not only to me but to all those who have longed for his Appearing.

Final advice

9 Do your best to come and see me as soon as you can.
10 As it is, Demas has deserted me for love of this life and gone to Thessalonika, Crescens has gone to Galatia and
11 Titus to Dalmatia; •only Luke is with me. Get Mark to come and bring him with you; I find him a useful helper
12 in my work. •I have sent Tychicus to Ephesus. •When you
13 come, bring the cloak I left with Carpus in Troas, and the
14 scrolls, especially the parchment ones. •Alexander the coppersmith has done me a lot of harm; *the Lord will repay*

3 a. In Jewish tradition, the leaders of the Egyptian magicians and disciples of Balaam.

¹⁵ *him for what he has done.*ᵃ ·Be on your guard against
him yourself, because he has been bitterly contesting everything that we say.
¹⁶ The first time I had to present my defense, there was
not a single witness to support me. Every one of them
deserted me—may they not be held accountable for it.
¹⁷ But the Lord stood by me and gave me power, so that
through me the whole message might be proclaimed for all
the pagans to hear; and so I was *rescued from the lion's*
¹⁸ *mouth.*ᵇ ·The Lord will rescue me from all evil attempts
on me, and bring me safely to his heavenly kingdom. To
him be glory for ever and ever. Amen.

Farewells and final good wishes

¹⁹ Greetings to Prisca and Aquila, and the family of Onesi-
²⁰ phorus. ·Erastus remained at Corinth, and I left Trophi-
²¹ mus ill at Miletus. ·Do your best to come before the winter.
Greetings to you from Eubulus, Pudens, Linus, Claudia
and all the brothers.
²² The Lord be with your spirit. Grace be with you.

4 a. Ps 28:4 and 62:12; Pr 24:12   b. Ps 22:21

Titus

THE LETTER FROM PAUL
TO TITUS

Address

¹ **1** From Paul, servant of God, an apostle of Jesus Christ
to bring those whom God has chosen to faith and to
the knowledge of the truth that leads to true religion;
² and to give them the hope of the eternal life that was
³ promised so long ago by God. He does not lie ·and so, at
the appointed time, he revealed his decision, and, by the
command of God our savior, I have been commissioned
⁴ to proclaim it. ·To Titus, true child of mine in the faith
that we share, wishing you grace and peace from God the
Father and from Christ Jesus our savior.

The appointment of elders

⁵ The reason I left you behind in Crete was for you to
get everything organized there and appoint elders in every
⁶ town, in the way that I told you: ·that is, each of them
must be a man of irreproachable character; he must not
have been married more than once, and his children must
be believers and not uncontrollable or liable to be charged
⁷ with disorderly conduct. ·Since, as president, he will be
God's representative, he must be irreproachable: never an
arrogant or hot-tempered man, nor a heavy drinker or
⁸ violent, nor out to make money; ·but a man who is hospitable and a friend of all that is good; sensible, moral,
⁹ devout and self-controlled; ·and he must have a firm grasp
of the unchanging message of the tradition, so that he can
be counted on for both expounding the sound doctrine and
refuting those who argue against it.

Opposing the false teachers

¹⁰ And in fact you have there a great many people who
need to be disciplined, who talk nonsense and try to make

others believe it, particularly among those of the Circum-
11 cision. ·They have got to be silenced: men of this kind
ruin whole families, by teaching things that they ought
not to, and doing it with the vile motive of making money.
12 It was one of themselves, one of their own prophets, who
said,ᵃ "Cretans were never anything but liars, dangerous
13 animals and lazy": ·and that is a true statement. So you
will have to be severe in correcting them, and make them
14 sound in the faith ·so that they stop taking notice of Jewish
myths and doing what they are told to do by people who
are no longer interested in the truth.
15   To all who are pure themselves, everything is pure; but
to those who have been corrupted and lack faith, nothing
can be pure—the corruption is both in their minds and in
16 their consciences. ·They claim to have knowledge of God
but the things they do are nothing but a denial of him;
they are outrageously rebellious and quite incapable of
doing good.

Some specific moral instruction

1 2 It is for you, then, to preach the behavior which goes
2 with healthy doctrine. ·The older men should be reserved, dignified, moderate, sound in faith and love and
3 constancy. ·Similarly, the older women should behave as
though they were religious, with no scandalmongering and
no habitual wine-drinking—they are to be the teachers of
4 the right behavior ·and show the younger women how
they should love their husbands and love their children,
5 how they are to be sensible and chaste, and how to work
in their homes, and be gentle, and do as their husbands
tell them, so that the message of God is never disgraced.
6 In the same way, you have got to persuade the younger
7 men to be moderate ·and in everything you do make yourself an example to them of working for good: when you
are teaching, be an example to them in your sincerity and
8 earnestness ·and in keeping all that you say so wholesome
that nobody can make objections to it; and then any
opponent will be at a loss, with no accusation to make
9 against us. ·Tell the slaves that they are to be obedient to
their masters and always do what they want without any
10 argument; ·and there must be no petty thieving—they must
show complete honesty at all times, so that they are in
every way a credit to the teaching of God our savior.

The basis of the Christian moral life

11 'You see, God's grace has been revealed, and it has made
12 salvation possible for the whole human race ·and taught us
that what we have to do is to give up everything that does
not lead to God, and all our worldly ambitions; we must
be self-restrained and live good and religious lives here in
13 this present world, ·while we are waiting in hope for the
blessing which will come with the Appearing of the glory
14 of our great God and savior Christ Jesus.[a] ·He sacrificed himself for us in order to *set us free from all wickedness*[b] and *to purify a people so that it could be his very
own*[c] and would have no ambition except to do good.
15 Now this is what you are to say, whether you are giving
instruction or correcting errors; you can do so with full
authority, and no one is to question it.

General instruction for believers

1 **3** Remind them that it is their duty to be obedient to
the officials and representatives of the government; to
2 be ready to do good at every opportunity; ·not to go
slandering other people or picking quarrels, but to be
3 courteous and always polite to all kinds of people. ·Remem-
ber, there was a time when we too were ignorant, disobedient and misled and enslaved by different passions
and luxuries; we lived then in wickedness and ill-will,
hating each other and hateful ourselves.
4 But when the kindness and love of God our savior
5 for mankind were revealed, ·it was not because he was
concerned with any righteous actions we might have done
ourselves; it was for no reason except his own compassion
that he saved us, by means of the cleansing water of rebirth
6 and by renewing us with the Holy Spirit ·which he has
so generously poured over us through Jesus Christ our
7 savior. ·He did this so that we should be justified by his
grace, to become heirs looking forward to inheriting eter-
8 nal life. ·This is doctrine that you can rely on.

Personal advice to Titus

I want you to be quite uncompromising in teaching all
this, so that those who now believe in God may keep their

1 a. Attributed to the Cretan poet Epimenides of Knossos.
2 a. Or "our great God and our savior, Christ Jesus." b. Ps
130:8 c. Ex 19:5

minds constantly occupied in doing good works. All this
9 is good, and will do nothing but good to everybody. ·But
avoid pointless speculations, and those genealogies, and
the quibbles and disputes about the Law—these are useless
10 and can do no good to anyone. ·If a man disputes what
you teach, then after a first and a second warning, have
11 no more to do with him: ·you will know that any man
of that sort has already lapsed and condemned himself as
a sinner.

Practical recommendations, farewells and good wishes

12 As soon as I have sent Artemas or Tychicus to you, lose
no time in joining me at Nicopolis, where I have decided
13 to spend the winter. ·See to all the traveling arrangements for Zenas the lawyer and Apollos, and make sure
14 they have everything they need. ·All our people are to
learn to occupy themselves in doing good works for their
practical needs as well, and not to be entirely unproductive.
15 All those who are with me send their greetings. Greetings to those who love us in the faith. Grace be with you
all.

Philemon

THE LETTER FROM PAUL TO PHILEMON

Address

1 From Paul, a prisoner of Christ Jesus and from our brother Timothy; to our dear fellow worker Philemon, 2 our sister Apphia, our fellow soldier Archippus and the 3 church that meets in your house; ·wishing you the grace and the peace of God our Father and the Lord Jesus Christ.

Thanksgiving and prayer

4 I always mention you in my prayers and thank God 5 for you, ·because I hear of the love and the faith which you have for the Lord Jesus and for all the saints. 6 I pray that this faith will give rise to a sense of fellowship that will show you all the good things that we are able to 7 do for Christ. ·I am so delighted, and comforted, to know of your love; they tell me, brother, how you have put new heart into the saints.

The request about Onesimus

8 Now, although in Christ I can have no diffidence about 9 telling you to do whatever is your duty, ·I am appealing to your love instead, reminding you that this is Paul writing, an old man now and, what is more, still a prisoner of 10 Christ Jesus. ·I am appealing to you for a child of mine, whose father I became while wearing these chains: I mean 11 Onesimus. ·He was of no use to you before, but he will 12 be useful[a] to you now, as he has been to me. ·I am sending him back to you, and with him—I could say—a part of 13 my own self. ·I should have liked to keep him with me; he could have been a substitute for you, to help me while I am in the chains that the Good News has brought me.

a. A pun—"Onesimus" means "useful."

¹⁴ However, I did not want to do anything without your consent; it would have been forcing your act of kindness, ¹⁵ which should be spontaneous. ·I know you have been deprived of Onesimus for a time, but it was only so that ¹⁶ you could have him back for ever, ·not as a slave any more, but something much better than a slave, a dear brother; especially dear to me, but how much more to you, as a blood-brother as well as a brother in the Lord. ¹⁷ So if all that we have in common means anything to you, ¹⁸ welcome him as you would me; ·but if he has wronged you in any way or owes you anything, then let me pay for ¹⁹ it. ·I am writing this in my own handwriting: I, Paul, shall pay it back—I will not add any mention of your own ²⁰ debt to me, which is yourself. ·Well then, brother, I am counting on you, in the Lord; put new heart into me, in ²¹ Christ. ·I am writing with complete confidence in your compliance, sure that you will do even more than I ask.

A personal request. Good wishes

²²   There is another thing: will you get a place ready for me to stay in? I am hoping through your prayers to be restored to you.

²³   Epaphras, a prisoner with me in Christ Jesus, sends his ²⁴ greetings; ·so do my colleagues Mark, Aristarchus, Demas and Luke.

²⁵   May the grace of our Lord Jesus Christ be with your spirit.

THE LETTER TO THE
Hebrews

A LETTER ADDRESSED
TO A JEWISH-CHRISTIAN COMMUNITY

PROLOGUE

The greatness of the incarnate Son of God

1 At various times in the past and in various different ways, God spoke to our ancestors through the prophets; 2 but ·in our own time, the last days, he has spoken to us through his Son, the Son that he has appointed to inherit everything and through whom he made everything there 3 is. ·He is the radiant light of God's glory and the perfect copy of his nature, sustaining the universe by his powerful command; and now that he has destroyed the defilement of sin, he has gone to take his place in heaven at the 4 right hand of divine Majesty. ·So he is now as far above the angels as the title which he has inherited is higher than their own name.

I. THE SON IS GREATER THAN THE ANGELS

Proof from the scriptures

5 God has never said to any angel: *You are my Son, today I have become your father;*[a] or: *I will be a father to* 6 *him and he a son to me.*[b] ·Again, when he brings the First-born into the world, he says: *Let all the angels of God* 7 *worship him.*[c] ·About the angels, he says: *He makes his* 8 *angels winds and his servants flames of fire,*[d] ·but to his Son he says: *God, your throne shall last for ever and ever;* and: *his royal sceptre is the sceptre of virtue;* 9 *virtue you love as much as you hate wickedness. This*

1 a. Ps 2:7   b. 2 S 7:14   c. Dt 32:43   d. Ps 104:4

is why God, your God, has anointed you with the
10 *oil of gladness, above all your rivals.*ᵉ ·And again: *It is*
you, Lord, who laid earth's foundations in the beginning,
11 *the heavens are the work of your hands; ·all will vanish,*
12 *though you remain, all wear out like a garment; ·you will*
roll them up like a cloak, and like a garment *they will be*
changed. But yourself, you never change and your years
13 *are unending.*ᶠ ·God has never said to any angel: *Sit at*
my right hand and I will make your enemies a footstool
14 *for you.*ᵍ ·The truth is they are all spirits whose work
is service, sent to help those who will be the heirs of salvation.

An exhortation

1 We ought, then, to turn our minds more attentively than
2 before to what we have been taught, so that we do not
drift away. ·If a promise that was made through angelsᵃ
proved to be so true that every infringement and disobedi-
3 ence brought its own proper punishment, ·then we shall
certainly not go unpunished if we neglect this salvation
that is promised to us. The promise was first announced
by the Lord himself, and is guaranteed to us by those who
4 heard him; ·God himself confirmed their witness with
signs and marvels and miracles of all kinds, and by freely
giving the gifts of the Holy Spirit.

Redemption brought by Christ, not by angels

5   He did not appoint angels to be rulers of the world to
come, and that world is what we are talking about.
6 Somewhere there is a passage that shows us this. It runs:
What is man that you should spare a thought for him, the
7 *son of man that you should care for him? ·For a short*
while you made him lower than the angels; you crowned
8 *him with glory and splendor. ·You have put him in*
*command of everything.*ᵇ Well then, if he has *put him in*
command of everything, he has left nothing which is not
under his command. At present, it is true, we are not able
to see that *everything has been put under his command,*
9 but we do see in Jesus one who was *for a short while*
made lower than the angels and is now *crowned with*
glory and splendor because he submitted to death; by
God's grace he had to experience death for all mankind.
10   As it was his purpose to bring a great many of his sons
into glory, it was appropriate that God, for whom every-

thing exists and through whom everything exists, should make perfect, through suffering, the leader who would
11 take them to their salvation. ·For the one who sanctifies, and the ones who are sanctified, are of the same stock;
12 that is why he openly calls them *brothers* ·in the text: *I shall announce your name to my brothers, praise you in*
13 *full assembly;*[c] or the text: ·*In him I hope;* or the text: *Here I am with the children whom God has given me.*[d]

14 Since all the *children* share the same blood and flesh, he too shared equally in it, so that by his death he could take away all the power of the devil, who had power over
15 death, ·and set free all those who had been held in slavery
16 all their lives by the fear of death. ·For it was not the angels that he took to himself; he took to himself *descent*
17 *from Abraham.*[e] ·It was essential that he should in this way become completely like his brothers so that he could be a compassionate and trustworthy high priest of God's
18 religion, able to atone for human sins. ·That is, because he has himself been through temptation he is able to help others who are tempted.

II. JESUS THE FAITHFUL AND MERCIFUL HIGH PRIEST

Christ higher than Moses

1 **3** That is why all you who are holy brothers and have had the same heavenly call should turn your minds to Jesus, the apostle and the high priest of our religion.
2 He was *faithful* to the one who appointed him, just like
3 *Moses,* who stayed faithful *in all his house;* ·but he has been found to deserve a greater glory than Moses. It is the difference between the honor given to the man that
4 built the house and to the house itself. ·Every house is built by someone, of course; but God built everything that
5 exists. ·It is true that Moses was *faithful in the house* of God, as a servant, acting as witness to the things which
6 were to be divulged later; ·but Christ was faithful as a son, and as the master in the house. And we are his house, as

e. Ps 45:6-7   f. Ps 102:25-27   g. Ps 110:1
2 a. The Law.   b. Ps 8:4-6 (LXX)   c. Ps 22:22   d. This, and the previous text, are from Is 8:17-18.   e. Is 41:8-9

long as we cling to our hope with the confidence that we
glory in.

How to reach God's land of rest

⁷ The Holy Spirit says: *If only you would listen to him*
⁸ *today;* ·*do not harden your hearts, as happened in the*
Rebellion, on the Day of Temptation in the wilderness,
⁹ *when your ancestors challenged me and tested me, though*
¹⁰ *they had seen what I could do* ·*for forty years. That was*
why I was angry with that generation and said: How un-
¹¹ *reliable these people who refuse to grasp my ways!* ·*And*
so, in anger, I swore that not one would reach the place
¹² *of rest I had for them.*ᵃ ·Take care, brothers, that there
is not in any one of your community a wicked mind, so
¹³ unbelieving as to turn away from the living God. ·Every
day, as long as this "today" lasts, keep encouraging one
another so that none of you is *hardened* by the lure of
¹⁴ sin, ·because we shall remain co-heirs with Christ only if
we keep a grasp on our first confidence right to the end.
¹⁵ In this saying: *If only you would listen to him today;*
do not harden your hearts, as happened in the Rebellion,
¹⁶ those who *rebelled* after they had *listened* were all the
¹⁷ people who were brought out of Egypt by Moses. ·And
those who made God *angry for forty years* were the ones
who sinned and whose *dead bodies were left lying in the*
¹⁸ *wilderness.*ᵇ ·Those that he *swore would never reach the*
place of rest he had for them were those who had been
¹⁹ disobedient. ·We see, then, that it was because they were
unfaithful that they were not able to reach it.

¹ **4** Be careful, then: the promise of *reaching the place*
of rest he had for them still holds good, and none of
² you must think that he has come too late for it. ·We received the Good News exactly as they did; but hearing
the message did them no good because they did not share
³ the faith of those who listened. ·We, however, who have
faith, shall reach a place of rest, as in the text: *And so,*
in anger, I swore that not one would reach the place of
rest I had for them. God's work was undoubtedly all
⁴ finished at the beginning of the world; ·as one text says,
referring to the seventh day: *After all his work God rested*
⁵ *on the seventh day.*ᵃ ·The text we are considering says:
⁶ *They shall not reach the place of rest I had for them.* ·It
is established, then, that there would be some people who
would reach it, and since those who first heard the Good

7 News failed to reach it through their disobedience, ·God fixed another day when, much later, he said "today" through David in the text already quoted: *If only you*
8 *would listen to him today; do not harden your hearts.* ·If Joshua had led them into this place of rest, God would not
9 later on have spoken so much of another day. ·There must still be, therefore, a place of rest reserved for God's people,
10 the seventh-day rest, ·since to *reach the place of rest* is to
11 *rest after your work,* as God did after his. ·We must therefore do everything we can to *reach this place of rest,* or some of you might copy this example of disobedience and be lost.

The word of God and Christ the priest

12 The word of God is something alive and active: it cuts like any double-edged sword but more finely: it can slip through the place where the soul is divided from the spirit, or joints from the marrow; it can judge the secret
13 emotions and thoughts. ·No created thing can hide from him; everything is uncovered and open to the eyes of the one to whom we must give account of ourselves.
14 Since in Jesus, the Son of God, we have the supreme high priest who has gone through to the highest heaven, we must never let go of the faith that we have professed.
15 For it is not as if we had a high priest who was incapable of feeling our weaknesses with us; but we have one who has been tempted in every way that we are, though he is
16 without sin. ·Let us be confident, then, in approaching the throne of grace, that we shall have mercy from him and find grace when we are in need of help.

Jesus the compassionate high priest

1 5 Every high priest has been taken out of mankind and is appointed to act for men in their relations with God,
2 to offer gifts and sacrifices for sins; and so ·he can sympathize with those who are ignorant or uncertain because
3 he too lives in the limitations of weakness. ·That is why he has to make sin offerings for himself as well as for the
4 people. ·No one takes this honor on himself, but each
5 one is called by God, as Aaron was. ·Nor did Christ give himself the glory of becoming high priest, but he had it

3 a. Ps 95   b. Nb 14:29
4 a. Gn 2:2

from the one who said to him: *You are my son, today I have*
⁶ *become your father,*ᵃ ·and in another text: *You are a priest*
⁷ *of the order of Melchizedek, and for ever.*ᵇ ·During his life
on earth, he offered up prayer and entreaty, aloud and in silent tears, to the one who had the power to save him out of
death, and he submitted so humbly that his prayer was
⁸ heard. ·Although he was Son, he learned to obey through
⁹ suffering; ·but having been made perfect, he became for all
¹⁰ who obey him the source of eternal salvation ·and was acclaimed by God with the title of high priest *of the order of
Melchizedek.*

III. THE AUTHENTIC PRIESTHOOD
OF JESUS CHRIST

Christian life and theology

¹¹ On this subject we have many things to say, and they are
difficult to explain because you have grown so slow at under-
¹² standing. ·Really, when you should by this time have become
masters, you need someone to teach you all over again the
elementary principles of interpreting God's oracles; you have
¹³ gone back to needing milk, and not solid food. ·Truly, anyone who is still living on milk cannot digest the doctrine of
¹⁴ righteousness because he is still a baby. ·Solid food is for
mature men with minds trained by practice to distinguish
between good and bad.

The author explains his intention

¹ 6 Let us leave behind us then all the elementary teaching
about Christ and concentrate on its completion, without
going over the fundamental doctrines again: the turning
² away from dead actions and toward faith in God; ·the teaching about baptisms and the laying on of hands; the teaching
about the resurrection of the dead and eternal judgment.
³ This, God willing, is what we propose to do.
⁴ As for those people who were once brought into the
light, and tasted the gift from heaven, and received a
⁵ share of the Holy Spirit, ·and appreciated the good mes-
⁶ sage of God and the powers of the world to come ·and
yet in spite of this have fallen away—it is impossible for
them to be renewed a second time. They cannot be repentant if they have wilfully crucified the Son of God and

7 openly mocked him. •A field that has been well watered by frequent rain, and gives the crops that are wanted by the owners who grew them, is given God's blessing;
8 but one that grows brambles and thistles is abandoned, and practically cursed. It will end by being burned.

Words of hope and encouragement

9 But you, my dear people—in spite of what we have just said, we are sure you are in a better state and on the way
10 to salvation. •God would not be so unjust as to forget all you have done, the love that you have for his name or the services you have done, and are still doing, for the
11 saints.[a] •Our one desire is that every one of you should go on showing the same earnestness to the end, to the per-
12 fect fulfillment of our hopes, •never growing careless, but imitating those who have the faith and the perseverance to inherit the promises.
13 When God made the promise to Abraham, he *swore by his own self*, since it was impossible for him to swear
14 by anyone greater: •*I will shower blessings on you and*
15 *give you many descendants.*[b] •Because of that, Abraham
16 persevered and saw the promise fulfilled. •Men, of course, swear an oath by something greater than themselves, and between men, confirmation by an oath puts an end to all
17 dispute. •In the same way, when God wanted to make the heirs to the promise thoroughly realize that his purpose was
18 unalterable, he conveyed this by an oath; •so that there would be two unalterable things in which it was impossible for God to be lying, and so that we, now we have found safety, should have a strong encouragement to take a firm
19 grip on the hope that is held out to us. •Here we have an anchor for our soul, as sure as it is firm, and reaching
20 right *through beyond the veil*[c] •where Jesus has entered before us and on our behalf, to become a high *priest of the order of Melchizedek, and for ever.*

5 a. Ps 2:7 b. Ps 110:4
6 a. The same phrase is used in Rm and 2 Co about a collection of money made for the church in Jerusalem. b. Gn 22
c. Lv 16:2

A. CHRIST'S PRIESTHOOD HIGHER THAN
LEVITICAL PRIESTHOOD

Melchizedek[a]

[1] You remember that *Melchizedek, king of Salem, a priest of God Most High, went to meet Abraham who was on his way back after defeating the kings,* and [2] *blessed him;* ·and also that it was to him that Abraham gave *a tenth of all that he had.* By the interpretation of his name, he is, first, "king of righteousness" and also [3] *king of Salem,* that is, "king of peace"; ·he has no father, mother or ancestry, and his life has no beginning or ending; he is like the Son of God. He remains a priest for ever.

Melchizedek accepted tithes from Abraham

[4] Now think how great this man must have been, if the patriarch *Abraham paid him a tenth of the treasure he* [5] *had captured.*[b] ·We know that any of the descendants of Levi who are admitted to the priesthood are obliged by the Law to take tithes from the people, and this is taking them from their own brothers although they too are de- [6] scended from Abraham. ·But this man, who was not of the same descent, took his tenth from Abraham, and he [7] gave his blessing to the holder of the promises. ·Now it is indisputable that a blessing is given by a superior to [8] an inferior. ·Further, in the one case it is ordinary mortal men who receive the tithes, and in the other, someone [9] who is declared to be still alive. ·It could be said that Levi himself, who receives tithes, actually paid them, in [10] the person of Abraham, ·because he was still in the loins of his ancestor when *Melchizedek came to meet him.*

From levitical priesthood to the priesthood of Melchizedek

[11] Now if perfection had been reached through the leviti- cal priesthood because the Law given to the nation rests on it, why was it still necessary for a new priesthood to arise, one *of the same order as Melchizedek*[c] not counted [12] as being "of the same order as" Aaron? ·But any change in the priesthood must mean a change in the Law as well. [13] So our Lord, of whom these things were said, belonged

to a different tribe, the members of which have never
¹⁴ done service at the altar; ·everyone knows he came from
Judah, a tribe which Moses did not even mention when
dealing with priests.

The abrogation of the old Law

¹⁵   This[d] becomes even more clearly evident when there
¹⁶ appears a second Melchizedek, who is a priest ·not by
virtue of a law about physical descent, but by the power
¹⁷ of an indestructible life. ·For it was about him that the
prophecy was made: *You are a priest of the order of*
¹⁸ *Melchizedek, and for ever.* ·The earlier commandment is
thus abolished, because it was neither effective nor useful,
¹⁹ since the Law could not make anyone perfect; but now
this commandment is replaced by something better—the
hope that brings us nearer to God.

Christ's priesthood is unchanging

²⁰   What is more, this was not done without the taking of
an oath. The others, indeed, were made priests without
²¹ any oath; ·but he with an oath sworn by the one who
declared to him: *The Lord has sworn an oath which he*
will never retract: you are a priest, and for ever.[e]
²² And it follows that it is a greater covenant for which
²³ Jesus has become our guarantee. ·Then there used to be a
great number of those other priests, because death put an
²⁴ end to each one of them; ·but this one, because he re-
²⁵ mains *for ever*, can never lose his priesthood. ·It follows,
then, that his power to save is utterly certain, since he is
living for ever to intercede for all who come to God
through him.

The perfection of the heavenly high priest

²⁶   To suit us, the ideal high priest would have to be holy,
innocent and uncontaminated, beyond the influence of
²⁷ sinners, and raised up above the heavens; ·one who would
not need to offer sacrifices every day, as the other high
priests do for their own sins and then for those of the

7 a. Gn 14, from which the following quotation is made, is
silent about any ancestors or descendants of Melchizedek, and
about "the beginning and ending" of his life. b. The regular
tithe paid to levitical priests was a tenth. c. Ps 110:4 d. What
has been said in v. 12. e. Ps 110:4

people, because he has done this once and for all by of-
28 fering himself. ·The Law appoints high priests who are
men subject to weakness; but the promise on oath, which
came after the Law, appointed the Son who is made perfect
for ever.

B. THE SUPERIORITY OF THE WORSHIP, THE SANCTUARY AND THE MEDIATION PROVIDED BY CHRIST THE PRIEST

The new priesthood and the new sanctuary

1 The great point of all that we have said is that we
have a high priest of exactly this kind. He has his
place *at the right* of the throne of divine Majesty in the
2 heavens, ·and he is the minister of the sanctuary and of
the true *Tent* of Meeting which *the Lord*, and not any
3 man, *set up.*ᵃ ·It is the duty of every high priest to offer
gifts and sacrifices, and so this one too must have some-
4 thing to offer. ·In fact, if he were on earth, he would not
be a priest at all, since there are others who make the
5 offerings laid down by the Law ·and these only maintain
the service of a model or a reflection of the heavenly
realities. For Moses, when he had the Tent to build, was
warned by God who said: *See that you make everything
according to the pattern shown you on the mountain.*ᵇ

Christ is the mediator of a greater covenant

6 We have seen that he has been given a ministry of a
far higher order, and to the same degree it is a better
covenant of which he is the mediator, founded on better
7 promises. ·If that first covenant had been without a fault,
there would have been no need for a second one to replace
8 it. ·And in fact God does find fault with them; he says:

*See, the days are coming—it is the Lord who speaks—
when I will establish a new covenant
with the House of Israel and the House of Judah,*
9 *but not a covenant like the one I made with their ancestors
on the day I took them by the hand
to bring them out of the land of Egypt.
They abandoned that covenant of mine,
and so I on my side deserted them. It is the Lord who
speaks.*

10 *No, this is the covenant I will make*
with the House of Israel
when those days arrive—it is the Lord who speaks.
I will put my laws into their minds
and write them on their hearts.
Then I will be their God
and they shall be my people.
11 *There will be no further need for neighbor to try to teach*
neighbor,
or brother to say to brother,
"Learn to know the Lord."
No, they will all know me,
the least no less than the greatest,
12 *since I will forgive their iniquities*
and never call their sins to mind.[c]

13 By speaking of a *new* covenant, he implies that the first
one is already old. Now anything old only gets more anti-
quated until in the end it disappears.

Christ enters the heavenly sanctuary

1 **9** The first covenant also had its laws governing worship, and its sanctuary, a sanctuary on this earth.
2 There was a tent which comprised two compartments:
the first, in which the lamp-stand, the table and the presentation loaves were kept, was called the Holy Place;
3 then beyond the second veil, an innermost part which
4 was called the Holy of Holies ·to which belonged the
gold altar of incense, and the ark of the covenant, plated
all over with gold. In this were kept the gold jar containing the manna, Aaron's branch that grew the buds,
5 and the stone tablets of the covenant. ·On top of it was
the throne of mercy, and outspread over it were the glorious cherubs. This is not the time to go into greater detail
about this.
6   Under these provisions, priests are constantly going into
7 the outer tent to carry out their acts of worship, ·but the
second tent is entered only once a year, and then only by
the high priest who must go in by himself and take the
blood to offer for his own faults and the people's.
8 By this, the Holy Spirit is showing that no one has the
right to go into the sanctuary as long as the outer tent re-

8 a. Nb 24:6 (LXX)   b. Ex 25:40   c. Jr 31:31-34

⁹ mains standing; ·it is a symbol for this present time. None of the gifts and sacrifices offered under these regulations can possibly bring any worshiper to perfection in his inner

¹⁰ self; ·they are rules about the outward life, connected with foods and drinks and washing at various times, intended to be in force only until it should be time to reform them.

¹¹ But now Christ has come, as the high priest of all the blessings which were to come. He has passed through the greater, the more perfect tent, which is better than the one made by men's hands because it is not of this created order;

¹² and he has entered the sanctuary once and for all, taking with him not the blood of goats and bull calves, but his own blood, having won an eternal redemption for us.

¹³ The blood of goats and bulls and the ashes of a heifer are sprinkled on those who have incurred defilement and

¹⁴ they restore the holiness of their outward lives; ·how much more effectively the blood of Christ, who offered himself as the perfect sacrifice to God through the eternal Spirit, can purify our inner self from dead actions so that we do our service to the living God.

Christ seals the new covenant with his blood

¹⁵ He brings a new covenant, as the mediator, only so that the people who were called to an eternal inheritance may actually receive what was promised: his death took place

¹⁶ to cancel the sins that infringed the earlier covenant. ·Now wherever a will is in question, the death of the testator

¹⁷ must be established; ·indeed, it only becomes valid with that death, since it is not meant to have any effect while

¹⁸ the testator is still alive. ·That explains why even the earlier covenant needed something to be killed in order to take

¹⁹ effect, ·and why, after Moses had announced all the commandments of the Law to the people, he took the calves' blood, the goats' blood and some water, and with these he sprinkled the book itself and all the people, using scarlet

²⁰ wool and hyssop; ·saying as he did so: *This is the blood*

²¹ *of the covenant that God has laid down for you.*ᵃ ·After that, he sprinkled the tent and all the liturgical vessels with

²² blood in the same way. ·In fact, according to the Law almost everything has to be purified*ᵇ* with blood; and if

²³ there is no shedding of blood, there is no remission. ·Obviously, only the copies of heavenly things can be purified in this way, and the heavenly things themselves have to be

²⁴ purified by a higher sort of sacrifice than this. ·It is not

as though Christ had entered a man-made sanctuary which was only modelled on the real one; but it was heaven itself, so that he could appear in the actual presence of God on
25 our behalf. ·And he does not have to offer himself again and again, like the high priest going into the sanctuary year
26 after year with the blood that is not his own, ·or else he would have had to suffer over and over again since the world began. Instead of that, he has made his appearance once and for all, now at the end of the last age, to do away
27 with sin by sacrificing himself. ·Since men only die once,
28 and after that comes judgment, ·so Christ, too, offers himself only once *to take the faults of many on himself,*[c] and when he appears a second time, it will not be to deal with sin but to reward with salvation those who are waiting for him.

SUMMARY: CHRIST'S SACRIFICE SUPERIOR TO THE SACRIFICES OF THE MOSAIC LAW

The old sacrifices ineffective

1 **10** So, since the Law has no more than a *reflection* of these realities, and no finished picture of them, it is quite incapable of bringing the worshipers to perfection, with the same sacrifices repeatedly offered year after year.
2 Otherwise, the offering of them would have stopped, because the worshipers, when they had been purified once,
3 would have no awareness of sins. ·Instead of that, the sins
4 are recalled year after year in the sacrifices. ·Bulls' blood and goats' blood are useless for taking away sins,
5 and this is what he said, on coming into the world:

You who wanted no sacrifice or oblation,
prepared a body for me.
6 *You took no pleasure in holocausts or sacrifices for sin;*
7 *then I said,*
just as I was commanded in the scroll of the book,
"God, here I am! I am coming to obey your will."[a]

8 Notice that he says first: *You did not want* what the Law lays down as the things to be offered, that is: *the sacrifices,*

9 a. Ex 24:8 b. Many instances are given in Lv. c. Is 53:12
10 a. Ps 40:6-8 (LXX)

the oblations, the holocausts and the sacrifices for sin, and
9 *you took no pleasure* in them; •and then he says: *Here I
am! I am coming to obey your will.* He is abolishing the
10 first sort to replace it with the second. •And this *will* was
for us to be made holy by the *offering* of his *body* made
once and for all by Jesus Christ.

The efficacy of Christ's sacrifice

11 All the priests stand at their duties every day, offering
over and over again the same sacrifices which are quite
12 incapable of taking sins away. •He, on the other hand, has
offered one single sacrifice for sins, and then taken his place
13 for ever, *at the right hand of God,* •where he is now waiting *until his enemies are made into a footstool for him.*[b]
14 By virtue of that one single offering, he has achieved the
15 eternal perfection of all whom he is sanctifying. •The Holy
Spirit assures us of this; for he says, first:

16   *This is the covenant I will make with them
        when those days arrive;*[c]

and the Lord then goes on to say:

        *I will put my laws into their hearts
        and write them on their minds.*
17   *I will never call their sins to mind,
        or their offenses.*

18 When all sins have been forgiven, there can be no more
sin offerings.

IV. PERSEVERING FAITH

The Christian opportunity

19 In other words, brothers, through the blood of Jesus we
20 have the right to enter the sanctuary, •by a new way which
he has opened for us, a living opening through the curtain,
21 that is to say, his body. •And we have the *supreme high
22 priest* over all *the house of God.* •So as we go in, let us be
sincere in heart and filled with faith, our minds sprinkled
and free from any trace of bad conscience and our bodies
23 washed with pure water. •Let us keep firm in the hope we
profess, because the one who made the promise is faithful.
24 Let us be concerned for each other, to stir a response in
25 love and good works. •Do not stay away from the meet-

ings of the community, as some do, but encourage each other to go; the more so as you see the Day drawing near.

The danger of apostasy

26 If, after we have been given knowledge of the truth, we should deliberately commit any sins, then there is no 27 longer any sacrifice for them. ·There will be left only the dreadful prospect of judgment and of *the raging fire* that 28 is to *burn rebels.*[d] ·Anyone who disregards the Law of Moses is ruthlessly *put to death on the word of two wit-* 29 *nesses or three;*[e] ·and you may be sure that anyone who tramples on the Son of God, and who treats *the blood of the covenant* which sanctified him as if it were not holy, and who insults the Spirit of grace, will be condemned to a 30 far severer punishment. ·We are all aware who it was that said: *Vengeance is mine; I will repay.*[f] And again: *The* 31 *Lord will judge his people.* ·It is a dreadful thing to fall into the hands of the living God.

Motives for perseverance

32 Remember all the sufferings that you had to meet after 33 you received the light, in earlier days; ·sometimes by being yourselves publicly exposed to insults and violence, and sometimes as associates of others who were treated in the 34 same way. ·For you not only shared in the sufferings of those who were in prison, but you happily accepted being stripped of your belongings, knowing that you owned some- 35 thing that was better and lasting. ·Be as confident now, 36 then, since the reward is so great. ·You will need endurance to do God's will and gain what he has promised.

37 Only *a little while now, a very little while,*
    and the one that is coming will have come; he will not delay.[g]
38 *The righteous man will live by faith,*
    but if he draws back, my soul will take no pleasure in him.[h]

39 You and I are not the sort of people who *draw back,* and are lost by it; we are the sort who keep *faithful* until our souls are saved.

b. Ps 110   c. From the long quotation from Jr 31 made in ch. 8.
d. Is 26:11 (LXX)   e. Dt 17:6   f. Dt 32:35-36   g. Is 26:20 (LXX)   h. Hab 2:3-4 (LXX)

The exemplary faith of our ancestors

¹ **11** Only faith can guarantee the blessings that we hope for, or prove the existence of the realities that at ² present remain unseen. ·It was for faith that our ancestors were commended.

³ It is by faith that we understand that the world was created by one word from God, so that no apparent cause can account for the things we can see.

⁴ It was because of his faith that Abel offered God a better sacrifice than Cain, and for that he was declared to be righteous when *God* made acknowledgment of *his offerings.* Though he is dead, he still speaks by faith.

⁵ It was because of his faith that Enoch was taken up and did not have to experience death: *he was not to be found because God had taken him.*ᵃ This was because before his assumption it is attested that *he had pleased God.* ⁶ Now it is impossible to please God without faith, since anyone who comes to him must believe that he exists and rewards those who try to find him.

⁷ It was through his faith that Noah, when he had been warned by God of something that had never been seen before, felt a holy fear and built an ark to save his family. By his faith the world was convicted, and he was able to claim the righteousness which is the reward of faith.

⁸ It was by faith that Abraham obeyed the call to *set out* for a country that was the inheritance given to him and his descendants, and that *he set out* without knowing where ⁹ he was going. ·By faith he arrived, *as a foreigner,* in the Promised Land, and lived there as if in a strange country, with Isaac and Jacob, who were heirs with him of the ¹⁰ same promise. ·They lived there in tents while he looked forward to a city founded, designed and built by God.

¹¹ It was equally by faith that Sarah, in spite of being past the age, was made able to conceive, because she believed that he who had made the promise would be faithful to it. ¹² Because of this, there came from one man, and one who was already as good as dead himself, *more descendants than could be counted, as many as the stars of heaven or the grains of sand on the seashore.*ᵇ

¹³ All these died in faith, before receiving any of the things that had been promised, but they saw them in the far distance and welcomed them, recognizing that they were only ¹⁴ *strangers and nomads on earth.* ·People who use such

terms about themselves make it quite plain that they are in
15 search of their real homeland. ·They can hardly have
meant the country they came from, since they had the
16 opportunity to go back to it; ·but in fact they were longing
for a better homeland, their heavenly homeland. That is
why God is not ashamed to be called their God, since he
has founded the city for them.

17 It was by faith that Abraham, *when put to the test, offered up Isaac.*^c He offered to sacrifice his only son even
18 though the promises had been made to him ·and he had
been told: *It is through Isaac that your name will be
19 carried on.*^d ·He was confident that God had the power
even to raise the dead; and so, figuratively speaking, he was
given back Isaac from the dead.

20 It was by faith that this same Isaac gave his blessing to
21 Jacob and Esau for the still distant future. ·By faith Jacob,
when he was dying, blessed each of Joseph's sons, *leaning
22 on the end of his stick as though bowing to pray.*^e ·It was
by faith that, when he was about to die, Joseph recalled
the Exodus of the Israelites and made the arrangements
for his own burial.

23 It was by faith that Moses, when he was born, *was hidden by his parents for three months;* they defied the royal
24 edict when they *saw* he was such a *fine* child. ·It was by
faith that, *when he grew to manhood,* Moses refused to be
25 known as the son of Pharaoh's daughter ·and chose to be
ill-treated in company with God's people rather than to
26 enjoy for a time the pleasures of sin. ·He considered that
the insults offered to the Anointed were something more
precious than all the treasures of Egypt, because he had
27 his eyes fixed on the reward. ·It was by faith that he left
Egypt and was not afraid of the king's anger; he held to his
28 purpose like a man who could see the Invisible. ·It was by
faith that he kept *the Passover* and sprinkled *the blood* to
prevent *the Destroyer* from touching any of the firstborn
29 sons of Israel. ·It was by faith they crossed the Red Sea
as easily as dry land, while the Egyptians, trying to do the
same, were drowned.

30 It was through faith that the walls of Jericho fell down
31 when the people had been round them for seven days. ·It

11 a. Gn 5:24 b. Gn 22:17, also quoted in Ex 32. c. Gn
22:1-14 d. Gn 21:12 e. Gn 47:31.

was by faith that Rahab the prostitute welcomed the spies
and so was not killed with the unbelievers.

³² Is there any need to say more? There is not time for me
to give an account of Gideon, Barak, Samson, Jephthah,
³³ or of David, Samuel and the prophets. ·These were men
who through faith conquered kingdoms, did what is right
and earned the promises. They could keep a lion's mouth
³⁴ shut, ·put out blazing fires and emerge unscathed from
battle. They were weak people who were given strength,
³⁵ to be brave in war and drive back foreign invaders. ·Some
came back to their wives from the dead, by resurrection;
and others submitted to torture, refusing release so that
³⁶ they would rise again to a better life. ·Some had to bear
being pilloried and flogged, or even chained up in prison.
³⁷ They were stoned, or sawn in half,ᶠ or beheaded; they
were homeless, and dressed in the skins of sheep and goats;
they were penniless and were given nothing but ill-
³⁸ treatment. ·They were too good for the world and they
went out to live in deserts and mountains and in caves and
³⁹ ravines. ·These are all heroes of faith, but they did not
⁴⁰ receive what was promised, ·since God had made provi-
sion for us to have something better, and they were not to
reach perfection except with us.

The example of Jesus Christ

¹ **12** With so many witnesses in a great cloud on every
side of us, we too, then, should throw off everything
that hinders us, especially the sin that clings so easily, and
² keep running steadily in the race we have started. ·Let us
not lose sight of Jesus, who leads us in our faith and brings
it to perfection: for the sake of the joy which was still in
the future, he endured the cross, disregarding the shame-
fulness of it, and *from now on has taken his place at the*
³ *right* of God's throne. ·Think of the way he stood such
opposition from sinners and then you will not give up for
⁴ want of courage. ·In the fight against sin, you have not yet
had to keep fighting to the point of death.

God's fatherly instruction

⁵ Have you forgotten that encouraging text in which you
are addressed as sons? *My son, when the Lord corrects*
you, do not treat it lightly; but do not get discouraged when
⁶ *he reprimands you.* ·*For the Lord trains the ones that he*
loves and he punishes all those that he acknowledges as

[7] his sons.[a] ·Suffering is part of your *training;* God is treat-
ing you as his *sons.* Has there ever been any son whose
[8] father did not *train* him? ·If you were not getting this
training, as all of you are, then you would not be *sons* but
[9] bastards. ·Besides, we have all had our human fathers who
punished us, and we respected them for it; we ought to be
even more willing to submit ourselves to our spiritual
[10] Father, to be given life. ·Our human fathers were thinking
of this short life when they punished us, and could only
do what they thought best; but he does it all for our own
[11] good, so that we may share his own holiness. ·Of course,
any punishment is most painful at the time, and far from
pleasant; but later, in those on whom it has been used, it
[12] bears fruit in peace and goodness. ·So *hold up your limp*
[13] *arms and steady your trembling knees*[b] ·and *smooth out*
the path you tread;[c] then the injured limb will not be
wrenched, it will grow strong again.

Unfaithfulness is punished

[14] *Always be wanting peace*[d] with all people, and the holi-
[15] ness without which no one can ever see the Lord. ·Be
careful that no one is deprived of the grace of God and
that no *root of bitterness should begin to grow and make*
[16] *trouble;*[e] this can poison a whole community. ·And be
careful that there is no immorality, or that any of you does
not degrade religion like Esau, *who sold his birthright* for
[17] one single meal. ·As you know, when he wanted to obtain
the blessing afterward, he was rejected and, though he
pleaded for it with tears, he was unable to elicit a change
of heart.

The two covenants

[18] What you have come to is nothing known to the senses:
not a *blazing fire,*[f] or a *gloom* turning to *total darkness,*
[19] or a *storm;* ·or *trumpeting thunder* or the *great voice*
speaking which made everyone that heard it beg that no
[20] more should be said to them. ·They were appalled at the
order that was given: *If even an animal touches the*

f. Some apocryphal books say that this was how King Manasseh
had Isaiah executed.
12 a. Ps 3:11-12 (LXX) b. Is 35:3 c. Pr 4:26 (LXX)
d. Ps 34:14 e. Dt 29:17 f. The quotations in vv. 18-20
are from Ex 19 (recalled in Dt 4).

²¹ mountain, *it must be stoned.* ·The whole scene was so terrible that Moses said: *I am afraid,ᵍ* and was trembling
²² with fright. ·But what you have come to is Mount Zion and the city of the living God, the heavenly Jerusalem where the millions of angels have gathered for the festival,
²³ with the whole Church in which everyone is a "firstborn son" and a citizen of heaven. You have come to God himself, the supreme Judge, and been placed with the spirits of
²⁴ the saints who have been made perfect; ·and to Jesus, the mediator who brings a new covenant and a blood for puri-
²⁵ fication which pleads more insistently than Abel's. ·Make sure that you never refuse to listen when he speaks. The people who refused to listen to the warning from a voice on earth could not escape their punishment, and how shall we escape if we turn away from a voice that warns us from
²⁶ heaven? ·That time his voice made the earth shake, but now he has given us this promise: *I shall make the earth shake once more and* not only the earth but *heaven as*
²⁷ *well.*ʰ ·The words *once more* show that since the things being shaken are created things, they are going to be
²⁸ changed, so that the unshakeable things will be left. ·We have been given possession of an unshakeable kingdom. Let us therefore hold on to the grace that we have been given and use it to worship God in the way that he finds
²⁹ acceptable, in reverence and fear. ·For our *God* is a *consuming fire.*ᶦ

APPENDIX

Final recommendations

¹₂ 13 Continue to love each other like brothers, ·and remember always to welcome strangers, for by doing this, some people have entertained angels without know-
⁸ ing it. ·Keep in mind those who are in prison, as though you were in prison with them; and those who are being badly
⁴ treated, since you too are in the one body. ·Marriage is to be honored by all, and marriages are to be kept undefiled, because fornicators and adulterers will come under God's
⁵ judgment. ·Put greed out of your lives and be content with whatever you have; God himself has said: *I will not*
⁶ *fail you or desert you,*ᵃ ·and so we can say with confidence: *With the Lord to help me, I fear nothing: what can man do to me?*ᵇ

Faithfulness

7   Remember your leaders, who preached the word of God
to you, and as you reflect on the outcome of their lives,
8 imitate their faith. ·Jesus Christ is the same today as he was
9 yesterday and as he will be for ever. ·Do not let yourselves
be led astray by all sorts of strange doctrines: it is better
to rely on grace for inner strength than on dietary laws
10 which have done no good to those who kept them. ·We
have our own altar from which those who serve the
11 tabernacle have no right to eat. ·The bodies of the animals
whose blood is brought into the sanctuary by the high priest
for the atonement of sin are burned outside the camp,[o]
12 and so Jesus too suffered outside the gate to sanctify the
13 people with his own blood. ·Let us go to him, then, *outside*
14 *the camp,* and share his degradation. ·For there is no eternal city for us in this life but we look for one in the life to
15 come. ·Through him, *let us offer God* an unending *sacrifice of praise,*[d] a verbal sacrifice that is offered every time
16 we acknowledge his name. ·Keep doing good works and
sharing your resources, for these are sacrifices that please
God.

Obedience to religious leaders

17   Obey your leaders and do as they tell you, because they
must give an account of the way they look after your souls;
make this a joy for them to do, and not a grief—you your-
18 selves would be the losers. ·We are sure that our own
conscience is clear and we are certainly determined to be-
19 have honorably in everything we do; pray for us. ·I ask
you very particularly to pray that I may come back to you
all the sooner.

EPILOGUE

News, good wishes and greetings

20   I pray that the God of peace, *who brought* our Lord
Jesus *back*[e] from the dead *to become the great Shepherd*

g. Dt 9:19   **h.** Hg 2:6, probably influenced also by Ps 68:8.
i. Dt 4:24
13 a. Dt 31:6   **b.** Ps 118:6; Ps 27:1   **c.** Lv 16:27   **d.** Ps 50:14
e. Is 63:11

of the sheep[f] by the blood that sealed an eternal covenant,[g]
21 may make you ready to do his will in any kind of good action; and turn us all into whatever is acceptable to himself through Jesus Christ, to whom be glory for ever and ever, Amen.

22 I do ask you, brothers, to take these words of advice kindly; that is why I have written to you so briefly.

23 I want you to know that our brother Timothy has been set free. If he arrives in time, he will be with me when I 24 see you. ·Greetings to all your leaders and to all the saints. 25 The saints of Italy send you greetings. ·Grace be with you all.

f. Ezk 34:23   g. Ezk 37:26

INTRODUCTION TO
The Letters to All Christians

Seven letters not written by Paul are included in the New Testament and these, because they were addressed to the Church at large, have been known as "the catholic epistles." The three of them attributed to John have been briefly introduced in the introductory note to John's Gospel.

James

The traditional attribution of this letter to "James, the brother of the Lord," is supported by internal evidence. Though it was written in Greek, the letter is full of hebraisms and its style of argument is characteristically semitic, and it was clearly intended for Jewish converts so familiar with the Old Testament that they would understand allusions to it without direct quotation. It is more a sermon than a letter and consists largely of moral exhortations, laying particular stress on the practical "good works" expected of Christians and re-presenting much of the Jewish Wisdom tradition. It takes a different point of view from Paul's on the problem of relating faith to works, and may either be earlier than Galatians-Romans and written as early as A.D. 49, or it may be a rejoinder to what Paul had written and be placed at 57 or 58.

Jude

This is also a letter to Jewish Christians, probably written between A.D. 70 and 80. It denounces certain false teachers and threatens them with the punishments promised by Jewish tradition, and it quotes from apocryphal Jewish writings.

1 Peter. 2 Peter

1 Peter has from the earliest times been accepted as written by the apostle, though it may not have been first composed as a single letter. It is addressed to Christian churches largely made up of converts from paganism, and is in quite good Greek, perhaps through the help of the disciple Silvanus mentioned in it as secretary. The letter reflects a time of trial through which the churches were passing and contains much

practical teaching under the dominating theme of fortitude in persecution.

2 Peter seems to date from later than Peter's death, though the writer may have had some claim to represent Peter and was possibly a disciple of his. One possibility is that he filled out one of Peter's writings by adopting the letter of Jude to make a chapter (ch. 2).

THE LETTER OF
James

Address and greetings

1 ¹ From James, servant of God and of the Lord Jesus Christ. Greetings to the twelve tribes of the Dispersion.*ᵃ*

Trials a privilege

² My brothers, you will always have your trials but, when ³ they come, try to treat them as a happy privilege;*ᵇ* ·you understand that your faith is only put to the test to make ⁴ you patient, ·but patience too is to have its practical results so that you will become fully developed, complete, with nothing missing.

⁵ If there is any one of you who needs wisdom, he must ask God, who gives to all freely and ungrudgingly; it ⁶ will be given to him. ·But he must ask with faith, and no trace of doubt, because a person who has doubts is like the ⁷ waves thrown up in the sea when the wind drives. ·That ⁸ sort of person, in two minds, wavering between going different ways, must not expect that the Lord will give him anything.

⁹ It is right for the poor brother to be proud of his high ¹⁰ rank, ·and the rich one to be thankful that he has been humbled, because riches last no longer than *the flowers in* ¹¹ *the grass;* ·the scorching sun comes up, and *the grass withers, the flower falls;ᶜ* what looked so beautiful now disappears. It is the same with the rich man: his business goes on; he himself perishes.

¹² *Happy the man who stands firmᵈ* when trials come. He has proved himself, and will win the prize of life, the crown that the Lord has promised to those who love him.

1 a. In O.T. days the "Dispersion" (*diaspora*) meant the Jews who had emigrated from their own country. The writer is using it here to mean the Jewish-Christians, living in the Graeco-Roman world. b. "happy privilege" is a pun on the greeting formula in v. 1. c. Is 40:6-7 d. Dn 12:12

Temptation

13 Never, when you have been tempted, say, "God sent the
    temptation"; God cannot be tempted to do anything wrong,
14 and he does not tempt anybody. •Everyone who is tempted
15 is attracted and seduced by his own wrong desire. •Then
    the desire conceives and gives birth to sin, and when sin
    is fully grown, it too has a child, and the child is death.
16
17 Make no mistake about this, my dear brothers: •it is all
    that is good, everything that is perfect, which is given us
    from above; it comes down from the Father of all light;
    with him there is no such thing as alteration, no shadow of
18 a change. •By his own choice he made us his children by
    the message of the truth so that we should be a sort of
    first-fruits of all that he had created.

True religion

19 Remember this, my dear brothers: be *quick to listen*[e]
20 but *slow* to speak and slow to rouse your temper; •God's
21 righteousness is never served by man's anger; •so do away
    with all the impurities and bad habits that are still left in
    you—accept and submit to the word which has been planted
22 in you and can save your souls. •But you must do what
    the word tells you, and not just listen to it and deceive
23 yourselves. •To listen to the word and not obey is like look-
24 ing at your own features in a mirror and then, •after a
    quick look, going off and immediately forgetting what you
25 looked like. •But the man who looks steadily at the per-
    fect law of freedom and makes that his habit—not listening
    and then forgetting, but actively putting it into practice—
    will be happy in all that he does.
26 Nobody must imagine that he is religious while he still
    goes on deceiving himself and not keeping control over
    his tongue; anyone who does this has the wrong idea of
27 religion. •Pure, unspoiled religion, in the eyes of God our
    Father is this: coming to the help of orphans and widows
  · when they need it, and keeping oneself uncontaminated by
    the world.

Respect for the poor

1   My brothers, do not try to combine faith in Jesus
2   Christ, our glorified Lord, with the making of distinc-
    tions between classes of people. •Now suppose a man
    comes into your synagogue,[a] beautifully dressed and with
    a gold ring on, and at the same time a poor man comes

8 in, in shabby clothes, ·and you take notice of the well-dressed man, and say, "Come this way to the best seats"; then you tell the poor man, "Stand over there" or "You

4 can sit on the floor by my foot-rest." ·Can't you see that you have used two different standards in your mind, and turned yourselves into judges, and corrupt judges at that?

5   Listen, my dear brothers: it was those who are poor according to the world that God chose, to be rich in faith and to be the heirs to the kingdom which he promised to

6 those who love him. ·In spite of this, you have no respect for anybody who is poor. Isn't it always the rich who are against you? Isn't it always their doing when you are

7 dragged before the court? ·Aren't they the ones who insult the honorable name to which you have been dedicated?

8 Well, the right thing to do is to keep the supreme law of scripture: *you must love your neighbor as yourself;*[b]

9 but as soon as you make distinctions between classes of people, you are committing sin, and under condemnation for breaking the Law.

10   You see, if a man keeps the whole of the Law, except for one small point at which he fails, he is still guilty of

11 breaking it all. ·It was the same person who said, *"You must not commit adultery"* and *"You must not kill."*[c] Now if you commit murder, you do not have to commit adultery

12 as well to become a breaker of the Law. ·Talk and behave like people who are going to be judged by the law of free-

13 dom, ·because there will be judgment without mercy for those who have not been merciful themselves; but the merciful need have no fear of judgment.

Faith and good works

14   Take the case, my brothers, of someone who has never done a single good act but claims that he has faith. Will

15 that faith save him? ·If one of the brothers or one of the sisters is in need of clothes and has not enough food to live

16 on, ·and one of you says to them, 'I wish you well; keep yourself warm and eat plenty', without giving them these

17 bare necessities of life, then what good is that? ·Faith is like that: if good works do not go with it, it is quite dead.

e. Si 5:11
2 a. Jewish Christians may still have been attending synagogues, or the writer may have adopted this word for the Christian assembly. b. Lv 19:18 c. Ex 20

¹⁸   This is the way to talk to people of that kind: You say
you have faith and I have good deeds; I will prove to you
that I have faith by showing you my good deeds—now you
prove to me that you have faith without any good deeds
¹⁹ to show. ·You believe in the one God—that is creditable
enough, but the demons have the same belief, and they
²⁰ tremble with fear. ·Do realize, you senseless man, that
²¹ faith without good deeds is useless. ·You surely know
that Abraham our father was justified by his deed, because
²² he *offered his son Isaac on the altar?*[d] ·There you see it:
faith and deeds were working together; his faith became
²³ perfect by what he did. ·This is what scripture really means
when it says: *Abraham put his faith in God, and this was
counted as making him justified;*[e] and that is why he was
called "the friend of God."
²⁴   You see now that it is by doing something good, and
²⁵ not only by believing, that a man is justified. ·There is
another example of the same kind: Rahab the prostitute,
justified by her deeds because she welcomed the messen-
²⁶ gers and showed them a different way to leave. ·A body
dies when it is separated from the spirit, and in the same
way faith is dead if it is separated from good deeds.

Uncontrolled language

¹ **3** Only a few of you, my brothers, should be teachers,
bearing in mind that those of us who teach can expect
a stricter judgment.
²   After all, every one of us does something wrong, over
and over again; the only man who could reach perfection
would be someone who never said anything wrong—he
³ would be able to control every part of himself. ·Once we
put a bit into the horse's mouth, to make it do what we
⁴ want, we have the whole animal under our control. ·Or
think of ships: no matter how big they are, even if a gale
is driving them, the man at the helm can steer them any-
⁵ where he likes by controlling a tiny rudder. ·So is the
tongue only a tiny part of the body, but it can proudly
claim that it does great things. Think how small a flame
⁶ can set fire to a huge forest; ·the tongue is a flame like
that. Among all the parts of the body, the tongue is a whole
wicked world in itself: it infects the whole body; catching
fire itself from hell, it sets fire to the whole wheel of crea-
⁷ tion. ·Wild animals and birds, reptiles and fish can all be
⁸ tamed by man, and often are; ·but nobody can tame the

tongue—it is a pest that will not keep still, full of deadly
9 poison. ·We use it to bless the Lord and Father, but we
also use it to curse men who are made in God's image:
10 the blessing and the curse come out of the same mouth.
11 My brothers, this must be wrong—does any water supply
give a flow of fresh water and salt water out of the same
12 pipe? ·Can a fig tree give you olives, my brothers, or a
vine give figs? No more can sea water give you fresh
water.

Real wisdom and its opposite

13 If there are any wise or learned men among you, let
them show it by their good lives, with humility and wisdom
14 in their actions. ·But if at heart you have the bitterness
of jealousy, or a self-seeking ambition, never make any
claims for yourself or cover up the truth with lies—
15 principles of this kind are not the wisdom that comes down
from above: they are only earthly, animal and devilish.
16 Wherever you find jealousy and ambition, you find dis-
harmony, and wicked things of every kind being done;
17 whereas the wisdom that comes down from above is es-
sentially something pure; it also makes for peace, and is
kindly and considerate; it is full of compassion and shows
itself by doing good; nor is there any trace of partiality
18 or hypocrisy in it. ·Peacemakers, when they work for
peace, sow the seeds which will bear fruit in holiness.

Disunity among Christians

1 **4** Where do these wars and battles between yourselves
first start? Isn't it precisely in the desires fighting inside
2 your own selves? ·You want something and you haven't
got it; so you are prepared to kill. You have an ambition
that you cannot satisfy; so you fight to get your way by
force. Why you don't have what you want is because you
3 don't pray for it; ·when you do pray and don't get it, it
is because you have not prayed properly, you have prayed
for something to indulge your own desires.
4 You are as unfaithful as adulterous wives; don't you
realize that making the world your friend is making God
your enemy? Anyone who chooses the world for his friend
5 turns himself into God's enemy. ·Surely you don't think
scripture is wrong when it says: the spirit which he sent to

d. Gn 22:9   e. Gn 15:6

⁶ live in us wants us for himself alone? ·But he has been even more generous to us, as scripture says: *God opposes* ⁷ *the proud but he gives generously to the humble.*ᵃ ·Give in to God, then; resist the devil, and he will run away from ⁸ you. ·The nearer you go to God, the nearer he will come to you. Clean your hands, you sinners, and clear ⁹ your minds, you waverers. ·Look at your wretched condition, and weep for it in misery; be miserable instead of ¹⁰ laughing, gloomy instead of happy. ·Humble yourselves before the Lord and he will lift you up.

¹¹   Brothers, do not slander one another. Anyone who slanders a brother, or condemns him, is speaking against the Law and condemning the Law. But if you condemn the Law, you have stopped keeping it and become a judge ¹² over it. ·There is only one lawgiver and he is the only judge and has the power to acquit or to sentence. Who are you to give a verdict on your neighbor?

A warning for the rich and the self-confident

¹³   Here is the answer for those of you who talk like this: "Today or tomorrow, we are off to this or that town; we are going to spend a year there, trading, and make some ¹⁴ money." ·You never know what will happen tomorrow: you are no more than a mist that is here for a little while ¹⁵ and then disappears. ·The most you should ever say is: "If it is the Lord's will, we shall still be alive to do this or ¹⁶ that." ·But how proud and sure of yourselves you are now! ¹⁷ Pride of this kind is always wicked. ·Everyone who knows what is the right thing to do and doesn't do it commits a sin.

¹/² 5 Now an answer for the rich. Start crying, weep for the miseries that are coming to you. ·Your wealth is all ³ rotting, your clothes are all eaten up by moths. ·All your gold and your silver are corroding away, and the same corrosion will be your own sentence, and eat into your body. It was a burning fire that you stored up as your ⁴ treasure for the last days. ·Laborers mowed your fields, and you cheated them—listen to the wages that you kept back, calling out; realize that the cries of the reapers have ⁵ reached the ears of the Lord of hosts. ·On earth you have had a life of comfort and luxury; in the time of slaughter ⁶ you went on eating to your heart's content. ·It was you who condemned the innocent and killed them; they offered you no resistance.

A final exhortation

7 Now be patient, brothers, until the Lord's coming. Think of a farmer: how patiently he waits for the precious fruit of the ground until it has had the autumn rains and the
8 spring rains! ·You too have to be patient; do not lose heart,
9 because the Lord's coming will be soon. ·Do not make complaints against one another, brothers, so as not to be brought to judgment yourselves; the Judge is already to
10 be seen waiting at the gates. ·For your example, brothers, in submitting with patience, take the prophets who spoke
11 in the name of the Lord; ·remember it is those who had endurance that we say are the blessed ones. You have heard of the patience of Job, and understood the Lord's purpose, realizing that *the Lord is kind and compassionate.*[a]
12 Above all, my brothers, do not swear by heaven or by the earth, or use any oaths at all. If you mean "yes," you must say "yes"; if you mean "no," say "no." Otherwise you make yourselves liable to judgment.
13 If any one of you is in trouble, he should pray; if any-
14 one is feeling happy, he should sing a psalm. ·If one of you is ill, he should send for the elders of the church, and they must anoint him with oil in the name of the Lord and pray
15 over him. ·The prayer of faith will save the sick man and the Lord will raise him up again; and if he has committed
16 any sins, he will be forgiven. ·So confess your sins to one another, and pray for one another, and this will cure you; the heartfelt prayer of a good man works very powerfully.
17 Elijah was a human being like ourselves—he prayed hard for it not to rain, and no rain fell for three-and-a-half
18 years; ·then he prayed again and the sky gave rain and the earth gave crops.
19 My brothers, if one of you strays away from the truth,
20 and another brings him back to it, ·he may be sure that anyone who can bring back a sinner from the wrong way that he has taken will be saving a soul from death and *covering up a great number of sins.*[b]

4 a. Pr 3:34 (LXX)
5 a. Ps 103:8   b. Pr 10:12

1 Peter

THE FIRST LETTER OF PETER

Address. Greetings

¹ Peter, apostle of Jesus Christ, sends greetings to all those living among foreigners in the Dispersion of Pontus, Galatia, Cappadocia, Asia and Bithynia, who have been ² chosen, ·by the provident purpose of God the Father, to be made holy by the Spirit, obedient to Jesus Christ and sprinkled with his blood. Grace and peace be with you more and more.

Introduction. The salvation of Christians

³ Blessed be God the Father of our Lord Jesus Christ, who in his great mercy has given us a new birth as his sons, by raising Jesus Christ from the dead, so that we have a sure ⁴ hope ·and the promise of an inheritance that can never be spoiled or soiled and never fade away, because it is being ⁵ kept for you in the heavens. ·Through your faith, God's power will guard you until the salvation which has been ⁶ prepared is revealed at the end of time. ·This is a cause of great joy for you, even though you may for a short time ⁷ have to bear being plagued by all sorts of trials; ·so that, when Jesus Christ is revealed, your faith will have been tested and proved like gold—only it is more precious than gold, which is corruptible even though it bears testing by fire—and then you will have praise and glory and honor. ⁸ You did not see him, yet you love him; and still without seeing him, you are already filled with a joy so glorious ⁹ that it cannot be described, because you believe; ·and you are sure of the end to which your faith looks forward, that is, the salvation of your souls.

The hope of the prophets

¹⁰ It was this salvation that the prophets were looking and searching so hard for; their prophecies were about the ¹¹ grace which was to come to you. ·The Spirit of Christ which was in them foretold the sufferings of Christ and

the glories that would come after them, and they tried to find out at what time and in what circumstances all this
12 was to be expected. •It was revealed to them that the news they brought of all the things which have now been announced to you, by those who preached to you the Good News through the Holy Spirit sent from heaven, was for you and not for themselves. Even the angels long to catch a glimpse of these things.

A call to sanctity and watchfulness

13 Free your minds, then, of encumbrances; control them, and put your trust in nothing but the grace that will be
14 given you when Jesus Christ is revealed. •Do not behave in the way that you liked to before you learned the truth;
15 make a habit of obedience: •be holy in all you do, since
16 it is the Holy One who has called you, •and scripture says: *Be holy, for I am holy.*[a]
17 If you are acknowledging as your Father one who has no favorites and judges everyone according to what he has done, you must be scrupulously careful as long as you
18 are living away from your home. •Remember, the ransom that was *paid to free you*[b] from the useless way of life your ancestors handed down was not paid in anything
19 corruptible, neither in *silver* nor gold, •but in the precious
20 blood of a lamb without spot or stain, namely Christ; •who, though known since before the world was made, has been revealed only in our time, the end of the ages, for your
21 sake. •Through him you now have faith in God, who raised him from the dead and gave him glory for that very reason —so that you would have faith and hope in God.

Love

22 You have been obedient to the truth and purified your souls until you can love like brothers, in sincerity; let your
23 love for each other be real and from the heart—•your new birth was not from any mortal seed but from the everlasting
24 word of the living and eternal God. •*All flesh is grass and its glory like the wild flower's. The grass withers, the*
25 *flower falls,* •*but the word of the Lord remains for ever.*[c] What is this word? It is the Good News that has been brought to you.

1 a. Lv 19:2 . b. Is 52:3   c. Is 40:6-8

Integrity

¹ Be sure, then, you are never spiteful, or deceitful, or hypocritical, or envious and critical of each other.
² You are new born, and, like babies, you should be hungry for nothing but milk—the spiritual honesty which will help
³ you to grow up to salvation—·now that you have *tasted the goodness of the Lord.*ᵃ

The new priesthood

⁴ He is the living stone, rejected by men but chosen by
⁵ God and precious to him; set yourselves close to him ·so that you too, the holy priesthood that offers the spiritual sacrifices which Jesus Christ has made acceptable to God,
⁶ may be living stones making a spiritual house. ·As scripture says: *See how I lay in Zion a precious cornerstone that I have chosen* and *the man who rests his trust on it*
⁷ *will not be disappointed.*ᵇ ·That means that for you who are believers, it is precious; but for unbelievers, *the stone*
⁸ *rejected by the builders has proved to be the keystone,*ᶜ ·*a stone to stumble over, a rock to bring men down.*ᵈ They stumble over it because they do not believe in the word; it was the fate in store for them.
⁹ But you are *a chosen race, a royal priesthood, a consecrated nation, a people set apart*ᵉ to sing the praises of God who called you out of the darkness into his wonderful
¹⁰ light. ·Once you were *not a people*ᶠ at all and now you are the People of God; once you were *outside the mercy* and now *you have been given mercy.*

The obligations of Christians: toward pagans

¹¹ I urge you, my dear people, while you are *visitors and pilgrims*ᵍ to keep yourselves free from the selfish passions
¹² that attack the soul. ·Always behave honorably among pagans so that they can see your good works for themselves and, when the day of reckoning comes, give thanks to God for the things which now make them denounce you as criminals.

Toward civil authority

¹³ For the sake of the Lord, accept the authority of every social institution: the emperor, as the supreme authority,
¹⁴ and the governors as commissioned by him to punish crim-
¹⁵ inals and praise good citizenship. ·God wants you to be

good citizens, so as to silence what fools are saying in their
16 ignorance. ·You are slaves of no one except God, so behave like free men, and never use your freedom as an
17 excuse for wickedness. ·Have respect for everyone and
love for our community; fear God and honor the emperor.

Toward masters

18 Slaves must be respectful and obedient to their masters,
not only when they are kind and gentle but also when they
19 are unfair. ·You see, there is some merit in putting up with
the pains of unearned punishment if it is done for the sake
20 of God ·but there is nothing meritorious in taking a beating patiently if you have done something wrong to deserve
it. The merit, in the sight of God, is in bearing it patiently
when you are punished after doing your duty.
21 This, in fact, is what you were called to do, because
Christ suffered for you and left an example for you to
22 follow the way he took. ·He had not done anything wrong,
23 and *there had been no perjury in his mouth.*[h] ·He was
insulted and did not retaliate with insults; when he was
tortured he made no threats but he put his trust in the
24 righteous judge. ·He was *bearing our faults* in his own
body on the cross, so that we might die to our faults and
live for holiness; *through his wounds you have been healed.*
You had *gone astray like sheep* but now you have come
back to the shepherd and guardian[i] of your souls.

In marriage

1 **3** In the same way, wives should be obedient to their
husbands. Then, if there are some husbands who have
not yet obeyed the word, they may find themselves won
over, without a word spoken, by the way their wives be-
2 have, ·when they see how faithful and conscientious they
3 are. ·Do not dress up for show: doing up your hair, wear-
4 ing gold bracelets and fine clothes; ·all this should be inside, in a person's heart, imperishable: the ornament of a
sweet and gentle disposition—this is what is precious in the
5 sight of God. ·That was how the holy women of the past
dressed themselves attractively—they hoped in God and were

2 a. Ps 34:8 b. Is 28:16 c. Ps 18:22 d. Is 8:14 e. Is
43:20-21 f. Ho 1:9; the two other quotations in this sentence
are allusive references to Ho 2. g. Ps 39:12 h. This quotation,
and the others in this paragraph, are from Is 53. i. *episcopos*.

6 tender and obedient to their husbands; ·like Sarah, who was obedient to Abraham, and called him her *lord*. You are now her children, as long as you live good lives and do not give way to fear or worry.

7 In the same way, husbands must always treat their wives with consideration in their life together, respecting a woman as one who, though she may be the weaker partner, is equally an heir to the life of grace. This will stop anything from coming in the way of your prayers.

Toward the brothers

8 Finally: you should all agree among yourselves and be sympathetic; love the brothers, have compassion and be self-effacing. ·Never pay back one wrong with another, or an angry word with another one; instead, pay back with a blessing. That is what you are called to do, so that you

10 inherit a blessing yourself. ·Remember: *Anyone who wants to have a happy life and to enjoy prosperity must banish malice from his tongue, deceitful conversation from his*

11 *lips;* ·*he must never yield to evil but must practice good;*

12 *he must seek peace and pursue it.* ·*Because the face of the Lord frowns on evil men, but the eyes of the Lord are turned toward the virtuous, his ears to their cry.*[a]

In persecution

13 No one can hurt you if you are determined to do only

14 what is right; ·if you do have to suffer for being good, you will count it a blessing. *There is no need to be afraid or*

15 *to worry about them.*[b] ·Simply reverence the Lord[c] Christ in your hearts, and always have your answer ready for people who ask you the reason for the hope that you all

16 have. ·But give it with courtesy and respect and with a clear conscience, so that those who slander you when you are living a good life in Christ may be proved wrong in

17 the accusations that they bring. ·And if it is the will of God that you should suffer, it is better to suffer for doing right than for doing wrong.

The resurrection and "the descent into hell"

18 Why, Christ himself, innocent though he was, had died once for sins, died for the guilty, to lead us to God. In the body he was put to death, in the spirit he was

19 raised to life, ·and, in the spirit, he went to preach to the

20 spirits in prison. ·Now it was long ago, when Noah was

still building that ark which saved only a small group of
eight people "by water," and when God was still waiting
21 patiently, that these spirits refused to believe. ·That water
is a type of the baptism which saves you now, and which
is not the washing off of physical dirt but a pledge made
to God from a good conscience, through the resurrection
22 of Jesus Christ, ·who has entered heaven and is at God's
right hand, now that he has made the angels and Dominations and Powers his subjects.

1   Think of what Christ suffered in this life, and then arm
    yourselves with the same resolution that he had: anyone
who in this life has bodily suffering has broken with sin,
2 because for the rest of his life on earth he is not ruled by
3 human passions but only by the will of God. ·You spent
quite long enough in the past living the sort of life that
pagans live, behaving indecently, giving way to your passions, drinking all the time, having wild parties and drunken
orgies and degrading yourselves by following false gods.
4 So people cannot understand why you no longer hurry off
with them to join this flood which is rushing down to ruin,
5 and then they begin to spread libels about you. ·They will
have to answer for it in front of the judge who is ready to
6 judge the living and the dead. ·And because he is their
judge too, the dead had to be told the Good News as well,
so that though, in their life on earth, they had been through
the judgment that comes to all humanity, they might come
to God's life in the spirit.

The revelation of Christ is close

7   Everything will soon come to an end, so, to pray better,
8 keep a calm and sober mind. ·Above all, never let your
love for each other grow insincere, since *love covers over*
9 *many a sin.*ᵃ ·Welcome each other into your houses with-
10 out grumbling. ·Each one of you has received a special
grace, so, like good stewards responsible for all these different graces of God, put yourselves at the service of others.
11 If you are a speaker, speak in words which seem to come
from God; if you are a helper, help as though every action was done at God's orders; so that in everything God
may receive the glory, through Jesus Christ, since to him
alone belong all glory and power for ever and ever. Amen.

3 a. Ps 34:12-16   b. Is 8:12-13 (LXX)   c. Pr 3:25
4 a. Pr 10:12

Recapitulation

¹² My dear people, you must not think it unaccountable that you should be tested by fire. There is nothing extraor-
¹³ dinary in what has happened to you. ·If you can have some share in the sufferings of Christ, be glad, because you will enjoy a much greater gladness when his glory is
¹⁴ revealed. ·It is a blessing for you when they insult you for bearing the name of Christ, because it means that you have the Spirit of glory, the Spirit of God resting on you.
¹⁵ None of you should ever deserve to suffer for being a
¹⁶ murderer, a thief, a criminal or an informer; ·but if any-one of you should suffer for being a Christian, then he is not to be ashamed of it; he should thank God that he has
¹⁷ been called one. ·The time has come for the judgment to begin at the household of God; and if what we know now is only the beginning, what will it be when it comes down
¹⁸ to those who refuse to believe God's Good News? *If it is hard for a good man to be saved, what will happen to the
¹⁹ wicked and to sinners?*[b] ·So even those whom God al-lows to suffer must trust themselves to the constancy of the creator and go on doing good.

Instructions: to the elders

¹ 5 Now I have something to tell your elders: I am an elder myself, and a witness to the sufferings of Christ, and with you I have a share in the glory that is to be re-
² vealed. ·Be the shepherds of the flock of God that is en-trusted to you: watch over it, not simply as a duty but gladly, because God wants it; not for sordid money, but
³ because you are eager to do it. ·Never be a dictator over any group that is put in your charge, but be an example
⁴ that the whole flock can follow. ·When the chief shepherd appears, you will be given the crown of unfading glory.

To the faithful

⁵ To the rest of you I say: do what the elders tell you, and all wrap yourselves in humility to be servants of each other, because *God refuses the proud and will always favor*
⁶ *the humble.*[a] ·Bow down, then, before the power of God
⁷ now, and he will raise you up on the appointed day; ·*un-load* all *your worries on to him,*[b] since he is looking after
⁸ you. ·*Be calm but vigilant,* because your enemy the devil is prowling round like a roaring lion, looking for someone

⁹ to eat. ·Stand up to him, strong in faith and in the knowledge that your brothers all over the world are suffering
¹⁰ the same things. ·You will have to suffer only for a little
while: the God of all grace who called you to eternal glory
in Christ will see that all is well again: he will confirm,
¹¹ streng*hen and support you. ·His power lasts for ever and
ever. Amen.

Last words. Greetings

¹² I write these few words to you through Silvanus, who
is a brother I know I can trust, to encourage you never
to let go this true grace of God to which I bear witness.
¹³ Your sister in Babylon, who is with you among the
chosen, sends you greetings; so does my son, Mark.
¹⁴ Greet one another with a kiss of love.
Peace to you all who are in Christ.

b. Pr 11:31 (LXX)
5 a. Pr 3:34 (LXX). **b.** Ps 55:22

2 Peter

THE SECOND LETTER OF PETER

Greetings

1 ¹ From Simeon Peter, servant and apostle of Jesus Christ; to all who treasure the same faith as ourselves, given through the righteousness of our God and savior Jesus ² Christ. ·May you have more and more grace and peace as you come to know our Lord more and more.

A call to Christian living, and its reward

³ By his divine power, he has given us all the things that we need for life and for true devotion, bringing us to know God himself, who has called us by his own glory and good-
⁴ ness. ·In making these gifts, he has given us the guarantee of something very great and wonderful to come: through them you will be able to share the divine nature and to
⁵ escape corruption in a world that is sunk in vice. ·But to attain this, you will have to do your utmost yourselves, add-ing goodness to the faith that you have, understanding to
⁶ your goodness, ·self-control to your understanding, patience
⁷ to your self-control, true devotion to your patience, ·kind-ness toward your fellow men to your devotion, and, to
⁸ this kindness, love. ·If you have a generous supply of these, they will not leave you ineffectual or unproductive: they will bring you to a real knowledge of our Lord Jesus Christ.
⁹ But without them a man is blind or else short-sighted; he
¹⁰ has forgotten how his past sins were washed away. ·Broth-ers, you have been called and chosen: work all the harder to justify it. If you do all these things there is no danger
¹¹ that you will ever fall away. ·In this way you will be granted admittance into the eternal kingdom of our Lord and savior Jesus Christ.

The apostolic witness

¹² That is why I am continually recalling the same truths to you, even though you already know them and firmly
¹³ hold them. ·I am sure it is my duty, as long as I am in

14. this tent, to keep stirring you up with reminders, ·since I know the time for taking off this tent is coming soon, as
15 our Lord Jesus Christ foretold to me. ·And I shall take great care that after my own departure you will still have a means to recall these things to memory.
16 It was not any cleverly invented myths that we were repeating when we brought you the knowledge of the power and the coming of our Lord Jesus Christ; we had
17 seen his majesty for ourselves. ·He was honored and glorified by God the Father, when the Sublime Glory itself spoke to him and said, "This is my Son, the Beloved; he
18 enjoys my favor." ·We heard this ourselves, spoken from heaven, when we were with him on the holy mountain.*a*

The value of prophecy

19 So we have confirmation of what was said in prophecies; and you will be right to depend on prophecy and take it as a lamp for lighting a way through the dark until the dawn
20 comes and the morning star rises in your minds. ·At the same time, we must be most careful to remember that the interpretation of scriptural prophecy is never a matter for
21 the individual. ·Why? Because no prophecy ever came from man's initiative. When men spoke for God it was the Holy Spirit that moved them.

False teachers

1 2 As there were false prophets in the past history of our people, so you too will have your false teachers, who will insinuate their own·disruptive views and disown the Master who purchased their freedom. They will destroy
2 themselves very quickly; ·but there will be many who copy their shameful behavior and the Way of Truth will be
8 brought into disrepute on their account. ·They will eagerly try to buy you for themselves with insidious speeches, but for them the Condemnation, pronounced so long ago, is
4 at its work already, and Destruction is not asleep. ·When angels sinned, God did not spare them: he sent them down to the underworld and consigned them to the dark underground caves to be held there till the day of Judgment.
5 Nor did he spare the world in ancient times: it was only Noah he saved, the preacher of righteousness, along with seven others, when he sent the Flood over a disobedient

1 a. At the transfiguration; Mt 17, Mk 9, Lk 9.

6 world. ·The cities of Sodom and Gomorrah, these too he
condemned and reduced to ashes; he destroyed them completely, as a warning to anybody lacking reverence in the
7 future; ·he rescued Lot, however, a holy man who had
been sickened by the shameless way in which these vile
8 people behaved—·for that holy man, living among them,
was outraged in his good soul by the crimes that he saw
9 and heard of every day. ·These are all examples of how
the Lord can rescue the good from the ordeal, and hold
the wicked for their punishment until the day of Judgment,
10 especially those who are governed by their corrupt bodily
desires and have no respect for authority.

The punishment to come

Such self-willed people with no reverence are not afraid
11 of offending against the glorious ones, ·but the angels in
their greater strength and power make no complaint or
12 accusation against them in front of the Lord. ·All the same,
these people who only insult anything that they do not
understand are not reasoning beings, but simply animals
born to be caught and killed, and they will quite certainly
destroy themselves by their own work of destruction,
13 and get their reward of evil for the evil that they do. They
are unsightly blots on your society: men whose only object
is dissipation all day long, and they amuse themselves deceiving you even when they are your guests at a meal;
14 with their eyes always looking for adultery, men with an
infinite capacity for sinning, they will seduce any soul which
is at all unstable. Greed is the one lesson their minds have
15 learned. They are under a curse. ·They have left the right
path and wandered off to follow the path of Balaam son
16 of Beor, who thought he could profit best by sinning, ·until
he was called to order for his faults. The dumb donkey put
a stop to that prophet's madness when it talked like a man.
17 People like this are dried-up rivers, fogs swirling in the
wind, and the dark underworld is the place reserved for
18 them. ·With their high-flown talk, which is all hollow, they
tempt back the ones who have only just escaped from paganism, playing on their bodily desires with debaucheries.
19 They may promise freedom but they themselves are slaves,
slaves to corruption; because if anyone lets himself be dom-
20 inated by anything, then he is a slave to it; ·and anyone
who has escaped the pollution of the world once by com-

ing to know our Lord and savior Jesus Christ, and who
then allows himself to be entangled by it a second time and
mastered, will end up in a worse state than he began in.
21 It would even have been better for him never to have
learned the way of holiness, than to know it and afterward
22 desert the holy rule that was entrusted to him. ·What he
has done is exactly as the proverb rightly says: *The dog
goes back to his own vomit[a]* and: When the sow has been
washed, it wallows in the mud.

The Day of the Lord; the prophets and the apostles

1 3 My friends, this is my second letter to you, and in both
of them I have tried to awaken a true understanding in
2 you by giving you a reminder: ·recalling to you what was
said in the past by the holy prophets and the commandments of the Lord and savior which you were given by
the apostles.

3   We must be careful to remember that during the last
days there are bound to be people who will be scornful, the
kind who always please themselves what they do, and they
4 will make fun of the promise ·and ask, "Well, where is this
coming? Everything goes on as it has since the Fathers
5 died, as it has since it began at the creation." ·They are
choosing to forget that there were heavens at the beginning, and that the earth was formed by the word of God
6 out of water and between the waters, ·so that the world
of that time was destroyed by being flooded by water.
7 But by the same word, the present sky and earth are destined for fire, and are only being reserved until Judgment
day so that all sinners may be destroyed.

8   But there is one thing, my friends, that you must never
forget: that with the Lord, "a day" can mean a thousand
9 years, and *a thousand years is like a day.[a]* ·The Lord is
not being slow to carry out his promises, as anybody else
might be called slow; but he is being patient with you all,
wanting nobody to be lost and everybody to be brought
10 to change his ways. ·The Day of the Lord will come like a
thief, and then with a roar the sky will vanish, the elements will catch fire and fall apart, the earth and all that
it contains will be burned up.

2 a. Pr 26:11
3 a. Ps 90:4

Conclusion and doxology

11 Since everything is coming to an end like this, you should
12 be living holy and saintly lives ·while you wait and long
for the Day of God to come, when the sky will dissolve in
13 flames and the elements melt in the heat. ·What we are
waiting for is what he promised: the new heavens and new
earth, the place where righteousness will be at home.
14 So then, my friends, while you are waiting, do your best
to live lives without spot or stain so that he will find you
15 at peace. ·Think of our Lord's patience as your opportunity to be saved: our brother Paul, who is so dear to
us, told you this when he wrote to you with the wisdom
16 that is his special gift. ·He always writes like this when he
deals with this sort of subject, and this makes some points
in his letter hard to understand; these are the points that
uneducated and unbalanced people distort, in the same
way as they distort the rest of scripture—a fatal thing for
17 them to do. ·You have been warned about this, my friends;
be careful not to get carried away by the errors of unprin-
cipled people, from the firm ground that you are standing
18 on. ·Instead, go on growing in the grace and in the knowledge of our Lord and savior Jesus Christ. To him be
glory, in time and in eternity. Amen.

1 John

THE FIRST LETTER OF JOHN

INTRODUCTION

The incarnate Word

1 ¹ Something which has existed since the beginning,
that we have heard,
and we have seen with our own eyes;
that we have watched
and touched with our hands:
the Word, who is life—
this is our subject.

² That life was made visible:
we saw it and we are giving our testimony,
telling you of the eternal life
which was with the Father and has been made visible
to us.

³ What we have seen and heard
we are telling you
so that you too may be in union with us,
as we are in union
with the Father
and with his Son Jesus Christ.

⁴ We are writing this to you to make our own joy complete.

I. WALK IN THE LIGHT

⁵ This is what we have heard from him,
and the message that we are announcing to you:
God is light; there is no darkness in him at all.

⁶ If we say that we are in union with God[a]

1 a. In the translation, "God" or "Christ" has been used in several places, where the Greek has a simple pronoun, in order to
make the writer's meaning clear.

while we are living in darkness,
we are lying because we are not living the truth.
7 But if we live our lives in the light,
as he is in the light,
we are in union with one another,
and the blood of Jesus, his Son,
purifies us from all sin.

First condition: break with sin

8 If we say we have no sin in us,
we are deceiving ourselves
and refusing to admit the truth;
9 but if we acknowledge our sins,
then God who is faithful and just
will forgive our sins and purify us
from everything that is wrong.
10 To say that we have never sinned
is to call God a liar
and to show that his word is not in us.

1 2 I am writing this, my children,
to stop you sinning;
but if anyone should sin,
we have our advocate with the Father,
Jesus Christ, who is just;
2 he is the sacrifice that takes our sins away,
and not only ours,
but the whole world's.

Second condition: keep the commandments, especially the law of love

3 We can be sure that we know God
only by keeping his commandments.
4 Anyone who says, "I know him,"
and does not keep his commandments,
is a liar,
refusing to admit the truth.
5 But when anyone does obey what he has said,
God's love comes to perfection in him.
We can be sure
that we are in God
6 only when the one who claims to be living in him
is living the same kind of life as Christ lived.
7 My dear people,

this is not a new commandment that I am writing to
tell you,
but an old commandment
that you were given from the beginning,
the original commandment which was the message
brought to you.

8 Yet in another way, what I am writing to you,
and what is being carried out in your lives as it was
in his,
is a new commandment;
because the night is over
and the real light is already shining.

9 Anyone who claims to be in the light
but hates his brother
is still in the dark.

10 But anyone who loves his brother is living in the light
and need not be afraid of stumbling;
unlike the man who hates his brother and is in the
darkness,

11 not knowing where he is going,
because it is too dark to see.

Third condition: detachment from the world

12 I am writing to you, my own children,
whose sins have already been forgiven through his
name;

13 I am writing to you, fathers,
who have come to know the one
who has existed since the beginning;
I am writing to you, young men,
who have already overcome the Evil One;

14 I have written to you, children,
because you already know the Father;
I have written to you, fathers,
because you have come to know the one
who has existed since the beginning;
I have written to you, young men,
because you are strong and God's word has made its
home in you,
and you have overcome the Evil One.

15 You must not love this passing world
or anything that is in the world.
The love of the Father cannot be
in any man who loves the world,

16 because nothing the world has to offer
    —the sensual body,
    the lustful eye,
    pride in possessions—
    could ever come from the Father
    but only from the world;
17 and the world, with all it craves for,
    is coming to an end;
    but anyone who does the will of God
    remains for ever.

Fourth condition: be on guard against the enemies of Christ

18 Children, these are the last days;
    you were told that an Antichrist must come,
    and now several antichrists have already appeared;
    we know from this that these are the last days.
19 Those rivals of Christ came out of our own number,
        but they had never really belonged;
    if they had belonged, they would have stayed with us;
    but they left us, to prove that not one of them
    ever belonged to us.
20 But you have been anointed by the Holy One,
    and have all received the knowledge.
21 It is not because you do not know the truth that I am
        writing to you
    but rather because you know it already
    and know that no lie can come from the truth.
22 The man who denies that Jesus is the Christ—
    he is the liar,
    he is Antichrist;
    and he is denying the Father as well as the Son,
23 because no one who has the Father can deny the Son,
    and to acknowledge the Son is to have the Father as
        well.
24 Keep alive in yourselves what you were taught in the
        beginning:
    as long as what you were taught in the beginning is
        alive in you,
    you will live in the Son
    and in the Father;
25 and what is promised to you by his own promise
    is eternal life.

26   This is all that I am writing to you about the people
            who are trying to lead you astray.
27   But you have not lost the anointing that he gave you,
        and you do not need anyone to teach you;
        the anointing he gave teaches you everything;
        you are anointed with truth, not with a lie,
        and as it has taught you, so you must stay in him.
28   Live in Christ, then, my children,
        so that if he appears, we may have full confidence,
        and not turn from him in shame
        at his coming.
29.   You know that God is righteous—
        then you must recognize that everyone whose life is
                righteous
        has been begotten by him.

II. LIVE AS GOD'S CHILDREN

1   Think of the love that the Father has lavished on us,
3   by letting us be called God's children;
        and that is what we are.
        Because the world refused to acknowledge him,
        therefore it does not acknowledge us.
2   My dear people, we are already the children of God
        but what we are to be in the future has not yet been
                revealed;
        all we know is, that when it is revealed
        we shall be like him
        because we shall see him as he really is.

First condition: break with sin

3   Surely everyone who entertains this hope
        must purify himself, must try to be as pure as Christ.
4   Anyone who sins at all
        breaks the law,
        because to sin is to break the law.
5   Now you know that he appeared in order to abolish sin,
        and that in him there is no sin;
6   anyone who lives in God does not sin,
        and anyone who sins
        has never seen him or known him.
7   My children, do not let anyone lead you astray:
        to live a holy life

is to be holy just as he is holy;
8 to lead a sinful life is to belong to the devil,
   since the devil was a sinner from the beginning.
   It was to undo all that the devil has done
   that the Son of God appeared.
9 No one who has been begotten by God sins;
   because God's seed remains inside him,
   he cannot sin when he has been begotten by God.

Second condition: keep the commandments, especially the law of love

10 In this way we distinguish the children of God
    from the children of the devil:
    anybody not living a holy life
    and not loving his brother
    is no child of God's.
11 This is the message
    as you heard it from the beginning:
    that we are to love one another;
12 not to be like Cain, who belonged to the Evil One
    and cut his brother's throat;
    cut his brother's throat simply for this reason,
    that his own life was evil and his brother lived a good
         life.
13 You must not be surprised, brothers, when the world
         hates you;
14 we have passed out of death and into life,
    and of this we can be sure
    because we love our brothers.
15 If you refuse to love, you must remain dead;
    to hate your brother is to be a murderer,
    and murderers, as you know, do not have eternal life
         in them.
16 This has taught us love—
    that he gave up his life for us;
    and we, too, ought to give up our lives for our brothers.
17 If a man who was rich enough in this world's goods
    saw that one of his brothers was in need,
    but closed his heart to him,
    how could the love of God be living in him?
18 My children,
    our love is not to be just words or mere talk,
    but something real and active;
19 only by this can we be certain

that we are children of the truth
and be able to quieten our conscience in his presence,
20   whatever accusations it may raise against us,
because God is greater than our conscience and he
knows everything.
21   My dear people,
if we cannot be condemned by our own conscience,
we need not be afraid in God's presence,
22   and whatever we ask him,
we shall receive,
because we keep his commandments
and live the kind of life that he wants.
23   His commandments are these:
that we believe in the name of his Son Jesus Christ
and that we love one another
as he told us to.
24   Whoever keeps his commandments
lives in God and God lives in him.
We know that he lives in us
by the Spirit that he has given us.

Third condition: be on guard against the enemies of Christ and against the world

1 **4** It is not every spirit, my dear people, that you can trust;
test them, to see if they come from God;
there are many false prophets, now, in the world.
2   You can tell the spirits that come from God by this:
every spirit which acknowledges that Jesus the Christ
has come in the flesh
is from God;
3   but any spirit which will not say this of Jesus
is not from God,
but is the spirit of Antichrist,
whose coming you were warned about.
Well, now he is here, in the world.
4   Children,
you have already overcome these false prophets,
because you are from God and you have in you
one who is greater than anyone in this world;
5   as for them, they are of the world,
and so they speak the language of the world
and the world listens to them.
6   But we are children of God,

and those who know God listen to us;
those who are not of God refuse to listen to us.
This is how we can tell
the spirit of truth from the spirit of falsehood.

III. LOVE AND FAITH

Love

7   My dear people,
let us love one another
since love comes from God
and everyone who loves is begotten by God and knows
    God.
8   Anyone who fails to love can never have known God,
because God is love.
9   God's love for us was revealed
when God sent into the world his only Son
so that we could have life through him;
10   this is the love I mean:
not our love for God,
but God's love for us when he sent his Son
to be the sacrifice that takes our sins away.
11   My dear people,
since God has loved us so much,
we too should love one another.
12   No one has ever seen God;
but as long as we love one another
God will live in us
and his love will be complete in us.
13   We can know that we are living in him
and he is living in us
because he lets us share his Spirit.
14   We ourselves saw and we testify
that the Father sent his Son
as savior of the world.
15   If anyone acknowledges that Jesus is the Son of God,
God lives in him, and he in God.
16   We ourselves have known and put our faith in
God's love toward ourselves.
God is love
and anyone who lives in love lives in God,
and God lives in him.
17   Love will come to its perfection in us

when we can face the day of Judgment without fear;
because even in this world
we have become as he is.

18   In love there can be no fear,
but fear is driven out by perfect love:
because to fear is to expect punishment,
and anyone who is afraid is still imperfect in love.

19   We are to love, then,
because he loved us first.

20   Anyone who says, "I love God,"
and hates his brother,
is a liar,
since a man who does not love the brother that he
          can see
cannot love God, whom he has never seen.

21   So this is the commandment that he has given us,
that anyone who loves God must also love his brother.

1 **5** Whoever believes that Jesus is the Christ
has been begotten by God;
and whoever loves the Father that begot him
loves the child whom he begets.

2   We can be sure that we love God's children
if we love God himself and do what he has commanded
          us;

3   this is what loving God is—
keeping his commandments;

4   and his commandments are not difficult,
because anyone who has been begotten by God
has already overcome the world;
this is the victory over the world—
our faith.

Faith

5   Who can overcome the world?
Only the man who believes that Jesus is the Son of God:

6   Jesus Christ who came by water and blood,[a]
not with water only,
but with water and blood;
with the Spirit as another witness—
since the Spirit is the truth—

5 a. The water and the blood from the side of Jesus, Jn 19:34,
are here used as figures of his "coming" to all Christians,
through the water of baptism and through his sacrificial death.

7   so that there are three witnesses,
8   the Spirit, the water and the blood,
    and all three of them agree.
9   We accept the testimony of human witnesses,
    but God's testimony is much greater,
    and this is God's testimony,
    given as evidence for his Son.
10   Everybody who believes in the Son of God
    has this testimony inside him;
    and anyone who will not believe God
    is making God out to be a liar,
    because he has not trusted
    the testimony God has given about his Son.
11   This is the testimony:
    God has given us eternal life
    and this life is in his Son;
12   anyone who has the Son has life,
    anyone who does not have the Son does not have life.

Conclusion

13   I have written all this to you
    so that you who believe in the name of the Son of God
    may be sure that you have eternal life.

ENDING

Prayer for sinners

14   We are quite confident that if we ask him for anything,
    and it is in accordance with his will,
    he will hear us;
15   and, knowing that whatever we may ask, he hears us,
    we know that we have already been granted what we
            asked of him.
16   If anybody sees his brother commit a sin
    that is not a deadly sin,
    he has only to pray, and God will give life to the sinner
    —not those who commit a deadly sin;
    for there is a sin that is death,
    and I will not say that you must pray about that.
17   Every kind of wrong-doing is sin,
    but not all sin is deadly.

Summary of the letter

18   We know that anyone who has been begotten by God
      does not sin,
      because the begotten Son of God protects him,
      and the Evil One does not touch him.

19   We know that we belong to God,
      but the whole world lies in the power of the Evil One.

20   We know, too, that the Son of God has come,
      and has given us the power
      to know the true God.
      We are in the true God,
      as we are in his Son, Jesus Christ.
      This is the true God,
      this is eternal life.

21   Children, be on your guard against false gods.

2 John

THE SECOND LETTER OF JOHN

¹ From the Elder: my greetings to the Lady, the chosen one,ᵃ and to her children, she whom I love in the truth—and I am not the only one, for so do all who have come ² to know the truth—·because of the truth that lives in us ³ and will be with us for ever. ·In our life of truth and love, we shall have grace, mercy and peace from God the Father and from Jesus Christ, the Son of the Father.

The law of love

⁴ It has given me great joy to find that your children have been living the life of truth as we were commanded by ⁵ the Father. ·I am writing now, dear lady, not to give you any new commandment, but the one which we were given at the beginning, and to plead: let us love one another. ⁶ To love is to live according to his commandments: this is the commandment which you have heard since the beginning, to live a life of love.

The enemies of Christ

⁷ There are many deceivers about in the world, refusing to admit that Jesus Christ has come in the flesh. They ⁸ are the Deceiver; they are the Antichrist. ·Watch yourselves, or all our work will be lost and not get the reward ⁹ it deserves. ·If anybody does not keep within the teaching of Christ but goes beyond it, he cannot have God with him: only those who keep to what he taught can have the ¹⁰ Father and the Son with them. ·If anyone comes to you bringing a different doctrine, you must not receive him in ¹¹ your house or even give him a greeting. ·To greet him would make you a partner in his wicked work.
¹² There are several things I have to tell you, but I have thought it best not to trust them to paper and ink. I hope instead to visit you and talk to you personally, so that our joy may be complete.
¹³ Greetings to you from the children of your sister,ᵇ the chosen one.

1 a. The local church to which the letter is addressed.   b. The local church from which the letter is sent.

3 John

THE THIRD LETTER OF JOHN

1 From the Elder: greetings to my dear friend Gaius,
2 whom I love in the truth. ·My dear friend, I hope everything is going happily with you and that you are as well
3 physically as you are spiritually. ·It was a great joy to me when some brothers came and told of your faithfulness to
4 the truth, and of your life in the truth. ·It is always my greatest joy to hear that my children are living according to the truth.

5 My friend, you have done faithful work in looking after these brothers, even though they were complete strangers
6 to you. ·They are a proof to the whole Church of your charity and it would be a very good thing if you could help them on their journey in a way that God would approve.
7 It was entirely for the sake of the name that they set out,
8 without depending on the pagans for anything; ·it is our duty to welcome men of this sort and contribute our share to their work for the truth.

Beware of the example of Diotrephes

9 I have written a note for the members of the church, but Diotrephes, who seems to enjoy being in charge of it,
10 refuses to accept us. ·So if I come, I shall tell everyone how he has behaved, and about the wicked accusations he has been circulating against us. As if that were not enough, he not only refuses to welcome our brothers, but prevents the other people who would have liked to from doing it,
11 and expells them from the church. ·My dear friend, never follow such a bad example, but keep following the good one; anyone who does what is right is a child of God, but the person who does what is wrong has never seen God.

Commendation of Demetrius

12 Demetrius has been approved by everyone, and indeed by the truth itself. We too will vouch for him and you know that our testimony is true.

Epilogue

13 There are several things I had to tell you but I would
14 rather not trust them to pen and ink. ·However, I hope to
15 see you soon and talk to you personally. ·Peace be with
you; greetings from your friends; greet each of our friends
by name.

THE LETTER OF
Jude

Address

1 From Jude, servant of Jesus Christ and brother of James;
to those who are called, to those who are dear to God
2 the Father and kept safe for Jesus Christ, ·wishing you all
mercy and peace and love.

The reason for this letter

3 My dear friends, at a time when I was eagerly looking
forward to writing to you about the salvation that we all
share, I have been forced to write to you now and appeal
to you to fight hard for the faith which has been once and
4 for all entrusted to the saints. ·Certain people have in-
filtrated among you, and they are the ones you had a
warning about, in writing, long ago, when they were condemned for denying all religion, turning the grace of our
God into immorality, and rejecting our only Master and
Lord, Jesus Christ.

The false teachers: the certainty of their punishment

5 I should like to remind you—though you have already
learned it once and for all—how the Lord rescued the nation from Egypt, but afterward he still destroyed the men
6 who did not trust him. ·Next let me remind you of the
angels who had supreme authority but did not keep it and
left their appointed sphere;[a] he has kept them down in the
dark, in spiritual chains, to be judged on the great day.
7 The fornication of Sodom and Gomorrah and the other
nearby towns was equally unnatural, and it is a warning
to us that they are paying for their crimes in eternal fire.

Their violent language

8 Nevertheless, these people are doing the same: in their
delusions they not only defile their bodies and disregard

a. Briefly mentioned in Gn 6:1-2, but elaborated in *The Book
of Enoch.*

⁹ authority, but abuse the glorious angels as well. ·Not even the archangel Michael, when he was engaged in argument with the devil about the corpse of Moses, dared to denounce him in the language of abuse; all he said was, "Let ¹⁰ the Lord correct you." ·But these people abuse anything they do not understand; and the only things they do understand—just by nature like unreasoning animals—will turn out to be fatal to them.

Their vicious behavior

¹¹ May they get what they deserve, because they have followed Cain; they have rushed to make the same mistake as Balaam and for the same reward; they have rebelled ¹² just as Korah did—and share the same fate. ·They are a dangerous obstacle to your community meals, coming for the food and quite shamelessly only looking after themselves. They are like clouds blown about by the winds and bringing no rain, or like barren trees which are then up- ¹³ rooted in the winter and so are twice dead; ·like wild sea waves capped with shame as if with foam; or like shooting ¹⁴ stars bound for an eternity of black darkness. ·It was with them in mind that Enoch, the seventh patriarch from Adam, made his prophecy when he said, "I tell you, the Lord will ¹⁵ come with his saints in their tens of thousands, ·to pronounce judgment on all mankind and to sentence the wicked for all the wicked things they have done, and for all the defiant things said against him by irreligious sin- ¹⁶ ners." ·They are mischief-makers, grumblers governed only by their own desires, with *mouths full of boastful talk*, ready with flattery for other people when they see some advantage in it.

A warning

¹⁷ But remember, my dear friends, what the apostles of ¹⁸ our Lord Jesus Christ told you to expect. ·"At the end of time," they told you "there are going to be people who sneer at religion and follow nothing but their own desires ¹⁹ for wickedness." ·These unspiritual and selfish people are nothing but mischief-makers.

The duties of love

²⁰ But you, my dear friends, must use your most holy faith as your foundation and build on that, praying in the Holy ²¹ Spirit; ·keep yourselves within the love of God and wait

for the mercy of our Lord Jesus Christ to give you eter-
22 nal life. ·When there are some who have doubts, reassure
23 them; ·when there are some to be saved from the fire, pull
them out; but there are others to whom you must be kind
with great caution, keeping your distance even from outside clothing which is contaminated by vice.

Doxology

24 Glory be to him who can keep you from falling and
bring you safe to his glorious presence, innocent and happy.
25 To God, the only God, who saves us through Jesus Christ
our Lord, be the glory, majesty, authority and power, which
he had before time began, now and for ever. Amen.

INTRODUCTION TO
The Book of Revelation

A "Revelation" (called *Apocalypse*, from the Greek term) is a distinct literary form; apocalyptic writing was very popular in some Jewish circles at the beginning of the Christian era. The framework of a Revelation is always a vision of hidden supernatural events; the language in which the vision is described is richly symbolic and so allusive that the message can be interpreted in more ways than one.

Thus the Book of Revelation is not to be accepted simply as an allegory which can be directly translated into other terms. It contains the author's vision of heaven and of the vindication of the Christian martyrs in the world to come, but it must be understood first and foremost as a tract for the times, written to increase the hope and determination of the Church on earth in a period of disturbance and bitter persecution, and prophesying the certain downfall and destruction of the Roman imperial power. The imagery, largely drawn from the Old Testament, especially Daniel, allows the author to allude to the enemy, Rome, under the disguise of the old enemy, Babylon; and to present the happenings of his own day, seen by their reflections in the heavens, as recapitulations or fulfillments of the great events of Israel's past.

The text contains difficulties: there are repetitions and interruptions, and there are passages out of context. One promising hypothesis is that the strictly prophetic part of the book is made up of two different "apocalypses" written at different times and later conflated. The author cannot be identified with the author of the Gospel according to John, but we can say that the book was written inside the evangelist's immediate circle and is pervaded by his doctrine. Its date is generally estimated as A.D. 95, but there are some who believe that parts, at least, were composed as early as Nero's time, shortly before A.D. 70.

THE BOOK OF

Revelation

Prologue

¹ **1** This is the revelation given by God to Jesus Christ so
that he could tell his servants about the *things which are*
now *to take place*ᵃ very soon; he sent his angel to make
² it known to his servant John, ·and John has written down
everything he saw and swears it is the word of God guar-
³ anteed by Jesus Christ. ·Happy the man who reads this
prophecy, and happy those who listen to him, if they treasure all that it says, because the Time is close.

I. THE LETTERS TO THE CHURCHES OF ASIA

Address and greetingᵇ

⁴ From John, to the seven churches of Asia: grace and
peace to you from him who is, who was, and who is to
come, from the seven spirits in his presence before his
⁵ throne, ·and from Jesus Christ, *the faithful witness, the
First-born* from the dead, *the Ruler of the kings of the
earth.* He loves us and has washed away our sins with his
⁶ blood, ·and made us a *line of kings, priests to serve* his
God and Father; to him, then, be glory and power for
⁷ ever and ever. Amen. ·It is he who *is coming on the
clouds;* everyone will see him, even *those who pierced him,*
and *all the races of the earth will mourn over him.* This
⁸ is the truth. Amen. ·"I am the Alpha and the Omega"
says the Lord God, who is, who was, and who is to come,
the Almighty.

The beginning of the vision

⁹ My name is John, and through our union in Jesus I
am your brother and share your sufferings, your kingdom,

1 a. Dn 2:28   b. This section contains many O.T. allusions to
the time of the Messiah. The five direct quotations printed in
italic are from: Ps 89:37,27; Is 55:4; Ex 19:6; Dn 7:13; and
Zc 12:10, 14.

and all you endure. I was on the island of Patmos*º* for
10 having preached God's word and witnessed for Jesus; ·it
was the Lord's day and the Spirit possessed me, and I
heard a voice behind me, shouting like a trumpet,
11 "Write down all that you see in a book, and send it to the
seven churches of Ephesus, Smyrna, Pergamum, Thyatira,
12 Sardis, Philadelphia and Laodicea." ·I turned round to see
who had spoken to me, and when I turned I saw seven
13 golden lamp-stands ·and, surrounded by them, a figure
like a Son of man,ᵈ dressed in a long robe tied at the
14 waist with a *golden girdle.* ·*His head* and *his hair* were
white as white wool or as snow, *his eyes* like a *burning*
15 flame, ·*his feet like burnished bronze* when it has been
refined in a furnace, and *his voice like the sound of the*
16 *ocean.ᵉ* ·In his right hand he was holding seven stars, out
of his mouth came a sharp sword, double-edged, and his
face was like the sun shining with all its force.
17   When I saw him, I fell in a dead faint at his feet, but
he touched me with his right hand and said, "Do not be
afraid; it is I, *the First* and *the Last;* I am the Living One,
18 I was dead and now I am to live for ever and ever, and
19 I hold the keys of death and of the underworld. ·Now
write down all that you see of present happenings and
20 *things that are still to come.ᶠ* ·The secret of the seven stars
you have seen in my right hand, and of the seven golden
lamp-stands is this: the seven stars are the angels of the
seven churches, and the seven lamp-stands are the seven
churches themselves.

1. Ephesus

1 **2** "Write to the angel of the church in Ephesus and say,
'Here is the message of the one who holds the seven
stars in his right hand and who lives surrounded by the
2 seven golden lamp-stands: ·I know all about you: how
hard you work and how much you put up with. I know
you cannot stand wicked men, and how you tested the
impostors who called themselves apostles and proved they
3 were liars. ·I know, too, that you have patience, and have
4 suffered for my name without growing tired. ·Nevertheless,
I have this complaint to make; you have less love now
5 than you used to. ·Think where you were before you fell;
repent, and do as you used to at first, or else, if you will
not repent, I shall come to you and take your lamp-stand

⁶ from its place. ·It is in your favor, nevertheless, that you
⁷ loathe as I do what the Nicolaitans are doing. ·If anyone
has ears to hear, let him listen to what the Spirit is saying
to the churches: those who prove victorious I will feed
from the tree of life set in God's *paradise.'ᵃ*

2. Smyrna

⁸ "Write to the angel of the church in Smyrna and say,
'Here is the message of *the First* and *the Last,* who was
⁹ dead and has come to life again: ·I know the trials you
have had, and how poor you are—though you are rich—
and the slanderous accusations that have been made by
the people who profess to be Jews but are really mem-
¹⁰ bers of the synagogue of Satan. ·Do not be afraid of the
sufferings that are coming to you: I tell you, the devil is
going to send some of you to prison *to test you,* and you
must face an ordeal for *ten days.*ᵇ Even if you have to
die, keep faithful, and I will give you the crown of life for
¹¹ your prize. ·If anyone has ears to hear, let him listen to
what the Spirit is saying to the churches: for those who
prove victorious there is nothing to be afraid of in the
second death.'

3. Pergamum

¹² "Write to the angel of the church in Pergamum and say,
'Here is the message of the one who has the sharp sword,
¹³ double-edged: ·I know where you live, in the place where
Satan is enthroned, and that you still hold firmly to my
name, and did not disown your faith in me even when
my faithful witness, Antipas, was killed in your own town,
where Satan lives.ᶜ
¹⁴ Nevertheless, I have one or two complaints to make:
some of you are followers of Balaam, who taught Balak
to set a trap for the Israelites so that they committed adul-
¹⁵ tery by eating food that had been sacrificed to idols; ·and
among you, too, there are some as bad who accept what
¹⁶ the Nicolaitans teach. ·You must repent, or I shall soon

c. Patmos (10m. × 5m.) was used by the Romans as a penal
colony. d. The messianic figure in Dn; the descriptive quotations which follow are from Dn 7 and 10. e. Ezk 43:2 f. Dn
2:28
2 a. Gn 2:9 b. I.e. of short duration. c. I.e. "where emperor-
worship is practiced."

come to you and attack these people with the sword out
¹⁷ of my mouth. ·If anyone has ears to hear, let him listen
to what the Spirit is saying to the churches: to those who
prove victorious I will give the hidden manna and a white
stone^d—a stone with *a new name* written on it, known only
to the man who receives it.'

4. Thyatira

¹⁸   "Write to the angel of the church in Thyatira and say,
'Here is the message of the Son of God who has eyes like
¹⁹ a burning flame and feet like burnished bronze: ·I know
all about you and how charitable you are; I know your
faith and devotion and how much you put up with, and
²⁰ I know how you are still making progress. ·Nevertheless,
I have a complaint to make: you are encouraging the
woman Jezebel^e who claims to be a prophetess, and by
her teaching she is luring my servants away to commit the
adultery of eating food which has been sacrificed to idols.
²¹ I have given her time to reform but she is not willing to
²² change her adulterous life. ·Now I am consigning her to
bed, and all her partners in adultery to troubles that will
test them severely, unless they repent of their practices;
²³ and I will see that her children die, so that all the churches
realize that it is I who *search heart and loins and give each
²⁴ one of you what your behavior deserves.*^f ·But on the
rest of you in Thyatira, all of you who have not accepted
this teaching or learned the secrets of Satan, as they are
²⁵ called, I am not laying any special duty; ·but hold firmly
²⁶ on to what you already have until I come. ·To those who
prove victorious, and keep working for me until the end,
²⁷₂₈ *I will give* the ·authority over *the pagans*^g ·which I myself
have been given by my Father, *to rule them with an iron
sceptre and shatter them like earthenware.* And I will give
²⁹ him the Morning Star.^h ·If anyone has ears to hear, let him
listen to what the Spirit is saying to the churches.'

5. Sardis

¹ **3** "Write to the angel of the church in Sardis and say,
'Here is the message of the one who holds the seven
spirits of God and the seven stars: I know all about you:
² how you are reputed to be alive and yet are dead. ·Wake
up; revive what little you have left: it is dying fast. So far
I have failed to notice anything in the way you live that
³ my God could possibly call perfect, ·and yet do you re-

member how eager you were when you first heard the message? Hold on to that. Repent. If you do not wake up, I shall come to you like a thief, without telling you at what
4 hour to expect me. ·There are a few in Sardis, it is true, who have kept their robes from being dirtied, and they are
5 fit to come with me, dressed in white. ·Those who prove victorious will be dressed, like these, in white robes; I shall not blot their names out of the book of life, but acknowledge their names in the presence of my Father and his
6 angels. ·If anyone has ears to hear, let him listen to what the Spirit is saying to the churches.'

6. Philadelphia

7   "Write to the angel of the church in Philadelphia and say, 'Here is the message of the holy and faithful one who *has the key of David*, so that *when he opens, nobody can*
8 *close, and when he closes, nobody can open:*[a] ·I know all about you; and now I have opened in front of you a door that nobody will be able to close—and I know that though you are not very strong, you have kept my com-
9 mandments and not disowned my name. ·Now I am going to make the synagogue of Satan—those who profess to be Jews, but are liars, because they are no such thing—I will make them come and *fall at your feet*[b] and admit that
10 *you are* the people *that I love.*[c] ·Because you have kept my commandment to endure trials, I will keep you safe in the time of trial which is going to come for the whole
11 world, to test the people of the world. ·Soon I shall be with you: hold firmly to what you already have, and let
12 nobody take your prize away from you. ·Those who prove victorious I will make into pillars in the sanctuary of my God, and they will stay there for ever; I will inscribe on them the name of my God and the name of the city of my God, the new Jerusalem which comes down from my
13 God in heaven, and my own new name as well. ·If anyone has ears to hear, let him listen to what the Spirit is saying to the churches.'

d. The manna hidden by Jeremiah (2 M 2:4-8), to be the food of those who are saved in the heavenly kingdom; the white stone is a badge or token of admittance or membership.   e. By this name the writer is indicating a prophetess of the Nicolaitan sect.   f. Jr 11:20   g. Ps 2:8-9   h. Symbol of power and thus of the resurrection.
3 a. Is 22:22   b. Is 45:14   c. Is 43:4

7. Laodicea

14 "Write to the angel of the church in Laodicea and say, 'Here is the message of the Amen, the faithful, the true 15 witness, the ultimate source of God's creation: ·I know all about you: how you are neither cold nor hot. I wish you 16 were one or the other, ·but since you are neither, but 17 only lukewarm, I will spit you out of my mouth. ·You say to yourself, "I am rich, I have made a fortune, and have everything I want," never realizing that you are wretchedly 18 and pitiably poor, and blind and naked too. ·I warn you, buy from me the gold that has been tested in the fire to make you really rich, and white robes to clothe you and cover your shameful nakedness, and eye ointment to put 19 on your eyes so that you are able to see. ·I *am* the one *who reproves and disciplines all those he loves:*[d] so repent in 20 real earnest. ·Look, I am standing at the door, knocking. If one of you hears me calling and opens the door, I will 21 come in to share his meal, side by side with him. ·Those who prove victorious I will allow to share my throne, just as I was victorious myself and took my place with my 22 Father on his throne. ·If anyone has ears to hear, let him listen to what the Spirit is saying to the churches.' "

II. THE PROPHETIC VISIONS

A. THE PRELUDE TO THE GREAT DAY

God entrusts the future of the world to the Lamb

1 4 Then, in my vision, I saw a door open in heaven and heard the same voice speaking to me, the voice like a trumpet, saying, "Come up here: I will show you *what is to* 2 *come* in the future." ·With that, the Spirit possessed me and I saw a throne standing in heaven, and the *One* who 3 was *sitting on the throne,* ·and the Person sitting there looked like a diamond and a ruby. There was a rainbow encircling the throne, and this looked like an emerald.[a] 4 Round the throne in a circle were twenty-four thrones, and on them I saw twenty-four elders sitting, dressed in 5 white robes with golden crowns on their heads. ·Flashes of lightning were coming from the throne, and the sound of peals of thunder, and in front of the throne there were

seven flaming lamps burning, the seven Spirits of God. [6] Between the throne and myself was a sea that seemed to be made of glass, like crystal. *In the center*, grouped round the throne itself, were *four animals[b] with many eyes*, in front and behind. [7] *The first* animal was like *a lion, the second* like *a bull, the third* animal had *a human face*, [8] and *the fourth* animal was like a flying *eagle*. *Each* of the four animals had *six wings* and *had eyes all the way round* as well as inside; and day and night they never stopped singing:

> "Holy, Holy, Holy
> is the Lord God, the Almighty;
> he was, he is and he is to come."

[9] Every time the animals glorified and honored and gave thanks to the One sitting on the throne, *who lives for ever* [10] *and ever*, the twenty-four elders prostrated themselves before him to worship the One *who lives for ever and ever*, and threw down their crowns in front of the throne, saying, [11] "You are our Lord and our God, you are worthy of glory and honor and power, because you made all the universe and it was only by your will that everything was made and exists."

[1] **5** I saw that in the right hand of the One sitting on the throne there was *a scroll that had writing on back and* [2] *front[a]* and was sealed with seven seals. Then I saw a powerful angel who called with a loud voice, "Is there anyone worthy to open the scroll and break the seals of [3] it?" But there was no one, in heaven or on the earth or under the earth, who was able to open the scroll and read [4] it. I wept bitterly because there was nobody fit to open the [5] scroll and read it, but one of the elders said to me, "There is no need to cry: *the Lion* of the tribe *of Judah, the Root[b]* of David, has triumphed, and he will open the scroll and the seven seals of it."

[6] Then I saw, standing between the throne with its four animals and the circle of the elders, a Lamb that seemed

d. Pr 3:12
4 a. For many of the descriptive details in this scene the writer draws on Ezk 1 and 10 and Is 6.   b. The angels or "principles" which direct the physical world. Since Irenaeus, these four creatures have been used as symbols of the four evangelists.
5 a. Ezk 2:9   b. Gn 49:9; Is 11:10

to have been sacrificed; it had seven horns, and it had seven eyes, which are the seven Spirits God has *sent out all*
7 *over the world.*[c] ·The Lamb came forward to take the scroll from the right hand of the One sitting on the throne,
8 and when he took it, the four animals prostrated themselves before him and with them the twenty-four elders; each one of them was holding a harp and had a golden bowl full of incense made of the prayers of the saints.
9 They sang a new hymn:

> "You are worthy to take the scroll
> and break the seals of it,
> because you were sacrificed, and with your blood
> you bought men for God
> of every race, language, people and nation
10 and made them *a line of kings and priests,*[d]
> to serve our God and to rule the world."

11 In my vision, I heard the sound of an immense number of angels gathered round the throne and the animals and the elders; there were *ten thousand times ten thousand of*
12 *them*[e] and *thousands upon thousands,* ·shouting, "The Lamb that was sacrificed is worthy to be given power, riches, wisdom, strength, honor, glory and blessing."
13 Then I heard all the living things in creation—everything that lives in the air, and on the ground, and under the ground, and in the sea, crying, "To the One who is sitting on the throne and to the Lamb, be all praise, honor, glory
14 and power, for ever and ever." ·And the four animals said, "Amen"; and the elders prostrated themselves to worship.

The Lamb breaks the seven seals

1 6 Then I saw the Lamb break one of the seven seals, and I heard one of the four animals shout in a voice like
2 thunder, "Come." ·Immediately a white horse appeared, and the rider on it was holding a bow; he was given the victor's crown and he went away, to go from victory to victory.
3 When he broke the second seal, I heard the second
4 animal shout, "Come." ·And out came another horse, bright red, and its rider was given this duty: to take away

peace from the earth and set people killing each other. He was given a huge sword.

5   When he broke the third seal, I heard the third animal shout, "Come." Immediately a black horse appeared, and
6 its rider was holding a pair of scales; ·and I seemed to hear a voice shout from among the four animals and say, "A ration of corn for a day's wages, and three rations of barley for a day's wages, but do not tamper with the oil or the wine."

7   When he broke the fourth seal, I heard the voice of the
8 fourth animal shout, "Come." ·Immediately another horse appeared, deathly pale, and its rider was called Plague, and Hades followed at his heels.

They were given authority over a quarter of the earth, *to kill by the sword, by famine, by plague and wild beasts.*[a]

9   When he broke the fifth seal, I saw underneath the altar the souls of all the people who had been killed on account
10 of the word of God, for witnessing to it. ·They shouted aloud, "Holy, faithful Master, how much longer will you wait before you pass sentence and take vengeance for
11 our death on the inhabitants of the earth?" ·Each of them was given a white robe, and they were told to be patient a little longer, until the roll was complete and their fellow servants and brothers had been killed just as they had been.

12   In my vision, when he broke the sixth seal, there was a violent earthquake and the sun went as black as coarse
13 sackcloth; the moon turned red as blood all over, ·and *the stars of the sky fell*[b] on to the earth *like figs* dropping from
14 a fig tree when a high wind shakes it; ·the *sky disappeared like a scroll rolling up* and all the mountains and islands
15 were shaken from their places. ·Then all the earthly rulers, the governors and the commanders, the rich people and the men of influence, the whole population, slaves and citizens, took to the mountains *to hide in caves and among*
16 *the rocks.*[c] ·They said to the mountains[d], and the rocks, "*Fall on us* and hide us away from the One who sits on
17 the throne and from the anger of the Lamb. ·For *the Great Day of his anger* has come, *and who can survive it?*"[e]

c. Zc 4:10   d. Is 61:6   e. Dn 7:10
6 a. Ezk 14:21   b. Is 34:4   c. Ho 10:8   d. Is 2:10,18,19
e. Jl 2:11; 3:4

God's servants will be preserved

1 7 Next I saw four angels, standing at *the four corners of the earth,*[a] holding the four winds of the world back to keep them from blowing over the land or the sea or in the 2 trees. ·Then I saw another angel rising where the sun rises, carrying the seal of the living God; he called in a powerful voice to the four angels whose duty was to devastate land 3 and sea, ·"Wait before you do any damage on land or at sea or to the trees, until we have put the *seal on the fore-*4 *heads*[b] of the servants of our God." ·Then I heard how many were sealed: a hundred and forty-four thousand,[c] out of all the tribes of Israel.

5 From the tribe of Judah, twelve thousand had been sealed; from the tribe of Reuben, twelve thousand; from 6 the tribe of Gad, twelve thousand; ·from the tribe of Asher, twelve thousand; from the tribe of Naphtali, twelve thousand; from the tribe of Manasseh, twelve thousand; 7 from the tribe of Simeon, twelve thousand; from the tribe of Levi, twelve thousand; from the tribe of Issachar, twelve 8 thousand; ·from the tribe of Zebulun, twelve thousand; from the tribe of Joseph, twelve thousand; and from the tribe of Benjamin, twelve thousand were sealed.

The rewarding of the saints

9 After that I saw a huge number, impossible to count, of people from every nation, race, tribe and language; they were standing in front of the throne and in front of the Lamb, dressed in white robes and holding palms in 10 their hands. They shouted aloud, ·"Victory to our God, 11 who sits on the throne, and to the Lamb!" ·And all the angels who were standing in a circle round the throne, surrounding the elders and the four animals, prostrated themselves before the throne, and touched the ground with 12 their foreheads, worshiping God ·with these words, "Amen. Praise and glory and wisdom and thanksgiving and honor and power and strength to our God for ever and ever. Amen."

13 One of the elders then spoke, and asked me, "Do you know who these people are, dressed in white robes, and 14 where they have come from?" ·I answered him, "You can tell me, my lord." Then he said, "These are the people who have been through the great persecution,[d] and because they have washed their robes white again in the blood of

15 the Lamb, ·they now stand in front of God's throne and
serve him day and night in his sanctuary; and the One who
16 sits on the throne will spread his tent over them. ·*They
will never hunger or thirst again; neither the sun nor
17 scorching wind will ever plague them,* ·because the Lamb
who is at the throne *will be their shepherd and will lead
them to springs of living water;*[e] and *God will wipe away
all tears from their eyes.*"[f]

The seventh seal

1 Ω The Lamb then broke the seventh seal, and there was
  silence in heaven for about half an hour.[a]

**The prayers of the saints bring the coming of the Great
Day nearer**

2 Next I saw seven trumpets being given to the seven
3 angels who stand in the presence of God. ·Another angel,
who had a golden censer,[b] came and stood at the altar.[c]
A large quantity of incense was given to him to offer with
the prayers of all the saints on the golden altar that stood
4 in front of the throne; ·and so from the angel's hand the
smoke of the incense went up in the presence of God and
5 with it the prayers of the saints. ·Then the angel took the
censer and *filled it with the fire* from the altar, which he
then threw down on to the earth; immediately there came
peals of thunder and flashes of lightning, and the earth
shook.

The first four trumpets

6 The seven angels that had the seven trumpets now made
7 ready to sound them. ·The first blew his trumpet and,
with that, hail and fire, mixed with blood, were dropped
on the earth; a third of the earth was burned up, and a
third of all trees, and every blade of grass was burned.
8 The second angel blew his trumpet, and it was as though a
great mountain, all on fire, had been dropped into the sea:

7 a. Ezk 7:2 b. Ezk 9:4 (see also Is 44:5). c. Twelve (the
sacred number) squared and multiplied by a thousand, representing the totality of the faithful. d. Under Nero. e. Is
49:10 f. Is 25:8
8 a. An awed silence; the "coming of Yahweh" is preceded by
silence in the prophetic writings. b. In the shape of a shovel:
the flat incense-vessel was also used for carrying live coals from
the altar on which offerings were burned. c. The altar of incense.

⁹ a third of the sea turned into blood, ·a third of all the living things in the sea were killed, and a third of all ships
¹⁰ were destroyed. ·The third angel blew his trumpet, and a
huge star fell from the sky, burning like a ball of fire, and it
¹¹ fell on a third of all rivers and springs; ·this was the star
called Wormwood, and a third of all water turned to bitter wormwood, so that many people died from drinking it.
¹² The fourth angel blew his trumpet, and a third of the sun
and a third of the moon and a third of the stars were
blasted, so that the light went out of a third of them and
for a third of the day there was no illumination, and the
same with the night.
¹³   In my vision, I heard an eagle, calling aloud as it flew
high overhead, "Trouble, trouble, trouble, for all the people on earth at the sound of the other three trumpets which
the three angels are going to blow."

The fifth trumpet

¹ **9** Then the fifth angel blew his trumpet, and I saw a star*
that had fallen from heaven on to the earth, and he was
given the key to the shaft leading down to the Abyss.*
² When he unlocked the shaft of the Abyss, *smoke poured
up out of the Abyss like the smoke from a huge furnace*
³ so that the sun and the sky were darkened by it, ·and out
of the smoke dropped locusts which were given the powers
⁴ that scorpions have on the earth: ·they were forbidden to
harm any fields or crops or trees and told only to attack
any men who were without God's seal on their foreheads.
⁵ They were not to kill them, but to give them pain for five
months, and the pain was to be the pain of a scorpion's
⁶ sting. ·When this happens, *men will long for death and
not find it anywhere;* they will want to die and death will
evade them.
⁷   To look at, these locusts were *like horses armored for
battle;* they had things that looked like gold crowns on
⁸ their heads, and faces that seemed human, ·and hair like
⁹ women's hair, and *teeth like lions' teeth.* ·They had body-
armor like iron breastplates, and the noise of their wings
sounded like a great charge of horses and chariots into
¹⁰ battle. ·Their tails were like scorpions', with stings, and
it was with them that they were able to injure people for
¹¹ five months. ·As their leader they had their emperor, the
angel of the Abyss, whose name in Hebrew is Abaddon, or
Apollyon* in Greek.

12   That was the first of the troubles; there are still two
more to come.

The sixth trumpet

13   The sixth angel blew his trumpet, and I heard a voice
come out of the four horns of the golden altar in front of
14 God. ·It spoke to the sixth angel with the trumpet, and
said, "Release the four angels that are chained up at the
15 great river Euphrates." ·These four angels had been put
there ready for this hour of this day of this month of this
year, and now they were released to destroy a third of the
16 human race. ·I learned how many there were in their army:
17 twice ten thousand times ten thousand mounted men. ·In
my vision I saw the horses, and the riders with their breastplates of flame color, hyacinth-blue and sulphur-yellow;
the horses had lions' heads, and fire, smoke and sulphur
18 were coming out of their mouths. ·It was by these three
plagues, the fire, the smoke and the sulphur coming out of
their mouths, that the one third of the human race was
19 killed. ·All the horses' power was in their mouths and their
tails: their tails were like snakes, and had heads that were
20 able to wound. ·But the rest of the human race, who
escaped these plagues, refused either to abandon *the things
they had made with their own hands*[g]—the *idols made of
gold, silver, bronze, stone and wood*[h] that can neither see
21 nor hear nor move—or to stop worshiping devils. ·Nor
did they give up their murdering, or witchcraft, or fornication or stealing.

The imminence of the last punishment

1 **10** Then I saw another powerful angel coming down
from heaven, wrapped in a cloud, with a rainbow
over his head; his face was like the sun, and his legs were
2 pillars of fire. ·In his hand he had a small scroll, unrolled;
he put his right foot in the sea and his left foot on the land
3 and he shouted so loud, it was *like a lion roaring*. At this,
4 seven claps of thunder made themselves heard ·and when
the seven thunderclaps had spoken, I was preparing to
write, when I heard a voice from heaven say to me, "Keep

9 a. A fallen angel. b. Where fallen angels were imprisoned,
to be released only to their final punishment. c. Ex 19:18
d. Jb 3:21   e. The descriptive details in vv. 7-9 owe much to
Jl 1 and 2. f. "Destruction." g. Is 17:8 h. Dn 5:4

the words of the seven thunderclaps secret and do not write
⁵ them down." ·Then the angel that I had seen, standing on
the sea and the land, *raised his right hand to heaven,*ᵃ
⁶ and *swore by the One who lives for ever* and ever, *and
made heaven and all that is in it,* and *earth and all it
bears,* and *the sea and all it holds,*ᵇ "The time of waiting is
⁷ over; ·at the time when the seventh angel is heard sound-
ing his trumpet, God's secret intention will be fulfilled,
just as he announced in the Good News told to *his servants
the prophets.*"

The seer eats the small scroll

⁸   Then I heard the voice I had heard from heaven speaking to me again. "Go," it said "and take that open scroll
⁹ out of the hand of the angel standing on sea and land." ·I
went to the angel and asked him to give me the small scroll,
and he said, "Take it and eat it; it will turn your stomach
¹⁰ sour, but in your mouth it will taste as sweet as honey." ·So
I took it out of the angel's hand, and swallowed it; it was
as sweet as honey in my mouth, but when I had eaten it
¹¹ my stomach turned sour. ·Then I was told, "You are to
prophesy again, this time about many different nations and
countries and languages and emperors."

The two witnesses

¹¹   Then I was given a long cane as a measuring rod,
and I was told, "Go and measure God's sanctuary,
² and the altar, and the people who worship there; ·but leave
out the outer court and do not measure it, because it has
been handed over to pagans—they will trample on the holy
³ city for forty-two months.ᵃ ·But I shall send my two witnesses to prophesy for those twelve hundred and sixty days,
⁴ wearing sackcloth. ·These are the *two olive trees*ᵇ and
the two lamps *that stand before the Lord of the world.*ᶜ
⁵ Fire can come from their mouths and consume their
enemies if anyone tries to harm them; and if anybody does
try to harm them he will certainly be killed in this way.
⁶ They are able to lock up the sky so that it does not rain
as long as they are prophesying; they are able to turn water
into blood and strike the whole world with any plague as
⁷ often as they like. ·When they have completed their witnessing, the beast that comes out of the Abyss *is going to
make war on them and overcome them*ᵈ and kill them.

8 Their corpses will lie in the main street of the Great City
known by the symbolic names Sodom and Egypt, in which
9 their Lord was crucified.[e] ·Men out of every people, race,
language and nation will stare at their corpses, for three-
10 and-a-half days, not letting them be buried, ·and the people of the world will be glad about it and celebrate the
event by giving presents to each other, because these two
prophets have been a plague to the people of the world."
11   After the three-and-a-half days, *God breathed life into
them and they stood up,[f]* and everybody who saw it hap-
12 pen was terrified; ·then they heard a loud voice from
heaven say to them, "Come up here," and while their
enemies were watching, they went up to heaven in a cloud.
13 Immediately, there was a violent earthquake, and a
tenth of the city collapsed; seven thousand persons[g] were
killed in the earthquake, and the survivors, overcome with
fear, could only praise the God of heaven.

The seventh trumpet

14   That was the second of the troubles; the third is to come
quickly after it.
15   Then the seventh angel blew his trumpet, and voices
could be heard shouting in heaven, calling, "The kingdom
of the world has become the kingdom of our Lord and his
16 Christ, and he will reign for ever and ever." ·The twenty-
four elders, enthroned in the presence of God, prostrated
themselves and touched the ground with their foreheads
17 worshiping God ·with these words, "We give thanks to
you, Almighty Lord God, He-Is-and-He-Was, for using
18 your great power and beginning your reign. ·*The nations
were seething with rage[h]* and now the time has come for
your own anger, and for the dead to be judged, and for
your servants the prophets, for the saints and for all who

10 a. Dt 32:40   b. Ne 9:6
11 a. This period, taken from Dn, is used as the symbol for any
time of persecution.   b. Zc 4:3,14, where they symbolize Joshua
and Zerubbabel; here they probably represent Peter and Paul.
c. 2 K 1:10   d. Dn 7:21   e. The "Great City" or "Babylon" in
this book is Rome, whose actions were identified with Sodom's
rejection of God's messengers and Egypt's oppression of God's
people. The words "in which their Lord was crucified" may be a
gloss, or may be justified by the responsibility of the Roman
authority for the crucifixion.   f. Ezk 37:5,10   g. That is, a
great number of all classes.   h. Ps 2:1,5

worship you, small or great, to be rewarded. The time has come to destroy those who are destroying the earth."

19 Then the sanctuary of God in heaven opened, and the ark of the covenant could be seen inside it. Then came flashes of lightning, peals of thunder and an earthquake, and violent hail.

The vision of the woman and the dragon

1 **12** Now a great sign appeared in heaven: a woman, adorned with the sun, standing on the moon, and 2 with the twelve stars on her head for a crown: •She was pregnant, and in labor, crying aloud in the pangs of child- 3 birth. •Then a second sign appeared in the sky, a huge red dragon which had seven heads and ten horns, and each of 4 the seven heads crowned with a coronet. •Its tail dragged a third of *the stars from the sky and dropped them to the earth,ᵃ* and the dragon stopped in front of the woman as she was having the child, so that he could eat it as soon as 5 it was born from its mother. •The woman brought *a male child into the world,* the son who was *to rule all the nations with an iron sceptre,ᵇ* and the child was taken straight up 6 to God and to his throne, •while the woman escaped into the desert, where God had made a place of safety ready, for her to be looked after in the twelve hundred and sixty days.

7 And now war broke out in heaven, when Michael with his angels attacked the dragon. The dragon fought back 8 with his angels, •but they were defeated and driven out of 9 heaven. •The great dragon, the primeval serpent, known as the devil or Satan, who had deceived all the world, was hurled down to the earth and his angels were hurled down 10 with him. •Then I heard a voice shout from heaven, "Victory and power and empire for ever have been won by our God, and all authority for his Christ, now that the persecutor, who accused our brothers day and night before 11 our God, has been brought down. •They have triumphed over him by the blood of the Lamb and by the witness of their martyrdom, because even in the face of death they 12 would not cling to life. •Let the heavens rejoice and all who live there; but for you, earth and sea, trouble is coming— because the devil has gone down to you in a rage, knowing that his days are numbered."

13 As soon as the devil found himself thrown down to the earth, he sprang in pursuit of the woman, the mother of

14 the male child, ·but she was given a huge pair of eagle's wings to fly away from the serpent into the desert, to the place where she was to be looked after for *a year and*
15 *twice a year and half a year.*[o] ·So the serpent vomited water from his mouth, like a river, after the woman, to
16 sweep her away in the current, ·but the earth came to her rescue; it opened its mouth and swallowed the river thrown
17 up by the dragon's jaws. ·Then the dragon was enraged with the woman and went away to make war on the rest of her children, that is, all who obey God's commandments and bear witness for Jesus.

The dragon delegates his power to the beast

18/1 I was standing on the seashore. **13** Then I saw *a beast emerge from the sea:*[a] it had seven heads and ten horns, with a coronet on each of its ten horns, and its heads were
2 marked with blasphemous titles.[b] ·I saw that the beast *was like a leopard*, with paws like *a bear* and a mouth like *a lion;*[c] the dragon had handed over to it his own power
3 and his throne and his worldwide authority. ·I saw that one of its heads seemed to have had a fatal wound but that this deadly injury had healed and, after that, the whole
4 world had marveled and followed the beast. ·They prostrated themselves in front of the dragon because he had given the beast his authority; and they prostrated themselves in front of the beast, saying, "Who can compare
5 with the beast?[d] How could anybody defeat him?" ·For forty-two months the beast was allowed *to mouth its boasts*[e] and blasphemies and to do whatever it wanted;
6 and it mouthed its blasphemies against God, against his name, his heavenly Tent and all those who are sheltered
7 there. ·It was allowed *to make war against the saints and conquer them, and given power* over every race, people,
8 language and nation; ·and all people of the world will worship it, that is, everybody whose name has not been written down since the foundation of the world in the book of life
9 of the sacrificial Lamb. ·If anyone has ears to hear, let him
10 listen: ·*Captivity for those who are destined for captivity;*

12 a. Dn 8:10   **b.** Ps 2:9   **c.** Dn 7:25. Cf. 11:3.
13 a. Dn 7:3   **b.** Seven heads represent a succession of seven Roman emperors; ten crowned horns are ten subject kings. **c.** Dn 7:4-6   **d.** A parody of the name Michael, "Who-can-compare-with-God?"   **e.** Dn 7:8,11

the sword for those who are to die by the sword.[f] This is
why the saints must have constancy and faith.

The false prophet as the slave of the beast

11   Then I saw a second beast;[g] it emerged from the
ground; it had two horns like a lamb, but made a noise like
12 a dragon. ·This second beast was servant to the first beast,
and extended its authority everywhere, making the world
and all its people worship the first beast, which had had the
18 the fatal wound and had been healed. ·And it worked great
miracles, even to calling down fire from heaven on to the
14 earth while people watched. ·Through the miracles which
it was allowed to do on behalf of the first beast, it was
able to win over the people of the world and persuade
them to put up a statue in honor of the beast that had
15 been wounded by the sword and still lived. ·It was allowed to breathe life into this statue, so that the statue of
the beast was able to speak, and to have *anyone who re-*
16 *fused to worship the statue of the beast*[h] put to death. ·He
compelled everyone—small and great, rich and poor, slave
and citizen—to be branded on the right hand or on the
17 forehead, ·and made it illegal for anyone to buy or sell
anything unless he had been branded with the name of the
beast or with the number of its name.
18   There is need for shrewdness here: if anyone is clever
enough he may interpret the number of the beast: it is the
number of a man, the number 666.[i]

The companions of the Lamb

1   **14** Next in my vision I saw Mount Zion, and standing on
it a Lamb who had with him a hundred and forty-
four thousand people, all with his name and his Father's
2 name written on their foreheads. ·I heard a sound coming
out of the sky like the sound of the ocean or the roar of
thunder; it seemed to be the sound of harpists playing their
8 harps. ·There in front of the throne they were singing a
new hymn in the presence of the four animals and the
elders, a hymn that could only be learned by the hundred
and forty-four thousand who had been redeemed from the
4 world. ·These are the ones who have kept their virginity[a]
and not been defiled with women; they *follow* the Lamb
wherever he goes; they have been redeemed from amongst
men to be *the first-fruits for God*[b] and for the Lamb.

⁵ They never *allowed a lie to pass their lips°* and no fault can be found in them.

Angels announce the day of Judgment

⁶ Then I saw another angel, flying high overhead, sent to announce the Good News of eternity to all who live on the ⁷ earth, every nation, race, language and tribe. ·He was calling, "Fear God and praise him, because the time has come for him to sit in judgment; worship *the maker of heaven and earth and sea°* and every water-spring."

⁸ A second angel followed him, calling, *"Babylon has fallen, Babylon the Great has fallen,°* Babylon which gave the whole world *the wine of* God's *anger* to drink."

⁹ A third angel followed, shouting aloud, "All those who worship the beast and his statue, or have had themselves ¹⁰ branded on the hand or forehead, ·will be made to drink the wine of God's fury which is ready, undiluted, in his cup of anger; in *fire and brimstone′* they will be tortured in ¹¹ the presence of the holy angels and the Lamb ·and *the smoke* of their torture *will go up for ever°* and ever. There will be no respite, *night or day*, for those who worshiped the beast or its statue or accepted branding with its name." ¹² This is why there must be constancy in the saints who keep ¹³ the commandments of God and faith in Jesus. ·Then I heard a voice from heaven say to me, "Write down: Happy are those who die in the Lord! Happy indeed, the Spirit says; now they can rest for ever after their work, since their good deeds go with them."

The harvest and vintage of the pagans

¹⁴ Now in my vision I saw a white *cloud* and, *sitting on it, one like a son of man* with a gold crown on his head and ¹⁵ a sharp sickle in his hand. ·Then another angel came out of the sanctuary, and shouted aloud to the one sitting on

f. Jr 15:2 g. Also called "the false prophet," 16:13; 19:20; 20:10. h. Dn 3:5-7,15 i. Codes and riddles were made in both Greek and Hebr. by using numbers for letters, according to their order in the alphabet. Some commentators have claimed that 666 is the total of the number-values of "Nero Caesar."

14 a. As so often in the O.T., "virginity" stands for faithfulness, and "adultery" or "fornication" for idolatry. b. Jr 2:2-3 c. Zp 3:13 d. Ex 20:11 e. Is 21:9. The *wine of* God's *anger* is a phrase from Is 51:17, also used in Jr 25:15f. f. Gn 19:28 g. Is 34:9-10

the cloud, "*Put your sickle in* and reap: harvest time has
16 come and *the harvest* of the earth *is ripe*."[h] ·Then the
one sitting on the cloud set his sickle to work on the earth,
and the earth's harvest was reaped.

17   Another angel, who also carried a sharp sickle, came
18 out of the temple in heaven, ·and the angel in charge of
the fire left the altar and shouted aloud to the one with the
sharp sickle, "Put your sickle in and cut all the bunches
19 off the vine of the earth; all its grapes are ripe." ·So the
angel set his sickle to work on the earth and harvested the
whole vintage of the earth and put it into a huge winepress,
20 the winepress of God's anger, ·outside the city, where it
was trodden until the blood that came out of the winepress
was up to the horses' bridles as far away as sixteen hundred
furlongs.

The hymn of Moses and the Lamb

1 **15** What I saw next, in heaven, was a great and wonderful sign: seven angels were bringing the seven
plagues that are the last of all, because they exhaust the
2 anger of God. ·I seemed to see a glass lake suffused with
fire, and standing by the lake of glass, those who had
fought against the beast and won, and against his statue
and the number which is his name. They all had harps
3 from God, ·and they were singing the hymn of Moses, the
servant of God, and of the Lamb:

"How great and wonderful are all your works,
Lord God Almighty;
just and true are all your ways,
King of nations.
4 *Who would not revere* and *praise your name, O Lord?*
You alone are holy,
and all the pagans will come and adore you
for the many acts of justice you have shown."[a]

The seven bowls of plagues

5   After this, in my vision, the sanctuary, the Tent of the
6 Testimony, opened in heaven, ·and out came the seven
angels with the seven plagues, wearing pure white linen,
7 fastened round their waists with golden girdles. ·One of the
four animals gave the seven angels seven golden bowls
filled with the anger of God who lives for ever and ever.
8 *The smoke from the glory* and the power *of God filled the*

temple so that no one could go into it[b] until the seven plagues of the seven angels were completed.

16 Then I heard a voice from the sanctuary shouting to the seven angels, "Go, and empty the seven bowls of God's anger over the earth."

2 The first angel went and emptied his bowl over the earth; at once, on all the people who had been branded with the mark of the beast and had worshiped its statue, there came disgusting and virulent sores.

3 The second angel emptied his bowl over the sea, and it turned to blood, like the blood of a corpse, and every living creature in the sea died.

4 The third angel emptied his bowl into the rivers and 5 water-springs and they turned into blood. ·Then I heard the angel of water say, "You are the holy He-Is-and-He- 6 Was, the Just One, and this is a just punishment: ·they spilt the blood of the saints and the prophets, and blood is what you have given them to drink; it is what they deserve." 7 And I heard the altar itself say, "Truly, Lord God Almighty, the punishments you give are true and just."

8 The fourth angel emptied his bowl over the sun and it 9 was made to scorch people with its flames; ·but though people were scorched by the fierce heat of it, they cursed the name of God who had the power to cause such plagues, and they would not repent and praise him.

10 The fifth angel emptied his bowl over the throne of the beast and its whole empire was plunged into darkness. Men 11 were biting their tongues for pain, ·but instead of repenting for what they had done, they cursed the God of heaven because of their pains and sores.

12 The sixth angel emptied his bowl over the great river Euphrates; all the water dried up so that a way was made 13 for the kings of the East[a] to come in. ·Then from the jaws of dragon and beast and false prophet I saw three foul 14 spirits come; they looked like frogs ·and in fact were demon spirits, able to work miracles, going out to all the kings of the world to call them together for the war of the

h. Jl 4:13; Am 8:2

15 a. This hymn is nearer to the Psalms than to the Song of Moses in Ex 15. The two direct quotations are from Jr 10 and Ps 86; the opening of it is reminiscent of Ps 92 and 98. b. 1 K 8:10-11

16 a. Of Parthia, the savage enemy dreaded by the Roman world.

[15] Great Day of God the Almighty.—·This is how it will be: I shall come like a thief. Happy is the man who has stayed awake and not taken off his clothes so that he does not go [16] out naked and expose his shame.—·They called the kings together at the place called, in Hebrew, Armageddon.[b]

[17] The seventh angel emptied his bowl into the air, and a voice shouted from the sanctuary, "The end has come." [18] Then there were flashes of lightning and peals of thunder and the most violent earthquake *that anyone has ever seen* [19] *since there have been* men *on the earth.*[c] ·The Great City was split into three parts and the cities of the world collapsed; Babylon the Great was not forgotten: God made [20] her drink the full winecup of his anger. ·Every island [21] vanished and the mountains disappeared; ·and hail, with great hailstones weighing a talent each, fell from the sky on the people. They cursed God for sending a plague of hail; it was the most terrible plague.

B. THE PUNISHMENT OF BABYLON

The famous prostitute

[1] **17** One of the seven angels that had the seven bowls came to speak to me, and said, "Come here and I will show you the punishment given to the famous prosti- [2] tute[a] *who* rules *enthroned beside abundant waters,*[b] ·the one with whom all the kings of the earth have committed fornication, and who has made all the population of the [3] world drunk with the wine of her adultery"[c] ·He took me in spirit to a desert, and there I saw a woman riding a scarlet beast which had seven heads and ten horns and had [4] blasphemous titles written all over it. ·The woman was dressed in purple and scarlet, and glittered with gold and jewels and pearls, and she was holding a gold winecup [5] filled with the disgusting filth of her fornication; ·on her forehead was written a name, a cryptic name: "Babylon the Great, the mother of all the prostitutes and all the [6] filthy practices on the earth." ·I saw that she was drunk, drunk with the blood of the saints, and the blood of the martyrs of Jesus; and when I saw her, I was completely [7] mystified. ·The angel said to me, "Don't you understand? Now I will tell you the meaning of this woman, and of the beast she is riding, with the seven heads and the ten horns.

The symbolism of the beast and the prostitute

8   "The beast you have seen once was and now is not;[d] he is yet to come up from the Abyss, but only to go to his destruction. And the people of the world, whose names have not been written since the beginning of the world in the book of life, will think it miraculous when they see how the beast once was and now is not and is still to come.

9   Here there is need for cleverness, for a shrewd mind; the seven heads are the seven hills, and the woman is sitting on them.

10   "The seven heads are also seven emperors. Five of them have already gone, one is here now, and one is yet to

11   come; once here, he must stay for a short while. ·The beast, who once was and now is not, is at the same time the eighth and one of the seven, and he is going to his destruction.

12   "The ten horns are ten kings[e] who have not yet been given their royal power but will have royal authority only for a single hour and in association with the beast.

13   They are all of one mind in putting their strength and their

14   powers at the beast's disposal, ·and they will go to war against the Lamb; but the Lamb is the Lord of lords and the King of kings,[f] and he will defeat them and they will be defeated by his followers, the called, the chosen, the faithful."

15   The angel continued, "The waters you saw, beside which the prostitute was sitting, are all the peoples, the popula-

16   tions, the nations and the languages. ·But the time will come when the ten horns and the beast will turn against the prostitute, and strip off her clothes and leave her naked;[g] then they will eat her flesh and burn the remains in

17   the fire. ·In fact, God influenced their minds to do what he intended, to agree together to put their royal powers at the

b. "Megiddo mountains"; Josiah's defeat at Megiddo, 2 K 23:29f, made this place a symbol of military disaster, cf. Zc 12:11. c. Dn 12:1

17 a. Rome. b. Jr 51:13, a literal description of Babylon, here applied metaphorically, as the author explains in v. 15. c. I.e. the idolatry of emperor-worship. d. The popular belief that Nero would return from the dead at the head of a Parthian army accounts for this parody of the divine title. e. Dn 7:24; here they are kings of the satellite nations. f. Dn 10:17 g. Ezk 16:37f

beast's disposal until the time when God's words should be
18 fulfilled. ·The woman you saw is the great city which has
authority over all the rulers on earth."

An angel announces the fall of Babylon

1 **18** After this, I saw another angel come down from
heaven, with great authority given to him; *the earth*
2 *was lit up with his glory.*ᵃ ·At the top of his voice he
shouted, "*Babylon has fallen,* Babylon the Great has fallen,
and has become *the haunt of devils*ᵇ and a lodging for
3 every foul spirit and dirty, loathsome bird. ·All the nations
have been intoxicated by the wine of her prostitution; every
king in the earth has committed fornication with her, and
every merchant grown rich through her debauchery."

The people of God summoned away

4 A new voice spoke from heaven; I heard it say, "Come
out, my people, away from her, so that you do not share
5 in her crimes and have the same plagues to bear. ·*Her sins
have reached up to heaven,*ᶜ and God has her crimes in
6 mind: ·*she is to be paid in her own coin.*ᵈ She must be
paid double the amount she exacted. She is to have a
7 doubly strong cup of her own mixture. ·Every one of her
shows and orgies is to be matched by a torture or a grief.
*I am the queen on my throne, she says to herself,*ᵉ and *I*
8 *am no widow* and shall never be in mourning. ·For that,
within a single day, the plagues will fall on her: disease
and mourning and famine. She will be burned right up.
The Lord God has condemned her, and he has great
power."

The people of the world mourn for Babylon

9 There will be mourning and weeping for her by the
kings of the earth who have fornicated with her and lived
with her in luxury. They see the smoke as she burns,
10 while they keep at a safe distance from fear of her agony.
They will say:

> "Mourn, mourn for this great city,
> Babylon, so powerful a city,
> doomed as you are within a single hour."

11 There will be weeping and distress over her among all the
traders of the earth when there is nobody left to buy their
12 cargoes of goods; ·their stocks of gold and silver, jewels

and pearls, linen and purple and silks and scarlet; all the sandalwood, every piece in ivory or fine wood, in bronze
13 or iron or marble; ·the cinnamon and spices, the myrrh and ointment and incense; wine, oil, flour and corn; their stocks of cattle, sheep, horses and chariots, their slaves, their human cargo.

14 "All the fruits you had set your hearts on have failed you; gone for ever, never to return, is your life of magnificence and ease."

15 The traders who had made a fortune out of her will be standing at a safe distance from fear of her agony, mourn-
16 ing and weeping. ·They will be saying:

"Mourn, mourn for this great city;
for all the linen and purple and scarlet that you wore,
for all your finery of gold and jewels and pearls;
17 your riches are all destroyed within a single hour."

All the captains and seafaring men, sailors and all those who make a living from the sea will be keeping a safe
18 distance, ·watching the smoke as she burns, and crying
19 out, "Has there ever been a city as great as this!" ·They will throw dust on their heads and say, with tears and groans:

"Mourn, mourn for this great city
whose lavish living has made a fortune
for every owner of a sea-going ship;
ruined within a single hour.

20 "Now heaven, celebrate her downfall, and all you saints apostles and prophets: God has given judgment for you against her."

21 Then a powerful angel picked up a boulder like a great millstone, and as he hurled it into the sea, he said, "That is how the great city of Babylon is going to be hurled down, never to be seen again.

22 "Never again in you, Babylon,
will be heard the song of harpists and minstrels,
the music of flute and trumpet;
never again will craftsmen of every skill be found
or *the sound of the mill* be heard;
23 never again will shine *the light of the lamp,*

18 a. Ezk 43:2 b. Is 34:11f c. Jr 51:9 d. Jr 50:15 e. Is 47:8 f. Jr 25:10

> never again will be heard
> *the voices of bridegroom and bride.*
> Your traders were the princes of the earth,
> all the nations were under your spell.

24 In her you will find the blood of prophets and saints, and all the blood that was ever shed on earth."

Songs of victory in heaven

1 **19** After this I seemed to hear the great sound of a huge crowd in heaven, singing, "Alleluia! Victory and 2 glory and power to our God! ·He judges fairly, he punishes justly, and he has condemned the famous prostitute who corrupted the earth with her fornication; he has 3 avenged his servants that she killed." ·They sang again, "Alleluia! *The smoke* of her *will go up for ever* and ever." 4 Then the twenty-four elders and the four animals prostrated themselves and worshiped God seated there on his throne, and they cried, "Amen, Alleluia." 5 Then a voice came from the throne; it said, "Praise our God, you servants of his and *all who, great or small,* 6 *revere him*." ·And I seemed to hear the voices of a huge crowd, like the sound of the ocean or the great roar of thunder, answering, "Alleluia! The reign of the Lord our 7 God Almighty has begun; ·let us be glad and joyful and give praise to God, because this is the time for the mar- 8 riage of the Lamb. ·His bride is ready, and she has been able to dress herself in dazzling white linen, because her 9 linen is made of the good deeds of the saints." ·The angel said, "Write this: Happy are those who are invited to the wedding feast of the Lamb," and he added, "All the things 10 you have written are true messages from God." ·Then I knelt at his feet to worship him, but he said to me, "Don't do that: I am a servant just like you and all your brothers who are witnesses to Jesus. It is God that you must worship." The witness Jesus gave is the same as the spirit of prophecy.

C. THE DESTRUCTION OF THE PAGAN NATIONS

The first battle of the End

11 And now I saw heaven open, and a white horse appear; its rider was called Faithful and True; he is *a judge* 12 *with integrity,*[a] a warrior for justice. ·His eyes were flames

of fire, and his head was crowned with many coronets; the
¹³ name written on him was known only to himself, *·his cloak
was soaked in blood.*[b] He is known by the name, The
¹⁴ Word of God. ·Behind him, dressed in linen of dazzling
¹⁵ white, rode the armies of heaven on white horses. ·From
his mouth came a sharp sword to strike the pagans with;
·he is the one *who will rule them with an iron sceptre,*[c]
·and tread out the wine of Almighty God's fierce anger.
¹⁶ On his cloak and on his thigh[d] there was a name written:
The King of kings and the Lord of lords.
¹⁷   I saw an angel standing in the sun, and he shouted aloud
to all the birds that were flying high overhead in the sky,
"Come here. *Gather together at the great feast*[e] that
¹⁸ God is giving. *·There will be the flesh* of kings for you,
and the flesh of great generals and heroes, the flesh of
horses and their riders and of all kinds of men, citizens
and slaves, small and great."
¹⁹   Then I saw the beast, with all the kings of the earth
·and their armies, gathered together to fight the rider and
²⁰ his army. ·But the beast was taken prisoner, together with
the false prophet who had worked miracles on the beast's
behalf and by them had deceived all who had been branded
with the mark of the beast and worshiped his statue. These
two were thrown alive into the fiery lake of burning sul-
²¹ phur. ·All the rest were killed by the sword of the rider,
which came out of his mouth, and *all the birds were gorged*
with their flesh.

The reign of a thousand years

¹ **20** Then I saw an angel come down from heaven with
the key of the Abyss in his hand and an enormous
² chain. ·He overpowered the dragon, that primeval serpent
which is the devil and Satan, and chained him up for a
³ thousand years. ·He threw him into the Abyss, and shut the
entrance and sealed it over him, to make sure he would
not deceive the nations again until the thousand years had
passed. At the end of that time he must be released, but
only for a short while.
⁴   Then I saw some thrones, and I saw *those who are*
given the power to be judges[a] take their seats on them. I

19 a. Is 11:4   b. Is 63:1   c. Ps 2:9   d. I.e. the place where
he wears his sword; so, perhaps, "on his sword."   e. Ezk 39:17
20 a. Dn 7:22

saw the souls of all who had been beheaded for having witnessed for Jesus and for having preached God's word, and those who refused to worship the beast or his statue and would not have the brand-mark on their foreheads or hands; they came to life, and reigned with Christ for a
⁵ thousand years. ·This is the first resurrection; the rest of the dead did not come to life until the thousand years were
⁶ over. ·Happy and blessed are those who share in the first resurrection; the second death cannot affect them but they will be priests of God and of Christ and reign with him for a thousand years.

The second battle of the End

⁷ When the thousand years are over, Satan will be re-
⁸ leased from his prison ·and will come out to deceive all the nations in the four quarters of the earth, *Gog and Magog*,ᵇ and mobilize them for war. His armies will be
⁹ as many as the sands of the sea; ·they will come swarming over the entire country and besiege the camp of the saints, which is the city that God loves. But *fire will come down*
¹⁰ *on them from heaven*ᶜ and consume them. ·Then the devil, who misled them, will be thrown into the lake of fire and sulphur, where the beast and the false prophet are, and their torture will not stop, day or night, for ever and ever.

The punishment of the pagans

¹¹ Then I saw a great white throne and the One who was sitting on it. In his presence, earth and sky vanished, leaving
¹² no trace. ·I saw the dead, both great and small, standing in front of his throne, while the book of life was opened, and *other books opened* which were the record of what they had done in their lives, by which the dead were judged.
¹³
¹⁴ The sea gave up all the dead who were in it; ·Death and Hades were emptied of the dead that were in them; and every one was judged according to the way in which he had lived. Then Death and Hades were thrown into the burning lake. This burning lake is the second death;
¹⁵ and anybody whose name could not be found written in the book of life was thrown into the burning lake.

D. THE JERUSALEM OF THE FUTURE

The heavenly Jerusalem

1 **21** Then I saw *a new heaven and a new earth;*[a] the first heaven and the first earth had disappeared now, 2 and there was no longer any sea. ·I saw the holy city, and the new Jerusalem, coming down from God out of heaven, as beautiful as a bride all dressed for her husband. 3 Then I heard a loud voice call from the throne, "You see this city? Here God lives among men. He will make *his home among them; they shall be his people,*[b] and he will 4 be their God; his name is *God-with-them.* ·*He will wipe away all tears from their eyes;*[c] there will be no more death, and no more mourning or sadness. The world of the past has gone."

5 Then the One sitting on the throne spoke: "Now I am making the whole of creation new" he said. "Write this: 6 that what I am saying is sure and will come true." ·And then he said, "It is already done. I am the Alpha and the Omega, the Beginning and the End. I will give water 7 from the well of life free to anybody who is thirsty; ·it is the rightful inheritance of the one who proves victorious; 8 and *I will be his God* and *he a son to me.*[d] ·But the legacy for cowards, for those who break their word, or worship obscenities, for murderers and fornicators, and for fortune-tellers, idolaters or any other sort of liars, is the second death in the burning lake of sulphur."

The messianic Jerusalem

9 One of the seven angels that had the seven bowls full of the seven last plagues came to speak to me, and said, "Come here and I will show you the bride that the Lamb 10 has married." ·*In the spirit, he took me to the top of an enormous high mountain*[e] and showed me Jerusalem, the 11 holy city, coming down from God out of heaven. ·It *had all the radiant glory of God*[f] and glittered like some pre- 12 cious jewel of crystal-clear diamond. ·The walls of it were of a great height, and had twelve gates; at each of the twelve gates there was an angel, and over the gates were

b. Ezk 38:2   c. Ezk 38:22
21 a. Is 65:17   b. Ezk 37:27   c. Is 8:8 and 25:8   d. 2 S 7:14
e. Ezk 40:2   f. Is 60:1-2

¹³ written the names *of the twelve tribes of Israel;* •*on the east there were three gates, on the north three gates, on* ¹⁴ *the south three gates, and on the west three gates.*ᵍ •The city walls stood on twelve foundation stones, each one of which bore the name of one of the twelve apostles of the Lamb.

¹⁵   The angel that was speaking to me was carrying a gold measuring rod to measure the city and its gates and wall. ¹⁶ The plan of the city is perfectly square, its length the same as its breadth. He measured the city with his rod and it was twelve thousand furlongs in length and in breadth, and ¹⁷ equal in height. •He measured its wall, and this was a hundred and forty-four cubits high—the angel was using the ¹⁸ ordinary cubit. •The wall was built of diamond, and the ¹⁹ city of pure gold, like polished glass. •The foundations of the city wall were faced with all kinds of precious stone: the first with diamond, the second lapis lazuli, the third ²⁰ turquoise, the fourth crystal, •the fifth agate, the sixth ruby, the seventh gold quartz, the eighth malachite, the ninth topaz, the tenth emerald, the eleventh sapphire and ²¹ the twelfth amethyst. •The twelve gates were twelve pearls, each gate being made of a single pearl, and the main street of the city was pure gold, transparent as glass. ²² I saw that there was no temple in the city since the Lord God Almighty and the Lamb were themselves the ²³ temple, •and the city did not need the sun or the moon for light, since it was lit by the radiant glory of God and ²⁴ the Lamb was a lighted torch for it. •*The pagan nations will live by its light*ʰ and the kings of the earth will bring ²⁵ it their treasures. •*The gates of it will never be shut by* ²⁶ *day*—and there will be no night there—and *the nations will* ²⁷ *come, bringing their treasure and their wealth.* •Nothing unclean may come into it: no one who does what is loathsome or false, but only those who are listed in the Lamb's book of life.

¹   **22**   Then the angel showed me the river of life, rising from the throne of God and of the Lamb and flow- ² ing crystal-clear •down the middle of the city street. *On either side of the river were the trees of life, which bear twelve crops of fruit in a year, one in each month, and the leaves of which are the cure for the pagans.*ᵃ

³   *The ban will be lifted.*ᵇ The throne of God and of the Lamb will be in its place in the city; his servants will wor- ⁴ ship him, •they will see him face to face, and his name

5 will be written on their foreheads. ·It will never be night again and they will not need lamplight or sunlight, because the Lord God will be shining on them. They will reign for ever and ever.

6   The angel said to me, "All that you have written is sure and will come true: the Lord God who gives the spirit to the prophets has sent his angel to reveal to his servants

7 *what is soon to take place.* ·Very soon now, I shall be with you again." Happy are those who treasure the prophetic message of this book.

8   I, John, am the one who heard and saw these things. When I had heard and seen them all, I knelt at the feet of the angel who had shown them to me, to worship him;

9 but he said, "Don't do that: I am a servant just like you and like your brothers the prophets and like those who treasure what you have written in this book. It is God that you must worship."

10   This, too, he said to me, "Do not keep the prophecies
11 in this book a secret, because the Time is close. ·Meanwhile let the sinner go on sinning, and the unclean continue to be unclean; let those who do good go on doing good,
12 and those who are holy continue to be holy. ·Very soon now, I shall be with you again, *bringing the reward to be given to every man according to what he deserves.*[c]
13 I am the Alpha and the Omega, *the First and the Last,*
14 the Beginning and the End. ·Happy are those who will have washed their robes clean, so that they will have the right to feed on the tree of life and can come through the
15 gates into the city. ·These others must stay outside: dogs, fortune-tellers, and fornicators, and murderers, and idolaters, and everyone of false speech and false life."

EPILOGUE

16   I, Jesus, have sent my angel to make these revelations to you for the sake of the churches. I am of David's line, the root of David and the bright star of the morning.
17   The Spirit and the Bride say, "Come." Let everyone who listens answer, "Come." *Then let all who are thirsty*

g. Ezk 48:31-35   h. Is 60:3
22 a. Ezk 47:12   b. Zc 14:11   c. Ps 62:12

come:[d] all who want it may *have the water* of life, *and have it free.*

[18] This is my solemn warning to all who hear the prophecies in this book: if anyone adds anything to them, God will add to him every plague mentioned in the book;

[19] if anyone cuts anything out of the prophecies in this book, God will cut off his share of the tree of life and of the holy city, which are described in the book.

[20] The one who guarantees these revelations repeats his promise: I shall indeed *be with you* soon. Amen; come, Lord Jesus.

[21] May the grace of the Lord Jesus be with you all. Amen.

d. Is 55:1

CHRONOLOGICAL TABLE

	B.C.	The census of Lk 2:1f? Cf. the *lapis Venetus* inscription, undated, giving evidence of a census in Apamea (Syria) by order of Quirinius "legate in Syria." Cf. Lk 2:2
		Birth of JESUS, about 7-6(?)
QUINTILIUS VARUS, legate in Syria: 6-4		
		End of March, beginning of April, 4 B.C., death of Herod at Jericho. Archelaus takes his body to the Herodion
ARCHELAUS ethnarch of Judaea and Samaria: 4 B.C.-6 A.D.		
HEROD ANTIPAS tetrarch of Galilee and Peraea: 4 B.C.-39 A.D.		
PHILIP tetrarch of Gaulanitis, Batanaea, Trachonitis, Auranitis and the district of Paneas (Ituraea): 4 B.C.-34 A.D.	A.D. 1	Between 5 and 10, birth of Paul at Tarsus; pupil of Gamaliel the Elder, Ac 22:3, cf. 5:34
6, Augustus deposes Archelaus who is exiled to Vienne (Gaul)		
6-41, Judaea a procuratorial province (with Caesarea as the capital)		
6, according to Josephus, QUIRINIUS legate in Syria(?)		
14 (19th August), death of Augustus. TIBERIUS emperor: 14-37		Valerius Gratus deposes Annas. Three other high priests follow, then JOSEPH CALLED CAIAPHAS: 18-36
VALERIUS GRATUS procurator: 15-26		
17-19, GERMANICUS, adopted son of Tiberius, in the East		About 27, Herod Antipas, married to the daughter of Aretas, marries Herodias, the wife of his

	A.D.	
		brother Herod (son of Mariamne II)
26-36, PONTIUS PILATE procurator		Autumn of 27, the preaching of JOHN THE BAPTIST and the beginning of the ministry of Jesus. Cf. Lk 3:2 +
The 15th year of Tiberius, Lk 3:1: 19th August 28 or 18th August 29, but according to the Syrian calculation: Sept.-Oct. 27 to Sept.-Oct. 28		30, on the eve of the Passover, i.e. 14th Nisan, a Friday, death of Jesus, Jn 19:31f. (The Passover fell on the Saturday, 8th April in 30 and 4th April in 33: the second date is too late, cf. Jn 2:20). Cf. Mt 26:17 +
		30, Pentecost, outpouring of the Spirit on the Church, Ac 2. The first community, Ac 2:42, etc.
CALIGULA emperor: 37-41		36-37, winter (?), martyrdom of Stephen and dispersion of part of the community. A little later, conversion of PAUL. Cf. Ac 9:1+
39, Caligula exiles Antipas to the Pyrenees and gives his tetrarchy to Agrippa I		Paul in "Arabia," then in Damascus, Ac 9:19f; Ga 1:17f
		About 39, Paul escapes from Damascus, 2 Co 11:32f, and makes a first visit to the elders of the Church, Ga 1:18f (Cephas and James the brother of the Lord); Ac 9:25f
41-54, CLAUDIUS emperor. Agrippa I, now in Rome, contributes to his success; Claudius concedes him Judaea and Samaria. His brother Herod becomes king of Chalcis (41-48) and marries Berenice (daughter of Agrippa)		About 43, Paul and Barnabas at Antioch which becomes the center for the hellenistic Christians. PETER in Samaria (Simon the magician) and in the coastal plain (the centurion Cornelius)
44, spring. On the death of Herod Agrippa, Judaea again becomes a procuratorial province, 44-66		43 or 44, before the Passover, Agrippa I orders the beheading of JAMES, BROTHER OF JOHN (James the Great); during the feast he imprisons Peter, Ac 12

A.D. Between 45 and 49, 1st mission by Paul: Antioch, Cyprus, Antioch in Pisidia, Lystra, . . .Antioch, Ac 13:1f

About 48, famine in Judaea, worsened by the sabbatical year 47/48. Visit to Jerusalem, by HELEN, queen of Adiabene, a convert to Judaism: she brings relief to the population

AGRIPPA II, son of Agrippa I, king of Chalcis 48-53. In 49 he is named inspector of the Temple, with the right to nominate the high priest

49, Claudius "drives from Rome the Jewish agitators stirred up by Chrestos" (Suetonius), cf. Ac 18:2

48-49, prophecy of Agabus and the aid given to the community at Jerusalem by that of Antioch. The council of Jerusalem: converts from paganism exempt from the Law, Ac 15:5f; Ga 2:1f

About the year 50, the oral tradition of the gospel is put into written form: the Aramaic Matthew, and the complementary collection. The Letter of James (or about 58)

50-52, 2nd mission by Paul: Lystra (Timothy), Phrygia, Galatia, Philippi, Thessalonika, Athens (sermon on the Areopagus)

Winter of 50 to summer of 52, Paul in Corinth: the Letters to the Thessalonians; and, in the spring of 52, summoned to appear before Gallio. Summer 52, he goes to Jerusalem, Ac 18:22, and then to Antioch

53-58, 3rd mission by Paul; APOLLOS at Ephesus and then at Corinth

54-68, NERO emperor

55, Nero adds a part of Galilee and Peraea to the kingdom of Agrippa

54-57, after passing through Galatia and Phrygia, Paul stays at Ephesus for 2¼ years. After 56(?), Letter to the Philippians. About Passover 57, 1 Corinthians. Then a quick visit to Corinth, 2 Co 12:14. Return to Ephesus and Letter to the Galatians

End of 57, passes through Macedonia. 2 Corinthians

A.D. Winter 57-58, at Corinth, Ac 20:3, cf. 1 Co 16:6; Letter to the Romans

Passover 58, at Philippi, Ac 20:6, then, by sea, to Caesarea (Philip and Agabus)

Summer 58, in Jerusalem. JAMES THE BROTHER OF THE LORD heads the Judaeo-Christian community; his Letter to the Jews of the Dispersion (or possibly before 49)

Autumn of 60, Paul's voyage to Rome, the storm, he winters in Malta

61-63, Paul in Rome under military guard. His apostolate, Letters to Colossians, Ephesians, Philemon (and to Philippians?)

62, the High Priest Anan has James the brother of the Lord stoned to death (after the death of Festus and before the arrival of Albinus). SIMEON, son of Cleophas and of Mary (sister-in-law of the mother of Jesus), succeeded James as head of the church of Jerusalem (Eusebius)

63, Paul is set free, and possibly goes to Spain, Rm 15:24f

64, July, burning of Rome and persecution of the Christians

About 64, 1 Peter and the gospel of Mark

64 (or 67), martyrdom of Peter in Rome

About 65, Paul at Ephesus, 1 Tm 1:3; in Crete, Tt 1:5; in Macedonia, whence he sends his 1st Letter to Timothy, 1 Tm 1:3; and probably Titus

The Greek gospel of Matthew; the gospel of Luke and the Acts of the Apostles: before 70? or about 80?

About 67, Letter to the Hebrews. Paul, a prisoner in Rome, writes 2 Timothy. A little later he is beheaded

A.D.

68, April, GALBA emperor

68, June, suicide of Nero

69, January, OTHO proclaimed Emperor by the Praetorians and VITELLIUS by the legions in Germany

69-79, VESPASIAN emperor. He entrusts the siege of Jerusalem to Titus

End of 69, Vespasian in sole command of the empire

70, Passover. Many pilgrims in Jerusalem. Titus lays siege to the city with four legions. Tiberius Alexander is second in command

70, 29th August, capture of the Inner Court and burning of the Temple (the 10th of Loos, i.e. the 10th of the 5th month, the day when Nebuzaradan set fire to the first Temple, Jr 52:12 and Josephus)

70, end of the year, Judaea an imperial province; under the rule of the legate of the Xth Legion based in Jerusalem. Caesarea a Roman colony

70, Sept., capture of the Upper City and the palace of Herod. The inhabitants killed, sold into slavery or condemned to hard labor

70-80, the Letter of Jude, then 2 Peter. 2 Esdras (apocryphal). About 78, the Jewish War (Josephus)

79-81, TITUS emperor

About 95, John exiled to Patmos. Final text of Revelation. Letter of St Clement, bishop of Rome, to the Corinthians

81-96, DOMITIAN emperor. Brother of Titus

Gospel of John; then 1 John (3 John and 2 John are possibly earlier). He opposes Cerinthus and his Docetism

96-98, NERVA emperor

98-117, TRAJAN emperor

100   At the beginning of Trajan's reign, death of John at Ephesus

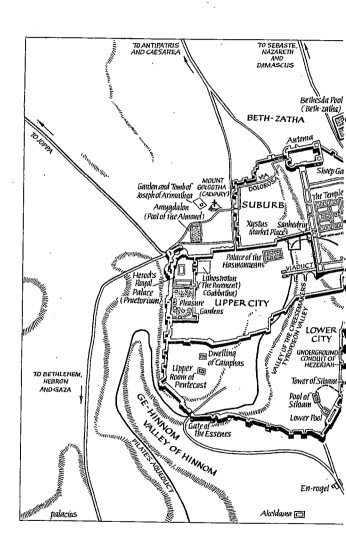

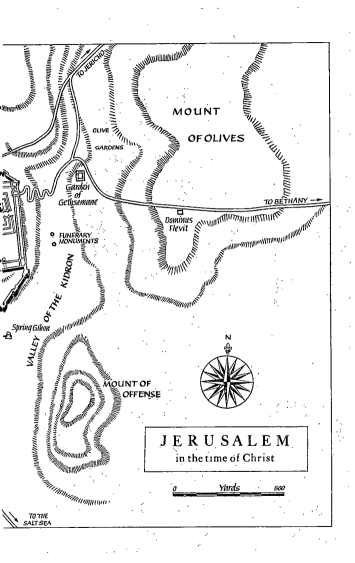

TO JERICHO

MOUNT

OF OLIVES

OLIVE
GARDENS

Garden
of
Gethsemane

TO BETHANY

Dominus
Flevit

FUNERARY
MONUMENTS

VALLEY OF THE KIDRON

Spring Gihon

MOUNT OF
OFFENSE

N

JERUSALEM
in the time of Christ

0   Yards   500

TO THE
SALT SEA

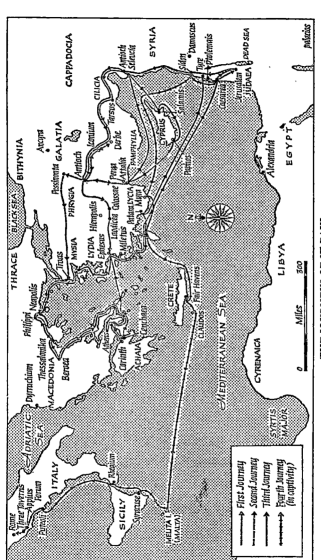

THE JOURNEYS OF ST PAUL

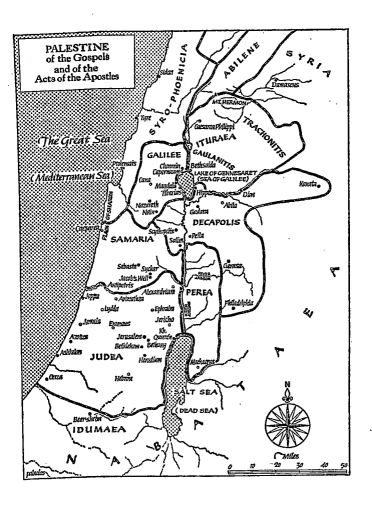

PALESTINE
of the Gospels
and of the
Acts of the Apostles

NOTES